Mallorca
& Menorca

timeout.com

Mallorca & Menorca

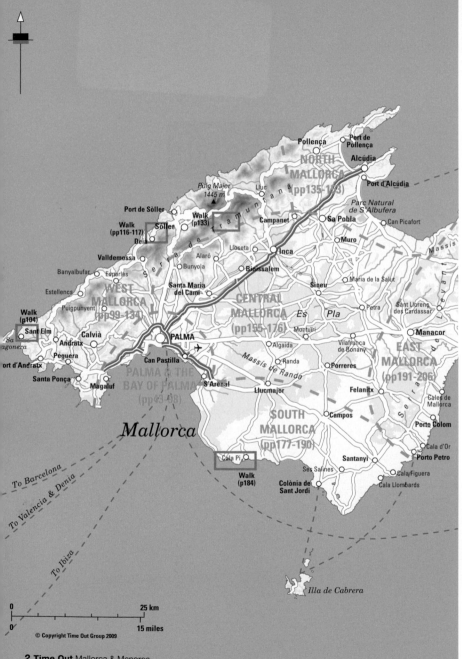

Puig Major
1445 m

Port de Sóller

Walk
(pp116-117)

Sóller

Walk
(p133)

Deià

Valldemossa

Banyalbufar

Esporles

Estellencs

Puigpunyent

Walk
(p104)

Sant Elm

Sa
Dragonera

Andratx

Port d'Andratx

Péguera

Santa Ponça

Magaluf

Calvià

Can Pastilla

PALMA & THE
BAY OF PALMA
(pp43-98)

Mallorca

PALMA

S'Arenal

WEST
MALLORCA
(pp99-134)

Santa Maria
del Camí

Alaró

Bunyola

Lloseta

Binissalem

Inca

Campanet

Sa Pobla

Muro

Llubí

NORTH
MALLORCA
(pp135-153)

Pollença

Port de
Pollença

Alcúdia

Port d'Alcúdia

Parc Natural
de S'Albufera

Can Picafort

Maria de la Salut

Sineu

Petra

CENTRAL
MALLORCA
(pp155-176)

Es   Pla

Montuïri

Algaida

Randa

Massís de Randà

Vilafranca
de Bonany

Porreres

Sant Llorenç
des Cardassar

Manacor

EAST
MALLORCA
(pp191-205)

Massís de Llevant

Serra de Llevant

Cales de
Mallorca

Porto Colom

Cala d'Or

Porto Petro

Llucmajor

Campos

Felanitx

SOUTH
MALLORCA
(pp177-190)

Cala Pi

Walk
(p184)

Colònia de
Sant Jordi

Ses Salines

Santanyí

Cala Figuera

Cala Llombards

Serra de Tramuntana

To Barcelona

To Valencia & Denia

To Ibiza

Illa de Cabrera

0   25 km
0   15 miles

© Copyright Time Out Group 2009

2 Time Out Mallorca & Menorca

To Barcelona

MENORCA
(pp207-258)

Fornells

Cala Morell
Port d'Addaia

Ciutadella
Cala en Blanes
Ferreries
Es Mercadal
Walk (p242)

Cala Blanca
Es Migjorn Gran

Cala Galdana
Alaior

Sant Tomàs
Son Bou
Maó
Es Castell

Sant Climent
Cala en Porter
Sant Lluís

Menorca

d'Artà

Walk (pp204-205)

Cala Ratjada
Artà
Capdepera

Son Servera
Cala Millor

Portocristo

M E D I T E R R A N E A N   S E A

Dublin
Rep. of Ireland
United Kingdom
Netherlands
Berlin
Poland

London
Amsterdam
Germany

Brussels
Belgium
Luxembourg
Prague
Czech Republic

Paris
Vienna
Austria
Budapest
Hungary

Atlantic
Bern
Switz.
Slovenia
Croatia

Ocean
France
Italy
Bosnia

Rome

Spain

Portugal
Madrid
Mallorca
Menorca

Lisbon
M e d i t e r r a n e a n   S e a

Algiers
Tunis
Algeria
Tunisia

Time Out Mallorca & Menorca **3**

Time Out Guides Ltd
Universal House
251 Tottenham Court Road
London W1T 7AB
United Kingdom
Tel: +44 (0)20 7813 3000
Fax: +44 (0)20 7813 6001
Email: guides@timeout.com
www.timeout.com

Published by Time Out Guides Ltd, a wholly owned subsidiary of Time Out Group Ltd.
Time Out and the Time Out logo are trademarks of Time Out Group Ltd.

© Time Out Group Ltd 2009
Previous editions 2004, 2006.

10 9 8 7 6 5 4 3 2 1

This edition first published in Great Britain in 2009 by Ebury Publishing.
A Random House Group Company
20 Vauxhall Bridge Road, London SW1V 2SA

Random House Australia Pty Ltd 20 Alfred Street, Milsons Point, Sydney, New South Wales 2061, Australia

Random House New Zealand Ltd 18 Poland Road, Glenfield, Auckland 10, New Zealand

Random House South Africa (Pty) Ltd Isle of Houghton, Corner Boundary Road & Carse O'Gowrie, Houghton 2198, South Africa

Random House UK Limited Reg. No. 954009

For further distribution details, see www.timeout.com.

ISBN: 978-1-84670-053-8

A CIP catalogue record for this book is available from the British Library.

Printed and bound by Firmengruppe APPL, aprinta druck, Wemding, Germany.

The Random House Group Limited supports The Forest Stewardship Council (FSC), the leading international forest certification organisation. All our titles that are printed on Greenpeace approved FSC certified paper carry the FSC logo. Our paper procurement policy can be found at http://www.rbooks.co.uk/environment.

Time Out carbon-offsets its flights with Trees for Cities (www.treesforcities.org).

Contents

Introduction

While they haven't completely shaken their reputations for soulless resorts and lairy hedonism – with some justification, it has to be said – the two largest islands of the Balearic archipelago have nonetheless experienced something of an image transformation over the past decade. Palma is now a firm fixture on 'top city breaks' lists in Sunday travel supplements, and many visitors are being seduced by the islands' growing reputations for outdoor activities, quality places to stay and eat and stunning beaches. With enticing natural attractions and forward-thinking authorities, especially in Mallorca's case, the image transformation hasn't been too problematic. Millions have been invested in cleaning up the streets and improving counter-resort culture tourist infrastructures, such as hiking and cycling routes, upmarket rural and metropolitan accommodation, yachting facilities and conference centres, while legislation has been brought in to curb late-night booze-driven behaviour.

This embracement of more 'civilised' tourism isn't actually anything new in Mallorca: in the 1920s, the glitterati, including Elizabeth Taylor and Audrey Hepburn, poured in to swan about the Hotel Formentor, while artists, hippies and writers, such as the late Robert Graves, have been cavorting around the west coast, and in particular the village of Deià, for decades.

While those in search of summer sun, late-night cocktails and English pubs will still find what they're after, visit off-season and the vibe is far more wholesome. In winter, spring or autumn, you're more likely to come across lycra-clad cyclists skimming along the interior, hikers scaling the peaks of the Tramuntana and metropolitan sophisticates keen to sample the tapas bars of Palma's perfectly preserved old town. Mallorca's capital is in fact a gem of a city, often likened to its big sister Barcelona, yet without the tourist droves (or pickpockets).

If you really want to escape, though, Menorca is the place. With a somnolent interior, some outstandingly beautiful, undeveloped beaches and a couple of tiny port towns, it's one of the Mediterranean's most manageable island destinations, and a real treat for divers.

So, two small islands but a wealth of different possible experiences. The question now is whether such tourism-reliant destinations can weather the storm in these economically challenged times. *Anna Norman & Patrick Welch, Editors*

Around the Islands

PALMA & THE BAY OF PALMA

If you had a list of desirable attributes for any city, few ticks would be missing on Palma's checklist, from stylish hotels and decent restaurants to a compact layout and interesting architecture. The surrounding Bay of Palma has been scarred by the tourism excesses to which the capital has made few concessions. Yet white sand beaches, yachting facilities and nightclubs draw in the crowds.
▶ For more, see pp43-98.

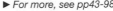

WEST MALLORCA

The rugged peaks of the Serra de Tramuntana flank the whole of the west coast, blocking large-scale tourist development. This region is certainly not free from tourists, but they tend to be of a more rarefied cast, often keen to head into the mountains for some soul-cleansing hiking. The area contains some of the choicest places to stay and eat, and some of the smartest and most atmospheric villages.
▶ For more, see pp99-134.

NORTH & CENTRAL MALLORCA

The Northern towns of Alcúdia and Pollença are among Mallorca's most appealing, and make great holiday bases. South of here, the central plain, Es Pla, is the island's agricultural heartland, and largely unknown by tourists. A growing wave of excellent *agroturismos* – along with an improving wine industry – are, however, starting to beckon in visitors wanting to escape the crowds.
▶ For more, see pp135-176.

EAST & SOUTH MALLORCA

On the east coast, you'll find a number of popular family resorts that may lack character but are at least not as environmentally offensive as they could be. In contrast, the wind-whipped southern coast is largely undeveloped; though flat and barren, it does possess a certain wild, melancholic beauty. The pristine islands of the Cabrera national park, a short boat trip away, are a must-do in this area.
▶ For more, see pp177-206.

MENORCA

Outside of its two large towns, Maó and Ciutadella – wonderful pint-sized ports worthy of a couple of days exploring – Menorca is more relaxed and quieter than Mallorca. It lacks the dramatic geography of the Tramuntana, but it is also largely free of frenzied overdevelopment, with paradisiacal beaches, a handful of excellent rural hotels and – often a surprise to visitors – prehistoric ruins.
▶ For more, see pp207-258.

Best of the Islands

BEACH LIFE
Mallorca has its fair share of fine (if over-populated) beaches, but few can compare to the idyllic coves that crenellate the Menorcan coast. Many can only be reached on foot, and with their fine bleached sands and pellucid shallow waters, it doesn't take a great leap of imagination to fancy yourself in the Caribbean. The twin beaches of **Cala Macarella** and **Cala Macarelleta**, and **Cala en Turqueta** (for all, *see p230*) in the southern part of the island are some of the best. Divers, meanwhile, are spoilt in Menorca, with visibility of up to 30 metres (100 feet) and water temperatures of up to 25 degrees celsius during high season.

HIGH PEAKS
The Serra de Tramuntana mountain range, stretching down Mallorca's west coast, is the island's most spectacular natural asset, offering memorable climbing, hiking, cycling and birdwatching, and little tourist development. A good introductory hike is the route up to the ruined monastery of **La Trapa** (*see p104*) in the south-west; more experienced trekkers should try the popular **Tossals Verds** (*see p133*) route. If you prefer to see the *serra* from the comfort of a car, a drive along the coastal road from **Port d'Andratx** (*see p103*) to **Sóller** (*see p122*) should not be missed, with some of the most dramatic scenery to be found in Europe.

WORKS OF ART
Palma's art scene has notably improved over the past few years, with the opening of modern and contemporary art mecca **Es Baluard** (*see p68*) in 2004, and with the strengthening of its popular **Nit de l'Art** (*see p41*) in September. **Miró**'s time in Palma is underdocumented outside of Mallorca; the Catalan artist had several prolific years of artistic creation in his studio

on the outskirts of the city, which can be visited (*see p78*). Outside of the Mallorcan capital, there's an unlikely and original art find in the form of the **Fundación Yannick y Ben Jakober** (*see p152*) on the Bay of Alcúdia, while the village of **Deià** is something of an enclave for expat artists; its renowned hotel **La Residencia** (*see p121*) showcases quality local work in its in-house **Tafona Gallery**.

LOCAL INDUSTRY

The islands' local industries (aside from tourism) are deeply connected with national identity, being centered around heritage crafts such as shoe-making, glass-making and the production of local foodstuff, such as the emblematic *ensaïmada* pastry and *sobrassada* sausage – both of which are unmissable for foodies. **Town markets** are a good way of appreciating

local products, with some of the best ones to be found in Palma, Alcúdia, Artà, Sineu, Inca, Bunyola and Santanyí. Mallorca's wine industry is a growing sector, with tasting tours available in the island's main vineyard region of **Binissalem** (*see p162* **Biniculture**), while gin has been the tipple of choice in Menorca since British rule in the 18th century; Maó's **Gin Xoriguer** factory (*see p214*) runs tours. And for a trip back in time, to when citrus growers on the west coast used to take their products to Palma's markets, take a trip on the old-school **Palma–Sóller train** (*see p126* **Ticket to Ride**).

PLACES TO STAY

No region of Spain has more classy hotels than Mallorca. In an attempt to lure more upmarket, higher-spending visitors, the island is now covered with a network of sleek places to stay – from urban designer hotels, such as the **Puro Hotel** (*see p88*), **Hotel Tres** (*see p88*; *pictured left*) and newcomer **Hotel Santa Clara** (*see p87*) in Palma, to luxury-rustic *agroturismos* (*see p172*). On the other end of the scale are the island's spectacularly located monastries, such as the **Santuari de Sant Salvador** (*see p195*) and the **Santuari Nostra Senyora des Puig** (*see p142*), which offer some of the cheapest and most spiritually satisfying lodgings on the island. Don't expect frills: just simplicity, utter tranquility and views to die for.

RUINS AND CAVES

Nowhere in Europe has a greater concentration of prehistoric sites than Menorca. More than 100 are scattered over the tiny island. Their typical structures of lookout tower (talayot) and T-shaped shrine (taula), as in the **Talatí de Dalt** and **Trépuco** (for both, *see p221*), are unique.

Mallorca has its own astonishing structures in the form of cave systems, with the most astounding, such as the **Coves del Drac** (*see p200*), to be found

along the east coast. Dripping with multi-hued stalactites and lined with silent underground lakes, they make for an otherwordly experience, which even their thorough commercialisation can't spoil.

Time Out

Mallorca
& Menorca

Editorial
Editors Anna Norman & Patrick Welch
Listings Editors Alex Phillips, Roberto Rama,
    Rodolfo Schmidt, Dylan Simanowitz
Proofreader Tamsin Shelton
Indexer Ismay Atkins

Managing Director Peter Fiennes
Editorial Director Ruth Jarvis
Series Editor Will Fulford-Jones
Business Manager Dan Allen
Editorial Manager Holly Pick
Assistant Management Accountant Ija Krasnikova

Design
Art Director Scott Moore
Art Editor Pinelope Kourmouzoglou
Senior Designer Henry Elphick
Graphic Designers Kei Ishimaru, Nicola Wilson
Advertising Designer Jodi Sher

Picture Desk
Picture Editor Jael Marschner
Deputy Picture Editor Lynn Chambers
Picture Researcher Gemma Walters
Picture Desk Assistant Marzena Zoladz
Picture Librarian Christina Theisen

Advertising
Commercial Director Mark Phillips
International Advertising Manager Kasimir Berger
International Sales Executive Charlie Sokol
Advertising Sales (Mallorca) Margarita Calderón
    Blanco

Marketing
Marketing Manager Yvonne Poon
**Sales & Marketing Director, North America
    & Latin America** Lisa Levinson
Senior Publishing Brand Manager Luthfa Begum
Marketing Designer Anthony Huggins

Production
Group Production Director Mark Lamond
Production Manager Brendan McKeown
Production Controller Damian Bennett
Production Coordinator Julie Pallot

Time Out Group
Chairman Tony Elliott
Group General Manager/Director Nichola Coulthard
Time Out Communications Ltd MD David Pepper
Time Out International Ltd MD Cathy Runciman
**Time Out Magazine Ltd Publisher/
    Managing Director** Mark Elliott
Group IT Director Simon Chappell
Head of Marketing Catherine Demajo

Contributors

Introduction Anna Norman & Patrick Welch. **History** Jonathan Cox. **Mallorca & Menorca Today** Jonathan
Cox & Tara Stevens. **Food & Drink** Jonathan Cox. **Outdoor Pursuits** Anna Norman & Patrick Welch.
Calendar Jonathan Cox (*Art Attack* Anna Norman). **Palma** Anna Norman. **The Bay of Palma** Tara Stevens.
West Mallorca Anna Norman (Valldemossa, Port de Sóller & Northern Serra Patrick Welch). **North Mallorca**
Patrick Welch. **Central Mallorca** Tara Stevens. **South Mallorca** Tara Stevens. **East Mallorca** Tara Stevens.
Menorca Patrick Welch. **Directory** Jonathan Cox.

Maps JS Graphics (john@jsgraphics.co.uk). Maps are based on material suppled by Netmaps.

Photography Karl Blackwell, except: pages 5, 72 (top right) Anna Norman; pages 7 (bottom left), 14, 20,
21, 134, 257 Jonathan Cox; pages 7 (bottom right), 251 Fundacio Desti Menorca; page 9 (middle) Hotel Tres;
page 19 Bridgeman Art Library; pages 25, 114, 115 Orient-Express Hotels (UK) Ltd; pages 26, 72 (bottom right),
83, 120, 126 Max Sloman; page 37 Fomento del Turismo de Mallorca; page 39 Gerado Cañellas, Jazz Voyeur
Festival; pages 72 (left), 84, 86, 120 (bottom right), 124 Rodolfo Schmidt; page 96 Thomas Reiner/BCM; page
110 Alix Cordell; page 194 AFP/Getty Images; page 204 Tara Stevens. The following images were provided by
the featured establishments: pages 97, 161, 172, 173, 182, 238, 242, 253.

The editors would like to thank Lanny Aldrich, Gabriella Cerretti and Doug Goodman at Reis de Mallorca, Ellie
Collins, Alix Cordell, Sally Davies, Alex Phillips, Rodolfo Schmidt, Anna Skidmore at Foment del Turisme de Mallorca,
Max Sloman, Alex Smith; and all the contributors to previous editions of *Time Out Mallorca & Menorca*, whose work
forms the basis for parts of this book, as well as readers who wrote in with feedback on the previous editions.

About the Guide

GETTING STARTED

All the individual areas start with maps, background history and sightseeing highlights, followed by details on where to eat, drink and stay (in bigger towns, these venues have been marked on the maps with coloured bullets like this: ❶), and tourist information. We also give travel directions; however, note that public transport options around inland rural areas are very limited.

THE ESSENTIALS

For practical information, including visas, disabled access, emergency numbers, useful websites and local transport, see the Directory. It begins on page 260.

THE LISTINGS

All listings were checked and correct at press time. However, arrangements can alter at any time, and economic conditions can cause prices to change rapidly.

The very best venues, the must-sees and must-dos, have been marked with a red star (★). We've also marked sights that offer free admission with a FREE symbol, and budget restaurants with a € symbol. Restaurant prices are denoted by euro symbols: € means under €20 for a full meal with drinks; €€ between €20 and €30; €€€ between €30 and €40; and €€€€ over €40.

THE LANGUAGE

The islands are bilingual: everybody who speaks Catalan (or rather, its dialects *mallorquí* and *menorquí*) will also speak Spanish. Many also speak English (and often German). That said, a little of the local lingo goes a long way. For a language primer, see pp271-272; there's also help with restaurant vocabulary on pages 28-33.

PHONE NUMBERS

The area code for the Balearics is 971. From outside Spain, dial your country's international access code (00 from the UK, 011 from the US), followed by the Spanish country code (34) and the nine-digit number. For more on phones, see p269.

FEEDBACK

We welcome feedback on this guide, including suggestions for future editions. Please email us at guides@timeout.com.

Time Out Guides

Founded in 1968, Time Out has grown from humble beginnings into the leading resource for anyone wanting to know what's happening in the world's greatest cities. Alongside our influential weeklies in London, New York and Chicago, we publish more than 20 magazines in cities as varied as Beijing and Beirut; a range of travel books, with the City Guides now joined by the newer Shortlist series; and an information-packed website. The company remains proudly independent, still owned by Tony Elliott four decades after he launched *Time Out London*.

Written by experts and illustrated with original photography, our books also retain their independence. No business has been featured because it has advertised, and all restaurants and bars are visited and reviewed anonymously.

ABOUT THE EDITORS

Anna Norman is a staff editor at Time Out Guides. She has also edited guides to Florence and London shops. She speaks fluent Spanish, having spent extended periods of time in Argentina and Cuba. **Patrick Welch** has lived in Spain, Brazil, Ecuador and France, and speaks French, Spanish and Portuguese. He has worked on various Time Out guidebooks, and also writes for *Time Out London*.

A full list of the book's contributors can be found opposite.

Airline flights are one of the biggest producers of the global warming gas CO_2. But with **The CarbonNeutral Company** you can make your travel a little greener.

Go to **www.carbonneutral.com** to calculate your flight emissions then 'neutralise' them through international projects which save exactly the same amount of carbon dioxide.

Contact us at **shop@carbonneutral.com** or call into the office on **0870 199 99 88** for more details.

CarbonNeutral®flights

In Context

S'Algar.
See p227.

History

A tale of almost non-stop invasions
– from Phoenicians to package tourists.

TEXT: JONATHAN COX

The Balearics' embrace of mass tourism in the 20th century has simply been the latest wave in a long history characterised by invasion and integration: the Greeks, the Carthaginians, the Romans, the Byzantines, the Moors and the British – as well as a plethora of pirates along the way – have all left their mark on the islands' cultural and social heritage. The tourism phenomenon of the 20th century was an important step in tackling the economic decline and poverty that had blighted the Balearics since the 15th century; yet visitors to Mallorca and Menorca who are aware only of its modern-day associations are often surprised by the references to the islands' early history, and in particular by the high number of important prehistoric ruins to be found here – especially in Menorca, home to dozens of Talayotic Period ruins.

PREHISTORIC BALEARICS

The Balearics, and Menorca in particular, are remarkably rich in prehistoric ruins. Humans first reached the islands some time before 4000 BC; just how long before is a matter of considerable controversy. Some archaeologists claim to have found evidence of human presence in Mallorca from around 5600 BC; others believe there's no reliable proof before the start of the fourth millennium BC. Whatever the truth is, it seems that, for reasons unknown, man arrived relatively late in the Balearics – most of the Mediterranean islands had been settled by the seventh or even eighth millennium BC.

Equally, no one knows why the first settlers appeared. Perhaps the islands were happened upon by chance by fishermen or traders, who precipitated a larger migration of people driven from Iberia or the south of France by hunger.

These earliest inhabitants found shelter in caves, establishing what has become known as the Balearic cave culture. A major food source was undoubtedly *Myotragus Balearicus* – a stumpy, endemic goat-like animal – and it's possible that its extinction by 3000 BC was due to over-hunting by man. Some historians believe that the early islanders tried to domesticate *Myotragus*; they certainly made an attempt to establish primitive agriculture.

Given the islands' prominent position in the western Mediterranean, they inevitably attracted the attention of the seafaring people of the region. From around 2500 BC to 1400 BC the first settlements outside caves appear – all inland, indicating the constant danger of pirate attack (a problem throughout Balearic history).

But not all interaction was violent. Ceramic technology came to the islands, domesticated animals were imported and, around the middle of the second millennium BC, the advanced Beaker culture (so named after their practice of burying distinctive bell-shaped ceramic beakers with their dead) was becoming influential. It also brought knowledge of metallurgical techniques to the islands.

The coming of the Beaker culture ushered in the Bronze Age. Gradually, a more sophisticated society developed with more efficient farming and improved metalworking, leading to population growth and social differentiation. This era is known as the Talayotic Period (c1400-c800 BC) in the Balearics, after the distinctive talayots (from the Arabic word 'atalaya', meaning 'watchtower'), unusual stone towers dating from this period that can still be seen scattered across the islands, especially in Menorca. The only similar structures have been found in Sardinia, suggesting that the two island cultures might share the same root.

Talayotic culture reached its apogee on Menorca. Here, and only here, are found the mysterious taulas (meaning 'tables' in Catalan) – huge T-shaped structures consisting of one stone lain flat on top of another upright stone. The other distinctive structures from this period are navetas – long, apsidal constructions, shaped like the prow of a boat with a large opening at one end and drystone walls that were possibly covered with twigs, leaves and dry mud.

For more on the design and possible functions of prehistoric structures, and where to find the best examples, *see p21* **Site-seeing guide**.

Though trade increased in the Post-Talayotic Period (Iron Age, c800-c123 BC), this was generally a time of cultural and economic decline in the Balearics, with the quality of pottery, architecture and agricultural techniques all suffering. There was, though, greater contact with the outside world (evidence of bull cults on the islands provides a link with other islands, such as Sardinia and Malta, with similar cults), and the influence of other Mediterranean peoples on the Balearics during this period was becoming increasingly important.

PHOENICIANS, GREEKS, CARTHAGINIANS AND ROMANS

The Phoenicians (maritime traders from the eastern Mediterranean) established a presence on the Balearics around the turn of the first millennium BC, though they seem to have considered the islands as staging posts rather than places for settlement. They did, however, construct an outpost at Sanisera on northern Menorca, and some artefacts have been found at Alcúdia, but there is no evidence of other Phoenician towns.

From around 800 BC, the Greeks became dominant in the region, but, again, very little evidence of their presence in the Balearics has been found. The Greeks called the islands Gimnesias – alluding to the inhabitants' scant clothing (athletes in the Greek gymnasion exercised naked).

The city of Carthage had been founded by the Phoenicians in North Africa in the ninth century BC, and, as Greek influence waned in the seventh century BC, so the Carthaginians became the major regional power. They colonised Ibiza in 654 BC, but, like the Phoenicians and Greeks before them, seem to have regarded Mallorca and Menorca merely as stepping stones, founding no more than trading posts.

Both Greeks and Carthaginians valued the islanders as mercenaries. The collective name of the islands probably derives from the Greek verb 'ballein', meaning 'to throw'. They became known as the Balearides. It seems that the islands faced little concerted external aggression throughout most of this period – there is no evidence of the fortification of settlements on Mallorca and Menorca from before 300 BC.

After the defeat of the Carthaginian general Hannibal by the emergent Romans at the Battle of Zama in 202 BC, the Carthaginians withdrew from Mallorca and Menorca, ushering in a period of relative independence for the islanders, who were then free to develop a passion for piracy relatively unchecked. Such was the menace that they posed to shipping in the region that the Romans were spurred to take Ibiza in 146 BC and then, under Quintus Metellus, Mallorca and Menorca in 123 BC, initiating 500 years of Roman hegemony. At this time the islands were dubbed Balearis Major (Mallorca) and Balearis Minor (Menorca).

The Romans rapidly introduced the infrastructure and trappings of their civilisation, founding towns at Pollentia (on the site of modern Alcúdia, not to be confused with modern-day Pollença, which appropriated the Roman name at a later date) and Palmeria (the name referring to the palm of victory) at present-day Palma. They also developed the old Phoenician settlement of Sanisera on Menorca as a port, and Port Magonum (Maó) as a bureaucratic centre. Roads, theatres, villas and temples were built; the interior was planted with olive groves, fig trees, grain fields and vineyards; and the economy boomed. The togas of Alcúdia became famed throughout the Roman Empire for their chic designs.

Throughout most of the Roman era, the Balearics formed part of the province of Tarraconensis (based around Tarragona on the Iberian mainland). In AD 404 the islands become a province in their own right, but by this time Roman dominance in Western Europe was crumbling before an onslaught of warlike tribes sweeping west and south.

VANDALS, BYZANTINES AND MOORS

One such tribe, the Vandals, led by Gesoric, brought a violent end to Roman rule in the Balearics in 425, obliterating almost all evidence of Roman civilisation. As adherents of Arianism (a Christian creed based on the distinctiveness of the figures of Christ and God, and thus denying their presence in the Trinity), the Vandals also made a point of destroying all signs of orthodox Christianity at the time. Hence the lack of Roman remains and early churches on the islands.

In 533 the Vandals were defeated in North Africa by the Byzantines under Belisarius, leading to Emperor Justinian I annexing the Balearics. But such a far-flung outpost of the Byzantine Empire was never easy to maintain, and it had been all but abandoned by the end of the seventh century.

As Byzantine power in the Mediterranean diminished, so the dynamic forces of Islam swept in from the east. In 711, the Moors (Arab and Berber tribes) of North Africa crossed the Straits of Gibraltar and invaded the European mainland. Defeating the Visigoths under Roderic, they proceeded to overrun the Iberian peninsula with remarkable speed. Although there had been large-scale Moorish attacks on Mallorca in 707-8, and again in 798, the Moors regarded the Balearics more as a source of booty than as a potential part of their empire.

'The Moors introduced almonds, apples, pears, peaches, pomegranates and new varieties of olive.'

After the latter raid the islanders appealed to the Holy Roman Emperor Charlemagne for protection, but this brought only temporary relief. As in the lawless preceding centuries, the Balearics, strategically placed as they were, continued to be a base for pirates and a target for marauders. The islands even suffered a seemingly unlikely attack by Vikings in 859. And although it seemed like everybody wanted their piece of the pie it wasn't until almost 200 years after their invasion of Spain that the Moors finally decided it might be about time to try and conquer the islands.

According to legend, a Moorish merchant, Isman al-Khaulani, was washed up on Mallorca after a storm. When he returned to Spain he extolled the beauty and potential of the island to the Emir of Córdoba and convinced him that it would be easy to annex Mallorca as part of al-Andalus. Khaulani himself headed the successful expedition in 902 and became the first wali (governor) of Mallorca, building the Almudaina (government palace) by the sea in Palma, which the Moors named Medina Mayurka.

Agriculture and infrastructure on the islands were a shambles after centuries of raiding and neglect. The Moors' most important contribution to the Balearics was (as in the rest of their empire) to hugely improve irrigation, bringing water from the mountains to the fertile but parched plains. They also introduced almonds, apples, pears, apricots, peaches, pomegranates, cherries and new varieties of olive. Estates and grand houses were built in the foothills of the Serra de Tramuntana, and villages were founded across the plain (many still have names of Arabic origin: for example, Deià is from 'daia', meaning 'village'; Algaida comes from the word for forest; Banyalbufar means 'vineyard by the sea'; and anywhere with an 'al-' or 'bini-' prefix derives from Arabic).

The 11th century was a time of peace, prosperity and relative cultural and religious harmony in the Balearics, with the islands too remote from the power centres of al-Andalus to play any part in the power struggles there. Palma, then known as Medina Maqurqa, contained 14 mosques, several synagogues and a couple of churches.

In 1076, al-Mu'tada proclaimed the independent Kingdom of the Balearics, breaking away from al-Andalus and ushering in the rule of the less tolerant Amortadha dynasty from North Africa. Christian islanders were persecuted and local shipping raided, prompting an invasion by Pisan, Genoese, Provençal and Catalan forces led by Ramón Berenguer III, Count of Barcelona, in 1114-15. The Christian armies took Ibiza and Palma, but Moorish reinforcements arrived from the mainland, forcing the Christians to evacuate the islands.

After this episode the more tolerant Almoravid tribe took over in the Balearics (and in al-Andalus), causing an improvement in the economic situation, down largely to an increase in trade and, something everybody had been waiting for: a decrease in piracy. When the Almohad dynasty overthrew the Almoravids in North Africa and southern Spain in the mid 12th century, the Balearics were the only Almoravid kingdom to survive. In 1184, the Almohads attempted, and failed, to take Mallorca, sparking a period of unprecedented Mallorcan influence in North Africa as successive rulers of the islands rampaged through present-day Morocco, Tunisia and Algeria, proving to be a major thorn in the side of the powerful Almohad ruler al-Mansur, before his successor al-Nassir eventually succeeded in conquering the Balearics in 1203.

The pendulum of tolerance once again swung back – Christians were forced to convert to Islam, and piracy of shipping and raids against the mainland once again became major problems for other local powers. When the Emir of Mallorca captured some of his ships in 1228, Jaume (Jaime or James) I, King of the newly united Aragón and Catalunya, was spurred to punish the insult and launch an invasion (he also fancied harnessing the island's wine production and agriculture).

IN CONTEXT

'Columbus's voyages to the Americas meant the focus of trade shifted to the Atlantic.'

THE RECONQUEST AND THE KINGDOM OF MALLORCA

Jaume set sail in 1229 with 143 ships and landed at Santa Ponça in south-west Mallorca (a stone cross marks the spot where the first noble came ashore). He beat the Moorish force sent to meet his army and proceeded to besiege Palma. After three months, on 31 December, the city fell, though it was another three years before the last of the Moorish resistance on the island was crushed. Pushed back to North Africa, the Moors continued to raid the Balearics for centuries afterwards.

While Jaume took Mallorca by force (earning himself the sobriquet 'the Conqueror') and Ibiza by subcontracting the dirty work (to Don Pedro, Crown Prince of Portugal, the Count of Roussillon and the Archbishop of Tarragona), he gained Menorca by guile. As another full-scale invasion was not financially viable, he sent bullish envoys to Menorca in 1232, while ordering the lighting of hundreds of fires across the north-east of Mallorca facing Menorca, creating the illusion of an immense army encamped just across the water. The trick worked and the Menorcan Moors capitulated. Their reward was a relatively tolerant regime for the next 50 years under which they were allowed to retain control of their own government while becoming vassals of Jaume.

On Mallorca, however, the Moors received far harsher treatment. The island was divided up (the repartiment) between Jaume's supporters, and almost all traces of Moorish buildings were eradicated (accounting for the paucity of remains today – Menorca was initially spared this, but a similar policy was later introduced there too). However, at the same time, Jaume introduced the Carta de Població (People's Charter – a progressive decree guaranteeing equality before the law), exempted the island from taxation to encourage Catalan immigration and protected Jewish residents in an attempt to encourage trade.

Another of Jaume's innovations was the establishment of a form of Mallorcan government that lasted until the 16th century. It consisted of six jurats (adjudicators), made up of two knights, two merchants, one noble and one peasant, who elected their successors annually.

Before his death, Jaume made the fateful decision to divide his kingdom between his two sons. Jaume II received the Balearics, Roussillon and Montpellier, while Pere (Pedro) II was given Aragón, Catalunya and Valencia. When their father died in 1276, it soon became clear that Pere had no intention of giving up part of what he saw as his rightful realm, bullying Jaume II into submission as his vassal and thereby throwing Jaume into the arms of the French.

When Pere discovered his brother's scheming he vowed to invade Mallorca, though his sudden death left this to his notoriously brutal son Alfons (Alfonso) III. Palma was captured in 1285, Jaume II deposed, and Alfons proceeded to conquer the rest of the island (and, in 1287, Menorca) with a violence that was notable even for the times. Not being the most compassionate of leaders by any stretch of the imagination, on Menorca, Alfons enslaved those Moors who couldn't afford to buy their freedom and threw the old, the sick and the infirm into the sea. All traces of Moorish architecture were eradicated and the capital, Medina Minurka, was renamed Ciutadella.

Following his early death in 1291, Alfons was succeeded by his level-headed brother Jaume, King of Sicily, who had rather more respect for the settlement of Jaume I. In 1298, the partition was restored, with Jaume ruling over Aragón, Catalunya and Valencia, and his uncle Jaume II put back in charge of Mallorca and Menorca. The latter made Sineu his residence and founded a number of towns, including Manacor, Llucmajor, Felanitx and Petra.

The islands prospered, developing their potential as a key trading post in the western Mediterranean and fostering home-grown textile and shipbuilding industries. Jaume II's chief architectural legacy is Palma's stunning cathedral (though it took 500 years to complete). There's some irony in the fact that, built as it was on the site of a demolished mosque, it actually faces Mecca rather than Jerusalem. He also commenced the building of the castle of Bellver outside Palma and was patron to the great Mallorcan poet, scholar, missionary and philosopher Ramón Llull (1235-c1315), a legendary local figure who transformed himself from libidinous womaniser to ascetic saint, eventually dying as a martyr to his goal of converting the Moors (and Jews) to Christianity through reason. The story surrounding his death is that he was stoned by an angry crowd of Muslims in Algeria, although this is unverified. What is certain is that Llull is viewed as a local hero and/or a saint by many on Mallorca and Menorca, and in Catalunya. (On his name day, 29 March, there is a pilgrimage to his grave in Sant Francesc church in Palma.)

Jaume II was succeeded by his sickly son Sanç (Sancho) I in 1311, and then Sanç's ten-year-old nephew Jaume III in 1324. Yet Aragón had a technically stronger claim to the Mallorcan crown than Jaume III, and relations gradually deteriorated until Pere IV of Aragón invaded the Balearics, driving Jaume III out to Roussillon on the mainland. When Jaume attempted to retake Mallorca, he was killed at the Battle of Llucmajor in 1349 and the Balearics lost their independence forever.

UNIFICATION WITH SPAIN AND A LONG DECLINE

It was not until the tourism boom of the last few decades that the Balearics were to again enjoy the level of prosperity they did under Jaume II. As the islands fell under the sway of the Crown of Aragón, so the focus for the nobility moved to the mainland. This, combined with shifting trading conditions (the Portuguese discovered the route to the Indies via the Cape of Good Hope just as the overland routes to the Far East via the Mediterranean became blocked by the growth of Turkish power), meant that the Balearics gradually regressed into a cultural and economic backwater. They became an even smaller cog in an ever bigger machine when the marriage of Fernando V of Aragón and Isabel I of Castilla in 1479 united Christian Spain, and then Columbus's voyages to the Americas in the 1490s

George Sand and Frédéric Chopin. *See p23.*

IN CONTEXT

Site-seeing Guide

The islands' many prehistoric sites share several distinctive features.

TALAYOTS

Talayots are conical, elliptical or quadrangular towers made from small and medium-sized rocks, tapering gradually as they rise. Sizes vary, as do states of dilapidation. The purpose of talayots is subject to debate, though they are believed to have been used as defensive towers or watchtowers, or perhaps a combination of both, since they are often found on high ground and, in some cases, form part of a settlement's defensive wall. Early Balearic islanders were renowned throughout the Mediterranean for their skill with a sling, and the talayots would have given a great height advantage for warding off marauders. It's also possible that the use of talayots changed over time, with some doubling as dwellings or storehouses.

Examples: Mallorca – **Capacorb Vell** (*see p183*), **Hospitalet Vell** (*see p203*); Menorca – **Torre d'en Gaumés** (*see p230*), **Torralba d'en Salort** (*see p221*), **Trépuco** (*see p221*).

TAULAS

Talayots are found on both Mallorca and Menorca, but a unique feature of Menorcan prehistoric sites is the taula, which is often found close to a talayot. This high, altar-like structure consists of two large rectangular rocks, one with a groove cut into it so that it can snugly balance on top of the other to form a 'T'. In some cases, a third, narrow rock stands behind the upright to act as a support, while in others this function is fulfilled, almost symbolically, by a narrow rib carved into the back of the upright.

Taulas undoubtedly had religious significance and are found at the centre of small, usually horseshoe-shaped walled sanctuaries. To the right of the entrance there is often an altar (though these are difficult to identify these days), and large amounts of ash, charred bones and broken amphorae have been found in many, indicating ritual of some sort. Whether the enclosures were covered with a roof or not is subject to some dispute, though, given the height of

Talayot.

Taula.

Naveta.

some of the taulas and the absence of any supporting evidence, this is unlikely.

Examples: Menorca – **Talatí de Dalt** (*see p221*), **Trépuco** (*see p221*), **Torralba d'en Salort** (*see p221*), **Torretrencada** (*see p256*).

NAVETAS

Dating from an earlier era than taulas, navetas are long stone chambers, shaped like the prow of a ship. Some were dwellings (central fireplaces and hearths have been found in many), while others served funerary purposes. This latter type often consists of two chambers, one on top of the other, with a small entrance hall connecting the two.

Examples: Menorca – **Naveta d'es Tudons** (*see p256*), **Rafal Rubí** (*see p221*).

HOUSES, CYCLOPEAN WALLS AND HYPOSTYLE CHAMBERS

Talayots and taulas are usually found at the centre of a settlement featuring one or more stone houses. These houses are generally small, low and little more than man-made caves, with cyclopean walls (made of irregular-sized rocks, without mortar). A wall made in this manner often encircled settlements. Several villages also contain cisterns for rainwater collection carved into the rock. Another common feature is the hypostyle chamber, which may have been used for storage. Its name refers to the use of one or more pillars made of several individual rocks, supporting a roof of stone slabs. This was probably then covered with sticks and vegetation to fill in the gaps.

Examples: Menorca – **Torralba d'en Salort** (hypostyle room; *see p221*), **Torre d'en Gaumés** (hypostyle room; *see p230*), **Son Catlar** (cyclopean encircling wall; *see p256*).

BARRACAS AND PONTS

On Menorca, and particularly at the western end of the island, you will spot circular and rectangular step pyramids specking the countryside. Yet more prehistoric structures, you may suspect, but these actually only date from the mid 19th century, and are (aesthetically rather pleasing) cattle shelters. The circular version is known as a barraca, while the rectangular type is called a pont.

Examples: They are numerous around Ciutadella, particularly heading towards Punta Nati (*see p258*).

meant the focus of European trade shifted almost immediately from the Mediterranean to the Atlantic. To compound the problem, the Spanish Crown forbade the Balearics and Catalunya from trading with the New World.

As the Balearics' wealth slowly evaporated and many of her more dynamic nobles and merchants moved elsewhere, so internal tensions within the declining islands simmered and bubbled. Often it was the Jews who were blamed, sometimes it was the ruling classes. High taxes and shortages of grain eventually ignited a peasants' rebellion in 1521 that led to the capture of Palma and a long period of instability before Charles V (King of Spain and Holy Roman Emperor) restored order. He negotiated the surrender of Palma, and then promptly reneged on his liberal promises, executing hundreds of the rebels.

The 16th century was also a time of renewed aggression from North African and Turkish pirates. The Moors had finally been expelled from Spain in 1492 and this, combined with the increasing presence of the Turks in the Mediterranean, meant that the Balearics were the victims of repeated attacks from Muslim raiders, particularly around the middle of the century. Menorca suffered even more than Mallorca. The notorious Barbarossa sacked Maó in 1535, and the Turks all but obliterated Ciutadella in 1558, taking away 1,000 of its citizens as slaves to Constantinople; such was the devastation that the official sent to rebuild the town initially had to live in a cave. The defeat of the Turks at the naval Battle of Lepanto in 1571 reduced the frequency of the raids, but they continued on and off until the 18th century.Economic matters didn't improve in the 17th and 18th centuries, with plague and emigration depressing the population.

THE 18TH CENTURY AND THE STRUGGLE FOR MENORCA

The power vacuum in the Mediterranean came to be filled increasingly by the British, whose merchant and Royal Navy ships became more and more common around the Balearics in the latter half of the 17th century. Always on the lookout for promising harbours, they saw little of value in Mallorca, but the superb anchorage at Maó on Menorca did catch their eye.

When the Spanish throne fell vacant, the War of the Spanish Succession (1701-14) provided the excuse for the British to take Menorca in 1708, and the following century saw three periods of occupation, only ending when the British renounced their claim to the island in 1802. The Mallorcans had, unfortunately, picked the losing claimant to the throne, and the victor, Philip of Anjou, extracted his revenge by abolishing many of the island's historic privileges, including the right to call itself a kingdom.

For Menorca, however, the 18th century was a time of resurgent hope and prosperity, thanks to the island's importance to the British. True, a foreign power was in charge, but the changes wrought by the occupiers unquestionably improved living conditions for the islanders and brought them into the mainstream of European trade and culture.

The first period of occupation (until 1756) was dominated by the efficiency and benevolence of Menorca's British Governor, Richard Kane (1662-1736). He may have alienated the local aristocracy by moving the capital from Ciutadella to Maó, but he did much to stimulate economic and agricultural growth, as well as improving internal communications (particularly by building a new road between Maó and Ciutadella) and initiating social programmes, including organising the moving of all the public gallows from central squares to the outskirts of each town; shipping prostitutes and undesirables back to the mainland; and ordering the streets and public water cisterns to be cleaned regularly.

At the outbreak of the Seven Years War in 1756, thanks to a mix of complacency and timidity, the French took Menorca from Britain, founding the town of Sant Lluís during their occupation. The island returned to the British at the end of the war in 1763, and there followed a harsher, less productive period of occupation until Menorca was again invaded in 1781, this time by a French-Spanish army, and reverted to Spanish rule. A final period of British occupation from 1798 to 1802 ended with the Treaty of Amiens and the permanent reversion of Menorca to Spanish rule, and to the status of economic and strategic backwater.

'For the islanders tourism has, inevitably, been something of a mixed blessing.'

Mallorca, meanwhile, had slipped into isolation and stagnation. Despite the frequent conflicts that convulsed much of the rest of Europe during the following two centuries, survival was the main concern for the desperately poor inhabitants of the Balearics, many of whom chose to emigrate to the Iberian peninsula or the Americas. One such making the latter journey was the Franciscan friar Junípero Serra (1713-84), born in the central Mallorcan village of Petra, who played a major role in the settlement of California (*see p170* Es Pla).

THE 19TH CENTURY
In the 19th century, romantic travellers were 'rediscovering' Spain, captivated and repelled in equal measure by what many of them (rather patronisingly) saw as an unspoilt (read: primitive) pre-industrial society. An added dash of exoticism was provided by Spain's rich Moorish architectural legacy.

Less easily accessible, and notably lacking in Moorish remains, Mallorca and Menorca didn't feature on the itineraries of many 19th-century travellers. It's for this reason that the visit of the French writer George Sand and her companion, the composer Frédéric Chopin, in 1838-9 is still so loudly proclaimed in all of Mallorca's tourist literature, despite the fact that they passed a miserable winter in Valldemossa, enjoying the scenery but railing against the ignorance of the natives, the food and wine, and the poverty of the island. (Sand's account of their time in Mallorca is detailed in her hugely entertaining and 'perhaps unintentionally unfair account' of their sojourn, *A Winter in Majorca*, which is ironically now prominently on sale in a number of editions and languages all over the island.)

In contrast, a foreigner held in far greater esteem locally is Archduke Ludwig Salvator (1847-1915), the black sheep of the stuffy Austrian Habsburg dynasty, who fell in love with Mallorca on his first visit, barely 20 years old, in 1867. A pioneering ecologist and naturalist, he returned to live on the island's west coast and devoted 22 years of study to compiling his nine-volume *Die Balearen (The Balearics)*, which detailed every aspect of life on the islands. At a time when charcoal burners were deforesting much of Mallorca, the Archduke forbade any cutting down of trees on the lands that he bought there. Olive trees were particularly precious to him, and even when they had passed their best fruit-bearing years, he refused to uproot them. (Mallorca's first nature reserve, the Son Moragues park, was one of his legacies to the island.)

It wasn't until the end of the 19th century that the economic situation on the islands began to pick up. Agriculture slowly started to modernise, and almond production in particular became profitable, while awareness of Catalan culture (reflecting developments in Catalunya) grew, instilling a new pride in Palma's small bourgeoisie and intellectual community. The clutch of fine *modernista* (Catalan art nouveau) buildings in the city is testament to the growing reintegration of the Balearics into European trends in the arts.

But it was to prove a false dawn for the islands. In the last decade of the century phylloxera swept through the Balearics, destroying the emergent wine industry, while the loss of Spain's remaining colonies – Cuba, Puerto Rico and the Philippines – devastated local shipbuilding. Another wave of emigration followed.

THE EARLY 20TH CENTURY AND THE CIVIL WAR
During the first few decades of the 20th century, both Mallorca and Menorca remained economically backward and deeply conservative. Mallorca did produce two nationally important figures during this time, however: the conservative politician and five times Spanish Prime Minister Antoni Maura (who spent all of his political life in Madrid), and

IN CONTEXT

the financier Joan March (1880-1962) who, in true rags-to-riches fashion, was born into poverty in Santa Margalida, yet rose to become the third richest man in the world.

The private Mallorca Tourist Board (Fomento del Turismo de Mallorca) was founded as long ago as 1905 (it still exists today), aiming not just to promote the island as a destination, but to improve its primitive internal communications. Its first project was building a road from Estellencs to Andratx. In 1908, it published the first tourist guide to the island, though tourism remained of minor importance for some decades to come.

The Balearics came through the Spanish Civil War (1936-39) relatively unscathed, with very little fighting taking place on the islands. This was despite the fact that Mallorca and Menorca found themselves on different sides of the conflict. General Goded secured Mallorca for the Nationalist rebels, but General Bosch was not so lucky on Menorca; his troops refused to abandon the Republican government and mutinied. At the end of the war Menorca was isolated as the last outpost of the Republicans. A potential bloodbath was avoided, thanks in large part to the British, who helped negotiate the surrender of the island from HMS *Devonshire*.

THE TOURISM BOOM

Just before the start of the Civil War there appeared the first signs of what was to revolutionise the economy of the Balearics in the second half of the 20th century. In 1929, the Argentinian poet and dandy Adam Diehl opened the Hotel Formentor in north-west Mallorca, attracting socialites and celebrities from the outset, including Churchill, Edward VIII and Charlie Chaplin. Soon Mallorca was becoming well known as a luxury tourist destination – three classy hotels were built in Palma in the early 1930s, and a British presence began to develop on the Bay of Palma.

Between 1936 and 1945 tourism all but ceased. Then, in 1950, the UN lifted its sanctions on Spain; 100,000 tourists visited the island that year, the figure doubling during the following year. The boom in the tourism industry in the Balearics was, however, largely a 1960s phenomenon. One of the chief attractions for holidaymakers was that the islands were considerably cheaper than most European destinations. This coincided with the development of commercial air travel and all-in package holidays.

Palma's Son Sant Joan airport opened in 1960 and, almost immediately, the number of visitors arriving by air started to exceed the number coming by sea. Its growth was remarkable – two-thirds of a million passenger movements in 1960, a million by 1962, four million by 1969 and seven million by 1973. This translated as a rise in little over a decade from a third of a million to almost three million annual visitors. The global recession and oil crisis of 1974 came as a major shock. The tourism industry was devastated, and, for the first time, those involved in the all-but-uncontrolled expansion were given pause for thought. It slowly became clear that things couldn't continue as they had been. The economic boom wasn't sustainable indefinitely; environmental disaster was looming.

The last couple of decades (and particularly the last few years) have seen a slow acceptance of the need for more responsible development, for a less-is-more approach, encouraging higher-spending visitors with classier accommodation, and keeping a tighter lid on the boozed-up bucket-and-spaders.

For the islanders tourism has, inevitably, been a mixed blessing. In some parts what was once the least valuable land on the islands – the rocky and infertile coastal areas – suddenly became the most lucrative, earning its proprietors a fortune but on the downside so much of the work is seasonal that come winter, much of the workforce decamp back to mainland Spain. As a consequence, traditional life has been eroded, property prices are among the highest in Spain, and large swathes of the countryside have been permanently blighted by insensitive development. In 2008, international economic concerns were also already being felt on the islands, with many small businesses – especially in the tourism sector – reporting falling profits, and with a general feeling of financial concern.

Mass tourism made the Balearics and mass tourism threatens to destroy them. Solving this dilemma holds the key to the islands' future.

Testing times for a tourism-dependent economy.

TEXT: JONATHAN COX & TARA STEVENS

Mallorca & Menorca Today

In the first half of the 20th century, the Balearics were one of the poorest areas in Spain; by the end they were one of the richest. That change was almost entirely down to the rise of tourism, which now accounts for some 80 per cent of the islands' GDP. Such heavy reliance on one industry has been the cause of widespread apprehension among islanders in 2008, though, in light of the global economic situation, which has already presented a challenge to many businesses on the islands. Recent reports of an increase in the number of Mallorcans living on the poverty line suggest that the island's newly elevated image hides some darker truths.

However, the islands have seen hard times before, and their governments have so far been forward-thinking in the face of impending economic doom and gloom, especially in comparison to mainland Spain. Current measures include a cap on construction to prevent oversupply of apartments and high-rise hotels; better protection of natural resources; and investment in improving tourist facilities, from cycling routes to business services, in an effort to continue attracting upmarket visitors with euros to spend.

THE ISLANDS' NEW IMAGE

Mallorca's image, in particular, has experienced something of a turnaround in recent years, going from one stained with the excesses of package tours to one characterised by boutique hotels and Michelin-starred restaurants. This has been in no small part down to the efforts of its governments in the 1990s – first the Partido Popular (PP), and then, from 1999, the Socialist coalition. Over the past 15 years, legislation to restrict unchecked coastal development has been put in place, eyesore hotels have been torn down, and fancy marinas and smart new convention centres have sprang up. In addition, Catalan has been made the official first language, with the islands' Catalan names adopted on tourist literature, and local cultural, culinary and literary heritage has been rediscovered and promoted. Legislation has been brought in banning pub crawls, and a 3am closing time has been introduced in many tourist areas. There has also been a ban on any new-build hotels of fewer than three stars. Pla Mirall, a European Union-funded project that involved a general sprucing up of the islands, but in particular Palma and specifically its old town, was launched in the 1990s; old buildings were restored, roads fixed and streets smartened up.

There has also been a drive to improve and market the islands' boutique hotels and *agroturismos* (in 1994 there were 45 rural hotels and *agroturismos* in the Mallorcan interior; by 2008 that number had increased to over 200), as well as trekking and cycling opportunities in previously undersold regions. IBATUR (the Ministry for Tourism) has been attempting to re-establish the island as a quality year-round destination, and locals are realising that quality over quantity is better for the islands in the long run. You could call all this a return to roots. In the 1920s, when tourism first began to take off, Mallorca was mainly a winter escape for artists and writers.

Menorca, meanwhile, has been way ahead of the game when it comes to keeping tourism in check. A desire for preservation of its rural and cultural heritage led to UNESCO declaring the whole island a Biosphere Reserve back in 1993, in recognition of its extraordinary prehistoric heritage, the large number of plants and animals unique to the island and its largely unspoilt rural tradition. The idea behind the label is to limit the impact of mass-market tourism on an area – in Menorca's case, particularly its pristine beaches. Since then the Menorcan government has quietly and systematically created environmental areas that will eventually protect much of the island. In 2008, Mallorca applied for a place on UNESCO's 2009 World Heritage List for its Tramuntana mountain range. It was a blow not to get it, but it is a strong contender for 2010. The question is whether tourist numbers can sustain so many places to stay in the island's interior under the current economic climate.

Protesters in Palma's Plaça Major.

'Forbes recently voted the artists' enclave of Deià one of the best places to live in Europe.'

A SOCIETY IN FLUX

All of this change has required labour, of course, and a lot of it. During the 1990s, the islands began to encourage an influx of immigrant workers, mainly from Africa, as well as parts of Latin America. This was a shock for the predominantly white population, and inevitably led to the usual tensions and covert racism, with a rise in crime conveniently blamed on new workers. This has finally been officially addressed with the Immigrants Attention Plan, which emphasises integration, women's rights, education and employment. The government-run project Linguistic Integration was also launched in 2008, and, although it has some way to go in what is an inherently conservative society, it's a start.

However, there is concern that a downturn in the economy may put further pressure on race relations on the islands. Caritas Mallorca, a branch of the Confederation of Catholic Relief, reported in 2008 that 18 per cent of the Balearic population lives on the poverty line, and predicted that the figure could rise to 30 per cent in the next few years. Union-backed demonstrations are an increasing sight in cities, with protests about the islands' strict labour laws – which make it difficult for small businesses to be competitive through restrictions on opening hours and discounting – taking place in the past couple of years.

GOING FOR GOLD

There are many reasons to remain cheerful, however. European budget airline travellers made Mallorca the top destination in 2008, drawing in 4.9 million passengers (many of whom stayed in Palma, now one of Europe's most popular city break destinations). There has also been a 50 per cent increase in business travellers coming to the island for conventions and meetings in the last four years. And business magazine Forbes recently voted the artists' and celebrity enclave of Deià, on Mallorca's west coast, one of the best places to live in Europe. The islands have generally faired better than the rest of Spain in property market terms too; while the mainland has seen property prices drop by around nine per cent in the past year, the Balearics have only witnessed a fall of 4.4 per cent.

Meanwhile, the Mallorcan authorities push onwards with concrete plans to continue improving the island's upmarket tourism infrastructure. Palma's swanky new Congress Palace will open in the spring of 2011; designed by Spaniard Francisco Mangado as the contemporary architectural sister to the cathedral, with the same stunning views, it will boast facilities for more than 2,000 business travellers. This is complimented by the new Hilton Sa Torre Conference Centre in nearby Llucmajor, and, on the other side of the bay, the Blau Porto Petro Conference Centre.

Mallorca's first mega yacht facility is also scheduled for completion in Port Adriano in spring 2009; the commercial zone of gourmet restaurants, luxury shopping and a state-of-the-art sailing school is being designed by Philippe Starck. And Palma's Teatro Principal reopened its doors in 2007 after a six year closure and a €21-million refurbishment.

There's also been a huge push to promote the island as a favourite training ground for athletes, with Britain's cycling, swimming and sailing teams training here prior to the 2008 Beijing Olympics. Mallorca has 260 kilometres of dedicated cycling routes, attracting 87,000 cyclists a year, making it one of the top cycling destinations in Europe. It's also increasingly popular for professional golf tournaments – boasting 21 world-class greens – and for walkers, with recently established 'New Nordic' (hiking with sticks) routes around Alcúdia, and the signposting of ancient stonewall routes and coastal paths.

If Menorca struggles to compete on the business side, and is too gentle to attract hardcore sporting types, at least its pristine beauty and charm stand it in good stead as visitors, partly drawn by the new-found hype of its big sister, begin to discover its magic.

IN CONTEXT

Rustic traditions rule, with pork, pa amb oli and pastries still the mainstays of local cuisine.

TEXT: JONATHAN COX

Food & Drink

Mallorcan and Menorcan cuisine has its roots firmly in rustic traditions, with a sprinkling of Arab influences, and is based around the classic trinity of Mediterranean ingredients – olive oil, garlic and tomatoes. At first glance, there doesn't seem much to distinguish the regional cuisine of the Balearics from mainland Spanish cuisine. Scratch the surface, though, and you'll find it to be rich and varied, with some surprising flavour combinations and distinctive dishes.

Much of the islands' cuisine derives from 'peasant' food – local, simple and fresh, with many dishes slow-cooked at low temperatures in a shallow casserole dish known as a *greixonera*. For many years, such food was derided by visitors and better-off locals. But although the holiday resorts are often still characterised by a dispiriting morass of tacky eateries, island food has crept back on to other menus in the Balearics ever since Spain's autonomous regions began to rediscover their individual cultural heritages. You'll now find it, often with a contemporary gloss, at even the most upmarket establishments. And standards are high: five Mallorcan restaurants have Michelin stars.

> *'Nearly every bar and restaurant has a leg of air-dried ham on display, either on the bar or suspended in great shanks from the ceiling.'*

PORK

Along with all its variations, pork (*porc/cerdo*) is the most common meat on local dinner tables, and has been the staple meat on the islands for many years. Roast suckling pig is the centrepiece of most island fiestas, and even today many villages celebrate their annual *matances* – pig slaughter. This ancient ritual, which brings together everyone in the community, all but died out as tourism took hold on the islands, but has now been revived. If you're not averse to gallons of blood and some hideous squealing, it's worth catching.

Matances take place in winter, after the pig has been fattened up all year, and historically are intended to provide food for the family until spring. For this reason no part of the pig is left unused, and you'll find everything from offal to trotters and ears ending up in dishes, most famously in *frit Mallorquí/frito Mallorquín* – a flavoursome fry-up of potatoes, vegetables and a variety of pork (or lamb) unmentionables, spiked with wild fennel and mint. Another popular local dish is *llom/lomo con col*: pork loin stuffed with *sobrassada* (*see below*) and rolled in cabbage leaves, a dish that you'll find on the menus of many rural restaurants. Pork lard (*saïm/manteca*) and salted pork belly (*xuia/panceta*) are frequently used in Balearic dishes; the former is used in the spiral-shaped *ensaïmada*, the quintessential pastry of both islands.

Various breeds of pig are raised on the islands, but the distinctive local porker is a black variety (*porc negre Mallorquí*), and you'll find it served *fregit/frito* (fried) or *rostit/asada* (roasted), as *pilotes/albóndigas* (meatballs), *solomillo* (steak), *llom/lomo* (loin), *costelletes* (chops) and various types of sausage (*embotits/embutidos*), such as *sobrassada* (*see below*), *butifarra/butifarrón* (a black pudding-like sausage, flavoured with fennel and allspice or cinnamon), *camaiot* (a less bloody, fattier *butifarra*, made with diced rather than minced meat) and *salxitxó/salchichón* (like chorizo, but with black pepper rather than paprika).

Sobrassada/sobrasada is one of the Balearics' best-known products (*see also p84* **Made in Mallorca & Menorca**). This spreadable, rich, chorizo-like sausage is made of cured pork, paprika, salt and seasoning. It comes in all shapes and sizes, and in spicy and mild versions; it can be eaten raw, simply slathered on crusty bread, or cooked, sometimes with honey. There are around 40 registered makers of *sobrassada* on Mallorca, qualifying for the quality mark of the Indicació Geogràfica Protegida. The best (and by far the most expensive) variety is labelled '*Sobrassada de Mallorca de Cerdo Negro*' and is made from the island's indigenous black pig.

You'll also find that nearly every bar and restaurant has a leg of air-dried ham (*pernil salat/jamón*) on display, either on the bar or suspended in great shanks from the ceiling. The standard serrano ham (*pernil serrà/jamón serrano*) is the cheapest and is what usually ends up in baguette sandwiches (*bocadillos*). Ham from Jabugo in Andalucía is generally regarded as the finest and is the most expensive. This is the prized *pata negra*, or *jamón ibérico*, made from free-range black pigs fed only on acorns.

OTHER MEATS

Mallorcan lamb (*xai or be/cordero*) is another popular meat, often served in chunks, roasted with garlic and olive oil. Local breeds are small and sturdy animals, lending themselves perfectly to the slow cooking favoured locally. *Cordero lechal* (suckling lamb) is most commonly served as *palatillas* (shoulders) and *piernas* (legs), roasted over rosemary sprigs and garlic cloves in a gentle oven until tender.

IN CONTEXT

Beef (*bou/buey*), particularly veal (*vedella/ternera*), again comes in numerous forms on the islands, such as *solomillo* (steak), *estofat de vedella* (stew) and *fricandó* (casserole). It's likely to be imported.

Game, such as rabbit (*conill/conejo*), pheasant (*faisà/faisán*), partridge (*perdiu/perdiz*) and quail (*guatllere/cordoniz*), is also popular, and you'll find classic dishes such as *conill alioli* (chargrilled rabbit smothered with garlic mayonnaise), *conill encebollado* (rabbit stewed with onions, olive oil and white wine), *perdiu a la vinagreta* (partridge in a vinegar-based sauce) and *guatllere amb figes* (quail with figs) served in the interior of both Mallorca and Menorca. Snails (*caragols/caracoles*) are also very popular locally.

Chicken (*pollastre/pollo*) is not a particularly favoured meat on the islands, but you will sometimes find it combined with seafood or stuffed with prawns and cooked in cava.

FISH AND SEAFOOD

Seafood is, not surprisingly, enormously popular on Mallorca and Menorca. There is a local fishing industry, but it's small; demand is such that most fresh fish is imported, usually from Galicia. A classic Balearic dish is *caldereta de llagosta*, popular on both islands and originating from Fornells in the north of Menorca. It's a simple but rich and flavoursome spiny lobster stew, made with tomatoes and onions. (It's also ruinously expensive, with prices of around €40 per portion not unusual.) The lobster for this dish is usually imported, but if you order it from June to August you could be in luck and get a local creature.

Local fish (*peix/pescados*) include dolphin fish (*llampuga/lampuga* – a great-tasting seasonal fish with only a very short season from late August to October), sea bass (*llop/lubina*), sea bream (*besuc/besugo*), monkfish (*rap/rape*), grouper (*anfós or nero/ mero*), gilthead bream (*orada* or *daurada/dorada*) and red scorpion fish (*cap roig*), which you'll find served in a variety of ways, the most popular of which is simply *a la plantxa/a la plancha* (grilled on a hot metal plate), usually with a splash of olive oil, garlic and parsley. More elaborate methods include *al forn/al horno* (baked), which is usually confined to sea bass baked in salt. Other popular fish are anchovies (*boquerónes/anchovas*), sardines (*sardinas* or *alatxas/sardinas* or *alachas*), John Dory (*gall/gallo de San Pedro*) and red mullet (*molls/salmonetes*).

Octopus (*pop/pulpo*) is usually prepared Galician-style *a la feria*, lightly grilled and sprinkled with rock salt, oil and paprika and served on a wooden platter. Eels (*anguiles*), found in the S'Albufera marshes in northern Mallorca, are an island delicacy and pop up in a number of dishes, including *greixonera d'anguiles* (eel stew) and *espinagada*, an eel and spinach pasty-type delicacy from Sa Pobla. Mussels (*musclos/mejillones*) are usually *al vapor* (steamed) or *marinera* (in a light cream sauce). Crab (*cranc/cangrejo*) is not native, but is available in the more upmarket restaurants, as is lobster (*llamàntol/ bogavante*). Cockles (*escopinyes/berberechos*) and clams (*cloïsses/almejas*) are also commonplace on the islands.

The most popular (and inexpensive) seafood is often squid (*calamars/calamares*), which comes *a la romana* (fried in batter), *en su tinta* (in its own ink) or *farcits* (stuffed), and prawns (*gambes/gambas*), which are cooked in a variety of ways – particularly *al ajilla/ajo* (in garlic) and *a la plantxa*. Also ubiquitous is salt cod (*bacallà/bacalao*), which, when served *a la Mallorquina*, comes baked with layers of fried potatoes, tomatoes and swiss chard mixed with raisins, pine nuts, spring onions and olive oil. It's also a popular choice in many tapas bars, often coming in the form of *croquetas de bacalao* (salt-cod croquettes).

VEGETABLES, RICE & PASTA

Compared with the Spanish mainland, vegetables (*verdures/legumbres*) do at least play a part in local cuisine, rather than being consigned to a side dish. Having said that, vegetarians and vegans are not particularly well catered for and you'll find just a handful of vegetarian restaurants on the islands. It's also worth noting that many ostensibly vegetable-only dishes and salads come sprinkled with bits of *jamón*.

Sobrassada shop, Palma.

The tomato (*tomàquet* or *tomàtiga/tomate*) is probably the most ubiquitous vegetable, used as the basis for many local dishes, as well as being smeared on bread in *pa amb oli* (see p32) and as a staple in salads. The potato (*patate/patata*) is used in hearty *frito* dishes and crops up in *tumbet*, the characteristic local dish of aubergine (*albergínia/ berenjena*), potato and courgette (*carabassó/calabacín*), lightly fried in olive oil, then layered with a freshly made tomato sauce and finished off in the oven. On Menorca it is often made with pumpkin.

Other commonly encountered vegetables include the onion (*ceba/cebolla*), artichoke (*carxofa/alcachofa*), mushroom (*xampinyons/champiñones*), asparagus (*espàrrec/ espárrago*), cabbage (*col*), cauliflower (*colflori/coliflor*), carrot (*pastanaga/zanahoria* – the local variety is purple), red and green pepper (*pebre/pimiento*), Swiss chard (*bledes/acelgas*) and spinach (*espinacs/espinacas*). The latter is the basis of a number of dishes, including *espinacs a la Catalana* (spinach, raisins and pine nuts). A popular starter is *escalivada*, a grilled pepper and aubergine salad, while summer sees the appearance of *trempó*, a huge salad based on onion, pale green peppers and tomatoes and any number of other ingredients.

Northern Mallorca's S'Albufera marshes are famous for their rice (*arròs/arroz*). *Arròs bomba* is a round Spanish variety that has excellent cooking qualities and a robust flavour. It is perfect for *arròs brut*, a rustic dish of meat, game and vegetables flavoured with *sobrassada* and *butifarra*; *arròs negro*, a spectacular black rice dish flavoured with cuttlefish and coloured with its ink; or Spain's most famous dish, paella.

Pasta, traditionally cheaper than rice, became widespread on the impoverished islands before tourism transformed the economy of the Balearics, and remains a staple today. The most popular shape is *fideus*, looking like short bits of spaghetti.

FRUIT AND NUTS

Locals are more likely to end a meal with a bowl of fruit than a dessert. The islands produce excellent figs (*figas/higos*), oranges (*taronjas/naranjas*), almonds (*ametllas/almendras*), apricots (*albercocs/albaricoques*), apples (*pomas/manzanas*), pomegranates (*magranas/granadas*) and melons (*melós/melones*).

CHEESE AND MAYONNAISE

The British left a lasting legacy on the Menorcan diet with the introduction of Friesian cattle. This breed produces, among other dairy products, Menorcan cheese (*formatge/queso*), a mixture of sun-ripened herbs and sea salt, coated with oil and paprika, and mixed with cream. Known generically as *queso Mahón*, its unique taste has been honoured with a *Denominació de Origen*, testifying to its quality. It comes in semi- and fully cured varieties. Mallorca produces a similar cheese in Campos, but it does not have the same piquancy as *queso Mahón*.

Menorca's capital Maó (or Mahón as it was previously known) also gave its name to mayonnaise, the classic emulsion of olive oil and raw egg yolks. It probably owes its origin to the culinary experimentation of the French occupiers of Menorca in the mid 18th century (*see also p210*).

BREAD AND OLIVE OIL

Simple dishes are often the best, and *pa amb oli* (pronounced 'pámbolly'), the most common light lunch in Mallorca, is a case in point: local brown bread (*pa Mallorquí*) and

Ensaïmadas.

'Ask a Mallorcan or Menorcan what foodstuff best represents the islands and they are most likely to reply, "the ensaïmada".'

olive oil. To refine it slightly, the bread is rubbed with garlic and tomato, and in many places you'll find it served with a variety of toppings – such as *jamón*, *chorizo* and local cheeses – making a meal in itself. Bread is also the centrepiece of another famed Mallorcan dish: *sopes mallorquines/sopas mallorquinas*. This typically robust winter stew made from stale bread and braised vegetables is, despite its name, not a soup, as the bread absorbs all the liquid. (In Catalan '*sope*' refers not to the soup, but to the slices of bread.)

Olive oil, meanwhile, is fast becoming Mallorca's 'liquid gold', following a push by producers in recent years, with Denomination of Origin regulations now ensuring consistently high standards, and with *oleoturismo* (olive oil tourism) a growing trend.

PASTRIES AND DESSERTS

Ask a Mallorcan or Menorcan what foodstuff best represents the islands and they are likely to reply, 'the ensaïmada', Spain's answer to the croissant (*see also p84* **Made in Mallorca & Menorca**). This versatile, light, fluffy-textured spiral pastry is dusted with icing sugar and comes in a variety of sizes, from bite-sized portions to the cake-sized ones you see people lugging on to planes. Locals eat *ensaïmadas* at breakfast, spread them with *sobrassada* as a savoury snack or serve them stuffed with nuts and fruits and covered in cream as a dessert. Other popular sweet pastries are *bunyols* (doughnuts) and *robiols* and *crespells* (both particularly popular at Easter).

Savoury pastries include the pies found throughout Spain known as *empanadas*, which come with various fillings, and *cocarroi*, the most typical version of which is filled with Swiss chard, raisins and pine nuts. The islands also have their own version of pizza (*coca*), differing from its Italian cousin in never having a tomato sauce base or cheese or meat toppings – its most popular form is covered in peppers. A sweet version of *coca* is made in Valldemossa.

Popular desserts include *greixonera de brosat*, a cream cheese tart, and *gató de almendra*, a light almond sponge cake. You might also want to try *granissats*, crushed ice flavoured with citrus fruit. Every *patisseria* and *xocolaterie* is stuffed full of local sweets such as chocolate and nougat. Generally, though, you'll see the same unimaginative desserts in the Balearics as you will throughout Spain. Most establishments will offer flan (crème caramel), *arroz con leche* (cold rice pudding), *natillas* (cold custard), *helado* (ice-cream; the local Menorcan brand, sold all over Spain), fresh fruit and a plate of cheese with *membrillo* (quince jelly).

DRINK

Local wine has enjoyed something of a renaissance of late and, though most cannot match an established Rioja, they hold their own well. *See p162* **Biniculture**.

Mallorca has a long tradition of making anise-based herbal liqueurs (*herbes/hierbas*), with production centred on the town of Bunyola. There are three broad types – *dolces* (sweet), *seques* (dry) and *mesclades* (a mix of both).

Menorca is famous for its gin production, which was introduced by the British during their 18th-century occupation of the island. The most famous brand is Xoriguer, which comes from the distillery of the same name in Maó. It's served up in a variety of ways, the most popular being *pomada*, gin with cloudy lemonade; the perfect refreshing drink for a hot Balearic summer's day.

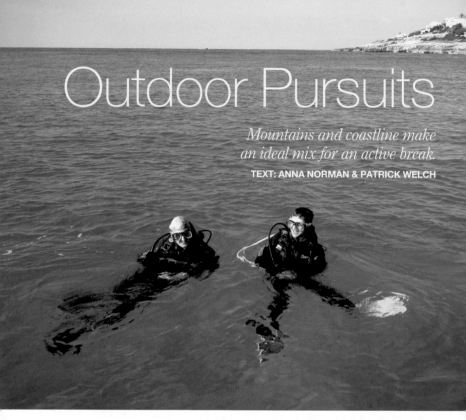

Outdoor Pursuits

Mountains and coastline make
an ideal mix for an active break.

TEXT: ANNA NORMAN & PATRICK WELCH

From the air they might look small and parched, and from the beach they may appear rather marred by whitewashed concrete and parasols. But if you head away from the built-up resorts, Mallorca and Menorca reveal an unexpected profusion of often dramatic landscapes, as well as a wealth of flora and notable fauna in the form of birdlife.

The islands are the visible high points of submerged mountains, a continuation of the Andalucían range in mainland southern Spain, with one dramatic set of peaks remaining – the Serra de Tramuntana, a towering, craggy 90-kilometre (56-mile) long chain of mountains that lies along Mallorca's west coast. With dramatic cliff-faces and challenging terrain, as well as forests of holm oak and pines, beautiful sea views and (further inland) an increasing number of vineyards, this is nirvana for walkers, cyclists and climbers.

Menorca is less than a fifth the size of Mallorca, but has more than 200 kilometres (125 miles) of coastline and some of the best diving in the Med. Its small size makes it easily accessible and thus particularly appealing for less ambitious, more low-key hikers and cyclists.

GETTING STARTED

The Mallorcan government is behind a drive to promote cyclotourism and hiking, in particular, as part of its plan to encourage a 'better breed' of tourist to the island. More and more operators and information are appearing around the island. The websites www.infomallorca.net, www.illesbalears.es and www.mallorcaweb.com have information on bike hire and other sports equipment rental, with PDF versions of brochures that can be downloaded. For info on outdoor activities in Menorca, visit www.enmenorca.org, which has information in English about everything from sailing to horseriding to hiking.

Only relatively recently have the Balearic governments shown an awareness of the fragility of the islands' ecosystems, prompted by a science and conservation NGO founded in 1973 – GOB, the **Grup Balear d'Ornitologia i Defensa de la Naturalesa** (www.gobmallorca.com). There are eight higher-status conservation areas, known as **Parcs Naturals**: seven are on or just off Mallorca, with the other (S'Albufera des Grau; *see p240*) on Menorca. The GOB wants the whole of the Serra de Tramuntana to become a Parc Natural, but there are conflicting interests in such a tourism-dependent archipelago.

A number of UK-based companies offer all-in adventure and walking holidays to Mallorca. One of the best is **Tall Stories** (Brassey House, New Zealand Avenue, Walton-on-Thames, Surrey KT12 1QD, from the UK 01932 252002, www.tallstories.co.uk), which runs one-week multi-sport trips in northern Mallorca, featuring coasteering (scrambling, abseiling and climbing around the coast), as well as sea kayaking, snorkelling, diving, canyoning and sailing. Other good companies include **Explore** (1 Frederick Street, Aldershot, Hampshire GU11 1LQ, from the UK 0870 333 4001, www.explore.co.uk), which organises week-long walking holidays in the Tramuntana mountains, and **Headwater** (The Old School House, Chester Road, Castle, Northwich, Cheshire CW8 1LE, from the UK 01606 720033, www.headwater.com), which offers cycling and walking trips. **Balearic Discovery** (C/Jaime Solivellas 11, Selva, 971 87 53 95, www.balearicdiscovery.com) tailor-makes holidays that include caving, ballooning, canyoning, cycling, deep-sea fishing, diving, riding and parapenting (leaping off the side of a mountain).

HIKING & CLIMBING

The Serra de Tramuntana in Mallorca is walking and climbing paradise, with well-marked trails, mountain refuges in which to spend the night and spectacular views at every turn. Throughout the guide we've highlighted a selection of short walks on both the islands that make an ideal afternoon's excursion or day's slow trek. As well as wonderful vistas, the islands are home to a considerable range of landscapes and flora, which are best experienced on foot. On both islands, but especially on Menorca, look out for wild flowers – orchids, poppies and gladioli – and patches of wild asparagus, heather, myrtle and bramble. In places like Menorca's Cala Galdana gorge – a great place for twitchers (*see p230*) – the air is filled with the sweet scent of flowers and plants, with photogenic beauties like the pig's ear and sawfly species of orchid, which in turn attract hordes of butterflies and bees. Many hikers visit Mallorca from late January to early March to coincide with the almond blossom; almonds are an important crop in the Balearics, and the island's four million almond trees are a beautiful sight when in bloom.

Popular routes on Mallorca include the well-signalled **Pedra en Sec** (Dry Stone) route and the **Artà-Lluc** path (the latest route to be signposted) in the Tramuntana mountains, and plans are in place, as part of the government's drive to promote hiking tourism, to mark out a route between the district of Andratx, on the western side of the mountain range, and the district of Pollença, on the eastern edge. Maps and information on these and other routes can be found on the website of the **Consell de Mallorca**; visit www.conselldemallorca.net/mediambient/pedra. **Sóller**, with its awesome backdrop of encircling peaks, is a popular base for hikers; its home to English-run operator **Tramuntana Tours** (C/Lluna 72, 971 63 24 23, www.tramuntanatours.com), which, as well as selling a comprehensive selection of hiking (and cycling) gear, can also organise guided treks and cycling tours.

IN CONTEXT

CYCLING

Cycling is now very popular on the islands, with the Balearic archipelago receiving around 80,000 cyclotourists a year. Most head to Mallorca: to its flat interior and to the mountains of the Serra de Tramuntana, a more adventurous route, with steep climbs and incredible views. The Serra de Llevant's lower peaks, in the east of Mallorca, are less challenging and more accessible for the novice. There is a well-signposted network of cycling routes on the island, with some 1,250 kilometres of road that's now been adapted for bikes; around 675 kilometres of these tracks are on secondary or minor roads.

Menorca's flatter terrain makes it less challenging for the serious cyclist, but offers some lovely routes to small coves. Be warned: cycling in the high summer heat is inadvisable.

For further information and route maps get hold of the **Guia del Ciclista** map from tourist offices. The website www.balearnet.com/mallorca/biking.htm details ten circular cycling routes on Mallorca.There are bike rental places all over the islands, including **Velo Sport Team Mallorca** (971 58 05 41, mobile 626 27 29 09, www.velosportmallorca.com), which can deliver bikes anywhere on Mallorca (call in advance). Many rural hotels and *agroturismos* also have bikes for guests to use.

GOLF

Golf is big business in Mallorca, and growing (there's also one course on Menorca). Book tee times well in advance during the official season (October to May), and in summer aim for an early tee. Wear a decent pair of shorts/trousers and a collared shirt (ladies too). Most courses don't ask to see a handicap certificate but it's something you should have just in case (Golf Andratx does like to see them). Most courses have clubs for hire and there are several driving ranges. If you're new to the game, there are good academies at the Marriott and Son Vida. For reservations and further info, see www.mallorcaonline.com, www.allspaingolf.com and www.magoco.com; and for a list of golf courses, see p263.

HORSERIDING

Horsemanship on the Balearics is well established and both Mallorca and Menorca have their own recognised thoroughbreds; Menorca, in particular, is nigh-on equine-obsessed and its black pure breeds take centre stage in most public celebrations. (They are somewhat hot-blooded, and infamous for their stamping and snorting, however; you'd have to be a loon to try and ride one.)

'There's a network of cycling routes on Mallorca, with 1,250 kilometres of road adapted for bikes.'

Horseriding is popular on both islands, and there are numerous stables and schools where you can have lessons and hire horses. Most schools offer ponies for kids, guides for tours and schooling for the rusty or novices, and both islands are criss-crossed with bridle paths, though the terrain varies enormously. The Tramuntana's lower slopes and those of the Serra de Llevant offer the best terrain for trekking on Mallorca. Menorca's flatter landscape lends itself to easy riding, particularly on the Camí de Cavalls bridle path.

For general information and a list of all riding clubs on the islands, contact the **Federació Hípica de les Illes Balears** (Recinto Ferial d'Es Mercadal, Menorca, 971 15 42 25, www.hipicabaleares.com). A list of the riding stables can be found on *p263*.

BIRDWATCHING & WILDLIFE

In terms of fauna, these days you'll be lucky to spy a semi-feral goat, and even then it will be ringing a bell so that the owner can find it when milking or market day comes around. Inedible fauna has been almost wiped out, first by farmers and then by tourism-related schemes, and the best you can hope for is a field rat, maybe a weasel, or if you are really lucky, a genet (a small wild cat). Birdlife, however, has to some extent managed to fly above and around much of the impact of *Homo sapiens turisticus*.

Keen twitchers tell of seeing up to 60 species of bird while on two-week holidays. As well as the European standards – sparrows, doves, ducks and the like – there are also purple, grey and night herons, greater flamingos, several varieties of plover, egrets and reed warblers, all of them happy residents of, or migrants to, the remaining *albuferas* (marshlands). There have also been sightings of the ultra-rare black vulture – especially around the highest peaks of the Tramuntana – as well as Audouin's gull, moustached warbler and marmora's warbler.

If you've only got time for one birding stop, **Pollença** in Mallorca is a wise option. The nearby **S'Albufera** marsh (*see p142*), the mountains of the Serra de Tramuntana and the cliffs and open seas off Formentor provide three typical habitats for Balearic birds. The

small museum at S'Albufera is a useful introduction to the charms and challenges of the resilient Mallorcan wetlands, while the park's website provides a list of species sighted locally every two weeks. Alternatively, on Menorca, the four-kilometre stretch of waterland on the eastern coast – comprising **S'Albufera des Grau** (*see p240*), **Illa d'en Colom** (*see p240*) and **Cap de Favaritx** (*see p241*) – is an attractive setting for spotting birds.

SAILING & WATERSPORTS

For many visitors, this is what Mallorca and Menorca are all about. Mallorca alone has 20,000 berths available in 30 marinas; Menorca has six marinas. For information on marinas, get hold of a copy of the leaflet *España Nautica: Baleares* from tourist offices.

Some of the biggest yachts in the world berth here, including that of the King of Spain, who times his annual visit for August's **Copa del Rey** (King's Cup), the most prestigious Mediterranean sailing event in the calendar. Menorca runs a number of regattas year-round, including the well-known **Almirante Ferragut de Snipes National Trophy**, organised by four local clubs.

There are countless sailing clubs on both islands and spots where you can rent a boat for a day or longer. The **Escuela Nacional de Vela de Calanova** (Avda. Joan Miró 327, Palma, 971 40 25 12, www.calanova.caib.es) and **Sail & Surf Pollença** (Passeig Sara Legui 134, Pollença, 971 86 53 46, www.sailsurf.de) are the top sailing schools on the islands. The latter also offers windsurfing for beginners. The **Federación Balear de Vela** (Balearics Sailing Federation, C/Joan Miró 327, Palma, 971 40 24 12, www.federacion balearvela.org) has information about sailing in the islands. Those planning to base themselves in or around Palma should check out www.realclubnauticopalma.com.

DIVING

The diving off Mallorca is not spectacular. Expect the usual Mediterranean topography of granite boulders and seaweed, with sparse marine life – the odd octopus, moray eel and some local fish species. Perhaps the best spot is around the island of **Sa Dragonera** *see p106*) off the south-west tip, where the water is crystal clear.

Menorca, however, is a completely different story, and offers some of the finest diving in the Med, with visibility of up to 30 metres (100 feet). The best time to go is late in the high season – mid August and September – when the sea has warmed sufficiently and you'll find temperatures of up to 25 degrees centigrade. All the diving centres offer 'try dives', but more experienced divers will inevitably get the more out of the organised trips. There's *Francisquita*, a fully intact cargo ship sitting at 50 metres (164 feet) deep; the *Malakoff* wreck, a British-built steamer that made her final voyage in 1928, and the world-famous Cathedral Cavern, a vast cave with a dramatic turquoise entrance and boulder-strewn floor.

For more information, contact the **Federación Balear de Actividades Subacuáticas** (C/Joan Miro 327, 971 70 87 85, www.fbdas.com); its Menorcan branch is at C/Camí de Baix, Ciutadella (971 38 39 18).

Calendar

Traditional festivities still make up the bulk of the Balearic calendar.

Mallorca and Menorca are not destinations where you can expect to find vibrant international cultural scenes, with both islands having jumped almost overnight from isolated agricultural backwaters to mass market tourist destinations. The old seasonal cycles tied to patron saints, along with Easter, Christmas and New Year, still underlie most popular mass gatherings. Semana Santa is still a cultural and social highlight with its warm-up Carnaval, a subdued affair in comparison with its Latin American counterparts, although Palma's Sa Rua procession, just before Lent, attracts as many as 25,000 spectators and 5,000 participants who dance down the streets.

In the past decade, however, various music festivals have sprung up across the islands; summer's Pollença music festival is especially well regarded, while Palma's Jazz Voyeur festival now attracts high-profile names. Events such as these are in keeping with the islands' drive to move tourism away from the lairy hedonism that has tarred their reputations for years. You won't find the myriad rock festivals that you'll find over on the mainland. What you will find, though, is ballet, opera, a lot of jazz, internationally renowned boating regattas and, in Mallorca, a first-class art festival: Nit de l'Art.

Calendar

January-March

Los Reyes Magos

Across Spain. **Date** 6 Jan.
Spaniards celebrate *Los Reyes Magos* (The Magi), preceded the night before in Palma by the *Cabalgata de los Reyes Magos* (Horse Ride of the Magi); three costumed figures arrive by sea into the harbour, lit up by flaming torches and fireworks, and lead a procession to Plaça Cort.

Beneides de Sant Antoni

Sa Pobla. **Date** Jan.
Among the most lavish in dress and dramatic effect of all the saintly festivals is the Beneides de Sant Antoni (St Anthony's Eve, 16 Jan) in Sa Pobla (also at Artà, Manacor and Sant Joan) – with bonfires to burn away sin, pig sacrifices and brass bands. It's also a major event in Maó, where St Anthony is the patron saint.

Fira del Fang

Marratxi. **Date** Mar.
Marratxi is the location for the Fira del Fang (Ceramics Fair), with displays of bowls, pots, pipes and the *siurells* – white figurines decorated with colourful dots – that inspired Miró. Handicraft fairs often accompany food events, and many villages host agricultural-artisanal fairs, especially in September, when Manacor, Felanitx, Petra and Alaró all show off their wares.

Festa del Pa i del Peix

Palma. **Date** Mar/Apr.
The Festival of Bread and Fish commemorates the feeding of the 5,000, and takes place on the last Sunday before Easter.

Bullfighting season

Across Spain. **Date** Mar-Oct.
The bullfighting season kicks off in March, and there is an irregular calendar of fights between March and October. There are bullrings at Palma (a 14,000-seater built in 1929; *see p82*), Muro (971 53 73 29), Alcúdia (971 54 79 03), Inca (971 50 00 87) and Felanitx (971 58 05 57), presenting both experienced matadors and *novilleros* (novices). Responding to the tourist market, Alcúdia hosts mock bullfights on Thursdays with no blood-letting.

Semana Santa

Across Spain. **Date** 5-13 Apr 2009; 28 Mar-4 Apr 2010.
Palm Sunday marks the beginning of Semana Santa, and there are processions in all the parishes, with Palma's endless march around the Rambla de los Duques de Palma (prior to High Mass) by far the most impressive. On Good Friday, Christ figures in all the parishes are symbolically buried in sepulchres – Pollença's *Davallament* (Descent from the Cross) ceremony is the one to see.

April-June

Jazz Voyeur Festival

Palma (971 90 52 92/www.jazzvoyeur festival.com). **Date** Apr-Dec.
A hugely popular jazz-slanted event, the Jazz Voyeur Festival was held for the first time in 2004 and was so successful it was extended over nine months in 2008, featuring Diana Krall, Cuban jazz masters Bebo and Chucho Valdes, and Mississippi Mass Gospel. Concerts are held at venues such as Calvia's Casino and the Auditorium (*see p82*) and Jazz Voyeur club (*see p79*) in Palma.

Feast of Trinity

Across Spain. **Date** May/June.
The Feast of Trinity, the week before Whit Sunday, traditionally marked the beginning of the fishing season. In Port d'Alcúdia this is maintained with a festival honouring St Peter – the Galilean fisherman-disciple – and at the end of June in Maó, games, dancing and old sailing boats celebrate the same feast day.

Deia's Classical Music Festival

Deia (971 63 91 78/mobile 678 98 95 36/ www.dimf.com/www.soundpost.org). **Date** May-Sept.
A series of concerts held at Son Maroig (*see p119*), which belonged to Archduke Ludwig Salvator (known locally as Luis Salvator; *see p23*), featuring world-class orchestras and soloists.

Ball de les Àguiles

Pollença. **Date** 11 June.
Pollença is the setting for a major Corpus Christi procession through the streets called the *Ball de les Àguiles* (Dance of the Eagles).

Sant Joan de Missa

Ciutadella. **Date** late June.
Menorca's religious parties are characterised by the presence of horses, the symbol of *festes* on the island. Equestrian performances called *jaleos* – with horses rearing up in the town's squares and charging down the streets – are set to the beat of a tambor.

Mallorca Ballet Season

Auditorium de Palma, Palma (www.auditorium-pm.com). **Date** June-Feb.
The Auditorium de Palma's ballet season (www.temporadadeballet.es) attracts major classical companies from overseas, as well as new and experimental dance troupes from the islands.

July-Sept

Bellver Festival

Palma (www.simfonicadebalears.com). **Date** July.
Palma's castle provides a backdrop for a series of concerts throughout July and August.

IN CONTEXT

Art Attack Nit de l'Art

Art boffins, people-watching and cava quaffing – welcome to 'Art Night'.

Now in its 11th year, the Mallorcan capital's annual **Nit de l'Art** (Art Night; *see p42*) – where around 30 galleries, cultural institutions and museums open their doors to the public in the evening for free – is a sure sign that the capital's art scene is finally making waves, in a city that's still rather lacklustre when it comes to cultural events. Record numbers of *Palmesanos* – as well as Mallorcans from all over the island – turned out for the event in 2008.

Over the past few years, the event, which is held on the third Thursday of September and organised mainly by the Associació Independent de Galeries d'Art de Balears (AIGAB) and Art Palma Contemporani Associació de Galeristes, has gone from strength to strength. There's now more high-profile contemporary work – both home-grown and foreign – than ever before, as well as a range of street performances and installations alongside the art shows.

Nit de l'Art 2008 saw tango dancing on 'Es Born', art and craft fairs in Plaça Mercat, interactive video installations on C/Unió and live musicians at various spots around the city. It generated quite a buzz; as one *palmesano* put it, 'Not much happens in Palma, but on Nit de l'Art it's like Madrid!' And, indeed, 'Art Night' does feel like a smaller version of the Spanish capital's 'Noche en Blanco', with what seems like the whole city out on the streets, hopping from gallery to gallery, to bar to gallery until midnight.

Galleries at the heart of the action, and where the cava and artistic banter flow freely, include **El Casal Solleric** (Passeig des Born 27, 971 72 20 92), **Es Baluard** (*see p61*), **Sala Pelaires** (C/Pelaires 5, www.pelaires.com), **Joanna Kunstmann** (C/Sant Feliu 18, www.kunstmann.com) and **Galería Maior Palma** (C/Can Sales 10, www.galeriamaior.com); the latter hosted one of 2008's highlights – Antonio Gonzales Paucar's 'Rites of Passage' exhibition, part-curated by Rebecca Horn. Hot streets to hang out on, meanwhile, include **C/Sant Feliu** – housing the most high-profile commercial galleries – **C/Unió** and **C/Pelaires**. La 5a Puñeta (*see p67*) is a popular munching spot for local creatives on the night, for its canapé-like *pintxos*, decent, affordable *copas de vino* and arty vibe. But the real attraction of Nit de l'Art lies in its community feel, with teenagers, artists, designers, tourists and grannies all joining in on the action.

If you can't be in town for the night itself, most exhibitions stay on into the autumn. Since 2007, Nit de l'Art has coincided with Palma's International Art Week, consisting of the Jam Art and Art Cologne fairs; however, it was uncertain whether these would run again after 2008. For up-to-date info, visit www.jamart mallorca.com.

IN CONTEXT

Carro Triunfal

Valldemossa. **Date** July.

If you like religion with your roots music, check out Valldemossa's Carro Triunfal on 28 July – with requisite country folk, donkeys and torch-bearing slaves.

Verge del Carme

Across the islands. **Date** July.

Port d'Andratx is the setting for arguably the most impressive celebration of the patron saint of seafarers and fishermen (Our Lady of Mount Carmel) on 15-17 July, with hundreds of traditional *llaüts* bobbing in the harbour, illuminated by torches.

International Folklore Festival

Sóller (www.soller.es). **Date** end of July.

Sóller's International Folklore Festival has been going for over 20 years, while Villafranca is a recognised centre for Mallorcan folk, with the scene given a lift by local folk artist-entrepreneur Tomeu Penya.

Copa del Rey

Palma (971 72 68 48, www.copadelrey audimapre.com. **Date** July-Aug.

The Copa del Rey (King's Cup) is arguably the most important regatta in the Mediterranean. Then comes the Regatta Princesa Sofia, held every year during Easter week (www.trofeoprincesasofia.org).

Menorca Opera Season

Teatre Principal, Maó. **Date** July-Aug.

Maó's Teatre Principal (*see p210*) is the venue for Menorca's diminutive opera season (three or four performances in July and August).

Festival de Pollença

Pollença (971 53 31 11/53 40 11/ www.festivalpollença.org). **Date** July-Aug.

The biggest classical festival is at the Claustre del Convento Santo Domingo. Established in 1962, past festival headliners have included Yehudi Menuhin, Viktoria Mullova and the St Petersburg Philharmonic.

Festival Chopin

Valldemossa (www.festivalchopin.com). **Date** Aug.

Chopin's stay in Valldemossa is recalled at the annual Festival Chopin (Aug) with shows by first-class virtuosi. Jean-Philippe Collard and Andrei Gavrilov were the stars of the 2008 festival.

International Jazz Festival Sa Pobla

Sa Pobla (971 54 41 11/www.ajsapobla.net/jazz). **Date** Aug.

This long-established festival drew in the likes of John Zorn and Nicholas Payton in 2008.

Mare de Déu dels Àngels

Across Spain. **Date** Aug.

Mock battles across the islands commemorate the fight between Moors and Christians. It's a lively pantomime ruckus with wooden swords, pitchforks and turbaned pirates. Pollença is the best place to see it (on 2 Aug). There are also re-enactments on the dates of other battles in Pollença (30 May 1550), Es Firó (11 May 1561) and at Andratx (2 Aug 1578).

International Balearic Islands Dance Festival

Cala Millor (971 58 73 73/ www.dansamaniga.com). **Date** Aug-Dec.

Started in 2000, the *Dansamaniga* festival provides a range of alternative dance performances. The festival is held in the Auditorium at Cala Millor.

Lluc Pilgrimage

Lluc. **Date** 12 Sept.

The Lluc pilgrimage to the *Moreneta* (Black Madonna) is the biggest pilgrimage on the island, and an ideal opportunity to visit the wild setting of the monastery amid the Tramuntana mountains.

Nit de l'Art

Around Palma. **Date** 3rd Thur of Sept.

See p41 **Art Attack**.

Festa d'es Vermar

Binissalem. **Date** late Sept.

The Festa d'es Vermar in late September is Binissalem's main wine festival. As well as the obligation to honour Dionysus by quaffing quantities of the ever-improving *vino* from Mallorca's best-known DOC, goat meat dishes are served before fireworks and a singing, dancing street party.

October-December

Sóller Classical Music Festival

Sóller (www.festivalportdesoller.com). **Date** Oct.

Concerts are held at weekends through the month in Santa Catalina, a former monastery.

Palma Opera Season

Auditorium de Palma and Teatre Principal (www.teatreprincipal.com), Palma. **Date** Nov.

The Teatre Principal reopened in 2007 after a mammoth six-year refurbishment; it has now returned to being the main host for Palma's opera season, which it previously had hosted since 1984. The Auditorium de Palma (*see p82*), meanwhile, celebrated its 12th opera season in 2008.

Christmas

Across Spain. **Date** Dec.

Christmas (*Nadal* in Mallorcan, *Navidad* in Spanish) is the other obvious religious bonanza after Easter. It's a family affair when even backsliders and apostates make it to mass. There are nativity plays and carol services from mid December on, with children once again taking centre stage. Christmas Eve is normally a big gathering of various relatives around a ginormous amount of food.

Palma

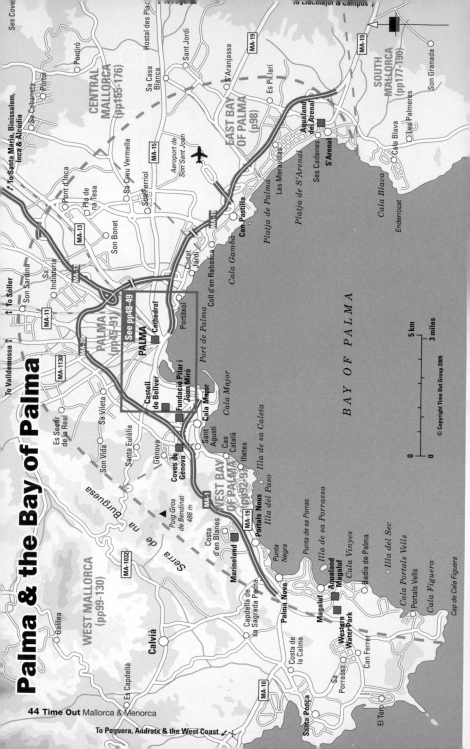

Palma & the Bay of Palma

To Santa María, Binissalem, Incar & Alcúdia

To Sóller

To Valldemossa

To Peguera, Andratx & the West Coast

Ses Covet

To Llucmajor & Campos T

Hostal des Plz

Sant Jordi

Sa Casa Blanca

S'Aranjassa

Es Pil·lari

Son Granada

Les Palmeres

SOUTH MALLORCA (pp177-190)

CENTRAL MALLORCA (pp155-176)

MA-19

MA-19

MA-19

Aqualand del Arenal

S'Arenal

Ses Cadenes

Las Meravilles

Cala Blava

Enderrocat

EAST BAY OF PALMA (p98)

Can Pastilla

Platja de Palma

Platja de S'Arenal

Cala Blava

Pontiró

Pòrtol

Sa Cabaneta

Pontiró

Sa Vileta

Aeroport de Son Sant Joan

Son Ferriol

Sant Jordi

Sa Creu Vermella

Pla de na Tesa

Pont d'Inca

Son Bonet

MA-13

MA-15

Ciutat Jardí

Cala Gamba

Coll d'en Rabassa

Cala Major

Illa de sa Caleta

Portitxol

Port de Palma

BAY OF PALMA

BADIA DE PALMA

See pp48-49

PALMA (pp45-91)

PALMA

Cathedral

Castell de Bellver

Fundació Pilar i Joan Miró

Cala Major

Son Sardina

MA-11

Sa Indioteria

MA-20

MA-1130

Es Secar de la Real

Son Vida

Santa Eulàlia

Gènova

Coves de Gènova

Son Vida

Cala Major

Sant Agustí

Cas Català

Illetes

WEST MALLORCA (pp99-130)

Serra de na Burguesa

Puig Gros de Bendinat 486 m

Costa d'en Blanes

Portals Nous

WEST BAY OF PALMA (pp92-97)

MA-19

Illa del Paso

Illa de sa Porrassa

Punta de sa Porras

Punta Negra

Badia de Palma

Illa de sa Porrassa

Cala Vinyes

Illa del Sec

Cala Portals Vells

Portals Vells

Cala Figuera

Cap de Cala Figuera

Marineland

Aqualand Magaluf

Magaluf

Palma Nova

Capdellà de sa Sagrada Pedra

Western Water Park

Costa de la Calma

Can Ferrer

Sa Porrassa

Calvià

Galilea

Es Capdellà

MA-1032

MA-10

Santa Ponça

El Toro

Illa del Sec

0   5 km

0   3 miles

© Copyright Time Out Group 2009

Palma

All the ingredients for a perfect city break.

Although many tourists to Mallorca still never set foot in its cosmopolitan capital – heading straight from airport to resort – the growing number that do are normally pleasantly surprised by its assured character and sophistication. As well as varied and characterful eating opportunities and an impressive number of boutique hotels for such a small city, you'll also find frenetic shopping streets, fine *modernista* architecture, cool seafront bars and an expanding contemporary art scene; think of it as a sort of mini-Barcelona, but without the suffocating tourist droves and related street crime. For, despite the exponential development of the wide bay that it dominates, this city of a third of a million people remains resolutely Spanish (or, as the locals would insist, *Mallorquí*) and in most of the city's cafés, restaurants and bars you'll find as many locals as visitors.

And thanks to the tourist cash over the past decades, coupled with a drive by the government to attract a more upmarket (and moneyed) visitor, Palma's infrastructure has been hugely improved, making it a supremely liveable city. Add in the fine museums and churches, markets and mansions and the pleasure of simply wandering its ancient streets – as well as the ease of getting out into mountains or to the sea – and it's easy to see why Palma has become one of Europe's most popular weekend break destinations.

HISTORY

Although there were prehistoric villages in the vicinity of modern-day Palma (including Son Oms, which was scandalously bulldozed in the 1970s to build a second airport runway), there's no evidence of settlement on the site of Palma itself before the Roman invasion of 123 BC. The Romans founded the city of Palmeria on the hill now occupied by the Almudaina palace, which remained the centre of government ever after, but it wasn't substantially developed until the arrival of the Moors in AD 902. Renaming it Medina Mayurka, they constructed the first Palau de l'Almudaina, with a mosque next door on the site of the present cathedral. Other mosques were built, as well as public baths and a new city wall that enclosed a far greater area than that constructed by the Romans (which, nevertheless, stood intact until the 13th century). This was to define the extent of the city right up to the 20th century.

Following the 13th-century Christian conquest of Jaume I, his son Jaume II built a new Palau de l'Almudaina, a cathedral on the site of the main mosque, the first city docks and the Castell de Bellver to define the renamed Ciutat (city) de Mallorca. Although the Moorish street plan was unaltered, almost all Arabic architecture was eradicated as the city took on a Gothic look.

Moorish walls were replaced by Renaissance fortifications in the 16th century, and these stood until the first decade of the 20th, when population growth finally forced Palma out of its Moorish confines. Plans for the city's expansion were drawn up, though only adopted piecemeal, while in the centre fine *modernista* buildings were built.

The 1950s and, especially, the 1960s were a period of major economic growth in Palma, chiefly fuelled by the rapidly expanding tourist industry. Zoning was introduced on the outskirts, creating two big industrial estates (Son Castello and Can Valero), one educational area (Son Rapinya), two dedicated to healthcare (Son Dureta and Son Llatzer) and the tourist resorts along the bay to the west and east. The formation of a university in 1978 (which became the Universitat de les Illes Balears) ensured that the island's brightest young things weren't all lured to the mainland, and that Palma developed an agreeably youthful atmosphere.

Meanwhile, though, the fabric of the city centre had been neglected. It wasn't until the 1990s that the authorities finally acted, spending huge sums on restoring and cleaning up its medieval streets and diverting traffic around it. The result is as beguiling a city as you'll find on the Mediterranean.

SIGHTSEEING

Palma's heart is a pristine historic core, within which lie a clutch of compelling sights secreted among its (largely traffic-free) twisting medieval streets, including the all-dominant cathedral, a royal palace, galleries and museums, distinctive urban mansions, Gothic churches, as well as most of the best bars and restaurants and most interesting shopping streets. In contrast is the bland modern city fanning out inland from the old town, which offers few enticements for visitors. A bigger draw is the café-specked waterside, stretching from the Parc de la Mar in front of the cathedral east to the old fishing harbour of increasingly trendy Portitxol, and west below the impressive Castell de Bellver to the city's old port of Porto Pi.

Apart from a couple of sights, almost everything of interest in Palma falls inside the jagged semicircle of roads, collectively known as the Avingudes ('Avenues'), that zig-zag their way along the course of the old fortifications. Starting from the cathedral, the following text takes you around all the chief points of interest in the old city, and can be followed as a walk (a suggested route is marked on the map, pp50-51; allow a whole day, or, preferably, two).

The Catedral, Sa Calatrava & Sa Gerreria

Palma's two most significant and emblematic buildings sit side by side overlooking the sea. For almost 700 years the grand, towering form of the **Catedral de Palma** (known locally as La Seu; *see pp58-59* **Profile**) has loomed up

---

**INSIDE TRACK
CYCLE PATH**

When you tire of the city, it's well worth hiring a bike (*see p91*) and taking advantage of the cycle track that runs most of the way around the bay.

---

from the harbourside, dominating the old town and providing a beacon for sailors. Visitor numbers for the landmark building have increased since spring 2007, following the unveiling of a 300square-metre (3,225 square-foot) ceramic mural by renowned Mallorcan artist Miquel Barceló in St Peter's Chapel, the culmination of a seven-year project. The **Palau de l'Almudaina** (*see p54*), which has an even longer pedigree than the cathedral, started as a Moorish palace before being converted into a royal residence for Mallorca's Christian kings. A visit to the former is essential, but the latter is disappointingly lacking in atmosphere.

Nearby you'll find the specialist **Museu de Pepas** (Antique Doll Museum; *see p54*) and, around the other side of the cathedral, a posse of lurking horse and carriage drivers, keen to whisk you around the old town (the rates are fixed; ask before you jump aboard).

On the other side of the cathedral from the palace stands the newly restored **Palau Episcopal** (Bishop's Palace); started in 1238 and finished in 1616, it now houses the unexpectedly interesting **Museu Diocesà** (Diocesan Museum; *see p54*).

Directly below the cathedral is a stylishly designed outdoor performance space, shaded by a suspended roof. This, together with the temporary exhibition space contained within the ramparts here (C/Dalt Murada s/n, 971 72 87 39, open June-Sept 10am-1.45pm, 5-8.45pm Tue-Sat, 10am-1.45pm Sun, Oct-May 10am-5.45pm Tue-Sat, 10am-1.45pm Sun, free), is known as **Ses Voltes**. The walls themselves are part of the Renaissance fortifications begun in 1562, though this section wasn't completed until 1801.

Between the walls and the road running alongside the harbour is the **Parc de la Mar**, an artificial lake laid out in the 1980s in which the reflection of the cathedral shimmers (as it had in the sea before the harbourside was reclaimed). A café sits on the lake's far side and you'll see various pieces of sculpture dotted around its edges.

The narrow streets that meander eastwards from the cathedral are some of the city's most characterful. This district is known as **Sa Calatrava** and contains a number of diverting museums and mansions, including the island's most important museum, the **Museu de Mallorca** (*see p54*); if you have any interest in the island's prehistory, an hour here is time well spent.

Further down the same street (C/Portella) you'll find the **Casa Museu J Torrents Lladó** (*see p53*), a well-designed museum dedicated to the eponymous painter, set within his evocative rambling house. Just around the corner on C/Can Serra is the only significant Moorish structure that survives in Palma, the **Banys Àrabs** (Arab Baths; *see p52*). Beyond their rarity value, the remains of the baths aren't very exciting.

It's worth ducking down C/Santa Clara to look at the charming **Convent de Santa Clara**, a largely 13th-century Mallorcan Gothic structure (though its façade was altered in the 17th century). There are still a few nuns here, and the public can only access the church.

As you wander the old town streets you'll gaze into the courtyards of numerous patrician mansions, most of which were built in Renaissance style in the late 17th and early 18th centuries. One such, **Can Oleza**, stands not far from the Museu de Mallorca at C/Morey 9; it became something of a model for what would be seen as a typical Mallorcan patio, with its external staircase, flattened arches, Ionic columns, loggia and iron railings.

Around the corner on C/Almudaina is a stretch of the Roman city wall, visible through a gateway on the right, while straddling the lane is the **Arc de l'Almudaina**. The origins of the arch are late Roman, though it was successively remodelled by the Moors and the Christians.

At No.9 is another old mansion, **Can Bordils**, this one being medieval in origin (though it doesn't look it). It was altered by the Sureda family in the 16th century, and its patio dates from the 17th. Frustratingly, almost all of Palma's many mansions are closed to the public. The exception is the fascinating **Can Marquès** (*see p53*) just to the left on C/Zanglada, which offers guided tours around a grand house decorated much as it would have been in the early 20th century.

Emerging from the top end of C/Almudaina, handsome C/Palau Reial heads left back towards the cathedral and the Palau de l'Almudaina. At the palace end is **Palau March**, named after the phenomenally wealthy Mallorcan financier Bartomeu March, and now a permanent exhibition space (*see p55*). Further up the street is the **Círculo Mallorquín** building, now home to the **Parlament de les Illes Balears** (Balearic Parliament). Towards Plaça Cort is the neo-Gothic **Palau de Consell Insular de Mallorca**, built by local architect Joaquín Pavía in 1882 to house Mallorca's Island Council; it still meets here today.

Plaça Cort itself has been a key hub of the city since the 13th century, and is easily identified by the twisted thousand-year-old olive tree in its centre. It's dominated by the elegant 16th- to 17th-century Renaissance-Baroque **Ajuntament** (Town Hall). It's possible to visit the building by booking a guided tour. North-west of the *plaça*, a tangle of shop-lined pedestrianised streets wind down the hill towards Plaça Rei Joan Carles I, at the top of the Passeig des Born.

The short street C/Cadena leads to Plaça Santa Eulàlia and back into the medieval town. Looming over the square is the blocky neo-Gothic façade of older-than-it-looks **Santa Eulàlia** (*see p56*), which you can peruse from one of the many cafés scattered hereabouts.

Pedestrianised C/Convent de Sant Francesc leads eastwards from Santa Eulàlia to another of the old city's key churches, **Sant Francesc** (*see p56*), whose vast blank façade dominates the square of the same name. If you want to know more about Palma's many fine mansions, there's a map in the *plaça* (and at other locations around the city) that details the locations of most of the old town's best examples.

There's pleasant wandering to be had in the streets south of here. Take C/Pere Nadal and then turn left on to C/Monti-Sion, passing the elaborate Baroque church of **Monti-Sion** (open times of services) before reaching Plaça Sant Jeroni and the 17th-century church of **Sant Jeroni** (the tympanum shows St Jerome's desert tribulations; open times of services).

Just east of Sant Jeroni, bordering Plaça Porta d'Es Camp, is one of the very few remaining

PALMA

Sa Calatrava.

BANYS ARABS

Palma Overview

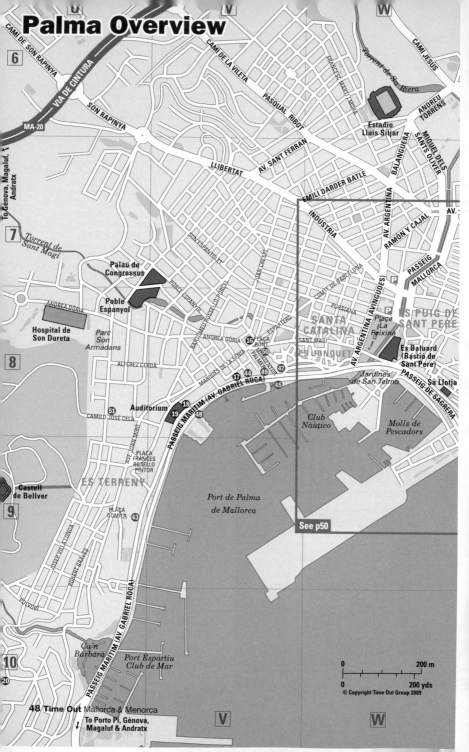

To Gènova, Magaluf, Andratx

MA-20

CAMI DE SON RAPINYA

VIA DE CINTURA

SON RAPINYA

Torrent de Sant Magi

Hospital de Son Dureta

Parc Son Armadans

ALFEREZ CERDÀ

ANDREA DÒRIA

Castell de Bellver

ES TERRENY

PLAÇA GOMILA

43

Ca'n Barbarà

Port Esportiu Club de Mar

PASSEIG MARITIM (AV. GABRIEL ROCA)

CAMI DE LA VILETA

PASQUAL RIBOT

FRANCESC MARTI TADRA

Torrent de Sa Riera

CAMI JESUS

ANDREU TORRENS

Estadio Lluis Sitjar

MIQUEL DELS SANTS OLIVER

BALANGUERA

LLIBERTAT

AV. SANT FERRAN

EMILI DARDER BATLE

INDUSTRIA

AV. ARGENTINA

RAMON Y CAJAL

AV.

PASSEIG MALLORCA

P

SON ESPANYOLET

Palau de Congressos

Poble Espanyol

POBLE ESPANYOL

BARTOMEU ROSELLO PORCEL

JOAN CRESPÍ

COMTE DE BARCELONA

PURSIANA

SANTA CATALINA

ES PUIG DE SANT PERE

P

Plaça La Feixina

ANDREA DÒRIA

ESPARTERO

SANT MAGI

ES JONQUET

16 PLAÇA PONT

PASSENDER

25 50

PALMERAS

AV. ARGENTINA (AVINGUDES)

Es Baluard (Bàstió de Sant Pere)

MARQUES DE LA SENIA

47

PASSEIG DE SAGRERA

Sa Llotja

17 44 49
45

Jardines de San Telmo

PASSEIG DE SAGRERA

Auditorium

51

CAMILO JOSÉ CELA

18

19 48

AV. JOAN MIRO

JOSEP VILADONGA

ROBERT GRAVES

PROVIDRI

PLAÇA FRANCES ROSELLO PINTOR

Club Nàutico

Molls de Pescadors

Port de Palma de Mallorca

See p50

0   200 m
0   200 yds
© Copyright Time Out Group 2009

To Porto Pi, Gènova, Magaluf & Andratx

To Valldemossa

FRANCESC SUAU

CAPITAN SALOM

AVINGUDA ARQUITECTE

JOSEP BALAGUER MUSIC

Plaça de
Toros

DE CINTURA

To Inca

JOSÉ
ALEMAN
Y VICH

GENERAL RIERA

AUSIÀS MARCH

ARAGÓ

6

LLUIS VIVES

PARE BARTOMEU POU

JAUME BALMES

ANTONI MARQUÈS

31 DE DESEMBRE

FRANCESC
SANCHO

GABRIEL
MAURA

JOSEP DARDER, METGE

AV COMTE
DE SALLENT

ARXIDUC
LLUIS SALVADOR

ARAGÓ

TORCUATO LUCA
DE TENA

ARQUEBISBE ASPAREG

ADRIÀ FERRAN

FERREOL PALLARES

7

AVE ALEMANYA

AV-JOAN MARCH

Parc de
les Estacions

FAUST MORELL

PORTUGAL

Sóller Line
Train Station

Inca Line
Train Station

NICOLAU DE PACS

GABRIEL
LLABRES

P

PLAÇA
ESPANYA

AV. ALEXANDRE ROSSELLÓ

FRANCESC PI
MARGALL

La
Misericòrdia

Mercat
d'Olivar

SANT MIQUEL

P

ARAGÓ

NUREDDUNA

CAMÍ DE MANACOR

CAMÍ DE MANACOR

To Manacor

AUDA JAUME III

Teatre
Principal

P

UNIÓ

PLAÇA
MERCAT

PLAÇA
MAJOR

SINDICAT

(AVINGUDES) AV. GABRIEL ALOMAR I VILLALONGA

GENERAL RICARDO ORTEGA

8

CENTRE

SA LLOTJA

Parlament de
les Illes Balears
Ajuntament

Santa Eulàlia

Sant
Francesc

JERONI POU

MANUEL AZAÑA

Parc de
Kristian
Krekovic

Museu
Krekovic

To Airport, Lluchmajor,
Platja de Palma

Palau de
l'Almudaina
Catedral

Palau
Episcopal

SA CALATRAVA

PÉREZ GALDÓS

AVINGUDA DE MÈXIC

P

Ses Voltes

Parc de
la Mar

Parc de
la Mar

JOAN
MARAGALL

AUTOPISTA DE LEVANTE

MA-19

AUTOPISTA DE LEVANTE

9

See p51

Platja de Can Pere Antoni

Portitxol

To Ciutat Jardi

21
52

Bay of Palma

10

❶ Where to stay pp86-90
❶ Where to eat & drink pp63-79

X

Y

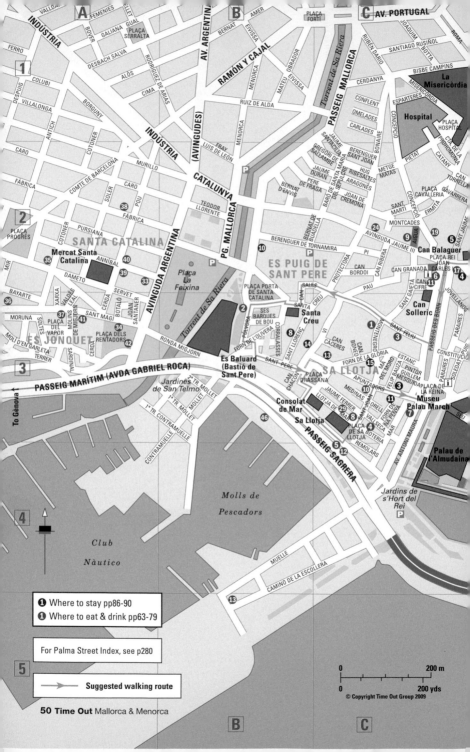

Central Palma

PALMA

stretches of tenth- to 12th-century **Moorish Wall** (Murada Àrab), while C/Temple runs north from Plaça Sant Jeroni, past a gateway that leads off to the right to the **Temple** (Templar Chapel; open 10am-noon Tue-Thur, free). Once part of a compound belonging to the Knights Templar, and then taken over by the Knights Hospitaller in the early 14th century, this rather dingy church maintains certain Gothic and Romanesque features, though it was much altered in the late 19th century.

Continuing north from the Temple, through Plaça Pes de la Palla and along C/Bosc, brings you to one of the most recently refurbished neighbourhoods of the old town, **Sa Gerreria**, the area contained between C/Sindicat and C/Monti-Sion, and the centre of which is marked by **Plaça de l'Artesania**. The local government has injected some 100 million euros into this area over the past decade, smartening up the streets and commissioning the construction of new residential and commercial buildings. The area has become popular with local artists and artisans, being home to the somewhat self-conscious 'Centre Artesanal' (Artisans' Centre), consisting of a school for trade crafts, **Escola d'Oficis Artesans** (C/Gerreria 6, 971 71 77 17) and a number of shops and workshops on the surrounding streets selling pottery, glassware, jewellery, wood and paper products, leather goods, textiles, wicker baskets, food and wine. (Most are open 10am-2pm, 4.30-8pm Mon-Fri, 10am-2pm Sat.) Sa Gerreria was the city's commercial centre centuries ago, so its recent regeneration plays on its heritage. Not all on sale is wildly desirable, but there's enough quality to make for a half hour's browsing.

Around ten minutes' walk east of here into the new town is the **Parc Kristian Krekovic** and the **Museu Krekovic** (*see p54*), devoted to the Croatian-born painter Kristian Krekovic and to Peru, where he spent much of his life before passing his final years in Palma.

C/Morer runs from here west to Plaça Josep Maria Quadrado, which is bordered at one end by the back of Sant Francesc (*see p56*) and at the other, on a corner site, by the lively façade of **Can Barceló**, a large *modernista* mansion. Continuing west along C/Can Savella takes you past the huge courtyard and grandiose split staircase of **Can Vivot** (No.4), an impressive mansion built on medieval foundations by Valencian Jaume d'Espinosa for Joan Sureda i Villalonga around 1725. Its design was much copied elsewhere in Palma. It's worth detouring up parallel C/Can Sanç, where you'll find 300-year-old **C'an Joan de s'Aigo** (*see p69*), a classic Palman café.

Banys Àrabs

C/Can Serra 7 (971 72 15 49). **Open** *Jan-Mar* 9am-5.45pm daily. *Apr-Dec* 9am-7.30pm daily. **Admission** €2; free reductions. **No credit cards. Map** p51 D4.

Such was the zeal of the Christian conquerors of Mallorca in the 13th century that almost every architectural trace of the 300-year presence of the Moors on the island was eradicated. A rare exception is the Arab Baths (Baños Arabes in Castilian), which date from the tenth century and probably once formed part of the palace of a wealthy official. Its layout is identical to that of bath houses in other Moorish cities of the time, with a tepidarium (warm room) alongside a grander caldarium (hot room). The latter is a square room topped with a half-orange dome

Plaça Cort. See p47.

supported by 12 pillars. In truth, you're unlikely to be inspired by the remains (Palau de l'Almudaina baths are more evocative), but the small gardens are a shady spot to escape the heat.

Can Marquès

C/Zanglada 2A (971 71 62 47/www.canmarques. net). **Open** 10am-3pm Mon-Fri. **Admission** €6; €5 reductions. **No credit cards. Map** p51 D3.

The old city of Palma is littered with grand old mansions, many of which offer tantalising glimpses of their interior patios but allow no further access. Can Marquès is the exception. Admission isn't cheap, but the mandatory guided tours are excellent. The origins of the house are in the 14th century, but it attained its current form when the wealthy coffee baron Don Martín Marquès bought it on his return from Puerto Rico in 1906. He renovated it in an intriguing blend of backward-looking, heavy-duty dark furniture and furnishings, with light and playful contemporary *modernista* touches (the fluid lines of the doors are delightful). Piped sounds add life to the rooms, which include a reception room, ballroom, kitchen, family dining room (with art deco touches), private chapel, study and the lady of the house's bedroom, while some modern art exhibitions show that the current owners don't want Can Marquès to remain a static museum piece. Although parts of the original house are now private apartments, the rooms that have been restored offer a fascinating glimpse into the life of a wealthy family in Palma a century ago.

Casa Museu J Torrents Lladó

C/Portella 9 (971 72 98 35/www.torrentsllado. com). **Open** *June-Sept* 11am-7pm Tue-Fri; 10am-2pm Sat. *Oct-May* 10am-6pm Tue-Fri; 10am-2pm Sat. **Admission** €3; free-€1.80 reductions. **Credit** AmEx, MC, V. **Map** p51 D4.

Open to the public since 2002, the former home and studio of the massively bearded painter Joaquin Torrents Lladó (1946-93), who lived most of his life on Mallorca, is well worth a visit, even if you're not a fan of his style (or if you've never heard of him). He achieved fame by the late 1970s for his precise, sober, Baroque-influenced portraits (many of jet-eyed, dark-haired beauties gazing intently out of the canvas). Yet his interests were far wider, encompassing the graphic arts, theatre set design, industrial design and teaching (he founded three art schools that aimed to break the monopoly of the prevalent dry academic schools). Around 100 of his works are on display – among the best are his penetrating self-portraits, while his rather gaudy Mediterranean landscapes are more of an acquired taste. The real highlight, though, is his stunning studio, stretching over two storeys. Lined in dark wood, with Persian rugs on the floor, floor-to-ceiling mirrors down one side and a snug sitting area under the staircase up to the library, it was designed for relaxing in as well as working. A grand player-piano tinkling away adds to the atmosphere. Elsewhere, look out for the piece of paper on which Robert Graves enigmatically wrote: 'Joaquin Torrents is a painter. Most painters think they are painters, but Joaquin Torrents really is a painter.'

PALMA

Plaça Santa Eulàlia. See p47.

PALMA

★ Catedral de Palma

Plaça de l'Almoina s/n (971 72 31 30). **Open**
Apr, May, Oct 10am-5.15pm Mon-Fri; 10am-
2.15pm Sat. *June-Sept* 10am-6.15pm Mon-Fri;
10am-2.15pm Sat. *Nov-Mar* 10am-3.15pm
Mon-Fri; 10am-2.15pm Sat. **Admission** €4.
No credit cards. Map p51 D4.
See pp58-59 **Profile**.

Museu Diocesà

C/Mirador 5 (971 72 38 60). **Open** 10am-
2pm Mon-Sat. **Admission** €3; €1 reductions.
No credit cards. Map p51 E4.
The Museu Diocesà moved back into a wing of the
former Palau Episcopal in April 2007, following a
large-scale renovation of the building. It displays a
well-organised and enjoyable collection of religious
art (although, sadly, the excellent English-language
guide that was previously included in the admission
price is now only available in Spanish and Catalan).
Notable paintings include a fine Flemish-style depiction of George slaying the dragon against the (ide-
alised) background of late 15th-century Palma
(1468-70) by Pere Niçard, a vivid 14th-century altarpiece by an unknown artist telling the story of St
Paul from the Chapel of St Paul in the Bishop's
Palace, and an anonymous altarpiece from around
the turn of the 13th century recounting the tale of
the Passion in 24 episodes.

Museu Krekovic

C/Ciutat de Querétaro 3 (971 24 94 09). **Open**
9.30am-1pm, 4-7pm Mon-Fri; 9.30am-1pm Sat.
Admission €1.80. **No credit cards. Map** p51 Z8.
The Croatian-born artist Kristian Krekovic lived
much of his life in Peru, before he moved to Palma
in 1960, dying in the city in 1985. This museum
holds around 150 paintings, as well as a variety of
handicrafts and exhibits related to Peru and the
Spanish presence in the country.

FREE Museu de Mallorca

*C/Portella 5 (971 71 75 40/www.museude
mallorca.es).* **Open** 10am-7pm Tue-Sat; 10am-
2pm Sun. **Admission** free. **No credit cards**.
Map p51 D4.
Created in 1961 (though it didn't open to the public
until 1976), the Museum of Mallorca is the island's
most wide-ranging museum, containing prehistoric
archaeological finds, Roman and Moorish relics, and
a decent spread of Gothic, Renaissance and Baroque

INSIDE TRACK
PAPIER-MACHE GIANTS

The Ajuntament (*see p47*) in Plaça
Cort houses the papier-mâché giants
that are always paraded around Palma
during important festivals.

---

art, as well as paintings and some graphic work and
industrial design from the 19th and 20th centuries.
Disappointingly, though, it doesn't really tell the
story of the island in any coherent way.

By far the most comprehensive and best thought-
out section of the museum is that devoted to prehistory. It occupies the atmospherically lit basement
and, although the English translation of the labelling
can be somewhat tortuous, it gives a decent explanation of the earliest phases of human habitation of
the island, including the mysterious, characteristic
talayots (conical or quadrangular stone structures)
and navetas (boat prow-shaped dwellings) that have
been found all over the island, plus the controversial
excavations of William Waldren in 1962 that appear
to put human habitation of Mallorca at least 2,000
years earlier than was previously thought. The highlights are the skeleton of the tiny antelope-goat
Myotragus balearicus that may have been driven to
extinction by early human settlers and a room of
miniscule statues (most of nude male warriors with
spear arm raised) that were probably used in cult
worship. Particularly beautiful is the head of the 'Bull
of Talapi', which looks more like a wistful gazelle.

Museu de Pepas

C/Palau Reial 27 (971 72 98 50). **Open**
10am-6pm Wed-Sun. **Admission** €3.50; €2.50
reductions. **Credit** AmEx, MC, V. **Map** p51 D3.
By definition, a Museum of Antique Dolls (Museo
Muñecas Antiguas in Castilian) is only likely to
appeal to those with an interest in antique dolls. The
private collection of Alicia Garcia-German, on the
first floor of an old house right by the cathedral, is
more than the tacky tourist trap you might expect
from the location. A couple of rooms are filled with
more than 500 antique dolls, including many rare
19th-century specimens from France and Germany.
The labelling is in Spanish only, but there's some
information on the museum's leaflet and the assistant can usually explain more.

Palau de l'Almudaina

*C/Palau Reial s/n (971 21 41 34/www.patromonio
nacional.es).* **Open** *Apr-Sept* 10am-5.45pm Mon-
Fri; 10am-1.15pm Sat. *Oct-Mar* 10am-1.15pm,
4-5.15pm Mon-Fri; 10am-1.15pm Sat. Guided
tours in English on request. **Admission** €3.20;
€2.30 reductions; free Wed. Guided tours €4.
No credit cards. Map p51 D3.
Ever since the conquering Romans built a fort on high
ground overlooking Palma harbour in 123 BC, the site
of the current Palau de l'Almudaina has been home
to the island's rulers and key officials; it remains the
official royal residence in Mallorca today. The
Vandals destroyed the Roman structure in the fifth
century AD and built their own castle here. This was,
in turn, converted into a Moorish alcazaba by the
Emir Isam el Jawlani when North African Arabs conquered the island in the early tenth century. When the
Christians wrestled Mallorca from the Moors in 1229,

One Day in Palma

How to get the most out of the capital if you only have 24 hours.

The Mallorcan capital has more than enough distractions to occupy you for two or three days, but if you can't spare that long, here are our suggestions on how you can get the essential feel of this beguiling city in one day. (You could attempt the walk marked on the map on pages 50-51, but frankly, attempt the whole thing in one go and you may feel you're on a route march.)

So, for a *fairly* relaxed day out, we suggest you start with the **Cathedral** (*see pp58-59*), Palma's most emblematic and important building. Get there when it opens at 10am or you'll feel you're drowning in a sea of tour groups. When you tire of craning your neck into the void above and puzzling over why Gaudí's contributions aren't more Gaudí-esque, then stroll along the front by the marina and have a coffee and an *ensaïmada* at one of the hip cafés that front the harbour (such as **Café Port Pesquer**; *see p75*).

While sipping, if you turn around you won't fail to notice the massive Bastió de Sant Pere, part of the city's fortifications. This huge bastion was converted into Palma's newest art museum, **Es Baluard** (*see p68*), in 2004. Its architecture is so stunning that it puts the art inside in the shade, but it shouldn't be missed. Head there next.

Lunch is probably beckoning now. To escape the crowds, head to **S'Eixerit** (*see p78*) in the the trendy port area of Portitxol, on the eastern side of the city, where you can enjoy top notch paella on a pleasant terrace looking out to sea. Afterwards, catch some rays on the cute, chilled-out beach there before taking the leisurely 25-minute stroll back to the centre of Palma.

Dusk should now be approaching, so it's time to take your pick from Palma's many and varied restaurants. If you opted for lunch at S'Eixerit, you might want to opt for a lighter dinner, in which case you should head to one of the city's excellent tapas bars: **La Bóveda** (*see p65*) has both a lively, authentic atmosphere and top-quality local food; arty newcomer **La 5a Puñeta** (*see p67*) offers a Basque version of tapas (*pintxos*); while **Tast** (*see p70*) should appeal if you like your restaurants slick and modern. If you want somthing more fancy (and expensive), however, then head to **Koldo Royo** (*see p77*).

After dinner, a stroll around the streets between Plaça Cort, Plaça Mayor and Plaça Mercat reveals the city's *modernista* architecture at its best – lit up and free of the tourist hoardes.

Feel like you've only scratched Palma's surface? Well, that's because you have. Go on, head back for second helpings.

PALMA

Jaume I used the palace as his main residence, though the building wasn't substantially altered until the reign of Jaume II, who remodelled it in Levantine Gothic style in the late 13th and early 14th centuries. Much of the palace's current appearance dates from this time, and, although it was altered on many subsequent occasions (and underwent a major restoration in the 1960s and '70s), its glory days were really over when the Kingdom of Mallorca was annexed to Aragón in 1349. Today, it is used for official functions and receptions, with tours available to visitors.

The palace is centred around two linked, but essentially separate, wings: the King's Palace (and the adjoining Great Hall) facing the sea and the Queen's Palace (meeting it at right angles), with a number of other buildings – the Royal Cellar, St Anne's Chapel, the Arab Baths, the Royal Procurator's Office – making up the ensemble. The Queen's Palace and the buildings on the north and east side of the palace are closed to the public (they are partly occupied by the regional military HQ). It's definitely worth paying for one of the audio guides at the entrance – the rooms are largely bare and scantily signed, so additional explanation, albeit a rather floral and longwinded one, is useful in bringing the place alive.

★ Palau March

C/Palau Reial 18 (971 71 11 22/www.fundb march.es). **Open** *Apr-Oct* 10am-6.30pm Mon-Fri; 10am-2pm Sat. *Nov-Mar* 10am-5pm Mon-Fri; 10am-2pm Sat. **Admission** €3.60; free under-12s. **No credit cards**. **Map** p50 C3.

The Palau March is a deceptively recent construction, built in the 1930s and '40s under Madrid architect Luis Gutiérrez Soto, who adopted a curiously historicist collection of styles. The grandiose result was for many years the March residence, becoming a cultural foundation in the 1990s and, in 2003, a fully fledged museum.

The terrace at the entrance, in itself an appealing space with wonderful views, holds an exceptional collection of sculptures, representing different movements in the medium, and including works by Rodin, Eduardo Chillida, Henry Moore, Andreu Alfaro and

Barbara Hepworth. The dynamic central piece by Xavier Corberó was created for Bartomeu March's residence in Cala Ratjada, with its dramatically positioned garden swooping down towards the sea, and loses a little of its impact in its new home.

The ground floor of the building used to house some fascinating temporary exhibitions, but these have been replaced by permanent works. The real highlight is the vast 18th-century Neopolitan nativity scene. Fantastically detailed, with scores of angels suspended overhead, the figures include three very varied and minutely observed retinues for the Three Kings, encompassing many ethnic groups.

On the first floor are collections showing the skill and artistry of Mallorcan cartographers, regarded as among the best in the world in medieval times.

FREE Santa Eulàlia

Plaça Santa Eulàlia 2 (971 71 46 25). **Open** 9am-1pm, 5.30-8.30pm Mon-Fri; times of services Sat, Sun. **Admission** free. **Map** p51 D3.
Santa Eulàlia was one of the first churches to be built following the Christian conquest of Mallorca

in 1229. A heavy-handed late 19th-century renovation altered the building's façade and added the belltower, but otherwise it's a remarkably harmonious 13th-century Gothic structure – the only one on the island (other than the cathedral) to have a nave flanked by two aisles. It's airy and spacious within, and would undoubtedly also be light if most of the windows were not bricked up. As it is, the interior appears something of a symphony in grey until your eyes adjust to the gloom. There are 15 chapels running along the walls of the nave and round the apse. Most of these contain doom-laden Baroque works of art – exceptions are the first on the right (if you're stood facing the altar), which features a delicate Gothic Flemish-style depiction of four saints, and the third on the left, which holds a subtle Death of the Virgin.

Sant Francesc

Plaça Sant Francesc 7 (971 71 26 95). **Open** 9.30am-12.30pm, 3.30-6pm Mon-Sat; 9.30am-12.30pm Sun. **Admission** €1. **No credit cards**. **Map** p51 E3.

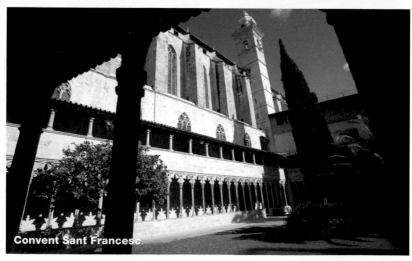

Convent Sant Francesc.

PALMA

The largely blank façade of what was wealthy medieval Palma's church of choice is not at all what you'd expect fronting a late 13th-century Gothic structure. The statue standing to the left of the door is of the mercilessly severe and ascetic missionary Junípero Serra (and a Native American boy), who founded many of the missions that would become the major cities of southern California in the 18th century while attempting to convert the native population to Catholicism.

To enter the church outside service times you have to pass through the convent to the right of the basilica, buy a ticket from the porter and turn left into the lovely 14th-century Gothic cloister. Another left turn at the end of the cloister brings you into the Stygian darkness of the church. Hit the 'Illuminación del Retablo' switch on the right as you enter and you'll at last be able to gasp at the huge, overblown (even for the Baroque) altarpiece. It's a tangle of gilt, polychrome statues and turquoise marbling, centred around a statue of St Francis (by Jaume Blanquer) flanked by Santa Clara and Santa Catalina. It's very difficult, however, to make out much detail in most of the 20 chapels spread around the nave and apse of the single-nave church. One of the better-lit is the first on the left behind the altarpiece. It contains the rather curious tomb of the theologian, poet, linguist and preacher Ramón Llull, one of Mallorca's most celebrated sons. Llull's effigy is positioned high on the right-hand wall and turned on its side, as if it's about to topple to the floor.

Plaça Major & Centre

If you are following the walk marked on pages 50-51, you'll find that if you stroll up C/Carnisseria you'll come to Plaça Salvador Coll and, to the right, the pedestrianised shopping street C/Sindicat. To the left along C/Bosseria is a conjunction of narrow streets at Plaça Marquès de Palmer, where two of the city's finest *modernista* buildings sit side by side: private residence **Can Rei** and former department store **L'Aguila**. Both date from the first decade of the 20th century; the former is the more flamboyant and sinuous (in the style of *modernisme*'s greatest exponent, Antoni Gaudí), the latter more geometrically patterned in the manner of Gaudí's contemporary Puig i Cadafalch. The top half of Can Rei's five storeys drips with multi-hued ceramic mosaic and flower motifs, and features a corner gallery and a two-storey hanging balcony decorated with a fierce-looking face flanked by two dragons. L'Aguila's olive-painted metal frame, expanses of glass and fluid balconies give way to a more extravagant structure as it rises. Red, green and white brickwork run up either side, and a huge arched window is topped with gilded and polychrome floral designs and metal spikes. *See also pp72-73* **Profile**.

INSIDE TRACK
SIGHTSEEING AT NIGHT

Many areas of the city are surprisingly quiet at night, and after-dark is a beautifully serene time for sightseeing; the cathedral is lit up and devoid of the throngs that attack it by day, and the *modernista* buildings on nearby narrow streets can be appreciated in their full glory.

There are more shopping opportunities in the tangle of streets (many pedestrianised) south-west of here leading off C/Jaume II.

Although arcaded **Plaça Major** has a certain superficial grandeur, it's actually disappointingly prosaic on closer inspection, and the haunt of mime artists (the sort who paint themselves green and then stand still), crooning hippies (the sort who belt out limp John Lennon covers) and cafés (the sort where you're ushered to a seat by over-pushy waiters). Still, the small handicrafts market held here most days is worth a look.

Leading north from Plaça Major, C/Sant Miquel is Palma's primary pedestrianised artery. Here you'll find shops aplenty, as well as the **Museu d'Art Espanyol Contemporani** (Museum of Contemporary Spanish Art; *see p60*) and the nearby ancient church of **Sant Miquel** (C/Sant Miquel 21, 971 71 54 55, 8am-1.30pm, 5-7.30pm Mon-Sat, 10am-12.30pm, 6-8pm Sun, free); particularly charming in the morning when the light falls through the rose window. Just north of here, the lovely little arcaded 18th-century oval courtyard of the church and hospital of **Sant Antoni** at No.30 is used as an exhibition space (hours vary).

Just past Sant Antoni, Plaça Olivar opens up to the right. Here you'll find central Palma's huge main food market, the **Mercat d'Olivar**, housed in a bright, airy new building. While it's had a lot of character revamped out of it, and now feels like a giant, odour-free supermarket, complete with cashpoints and signposts, it does at least serve its purpose with efficiency.

Towards C/Sant Miquel's northern end, Plaça Porta Pintada branches off right and fans out into thoroughly prosaic **Plaça Espanya**, adorned only by an equestrian statue of Jaume I, conqueror of Moorish Mallorca in 1229. This utterly undistinguished modern square is essentially a transport hub, containing a clutch of bus stops and Palma's two stations (one for the **Ferrocarril de Sóller** – *see p126* **Ticket to Ride** – and the other for services to Inca).

Running west from Plaça Porta Pintada is another wide pedestrianised shopping street,

PALMA

Profile Catedral de Palma

Gothic spendlour, Gaudí's input and a new mural result in an architectural marvel.

When Jaume I was ending more than three centuries of Moorish rule in Mallorca in 1229 he vowed to raze the city's Great Mosque and replace it with a Christian cathedral. However, though the mosque was converted for Christian use by the King (and the minaret replaced with a belltower), its external structure remained largely intact until Jaume II commenced work on a new cathedral in 1306. It was to take 300 years before the completion of the façade in 1601 marked the end of the project. In subsequent centuries it became obvious (from the frequently collapsing masonry) that the great height of the nave was putting too much strain on the supporting structure, leading to a major reconstruction that resulted in the soaring pinnacled buttresses that give the cathedral (*see p54*) its distinctive profile.

Of the building's three doors, the finest is without doubt the **Portal del Mirador** (1385-1430) on the south façade, designed by Pere Morey. It features delicate, Flemish-inspired figures of Old Testament patriarchs. In stark contrast, around the corner on the main façade is the inept **Portal Major**, a replacement for the door damaged in the 1851 earthquake. The third door, which faces Plaça Almoina, is the no-nonsense Gothic **Portal de l'Almoina** (1498) at the base of the belltower. Beside it is the current entrance to the cathedral, through its small museum.

As you enter one of the finest Gothic church interiors in Europe, your eyes are drawn upwards into the thrillingly vast central space. The nave rises to 44 metres (144 feet), supported by delicate octagonal columns that culminate in cross-ribbed

vaulting. The side aisles (lined by chapels) are a full 30 metres (98 feet) high, giving the interior an open, airy atmosphere that is enhanced by the light streaming through the huge rose window (with a diameter of more than 11 metres/36 feet) at the east end of the nave.

Credit for the ethereally light interior must go to **Antoni Gaudí**, the intensely religious and now ultra-famous Catalan architect, who supervised a major restoration between 1904 and 1914. There's little evidence here, though, of the iconoclastic eccentricities he displayed in many of his most famous works; instead Gaudí was largely concerned with returning the cathedral to its Gothic purity. He opened up the space by a number of modifications: moving the choir stalls from the centre of the cathedral to the walls of the **Royal Chapel** (in the apse of the nave), opening up the rose window and eight windows in the Royal Chapel (many had been closed or obscured by ornamental screens) and removing the Baroque High Altar, replacing it with a plain Byzantine-era altar table. Over the altar hangs a decidedly odd baldachin (canopy) in the shape of an octagonal crown, decorated with symbols of the Eucharist. Its somewhat tatty appearance is down to the fact that it is made from cardboard, paper and wood, and was only meant to be a provisional model.

The chapels running down the sides of the aisles have taken on new interest since the intervention of celebrated abstract Mallorcan artist **Miquel Barceló**, whose three-dimensional 300-square-metre (3,225-square-foot) ceramic mural in the **Chapel of St Peter** was officially opened (by King Juan Carlos I and Queen Sofía of Spain) in February 2007. The surreal and colourful mural, which took seven years to complete, loosely depicts the Feeding of the Five Thousand, and has reportedly quintupled the cathedral's visitor numbers. Barceló also completed the five previously unfinished stained-glass windows.

The other notable chapels are that of **Corpus Christi**, to the left of the High Altar, and the **Trinity Chapel**. In the former, you'll see a gilded polychrome Baroque *reredos* of rare beauty and craftsmanship by local sculptor Jaume Blanquer. It dates from the first half of the 17th century and depicts in its three tiers the

Temptations of St Anthony, the *Presentation of Jesus in the Temple* and the *Last Supper*. The latter is situated behind the High Altar and, unfortunately, is not accessible to visitors. It was built by Jaume II in the early 14th century as a suitable resting place for the remains of his dynasty, but it was only in the 20th century that the chapel was finally used for this purpose – it now contains tombs to Jaume II and Jaume III by Frederic Marés.

The **Museu de la Catedral** is housed within three rooms: the lofty Vermells Sacristy holds various ecclesiastical bits and bobs, including a giant gilded silver monstrance dating from 1585; the austere Gothic chapterhouse features some fine paintings (particularly the early 14th-century Santa Eulàlia *reredos*) and the tomb of Bishop Gil Sánchez Muñoz; and the exuberant, elliptical Baroque chapterhouse, which was built at the beginning of the 18th century and contains a wildly over-the-top silver candelabra from that period, along with a piece of the Holy Cross and various saintly digits.

GAUDÍ'S LEGACY

Gaudí left his mark on the building by the contorted shapes of the metal railings in front of the altar; with the ceramic inlays framing the Bishop's Throne at the east end; and with the installation of electric lighting (very unusual in churches at that time).

INSIDE TRACK
SKATEBOARDING

You'll always find skaters and BMXers at the Sa Riera skatepark, the Passeig de Born and Plaça de Feixina – the latter's abundance of marble ledges, benches and steps make it one of the most visited spots in Europe. The ABM (Asociación Balear de Monopatín or Balearic Skateboard Association) is leading a campaign to officialise the square and turn it into a legitimate skate plaza.

C/Oms, which eventually hits the Rambla dels Ducs de Palma de Mallorca at an angle. La Rambla apes its more famous counterpart in Barcelona in style, with a central strolling boulevard lined with plane trees and flower stalls, if not in liveliness (or length).

At the southern end of the Rambla, the road sweeps round to the right in front of the hill crowned by Plaça Major to emerge in narrow Plaça Weyler, dominated by the majestic **Gran Hotel**. Designed by the Catalan architect Lluis Domènech i Muntaner, this was both Palma's first luxury hotel and the city's first *modernista* building when it opened in 1903. Despite its structural and decorative richness, polychrome ceramics, floral stonework and flowing ironwork, it's a highly disciplined work with not a touch of whimsy. It closed as a hotel in 1942 and is now home to the **Fundació La Caixa** (*see below*).

There's more evidence of *modernisme* opposite the Gran Hotel in the façade of the **Forn des Teatre** pâtisserie – a great place to pick up a *bocadillo* or *ensaïmada* – and on the conjoined Plaça Mercat, where two matching *modernista* buildings, **Casas Cassayas**, commissioned in 1908 by Josep Cassayas, stand.

C/Unió continues westwards from here, past **Can Balaguer**. Commissioned by the first Marquis of Reguer in the first half of the 18th century, this was the largest mansion in the city, before being bought and partitioned by the Blanes family of merchants in the 19th century. Further along is the pivotal **Plaça Rei Joan Carles I**. Locals and tourists congregate at the outdoor tables at long-established **Bar Bosch** (*see p67*) to catch up on the papers and indulge in some prime people-watching. Heading south from here in the direction of the sea is another tree-lined Rambla-like street, **Passeig des Born**, presided over by stone sphinxes and long Palma's premier promenading spot.

Just north of the *passeig*, on C/Sant Jaume, is the 14th- to 16th-century church of **Sant Jaume** (C/Sant Jaume 10, 971 72 43 75, open 11am-1.30pm, 5.30-8.30pm Mon-Fri, 11.30am-1.30pm, 5.30-9.30pm Sat, 9.30am-1.30pm, 7-9.30pm Sun, free), one of Palma's original four parish churches. C/Sant Jaume, and the small streets running off it, is home to several commercial art galleries and architectural firms.

Running parallel to C/Sant Jaume is C/Concepció, worth a stroll for its eighth-century fountain – the awkwardly restored **Font del Sepulcre**, and the **Sa Nostra** exhibition space opposite (C/Concepció 12, 971 72 52 10, open 11am-9pm Mon-Sat, free). As well as occasionally interesting exhibitions, it has a peaceful terrace-café on the first floor, open for lunch only.

Facing the Born, on the corner of C/Cifre, is **Can Solleric**, now a tourist info centre and contemporary art gallery (Passeig des Born 27, 971 72 20 92, open 10am-2pm, 5-9pm Tue-Sat, 10am-1.30pm Sun, free). Dating from 1763, this graceful mansion, with its five-arched loggia, is unusual in Palma in being a new construction (rather than being built on earlier foundations).

FREE Fundació La Caixa

Plaça Weyler 3 (971 17 85 00/www.fundacio. lacaixa.es). **Open** 10am-9pm Tue-Sat; 10am-2pm Sun. **Admission** free. **Map** p51 D2.
Run by the cultural foundation of the La Caixa savings bank, the former Gran Hotel now houses an exhibition space, café and bookshop specialising in design, travel and designer travel. Programming is organised in conjunction with the foundation's headquarters in Barcelona and, given the state of La Caixa's coffers, is normally excellent. On permanent display is a collection of important works, including vast, riotous oil paintings, by Catalan *modernista* Hermen Anglada Camarasa. Temporary shows often explore links between *modernisme* and other 20th-century movements in art, architecture and design.

★ FREE Museu d'Art Espanyol Contemporani

C/Sant Miquel 11 (971 71 35 15/www.march.es/ museupalma). **Open** 10am-6.30pm Mon-Fri; 10.30am-2pm Sat. **Admission** free. **Map** p51 E2.
The Museum of Contemporary Spanish Art offers a potted history of 20th-century Spanish art, with 70 paintings from the March Collection representing 52 different artists. The Mallorcan financier Joan March Ordinas set up the March Foundation in 1955 to promote science and culture, and this elegant 18th-century mansion (where March was born) has been home to paintings and sculptures from the Foundation's modern Spanish collection since 1990. It was extended in 1996, and again in 2003, and now offers a pristine setting in which to brush up on the finer points of Spanish art over the last century.

Although the collection begins with works by the biggest names (Miró, Gris, Dali and an important early painting by Picasso, *Tête de Femme*, from 1907), the focus is on four post-war movements: Dau al Set (Barcelona, 1948-53), Grupo Parpalló (Valencia, 1956-61), El Paso (Madrid, 1957-60) and the Grupo de Cuenca (Cuenca, 1960s). All in all it's a challenging, largely abstract collection, but enjoyable for anyone with an interest in 20th-century Spanish art. The museum also has excellent temporary exhibitions.

Es Puig de Sant Pere & Sa Llotja

The south-west quarter of the old town, stretching south of Avinguda Jaume III and west of the Passeig des Born and Passeig Antoni Maura, is one of the city's most atmospheric and appealing, containing both central Palma's main restaurant and bar area and quiet residential streets little altered in centuries. The higher part is known as **Es Puig de Sant Pere** (St Peter's Mount), and climbs up to the church of **Santa Creu** (one of Christian Palma's first four churches; C/San Lorenzo 4, 971 71 26 90, open Sept-June 10.30-11.30am, 6.30-7.30pm Mon-Fri, 6.30-7.30pm Sat, July, Aug 7.30-8.30pm daily, free) and the mighty 16th-century Renaissance **Bastió de Sant Pere**, now home to contemporary art museum **Es Baluard** (*see p68* **Art Attack**).

Immediately west of here are the narrow streets and squares of the area known informally as **Sa Llotja** (meaning 'Exchange'), containing a wealth of bars and restaurants. The name comes from the magnificent 15th-century turreted building that faces the sea close by. Sa Llotja is the masterpiece of Mallorcan architect Guillem Sagrera (who also worked on the cathedral) and the high point in Mallorcan Gothic architecture. Commissioned by the Guild of Merchants as a commercial exchange, it was constructed between 1426 and 1448 and combines elegance with practicality. Light pours in through the huge windows, while six delicate spiraling columns (linking up to ribbing in the vaults and often compared to palm trees) provide for a spacious, uncluttered interior. The building is now used for temporary art exhibitions (and is closed to the public at other times).

Almost adjacent to it is the **Consolat de Mar**, founded in the 14th century as a centre for dealing with legal issues concerning maritime trade. The current building is 17th-century and is now the HQ of the Balearic Government.

As the Passeig des Born heads towards the sea, it changes name to Avinguda Antoni Maura (named after the Palma-born five-time Prime Minister of Spain during the first three decades of the 20th century). Alongside the road run the shady **Jardins de s'Hort del Rei**, once part of the Almudaina palace.

★ Es Baluard, Museu d'Art Modern i Contemporani de Palma
Plaça Porta Santa Catalina 10 (971 90 82 00/ www.esbaluard.org). **Open** *Mid June-Sept* 10am-10pm Tue-Sun. *Oct-mid June* 10am-8pm Tue-Sun. **Admission** €6; €4.50 reductions. **Credit** AmEx, DC, MC, V. **Map** p50 B3.
See p68 **Art Attack**.

Passeig Marítim to Gènova

The multi-lane Avinguda Gabriel Roca (more popularly known as the **Passeig Marítim**) sweeps along Palma's harbourfront. Once you've negotiated your way across the traffic,

Plaça Major. *See p57.*

PALMA

you can enjoy the waterfront walk and cycle track that follows the harbour edge past the ferry pier, the luxury yachts in the marina, a clutch of cool cafés, fishermen mending their nets, and, in the early mornings, a daily fish auction. If you want to get out on the water, **Cruceros Marco Polo** operates hour-long boat trips around the harbour from close to the foot of the ferry pier (mobile 659 63 67 75, trips at 11am, 1pm, 2pm, 3pm & 4pm Mon-Sat, €10, free under-12s).

Inland from here, and west of the Bastió de Sant Pere, is the grid plan district of **Santa Catalina**, an area devoid of tourists but packed with good bars and restaurants; head here in the evening to eat and drink with the locals. The district's hub is the **Mercat Santa Catalina**, a fine food market, open Monday to Saturday from 7am until around 2.30pm (a little later on Saturdays).

Immediately south of Santa Catalina, sandwiched between C/Sant Magi and the Passeig Marítim, is the tiny district of **Es Jonquet**, a characterful tangle of little lanes and low houses that brings to mind Granada's Albaicín, and which is symbolised by its restored windmills overlooking the marina.

West of Santa Catalina is the weird **Poble Espanyol** (*see p63*), an enjoyably tacky scaled-down re-creation of famous Spanish buildings. More compelling, though, is the impressive **Castell de Bellver** (Bellver Castle; *see below*), crowning a hill on the west side of Palma. You can drive up here, but there's no public transport and the castle is a good half-hour's walk from the cathedral, the latter part of which is steeply uphill (504 steps lead up to the castle). It's worth the effort, though; the views over the city from the castle are wondrous, and the **Museu d'Història de la Ciutat** (City History Museum; *see below*) within is well worth a look.

Below the castle, the area known as **El Terreny** is currently one of the seediest parts of town though it was once the most fashionable nightlife district in Palma. As the city continues its inexorable rise, however, it's entirely possible that history will come full circle and that within a few years El Terreny will again be the place to be seen after dark.

Further west around the bay from the castle is the workaday suburb of **Gènova** (about five kilometres from the old town), home to the **Coves de Gènova** (*see below*), the **Fundació Pilar i Joan Miró** (*see p78* Art Attack) and a number of good restaurants (*see p77*).

Castell de Bellver & Museu d'Història de la Ciutat

C/Camilo José Cela s/n (971 73 06 57). **Open** *Apr-Sept* 8am-8.30pm Mon-Sat; 10am-7pm Sun. *Oct-Mar* 8am-7.15pm Mon-Sat; 10am-5pm Sun.

Museum closed Sun. **Admission** €2.10; €1.05 reductions. **No credit cards**. **Map** p50 U9.

Erected on the 'Puig de sa Mesquida' (hill of the mosque) in the first decade of the 14th century by Jaume II as a royal residence, this unusual castle retains its original design (the only modifications were made in the 16th century to allow it to take artillery). It's essentially circular, with a two-storey galleried central courtyard. The castle was rarely used as a royal home, and from the 18th century was employed as a military prison (graffiti on the walls attests to its long use as such). It now houses the Despuig Collection of Classical Sculpture, the chapel of Sant Marc and the excellent City History Museum, which tells the story of Palma from pre-historic times to the present.

Coves de Gènova

C/Barranc 45 (971 40 23 87). **Open** *July-Sept* 11am-1.30pm, 4-7pm Mon-Sat. *Oct-June* 10.30am-1pm, 4-5.30pm Tue-Sun. **Admission** €8; €4 reductions. **No credit cards**.

Guides take small groups down to a depth of 36m (118ft) in these caves, discovered in 1906. If you have been to any of the east coast caves, these more modest caverns probably won't impress, but they have the advantage of not heaving with coach parties. Tours last about 40 minutes.

★ Fundació Pilar i Joan Miró

C/Joan de Saridakis 29, Cala Major (971 70 14 20/http://miropalmademallorca.es). **Bus** 6. **Open** *Mid May-mid Sept* 10am-7pm Tue-Sat; 10am-3pm Sun. *Mid Sept-mid May* 10am-6pm Tue-Sat; 10am-3pm Sun. **Admission** €6; €3 reductions. **No credit cards**.

See p78 **Art attack**.

Mercat d'Olivar. See p57.

Poble Espanyol

*C/Poble Espanyol s/n (971 73 70 75). Bus 5
(to Son Dureta Hospital).* **Open** 9am-midnight
daily. **Admission** €5; €3 reductions. **No credit
cards. Map** p50 U/V8.

Opened in 1967, the 'Spanish Village' was designed
by the architect Fernando Chueca Goitia as an
open-air architectural museum-cum-theme park.
The idea was to reproduce many of the classic
buildings of Spain in one place. Thus, visitors enter
through the Bisagra Door (Toledo), passing
Madrid's Hermitage of St Anthony on their right
and the Alhambra's Patio of the Arrayanes
(Granada) on their left before skirting around the
church of Torralba de Ribota (Zaragoza) to reach
the generic main square. Sound tacky? Well, it is
(and the piped muzak floating from ubiquitous
speakers doesn't help), yet it's also rather fun, particularly for kids, and some of the buildings are
fairly convincing. After changing ownership a few
years ago, the Poble lost its quirky museums and
artisans' workshops to an increasingly commercial
selection of shops, bars and restaurants.

Portitxol & Ciutat Jardí

If you walk east along the harbourside from
the cathedral, within 25 minutes you'll come
to the hippest ports on the Bay of Palma.
Portitxol is up-and-coming, friendly and
full of young, sophisticated types. It's the old
fishing quarter and has retained its villagey
feel, with single- and double-storey fishermen's
cottages lining a coast that alternates between
narrow strips of sand and rocks. Sea-facing
fish restaurants and cafés offer everything
from designer restaurants to local *chiringuitos*.
If you are staying in Palma, lunch or dinner
here is a must.

As part of the makeover of Portitxol the
seafront has been beautified and the walk
from here to Ciutat Jardí – about 20 minutes
– is lovely. Do as trendy locals do and stop
at the small scallop-shaped beach east of the
Hotel Portixol, known affectionately as **Es
Portixolet**. Fringed by rock pools and backed
by wild olive trees, it's ideal for a little late
afternoon sunbathing before a cocktail and
a spot of tapas at one of the area's many bars
prior to heading out for dinner around 10pm.

Further along, **Ciutat Jardí** has seen a
number of cool new openings over the past
few years; it's a lovely spot in which to catch
some rays and then follow up the chilled-out
vibe with a drink overlooking the sea.

WHERE TO EAT & DRINK

Culinarily speaking, Palma ranks highly
compared with many Spanish cities, with
an impressive number of high-quality

INSIDE TRACK
SALVEM ES JONQUET

Many of the sweet little houses in Es
Jonquet were hung with '*Salvem Es
Jonquet*' ('Save Es Jonquet') banners
in the latter months of 2008; residents
have been campaigning to get the
neighbourhood and its emblematic
windmills cleaned up and restored as
part of the planned new seafront project,
which currently doesn't include Es
Jonquet. It remains to be seen how
the city council will respond.

restaurants. There is a wide choice too,
from spit-and-sawdust establishments serving
simple tapas to classic Mallorcan restaurants
and stylish modern eateries with prices to
match. You'll also find a smattering of decent
international restaurants including Chinese,
Japanese, Indian and Thai.

Palma has a thriving café society, which
takes in atmospheric old places where the
artists and intellectuals once met – though
now it's city workers and visitors sipping hot
chocolate and nibbling *ensaïmadas*. Palma's
keenness on 'doing coffee' is exemplified by
the rise of the trendy **Cappuccino** chain,
whose branches tend to occupy historically
interesting buildings (the newest, on C/Sant
Nicolau, is located in an old tailor's shop).
It's much loved by Palmesanos and visitors
alike for its good-quality, if pricey, breakfast
and lunch plates, mouth-watering cakes
and vast array of coffees and teas. The huge
C/Sant Miguel branch is the place to be seen
come teatime. For details of branches, visit
www.grupocappuccino.com.

In terms of food and drink, the city centre
can be broadly divided into four distinct areas:
Sa Llotja (west of the Palau de l'Almudaina),
where you'll find the highest concentration of
bars and pubs; **Centre**, which includes some
of the more traditional restaurants in the streets
of the old town and around Plaça Joan Carles I;
Santa Catalina (west of the old city walls),
with some of the best new restaurants and a
favourite with locals; and **Passeig Marítim**
(running along the harbourside), which is
generally touristy, but has a few gems.

If you are in Palma for just a couple of days,
you'll probably spend most of your time in and
around these areas. However, it's well worth
exploring some of the outer districts, including
the harbourside **Portitxol** and, a little further
along, the equally hip **Ciutat Jardí**, on the
city's eastern outskirts, and **Gènova**, which
lies in the hills on the city's west side.

PALMA

RIALTO
LIVING

Your lifestyle store in Palma

WE ARE OPEN MONDAY – SATURDAY 10.00 – 20.30
C/ SANT FELIU 3C, PALMA DE MALLORCA, TEL 971 71 33 31
www.rialtoliving.com

Sa Llotja

Sa Llotja (or, in Castilian, La Lonja), named after the former stock exchange that dominates the square of the same name, is a clutch of streets stretching back from the seafront up to C/Jaume III and flanked on the east by Passeig des Born and on the west by the Passeig de Mallorca. Despite being the most touristy district of Palma, it offers up a number of superb restaurants, tapas bars and cafés.

Aramis

C/Montenegro 1 (971 72 52 32). **Open** 1-3.30pm, 8-11pm Mon-Sat. **Average** €€€€. **Credit** AmEx, MC, V. **Map** p50 C3 ❶ **Mediterranean/international**
This sophisticated yet relaxed restaurant offers a sleek, modern setting for first-rate international food with an Italian leaning. Starters are along the lines of beef carpaccio. Move on to one of the pastas and risottos – including a delicate ravioli of chicken with saffron sauce – or something from the handful of fish dishes (such as bream with a red pepper sauce) or meat main courses (duck breast with potato gratin and date gravy is particularly good). The €13 lunch *menú* makes for a reasonably priced treat.

Es Baluard

Plaça Port de Santa Catalina 9 (971 71 96 09). **Open** 1-3.30pm, 8-10.30pm Mon-Sat. **Average** €€€. **Credit** AmEx, MC, V. **Map** p50 B2/B3 ❷ **Mallorcan**
From the same owners as the excellent Can Amer in Inca, Es Baluard specialises in Mallorcan dishes, both classic and contemporary. The decor is ineffably cool, with the restaurant done out like a typical Mallorcan kitchen, with big, colourful plates, chunky furniture and earthy tones. The food is all market-fresh and served in a modern, uncluttered style. Try the *champiñones con mariscos* (mushrooms stuffed with seafood) or a lamb dish. The wine list is impressive.

Bon Lloc

C/Sant Feliu 7 (971 71 86 17). **Open** 1-4pm Mon-Sat. **Average** €€. **Credit** MC, V. **Map** p50 C3 ❸ **Vegetarian**
Trading on its position as Palma's most established veggie restaurant, Bon Lloc charges €13.50 for its set lunch (there is no à la carte) of standard meat-free fare – carrot soup or lentil soup, courgette quiche or spinach tart and so on. Puddings are more creative and might include kefir with baked apple or a banana millefeuille. Service can be slightly frosty.

★ La Bóveda

C/Boteria 3 (971 72 00 26). **Open** 1.30-4pm, 8pm-midnight Mon-Sat. **Average** €€. **Credit** AmEx, DC, MC, V. **Map** p50 C3 ❹ **Tapas/Spanish**

A hugely popular old tapas joint in the heart of touristville Sa Llotja. With its rough stone floor, high ceiling (with lazily rotating fans), patterned wall tiles and galleried wine bodega, there's no shortage of character. Try a classic Mallorcan *pa amb oli* and the excellent seafood; the *jamón* is also as good as any you'll find in Palma (and so popular that one member of staff is employed solely to cut it), the cheese plates are excellent value and house Rioja is a steal.

Caballito de Mar

Passeig Sagrera 5 (971 72 10 74). **Open** *July-Sept* 1-4pm, 8pm-midnight daily. *Oct-June* 1-4pm, 8pm-midnight Tue-Sun. **Average** €€€€. **Credit** AmEx, DC, MC, V. **Map** p50 C4 ❺ **Mediterranean/international**
A top fish restaurant in a great spot beside Plaça Sa Llotja and over the road from the harbour. It's formal, and certainly not cheap, but if you are after superb seafood dishes in an idyllic setting, it's worth the splurge. It's difficult to know what to choose – oysters or langoustines to start, or a towering *paradilla de mariscos*. As a main, you might want to try *lubina al sal* (sea bass in salt), *caldereta de llagosta* (spiny lobster stew) or paella. If it's warm, you can sit outside on the *terraza*.

Café d'es Casal Solleric

Passeig des Born 27 (971 72 61 22). **Open** 7am-3am daily. **Average** €. **Credit** AmEx, MC, V. **Map** p50 C3 ❻ **Café**
Smart office workers choose to meet in this small modern café attached to the art gallery/tourist office at the top end of the street. There are croissants and *ensaimadas* for breakfast, along with excellent coffee, and *bocadillos* are available throughout the day. There are a few tables out front as it's also a good spot in which to pick up flyers for music events.

€ Café Lírico

Avda. Antoni Maura 6 (971 72 11 25). **Open** 7am-midnight Mon-Sat. **Average** €. **No credit cards. Map** p50 C3/C4 ❼ **Café**
Don't be put off by the garish pictures of pizza outside – this is one of the city's oldest and most congenial meeting places. Inside it seems like little has changed since the 1920s (probably because it hasn't), with marble-topped round tables, old wooden chairs and big mirrors on the walls. This is where

INSIDE TRACK
CIUTAT JARDI

Ciutat Jardí ('Ciudad Jardín' in Castellano) is fast becoming the trendiest spot in town, with lots of cool, boho-style bars, restaurants and sushi joints opening up; local scenesters flock here in the summer months.

PALMA

Deià's artistic community once met and where *palmesanos* of all ages still meet for a coffee and a game of pool. There's a *terraza* outside with views of the Almudaina palace.

Café La Lonja

C/Llotja del Mar 2 (971 72 27 99). Open 10am-1.30am daily. Closed Dec. Average €. Credit AmEx, MC, V. Map p50 C3 ❽ Café/bar
This lovely, relaxed bar across from Sa Llotja is actually a very convincing fake – its *modernista* flourishes, dark wood fittings, revolving doors and luggage racks were actually put together 20 or so years ago. Still, it's a cosy spot to nurse a daytime *café con leche* or a night-time glass of wine. There's also a good range of tapas and *garrotins* (small, thin *bocadillos*).

Ca'n Carlos

C/Aigua 5 (971 71 38 69). Open 1-4pm, 8-11pm Mon-Sat. Average €€. Credit AmEx, MC, V. Map p50 C2 ❾ Mallorcan
For Mallorcan cuisine both traditional and creative, served in a civilised setting by agreeably old-school waiters, you can't beat Ca'n Carlos. The menu is admirably short – start, perhaps, with a huge portion of *sepias* (cuttlefish) cooked with *sobrassada* or broad bean stew, before sinking your teeth into a choice steak; turbot with *arròs negre* or aubergine stuffed with monkfish. A reassuring proportion of the clientele are locals.

La Cueva

C/Apuntadors 5 (971 72 44 22). Open noon-midnight Mon-Sat. Closed Feb. Average €. Credit AmEx, DC, MC, V. Map p50 C3 ❿ International

A bright traditional tapas restaurant with *jamones* hanging from the ceiling and a stuffed bull's head on the wall. Specialities include *albóndigas* (meatballs), *riñones al jerez* (kidneys in sherry), grilled sardines and rabbit stew with onions.

★ El Pilón

C/Can Cifre 4 (971 71 75 90). Open 10am-midnight Mon-Sat. Average €€. Credit DC, V. Map p50 C2 ⓫ Tapas
Another excellent tapas bar, just off the top end of Born, it's less smart than La Bóveda (*see p65*) but with a bewildering array of tapas on offer in a wonderful vault-like setting. You can watch the food being prepared in the open kitchen, of which the seafood – *pulpo a la gallega* (Galician-style squid), *gambas, langostinos* – is particularly good and the prices are very reasonable. Highly recommended.

Taberna La Bóveda

Passeig Sagrera 3 (971 71 48 63). Open 1.30-4pm, 8.30pm-midnight Mon-Sat. Average €€. Credit AmEx, DC, MC, V. Map p50 C4 ⓬ Basque/Mallorcan
Bigger and brighter than its sister establishment (*see p65*), this one has as its main draw a large terrace, wildly popular with the city's expat German population. The food is typical: *gambas al ajillo* (prawns with garlic), *jamón* and the very tasty *dátiles con beicon* (dates wrapped in bacon), plus variations on *pa amb oli* (bread and oil). Prices are reasonable too.

Varadero

Moll Vell s/n (971 72 64 28). Open 9am-midnight Mon-Thur, Sun; 9am-3am Fri, Sat. Average €. Credit MC, V. Map p50 B5 ⓭ Tapas/international

Museu d'Art Espanyol Contemporani. *See p57.*

This is the place to meet for a pre-clubbing *copa* or two, where you can watch the sun set over the bay and enjoy a few plates of tapas. It's entirely surrounded by glass walls, giving views of the whole city, and on the cathedral side there's a terrace that juts into the sea. All-day opening means that Varadero is popular for breakfast and lunch, and it transforms into a club with good tunes on Friday and Saturday nights.

Centre

This area runs east of Passeig des Born to the Avingudas and includes the old town, Plaça Major and the streets running off it up to Plaça Espanya. It's the oldest part of town, made up of tiny, winding streets, and full of little bars and simple restaurants where you can grab a tapa or a quick meal at a reasonable price; just don't expect anything too stylish or fancy.

★ € La 5a Puñeta

Calle de les Caputxines 3 (971 71 15 71). **Open** noon-4pm, 7.30pm-midnight Tue-Sat. **Average** €. **Credit** MC, V. **Map** p51 D2 ⓭ **Tapas**
Hangout of choice for the city's artists and architects (there are several architecture firms in the surrounding backstreets), La 5a Puñeta is a cool, basic space specialising in *pinchos* – small slices of bread with a mix of ingredients on top (essentially the Spanish equivalent of Italian bruchetta) and a toothpick through the middle; the toothpicks are tallied up once you're ready to pay (€1.40 each). Choose from toppings such as red cabbage and goat's cheese and tuna with green chillies. There's a good selection of very reasonably priced wine to accompany them.

★ L'Antiquari

C/Arabi 5 (971 71 96 87). **Open** noon-2am Mon-Sat. **Average** €. **Credit** AmEx, MC, V. **Map** p51 E2 ⓯ **Café/bar/international**
It didn't take long for this relative newcomer to become a firm fave with the city's young, arty crowd. With its romantic location (beside the steps leading up to the church of Sant Miquel) and cosy interior (theatre posters, mismatched chairs and interesting flea market furnishings), it's a lovely spot in which to sit back with a glass of *vino* or a mug of hot chocolate and enjoy some live jazz. There are a couple of tables outside, and the place offers tasty snack-style food like quiche and sandwiches.

€ S'Arc

Plaça del Banc de l'Oli 13 (971 71 17 20). **Open** 9.30am-5pm Mon-Sat. **Average** €. **Credit** MC, V. **Map** p51 E2 ⓰ **Tapas**
Clean and new-looking, despite its beams and painted wooden tables, S'Arc has keenly priced *bocadillos*, tapas and more substantial dishes such as duck with berries, cod with *alioli* and *greixonera de brosat* – similar to a baked cheesecake, with

INSIDE TRACK
TAPAS TRAILS

In October every year, the Restaurateurs Association of Mallorca organises the popular 'TAPALMA' trails, providing visitors with four different tapas crawls around the city. Around 40 establishments take part, and routes normally cover Sa Llotja, Santa Catalina, the central area around Plaça Espanya and the harbour area of El Molinar. Maps showing participating restaurants can be obtained from hotels and tourist information centres, or downloaded from www.tapalma.es.

honey. There are plenty of decent wines available by the glass, a good weekday €9 lunch *menú*, and, on Saturdays, a special *cocido* (a traditional, slow-cooked *Madrileño* stew). The space suffers somewhat from its rather hidden location.

Bar Bosch

Plaça Rei Joan Carles I 6 (971 71 22 28). **Open** 7am-2am Mon-Sat; 8am-2am Sun. **Average** €. **No credit cards**. **Map** p50 C2 ⓱ **Mallorcan**
Largely unchanged since it first opened in 1936, this is where *palmesanos* meet to talk politics and where tourists meet to people-watch. While the interior suffers from industrial lighting, its terrace, with supremely comfortable chairs, is perennially popular and it can take an age to get served. Bar Bosch offers a limited range of reasonably priced tapas and *bocadillos*, as well as the sweet, non-alcoholic local almond beverage *granizado de almendra*.

Bodega Bellver

C/Can Serinyà 2 (971 72 47 96). **Open** 7pm-2am. Closed Aug. **Average** €. **No credit cards**. **Map** p51 D2 ⓲ **Bar**
A diminutive and ancient bar with a characterful owner, stuffed to the rafters with dusty bottles, football pennants and old wooden barrels, which somehow also manages to fit in a TV and a fruit machine. Peopled mainly by old men, it is nonetheless an unmissable and increasingly rare pocket of unreconstructed old Palma. Bellver serves meats and vegetables *a la plancha* (griddled).

€ El Burladero

C/Concepció 3B (971 71 34 59/www. burladero-restaurantes.com). **Open** noon-4pm, 8pm-midnight Mon-Sat. **Average** €. **Credit** MC, V. **Map** p50 C1/C2 ⓳ **Tapas**
A great way to experience an authentic Spanish tapas bar without the ham and the smoke. As well as the cutesily painted wooden tables and chairs – it wants for nothing in the way of folkloric decor – the

Art Attack Es Baluard

Palma's premier contemporary art gallery is also its coolest public space.

The words 'Palma' and 'art' were not commonly seen in the same sentence until a few years ago. True, the city has been home since 1990 to the 20th-century Spanish art collection of the Museu d'Art Espanyol Contemporani (*see p57*), but it has only been since the opening of the Palau March's sculpture collection (*see p47*) and, particularly, the unveiling of the superb **Es Baluard, Museu d'Art Modern i Contemporani de Palma** (*see p61*) in 2004 that the Mallorcan capital has been placed on the map for modern art lovers.

The project originated in 1997, when businessman Pere Serra offered to donate work from his collection to a new museum. Palma City Council, the Mallorca Island Council and the Balearic Government joined together to provide further works and to fund the development of the old Renaissance defences of the Bastió de Sant Pere, overlooking the marina.

Serra's collection of 20th-century art forms the core of Es Baluard's permanent collection, which starts with Mediterranean landscape painting of the early 20th century, including works by artists with connections to the island, such as Joan Miró and Santiago Rusiñol (who wrote *Majorca: The Island of Calm*).

More interesting is the series of female portraits and nudes from around 1910 to the 1970s, which includes fine works by Kees van Dongen and Mallorcan artist Juli Ramis (there's also a collection of ceramics by Picasso and a Magritte).

There then follows an examination of abstraction, with paintings by COBRA group artists Karel Appel and Asger Jorn. Drawings include work by Kandinsky, Gustav Klimt and Toulouse-Lautrec.

In addition to the permanent collection, there's always a temporary exhibition in the basement. A recent show devoted to private collections from the Balearics featured photography by local artists, and work from the prestigious animation studio at the University of the Balearic Islands.

However, in truth, the main reason for visiting Es Baluard is for the building rather than the art it contains. A team of architects that included Luis and Jaime García Ruiz, Vicente Tomás and Ángel Sánchez-Cantalejo have brilliantly incorporated the old fortifications within a thoroughly contemporary structure. It's a soothing, harmonious blending of old stone, glass and white concrete. The three-storey structure incorporates the old cistern that once supplied water to boats in the port of Palma, and each level is connected by interior balconies, skylights and ramps. The linking of interior and exterior spaces is particularly clever, with the roof featuring wonderful sight lines and a wooden walkway around the perimeter that allows visitors to fully appreciate the structure and purpose of the original fortifications.

Even if you don't want to go inside, don't pass by the chance to have a coffee or snack at the classy café; there are fine views from its wide stone terrace.

music is downtempo and the atmosphere relaxed. Traditional tapas are here in spades, but best are the small earthenware bowls filled with green beans and ham or chicken with mushrooms, cumin, garlic and onion, all served with robust *mallorquí* bread.

Café Colonial
C/Palau Reial 3 (971 72 68 04). **Open** 7am-7pm Mon-Fri; 7am-3pm Sat. **Average** €. **No credit cards**. **Map** p51 D3 ⑳ **Bar**
Not especially atmospheric, this modern café is nonetheless usefully situated just up from the cathedral, offering a wide selection of coffees and teas along with *empanadas*, *bocadillos* and salads.

Café del Gran Hotel
Plaça Weyler 3 (971 72 80 77). **Open** *June-Aug* 9am-10pm Mon-Sat; 9am-2pm Sun. *Sept-May* 9am-9pm Mon-Sat; 9am-2pm Sun. **Average** €. **Credit** MC, V. **Map** p51 D2 ㉑ **Tapas**
While its spartan bar and restaurant are at odds with the *modernista* splendour of the exterior of the Gran Hotel, its terrace is a nice spot for lunch, particularly in spring when the Judas trees are in blossom. As well as fancy tapas (tempura of langoustine and garlic shoots) there are main courses such as linguini with courgettes and gorgonzola, and chicken with aubergine ravioli.

Café Isla de Palma
C/Oms 32 (971 72 21 19). **Open** 8am-9pm Mon-Sat. **Average** €. **Credit** AmEx, DC, MC, V. **Map** p51 D1 ㉒ **Café**
This Palma institution can be found on a pedestrianised street about ten minutes' walk north of Plaça Major. It's a tiny, unpretentious café-cum-pub, festooned with plant pots outside and tiny paintings of Palma inside. Within its cosy confines you can enjoy a pint of Guinness, Häagen Dazs ice-cream, excellent coffee and a slice of cake. Though probably not all at the same time.

Ca'n Joan de s'Aigo
C/Ca'n Sanç 10 (971 71 07 59). **Open** 8am-9pm Mon, Wed-Sat. **Average** €. **No credit cards**. **Map** p51 E3 ㉓ **Café**
This wonderful old café, tucked away on a side street between Santa Eulàlia and Sant Francesc, is one of Palma's hidden gems. With more than 300 years of history, a pretty tiled floor, green glass chandeliers and a tinkling fountain in a plant-filled mini-patio, the atmosphere's a treat – as are the home-made ice-cream, hot chocolate, iced *horchata* (tiger nut milk) and pastries. There is another branch on C/Baró Santa Maria del Sepulcre (971 72 57 60).

Ca'n Miguel
Avda. Jaume III 6 (971 72 49 09). **Open** *Mar-Oct* 9.30am-9.45pm daily. *Nov-Feb* 10am-9pm daily. **No credit cards**. **Average** €. **Map** p50 C2 ㉔ **Ice-cream parlour**

A wickedly irresistible selection of home-made and preservative-free sorbets and ice-creams – including chocolate with Ceylon tea, date, and, weirdly, roquefort; try the basil, rose of Alexandria and rosemary. The almond biscuits are also made in house and are the perfect accompaniment.

Cappuccino Sant Miquel
C/Sant Miquel 53 (971 71 97 64). **Open** *June-Sept* 8.45am-11pm Mon-Sat. *Oct-May* 8.45am-10pm Mon-Sat. **Average** €. **Map** p51 E1/E2 ㉕ **Café**
This is the most attractive branch of this fashionable café chain, set in a former 18th-century palace and boasting original fittings and a lovely courtyard, redolent with orange blossom and with a tiled fountain in the centre. It does a huge selection of coffees and a range of sandwiches, salads and pastries; expect to pay premium prices. At night, despite the serried ranks of tables, it has a youthful, clubby atmosphere and has recently released its own lounge CD (which it shamelessly promotes at every opportunity).

★ € Celler Sa Premsa
Plaça Bisbe Berenguer de Palou 8 (971 72 35 29/ www.cellersapremsa.com). **Open** noon-4pm, 7.30-11.30pm Mon-Sat. **Average** €. **Credit** AmEx, DC, MC, V. **Map** p51 D1 ㉖ **Mallorcan**
Sa Premsa's vast, high-ceilinged dining room, open since 1958, is lined with huge wine barrels, strings of garlic, ancient bullfighting posters and old photos. It is much loved by tourists for its comprehensive (and comprehensible) list of classic *Mallorquí* dishes at rock-bottom prices.

La Cuchara
Pasaje Santa Catalina de Sena 4 (971 71 00 00/ www.lacuchara.com). **Open** 12.30-4.30pm, 7pm-midnight daily. **Average** €€€. **Credit** AmEx, DC, MC, V. **Map** p50 E1 ㉗ **Spanish/Mediterranean**
This unassuming place has garnered an enviable reputation among those in the know. The owner, Peter Newman, used to run the very popular English restaurant Samantha's in Gènova, but the emphasis here is on cuisine described as 'cocina castellana with an international influence'. The menu includes starters such as *chistorra* – superb chorizo-style sausage from the island – delicious *croquetas* and one of the best *pulpo a feira* (octopus with paprika) you'll ever taste. For mains, try the *lubina* (sea bass) or the rack of lamb, both of which are superb.

INSIDE TRACK
DRAUGHT BEER

As in the rest of Spain, draught beer in the Balearics is normally served in a 250ml glass. Ask for *'una caña'*.

PALMA

PALMA

Natural Fusion

Plaça del Olivar 7 (971 71 21 95). **Open** 9am-8.30pm Mon-Sat. **Average** €. **Credit** AmEx, DC, MC, V. **Map** p51 E2 **②** **Café/bar**
With a pleasant terrace setting on Plaça del Olivar, a stone's throw from one of the main shopping drags, this new café is all about clean lines and clean living, with white plastic tables and chairs and lots of fruit teas on the menu. The coffee is excellent.

Orient Express

C/Llotja de Mar 6 (971 71 11 83). **Open** 1.30-4pm, 8.30pm-midnight Mon-Fri; 8.30pm-midnight Sat. Closed Nov & Dec. **Average** €€. **Credit** AmEx, DC, MC, V. **Map** p50 C3 **②** **Oriental/international**
Charmingly decked out as a 1920s dining car, complete with battered leather suitcases, mahogany mirrors and luggage racks, Orient is primarily a crêperie, although you can also order risotto, stroganoff and an ostrich carpaccio. Crêpes are tasty and varied.

★ Es Parlament

C/Conquistador 11 (971 72 60 26). **Open** 1-4pm, 8-11pm Mon-Sat. **Average** €€€. **Credit** MC, V. **Map** p51 D3 **③** **Mediterranean**
An old favourite with Palma's politicos, due to its location right by the government buildings. In a candlelit setting with gilded mirrors, huge chandeliers and high ceilings, it lost a lot of its former starchiness under new ownership, and now serves dishes such as beetroot gazpacho, breaded monkfish with spiced apple and anchovy purée, and banana tatin.

★ El Refectori

C/Missió 7A (971 22 73 47/www.conventdela missio.com). **Open** 1-3.30pm, 8-10.30pm Mon-Fri; 8-10.30pm Sat. **Average** €€€€. **Credit** AmEx, DC, MC, V. **Map** p51 D1 **③** **International**
This is one of the finest restaurants in town. It's part of the hotel Convent de la Missió (*see p86*), so the design is minimalist, with a moody black and white backdrop of the salt mines of Ibiza across the back wall, water rushing down a granite screen, and a red rose on every table providing the only splash of colour. The creative cuisine is modern European with Spanish influences, and although it is at the top end of the price scale, the food is superb, as is the service.

THE BEST TAPAS BARS

For a classic selection and vibe
La Bóveda. *See p65*; **El Burladero**. *See p67*. **La Cueva** and **El Pilón**. *See p66*.

For something a bit different
APTC. *See p70*. **La 5a Puñeta**. *See p67*; **Es Pou de San Magí**. *See p75*. **Tast**. *See p70*.

★ Tast

C/Unió 2 (971 72 98 78). **Open** 12.30pm-midnight Mon-Sat. **Average** €. **Credit** DC, MC, V. **Map** p51 D2 **③** **Tapas/international**.
Despite the bright lighting and Spanish pop, this is a good bet for quality tapas made with supremely fresh ingredients, and a popular after-work spot for Palma's office workers. If you are hungry, try the *chuleton a la piedra* – a selection of meats cooked on a hot stone at your table. There's a solid selection of tapas, such as *pulpo a feira, gambas al ajillo* and *jamón*. Leave space for pud – the *tocino de cielo* a type of crème caramel) and the banana and white chocolate mousse are particularly moreish.

Santa Catalina

Until recent years Santa Catalina was somewhat run-down and shabby, but it's now enjoying a renaissance, fuelled by the large number of bars and trendy restaurants that have sprung up. Bounded on the east by Avinguda de la Argentina and to the west by C/Joan Crespi, the heart of Santa Catalina is the market of the same name and the streets running off it, notably C/Fabrica, where most of the best restaurants are located, Carrers Pursiana and Pou, and Plaça Progres.

★ APTC

C/Aníbal 11 (971 28 91 65). **Open** 1-3.45pm, 8-11.45pm Mon-Sat. **Average** €€. **Credit** MC, V. **Map** p50 A2 **③** **Tapas**
This reasonably priced nouveau Spanish tapas bar opened around five years' ago, serving up approachable fusion tapas and main meals (as diverse as veal lasagne, wok-sautéed chicken, and lamb kebab) in a smart, stylish yet friendly space – think contemporary art, pendant lights and chrome and plastic chairs. The *menús* feature several group sharing options, and there's a terrace at the back.

€ Diner

C/Sant Magí 23 (971 73 62 22). **Open** 6am-4am daily. **Average** €. **Credit** MC, V. **Map** p50 A3 **③** **North American**
A shrine to all that is good about the US of A, with juicy burgers, BLTs, Dixieland chicken, New York strip, bagels, peanut butter and jelly sandwiches and apple pie just like Mom used to make. The decor is everything it should be too: red leatherette banquettes; a 1954 Seeburg jukebox; chrome bar stools and enamelled '50s adverts, although it's looking a little tired now. Expect queues even at the most ungodly hours, such is Diner's deserved popularity.

★ Fabrica 23

C/Cotoner 42-44 (971 45 31 25/www.fabrica23. com). **Open** 1-3.30pm; 9-11.30pm Tue-Sat; 1-3.30pm Sun. **Average** €€€. **Credit** AmEx, MC, V. **Map** p50 A2 **③** **Mediterranean**

Portitxol. *See p63*.

PALMA

Profile Modernisme

Spain's decorative take on art nouveau can be found in droves in Palma and beyond.

George Sand may have ridiculed the poverty and insularity of 19th-century Mallorcan society in her book *A Winter in Majorca*, but by the end of that century a small but wealthy and increasingly outward-looking bourgeoisie had developed. The modernisation of agriculture and development of industry brought profits to the few, while a growing awareness of, and pride in, Catalan culture fuelled the moneyed classes with a desire to display their wealth and progressiveness in concrete form. In the early 1900s, *modernisme*, the Catalan take on art nouveau, came to Mallorca.

The most influential style in the applied arts and architecture in Europe from the 1890s, art nouveau was a Janus-faced movement, simultaneously looking into the past and the future. A love for decoration, for fluid, organic forms, was combined with a championing of new industrial techniques and materials, of concrete and iron and glass. The Balearics' cultural links with Catalonia provided the great Catalan exponents of *modernisme* (not to be confused with the ascetic, stripped-down Modernism movement that followed it) with a responsive secondary market for their architectural and decorative ideas.

The greatest name of *modernisme*, Catalan architect Antoní Gaudí i Cornet, came to Mallorca in 1904 to oversee the restoration of **Palma Cathedral** (*see pp58-59* **Profile**). Lovers of Gaudí's creations in Barcelona might be disappointed with the restraint he showed in Palma. An extremely religious man, he focused on restoring what he saw as the cathedral's lost Gothic purity, opening up the

space and introducing more light. There are characteristic flourishes in the baldachin (canopy) over the altar, however, and the contorted shapes of the flowing railings in front of it, as well as the bright ceramic inlays framing the Bishop's Throne.

Prize for first *modernista* building in Mallorca, however, goes to Gaudí's rival, Lluis Domènech i Montaner. In 1903, on Palma's Plaça Weyler, he built the city's first luxury hotel, the **Gran Hotel** (*pictured right*). It is a superb exercise in the balance of creativity and restraint, and the decorative stonework, ceramics and ironwork never threaten to detract from the building's structural integrity. Today, it is home to the **Fundació La Caixa**, which often puts on exhibitions exploring *modernisme*'s links with later movements in art, architecture and design.

Opposite the Gran Hotel is a more modest incarnation of

COMMON FEATURES
Modernisme prioritises curves over straight lines.

Decorative mosaics, sculptures and motifs feature heavily.

Iron grilles and stained glass are common.

modernisme in the lively façade of the little **Forn des Teatre** pâtisserie, while on Plaça Mercat stand **Casas Cassayas** (*pictured near left, top*) – two identical *modernista* apartment buildings, designed in 1908 by Josep Cassayas.

The other key site in Palma for lovers of *modernisme* is Plaça Marquès de Palmer, just south of Plaça Major. Here, side by side, rise two of the city's finest yet contrasting *modernista* buildings. **Can Rei** (*pictured near left, bottom*) was built as a private residence and is the most Gaudí-esque structure in the city; a riotous explosion of floral motifs and polychrome ceramic mosaics, dripping down five storeys to a hanging balcony decorated with a scowling face flanked by dragons. Next door, former department store **L'Aguila** (by Gaspar Bennàssar) is a far more measured and restrained work. Despite the coloured brickwork of its upper storeys (reminiscent of the style of the third great Catalan *modernista* architect,

Josep Puig i Cadafalch), its strict geometry, metal frame and large windows provide a far clearer link than Can Rei to the more severe architectural movements that were to follow art nouveau.

When Gaudí came over to work on the cathedral in Palma, he brought with him his talented pupil Joan Rubió i Bellver. Rubío made his mark, however, not in the capital but in Sóller (*see p122*). The town's successful citrus fruit export trade meant that there was plenty of money around to commission Rubió to give a *modernista* twist to the façade of **Sant Bartomeu** on the main square. Later (in 1912), he built the **Banco de Sóller** next door (*pictured far left*) – a rugged, fortress-like structure, lightened by playful iron window grilles – and his own house, **C'an Prunera** (1909-11) on nearby C/Lluna. There are a handful of other *modernista* mansions around Sóller, including one that is now provides a home for the **Museu Balear de Ciències Naturals & Jardí Botànic de Sóller**.

CAN CORBELLA
The intricate building on the corner of Palma's Plaça Cort and C/Sant Domingo is sometimes mistakenly thought to be *modernista*; it is in fact pre-*modernista* neo-Mudéjar architecture, with stained glass and horseshoe arches. It houses the fashion shop 19 (*see p83*).

PALMA

Fabrica's popularity is such that it recently moved to larger premises (it was previously called Fabrica 23 to match its original address just around the corner). The funky modern restaurant fuses traditional Mallorcan cuisine with contemporary European influences for a predominantly young crowd. The regularly changing menu features the likes of mozzarella quiche with aubergine and red peppers, and roast fillet of bacalao with crushed potatoes. Not to be confused with Veintetres, another restaurant that has now set up shop in Fabrica 23's original space.

Sa Llimona

C/Sant Magí 80 (971 28 00 23). **Open** 8pm-midnight Mon-Fri, Sun; 8pm-12.30am Sat. **Average** €. **Credit** MC, V. **Map** p50 A3 **36** Spanish

Sa Llimona is one of the best-known places in Palma for Mallorca's signature dish, *pa amb oli*, a peasant snack of coarse brown bread rubbed with tomato and garlic and drizzled with olive oil. Here, it has been refined to include a wide selection of toppings – *pato* (duck), *jamón serrano*, *jamón ibérico* – and various salads, including a typical Mallorcan *lombarda*, which comes with apple, carrots and walnuts.

Mangiafuoco

Plaça del Vapor 4 (971 45 10 72). **Open** 1.30-3.30pm; 8-11.30pm Mon, Tue, Thur-Sun. **Average** €€€. **Credit** MC, V. **Map** p50 A3 **37** Italian

An unexpectedly upmarket Italian restaurant, tucked away on this atmospheric little square in Es Jonquet. While there are ticks in all the boxes – red gingham tablecloths, family photographs, pages of pasta followed by a decent sprinkling of veal and

fish dishes – the ingredients are impeccably sourced, many of them imported from Italy, and cooked with flair by Italian chef Daniel.

Parrilla Asador Txakoli

C/Fabrica 14 (971 28 21 26). **Open** 1.30-3.30pm, 9-11.30pm Mon-Fri; 9-11.30pm Sat. **Average** €€€. **Credit** AmEx, MC, V. **Map** p50 A2 **38** Seafood/international

An excellent Basque-run place where the emphasis is on fish: the *besugo* (sea bream) and *merluza* (hake) are particularly special. The cooking is straight forward, although not cheap, and is served up in a split-level wooden dining room with a friendly atmosphere. A tapas bar next door serves a fine selection of tapas, *raciones* and salads, and has a dining room at the back for sit-down meals.

Pasteleria Madeleine

C/Annibal 17 (971 20 54 54). **Open** *July, Aug* 7.30am-3pm Mon-Fri; 8am-2pm Sat, Sun. *Sept-June* 8am-8pm Mon-Fri; 8am-3pm Sat, Sun. **Average** €. **No credit cards**. **Map** p50 A2 **39** Café

A nice spot for a cake and a cup of coffee after a browse around Santa Catalina market, Pasteleria Madeleine is also a good stop-off for freshly baked local breads, as well as *flautas*, pretzals, croissant, pastries and freshly made sandwiches (to take away or eat in). A small selection of local aperitifs and beer is also stocked.

★ € El Perrito

C/Annibal 20 (971 45 59 16). **Open** 8.30am-8pm Mon-Fri; 8.30am-5pm Sat, Sun. **Average** €. **No credit cards**. **Map** p50 A2 **40** Café

La Bóveda. *See p65.*

A lovely, arty little spot that's popular for brunch, with delicious local scones and fruit smoothies. Lunch fodder covers *bocadillos*, soups and salads and the likes of salmon quiche. It's right next to Santa Catalina food market, with tables on the pavement out front, and there's a relaxed buzz to the street on Saturday mornings.

★ Es Pou de San Magí

C/San Magí 67 (971 90 55 70). **Open** 7.30-11.30pm daily. **Average** €€. **Credit** MC, V. **Map** p50 A3 ④ **Basque**
Specialising in fish, meat and Basque cooking, the family-run, two-storey Es Pou de San Magí is one of the homelier restaurants in this neighbourhood, and always has a convivial vibe. All produce comes from nearby Santa Catalina market, and a frequently changing menu includes a range of tapas options (try the delicious salt cod croquettes) and some excellent meat and fish dishes.

★ Soho Urban Vintage Bar

Avda. Argentina 5 (971 45 47 19). **Open** 6.30pm-2am daily. **Average** €. **Credit** AmEx, DC, MC, V. **Map** p50 B2 ④ **Bar**
Opened in May 2005, the Vintage Bar has become an essential stop on the night-time circuit thanks to its new wave retro look – '70s wallpaper, armchairs, still-functioning telly and album covers over the bar – and its cocktails and exceptionally friendly vibe.

Passeig Marítim & around

This street (also known as Paseo Marítimo and officially Avinguda Gabriel Roca, but no one calls it that) is Palma's main waterside drag, running between Porto Pi and the cathedral. At the western end you'll find the city's main area for late nightlife with a number of *discotecas*, clubs and *discobares*; as you move east it's more restaurants, bars, pubs and cafés.

Bahía Mediterráneo

Passeig Marítim 33 (971 45 76 53/www. restaurantebahiamediterraneo.com). **Open** noon-midnight daily. **Average** €€€€. **Credit** AmEx, DC, MC, V. **Map** p48 U9 ④ **Mediterranean/international**
The setting here is breathtaking. You take a lift up from the street and are met with over-the-top opulence in what was once the finest hotel in all Palma. In winter, dine below the chandeliers and huge mirrors; in summer, the *terraza* has perhaps the best views in the city, looking out across the bay to the cathedral. The food concentrates on fish, with lovely dishes such as *lenguado con gambas* (sole with prawns) and fresh *langostinos*. Superb service from old-school waiters.

Baisakhi

Passeig Marítim 8 (971 73 68 06). **Open** *Sittings* 8pm, 11.30pm Tue-Sun.

**INSIDE TRACK
C/D'ANNIBAL**

The strip in front of Santa Catalina market is a lively, popular destination among locals and visitors for Saturday brunch or lunch, after the morning's food shopping.

Average €€€. **Credit** AmEx, DC, MC, V. **Map** p48 V8 ④ **Indian**
Palma's best-known and best-loved Indian restaurant offers a set menu (€32.90), including wine and lassi – and two sittings, at 8pm and 11.30pm. Wonderful surroundings – all tinkling music, wooden carvings and garlands of flowers – and a small army of friendly waiters.

Café Dàrsena

Passeig Marítim s/n (971 18 05 04). **Open** *July, Aug* 8am-midnight daily. *Sept-June* 7am-1am daily. **Average** €. **Credit** AmEx, DC, MC, V. **Map** p48 V8 ④ **Tapas/international**
Located right on the harbourfront, with views of the yachts, this is a stylish spot to have a pre-dinner drink or a long, lazy lunch, with its glass walls and canvas canopies outside.

Café Port Pesquer/El Pesquero

C/Moll de la Llotja s/n (971 71 52 20/www. cafeportpesquer.com). **Open** *Oct-May* 10am-midnight daily. *June-Sept* 10am-1pm Mon-Fri; 10am-3am Sat, Sun. **Average** €€. **Credit** AmEx, DC, MC, V. **Map** p50 B3 ④ **Spanish**
This chic harbourside café is certainly not one of the cheapest places in town, but its capacious decked terrace is a prime spot to while away a long sunny afternoon or evening. The *pa amb oli* with *jamón serrano* weighs in at a hefty price, but it's a very superior version, with olives and capers on the side, and is easily large enough for a light lunch for two. Good fish and seafood dishes are among the other options on the menu, and there's also a *menú del día* (Mon-Fri only).

Cappuccino Passeig Marítim

Passeig Marítim 1 (971 28 21 62). **Open** 8am-midnight Sun-Thur; 8am-2am Fri-Sun. **Average** €. **Credit** AmEx, MC, V. **Map** p48 V8 ④ **Café**
A prime spot on the harbourfront in which to see and be seen, with a large outdoor *terraza* and a glass-fronted area upstairs with great views across the bay.

Sa Cranca

Passeig Marítim 13 (971 73 74 47). **Open** 1-3.45pm, 8-11.45pm Tue-Sat; 1-3.45pm Sun. Closed Sept. **Average** €€. **Credit** AmEx, DC, MC, V. **Map** p48 V8 ④ **Spanish/Mallorcan**
Sa Cranca is an *arroceria*, which means that it specialises in rice dishes. There is a huge variety to choose from – seven different (and superb) paella

PALMA

dishes, including *valenciana* and *marisco*; *arròs a banda*, a Mallorcan speciality; and *arròs negre*, rice cooked in squid ink. Set on the first floor of one of the faceless office blocks that line this street, it has a great view of the harbour – reserve a table by the window.

★ Koldo Royo
Passeig Marítim 3 (971 73 24 35). **Open** 11.30am-3.30pm; 8-11.30pm daily. **Average** €€€€. **Credit** AmEx, MC, V. **Map** p48 V8 ㊾
Basque/Mediterranean
Basque chef Koldo Royo served his apprenticeship with the masters of Basque cooking before opening his own place in Mallorca and has earned a Michelin star for his efforts. He is now the leading proponent of the *nueva cocina vasca* (new Basque cuisine). Dishes include such gems as roasted scallops with mushrooms, loin of rabbit stuffed with plums, wild pigeon with plum purée and shallot vinaigrette, and sea bass with black sepia pasta. Try to get a window seat with lovely views of the bay, and make sure you reserve well in advance.

Samurai
C/Monsenyor Palmer 2 (971 73 78 37). **Open** 8pm-midnight Mon; 1-4pm, 8pm-midnight Tue-Sun. **Average** €€€. **Credit** AmEx, MC, V. **Map** p48 V8 ㊿ **Japanese**
A classily designed Japanese restaurant where the waiters sport traditional clothing and serve good sushi, tempura and sashimi. Sit at the bar around the *plancha* to enjoy the chefs putting on a show.

Shogun
C/Camilo José Cela 14B (971 73 57 48). **Open** 1-4pm, 7-11.30pm daily. **Average** €€. **Credit** AmEx, MC, V. **Map** p48 U8 ㉑ **Japanese**
Excellent Japanese cuisine served in stylish surroundings. Classic dishes employ market-fresh fish and good cuts of meat. The ambience is subtle and restrained, the service attentive and efficient.

Gènova

This area, a suburb just out of town to the west of the Castell de Bellver, is justly famous for its restaurants. If you are in Palma for more than a few days, it's worth the journey; about a 15-minute drive from the centre along C/Andrea Doria.

Sa Caseta
C/Martínez Vaquer 1 (971 40 42 81/www. sacaseta.com). **Open** 1pm-midnight Mon, Tue, Thur-Sun. **Average** €€€. **Credit** AmEx, DC, MC, V. **Mallorcan/Spanish**
For high-end dining, this is one of the best eating destinations in Gènova. There is a good-value tasting menu, consisting, perhaps, of snails, *frito Mallorquín* (generally offal), bacalao, suckling pig, almond cake, wine and cava.

Meson Ca'n Pedro 1
C/Rector Vives 4 (971 40 24 79/www.meson canpedro.com). **Open** 1-4pm, 7pm-midnight Wed-Sun. **Average** €€. **Credit** AmEx, DC, MC, V. **Mallorcan/international**
This spot is hugely popular, and one of the most famous of Mallorca's *asadores*, serving up huge piles of roast and grilled meats, such as suckling pig and lamb. Reportedly, it's the busiest restaurant on the island – the third busiest in Spain – so you may find that the focus is on quantity rather than quality. On the same street, there's also a Meson C'an Pedro 2 (971 70 21 62, 12.30pm-12.30am daily), which specialises in fish.

La Rueda
C/Rector Vives 11 (971 40 34 60). **Open** *July-Oct* 7.30-11.30pm Tue-Sun. *Nov-June* 1-3.30pm, 7.30-11.30pm Tue-Sun. **Average** €€. **Credit** MC, V. **International/Latin American**
Across the street from Ca'n Pedro, La Rueda has a lovely garden terrace and specialises in South American ingredients, creatively prepared. If you want *ceviche* (fish or seafood 'cooked' in fresh lime juice), you'll need to phone ahead to order; otherwise try the barbecued loin of beef for two.

Portitxol & Ciutat Jardí

Located around 25 minutes' walk east of the cathedral along the seafront, Portitxol's cutesy harbour and mix of the trendy and the trad is irresistible; there are more good seaside eateries further east in Ciutat Jardi, which is on its way to becoming the coolest spot in town.

★ Bar, Co
C/Vicari Joaquim Fuster 67, Portitxol (971 24 86 85). **Open** 1pm-midnight Tue-Sun. **Average** €€. **Credit** MC, V. **Asian/fusion**
Now in larger premises (the space that was formerly Minimar, just along from the previous restaurant), Bar, Co continues to defy expectations. Mexican owner Emilio Castrejón is passionate about sourcing and creating wonderful food and has consequently made this one of the city's most rewarding places to eat. Alongside an impressive wine list, the Asian-influenced menu includes fresh salads (such as seaweed and tofu) and specialities such as Korean *tortitas* (made with potato, onion, fermented soy beans and oyster sauce).

★ El Bungalow
C/Esculls 2, Ciutat Jardí (971 26 27 38). **Open** *Apr-mid Oct* 1.30-4pm, 8.30-11.30pm Tue-Sat; 1-4pm Sun. *Mid Oct-Mar* 1.30-4pm Tue-Sun. **Average** €€€. **Credit** DC, MC, V. **Spanish**
Set in a former fisherman's cottage separated by the coastal road from the modern apartment blocks behind, El Bungalow may offer simple food but it attracts an upmarket clientele. Even Michelin-starred

PALMA

chefs have praised its fresh fish and rice dishes (including paella), unobtrusive but efficient service and good prices. Waves gently lap up against the terrace.

Casa Fernando

C/Trafalgar 27, Ciutat Jardí (971 26 54 17/ www.restaurantecasafernando.com). **Open** 1-4pm, 7pm-midnight Tue-Sun. **Average** €€. **Credit** MC, V. **Seafood**

Recognisable by the *llaüt* (traditional Mallorcan boat) on its roof, Casa Fernando is one of the emblematic fish restaurants of this trendy zone, and popular with both tourists and locals, especially out of season when

El Bungalow (*see p77*) is closed. Both restaurants helped to put Ciutat Jardi on the culinary map.

★ S'Eixerit

C/Vicari Joaquim Fuster 73, Portitxol (971 27 37 81). **Open** 10am-midnight daily. **Average** €€. **Credit** MC, V. **Mallorcan/Mediterranean**

S'Eixerit is situated in an old house that has been converted into a delightful restaurant with plenty of cosy nooks filled with antiques, a gorgeous leafy garden and an open front terrace facing the sea. Locals flock here for the excellent-value lunchtime *menú* and paella.

Art Attack Fundació Pilar i Joan Miró

The Spanish artist's solid Mallorcan connections are surprisingly little known.

Though born in Catalonia, Joan Miró was always intimately connected to Mallorca. His mother was from the island, he spent many childhood holidays here and married a native, Pilar Juncosa, before settling at Son Abrines, near Cala Major (just west of Palma) in 1956 at the age of 63. At Palma's Fundació Pilar i Joan Miró (*see p62*) you'll find the three main buildings that make up the Pilar and Joan Miró Foundation, two of which are interesting in themselves as rare examples of modern architecture in Palma.

Miró commissioned his old friend, the architect Josep Lluís Sert, to design a studio for him, and the result, the **Sert Studio** (completed in 1955), is a synthesis of Mediterranean materials and techniques in harmony with its environment; it was a milestone in Sert's architectural career. However, the uninitiated have to take this on trust – it looks more like a light

industrial unit. The interior is filled with unfinished canvases and gives an insight into the way Miró worked, often on a number of pieces simultaneously.

The second building is **Son Boter**, a late 17th-century *possessió* (country house) that Miró bought in 1959 and used to work on extra large works and sculptures. Today, both studios are employed as venues for a range of courses and special projects.

After Miró's death (in 1983), his wife started planning an exhibition space and cultural centre in which to exhibit her late husband's work. She sold a few gouaches and commissioned Rafael Moneo to build the low-rise, horizontal-lined structure that is the Foundation's **headquarters**. It opened in 1992 and displays a rotating selection from the Foundation's 5,000 works, as well as some impressive temporary exhibitions from other artists.

PALMA

El Peñon

Isla de Chipre 43, Coll d'en Rabassa, Ciutat Jardí (971 26 04 28/www.elpenon1957.com). **Open** 9am-midnight daily. **Average** €. **Credit** MC, V. **Bar/Mediterranean**

A sexy little bar with one of the best settings in town, El Peñon has been here for over half a century and is currently enjoying something of a renaissance under its present managers, Juan and Miguel. With two terraces overlooking the sea, an additional rooftop space, chilled jazzy-electronic tunes (plus live jazz some nights) and good food to boot (served all day), this unpretentious spot is a winner. The Mediterranean menu includes lots of varieties of *pa amb oli* and seafood-based tapas, various paellas and popular barbecues in the summer months.

Portixol

C/Sirena 27, Portitxol (971 27 18 00/www. portixol.com). **Open** 7-11.30am, 1-4.30pm, 8pm-midnight daily. **Average** €€€€. **Credit** AmEx, DC, MC, V. **Map** p49 Z9 ⑫ **International**

The restaurant at the stylish Hotel Portixol (*see p90*) is as gastronomically savvy as you'd expect from a place that has featured in more designer accommodation guides than you've had sashimi dinners. Chilled sounds provide a relaxing background as you gaze out over the swimming pool and decide, perhaps, to go for the red curry and lemongrass soup with king prawns, followed by duck breast cooked perfectly pink, with a side order of asparagus tempura. The quality and (inevitably) the prices are high, the service is spot on and the vibe is Zen.

Wasabi Blue

C/Trafalgar 41, Ciutat Jardí (971 26 46 02/ www.wasabirestaurants.es). **Open** 1-4pm, 8-11pm Mon, Wed-Sat; 1-4pm Sun. **Average** €€€. **Credit** AmEx, MC, V. **Japanese**

All angles and glass, the super-cool Wasabi Blue offers up excellent sushi, with exciting rolls such as soft-shell crab and spicy tuna. A mixed platter of 38 different pieces costs €45. There is a sister restaurant in the similarly hip neighbourhood of Santa Catalina (C/Caro 16, 971 45 65 93).

NIGHTLIFE

Palma isn't blessed with the most exciting nightlife but it is reasonably active year-round and is particularly buzzing at weekends and during the summer months. In terms of pubs and bars, most of the action is around Sa Llotja, but many of these start closing at about 2am, so for late-night drinking and dancing you'll need to head to the Passeig Marítim where the city's glitziest *discobares* and *discotecas* are open until 5am or 6am. More laid-back and discerning drinkers head to the trendy districts of Ciutat Jardí and Portixol. Cala Estancia, further out on the East Bay, is home to **Puro Beach** (a

mix of Ibiza's Café del Mar, Miami Beach and a yoga retreat; *see p98*) that's popular with a style-conscious, designer-clothed crowd.

For listings of what's going on and where, including live bands and the alternative scene, pick up a copy of the free mags *Youthing*, and the English-language *Dígame* (www. digamemallorca.com), both of which you'll find in clothes shops, hotels and bars. There is also a *Guia del Ocio* available at *kioscos*, which gives details of more mainstream entertainment such as theatres, cinemas, exhibitions and restaurants.

Sa Llotja

This is the traditional heart of the city's pre-clubbing nightlife, popular with locals and tourists, where you'll find Irish pubs next to flamenco clubs and lager and sangria drunk with equal vigour. It's all packed into a very small area concentrated around C/Apuntadors, where almost every doorway leads into a pub or bar. Officially, most places are required by law to close at 2am, but you'll find that many will go on until 3am or 4am, particularly at weekends or in high season.

Ábaco (C/Sant Joan 1, 971 71 49 39, open 8pm-1am Thur, Mon-Thur, Sun; 8pm-3am Fri, Sat, closed 7 Jan-13 Feb) is Palma's most talked-about establishment (mainly by a fortysomething crowd), though you could quite easily walk past it if you didn't know it was there. Housed within an opulent mansion, it's an outrageously theatrical spot, with an indoor and outdoor patio full of flowers, cascading fruit, birds in cages, a fountain outside, classical music and an army of waiters to-ing and fro-ing with some of the largest (and most expensive) cocktails in Mallorca. The only pity is that tour groups regularly wander in for a gawp.

For some live music, head to the **Jazz Voyeur Club** (C/Apuntadors 5, open 8.30pm-1am Mon-Thur, Sun, 8.30pm-3am Fri, Sat), which replaced Café Barcelona in 2006 while continuing the former's solid trajectory. Run by Jazz Voyeur Festival honcho, the Argentinian Roberto Menéndez, it lays on live jazz, blues and soul from its atmospheric space (complete with audio-visuals, arty photography and a food menu) on most nights of the week.

Atlantico (C/Sant Feliu 12, open 6pm-2.30am Mon-Thur, Sun, 6pm-3am Fri, Sat) has a retro rock 'n' roll look, bedecked with memorabilia, and swings to the sound of Elvis and the Stones. **Agua** (C/Jaume Ferrer 6, mobile 607 54 32 77, 7pm-late daily) is less predictable music-wise, thanks to the multifarious musical tastes of US owners Richard and Lee; you're as likely to hear soft metal as chillout or jazz in the dark, narrow space. Nearby, **Duplex**

Lounge (C/Jaume Ferrer 14, no phone, 6pm-1am Mon-Thur, Sun, 6pm-3am Fri, Sat) is an altogether more mellow place, French-owned and specialising in cocktails, while on the next street down you'll find self-described 'underground club' **Bugulú** (C/Llotja de Mar 20, no phone), the city's best bet for rock, punk, mod and 1960s soul music. Regular theme nights dedicated to bands such as the Ramones keep local rockers' musical thirsts satiated.

For the less musically discerning, **La Bodeguita del Medio** (C/Vallseca 16, 971 71 78 32, open 8pm-1am Mon-Thur, Sun; 8pm-3am Fri, Sat) is an enjoyably tacky salsa dive; **O'Briens** (C/Sant Joan 7, 971 71 43 81, open 6pm-1am Mon-Thur, Sun, 6pm-3am Fri, Sat) is a popular Irish pub, full of British and Irish visitors, with Guinness and Kilkenny on tap; **MacGowan's** (C/del Mar 18, open 9pm-1am Mon-Thur, Sun, 9pm-3am Fri, Sat) offers more of the same, with pool and darts.

Santa Catalina

Some of Palma's alternative and rock clubs are concentrated in and around this area, including **Café Lisboa** (C/Sant Magí 33, no phone, open 11pm-2.30am Mon-Thur, 11pm-3.30am Fri, Sat) for rock and jazz, and **Rimanblu** (C/Fabrica 21, open June-mid Sept 9pm-3am Mon-Thur, 9pm-4am Fri, Sat, mid Sept-May 4pm-3am Mon-Thur, 4pm-4am Fri, 10pm-4am Sat), whose name is a mangled version of 'rhythm and blues' and gives you an idea of the type of music on offer. There are a number of clubs and bars along C/Industria.

Passeig Marítim & El Terreny

Passeig Marítim is popular with nightlife-loving tourists and locals, who have moved here since the Town Hall clamped down on late-night drinking in the Sa Llotja area. The area directly above Tito's (*see below*) is known as El Terreny, and used to be the trendiest part of town; it's centred on Plaça Gomila and Avda. Joan Miró, and is now pretty seedy. Around here is the centre of Palma's gay scene *(see below)*.

INSIDE TRACK
EL TERRENY

Although currently one of the most downtrodden parts of town, El Terreny was Palma's glitziest nightlife zone back in the 1950s. Nightclub **Tito's** (*see below*), which is still open today, played host to international stars such as Frank Sinatra and Liza Minelli.

Palma's late nightlife begins at the eastern end of the Passeig Marítim at **Hogan's** (C/Monsenyor Palmer 2, 971 28 96 64, open noon-3am daily), an Irish-style pub popular with Brits; it screens big football matches and has occasional live music. If you are after more of a pre-clubbing atmosphere, you need to move west along the Passeig past the big hotels, where the bars and *discobares* are situated. Bear in mind that few open before 10pm and most won't get going until midnight. One of the best is **Crazy Cow** (Passeig Marítim 33, 971 28 38 29, open June-Aug 10pm-5am daily, Sept-May 10pm-5am Wed-Sun), which has a *terraza* and plays house music and Spanish chart hits. For Latin sounds, lambada and cocktails try **Made in Brasil** (Passeig Marítim 27, mobile 670 37 23 90, open 8pm-3.45am Mon-Thur, Sun, 8pm-4am Fri, Sat).

Palma's *discotecas* are not like Ibiza's, despite the presence of Abraxos (the renamed Pacha; *see below*), so don't expect cutting-edge dance sounds – you'll find the music (perhaps with the exception of Abraxos) predominantly bland, bubblegum Spanish pop. The first of the big clubs is **Art Deco** (Plaça del Vapor 20, 971 73 34 95, open midnight-5.45am Thur-Sat), set back from Passeig Marítim and with a slightly older crowd. **Tito's** (Passeig Marítim s/n, 971 73 00 17, open July-Aug 11pm-6am daily, Sept-June 11pm-6am Fri-Sun) is the biggest in town, with glass lifts on the outside, six bars, a laser show, great views over the bay and commercial pop tunes. Opposite, **Level** (971 73 36 71, open 11pm-6am Fri-Sun) attracts well-heeled yachties to an outdoor setting with pool. Pacha-run **Abraxas** (Passeig Marítim 42, 971 45 59 08, www.abraxasmallorca.com, open June-Sept 11pm-6am Tue-Sat, Oct-May 11pm-6am Fri, Sat) is the granddaddy of them all, and plays a mix of house, techno and trance. Dress up to get in – the doormen operate a ruthless dress code. Towards the end of the harbour is **Mar Salada** (Moll de Pelaires s/n, 971 70 27 09, www.marsalada.net, open 11pm-6am Fri-Sat), another huge, late-night disco that plays current Spanish pop music.

Ca'n Barbarà

Beyond Abraxos and just before Club de Mar, you'll find a handful of stylish places spread round the inner marina area of Ca'n Barbarà offering an excellent alternative to the frantic atmosphere of the Passeig Marítim. **El Garito Café** (971 73 69 12, www.garitocafe.com, open 7.30pm-4am Tue-Sun) is a laid-back place with black and white floor tiles, pendant lights and a cool atmosphere. Electronic, soul, funk and jazz music comes

PALMA

La 5a Puñeta. *See p67.*

courtesy of big-name international DJs at weekends (Gilles Peterson kicked off its 30th anniversary in 2008) and occasional live music. It also puts on exhibitions and serves food (8pm-1am) and cocktails (until 4am). Just along, **113** (open 9pm-3am Mon-Thur, Sun, 9pm-4am Fri, Sat) is a more exclusive place, where the people are more designer cool and the house is easygoing. Inside, there is a huge central bar and two smaller ones, tiled columns and enormous comfy sofabeds. **Mosquito Coast** (971 40 52 15, open July, Aug 11.30pm-3am Mon-Thur, 11.30pm-4am Fri, Sat, Sept-June 11.30pm-3am Thur-Sat) is the biggest of the bars along here, with two floors reverberating to Spanish pop. Above here, Plaça Gomila is the destination for grungier sounds.

GAY & LESBIAN

For information on the gay scene (though only in Castilian or Catalan), check out www. mallorcagaymap.com or the **Ben Amics**

website (www.benamics.com) or give them a call (971 71 56 70, 9am-3pm Mon-Wed, 6-9pm Thur, Fri). Both websites have links to various bars, clubs, saunas and beaches, as well as to Palma's pride celebrations, which are in June.

Nightlife

El Terreny, below the Castell de Bellver, is at the heart of Palma's small gay scene, and you'll find a range of bars and clubs here and along the western end of Avda. Joan Miró, including **La Tasca** at No.41 (not specifically a gay bar, but in the heart of the gay zone), **Marcus Pub** at No.54 (971 28 61 44), **Dylan** at No.68 and **Status Pub** at No.38 (971 45 40 30). Bars on the streets off Avda. Joan Miró include **Isidoro** (C/Alvaro de Bazan 2) and the recently opened **Club Fem** (C/Joan Miró 64, mobile 610 80 58 44), both of which are popular with gay women. You'll also find a couple of places on C/Industria, to the north-east, including **Room Service** and **NPI** (also popular with lesbians). Both hotels below have well-frequented bars; the terrace bar at the **Rosamar** is the best place for outdoor people-watching. In summer 2008 the **Mythos** (www.mythospalma.com, no phone) bi-monthly boat parties saw gaggles of straight people struggling to get on board with all the boys, girls and trannies for a three-hour floating fiesta. Check the website for where to buy tickets. The majority of the gay clubs are also situated along Avda. Joan Miró and include **Heaven** in Plaça Gomila and two that are attracting an increasingly mixed crowd: **Black Cat** at No.75, and **La Demence** at No.36. **Tito's** (*see p80*) has a gay night, Made For House, on Sunday. You'll find saunas at the **Hotel Aries** (*see below*) and, in the centre of town, **Spartacus** (C/Sant Espirit 8B, 971 72 50 07).

Where to stay

The following places are exclusively gay. For the rest of the accomodation options, *see p86.*

Hotel Aries
C/Porras 3 (971 73 78 99/www.ariesmallorca .com). **Rates** €45 single; €55-€75 double; €80 suite. **Credit** DC, MC, V. **Map** p50 U9.
This gay hotel in the heart of El Terreny has a pretty roof terrace with jacuzzi, sunbeds and bar. Things can get a little hardcore in here, and the indoor pub (10pm-5am every night) features darkrooms and cabins, while the sauna (4-11pm), has a whirlpool, wet and dry sauna, showers, cabins, darkrooms and a porn room.

Rosamar
Avda. Joan Miró 74 (971 73 27 23/www.rosamar palma.com). **Rates** €45-€65 double; €95-€100 suite. **Credit** AmEx, DC, MC, V. **Map** p50 U9.
This privately run gay hotel in El Terreny is owned by gay couple Bill and Basilio. The atmosphere is laid-back and friendly, with an open-air evening bar used as a popular meeting place for gay crowds. There are two sun terraces with sunbeds and showers on the roof with views over the bay and the Castell de Bellver. There are 40 en suite bedrooms, some with balconies and views, other quieter ones at the back.

INSIDE TRACK
LASSALLE OPTICO

The eccentric owner of shop Lassalle Optico on C/Brossa (*see p83*) has sat among his wares – a jumble of vintage glasses frames (most in terrible condition) and retro toy cars – for decades. Pop in to the opticians – apparently Mallorca's oldest – to hear his accounts (in Spanish or English) of the history of the street.

ARTS & ENTERTAINMENT
Film

There are several cinemas in town, but the only one that shows films in their original language (VO) is **Multicines Renoir**, C/Emperatriz Eugenia 6 (971 29 73 01, www.cinesrenoir. com/www.cinentradas.com, tickets €4.50-€6.30).

Music

Live music can be seen in several bars and clubs across the city (*see p79* **Nightlife**). Classical concerts are usually performed in the **Auditorium** (*see below*). Rock bands and groups play in many of the venues in and around Plaça Gomila. For current listings, get hold of a copy of *Youthing* or *Digame*.

Theatre

Palma has a thriving drama scene. For full listings of what plays are on get *Guia del Ocio* at a *kiosco*. The main venues are:

Auditorium
Passeig Marítim 18 (971 73 53 28/tickets 971 73 47 35/www.auditoriumdepalma.com/ tickets www.servicaixa.com). **Tickets** €20-€50. **Credit** DC, MC, V. **Map** p50 V8.
Stages opera, dance, pop and classical concerts.

Teatro Municipal
Passeig de Mallorca 9B (971 73 91 48). **Performances** Wed-Sun. Closed July, Aug. **Tickets** €12-€20. **No credit cards. Map** p50 B2.
Features comedy, cabaret and small productions.

SPORT
Bullfighting

Plaça de Toros
Avda. Gaspar Bennuzar Arquitecte (971 75 16 39). **Tickets** phone for prices. **No credit cards. Map** p51 Y6.
Palma's bullring, built in 1929, is in the north of the city. The bullfighting season runs from March to October but *corridas* are not frequent, with about one a month, and it's rare to see a poster advertising one. Bulls are not reared on the island and have to be shipped in from the mainland, and bullfighting does not take centre stage in the social calendar. Tickets are not hard to come by: go to the ring itself and request *sol* (sun) or *sombra* (shade); *sol* is cheaper.

Football

Football does not command the same levels of obsession here as in the rest of Spain,

Celler Sa Premsa. *See p69.*

C/Brossa is one of Palma's most interesting, eclectic shopping streets. Leading off from the highest point of C/Sant Domingo, and identified by a vintage sign signalling 'Travesia Comercial', its shops get more interesting the nearer you get to Plaça Mercat. The last stretch houses the cream of the crop, with several shops that have been in business since the 19th century, plus more recent places selling trendy fashion items.

The biggest shopping complex is **Porto Pi**, at the western end of Passeig Maritim, with more than 100 shops and a food court. There are also two big branches of department store **El Corte Inglés**, one at Avda. Jaume III 15 and another at Avda. d'Alexandre Roselló 12-16 (971 77 01 77, www.elcorteingles.com).

Note that lots of shops in Palma still adhere to traditional opening times, so you may be disappointed if you head out for some credit card action between the hours of 1pm and 4.30pm; many, however, stay open till around 8pm.

Fashion

On Born you'll find a number of fashion shops, including **Caroline Herrera** and **Corner** for designer wares, and **Zara** and **H&M** representing the high street. The streets immediately east of Born, particularly those concentrated around Plaça Chopin, are where the high-end clothes and shoes boutiques are situated; **Elle** and **Escada** are on C/Can Veri, while on nearby C/Sant Nicolau you'll find Menorcan shoe brand **Jaime Mascaró** (No.3, 971 71 94 50; *see p238* **Profile**).

Highlights on C/Unió are Spanish brands **El Ganso** (No.15, 971 71 64 20), a small, on-trend company selling British-inspired gear (tartan coats, argyle knitwear, canvas tennis-style shoes) for both men and women, and **Bimba y Lola** (C/Unió 7, 971 71 78 53), with stylish and feminine clothes, handbags and shoes. Nearby C/Brossa is home to affordable contemporary jewellery shop Twins (No.5, 971 72 64 54), trendy streetwear and accessories shops Truco o Trato (No. 13, 971 42 50 34) and True Love (No.20, 971 71 66 43). Head right up to the top of C/Brossa, where it joins C/Sant Domingo, for 19 (Plaça de Cort 6, 971 72 00 27), in the beautiful neo-Mudéjar Can Corbella building; it stocks women's clothes from hip Parisian label Sessùn, organic cosmetics from local brand Oliveda and a range of accessories. It's one of the city's most stylish outlets.

More clothes and shoe shops can be found further north on C/Sant Miquel, including a branch of **Camper** at No.17 (971 72 62 54), the groovy footwear brand based in Inca and sold all over the world (cheaper end-of-lines can be picked up from the Camper outlets in Inca and at the Festival Park mall; *see p157*), and a

despite the fact that the town's team Real Club Deportivo Mallorca, or **Real Mallorca**, has often finished in the top half of the Primera Liga and has won the national cup and reached the final of the European Cup Winners' Cup. Many *Palmesanos* could be described fair-weather fans – keen to support the team when it's riding high, but quick to abandon it when it slips down the league. Real Mallorca has 18,000 registered fans and a big stadium (**Son Moix**, in the north of the city by the Via Cintura), which has a capacity of 24,000. English businessman Paul Davidson bought up the controlling share of the club in 2008. If you want to see a game, you shouldn't have too much difficulty getting a ticket. Most matches take place on a Sunday and you can buy tickets at the stadium.

Real Club Deportivo Mallorca

Son Moix, Cami dels Reis s/n (971 22 12 21/ www.rcdmallorca.es). **Tickets** €20-€42; €7-€15 reductions. **Credit** AmEx, DC, MC, V.

SHOPPING

Palma's shopping is concentrated in two main areas that run into each other: along **Passeig des Born** and the mainly pedestrianised streets running east towards Plaça Major and bounded by **C/Unio** (which also houses several decent shops itself); and the streets running east and north of Plaça Major, including **C/Sindicat**, **C/San Miquel** and **C/Oms**.

PALMA

Made in Mallorca & Menorca

Local industry is deeply entwined with national identity on the islands.

ALBARCAS

Albarcas are hand-produced sandals traditionally made with soles from recycled car tyres and with soft leather uppers. They originated in Menorca but can now be found all over the Balearics. That local companies such as Riudavets in Alaior, Menorca (www.riudavets menorca.com) and Ben Calçat in Sóller, Mallorca (www.ben calcat.es; *see p122*) take orders from all over the world is a slight mystery – unique they may be, but we can't help thinking that what's cool in Portitxol might not fly in Paris. That said, *espadrilles* have been cropping up on the feet of the most sneering of London hipsters lately, so who knows? If you like your shoes super flat, comfortable, colourful and with a simple structure, *albarcas* may be just your cup of tea. Ben Calçat's men's models are probably the most stylish.

GORDIOLA GLASS

Gordiola, the Mallorcan glass-making family, has been producing its colourful, translucent drinking glasses, tableware and Murano-style chandeliers since 1719. The collection is sold in the factory showroom in a castle-like factory in Agaida (*see p175*), as well as from its three shops in Palma. A sea of green, turquoise and ruby awaits you, as do high prices; avoid at all costs if you have a tendency towards clumsiness.

SOBRASSADA

You'll find these cured sausages on many a Balearic breakfast plate. They are a little like chorizo, though fatter, sweeter, softer and flavoured with spices such as thyme, rosemary or oregano. They are generally free of artificial colourings, taking their reddish, orange tone from the peppers, pork and fat. The most revered type is 'Sobrassada de Mallorca de Cerdo Negro', made from the the indigenous black pig.

ENSAÏMADAS

Produced in Mallorca since the 17th century, *ensaïmadas* are one of the island's most emblematic culinary items. Made from a pastry of strong flour, water, sugar, eggs and pork lard (the name stems from the Arabic word 'saïm', meaning pork fat), these spiral-shaped sweet breads have a light, airy texture and taste a bit like French brioche. They are sold whole in a variety of sizes, dusted with icing sugar and packaged in octagonal cardboard boxes. They sometimes contain fillings such as custard, almond purée, chocolate, pumpkin strands (known as angel hair), even *sobrassada*.

PALO, HIERBAS & MENORCAN GIN

Both Palo and Hierbas, the favoured liqueurs of many Mallorcan locals,

---

branch of Barcelona fashion house **Custo** at No.15 (971 22 83 47). On C/Oms, the stores are more downmarket, with tattoo parlours at either end and various cheap clothes stores.

Out on its own in Sa Calatrava, **Modanostra** (C/Pont i Vic 8B, 971 22 74 38) has hand-stitched clothes for women (skirts €30-€60).

The district of Santa Catalina is starting to become something of a destination for small boutique-style shops. **Cronopios** (C/Pou 33,

871 96 07 80), run by a super-friendly and helpful Argentinian, sells colourful trendy shoes and clothes for women and men, while **Nucandara** (C/Despuig 62, 971 22 27 33) is Palma's most stylish shoe shop, stocking footwear by Marc by Marc Jacobs, Melissa, les Lolites and more.

On C/Santo Domingo and the streets off it you'll find the best deals on high-class artificial **Majorica** pearls. Try **Sant Joan** (C/Jaime II

originated in the 16th century as medicinal concoctions. **Palo**, made with quinine, gentian and burnt sugar, is an aperitif that's popularly mixed with soda water, but which can also be drunk neat. (Mixed with milk we found it to taste a bit like Baileys). **Túnel**, the most famous brand, comes in a colourful, classically designed bottle. Aniseed-tasting, lime-green **Hierbas** – a digestif – is made with a variety of herbs, such as chamomile, fennel and rosemary, which are left to macerate for several months. It comes in sweet and dry versions.

Gin was introduced to Menorca by the British in the 18th century and is now an intrinsic part of the island's culture, with *pomada* – gin mixed with lemonade – the tipple of choice at Menorcan festivals. Menorcan gin is made with a wine base rather than a cereal one like Dutch and British gins, and is flavoured with juniper berries and herbs and stored in white oak barrels. The **Gin Xoriguer** (Menorca's most famous brand) factory in Maó runs tours (*see p213*).

FLOR DE SAL

Natural sea salt from South and South-eastern Mallorca's coastal salt plains has started to be harvested in recent years by several different companies, of which **Flor de Sal d'Es Trenc** (www.gustomundial.com) is the most famous. Its smart white tins of 'Flor de Sal' – fast being considered the cream of sea salts – appear in tourist shops everywhere. The salt is celebrated by gourmets for its rarity, delicate flavour and high percentage of trace elements. Buy it completely pure or flavoured with ingredients such as black olives or hibiscus flowers.

16, 971 71 16 15) for an excellent selection of bracelets, earrings and necklaces at good prices; for more pricey jewels try **Miro** on Plaça Rosari.

Food & drink

For traditional Mallorcan food and drink head to **Sobrasada** (C/Santo Domingo 1, 971 71 48 87), a tiny, picturesque place where you'll have to duck to get in for the number of chorizos

hanging from the ceiling. It has a wide selection of *sobrassada* and other sausages, herb liqueurs from Bunyola and various breads. (Note: the owner prefers you to make a purchase before taking photos.) **Forno del Sant Cristo** (C/Paraires 2, 971 712 649) is good for traditional Mallorcan *ensaïmadas* and liqueurs.

For an excellent selection of home-grown and international wines try **La Vinoteca** (C/Padre Bartolomé Pou 29, 971 76 19 32), which also has an export service, or smart Spanish chain **Vinus & Brindis** (C/Josep Tous i Ferrer 4, 971 72 23 04), near the Mercat de L'Olivar. Nearby, **La Favorita** (C/Sant Miquel 38A, 971 71 37 40) remains a reasonably priced deli specialising in *Mallorquí* products. Opened in 1872, **La Pajarita** (C/Sant Nicolas 4, 971 71 18 44) is two shops in one, with gorgeous displays for both *xarcuteria* and sweets.

Fosh Food (C/Blanquerna 6, 971 29 01 08, www.foshfood.com) is an upmarket deli owned by Michelin-starred British chef Marc Fosh of Reads (*see p158*), and is worth the trip up here just for the chocolates alone. Marc and other chefs also give cooking classes here; see the website for details.

For food markets, *see p86*.

Furniture & homewares

For traditional coloured glassware, head to the Palma outlets of the famed **Gordiola** factory (C/Victoria 2, 971 71 15 41 and C/Jaime II 14, 971 71 55 18) – but be prepared for high prices.

For artisanal wooden chairs, tables and homewares, head to **Muebles Bosch** (C/Brossa 10), in business since the 19th century, while **Un Mundo de Hamacas** (C/Forn del Racó, 971 22 76 02), next to Plaça Major, is the place for furniture of the less solid variety: the shop specialises in colourful hammocks.

C/Can Veri, in the centre, is home to several of the city's commercial art galleries, as well as upmarket homewares shop **Janer** (No.1, 971 72 76 74, www.janer.es). Other galleries are concentrated on the streets behind C/Unió, such as C/Sant Jaume, and on C/Sant Feliu and C/Santa Creu in Sa Llotja.

Rialto Living (C/Sant Feliu 3C, 971 49 53 16) is Palma's premier 'concept shop', with designer tableware, bedlinen and posh bathroom accessories – as well as fashion and fragrances – from high-end niche brands.

Books & maps

You'll find a broad range of second-hand English books, prints and maps at **Fiol Llibres** (C/Oms 45A, 971 72 14 28) and **Fine Books** (C/Morey 7, 971 72 37 97). For browsing new books in a contemporary space, head to **Literanta** (C/Can Fortuny 4A, 971 42 53 35), with lots of cult literature and design-led titles as well as an in-house café. **Librería Ripoll** (C/San Miguel 12 (971 72 13 55), meanwhile, is a good bet for antiquarian books and prints on Mallorca, as well as Vespa and Fiat 500 paraphernalia (mugs, fridge magnets, prints, notepads). For local and international maps, including some lovely antiquarian reprints, head to **La Casa del Mapa** (C/Sant Domingo 11, 971 22 59 45).

Markets

Craft markets are held at Plaça de les Meravilles (mid May-mid Oct 8pm-midnight daily) and Plaça Major (Jan, Feb 10am-2pm Fri, Sat, Mar-July, Oct-Dec 10am-8pm Mon, Fri, Sat, Aug, Sept 10am-8pm daily). There is also a Saturday **flea market** (8am-2pm) on the lower Avingudes, to the east of the cathedral area.

There are **food markets** at Plaça Olivar (7am-2pm Mon-Sat), Plaça Navegació (7am-2pm Mon-Sat) and Santa Catalina (Mercat Santa Catalina, corner of C/Anníbal and C/Cerda, 7am-2pm Mon-Sat).

WHERE TO STAY

Palma has a limited number of budget places to stay, but you are spoilt for choice if you are prepared to spend and want to relax in one of its boutique-style hotels, most of which are located in converted former *casas particulares*. The city is becoming increasingly popular as a year-round destination, thanks in no small part to the no-frills airlines, so you may find these places booked up well out of the traditional high season from June to September. From November to February you should be fine just turning up, but from Easter onwards and into October it's always worth ringing ahead. Most of the stylish accommodation is situated in the old town, with the bigger hotels strung along the Passeig Marítim.

Centre, Sa Llotja & Sa Calatrava

★ **Convent de la Missió**
C/Missió 7A (971 22 73 47/www.convent delamissio.com). **Rates** (incl breakfast) €230 double; €345-€390 suite. **Credit** AmEx, DC, MC, V. **Map** p51 D2 ❶
Don't be discouraged by the discreet entrance on a dingy backstreet, for this is one of Palma's most stylish hotels. The Convent de la Missió is ferociously minimalist in a way that cleverly evokes the seminary (part of the adjacent convent) once housed here. No expense has been spared on the comfort, however, and beds and pillows are of the best

Santa Catalina Market.

quality. The superior rooms and suites have hydro-massage and Bulgari toiletries, while downstairs there is a Turkish bath and spa. Video and DVD machines are available on request. The restaurant, El Refectori (*see p70*), is one of the finest in town.

★ Dalt Murada

C/Almudaina 6 (971 42 53 00/www.daltmurada. com). **Rates** €149 double; €255 suite. **Credit** AmEx, DC, MC, V. **Map** p51 D3 ❷

None of the many townhouses converted into luxury hotels retains as much character as this one, thanks to the efforts of the wonderfully welcoming Moragues family. They have left much of the antique furniture, tapestries and paintings (most by or of members of the family) just as they were, creating a uniquely intimate atmosphere. The penthouse suite is well worth splashing out on with a large terrace with splendid views. The lovely old dining room, with its original tiled floors, now serves as a breakfast and bar area, and sports an impressive and free DVD library. The number of rooms was expanded from nine to 14 in 2006 and all have jacuzzis.

Hostal Apuntadores

C/Apuntadors 8 (971 71 34 91/www.palma-hostales.com). **Rates** €35 single; €55-€70 double. **Credit** MC, V. **Map** p50 C3 ❸

If you are on a tight budget, want to be in the heart of the action and don't mind a bit of noise from the street, then this place is ideal; just don't expect too many mod cons. There are fantastic views from the roof terrace.

Hostal Brondo

C/Ca'n Brondo 1 (971 71 90 43/www.hostal brondo.net). **Rates** €40 single; €55-€70 double; €65 triple. **Credit** MC, V. **Map** p50 C2 ❹

Ten high-ceilinged rooms, decorated with putti, silk flowers and mahogany furniture, go for a song at Hostal Brondo. Room 6 is especially nice, with a galleried balcony, as is the attic room with sloping ceiling. At the top there is also a studio flat for three or four people for a minimum of three nights; it has a well-stocked kitchen and a veritable library of videos and DVDs.

Hotel Born

C/Sant Jaume 3 (971 71 29 42/www.hotelborn. com). **Rates** €52-€68 single; €76-€108 double. **Credit** AmEx, DC, MC, V. **Map** p50 C2 ❺

By far the best of the cheaper hotels in the centre, the Born occupies a great spot at the top of the main shopping drag. A former 16th-century palace belonging to the Marquis de Ferrandell, this all has the atmosphere of a four-star place, with a huge marble reception and its own palm-shaded courtyard where you eat breakfast. The clean, airy rooms all have baths, and some also have tiny balconies with views over the courtyard.

Hotel Ca Sa Padrina

C/Calle Tereses 2 (971 42 53 00/www.hotelcasa padrina.com). **Rates** €100-€120 double. **Credit** AmEx, DC, MC, V. **Map** p51 D2 ❻

The cheaper option from the owners of the esteemed Dalt Murada (*see above*) is an altogether different affair; the hotel has no reception or staff within the building, making it an attractive prospect for those who seek total privacy and independence, but rather soulless for others. You're given a code for the main door and your room when you book, and staff are on hand in the Dalt Murada (via an automatic phone line) to deal with any problems. Rooms are small and basic with traditional furnishings, all are spotlessly clean, the location is central and prices reasonable.

Hotel Regina

C/Sant Miquel 77 (971 71 37 03/www.hostal reginapalma.com). **Rates** €35 single; €70 double; €90 triple. **Credit** MC, V. **Map** p51 E1 ❼

Useful for the train and bus stations, the Regina has clean and simple ensuite rooms, enlivened by colourful hanging baskets suspended in the windows. Rooms overlooking the street can be noisy, but there is a roof terrace for a little respite in the sun.

★ Hotel San Lorenzo

C/Sant Llorenç 14 (971 72 82 00/www.hotelsan lorenzo.com). **Rates** €170-€240 double. **Credit** AmEx, DC, MC, V. **Map** p50 B3 ❽

A tasteful conversion of a 17th-century townhouse in the neighbourhood of San Pedro (near both Carrer Apuntadors and the Museu Es Baluard), with nine lovely rooms, each furnished differently; all have comfy beds, wooden-beamed ceilings and big bathrooms beautifully decorated with traditional Spanish tiles; the suite has its own rooftop *terraza*. There's a pretty pool tucked at the back surrounded by bougainvillea, and the bar is a convivial place for a nightcap. Staff are fairly formal but friendly.

★ Hotel Santa Clara

C/San Alonso 16 (971 72 92 31/www.hotel santaclarahotel.es). **Rates** €190 double. **Credit** AmEx, MC, V. **Map** p51 E4 ❾

Situated in the shadow of the Santa Clara Convent, this well-designed four-star became a welcome addition to the city's boutique hotel options when it opened in April 2008. The €5.5 million conversion of an old townhouse contains 20 rooms (11 superior suites, seven junior and two doubles), a spa and a terrace complete with sunbathing area and great views of the cathedral. Original stone walls and wood-beamed ceilings are combined with contemporary designer furnishings to create a minimalist feel.

Hotel Saratoga

Passeig Mallorca 6 (971 72 72 40/www.hotel saratoga.es). **Rates** €115 single; €165 double; €240 suite. **Credit** AmEx, DC, MC, V. **Map** p50 B2 ❿

PALMA

This big hotel has undergone a major refit in an attempt to keep up with its smaller, trendier neighbours. And in some ways it succeeds – the reception and patio area are stylish and the rooftop pool and bar are worth a visit for the wonderful views – but the bedrooms don't quite live up to the hype. There's nothing wrong with them; it's just you could be in any of Palma's huge hotels.

★ Hotel Tres

C/Apuntadors 3 (971 71 73 33/www.hoteltres. com). **Rates** (incl breakfast) €155 single; €215 double; €455 suite. **Credit** AmEx, DC, MC, V. **Map** p50 C3 ⓫

While the Portixol goes for a maritime art deco vibe and the Puro opts for ethno-chic, the Tres (the biggest of Palma's three principal boutique hotels) plumps for more of a classic contemporary look. There's an understated Scandinavian austerity to its clean lines and limited palette that's softened by the odd splash of colour and comforts such as luxuriant beds, sleek bathrooms and a DVD library. There's a bar, but no restaurant, although snacks are available, and the breakfast is a treat. The two rooftop terraces, one with a plunge pool and sauna, offer stupendous views over the city, from the cathedral to the mountains.

Palacio Ca Sa Galesa

C/Miramar 8 (971 71 54 00/www.palaciocasa galesa.com). **Rates** €209-€315 double. **Credit** AmEx, DC, MC, V. **Map** p51 D4 ⓬

For the ultimate in discreet refinement, you can't beat this gem of a hotel, located in a 16th-century mansion in the oldest part of the city, just a couple of minutes' walk from the cathedral. There are only 12 rooms (seven suites, five doubles) and each one is decorated with panache and named after a famous composer. Facilities include a roof terrace with fine views over Palma and a small heated indoor pool, which shares its atmospheric vaulted space with a sauna and mini-gym. Complimentary tea and cake is available from 4pm to 6pm in a replica of Monet's kitchen at Giverny, and the spoils of the honour bar (sherry is available free) can be enjoyed in the elegant lounge (with a log fire in winter).

★ Palau Sa Font

C/Apuntadors 38 (971 71 22 77/www.palausa font.com). **Rates** €90 single; €145-€205 double; €195-225 suite. Closed 3wks Jan. **Credit** AmEx, MC, V. **Map** p50 C3 ⓭

In a perfect location in the heart of town, the German-run Palau Sa Font blends classic Mallorcan architecture with contemporary design in a 16th-century former palace. The concept is 'art as part of everyday life', with colourful designer touches in the entrance and bar area; however, these belie the spartan nature of the 19 guest rooms: although a different original painting appears on the door of each, there are strangely no artworks in the rooms themselves. Rather thin walls can create noise problems too. On

Dalt Murada. *See p87.*

the first floor is a pretty terrace area with a plunge pool and sun loungers. Other draws include one of the best breakfast buffets in town and very friendly staff.

Pons

C/del Vi 8 (971 72 26 58). **Rates** €45-€50 double. **No credit cards. Map** p50 C3 ⓮

This simple one-star *hostal residencia* is in an old Palma house, with rooms arranged around a central courtyard just off the Passeig des Born. It's less noisy than the similarly priced Hostal Apuntadores.

★ Puro Hotel

C/Montenegro 12 (971 42 54 50/www.purohotel. com). **Rates** €165 single; €235 double; €551 suite. **Credit** AmEx, DC, MC, V. **Map** p50 C3 ⓯

Design mag heaven. Styling itself as an 'urban oasis', the Puro offers a blissed-out, ethno-hippie panacea to calm the weary metropolitan sophisticate. A chilled soundtrack wafts through the airy public spaces; strings of tiny shells cascade down the walls of the oriental-slanted restaurant; a massive white-feather light installation hovers over the hip bar. Bedrooms come equipped with broadband access, yoga mats, a flash audio/TV system and slate and dark-wood bathrooms boasting monsoon showers. It would all be a bit OTT if it wasn't so relaxing; there's also a plunge pool and huge double beds on the roof on which to recline and order chilled bubbly from down below.

A cheaper alternative to its four-star neighbours and offering the same priceless views over the Bay of Palma and an indoor pool.

Hotel Mirador
Passeig Marítim 10 (971 73 20 46/www.hotel mirador.es). **Rates** €84.10-€96.10 single; €100-€124 double. **Credit** AmEx, DC, MC, V. **Map** p48 V8
A comfortable high-rise hotel next door to the Tryp Bellver (*see below*), which is slightly cheaper but offers the same views and similar amenities, including a plunge pool (and indoor and outdoor pools, sauna and jacuzzi in an affiliated pool across the road) and good breakfasts. There are good deals to be had at weekends and out of season.

Hotel Tryp Bellver
Passeig Marítim 11 (971 73 51 42/www.sol melia.com). **Rates** €153-€230 double. **Credit** AmEx, DC, MC, V. **Map** p48 V8
The best of the big seafront hotels in the area, with a shade more character than the rest, a funky white exterior and curved stone balconies. The rooms are a decent size and all have balconies – try to get one on a high floor as the views are stunning. Pool, gym and all the mod cons you would expect.

Valparaiso Palace
C/Francisco Vidal Sureda 23 (971 40 03 00/www.grupotel.com). **Rates** €152-€163 single; €248-€270 double; €321-€1,017 suite. **Credit** AmEx, MC, V. **Map** p48 U10
A plush five-star place set in its own grounds below the Castell de Bellver. Great views across the entire bay and superb amenities, with three pools – two huge ones outside and another smaller indoor one – gym, *terraza*, restaurant and bar, but rooms are of a three-star standard.

Portitxol & Ciutat Jardí

There are really only three noteworthy places to stay on the eastern bay, all of them closeish to the city in Portitxol and Ciutat Jardí.

Hotel Ciutat Jardí
C/Illa de Malta 14, Ciutat Jardí (971 26 00 07/www.hciutatj.com). **Rates** €140-€270 double (closed mid Dec-mid Jan). **Credit** AmEx, MC, V.

Passeig Marítim & around

Big hotels tend to dominate this part of town. You shouldn't have too much difficulty getting a room if you want to stay here at the weekend, as they mainly cater for business travellers during the week and will often give discounted rates on Friday and Saturday nights.

AC Ciutat de Palma
Plaça Pont 3 (971 22 23 00/www.ac-hotels.com). **Rates** €90-€160 double. **Credit** AmEx, MC, V. **Map** p48 V8
The designers have gone for a minimalist look in the common areas, with a black, white and grey design, sliding Japanese-style doors and low, comfortable chairs. It's set around a simple, sun-drenched patio, with a small restaurant on one side and a bar on the other, which offers free drinks to residents. This theme is continued in the rooms, where even the mini-bar is free. The rooms don't quite achieve the same level of cool as the rest of the hotel, but they are a good size (especially the superior ones) and comfortable. The bathrooms are all marble, but with shower only.

Costa Azul
Passeig Marítim 7 (971 73 19 40). **Rates** €68-€74 single; €88-€109 double. **Credit** AmEx, DC, MC, V. **Map** p48 V8

> ### INSIDE TRACK
> ### CA, CA'N
>
> You'll notice that many restaurants, cafés and hotels start with the *Mallorquí* words 'ca' and 'ca'n' – the literal translation of which is 'house of' (the equivalent of the French 'chez').

The four-star Hotel Ciutat Jardí was built in 1921. It's a lovely looking pad with a distinctive colonial air about it, an eye-catching dome dominating the centre and grand palm trees shading the pool. The rooms, especially those with huge sweeping terraces overlooking the sea, are oases of calm. The suite is particularly impressive, with views of both the sea and the mountains from the glass living room and a bedroom in a cupola. Good for a romantic getaway.

★ Hotel Portixol

C/Sirena 27, Es Portixol (971 27 18 00/ www.portixol.com). **Rates** (incl breakfast) €135 single; €220-€420 double; €420 suite. **Credit** AmEx, DC, MC, V. **Map** p49 Z9 ㉑

A place for urban sophisticates, this Swedish-owned boutique hotel is stereotypically in Scando in design – minimal, calming and ultra-suave, with neat details like binoculars in your room for perusing the comings and goings at the port or simply gawping at people in the pool. The bedrooms are comfortable, while the brightly coloured mosaic-tiled bathrooms are a refreshing change from clinical white. Since the hotel is smack-bang in the middle of the marina it's worth paying extra for a room with a view. When the hotel opened in 1999, *Wallpaper** voted it one of its fave retreats. The owners opened Port de Sóller's Hotel Espléndido in 2005 (*see p130*).

Portofino Urban Sea Hotel

C/Trafalgar 24, Platja Ciutat Jardi (971 26 04 64/www.portofinourbanseahotel.com). **Rates** (incl breakfast) €90-€110 double. **Credit** AmEx, MC, V.

A basic, comfortable 73-room boutique hotel, painted turquoise blue and situated just a block from the beach. It also has its own swimming pool, restaurant and bar. Request a balcony when booking as not all rooms have one. It's handy for the airport and the centre of Palma. A sister hotel, Azul Playa (www.hotelazulplaya.com), is located down the road in Portitxol.

Son Vida

Son Vida is on the western outskirts of Palma, around 15 minutes' drive from the centre.

Arabella Sheraton Golf Hotel Son Vida

C/Vinagrella s/n, Costa d'en Blanes (971 78 71 00/www.luxurycollection.com). **Rates** €361-€385 double. **Credit** AmEx, DC, MC, V.

This beautifully designed, ultra-luxurious modern hotel is set in its own grounds below the Castillo Hotel Son Vida (*see below*). It boasts huge rooms with comfortable beds, thick carpets, marble bathrooms and balconies with views across the grounds. A grand reception area leads to all the amenities: large pool, fitness centre, spa and 18-hole golf course. The restaurant Plat d'Or offers superb cuisine, while another less formal dining room serves Mallorcan and Spanish dishes.

Castillo Hotel Son Vida

C/Raixa 2, Urb. Son Vida (971 79 00 00/ www.hotelsonvida.com). **Rates** €195-€410 double. **Credit** AmEx, DC, MC, V.

This hotel is regarded as one of the finest on the island. It is built around the remains of an old tower and set in extensive grounds overlooking the city. It's extremely luxurious in the old style – grand entrance hall, impeccable service, big wooden furniture and wall hangings – with an extraordinary *terraza* that affords breathtaking views over the city and harbour. Rooms vary: the best are high-ceilinged and have balconies, but those high up are without balconies and feel somewhat cramped. The hotel has an indoor pool, tennis courts, spa treatment and two 18-hole golf courses – one for exclusive use of guests and another it shares with the Arabella Sheraton (*see above*).

RESOURCES

Bike hire

Palma on Bike Centre *Plaça Salvador Coll 8 (971 71 80 62). Passeig Marítim. Avda. Gabriel Roca 15 (971 91 89 88).* Both *www.palma onbike.com*. **Open** *Centre* 10am-7pm Mon-Sat. *Passeig Marítim* 10am-7pm daily. **Rates** €4 1hr; €12-€16 1 day; €30-€42 3 days. A deposit of €100, or a credit card or a passport is required.

Internet

Babaloo *C/Verja 2, Santa Catalina (871 95 77 25/www.babaloointernet.com).* **Open** 10am-10pm Mon-Fri; 10am-2.30pm Sat; 3-10pm Sun. **No credit cards. Map** p51 A3.
CyberCentral *C/Soledat 4, Sa Llotja (971 71 29 27).* **Open** 9.30am-10pm Mon-Sat. **No credit cards. Map** p50 C3.

Police station

Avda. Sant Ferran 42 (971 22 55 00). **Map** p50 V7.

Post office

C/Constitució 6 (971 22 88 82). **Map** p50 C3.

Tourist information

902 10 23 65/www.palmavirtual.es
Casal Solleric *Passeig des Born 27 (971 72 96 34).* **Open** 9am-8pm daily. **Map** p50 C3.
Parc de las Estaciones office *Plaça Espanya (971 75 43 29).* **Open** 8am-8pm daily. **Map** p51 E1.
Plaça de la Reina *No.2 (971 71 22 16/ www.infomallorca.net).* **Open** 9am-8pm Mon-Fri; 9am-2pm Sat. **Map** p50 C3.

Regional tourist office, with information on the whole of Mallorca (albeit limited at times).

GETTING AROUND

By bike
If you're staying in Palma, it's well worth hiring a bike to explore the further reaches of the city, and to take advantage of the waterside cycle path that runs most of the way around the Bay of Palma. *See also p90.*

By bus
A range of bus routes circumnavigate Palma's old town (almost all passing through Plaça Espanya) and run along the coastal roads either side of the bay. The city tourist offices have maps of bus routes, but the most useful is the No.1, which runs from the airport (journeys to or from the airport cost €1.85) to Porto Pi, via Plaça Espanya, Passeig de Mallorca and the Passeig Marítim. The No.2 passes through the centre of the old city. Among the useful routes going further afield are the No.4 to Gènova, and the No.15 or No.25 along the Platja de Palma to S'Arenal. There are no buses to Calvià (for privately run buses, call Transport de les Illes Balears on 900 17 77 77 or visit www.tib.caib.es). Within the Greater Palma area there's a flat fare of €1.10, or you can buy a ten-journey pass at news kiosks for €8. For more information call 971 21 44 44 or visit www.mtpalma.es. Tourist buses (Palma City Sightseeing 971 22 04 28, www.mallorcatour.com) run on two routes every 20 minutes around the city (and as far as the Castell de Bellver). You can jump on or off the buses as many times as you want within a 24-hour period and there's an audio commentary (€13, €6.50 reductions, free under-8s).

By car
Palma is a very easy city to get around on foot, so don't even think about driving in the centre – you are much better off leaving your car in one of the city's numerous car parks. The most convenient one is underneath the Parc de la Mar (971 72 77 03), at the foot of the cathedral, which was extended a couple of years ago. A central alternative is below Plaça Major, accessed along C/Unió at the bottom of the Rambla.

By taxi
Taxis are cheap and plentiful – there are ranks at the bottom of Avda. Antoni Maura, on Passeig des Born and in Plaça Weyler. Alternatively, simply hail one with its green light on or call **Radio Taxi** (971 75 54 40), **Palma Taxi** (971 40 14 14) or **Fono Taxi** (971 72 80 81).

PALMA

Palau Sa Font. *See p88.*

The Bay of Palma

Some of Mallorca's best beaches – and its most notorious resort.

Despite a major clean-up and renovation programme by the island authorities, much of the Bay of Palma remains the Mallorca of package holiday legend: a land of boorish Brits, chips with everything and holiday rep TV shows.

The eastern side of the bay (more favoured by Germans) has been improved in recent years but, alas, much of the strip remains dreary. The western portion (dominated by the British) has been smartened up, with even the most notorious offender, Magaluf, almost presentable. The area does, however, have the best, longest, widest white-sand beaches on the island.

PALMA

West Bay of Palma

Mostly purpose-built for the onslaught of sunseekers from northern Europe, the West Bay, more than the east, seems to have modelled itself on the success of the Costa del Sol. Marbella exists in the form of **Portals Nous**, while echoes of Torremolinos can be found in Magaluf, and with them you also get two extremes of clientele: lager louts and demented teenagers in Magaluf, shameless snobs and C-list celebrities in Portals Nous.

These dubious qualities aside, what you do get are some affordable package deals, some reasonable dining, great beaches and easy access to the beautiful Tramuntana mountains and the west coast.

CALA MAJOR, SANT AGUSTI, CA'S CATALA & ILLETES

The first settlements you hit coming out of Palma heading west are **Cala Major**, **Sant Agustí** and **Ca's Català**, none of which are particularly interesting unless you savour the scenery of car rental offices, pizza joints and souvenir shops. (Cala Major, though, has an island of culture in the form of the **Fundació Pilar i Joan Miró** – *see p78* **Art Attack**).

Illetes has a couple of decent sandy cove beaches, flanked by sloping, pine-studded but heavily populated banks. It's a good base if you want a beach holiday within easy access of the city. Once off the main road, a right turn brings you to **Cala Comtesa**, with a substantial parking area and a scoop of sand that's quiet out of season. A left turn takes you to **Platja Illetes**; there's not as much parking here but better facilities – a bus stop (No.3 from Palma to Port Andratx), beach massages and a couple of restaurants just across the road from the sand. It also has a couple of laid-back beach clubs.

Where to stay, eat & drink

Most of the hotels along this stretch are block-booked by English and French travel agencies but there are good deals to be had.

In **Sant Agustí**, try **Hostal La Mimosa** (C/Suecia 5, 971 40 03 30, www.lamimosa.com, doubles incl breakfast €48-€56), which offers clean, simple accommodation; its best feature is a pool tucked away behind a walled garden.

Ca's Català is home to a better budget option, though: **Hostal Ca's Català** (Ctra. de Palma–Andratx, km7, 971 40 50 08, closed mid Oct-mid Apr, doubles incl breakfast around €55), decorated with mix-and-match junky antique furniture and old maps in the large lounge area, and with a pool.

Nearby, the exclusive **Hospes Maricel** (Ctra. de Palma–Andratx 11, 971 70 77 44, doubles €223-€465) offers a pocket of tranquillity and elegance, with a hip design, comfortable rooms, an infinity pool with chill-out area in the shade, a private jetty and coves cut into the rock where you can get a massage above the lapping water. The *'degustación'* breakfast is superb, which it should be given the hilarious price (€37.50). For family atmosphere and creature comforts though, nowhere in the area beats the **Hotel Bon Sol** (Paseo de Illetas 30, 971 40 21 11, www.hotelbonsol.es, doubles €166-€236), a labyrinthine hotel built into the cliffs with plush rooms, sea views, two pools, a private beach and spa all built into the price. A cosy living room peopled by knights in shining armour, free yoga classes and a restaurant that's buzzing every night make it a home-away-from-home for legions of return guests.

In terms of eating, **Avinguda Joan Miró**, the endless road running around the west of the bay, is lined with English pubs and countless places dishing up pizzas, ice-cream and anything with chips. There are a few pockets of civilisation, however.

In **Cala Major**, **Casa Tauro** (C/Miguel Rosselló Alemany 1, 971 40 01 04, closed Mon Nov-Mar, €€) is one of the oldest (opened 1981) and friendliest bistros in the area, with a pretty terrace surrounded by geraniums and dragon trees. Grilled meats and paellas are the order of the day here, with a bargain daily special. The slipway down to the beach is old Torremolinos in miniature, with a couple of ersatz Spanish places, such as flamenco bar **Al Andalus** (C/Gavina 7, 971 40 58 03, €€), which puts on a dinner and show on Thursdays and Sundays. Next door, Danish-owned restaurant **Los Laeros Ca Na Christina** (Avda. Joan Miró 275, mobile 656 75 58 56, closed Thur, mid Nov-Dec, €€) is a break from the norm, offering Danish food served on a charming bamboo roof terrace. And if you can't get through your holiday without a curry, there's **Nawaab** (Avda. Joan Miró 309, 971 40 16 91, 1pm-midnight daily, €€) in Sant Augustí, which has branches in Leeds, Huddersfield and Bradford.

Generally, things are a bit more refined in **Illetes**, though choices are fewer. Smart Mallorcan food can be found at **Restaurant Es Parral** (Passeig Illetes 75, 971 70 11 27, closed Dec & Jan, €€), which is a good dinner choice,

but the menu is a little heavy for lunch. The stunningly situated **Virtual Club** (Passeig Illetes 60, 971 70 32 35, closed mid Oct-Apr, €€€) serves *Franco-Mallorquí* cuisine to celebs and expat hipsters – with dishes such as turbot with hazelnuts and bacon, and lobster lasagne with star anise – on a terrace overlooking the sea. It also has a snack bar that knocks out club sandwiches, a nightclub in a cave and a marvellously handy dinghy collection service should you rock up in a yacht. If you don't, you can still taste the high life by hiring a sun lounger for €9 – the price includes water and fruit provided at intervals. Next door, **Las Terrazas Beach Club** (Avda. Illetes 52A, 971 40 10 31, closed Mon, www.balnearioilletes.com) is a sexy white-on-white alfresco lounge with those same heavenly views.

PORTALS NOUS & PALMA NOVA

Portals Nous has a jet-set reputation, but its reality is a little more economy than club class. The large marina, **Puerto Portals**, with its flashy restaurants and chic boutiques, does attract its share of celebrities, but they're more of the ilk of Peter Stringfellow than Claudia Schiffer. The main reason to come is for a swanky dinner and swankier shopping at the Blue Marlin mall. It also has two beaches. The one to the right of the marina as you face the sea is a grubby town beach adjoining **Marineland**, which features kid-pleasing dolphin and seal shows. The other, to the left facing a rocky islet, is used more by locals.

By contrast, **Palma Nova** is quieter and less chi-chi than Portals Nous, with more low-key beachfront cafés and bars and a wide swathe of sand shaded by mature umbrella pines. If you hop around the coast a little towards Portals Nous, you'll come across a couple of more secluded inlets, including the lovely **Son Caliu**, with its fat, pineapple-shaped palms, fine sand and gentle waters. Keep going beyond Portals Nous following signs to Cala Vinyes and you'll hit the secluded **Cala Falco** at the end of a dirt track. It's a little bit of paradise on this stretch of the *bahia* with a Hawaiian-style beach bar (group parties can be arranged, call Antonio on mobile 665 27 92 18; licence laws prevent any wild affairs, however) shaded by umbrella pines, jewel blue water and white powder sand.

Marineland

C/Garcilaso de la Vega 9, Costa de'n Blanes (971 67 51 25/www.aspro-ocio.es). **Open** *July, Aug* 9.30am-6pm daily. *Feb-June, Sept-mid Dec* 9.30am-5pm daily. Closed mid Dec-Jan. **Admission** €15-€21; €13.50 3-12s; free under-3s. **Credit** AmEx, MC, V.

THE BEST PALMA BEACHES

For avoiding the hordes
Cala Falco; *see p93.* **Cala Portals Vells**; *see p96.* **Son Caliu**; *see p93.*

For people-watching
Magaluf; *see p95.* **Portals Nous**; *see p93.*

For family fun
Can Pastilla; *see p98.* **Platja Illetes**; *see p92.*

PALMA

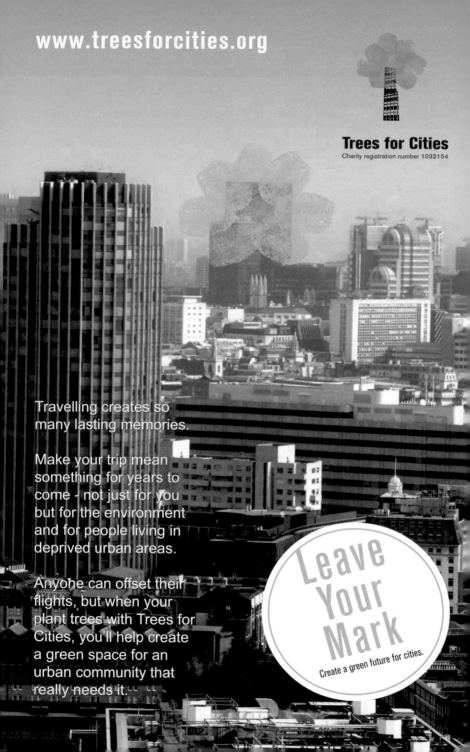

Where to stay, eat & drink

Portals Nous is definitely not the place to come if you're on a limited budget, unless you manage to bag a good package deal. The **Lindner Golf & Wellness Resort Portals Nous** (C/Arquitecte Francesc Casas 18, 971 70 77 77, www.lindnerhotels.com, doubles incl breakfast €160-€220) is an all-round four-star package in the style of a big-game hunting lodge, with something to please everyone – golf, spa, beauty salon, swimming pool, a kids' pavilion, crèche facilities, a snack bar and restaurant **Es Romaní** (closed lunch and all Tue, €€€). The Sunday jazz brunch attracts diners from all over.

Down on the waterfront, the four-star **Hotel Son Caliu** (Avda. Son Caliu 8, 971 68 22 00, www.soncaliu.com, closed 28 Nov-20 Jan, doubles incl breakfast €114-€159) has private access to a small, secluded cove, with mature subtropical gardens spilling on to the sand. Facilities include an indoor pool, sauna and tennis courts, and the large, comfortable rooms all have terraces or balconies.

A beautifully situated alternative is the lovely 52-room **Hotel Bendinat** (C/Andrès Ferret Sobral 1, 971 67 57 25, www.hotel bendinat.com, closed end Oct-early Apr, doubles incl breakfast €190-€280), which perches over a rocky cove within lovely terraced gardens that include a pool and access to the sea. The bedrooms are sleek and spacious with magical balconies overlooking the sea.

You'll find one of the highest concentrations of high-class restaurants in the area in Portals Nous, with something to suit everyone, but beware of elevated prices. The aptly named **Ritzi** (Puerto Portals 34-35, 971 68 41 04,www.ritzi-mallorca.com, daily from 7.30pm) is reassuringly chic with a menu to match, serving tuna carpaccio with wasabi mousse and ginger; sea bass on steamed bok choy with lemongrass; and rack of lamb on Barolo lentils. Next door, **Due** (971 67 73 37) offers more basic pizza and pasta dishes, and a lunchtime menu for €23.50, making it one of the port's more affordable options. Next door to this is **Spoon** (971 67 72 25, open 6pm-1am), serving Asian-inspired dishes such as Thai soup, wok scallops and sashimi; it's handy if you want to eat late. Top billing, however, goes to Michelin-starred **Tristán** (Puerto Portals, 971 67 55 47, www.grupo.com, closed lunch all Mon mid Oct-Apr and all Nov-Feb, €€€€), built around a small plaza and decked out like a footballer's wedding. The restaurant produces the sort of accomplished, overblown dishes beloved of Michelin inspectors but the bar is a little more laid-back, with a lighter menu offering the likes of prawn dim sum, and Wagyu burgers.

Tahini Sushi Bar & Restaurant (Puerto Portals 2, 971 67 60 25, €€€), owned by the Cappuccino chain (*see below*), is a Japanese restaurant that manages to make minimalism ostentatious with its decor of sleek black wood, bamboo canes and pebble and water features. **Cappuccino Puerto Portals** (Puerto Portals 1, 971 67 72 93, www.cafe-cappuccino.net, €€) is good for a daytime coffee and a spot of people-watching, with its large sunny terrace crammed with wicker chairs.

Beautifully situated next to a tiny church high above all the glitz of the port, at the end of a narrow quiet road leading from the town, is **Port'Alt** (C/Oratorio 1, 971 67 61 79, closed dinner Sun & all Mon, €€). The menu centres around steaks, duck magret and the like, and there is a large, leafy garden terrace on the headland overlooking the sea.

Heading towards Palma Nova, you'll find **Mood** (Ctra.Palma–Andratx km11, 971 67 94 02, www.moodbeach.com) a breath of fresh air after the pomp and poseurs of the port. Open year-round, it's a lively partygoers' paradise with a restaurant that wraps around the bay, a swimming pool and beach access, a barbecue, *chiringuito*, tennis, kids' water-slide, massage and just about every other service you can think of to keep the troops entertained. There are good-value nights throughout the week, such as €3 drinks on Mondays and cookery classes on Thursdays (€35 including lunch).

MAGALUF

Despite the clean-up a few years back, when the worst of the strip's hotels were demolished, Magaluf retains a personality that's overbearing to the point of being offensive. It's now largely high-rise three-star apart-hotels and depressingly English pubs and caffs, proudly declaring themselves 'Manchester owned and run' on the bunting that flies above the beachside terraces. It's basically Blackpool with guaranteed sun, and its very notoriety has made it a 'sight' in its own right. You wouldn't want to stay here, but it's worth spending half an hour of your time observing the curious phenomenon of mass tourism up close.

Magaluf does, though, score highly on the theme park stakes, with **Aqualand Magaluf** and its little cowboy brother the **Western Water Park** providing plenty of aquatic fun for the kids. Many of the hotels stage Vegas-style shows, or you could try the popular **Pirates Adventure** show, awash with 'Pirate Punch' and much swashbuckling.

The beach here may be permanently packed, but it's a beauty, offering powdery white sand, clear blue water and, offshore, the tiny **Isla de sa Porrassa** waiting to be explored.

PALMA

Aqualand Magaluf

*Ctra. Cala Figuera 1-23 (971 13 13 71/www.
aspro-ocio.es).* **Open** *July, Aug* 10am-6pm daily;
June, Oct 10am-5pm daily. Closed Nov-May.
Admission €21.50; €13.50 3-12s;
free under-3s. **Credit** AmEx, MC, V.

Pirates Adventure

*Ctra. Sa Porrassa 12 (971 13 04 11/www.
piratesadventure.com).* **Show times** call in
advance. Closed Nov-Mar. **Admission** €41-
€45.50; €23.50-€25 reductions. **Credit** MC, V.

Western Water Park

*Ctra. Cala Figuera 12-22 (971 13 12 03/
www.western-park.com).* **Open** *May* 10am-
5pm Mon-Fri, Sun. *June-Oct* 10am-6pm daily.
Closed Nov-Apr. **Admission** €22; €14 3-12s;
free under-3s. **Credit** AmEx, MC, V.

Where to stay, eat & drink

Nowhere to stay or eat can be recommended
in Magaluf (the whole place smells like a
fried-chicken joint), but if it's nightlife of a
questionable quality you're after, there are
pubs and bars galore and the biggest disco in
Europe: **BCM** (Avda. de S'Olivera 14, 971 13
26 09, www.bcm-planetdance.com, closed Oct-
Apr), a veritable temple to binge drinking,
which packs in 4,000 people a night in high

season. The main plaça, BCM Square, is named
after it and is filled with the 'trendiest pre-club
bars in town' – **Bobby's Tavern** and **Coyote
Ugly**, the US saloon-style theme bar. It's also
the best place in Mallorca to watch a match. And
if that's not enough to keep you entertained, you
can always try your luck at the **Gran Casino
Mallorca** (Urb. Sol de Mallorca s/n, 971 30 00
00, www.casinodemallorca.com).

CAP DE CALA FIGUERA

The West Bay's best-kept secret is located at
its westernmost tip; the two pretty beaches
here are a world away from the rammed sands
of Magaluf. Follow the road out of town along
the hard-baked, pine-studded landscape to
Cala Portals Vells with its V-shaped inlets.

El Mago is Mallorca's first official nudist
beach, carved out of the sandstone cliffs and
backed by aromatic pine forests and very
little development. There's a small port and
matchbox-sized boats.

From here you can walk around the cliffs
to **Portals Vells** and on to the **Cove de la
Mare de Déu** – a chapel built into the rock
by fishermen in the 15th century to give thanks
for a safe return home. The caverns are actually
the mines from where the rock was hewn to
build the chapel.

Continue another mile or so along the road
and you'll come to the headland, crowned by a
lighthouse, of **Cap de Cala Figuera**, giving
stunning views back across the bay.

Where to eat & drink

There are two *chiringuitos* on **Cap de Cala
Figuera**, one on each bay. **Es Repòs** (Platja
Portals Vells s/n, 971 18 04 92, closed lunch
July & Aug and all mid Oct-mid Mar) is the
friendliest and best. You can spend anything
from €6 to €60 here, depending on whether
you go for grilled *calamares* or spiny lobster
tail slathered in *alioli*. **Restaurante Playa
del Mago** on El Mago beach (971 18 07 66,
closed dinner and Nov-Mar) gets the shade
early, which you might want to bear in mind if
you're visiting in the cooler months of spring
or summer; it's very expensive for what it is
(€16 for squid rings), but it is hugely popular
for a lunchtime paella nevertheless.

RESOURCES

Internet

Magaluf *Galaxy, C/Lope de Vega Local 98
(971 13 15 33).*

Post office

Palma Nova *C/Na Boira 2 (971 68 00 06).*

BCM

Profile Palma Aquarium

Mallorca's newest aquarium is up there with the world's finest.

As one of the most eagerly anticipated projects in Mallorca for years, costing around €32 million, it's something of a relief that Palma Aquarium (*see p98*) has been lauded as a great success since its opening in 2007. Located in S'Arenal, and part of a strategy to spruce up a neighbourhood that had become beleaguered by the effects of mass tourism, the aquarium is by contrast a striking modern building.

Head curator Aharon Miroz worked for many years with French oceanographer Philippe Cousteau, son of Jacques Cousteau, and when Miroz insisted on making at least half of the aquarium Mediterranean, his critics thought he was mad. And yet he's pulled it off with a number of carefully gathered species of flora and fauna – 55 tanks in tota, containing around 700 different marine species.

The low-lit walk through the tanks resembles an underwater cavern, while 'Sea Secrets' labels reveal the mysteries of the deep (holy fish, for example, live in harems; if the male dies a female changes sex and becomes male).

The Indian Ocean section reveals disco pink corals, geometric Picasso trigger fish, prehistoric zebra fish and the graceful, slow-moving butterfly

fish. The old wife fish looks like two striped fish glued together, while blood shrimp and open meat coral lend a certain B-movie horror to the deep. Fact boxes around the tanks tell you that the Napoleon wrasse can grow up to two metres long, while the cleaner wrasse attracts queues of fish waiting for a good scrub down.

The Jungle is the largest rooftop garden in Spain, created by Simon and Victoria Arnold, who travel the world designing state-of-the-art aquariums. It replicates a tropical rainforest with waterfalls and ferocious piranhas, and also has its own micro-climate, allowing the tropical plants there to flourish.

After a stroll through a more serious Discovery Zone, which educates about the importance of protecting nature's most precious element – water – the grand finale is a stroll through the aquarium's eye-popping shark tank. It is the deepest in Europe, holding 3.5 million litres of water and designed so that sharks cruise in profile to your side, or a belly-view from above. There's even handy cushions provided to take the weight off your feet so you can sit back and simply absorb the sea. It is indeed a journey to the bottom of the ocean.

PALMA

GET IN
Those with PADI divers licences can organise a dive through the shark tanks.

DON'T MISS
The Jellyfish tank is surprisingly appealing, with subdued lighting and chilled out music.

PALMA

Tourist information

Illetes *OIT, Passeig Illetes 4 (971 40 27 39/www.calvia.com).* **Open** 9am-3pm Mon-Fri.
Magaluf *OIT, Avda. Pere Vaquer Ramis 1 (971 13 11 26/www.calvia.com).* **Open** 9am-6pm daily.
Palma Nova *OIT, Passeig de la Mar 13 (971 68 23 65/www.calvia.com).* **Open** 9am-6pm daily.

GETTING THERE

By bus
From Palma, the No.1 runs to Porto Pí, 3 to Cas Català, 6 to Sant Agustí, and the 20 to Palmanova.

East Bay of Palma

Favoured mainly by German package tourists, the East Bay starts well, having admirably retained some of its Mallorcan flavour. After that, alas, it's all downhill...

CAN PASTILLA TO S'ARENAL

Cala Estancia is becoming something of an extension of the seriously up-and-coming Ciutat Jardí, having smartened up in the last couple of years with the opening of hip hotels, restaurants and attractions, including the style-conscious beach club **Puro Beach** (C/Pagell 1, 971 74 47 44, www.purobeach.com) and the much-lauded **Palma Aquarium** (*see below and p97* **Profile**). **Can Pastilla**, the next stop along, still has some way to go in the style stakes but boasts five and a half kilometres of beach and watersports galore (particularly banana boating).

A footpath and cycle track stretches all the way to S'Arenal via encroaching apartment blocks and endless shops selling beach towels. If Magaluf points to Blackpool, **S'Arenal** is Frankfurt-on-Sea, albeit a sunny one. The beach may be long and wide, but there's little joy to be had in coming here, unless you're planning to visit **Aqualand del Arenal,** the area's waterpark.

Aqualand del Arenal
Autovia Palma–S'Arenal, km15, Exit 13 (971 44 00 00/www.aspro-ocio.es). **Open** *July, Aug* 10am-6pm daily. *May, June, Sept, Oct* 10am-5pm daily. Closed Nov-Apr. **Admission** €21.50; €13.50 3-12s; free under-3s. **Credit** AmEx, MC, V.

Palma Aquarium
C/Manuela de los Herreros i Sorà 21 (971 26 83 82/www.palmaaquarium.com). **Open** 10am-6pm daily (last entrance 5pm). **Admission** €19.50; €15 4-12s; free under-3s. **Credit** AmEx, MC, V. *See p97* **Profile**.

Where to stay, eat & drink

In **Cala Estancia**, the spanking new **Marina Luz** (971 49 24 00, www.marina-hotels.com, double €94-€228) was reformed last year in swish, minimalist nautical style and it's a bargain for the price. The terrace looks straight out to sea, while a colourful lounge, serving decent cocktails, provides a cheerful chill-out space in a storm. The place is open year-round. Beach club **Puro Beach** has all-white decor, beautiful staff and attention to detail, but, although also good for cocktails, the cooking can sometimes be disappointing. A better bet for dining is to head around the corner to **Anima Sea Lounge** (C/Pins 17, 971 74 54 37, www.animasealounge.com), which, while still hopelessly cool with its turquoise colour scheme and polka dot cut out furniture, takes itself a little less seriously. And the food is great: a kind of Mallorcan-Italian-Asian fusion – sounds irritating, tastes great.

Heading round the bay into **Can Pastilla** and towards **S'Arenal** there are plenty of three-star hotel options, although most are block-booked by German tour companies.

The classiest S'Arenal option is the **Mallorca Marriott Son Antem Golf Resort & Spa** (Ctra. Palma–Llucmajor, km3.4, 971 12 91 00, www.marriott.com, doubles incl breakfast €169-€218), a few kilometres out of town. The villa-style resort is set in acres of rolling countryside and offers two championship-level golf courses, holistic spa treatments and world-class dining.

A better choice if you want to party is the aptly named four-star **Hotel Gran Fiesta** (C/Marbella 28, 971 26 31 24, www.hmhotels.net, doubles incl breakfast €66-€144). Located just across the road from the beach, it has a sauna, two swimming pools and nightly entertainment laid on. For something cheap and cheerful, meanwhile, try the 30-room **Hotel Las 5 Islas** (C/San Cristóbal 38, 971 44 11 20, www.hotelsoldemallorca.com, doubles €25-€60 incl breakfast); all the rooms here have terraces, and a handful of them have sea views.

RESOURCES

Tourist information
S'Arenal *OIT, Plaça Reina Maria Cristina s/n (971 44 04 14/www.llucmajor.org).* **Open** *Apr-Oct* 8am-2.30pm Mon-Fri. Closed Nov-Mar.

GETTING THERE

By bus
From Palma, the Nos.15 and 23 run to S'Arenal, and the 17 runs as far as Can Pastilla.

West Mallorca

Sa Pedrissa.
See p121.

West Mallorca

BAY OF POLLENÇA

BAY OF ALCUDIA

ALCUDIA
Alcanada
Es Mal Pas
Port d'Alcúdia
Platja d'Alcúdia
Ses Fotges
S'Oberta

Port de Pollença
Cala Sant Vicenç
L'Horta
POLLENÇA
Can Singala
Can Felliu
Santa Margalida
Santa Margalida
Son Serra
Son Martí
Son Real

Puig de sa Talaia
MA-10
Puig Roig
Els Rafals
Can Felíu
Sa Pobla
Parc Natural de S'Albufera
Muro
MA-13

NORTHERN SERRA (pp137-154)
NORTH MALLORCA (pp135-153)

Morbiget
Son Marc
Puig Tomir
Coves de Campanet
Crestatx
Búger
Llubí
Maria de la Salut
Petra
MA-3300

Monestir de Lluc
Santuari de Sta...
Oratori de Sant Pere
Selva
Caimari
Mancor de la Vall
Inca
Sineu
Sencelles
Costitx
Sant Joan
Vilafranca de Bonany
FELANITX
MA-14

SOUTH MALLORCA (pp177-190)

CENTRAL MALLORCA (pp155-176)
Es Pla

Massanella
Puig Major 1445 m
Lloseta
Binissalem
Santa Maria del Camí
Algaida
Randa
Massís de Randa
Puig de Randa
MA-15

WEST COAST (pp109-130)

Sóller
Port de Sóller
Museu de la Mar Sóller
Deià
Son Marroig
Miramar
Valldemossa
Biniaraix
Fornalutx
Jardins d'Alfàbia
Bunyola
Orient
Alaró
Consell
Santa Eugènia

PALMA & THE BAY OF PALMA (pp63-99)

PALMA
Aeroport de Son Sant Joan
S'Arenal
Can Pastilla
Cala Major
Illetes
Portals Nous
Palma Nova
Magaluf
Cala Figuera

BAY OF PALMA

THE SOUTH-WEST (pp101-108)

La Granja
Esporles
Banyalbufar
Estellencs
Torre del Verger
Mirador de Ricardo Roca
Andratx
Port d'Andratx
Peguera
Santa Ponça
Calvià
Galilea
Puigpunyent

Sant Elm
PARC NATURAL DE SA DRAGONERA
Sa Dragonera
Cala d'Egos
Cap de sa Mola

10 km
5 miles
© Copyright Time Out Group 2009

The South-west

From overdeveloped coastal resorts to remote mountain villages.

As the coastal road heads west from Magaluf towards the family-oriented resorts of Peguera and Santa Ponça, the tone becomes more measured; these resorts are the quintessence of mass tourism – solid, efficient and almost entirely devoid of character. The landscape, though, is much more interesting, with the most jagged coastline in Mallorca; it's marked with numerous bays and coves, and fringed by tiny islands, the best-known of which is Sa Dragonera, a nature reserve and birdwatcher's paradise. There are a few pretty resorts in the area too, including Camp

de Mar with its sheltered bay and small beach; Port d'Andratx, an increasingly upmarket (although rather soulless) alternative for the moneyed crowd; and tiny Cala Fornells, a low-key resort set in a tiny bay.

Inland is a complete contrast, almost untouched by tourism and hiding some of the prettiest villages in this part of the island. The seat of local government is Calvià – once one of the poorest towns in Spain; now, thanks to tourism, one of the richest. The surrounding area is characterised by dense pine groves, *torrentes* and soaring peaks. Among them lie the villages of Puigpunyent and Galilea, tiny places less than half an hour from the coast but part of a Mallorca from another era.

SANTA PONÇA, PEGUERA, CALA FORNELLS & CAMP DE MAR

The autopista MA-1 becomes the MA-1013 just west of Magaluf. From here you can go south to thus-far unspoiled Portals Vells (*see p98*). Alternatively, you can head west, passing **Son Ferrer** and **El Toro** – two lifeless *urbanizaciones*, the latter of which has a small marina, **Port Adriano**, and a luxury hotel (Vista Port Adriano; *see p102*) – before running along a wild stretch of coast and reaching **Santa Ponça**, where Jaume I stepped ashore in 1229, planting his flag and marking the start of the Reconquest of the Balearics. The event is marked by a tall stone cross, carved with reliefs at its base, which stands on the headland at the southern tip of the bay, and the **Capilla de la Piedra Sagrada**, where the first Christian mass was held.

But no one comes to Santa Ponça for its historical significance – this is a resort plain and simple, favoured by Brits, dominated by a number of characterless package tour-packed

hotels and some truly hideous places to eat. Santa Ponça's saving grace is its beach, which is long, with fine white sand leading out into a clear, shallow bay.

Santa Ponça sprawls into Peguera, but to get there you will need to get back on the autopista MA-1. **Peguera** is less depressingly downmarket than Santa Ponça, with almost entirely German-run shops, restaurants and bratwurst stalls. The three beaches here (one marred by the high-rise hotel looming behind it) are well kept and there is a pleasant promenade and a part-pedestrianised main street, El Bulevar de Peguera, lined with tacky shops.

If you fancy a (tiny) beach, take a left at the roundabout just after the Bulevar and head to **Cala Fornells**, a pint-size and unexpectedly delightful little place on the other side of the bay. The road threads through **Aldea Cala Fornells**, where cute private villas tumble down the hillside in a picturesque, colourful jumble, before reaching Cala Fornells, with its postage stamp-sized sandy beach, some concreted rocks on which to sunbathe and two big hotels.

From Cala Fornells it's a short drive back on the MA-1A to **Camp de Mar**, nestled in a perfect little bay, with a small slice of beach and clear, calm waters. The setting is disfigured somewhat by three enormous hotels right on the seafront and, sprinkled over the pine-forested hills behind, a number of large private villas – Claudia Schiffer and Michael Schumacher are among their owners. There's little to do here other than laze around, which is, of course, why people come. A row of small shops on a pedestrianised street leads down to the sea and a number of decent restaurants, which, though mobbed during the day, are appealing at night, as many people eat in their hotels.

Where to stay, eat & drink

In **El Toro**, the five-star **Hotel Vista Port Adriano** (Urb. El Toro, Port Adriano, 971 23 73 23, www.hotelportadriano.com, doubles €280-€360 incl breakfast) has 56 doubles and 11 suites beside the marina. The rooms are simply designed with large beds, big balconies and lovely coastal views. There's a pool and a good restaurant.

The best choice in **Santa Ponça** is the **Hesperia Playas de Mallorca** (Gran Via del Puig Major 2, 971 69 33 66, www.hesperia-playasdemallorca.com, closed Nov-Apr, doubles €85-€120), a bright, modern hotel over the road from the beach. It's set around a large swimming pool and has good-sized rooms (all with balconies, and most with pool or sea views).

Cala Fornells. See p101.

The nicest spot to stay in **Peguera** is the three-star **Hotel Bahía** (Avda. Peguera 81, 971 68 61 00, www.hotelbahia.com, closed Nov-Mar, doubles €76-€81 incl breakfast), a very pretty place in its own grounds. It's great value for what you get: smartly designed air-conditioned rooms, indoor and outdoor pools, sauna, putting green and pool bar. Nice places to eat in Peguera aren't that forthcoming; tapas bar **Bar Eucalyptus** (C/Eucalyptus 6, 971 68 68 20, open noon-3pm, 7pm-midnight) is one of the best bets.

In **Cala Fornells**, **Hotel Petit Cala Fornells** (971 68 54 05, closed 30 Oct-19 Dec, doubles €90-€150) is a lovely spot with an upper *terraza* for drinks and views, and a lower one for dining. It has classily furnished rooms, some with four-poster beds and all with balconies.

There are a couple of good restaurants in **Aldea Cala Fornells**: **La Gran Tortuga** (971 68 60 23, closed Mon in Jan & Feb, all Dec) boasts a stunning setting, with a balcony and *terraza*, set round a swimming pool and with priceless views towards Cala Fornells. The pool bar serves light snacks (€); upstairs is the restaurant (€€€), which has some fine main dishes, including *bacalao gratinado* (baked salt cod with garlic) and a delicious *merluza a la Mallorquina* (Mallorcan-style hake); and **C'an Luís Mi Bodega** (C/Cala Fornells, 971 68 60 35, closed Wed and Dec & Jan, €), which serves tapas on a shaded terrace, and specialises in meat dishes, such as *cochinillo al horno* (roast piglet), as well as good-value paella.

The best place to stay in **Camp de Mar** (by a long shot) is the gigantic **Dorint** (C/Taula 2, 971 13 65 65, www.dorint.com, doubles €270-€385 incl breakfast), set beside an 18-hole golf course, just back from the beach. This is real five-star luxury, with extremely comfortable and big rooms, all with large balconies and views either of the golf course or the sea. There is a lovely pool and two superb restaurants, one serving traditional Mallorcan and Spanish cuisine, the other 'international'. It also has a large gym, an indoor pool, a spa and facilities for tennis and watersports.

On the beach you can choose from several resort-type hotels; **Grupotel Playa Camp de Mar** (971 23 50 25, www.grupotel.com, closed Jan-Apr, doubles €104-€208) is popular with British tourists, offering comfortable, characterless (mainly) sea-facing rooms, a large pool, jacuzzi and a tennis court; while **Hotel Camp de Mar** (971 23 52 00, www.campdemar.es, closed Oct-Apr, doubles €150 incl breakfast) is mainly used by German tourists and has a large swimming pool and sports centre with tennis and squash, games room, kids' playground, bike hire and scuba diving. In July and August, both these hotels are likely to be block-booked by tour operators, so ring ahead.

Camp de Mar.

Eating options in Camp de Mar include the **Petit Ambassador** (Camí de Salinar 1, 971 23 58 18, €€), which has a shady *terraza* affording great views of the beach and the bay, and specialises in fresh fish. **La Siesta** (C/Ses Dunes 5, 971 23 58 41, closed Nov-Feb, €€) serves traditional meaty Mallorcan cuisine; it has a pretty vine-covered terrace, again with pleasant views. **Arco Iris** (C/Ses Dunes 7, 971 23 51 61, closed Nov-Feb, €) is the best-value place along this stretch, with a more relaxed feel and lower prices that don't reflect any dip in the standard of the food. It specialises in paella of the Valencian and *marisco* (seafood) variety. The aptly named **Bar-Restaurante Illetas** (Passeig Illetas 75, 971 70 18 96, closed Nov-mid Feb, €) occupies the rock in the middle of the bay, and is reached by a walkway from the beach. Although the food here isn't the best quality (though it does serve a decent selection of reasonably priced fish and shellfish), it wins hands down for location.

Resources

Internet
Santa Ponça Ciber, Puig d'es Teix 7 (971 69 73 24). **Open** 10am-9pm Mon-Fri; 4-9pm Sat, Sun.

Post office
Peguera *C/Dragonera 1 (971 68 63 95).* **Santa Ponça** *Avda. Puig Major s/n (971 69 15 56).*

Tourist information
Peguera *OIT, C/Ratoli s/n (971 68 70 83/ omtpeguera@calvia.com).* **Open** 9am-6pm daily. **Santa Ponça** *OIT, Via Puig de Galatzo s/n (971 69 17 12/omtsantaponsa@calvia.com).* **Open** 9am-6pm Mon-Fri; 9am-2pm Sat, Sun.

PORT D'ANDRATX

The coastal road MA-1020 winds gently west from Camp de Mar, up through the pine-forested hills pock marked with huge villas, before reaching **Port d'Andratx**, a snug place built around a bay that is home to a marina, a working fishing fleet and a large number of restaurants and bars. This was once a quiet fishing village, but its proximity to Palma and picturesque setting have transformed it into one of the most popular spots along this part of the coast. Despite this, it retains an old-fashioned charm unlike many of the towns further east. However, speedy development in recent years now scars the hills that encircle the bay with identikit villas (though their twinkling lights look pretty at night).

The town's main artery is the harbourside road, which starts as Avda. Mateo Bosch and ends up as Avda. Almirante Riera Alemany. Most places of interest are along here, on parallel C/Isaac Peral and on the streets leading between the two, particularly around the tiny pedestrianised Plaça Almirante Oquendo. Port d'Andratx has plenty of small shops and a scattering of designer boutiques, reflecting the well-heeled clientele it attracts; look particularly on C/Isaac Peral and C/Cristófal Colom.

Where to eat & drink

Port d'Andratx is packed with places to eat. The café-pâtisserie **Consigna** (Avda. Mateo Bosch 19, 971 67 16 04, closed Nov, €), near the start of the harbourside road, is popular with locals and tourists, and a little further along you can enjoy the excellent coffee and salads at the town's branch of sleek café chain **Cappuccino** (Avda. Mateo Bosch 31, 971 67 22 14, €).

WEST MALLORCA

Walk La Trapa

A ruined monastery, lovely views, birdlife galore and a dip to wind-up.

Distance: 9km. Circular. **Time**: 3hrs (with possible extension).

The south-western tip of Mallorca is a wild and beautiful spot, and this walk, up to the ruined monastery of La Trapa, is one of the island's most popular hikes. A reasonable degree of fitness is required, as there's a long upward climb and then a descent that involves a fair amount of rock scrambling, but the phenomenal views of the coastline and the offshore island of Sa Dragonera more than compensate.

Start at the rough car park around two kilometres before you reach Sant Elm on the road from Andratx. (You'll pass a smarter car park at a cemetery 200 metres before the one you want.) Here you'll see a sign marking the **Camí Sa Font dels Morers** by a map showing the route to La Trapa. Head off on the wide track that leads gently downwards in the direction of Sant Elm.

After around ten minutes, the path splits at a sign saying 'Camí de Can Bolei'; you bear round to the right. The path winds through the valley, with rocky hills rising on both sides, until, after 15 minutes, you come to a T-junction in front of a couple of houses. You will return along the left-hand path to this spot later, but take the right turn now (marked 'Camí Coll dels Cairals'), looping around the back of the houses and then starting to climb the hill beyond. This is the start of a steady but tiring 45-minute ascent.

After about 20 minutes you reach a sign that says '**Reserva Natural La Trapa**' and, usually, a chain across the road, barring anyone foolish enough to have brought their vehicle this far. Continue, and, when you reach the top of the climb, you are rewarded with superb views. It can be very windy up here, but the mountain goats that you may see clearly aren't fazed by a bit of a breeze. It's worth scrambling up the rocks to your left for an even better vantage point, and a great view of the island of **Sa Dragonera**.

Down below you'll also see the ruins of **La Trapa**, to which you descend in five or so minutes. Trappist monks, fleeing from the chaos of the Peninsular War, arrived here in 1810, but were moved on by the Spanish government after only 14 years.

You can extend the walk at this point by continuing along the west coast (at the first hairpin bend as you come down to La Trapa,

there's a narrow path off to the right, marked with a sign to S'Arracó and Sant Elm).

Down at the monastery you'll probably see evidence of the restoration of the buildings being undertaken by the GOB environmental organisation, which has owned the La Trapa reserve since 1980. The reserve covers 75 hectares (187 acres). If you're a twitcher, you should look out for Marmora's warbler and Yelkouan shearwater (two species endemic to the Balearics), and also peregrine falcons and booted eagles. You'll probably have noticed the bent and broken skeletons of many trees in the area, the legacy of a major fire in 1994 that burned 1,300 hectares (3,241 acres) of land. GOB has done a great deal of work since then to replant the slopes.

Walk down past the monastery's restored mill house for more stunning, precipitous views over to Sa Dragonera, and down to the rocky cove of **Cala Basset** (overlooked by a watchtower). An inscribed stone here tells a cautionary tale – a young Mallorcan fell to his death at this spot in 1985.

When you've had your fill, climb back to just above the monastery and take the path to the right signed to Sant Elm, climbing up and over the headland, following the rough path marked by cairns and crimson paint splodges. It's a pretty tough, steep scramble.

Around 45 minutes after you set off from the monastery you reach a T-junction. To the right, through two posts, a walk of around a quarter of an hour will bring you down to Cala Basset, where you can swim on calm days. If you don't fancy a dip, take the left turn and continue on towards Sant Elm.

After seven or so minutes you come to another T-junction where a sign marks the **Camí Punta de sa Galera**. If you feel in need of refreshment, turn right and then immediately left after the abandoned, mural-spattered house C'an Tomeví, and within 20 minutes you'll be in Sant Elm where you'll find a number of seafront restaurant-bars. (From here, you can either retrace your steps to the T-junction of the paths or walk the couple of kilometres up the road towards Andratx to return to the car park.)

Otherwise, take the left turn, and within ten minutes you're back at the point by the two houses where you turned right just before beginning your ascent of the hill. Turn right here and retrace your steps to the car park. It should take around 25 minutes.

Most of the local restaurants specialise in seafood and there is not a great deal to choose between them. **Miramar** (Avda. Mateo Bosch 18, 971 67 16 17, €€€€) is perhaps the best (though a line of parked cars out front mars the view of the fishing fleet), although this is reflected in its prices (squid €22; paella €17). The shellfish is superb, and the three-course *menu del día* is reasonably priced at €18. **Rocamar** (Avda. Almirante Riera Alemany 27, 971 67 16 78, closed Wed in Oct and all Nov-Jan, €€€, lunch *menú* €16), a bit further on, is a more affordable alternative that also majors in shellfish. **Marisquería Galicia** (C/Isaac Peral 37, 971 67 27 05, closed 7 Jan-7 Feb, €€) is a Galician seafood restaurant where the atmosphere and prices are less touristy than those on the front; try the *pulpo à la Gallega* (Galician-style octopus).

There are several late-night bars about two-thirds of the way along the harbourfront, after the Hotel Brismar; most have terraces overlooking the bay. First up is **Tim's** (no phone), a small drinking den that serves English breakfasts and pasta, salads and hamburgers at lunchtime; **Majid's Bar del Mar** (Avda. Almirante Riera Alemany 8, 678 29 09 04) is next, offering salads and sandwiches during the day (you can't miss the painted life-size horses in the doorway); next is **Mitj y Mitj** (no phone), which plays club sounds until late and serves up pizzas, salads and *pa amb oli*; lastly there's **L'Habana** (971 67 26 08) – it doles out Cuban-inspired cocktails and a small selection of tapas.

Where to stay

Surprisingly, **Port d'Andratx** has relatively few places to stay. Built against the hill overlooking the bay, the German-managed **Hotel Villa Italia** (C/San Carlos 13, 971 67 40 11, www.hotelvillaitalia.com, doubles €275-€325, Suite Royal €750), as its name suggests, resembles a Tuscan *palazzo*, complete with stucco ceilings, Italianate marble fittings and Roman columns – it's all a touch Liberace. All rooms have balconies and great views; there are ten doubles and six suites – with round, tiled baths – and a split-level room at the top with views across the bay. Facilities include a pool, gym and good restaurant with a terrace.

The simple, old-style **Hotel Brismar** (C/Almirante Riera Alemany 6, 971 67 16 00, www.hotelbrismar.com, closed mid Nov-mid Dec, mid Jan-mid Feb, doubles €80-€95) enjoys a great location overlooking the marina, with its own private sundeck by the beach. It's clean and friendly, and half the rooms have balconies and views; those at the front can be a bit noisy on summer nights, though, as the town's late-night bars are right next door.

Set in its own grounds one street back from the main drag in a quiet location, the **Hostal Catalina Vera** (C/Isaac Peral 63, 971 67 19 18, closed Dec & Mar, doubles €65) is an excellent, friendly budget option, with loads of character. The breakfast room is filled with ceramic pots and pictures, the rooms are very clean and comfortable and all have their own shower room.

Resources

Internet
Port d'Andratx *Cyber, C/Sa Fábrica 10 (971 67 10 10).* **Open** 9am-midnight Mon-Sat.

Tourist information
Port d'Andratx *OMT, Edificio de la Lonja, Avda. Mateo Bosch (971 67 13 00).* **Open** *Oct, Mar* 9am-8pm Mon-Sat; 9am-2pm Sun. *Apr-Sept* 9am-8pm Mon-Sat; 9am-4pm Sun. Closed Nov-Feb.

ANDRATX, SANT ELM & SA DRAGONERA

Four kilometres inland from Port d'Andratx is **Andratx**, a sleepy place nestling among slopes of olives and almonds. Andratx's origins are Roman, when it was known as Andrachium. After the Reconquest, Jaume I made it his base, eventually ceding the area to the Bishop of Barcelona.

The town is dominated by the fortress-like church of **Santa Maria**, with huge walls built to deter would-be marauders. Clamber to the top for great views of the Port. The **Castell Son Mas**, an oft-fortified tower dating from the 15th century, was similarly constructed – there's a relief of one wild-haired pirate staring out to sea on the outer wall. It's also worth popping in to the **Centre Cultural Andratx**, lying just outside the town on the road to Es Capdellà, to check out one of the three annual contemporary art exhibitions and to see the modest but growing permanent collection; German artists feature heavily, and much of it is thought-provoking stuff.

The MA-1030 twists and turns westwards from Andratx through pretty countryside of pines and rocky outcrops, passing through the

WEST MALLORCA

INSIDE TRACK ANDRATX

It's worth timing your visit to Andratx for a Wednesday so that you can catch the local market. There are stalls selling fruit, vegetables and handicrafts – as always, haggling is essential.

nondescript hamlet of **S'Arracó**, before reaching **Sant Elm** and the coast. Despite its promising location on the map as the westernmost point on Mallorca, Sant Elm is an unprepossessing little resort, with two small, grey sand beaches that get very crowded on summer weekends. The setting, though – surrounded by forested hills and looking out towards the island of Sa Dragonera – is a treat, and there is a decent choice of places to eat.

Perhaps the biggest draw, however, is the chance to take a boat trip to virgin **Sa Dragonera** (Crucero Margarita, mobile 639 61 75 45, mobile 696 42 39 33, €10, €5 under-8); boats leave from the far end of Avda. Rei Jaume I, near El Pescador restaurant (first boat at 10.15am and every 30mins thereafter, last back Oct-Mar 3pm, Apr-Sept 4pm). This uninhabited four-kilometre-long island, named after its supposed similarity to the jagged back of a dragon, is an extension of the Tramuntana, and well known for its birdlife. Among the species you may spot are Eleanora's falcons, cormorants, Audouin's gulls, shags and petrels; it is also home to a large number of lizards. In the 15th century, one of the Balearics' most notorious pirates, Redbeard, used it as his base; today, it's a nature reserve and the protected area includes two smaller islands, Illa Mitjana and Es Pantaleu (the public can use the beach on the latter). You'll need to get permission to visit from the reception centre in Cala Lladó, where the boat drops you. You can't wander at will; the centre will give you details of permitted itineraries, which include hiking up the 312-metre- (1,024-foot-) high Puig de Na Popia and walking to the lighthouse at Cap des Llebeitx, the southernmost point of the island. **Parc Natural de Sa Dragonera** (971 18 06 32), based in Sant Elm, has information about the island.

A German-run scuba diving centre, **Scuba Activa** (Plaça Monsenyor Sebastian Grau 7, 971 23 91 02, www.scuba-activa.com, closed Nov-15 Mar), offers dives around Sa Dragonera.

**INSIDE TRACK
PORT D'ANDRATX**

If you're based in Port d'Andratx and planning a trip to Sant Elm or to the Sa Dragonera island, a great way to get there is by boat. Between March and mid November, a service runs to Sant Elm from Port d'Andratx at around 9am, returning at around 4pm; it's officially the **Sa Dragonera–Sant Elm** service, but as the boats dock at Port d'Andratx, you're able to board from here. Call 639 61 75 45 for information.

To the north-east of Sant Elm rise steep, rocky hills. Here lies the **Reserva Natural La Trapa**, centred on the ruined monastery of **La Trapa**. The reserve is only accessible on foot and the one-and-a-half-hour walk to reach it is one of the island's most popular hikes. One path starts out at the northern end of Sant Elm; a second one is detailed on *p108* **Walk**.

CCA Andratx

Ctra. Andratx–Es Capdellà, km1.5 (971 13 77 70/www.ccandratx.com). **Open** 10.30am-7pm Tue-Fri; 10.30am-4pm Sat, Sun. **Admission** €5. **Credit** MC, V.

Where to stay, eat & drink

There are two accommodation options in **Sant Elm**. The unattractive **Hotel Aquamarín** (C/Cala Conis 4, 971 23 90 75, www.universalhotels.es, closed Oct-Apr, doubles €45-€65 incl breakfast) sits between the two beaches; its rooms are basic and clean; all have balconies and most have sea views. The alternative is the **Hostal Dragonera** (Avda. Rei Jaume I 5, 971 23 90 86, www. hostaldragonera.net, closed mid Nov-Feb, doubles €50-€66), which offers simple, clean en suite rooms with tiled floors and views towards the island, and a decent restaurant with a lovely *terraza*.

The best place to eat is right at the end of the street that runs up from the beach. **El Pescador** (Avda. Jaime I 48, 971 23 91 98, €€) serves the freshest of catches from its own fishing boat, the *Caladent II*. Try the house special, a delicious light *lenguado* (sole), or the *paella de mariscos*. There are a number of other decent places along Avda. Rei Jaume I, including **Vista Mar** (No.46, 971 23 90 44, closed Mon and Nov-Mar, €€), which, true to its name, offers great sea views, and excellent fish dishes, and **Na Caragola** at No.23A (971 23 90 06, closed Wed and Nov-Jan, €€), which occupies a prime spot at the end of the street with a fine terrace affording views across to Sa Dragonera; it specialises in paella and fresh fish dishes at reasonable prices.

Resources

Police station
Andratx *C/Curia 1 (971 62 80 08).*

Post office
Andratx *Avda. Joan Carles I 20 (971 23 53 44).*

Tourist information
Andratx *OMT, Avda. Curia (971 262 80 19).* **Open** 8.30am-2.30pm Mon-Fri.

Port d'Andratx.

CALVIA, GALILEA & PUIGPUNYENT

The regional capital of **Calvià** lies in the foothills of the mountains, just ten minutes' drive inland from Santa Ponça and the coast, and yet is completely untouched by tourism – other than having grown fat on tourist euros, that is; note its gleaming, new-build town hall. Calvià now has one of the richest town councils in the whole of Spain – 40 years ago it was one of the poorest in Europe.

The town was founded in the 13th century, and the church that tops it, **Sant Joan Baptista** (open 10am-1.30pm daily, entry by donation) was begun in the same century, but not completed until 1896, after numerous remodellings. The exterior is notable for its slender belltowers and large Gothic window, and a Romanesque-style façade with a depiction of the Garden of Gethsemane; the interior has an enormous cockleshell emblem carved into the ceiling over the red marble altar. Outside in Plaça Església is a fountain, a shaded terrace looking out over the valley to the coast, and a mural depicting the history of the town.

Four kilometres west of Calvià is tiny **Es Capdellà**, from where the MA-1032 road follows a spectacularly winding course north-east up into the mountains. After around 20 minutes of driving you reach the village of **Galilea**, which spills dramatically down the slopes. This is one of the loveliest unspoiled spots in the area, with extraordinary views across the countryside and down to the coast. Galilea is topped by the **Parroquía de la Immaculada**, a chunky little church with a sundial carved into its outside wall.

From here, it's a further 20 minutes' drive to **Puigpunyent** (meaning 'pointed peak'),

another sleepy little place with an appealingly isolated feel (yet it's only 20 minutes from Palma). The village is spread along a small valley and dominated by the thrusting 1,027-metre (3,369-foot) peak of **Galatzó** – hence its name. It's best known for being home to one of the most luxurious hotels on the island, **Son Net** (*see p108*), a former private mansion owned by Count Ramón Zaforteza that dominates the village from a plateau above it. Puigpunyent itself has a lovely, relaxed rustic feel, although there's little to see beyond the 17th-century parish church and its outsize belltower in Plaça Leon XIII.

The source of the **Torrent Sa Riera** (at 23 kilometres/14 miles one of the longest on the island), which extends all the way to Palma, lies a couple of kilometres north from here.

From Puigpunyent, you can either head east along the MA-1041 to Palma, or north along the MA-1101 to Esporles, La Granja and the west coast (*see p110*).

Where to stay & eat

If you want to stay near **Calvià**, a kilometre south of the town is **Son Malero** (Camí de Son Malero s/n, 971 67 03 01, www.son malero.com, doubles €110 incl breakfast), boasting a pool and magnificent views; it has four double rooms, a suite and an apartment with its own terrace.

Calvià has a few decent places to eat, including **Restaurant Sant Joan** (Plaça Església 5, 971 67 09 27, closed Wed, €€), beside the church – a fairly smart place with a pretty *terraza* serving Norwegian/international cuisine from chef Martin Sween; **Mesón C'an Torrat** (C/Major 29-31, 971 67 06 82, closed Aug, all Tue, €€), which specialises in suckling

Parroquía de la Immaculada, Galilea. *See p107.*

pig; and **La Sala** (Edifici Ajuntament de Calvià, C/Julià Bujosa Sans, www.ava restauracio.com), near the town hall, a smart café-restaurant popular at lunchtime with the local business crowd.

In **Galilea**, **Scott's Galilea** (971 87 01 00, 0871 717 4227 in UK, www.scottsgalilea.com, €149-€230 for two people incl breakfast, minimum four-night stay) is not exactly a hotel, but more a luxurious collection of private studios and houses, refurbished and redesigned by George and Judy Scott, who run Scott's Hotel in Binissalem (*see p159*). Each of the seven studios and houses has a sitting room and kitchen, most have a fireplace and all enjoy south-facing terraces. The three houses are split-level, classily fitted and very private, and one can accommodate four people. The views from all the properties are some of the best on the island. There is also an outdoor pool and sauna.

Puigpunyent is home to the grand **Son Net** (971 14 70 00, www.sonnet.es, closed 15 Dec-14 Feb, doubles €193-€353). The reception area looks out on to the internal patio, with a small well at its centre (the hotel still uses water from it). Around the patio run corridors hung with genuine Chagall, Hockney and Warhol paintings, a small bar, gym and the original chapel. The grounds are extensive and perfectly kept, with fountains, huge old cypresses, a clay tennis court and an enormous pool surrounded by private cabañas and a poolside bar and restaurant. There are 31 rooms, all luxuriously fitted with big, comfortable beds and soft pillows, antique wooden furniture and marble

bathrooms. The bedrooms at the back, though comfy, are best avoided as they have no views; if you can afford it, go for a deluxe double (or one of the extraordinary suites, the best will set you back €1,284). The **Oleum** restaurant (€€€€) in the old olive-pressing room, complete with original press, and has an outdoor *terraza* overlooking the village. Chef Christian Rullan uses local produce to create refined, well-regarded Mediterranean dishes.

If your budget is slightly more modest, there's a good *agroturismo* a couple of kilometres from Puigpunyent; **Son Pont** (Ctra. Palma–Puigpunyent, km12.3, 971 71 95 27, www.son pont.com, doubles €98 incl breakfast) is a restored 17th-century Mallorcan house set in its own grounds, with four rooms and priceless mountain views. The place oozes old Mallorcan charm but benefits from modern day conveniences such as Wi-Fi in the communal areas and a great pool.

Puigpunyent has a number of decent eateries, including the arty **Sa Café Central** (C/Sa Riera 40, no phone) serving tapas and salads, and with sporadic live music, **La Vila** (Ctra. Galilea 2, 971 61 41 08), a modern pizza and pasta parlour, and the **Rose** restaurant (C/Ciutat 3, 971 61 43 60), run by an English couple.

Resources

Post office
Calvià *C/Serral 1 (971 67 06 27).*
Puigpunyent *C/Na Beltrana s/n (971 61 44 63).*

GETTING THERE
By bus
Hourly Transabus Balear (971 20 45 04, http://tib.caib.es) services run from Palma around the western Bay of Palma and on to Santa Ponça, Peguera, Camp de Mar, Andratx and Port d'Andratx. There are no longer services from Peguera to Valldemossa via Andratx, Estellencs and Banyalbufar; to reach these places by public transport, you now have to head back to Palma and take a bus from there.

INSIDE TRACK
'PORT' TOWNS

It's a common arrangement in Mallorca, and particularly in the South-west, to find towns set back from the coast, with their associated 'Port' nearby; this reflects the threat of pirate attack that has plagued the island through most of its history (pirate sorties were common in this area until the 18th century).

WEST MALLORCA

West Coast

Breathtaking settings that are the antithesis of the beach resorts.

The area of coastline that runs from Andratx to Sóller is isolated from the rest of the island by the Serra de Tramuntana, which falls steeply into the Mediterranean in a series of jagged cliffs and surf-battered coves. The spectacular precipices, pine-forested hills and shimmering blue of the sea give it an air of almost unworldly beauty that, thanks to the absence of sandy beaches and the unsuitability of the terrain for building, is almost pristine; tiny villages are all that dot the mountainsides. The majesty and peace of the mountains have drawn foreign writers and artists to this bit of the coast for many years, particularly to the lovely village of Deià, where Robert Graves was a pioneering expat.

Further along the coast, Port de Sóller offers a complete contrast to the brash resorts of the south, while inland the town of Sóller and the villages nearby – Fornalutx, one of Spain's prettiest, and the tiny hamlet of Biniaraix – have managed to retain their calm and character.

In contrast, the once-tranquil hamlet of Valldemossa, briefly home to Frédéric Chopin and George Sand, is too close to Palma and the Bay of Palma's bucket-and-spade resorts for its own good. Its setting is still beautiful, but this is one spot that has been overwhelmed by tourism.

ESTELLENCS, BANYALBUFAR & ESPORLES

A drive along the twisting new MA-10 coastal road from Andratx to Sóller is one of the great Mallorcan experiences. You won't find any more dramatic and sublime landscape in Europe than the dizzying, pine-clad slopes of the Tramuntana plunging hundreds of metres down into an azure sea.

There are a number of places to admire the view, the first of which (coming from Andratx) is the **Mirador de Ricardo Roca**, which is marked by a restaurant with a terrace and a viewpoint beyond it.

A further four kilometres brings you to the first settlement you encounter on this hostile coastline: **Estellencs**. It's a sweet, characterful place of small twisting lanes and chunky stone houses scattered across the terraced mountainside. The village's centre is marked by the small but lovely church of **Sant Joan Baptista** and a handful of café-restaurants. A two-kilometre-long track (marked 'Platja')

leads down from the main road to a postage stamp-sized shingly 'beach'; it doesn't get the sun until after midday, but the clear water and atmospheric surrounding landscape make for a wonderfully invigorating dip. There are a handful of good places to stay in the village and a couple of decent restaurants. A stunning walk to the next village along, Banyalbufar, is indicated by a sign off the main road on the Banyalbufar side of the village – it's a five-hour trek there and back, and you'll be rewarded by staggering views all the way.

A few kilometres further along the main road is another stunning spot, often known as the **Mirador de Ses Ànimes** (Viewpoint of the Souls) but signposted as **Mirador Torre del Verger**. The watchtower (which you can climb up) was built in 1579 as a lookout point to spot pirates and provides one of the finest views along this stretch of the coast. There's a plaque here commemorating the Habsburg Archduke Ludwig Salvator.

Banyalbufar lies just beyond the next bend (six kilometres from Estellencs), and is similarly

WEST MALLORCA

formed from a series of terraces created by the Moors, who built an elaborate series of channels, pipes and cisterns that still irrigate the fields. They named the village 'bany al buhar', which means 'vineyard by the sea', and produced wine, despite being forbidden to drink it. Vines were cultivated here until the 1870s, when the phylloxera virus wiped out the vineyards across the island, forcing the inhabitants to turn to tomatoes (which are still grown here today – the reservoirs on the lower slopes provide the fruit with water all year round). On the small square on the way into the village is the town hall and a squat church, the **Església de la Natividad**, which dates from the 15th century but whose twin domes were completed some 200 years later. Classical music concerts are held here once a month from June to October (visit www.banyalbahar.com for details). On the other side of the road is the **Baronia**, a beautiful mansion, once the feudal seat of the nobles who governed this region and now a hotel. Have a peek inside the old stone courtyard, below the main entrance to the hotel, for an idea of its former splendour. Further along the main street you'll find several cafés and restaurants and shops selling colourful ceramics and lace.

The MA-10 becomes increasingly winding and narrow as it leaves Banyalbufar, rising towards the junction with the PM104.

Just before here is a turning to **Port d'es Canonge**, which is made up of a nondescript *urbanización*, a handful of exquisitely restored private fincas (one owned by Richard Branson) and a couple of restaurants arranged around a shingly beach, but it's not really worth the half-hour hairpin drive to discover.

From here you can continue on for a further ten kilometres along the MA-10 to Valldemossa (*see p112*) or head south on the PM104 to Esporles and **La Granja**, a one-time Moorish farm that became a convent and then home to the Fortuny family. Today, it's an unsatisfying mishmash of everything from tedious collections of farm implements via children's toys and musical instruments to (for reasons unknown) torture equipment. There's precious little explanation, and, it's often heaving with coach parties, and, frankly, is not really worth the hefty admission price. If you'd hoped for a glimpse into how a wealthy Mallorcan family once lived, you're far better off heading for Els Calderers in the centre of the island (*see p171*). The gardens are nice, though.

From La Granja you can head south-west to **Puigpunyent** (*see p107*) or south-east for a couple of kilometres to **Esporles**, a very likeable village, just 20 minutes' drive from Palma, but with a refreshing middle-of-nowhere feel to it. The old quarter is centred on a

sizeable church dating from the 13th century; opposite is tiny Plaça d'Espanya and the town hall. The newer part of Esporles stretches south beside the raised pavement along the Passeig del Rei, which is home to numerous cafés, bars and restaurants. There's also a municipal swimming pool, a few cute pâtisseries and several banks.

La Granja

Ctra. Esporles–Puigpunyent, km2 (971 61 00 32/ www.lagranja.net). **Open** *June-Oct* 10am-7pm daily (last entry 6pm). *Nov-May* 10am-6pm (last admission 5pm). **Admission** €11-€13; €6-€7 reductions. **Credit** AmEx, DC, MC, V.

Where to stay, eat & drink

At the Mirador de Ricardo Roca, you'll find the restaurant **Es Grau** (Ctra. Andratx 98, 971 61 85 27, closed Thur and mid Nov-Jan, €€), which serves standard fare such as grills and fresh local fish on a terrace with breathtaking views.

In **Estellencs**, the two-star **Maristel** (C/Eusebi Pascual 10, 971 61 85 50, www. hotelmaristel.com, closed Nov-Jan, doubles

Estellencs.

€110-€140 incl breakfast) has unremarkable en suite rooms, but wondrous views and two pools; the **Hotel Nord** (Plaça Triquet 4, 971 14 90 06, www.hotelruralnord.com, closed Nov-Jan, doubles €88-€130 incl breakfast) is a lovely alternative, consisting of a typical Mallorcan house with eight air-conditioned rooms (three with terraces) decorated in traditional *Mallorquí* style. Excellent home-cooked local cuisine is available, served in an interior courtyard featuring an old olive oil mill. Or try the friendly family-run five-room **Sa Plana Petit Hotel** (C/Eusebi Pascual s/n, 971 61 86 66, www.saplana.com, closed 10 Dec-20 Jan, doubles €88-€100), which offers home cooking washed down by the owner's own wine, and there's a pool too.

For eating out, try the nicely located **Son Llarg** (Plaça Constitució 6, 971 61 85 64, closed Tue, €); the rustic spot was changing hands as this guide went to press, but the new locale will continue to serve traditional Mallorcan cuisine when it opens at the end of 2008. Alternatively, head next door to **Montimar** (Plaça Constitució 7, 971 61 85 76, closed Mon and Dec & Jan, €), a traditional place in a grand house with a pleasant terrace serving unadorned local dishes.

There are plenty of places to stay in **Banyalbufar**. The choicest is **Son Borguny** (C/Borguny 1, 971 14 87 06, www.sonborguny.com, doubles €95-€130 incl breakfast), signposted on the steps leading up from the main road. This 15th-century building has been tastefully converted into a hotel with eight rooms, each individually designed in Mallorcan style, with light fabrics, wooden furniture and floors, exposed beams and iron-framed beds. The 'Sol' and 'Luna' rooms are the best, with jacuzzis and stunning views. Dinners on request. **Mar i Vent** (C/Major 49, 971 61 80 00, www.hotelmarivent.com, closed Dec & Jan, doubles €98-€150 incl breakfast) is a good alternative, with 29 pretty rooms, all with great views, and a lovely *terraza* for an evening drink and a pool. **Hostal Baronia** (C/Baronia 16, 971 61 81 46, www.hbaronia.com, closed Nov-Mar, doubles €70 incl breakfast) occupies a former *palacio*, but is marred by the ugly modern extension stuck on the back. The en suite rooms are basic, but there's a large pool and lovely views. Down the hill from the main road you'll find the stylish hotel-restaurant **Ca Madò Paula** (C/Constitució 11, 971 14 87 17, www.camadopaula.com, doubles €110, restaurant closed Wed and Nov-Feb, €€), which has crisp rooms, and serves both classic and more adventurous dishes like ostrich steak with Cassis mustard. Right at the bottom of the village, the rooms at **Sa Coma** (Camí des Moli 3, 971 61 80 34, www.hotelsacoma.com,

closed Nov-Feb, doubles €112) are nothing to write home about, but the uninterrupted sea views certainly are.

There's plenty of choice for eating places in Banyalbufar. **Restaurante Son Tomás** (C/Baronia 17, 971 61 81 49, closed dinner Mon, all Tue and 15 Dec-1 Feb, €€€) is the best and most popular spot in town, located at the far end of the village as you approach from Estellencs. The emphasis is on fish: try the house special *peixado a la mallorquí* while gazing out at the view from the *terraza*. **Café Bellavista** (C/Comte Sallent 15, 971 61 80 04, closed Sun and Dec & Jan, €), at the other end of town, has similarly wonderful views from a lovely terrace, and serves sandwiches, cakes and artisanal ice-cream (try the walnut flavour). **Ca's Cosi** (C/Baronia 1-3, 971 61 82 45, closed Tue and Dec-Mar, €€) is a pleasant place halfway along the main street that serves simple pastas and local meats such as lamb. There's also a cute pizzeria, **Pegasón y el Pajarito Enmascarado** (Carrer Pont 2 Baixos, 971 14 87 13, €) just across the main road from the town hall (down a little slope), which serves good pizza and pasta dishes as well as tapas.

In **Port d'es Canonge**, **Ca'n Toni Moreno** (971 61 04 26, closed Mon and 20 Dec-20 Jan, €€€) is a prime spot for fresh fish; the *caldereta de langosta* (fish stew) is particularly fine.

In **Esporles**, the former Hostal Esporles – a lovely old building next to the church – has changed hands a couple of times over the past few years; it's now known as **L'Estada** (Plaça d'Espanya 8, 971 61 02 02, www.hotel estada.com, closed Nov, doubles €100-€130 incl breakfast, restaurant €€€), it has nine stylishly furnished, tranquil rooms (including a suite and a junior suite). There's also a sleek restaurant offering Mallorcan/Mediterranean cuisine.

For other eating options, wander along Passeig del Rei to **Es Brollador** (No.10, 971 61 05 39, closed Tue and Nov, €€), which has a lovely patio and fine local meats, including *cordero con miel* (lamb with honey) and *lechona frita* (suckling pig). **Café Passeig** (No.13, 971 61 92 44, closed Mon, €) is an old-style café, good for a tapa or pastry.

Four kilometres from Esporles is the classy **Posada del Marqués** (Es Verger, 971 61 12 30, www.posada-marques.com, doubles €194 incl breakfast, restaurant €€€), a handsome 16th-century stone house that's been converted into a four-star hotel, with 17 air-conditioned rooms (some with terraces), a pool and restaurant. It's signposted from the main road on the south side of the village.

Resources

Police station
Esporles *Plaça Espanya 1 (mobile 686 94 48 26)*.

Post office
Banyalbufar *Plaça de la Vila 2 (no phone)*. Esporles *Passeig del Rei 2 (971 61 91 37)*. Estellencs *C/Síquia 4, Baixos (no phone)*.

VALLDEMOSSA

The town of **Valldemossa** is now totally given over to tourism, albeit of the slightly more refined west coast variety – there's not a neon lilo or football pub in sight. That said, its proximity to Palma (18 kilometres/11 miles) and ease of access from the coastal resorts have made it popular with day-trippers and coach parties all day long, so if you want to see why many people consider it to be one of the prettiest towns on the island, come at night, or, better still, off-season.

The village's origins date from Moorish times; its name 'Vall d'en Musa' means 'valley of Musa', the Moorish owner of the original estate. By far its biggest draw for visitors is the **Real Cartuja de Valldemossa**, best known as the place where Frédéric Chopin and George Sand spent an infamous, bitter winter in 1838-9. Sand immortalised their stay in her book *A Winter in Majorca*, the thrust of which could be summed up with: 'love the landscapes, hate the natives (and

---

INSIDE TRACK
PORT DE VALLDEMOSSA

To escape the coach party hoards that descend on Valldemossa, take the long, narrow and winding road to the diminutive **Port de Valldemossa** (celebriphiles should note that Michael Douglas's humungous S'Estaca estate is off this road), which is little more than the stony beach, a scattering of houses, a couple of beach bars in season and one of the area's best fish restaurants, **Es Port** (*see p114*).

---

the weather)', but, despite its less than complimentary take on the place, you'll find it for sale all over the island, and all over the monastery too.

The Cartuja's origins stretch back to 1399, when it was founded by Carthusian monks, who lived here until they were expelled in 1835 (hence the fact that cells were going cheap when Sand and Chopin showed up). Visits start at the church, an uninspiring neo-classical structure tacked on to the main complex, notable only for a few frescoes painted by Goya's brother-in-law. Head straight through to the cloisters where you'll find the pharmacy – a pleasingly chaotic collection of potions preserved in delicate jars and painted wooden boxes, which the monks doled out to parishioners; it continued as the village chemist's until 1896. Next door, the Prior's Cell is reached through a small private chapel dedicated to **Santa Catalina Tomás** (*see p113*). Inside, there is a library where the monks would break their silence for a once-a-week chat, and the audience chamber, where the prior would meet guests, hung with numerous oil paintings and containing various penitential objects used for self-flagellation.

Cells two and four are where most visitors head; these were the ones inhabited by Chopin and Sand. They're a curious mishmash of objects: locks of hair, original scores, the piano on which the sickly Chopin composed the 'Raindrop' Prelude, love letters and a signed manuscript of *A Winter in Majorca*. But it's all slightly unsatisfying, and you get little insight into how the pair actually lived here. Wander out into the terrace gardens outside the cells for lovely views down the valley towards Palma.

Next door, the **Museu Municipal** gives a brief history of Archduke Ludwig Salvator on the ground floor; upstairs is dedicated to a small but impressive display of modern art, including paintings by Joan Miró, sketches by Picasso and etchings by Francis Bacon and Max Ernst. Double-back to get to King Sancho's Palace, which has several rooms to explore, full of paintings and knick-knacks; Nicaraguan poet Ruben Dario stayed here in the early part of the 20th century.

Adjoining the monastery complex is the pretty **Jardí de Joan Carles I**.

Valldemossa's other (though certainly lesser) tourist draw is the curious **Costa Nord** centre, initially funded by Michael Douglas, who has a house nearby (S'Estaca, one of the Archduke Ludwig Salvator's properties). The actor hoped that the centre would create 'a cultural bond between the island's inhabitants and those who visit it'. It's part restaurant-bar, part audio-visual show; the latter consists of a 15-minute history of Mallorca, followed by a less cursory and more interesting look at Archduke Ludwig

Salvator, his life and contribution to Mallorca. Frankly, it's a bit pricey for what you get. Douglas sold the centre to the Balearic Island Government in 2003, although he stays involved, not least in promoting the island at international tourism trade fairs.

In the lower part of the village is the church of **Sant Bartomeu**, dedicated to the life of Mallorca's only saint, **Santa Catalina Tomás**. She was born in Valldemossa in 1533 and worked on an estate near Bunyola, where she performed various miracles, before joining the Church at the age of 21. Throughout her life (she died of natural causes in 1574) she experienced countless mystical experiences and strange phenomena, and, according to *The Book of Saints*, 'during the last years of her life she was in continual ecstasy'. She was canonised in 1930, and lies in a shrine in the church of Santa Margalida in Palma, where celebrations dedicated to her take place on 28 July each year.

Six kilometres south of Valldemossa, heading towards Palma, is the **Lafiore** glass factory, which specialises in hand-blown reproduction antique Roman glassware. Visitors can watch glass-blowing demonstrations and spend their euros in the factory shop.

Costa Nord
Avda. Palma 6 (971 61 24 25/www.costanord. com). **Open** 9am-5pm daily. **Admission** €7.50; €6 reductions. **Credit** MC, V.

FREE Lafiore
Ctra. Palma–Valldemossa, km11, S'Esgleieta (971 61 01 40/www.lafiore.com). **Open** *Shop* 9.15am-8pm Mon-Fri; 9.15am-2pm, 3-6pm Sat. *Workshop* 9am-1pm, 2-5pm Mon-Fri; 9am-1pm, 2-4pm Sat. **Admission** free.

Real Cartuja de Valldemossa
Plaça de la Cartuja 11 (971 61 21 069). **Open** Jan, Dec 9.30am-3pm Mon-Sat. Feb, Nov 9.30am-5pm Mon-Sat; 10am-1pm Sun. Mar, Oct 9.30am-5.30pm Mon-Sat; 10am-1pm Sun. Apr-Sept 9.30am-6.30pm Mon-Sat; 10am-1pm Sun. **Admission** €8.50; €4 reductions; free under-10s. **Credit** AmEx, DC, MC, V.

Where to eat & drink

If you want a coffee and a snack, you could do worse than head for the branch of the fast-growing **Cappuccino** chain (Plaça Ramon Llull, 5, 971 61 60 59, www.grupocappuccino. com); though slightly pricey, it's perfectly located for a spot of people-watching. For something more substantial you're best off ignoring the centre's offerings and walking along the main road in the direction of Deià, where, beyond the main bus stop, you'll find two friendly restaurants side by side. **Can Pedro** (Avda. Arxiduc Lluís Salvador s/n, 971 61 21 70, closed Mon & dinner Sun, €€) offers hearty traditional food and Mallorcan wines in

WEST MALLORCA

Valldemossa.

INSIDE TRACK
GEORGE SAND

George Sand had little time for the locals during her time living on the west coast of Mallorca, seeing them as lazy, ignorant and devious; she semi-jokingly referred to them as 'monkeys'. Her book is sold in every tourist shop on the island.

a rustic dining room, while **Vesubio** (Avda. Arxiduc Lluís Salvador 23, 971 61 25 84, closed Wed and Jan, €) serves up good pizzas and pastas and is popular with local families – salads come a tad overdressed so it's worth asking for the vinaigrette separately.

For something truly special but not truly expensive try **Es Port** (971 61 61 94, www. geocities.com/restaurantesport, closed Wed in Feb, dinner Sept-June and all Nov & Dec, €€€) in **Port de Valldemossa**, seven kilometres from Valldemossa. Tucking into a vast mixed seafood grill for two on the terrace while taking in the sea views is one of the great Mediterranean dining experiences.

Another enjoyable restaurant, on the road between Valldemossa and Deià, is the popular **Ca'n Costa** (Ctra. Valldemossa–Deià, km2.5, 971 61 22 63, closed Tue, €€), another of the Archduke's numerous former properties along the coast. The interior is a wonderful old *tafona* (olive press room), within which decent, if not outstanding, Mallorcan food is served. The wine list is excellent and the family welcome is warm. This place is a big favourite for Sunday lunch with Mallorcan families from Palma.

The best place to drink when night falls is the bar and restaurant at the **Costa Nord** (Avda. Palma 6, 971 61 24 25, €€€).

Where to stay

The most celebrated place to stay in town is the **Hotel Valldemossa** (Ctra. Vieja de Valldemossa s/n, 971 61 26 26, www. valldemossahotel.com, doubles €320-€460 incl breakfast, restaurant €€€€), located in a former private house just outside Valldemossa on the old Palma road. What's a little odd, considering you'll see ads for it all over the island (the proprietor owns Mallorca's billboards), is that it has just 12 rooms. They all have private *terrazas* or patios, tiled floors, marble bathrooms and refined design; one has a four-poster bed. The views from the pool area and the dining room terrace are extraordinary. One note of caution: the lofty prices in the restaurant aren't always justified by the quality of conception and execution of the dishes.

A great alternative a half-hour stroll from town is **Cases de Ca's Garriguer** (Ctra. Valdemossa–Andratx, km3, 971 61 23 00, www. vistamarhotel.es, closed Nov-Mar, doubles €165-€175 incl breakfast), a tranquil old house that contains ten spacious, elegant rooms, seven with terraces and three with balconies; there's a sauna, and the views from the pool are lovely. Another pleasant place to stay, a couple of kilometres south of Valldemossa, is the verdant **Finca Son Brondo** (Ctra. Palma–Valldemossa, km14.3 & km15.2, 971 61 22 58, www.fincason brondo.com, doubles €150 incl breakfast), which has been in the same family since the 16th century and now offers six bedrooms, a pool and even a chapel, and which also has great views of the surrounding mountains.

A first-rate mid-range option in the heart of the village is the friendly **Es Petit Hotel de Valldemossa** (C/Uetam 1, 971 61 24 79, www. espetithotel-valldemossa.com, doubles €125-€170 incl breakfast, closed 2wks Nov), offering eight air-conditioned rooms (two with terraces) within a carefully restored stone townhouse; there's a big communal terrace with great views too. On the same street is the attractive and great-value **Ca'n Mario** (C/Uetam 8, 971 61 21 22, closed dinner Mon-Thur, Sun mid Oct-mid Dec & mid Jan-Mar and all mid Dec-mid Jan, €), a reassuringly old-fashioned, centrally located and economically priced restaurant serving decent food.

WEST MALLORCA

Resources

Police station
Valldemossa *C/Rei Sanxo I s/n (971 61 29 40).*

Post office
Valldemossa *C/Pintora Pilar Muntaner 3 (no phone).*

Tourist information
Valldemossa *OIT, Avda. Palma 7 (971 61 20 19/oficinaturismevalldemossa@yahoo.es).* **Open** Jan-Nov 9am-1.30pm, 3-5pm Mon-Fri; 10am-1pm Sat.

DEIA

The MA-10 continues along the coastline from Valldemossa, passing (after about eight kilometres), **Son Marroig**, the favourite estate of Archduke Ludwig Salvator. This impressive pile is just one of a number of properties the Archduke bought to preserve this part of the coastline (another, S'Estaca, is now owned by Michael Douglas; *see p112*). Only part of it is open to the public and, though visitors can admire the Archduke's voluminous library and hundreds of photos and paintings, there's very little English labelling and no attempt to tell his fascinating life story. Outside, sculpted gardens lead to the cliff edge, and include Ludwig Salvator's favourite spot for thought, the white

marble rotunda. From here you can see down to **Sa Foradada**, which means 'pierced rock' – it's just that, a jagged rock rising from the sea with a big hole through it.

A couple of kilometres back towards Valldemossa is another of the Archduke's old properties, the one-time monastery of **Miramar**, founded in 1276 by King Jaume II on the prompting of Ramón Llull as a missionary school. Both Miramar and Son Marroig passed to the family of his secretary Antoni Vives on the Archduke's death in 1915, and remain in its ownership today. A museum tells the story of the building.

Four kilometres further on from Son Marroig is one of the most celebrated villages on the island, **Deià**. It's an extraordinarily pretty place, and knows it. Honey-coloured houses nestle on the precipitous terraced slopes of the mountain, the **Puig des Teix**, which drop dramatically down to a tiny cove below.

Despite its renown, and being packed with (largely upmarket) hotels and restaurants (mostly along the main road, which doubles as the village high street), Deià stubbornly maintains its own character. Little further concession is made to tourists; car parking, for example, is minimal (there are eight or nine spaces outside the entrance to La Residencia hotel), and coaches are banned from stopping. Deià's history dates back to Moorish times, the Arabic name 'ad-daia' simply meaning

La Residencia. See p121.

WEST MALLORCA

Walk Around Deià

The Breathtaking scenery surrounding Deià merits this challenging hike.

Distance: 16km. Circular.
Time: 6hrs.

There are some very popular walks around the famously chic village of Deià, but the following long and fairly strenuous hike avoids the crowds for most of its length, climbing high above the village, then following the contours of the hills through coniferous forests before descending to the sea and returning to Deià along the cliff tops. It makes a fine day's walking, and has refreshment stops at the halfway point and at the end, where you can swim on fine days at Cala de Deià. Parking in Deià is nightmarish, which is why this walk starts in the sizeable car park down by the sea at Cala de Deià (if you don't have your own transport, start in Deià). This does mean that the first hour and a half or so is almost all climbing, but at least you get all the uphill out of the way at the beginning. If you want an easier, clearly signposted and more populated stroll, take the path to Sóller from the hamlet of **Lluc-Alcari**, a few kilometres north of Deià.

From the car park, walk up the road you've just come down, and turn right on to the path signed to Deià. It's a steep but beautiful 40-minute climb up to the village.

On reaching the main road through Deià, turn left and then right in front of **La Residencia** hotel (between the bus stop, the sign to the hotel and El Olivo restaurant).

Follow this road, going sharp left in front of the huge drystone retaining wall of a house, through a pair of metal gates, then on upwards as the road changes from metalled to rough concrete to track, then back to concrete. As it bends round to the left below another villa (about 20 minutes after setting off from Deià), take the wide track leading off to the right.

Five or so minutes later you pass a twisted tree trunk on your right, then, after another five minutes, take the track to the right of the highest of the villas that you'll come across, bearing left around the back of the property and climbing over a low drystone wall, before continuing along the path with a wire fence to your right.

You'll come to a drinking fountain with a brass tap. There's a route downwards here, indicated by red marks, but ignore it and continue upwards following the cairns and a set of red paint splodges.

Ca's Patró March. *See p121.*

After six or seven minutes you pass through a wire gate between two trees, and then, soon, through a gap in a stone wall.

At this point, you'll see a viewpoint towards the sea to your left (next to a stone hut), but the path continues straight on (marked by a cairn). Follow the cairns upwards, past another hut and up a succession of terraces.

Around 15 minutes later the path starts to level and you can enjoy precipitous views down to Deià and the sea as you walk into coniferous woodland. Pass through another gap in a stone wall, and bear round to the left (ignoring a steep uphill path).

The route becomes a little tricky to make out after this point, but around a quarter of an hour after passing through the stone wall you should find yourself walking along the top of a terrace. After a couple of minutes you come to a fork in the path, with the left fork heading downwards and the right gently upwards. There are purple splodges on a tree and a rock here. Take the right upward path.

Eight minutes later, just past a flat mossy area supported by a stone wall, the path swings left. One branch heads up, but continue on downwards on the main one to the left, past another raised mossy area. You may spot goats darting between the holm oaks. After five minutes you'll come across a huge pile of rocks and various stone foundations.

After this point the trail becomes wide and clear and then heads generally downwards, supported by a wall, with fine views down towards the sea.

Around 15 minutes after passing the big pile of rocks you'll come to a T-junction. The right path goes upwards, but take the left branch downwards, by another mossy-topped spot, some stone foundations and a huge boulder with a fissure running through it, and then through a wide gap between stone pillars, under a curious wooden construction over the path and round a metal gate with spikes on top of it.

The track is now wide enough for a four-wheel drive. Ignore an offshoot heading upwards and continue down. About a quarter of an hour after the T-junction you'll find yourself walking down through a series of terraces, punctuated with gnarled old olive trees and massive boulders. The track goes through a stone wall and you can enjoy the great views towards the mountains surrounding Sóller.

Pass through a large metal gate and immediately cross the signed **Deià–Sóller footpath** (you may well meet the first other walkers you've come across on this hike here). After a couple of minutes you'll arrive at a huge 300-year-old house, from which excellent quiche and fresh orange juice is dispensed to walkers (at a price).

From here, take the cobbled path downwards, turn sharp left by a ruined chapel (not towards Sóller) and continue down to the main **Deià–Sóller road**. Turn left along the road and after one minute, as the road bends left at a right angle, go right down the side road marked to '**Restaurant Bens d'Avall**'.

Keep heading downwards, following signs to the restaurant (ignoring a turn-off to the right). Eventually, you'll come to the restaurant (*see p124*), the terrace looks down the coastline towards Deià, and makes a good spot to take a break.

Most of the rest of the walk is back along the coast. Walk back up the road until you're above the restaurant car parking, looking for a place to scramble down to the right into the rainwater run-off trench and up on to the footpath on the other side. Turn right and head towards the sea.

Ten minutes later, as the track bends right to go down to the cove, you take the path to the left, where you'll see a red paint splodge, and continue up to walk alongside a wire fence. After five minutes go left up a wider track with a gate on the right, then climb over a stile in front of where the track has a chain across it.

The rest of the walk consists essentially of following the cairns and paint marks along the coast. Much of the ground is rough, and a fair amount of scrambling is involved, particularly around the many fallen trees.

You should arrive at **Cala de Deià** (where you can swim, and get a meal or drink at Ca's Patró March) around two hours after leaving the restaurant.

Cala de Deià.

'hamlet', and the Moors cultivated the slopes and terraced the land here, growing grapes and olives. The Reconquest saw the extension of farming to the higher slopes with the growing of citrus fruit and keeping of sheep and pigs. Like so many villages along this stretch of the coast, Deià grew with its back to the sea: protection against pirates and the north winds.

Today, the village has around 700 inhabitants, more than half of whom are foreigners. It has been attracting artists and writers for decades, the most famous being **Robert Graves**, who lived here for most of his life in Ca n'Alluny (meaning 'The Faraway House'), five minutes from the centre of Deià on the Deià–Sóller road; the house was acquired by the Fundació Robert Graves and turned into a museum, **La Casa de Robert Graves**, with the help of Graves's son William, opening to the public in summer 2006. Tours of the museum begin with a 15-minute documentary on Graves's life, while the house itself contains the poet's original furnishings and artefacts, including his typewriters, letters from various bigwigs, photographs and manuscripts. It may not reflect the place as it was when Graves was alive – reportedly full of bustle and mirth – but it's interesting all the same and the lovely garden, with its olive, carob and almond trees, is a highlight of a visit here. It was largely Graves's presence in Deià that drew in a stream of famous writers and actors to the village, including Anaïs Nin, Kingsley Amis, Anthony Burgess, Gabriel García Márquez, Mario Vargas Llosa, Ava Gardner and Alec Guinness. But Graves wasn't the first foreigner to fall for the village's charms – DH Lawrence, Arthur Rackham and composer Manuel de Falla all preceded him.

Graves's widow Beryl lived in Deià until her death in 2003. Of his sons, only Tomás, the youngest, still has a home here, and his house was on the market at the time that this guide was being updated; it seems the village's celebrity status has become a little overbearing. However, all three sons still regularly congregate in Deià to check on the house and play in the family band (Pa Amb'Oli), much to the delight of local residents.

There's still a vague air of bohemianism to Deià, albeit of a moneyed, Notting Hill kind these days, and, though some visitors find the place a little precious, its easygoing confidence continues to seduce many. It makes a great holiday base.

It doesn't take long to wander around. Head up the hill to the church of **Sant Joan Baptista**, where you'll see Graves's headstone under a tree towards the back left-hand corner of the churchyard (away from the entrance),

marked simply 'Robert Graves, Poeta, EPD' (*'En Paz Descanse'*, 'Rest In Peace'). The views from here are marvellous. Adjoining the church is a tiny museum (open 9am-7pm Sat, free), which has a few bits of Graves memorabilia. A nose around the tiny graveyard reveals ample evidence of Deià's bohemian heritage, with a corner on a lower terrace devoted to foreign artists and writers who were so captivated by the village that they never left it. Near the church is the lovely tranquil **Plaça de la Iglesia**.

If you're interested in Mallorcan prehistory, the **Deià Archaeological Museum** is worth a visit. Founded by American archaeologist William Waldren in 1962, it contains finds from several local sites, in particular that at Muleta near Sóller.

There are a good number of appealing shops in the village, such as **Nexus** (C/Arxiduc Lluís Salvador 9, 971 63 93 10) and **Islas** (C/Arxiduc Lluís Salvador 17, 971 63 91 44, closed mid Nov-mid Mar), whose long-term expat owners bring back some lovely clothes from their forays to South-east Asia (many of which they design themselves and get made up in Bali).

Decorative tiles, plates and jewellery are sold at **Deià Arte** (Plaça de la Iglesia 2, 971 63 91 26), while tasteful Mallorcan clothing, crafts and art are on sale at **Galeria Deià** (C/Arxiduc Lluís Salvador 3, 971 63 91 42), and there are further classy shops on the hill between the church and the main road. The **Tafona Gallery** within La Residencia hotel (*see p121*) has year-round shows of work by local artists.

To get down to the small beach (a mix of stone, shingle and a tiny patch of sand) of **Cala de Deià**, head along the road out of town towards Sóller, and turn left at the sign saying 'Depuradora' (there's a small sign to Cala de Deià too). It's a five-minute drive or 25-minute walk down to the cove, which has a couple of beautifully situated seasonal bar-restaurants.

Deià's arty heritage has left its mark on the village's cultural calendar. The **Deià International Music Festival** (mobile 678 98 95 36, www.dimf.com) was born nearly 30 years ago and offers a progamme of classical performances from local and international artists from March to September.

WEST MALLORCA

Deià. See p115.

La Casa de Robert Graves
Ctra. Deià–Sóller s/n (971 63 61 85/www.lacasa derobertgraves.com). **Open** *Apr-Oct* 10am-5pm (last admission 4.20pm) Mon-Fri; 10am-3pm Sat (last admission 2.20pm). *Nov-Mar* 9am-4pm (last admission 3.20pm) Mon-Fri; 9am-2pm (last admission 1.20pm) Sat. Opening times may be reduced in *Dec & Jan;* call or check website in advance. **Admission** €5; €2.50 under-12s. **Credit** MC, V.

FREE Deià Archaeological Museum
C/d'es Clot 4 (971 63 90 01). **Open** *June-Sept* 5-7pm Tue, Thur, Sun. *Oct-May* by appointment. Times vary; phone to check. **Admission** free.

Miramar
Ctra. Valldemossa–Deià s/n (971 61 60 73). **Open** 9.30am-4.30pm daily (closed some Sun and on stormy days). **Admission** €4; free under 12s. **No credit cards.**

Son Marroig
Ctra. Valldemossa–Deià s/n (971 63 91 58). **Open** Apr-Sept 9.30am-8pm Mon-Sat. Oct-Mar 9.30am-6pm Mon-Sat. **Admission** €3; free under-10s. **No credit cards.**

Where to eat & drink

There are a remarkable number of eating and drinking options in Deià, most of them excellent and most towards the pricey end of the scale. Probably the pick of the restaurants is **Es Racó d'es Teix** (C/Sa Vinya Vell 6, 971 63 95 01, www.esracodesteix.es, closed Mon, Tue and Dec, Jan, €€€€), run by Josef Sauerschell, the chef who earned El Olivo a Michelin star (which it no longer has) and then set up on his own, achieving the same feat at Es Racó. Expect perfectly conceived and executed Mallorcan dishes such as *lechona* (piglet), as well as a few modern Mediterranean options, served in a lovely old stone building or on a series of elegant terraces in summer. The place is referred to locally simply as 'Josef's'.

Another classy (if very expensive) dining spot is **El Olivo** (971 63 90 11, closed Jan, €€€€), within the trendy La Residencia hotel. This is a thoroughbred restaurant, from the slickly professional yet friendly staff (it was awarded the accolade of 'best dining room service in a hotel restaurant' by prestigious gastronomic organisation Madrid Fusión in 2008) and lushly romantic decor (candelabras abound) to the verve and quality of the imaginative modern European cooking. If you can stretch to the €80 five-course (plus 'surprise' dessert) Chef's Menu, you will be rewarded by the likes of asparagus cream with lobster ravioli.

Among the other local gems is **Sebastián** (C/Felipe Bauzá s/n, 971 63 94 17, closed lunch and all Wed, €€€), which offers superb meat dishes (including lamb with rosemary and honey, and wild boar in season) and a good range of fish and seafood – plus a couple of Asian dishes. The surroundings are elegant with a rustic touch. **Restaurante Jaime** (C/Arxiduc Lluís Salvador 22, 971 63 90 29, closed Mon and Jan, €€€) is another good bet; Jaime died in 2002, but his son Biel Payeras reinvented this Deià institution across the road from the original, serving a refined, modernised version of traditional Mallorcan food. Lovely terrace.

Up a narrow lane from the main road in a delightful tree-shaded setting is **Sa Vinya** (C/Sa Vinya Vella 3, 971 63 95 00, closed Tue and mid Nov-Feb, €€€). The international food is good and well presented in a clean, uncluttered style.

Other possibilities are **Sa Dorada** (C/Arxiduc Lluis Salvador 24, 971 63 93 18, €€), now in Argentinian hands, and **Restaurant Deià** (C/Felipe Bauzà 1, 971 63 92 65, €€), for Spanish cuisine; the place recently changed ownership.

If you don't want a major blow-out at major prices, try **El Barrigón Xelini** (C/Arxiduc

Lluís Salvador 19, 971 63 91 39, closed Mon and mid Dec-mid Jan, €€), a great modern tapas bar with bags of atmosphere, a wide range of reasonably priced dishes and a small *terraza*; it puts on live jazz in the winter months, every Saturday from 9pm.

Also on, or just off, the main drag are the unabashedly tourist-led **Las Palmeras** (C/Arxiduc Lluís Salvador 11, 971 63 90 16, closed Wed, €€), offering Mallorcan dishes and tapas and with a vine-covered terrace, Argentinian-run **Senset & Senseta** (C/Vinya Vella 1, 971 63 61 09, €), for sushi or grilled meats, and, just round the bend at the end of the street, the low-key **Sa Font Fresca** (C/Arxiduc Lluís Salvador 30, 971 63 94 41, closed Sun and Dec, €), a new café with a distinctly local feel (it's often packed with local men watching the game), a nice *terraza* and cheap, good quality coffee, sandwiches, home-made pizza and beer.

Patricia's (C/Felipe Bauzá 1, 971 63 91 99, closed Tue, Wed, €), which used to be owned by the same people as Sebastián, is now run by a British couple, who have turned it into a café serving sandwiches, simple salads and ice-creams at reasonable prices.

Down in the cove are a couple of wonderfully located restaurants that have been operating for decades. **Ca's Patró March** (971 63 91 37,

closed dinner Sept, Oct, Apr-June, dinner Mon-Thur, Sun July, Aug and all Nov-Mar, €€€) is an informal, though certainly not cheap, fish restaurant and bar (where you'll struggle to get a table for lunch in summer, thanks to all the luxury yachts mooring in the cala). It has been run by three generations of the March family and the present owner, Juan, often goes out before dawn to catch the fish for that day's meals. The other spot is the cheaper **Restaurante C'an Lluc** (mobile 649 19 86 18, closed Wed and Nov-Mar, €€), run by Francisca and her husband Jordi, whose cave-located kitchen knocks out great, simple Mallorcan home cooking and fish.

Sóller. *See p122.*

Ca'n Quet (Ctra. Valldemossa–Deià s/n, 971 63 91 96, closed Mon and Nov-Mar, €€€€), part of Es Molí hotel (*see below*), enjoys a sublime position, tucked into the side of the hill overlooking a stream, and the food is exceptional – lots of fresh local produce and a wide selection of fish, such as *rape asado con jamón* (roast monkfish with ham) and *merluza* (hake) with local mushrooms. Treat yourself to the cold white chocolate soup with fruits of the forest to finish.

In terms of drinking, most head straight to **Sa Fonda** (C/Arxiduc Lluís Salvador 5, no phone), the hub of village nightlife. Previous owner Tomao, who passed away recently, was something of a local legend, and his son now runs the show. First impressions may not suggest a rocking nightlife venue, but this is *the* place to come for sunset drinks and partying till dawn; there's lots of live music in summer (until midnight), and those in the know travel from all over the island to be here on Saturday nights. Tim Robbins, the Corrs and the Geldofs have all hung out here. Note, if you're coming from outside Deià, that it's often near-impossible to find a taxi willing to transport you out of the village after midnight.

Where to stay

Although Deià is known for its luxury hotels, there are places to stay to suit every budget and taste. Possibly the most celebrated hotel in Mallorca, the super-chic **La Residencia** (C/Son Canals s/n, 971 63 90 11, www.hotel-laresidencia.com, doubles €280-€685 incl breakfast) is a haven of indulgence and recuperation for the rich and (discretion-craving) famous, offering low-key luxury and an informal, thoroughly relaxed vibe. The decor of the 59 rooms (including 22 suites, three of which have their own private swimming pools) is contemporary-rustic with immense traditional Mallorcan dark wood beds and wardrobes, tiled floors, white linen, earth-toned bathrooms and paintings by local artists. There are three swimming pools (one indoor), sauna and steam room, outdoor jacuzzi, beauty salon, gym and two tennis courts. Note that there's a five-night minimum stay between April and October.

For all its charms, La Residencia can't promise much in the way of rooms with views. Not so **Es Molí** (Ctra. Valldemossa–Deià s/n, 971 63 90 00, www.esmoli.com, closed Nov- Apr, doubles €250-€310 incl breakfast), another exceptional hotel, offering some of the choicest vistas on this stretch of coast. It's set in luxuriant grounds, with a pool, tennis court and bar with picture windows overlooking the bay. There are 87 rooms, the best of which are sea-facing and have their own private terrace.

If you want somewhere more intimate, but with views that are, if anything, even better, try **Sa Pedrissa** (Ctra. Valldemossa–Deià, km74.5, 971 63 91 11, www.sapedrissa.com, closed 2wks Dec, double €128-€289 incl breakfast), just outside the village. Owner Sebastià Artigues's beautifully restored former olive mill is a four-star luxury haven in immaculate taste. The six rooms and three suites all have views either to Deià or the coast, and are wood-beamed and fitted to an extremely high standard, with soft pillows, big beds, comfy armchairs, terraces or balconies and marble-tiled bathrooms. The pool is at the edge of the grounds and looks across to the village, with a barbecue area behind. The kitchen is superb, serving local meats and fish, and you can choose to eat in the house itself, in an atmospheric dining room with original fittings, or on the *terraza* outside, which on a warm night is sublime.

A cheaper option is **S'Hotel d'es Puig** (C/Es Puig 4, 971 63 94 09, www.hoteldes puig.com, closed Dec-Feb, doubles €118-€140 incl breakfast), located in the heart of Deià on the road up to the church. This former *hostal* was where Anaïs Nin and Manuel de Falla would stay when holidaying in the village, and it also appears in one of Graves's works. Today, it has been tastefully refurbished and upgraded, with eight comfortable rooms with en suite showers, while retaining its original character. There's also a pool.

Hostal Villaverde (C/Ramón Llull 19, 971 63 90 37, www.hostalvillaverde.com, doubles €60-€80 incl breakfast), a very pretty budget option tucked below the church, has simple, clean rooms (some with terrace), an open courtyard and a lovely tree-covered *terraza* looking out to the coast.

If there is no room in Deià itself, try the **Hotel Costa d'Or** (C/Llucalcari s/n, 971 63 90 25, www.hoposa.es, closed Nov-Apr, doubles €129-€245 incl breakfast), a gorgeous hotel a couple of kilometres towards Sóller in the hamlet of Llucalcari. It's set in a pretty pine grove in a stunning position overlooking the sea. The rooms are simple (the ones to go

WEST MALLORCA

for are at the front with the views), and there's an outdoor pool, tennis court and bar.

Resources

Police station
Deià *Porxo 4 (971 63 90 77)*.

Post office
Deià *Via Arxiduc Lluís Salvador 30 (no phone)*.

SOLLER

Sóller, the major settlement on Mallorca's west coast, lies 11 kilometres north-east of Deià. With a magnificent backdrop of encircling high peaks, this relaxed town of little over 10,000 inhabitants makes a fine base for exploring the coast and the mountains, as well as being an enjoyable day-trip destination.

Until the four-kilometre-long tunnel between here and Palma opened in the mid 1990s, the only way to get to Sóller was over the top of the mountain, or by train on ancient rolling stock (*see p126* **Ticket to Ride**). And before the rail line opened in 1912, the journey from the capital – just 30 kilometres (19 miles) away – took the best part of a day. As a result, Sóller has historically turned its face to the west and the sea, setting up trade agreements for its lucrative citrus business with Barcelona and France in preference to Palma.

The citrus fruit groves that line the valley floor – the **Valle de los Naranjos** (Valley of the Oranges) – made its inhabitants rich in the late 19th and early 20th centuries, and account for the fanciful architecture and grand mansions dotted around the town. Citrus fruits, olives and handmade sausages are still produced here, and it's well worth spending some time exploring its winding streets, followed by a leisurely lunch in the central square, Plaça Constitució.

The square is dominated by the towering church of **Sant Bartomeu** (open 11am-1.15pm, 3-5.15pm Mon-Thur, 11am-1.15pm Fri, Sat, free), which was begun in the 13th century but is largely Baroque in style, with a neo-Gothic tower and a *modernista* (Catalan art nouveau) façade by a pupil of Gaudí's, **Joan Rubió i Bellver**. Rubió came over with Gaudí from Barcelona in 1904 when the great architect was invited to work on Palma Cathedral. Rubió busied himself in Sóller, finishing the church façade (in 1904), designing the building next door, the **Banco de Sóller** (in 1912; now the Santander Central Hispano bank – its rugged, rusticated exterior is lightened by the wonderfully intricate metalwork of its window grilles) and his own house, **Ca'n Prunera** (1909-11; C/Lluna 90), which has more striking ironwork and is alive with floral motifs. *See also pp72-73* **Profile**.

There is not much else in Sóller with regard to sights, but at the edge of town on the main road from Palma is another *modernista* mansion that is now home to the **Museu Balear de Ciències Naturals & Jardí Botànic de Sóller**, a small museum and botanic garden dedicated to the study and conservation of Balearic palaeontology and the evolution of native flora and fauna.

Sóller is pretty good for shopping, for a small town. C/Lluna, off Plaça Constitució, offers some of the best shops; for classy, imaginative jewellery, try **Arte Artesania** (C/Lluna 43, 971 63 17 32, www.arteartesania.com) or for genuine *albarcas*, sandals traditionally made with old car tyres (check the tread on the soles), go to **Ben Calçat** (C/Lluna 74, 971 63 28 74). You can pick up some interesting second-hand clothes and accessories at **La Bohème** (C/Bauza 11, no phone) and cute kids' toys at **Cavall Verd** (C/Bon Any 5, 971 63 35 17).

The municipal **market** (8am-1pm Mon-Sat), just north of the main square, isn't big on atmosphere, but you can find good meat, fish, fruit and veg here. Opposite is **Sa Fàbrica de Gelats** (Plaça Mercat, 971 63 17 08, www.gelatsoller.com), where more than 40 flavours of ice-cream are made, some using the valley's oranges and lemons. Market day is Saturday, when the centre is cordoned off from traffic and shops spill into the streets to join countless market stalls.

If you want to explore the spectacular mountains in the area, **Tramuntana Tours** (C/Lluna 72, 971 63 24 23, mobile 649 03 47 59, www.tramuntanatours.com) organises guided hikes and mountain bike tours – as well as sea kayaking, deep-sea fishing and canyoning excursions – or you can hire a bike and head off on your own. The company has an additional shop in Port de Sóller (Paseo de Traves 12).

Sóller celebrates a number of fiestas: Nit de San Antoni (16 Jan), Fira i Es Firó (2nd Sun & Mon in May), San Pere (29 June) and Sant Bartomeu (24 Aug).

INSIDE TRACK
SOLLER TUNNEL

If you find yourself travelling back and forth from Sóller to Palma a lot it's worth, at least once, planning a slightly longer journey time and taking **Coll de Sóller** – a 14-kilometre (nine-mile) series of hairpin bends that winds over the mountains. Not only are the views splendid, you'll save yourself the €4-euros-a-pop toll fee.

WEST MALLORCA

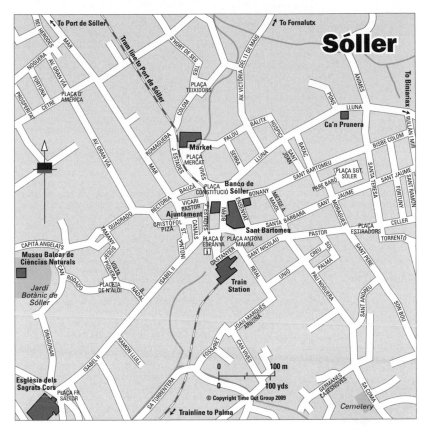

Sóller

WEST MALLORCA

Museu Balear de Ciències Naturals & Jardí Botànic de Sóller

Ctra. Palma–Port de Sóller, km30 (971 63 40 64/www.museucienciesnaturals.org). **Open** 10am-6pm Tue-Sat; 10am-2pm Sun. **Admission** €5; free under 10s. **No credit cards. Map** above.

Where to eat & drink

Sóller has an abundance of small bars and cafés, concentrated on and around Plaça Constitució. One of the less touristy is **Es Planet** (No.3, 971 63 45 70, €), where locals sip their morning coffees and later munch on *pa amb oli*, pizzas, salads, and hot and cold baguettes. **Café Sóller** (No.13, 971 63 00 10, €) is great for well-above-average salads and pasta dishes, and is pretty cool (in both senses) inside. Even hipper is **Bar España** (No.1, 971 63 00 04, €), in front of the Banco de Sóller. Once a grimy old spot, it has been taken over by the original owners' children and transformed into a sleek Barcelona-style joint that serves basic snacks. New addition to the square, **Cipriani's** (opposite Bar España) outdoor tables are much-coveted. The food is good too: try the crab salad or baked sea bass, for example, or if you're just after a tipple, then typical to Spain, its drinks are mixed stiff as you like.

For cheap fare and fresh fruit juices, try **Bar La Union 'Sa Botigueta'** (C/Jeroni Estades 9, 971 63 01 63, €), just off the main *plaça* (there's also an entrance on C/Born). If juice and superfoods are your thing, check out tiny Brazilian juice bar **Açai Café** (C/Rectoria 3, 971 63 18 18, www.acai-espana.com, closed Sun).

Surprisingly, the town isn't great for restaurants – most people head down to the places around the Port (*see p128*) or to the handful of excellent eateries just outside Sóller (booking is advisable for all of them).

Sa Teulera (Ctra. Lluc–Pollença s/n, 971 63 11 11, closed Wed and Feb, €€) is a delightful, informal, rustic restaurant that packs out with locals at weekends who come to enjoy great steaks, rabbit, quail and particularly *lechona* – suckling pig roasted over fires made with almond shells. If you're coming from the Deià road, turn right at the war memorial between Sóller and the Port, and the restaurant is on the left after a couple of kilometres.

More formal is **Ca'n Ai** (Camí Son Sales 50, 971 63 24 94, www.canai.com, closed Mon and Nov-Feb, €€€), an old country house with a garden, where first-rate Mallorcan and international dishes can be enjoyed. Look out for the signs close to the Sóller roundabout. You can also stay here (*see p125*).

Back five or so kilometres towards Deià a road leads off towards the coast and has a sign to **Bens d'Avall** (Urb. Costa de Deià s/n, 971 63 23 81, closed Sun dinner, Mon Mar-Oct and Mon-Fri Nov-Feb, €€€€). This classy place enjoys a spectacular coastal setting; its terrace is a dreamy spot for a long lunch or dinner. The food is contemporary and superb, but be prepared to pay heftily for it.

Where to stay

Recent years have witnessed an explosion of wonderful places to stay in and around Sóller, though most are towards the top end of the price scale.

Bar España. *See p123.*

Prize for poshest spot in town goes to the five-star **Gran Hotel Sóller** (C/Romaguera 18, 971 63 86 86, www.granhotelsoller.com, doubles €235-€332), a splendidly restored late 19th-century building that was a hotel in the 1960s and '70s, but reopened in its current incarnation in 2004. The 38 rooms are decorated in a clean, modern style, with plenty of local stone in evidence. Top selling points include a spa with indoor pool, and a rooftop pool with bar and fabulous views, and a superior Mediterranean restaurant, **Can Blau** (€€€).

Ca'n Roses (C/Quadrado 9, 971 63 22 99, www.canroses.com, closed Nov-mid Dec, doubles €150-€235 incl breakfast) is a supremely tasteful and relaxing hideaway, secreted down a side street close to the main square. A huge wooden door gives on to a patio around which there are eight light-filled rooms (some with terraces), beautifully designed, with steel beds, exposed wood beams and wooden floors. But it's the garden that will take your breath away: palms and orange trees shade a huge swimming pool.

A wonderful, deeply romantic place to stay in Sóller is the **Hotel Salvia** (C/Palma 18, 971 63 49 36, www.hotelsalvia.com, closed Nov-Feb, doubles €258-€368 incl breakfast), an effortlessly stylish conversion of an 18th-century townhouse, now a tiny but plush six-bedroom hotel (the whole place can be rented too). The pool and gardens are lovely, there are three honesty bars (so you can help yourself to whiskey and brandy), there are no children under 14 allowed and guests are given their own keys, all leading to the illusion that you own the place. If only.

C'an Quatre (Camí de Villalonga 16, 971 63 80 06, www.canquatre.com, closed mid Dec-mid Jan, doubles €120-€140) is yet another delightful place, just off the main square, but feeling like it's out in the countryside. There are six rooms (five with terraces) and four suites (also with terraces), all designed in rural style. It's set within its own grounds, with a pool and wonderful views of the mountains.

Other options include four-star **Ca'l Bisbe** (C/Bisbe Nadal 10, 971 63 12 28, www.hotel calbisbe.com, closed Nov-Jan, double €106-€126 incl breakfast), in the heart of the town, but with a big pool, and the more modest four-room **Ca'n Isabel** (C/Isabel 13, 971 63 80 97, www.canisabel.com, closed mid Nov-mid Feb, double €115-€145 incl breakfast), which, nevertheless, offers plenty of modern comforts (air-con, satellite TV, classy bathroom products).

Typically of Mallorca, once you veer away from the classy end of the accommodation scale, pickings are lean. Sóller does have a number of passable *pensiones*. **Margarita Trias Vives** (C/Reial 3, 971 63 42 14, www.sollernet.com/casamargarita, doubles €33-€60) is a basic but

The road to Fornalutx.

very friendly budget option in a central location handy for the square and the station; it has ten rooms, two with a terrace, three are en suite.

Another possibility is **El Guía** (C/Castanyer 2, 971 63 02 27, closed mid Nov-Feb, doubles €84 incl breakfast), just behind the station, which has a large courtyard and simple rooms.

On the road to Deià, **C'as Xorc** (Ctra. Sóller–Deià, km56.1, 971 63 82 80, www.casxorc.com, closed Nov-mid Mar, doubles €210-€330 incl breakfast, restaurant €€€) is a stunningly located oasis of indulgence that enjoys some unforgettable views of the valley and the mountains. The bedrooms are large, airy and not over-designed, and there's a fine restaurant and a lovely pool.

There are a number of other good *agroturismos* and *hoteles rurales* around Sóller. Among the best are **Ca n'Ai** (Camí Son Sales 50, 971 63 24 94, www.canai.com, closed Nov-Feb, doubles €225 incl breakfast), **Can Coll** (Camí de Can Coll 1, 971 63 32 44, www.cancoll.com, closed Nov-Feb, doubles €155-€262 incl breakfast) and **Ca's Sant** (Camí ses Fontenelles 34, 971 63 02 98, mobile 649 91 11 94, www.cassant.com, doubles €149-€184 incl breakfast).

Resources

Internet
Sóller *Forn de Campos, Avda. Jeroni Estades 9 (no phone/www.forndecampos.com).* **Map** p123.

Police station
Sóller *Plaça de Constitució 1 (971 63 41 41).* **Map** p123.

Post office
Sóller *C/Rectoria 7 (971 63 11 91).* **Map** p123.

Tourist information
Sóller *OIT, Plaça d'Espanya s/n (971 63 80 08/www.ajsoller.net).* **Open** 9.45am-1.30pm Mon-Fri; 9am-1pm Sat. **Map** p123.

FORNALUTX

Once voted the prettiest village in Spain, Fornalutx – a couple of kilometres east of Sóller – is still a lovely place to spend a couple of days. And, though like many of Mallorca's famously beautiful spots it's now almost antiseptically clean and well maintained, it still has charm. There's a small central square with a fountain and a set of steps where the residents celebrate the festival of Reyes Magos on 6 January by giving every child in the village a present. Beyond climbing the steps and having a drink in a café to recover, there's not actually anything to do here, and it's a well-worn stop-off on the tourist trail, so you'll have plenty of company.

From Fornalutx, it's about a 20-minute walk or a short drive to the even tinier, but equally pretty, hamlet of **Biniaraix**. There's a memorable walk from Biniaraix up the

Ticket to Ride

The scenic Palma–Sóller railway is a charming throwback to a bygone era.

A journey on the **Ferrocarril de Sóller** (Sóller Railway) is a must-do on any visit to Mallorca; if you're staying in Palma and make only one foray out of the city, this should be it. You'll be hard-pressed to find a local aboard the toytown-style service, and it's very unlikely it would still be operational were it not for the tourist trade; but this in no way detracts from what is a hugely enjoyable hour-long journey through the mountains, as well as the most convenient way of travelling between Palma and the west coast if you're holidaying without a car.

This 27-kilometre (17-mile) length of track (with one of the narrowest gauges in the world at 914 millimetres) opened in 1912, connecting the capital with Sóller. The new route cut journey times down from a whole day to just an hour and a quarter, thus allowing the citrus growers of Sóller to get to the Palma markets and back in one day.

Little has changed since then. Leaving from Palma, you need to head to the tiny station (marooned on C/Eusebio Estada, in the soulless expanse of the Plaça Espanya), reached through a wrought-iron gate. The ticket office still dispenses old-fashioned paper tickets and the carriages are largely constructed from wood with banquette-style seats, brass fittings and gaslights.

The first part of the journey out of Palma is not spectacular, and for the first ten minutes the track runs along the road like a city tram, before reaching the outskirts of Palma and then open countryside, with the peaks of the Tramuntana as a fantastic backdrop.

As you approach the first stop at Bunyola, olive fields give way to pine forests. Beyond the village the train enters the first of 12 tunnels, which become progressively longer, until it breaks through the mountains and emerges on the west side of the island. The views here are superb as the train wends its way over precarious bridges and across dry torrents, high above a valley rutted with terraces and dotted with old farmhouses. In the distance you can spot Sóller and the villages of Biniaraix and Fornalutx.

The last part of the journey, the approach to Sóller, is delightful: citrus groves crowd round the carriages, close enough to pull off a ripe lemon or orange. From the station, in Sóller's Plaça d'Espanya, you can jump on the equally atmospheric tram (€4) down to the sea at Port de Sóller (*see p126*).

Note that the services marked with an asterisk below make an additional stop at the Mirador del Pujol d'en Banya for five minutes to provide passengers with photo opportunities.

Ferrocarril de Sóller
Palma *C/Eusebio Estada 1 (971 75 20 51/www.trendesoller.com).* Sóller *Plaça d'Espanya 6 (971 63 03 91/902 36 47 11).* **Tickets** €10 single, €17 return. **No credit cards. Map** *Palma* p51 E1. *Sóller* p123. **Palma to Sóller** *Mar-Oct* 8am, 10.50am*, 12.15pm*, 1.30pm, 3.10pm, 7.30pm daily. *Nov-Feb* 8am, 10.50am*, 1.05pm, 3.10pm, 7.30pm daily. **Sóller to Palma** *Mar-Oct* 7am, 9.10am, 10.50am, 12.15pm, 2pm, 6.30pm (also 7pm Sat, Sun) daily. *Nov-Feb* 7am, 9.10am, 11.55am, 2.10pm, 6pm daily.

vertiginous *barranc* above the village by way of a cobbled path to the rounded, iron cross-topped peak of **L'Ofre** (1,090 metres/3,576 feet).

Where to stay & eat

Despite its diminutive size, **Fornalutx** excels at lovely small places to stay. **Ca'n Verdera** (C/Toros 1, 971 63 82 03, www.canverdera.com, closed mid Nov-Feb, doubles €160-€500 incl breakfast) is tucked behind the main *plaça* in a 150-year-old house (you'll need to park at the car park just beyond the square and walk up – call to reserve one of the hotel's private spaces). The rooms are clean and simple but the highlight is the huge penthouse suite, with its own *terraza* and views from the picture windows across the village and valley. (Note that most rooms don't have as spectacular views.) There's a small pool but the lush terrace deserves a special mention: owing to the vista, breakfast up here is one of the island's most memorable.

Petit Hotel (C/Alba 22, 971 63 19 97, www.fornalutxpetithotel.com, closed mid Nov-mid Feb, doubles €130 incl breakfast) is a former convent, sympathetically and stylishly converted, with just 11 rooms. All are individually designed in a modern style with space and light as key features. Bathrooms are a good size, with marble floors and fluffy towels. The suite is particularly lovely, with views over the terrace and valley. There's also a jacuzzi, sauna and swimming pool.

Near-neighbour **Ca'n Reus** (C/Alba 26, 971 63 11 74, www.canreushotel.com, doubles/incl breakfast €120-€150) occupies a characterful old townhouse that has been sympathetically restored. It's a deeply relaxing place – the reception is overflowing with plants and the British couple that run it are very friendly. Of the seven comfortable, sleek rooms, five have stunning views of the mountains. The garden room is particularly lovely: secluded, homely and leading straight out to the garden. Other pluses include a small pool, decked terrace, living-room area and the reputation for the best breakfast in town.

If you fancy self-catering (though with breakfast thrown in), then the Marroig family's **Sa Tanqueta** (Fina Colom, C/Sant Bernat s/n, 971 63 85 20, www.sa-tanqueta.com, closed Nov-Feb, 2-person apartment €128-€150, 4-person apartment €223-€255, incl breakfast) on the outskirts of the village offers 14 bright, contemporary one- and two-bed apartments sharing a communal pool; most have terraces and all have awesome views.

Eating options have been expanding in recent years in Fornalutx. On the road leading up out of the village, you'll find **Calzone** (C/Arbona Colóm 4, 971 63 03 68, closed Sun

and Dec-mid Jan), run by the same couple as Café Med (*see below*), and specialising in home-made pasta and pizzas – or try the tuna salad with fresh, lightly seared tuna steak. **Ca'n Antuna** (C/Arbona Colóm 8, 971 63 30 68, closed dinner Sun, all Mon and mid Nov-mid Dec, €€) is where King Juan Carlos and Queen Sofia have been known to pop in for informal, traditional Mallorcan cooking at its best: soups, lamb or pork and wine served in *jarras* (terracotta jugs). Sit outside on the vine-covered *terraza* for priceless views of the valley and village. The steak at €10 is a steal.

Es Turó (C/Arbona Colóm 6, 971 63 08 08, closed Thur and mid Dec-mid Feb, €€), a bit further down, offers more good, honest home cooking, with similar views.

On the road through the village, just beyond the main *plaça* is **Bella Vista** (C/Sant Bartolomé s/n, 971 63 15 90, closed Wed and 15 Nov-15 Jan, €€), which, true to its name, offers marvellous views of the valley and good Spanish/Mallorcan dishes, such as roast suckling pig and grouper with baked vegetables.

For simple but well-executed international fare, try **Café Med** (C/Sa Plaça 7, 971 63 09 00, closed lunch, all Sun and Dec & Jan, €€€). The beef carpaccio with capers and parmesan is as good as you'll find in Italy; the crab risotto with pan-fried salmon, a perfect summer dish.

Resources

Police station

Fornalutx *Vicari Solivellas 1 (971 63 19 01/mobile 620 96 30 34).*

Post office

Fornalutx *Bellavista 2 (971 63 05 05).*

PORT DE SOLLER

Four kilometres from Sóller, **Port de Sóller** lacks the brashness of the island's more famous resorts. Indeed, it feels more like a grown-up seaside retreat than a full-on resort, with none of the boozy, lads-on-the-lash vibe prevalent in the Bay of Palma, and with more atmosphere than resorts in the South-west. Its lone Burger King restaurant looks distinctly out of place.

The port curves in an arc around a pretty harbour, protected by cliffs either side, with a naval base at the north end and a couple of sandy beaches. Historically, it has always been Sóller's gateway to the rest of the world, acting as a departure point for boats laden with citrus fruits making their way to France and mainland Spain. It was also a magnet for pirates; in 1561 the port was razed in an attack, forcing the Sóllerics to fortify the harbour with huge stone jetties and lighthouses; hence, the bay comes almost round on itself. The whole episode is re-enacted with the chaotic, alcohol-fuelled *moros i cristianos* (Moors and Christians) fiesta in the second week of May.

Port de Sóller was never intended as a resort and only began to be developed after 1913, when the tramline from Sóller was built. The same open tram (€4 one way) makes the 20-minute journey today, terminating at the eastern end of the bay by the harbour and the best restaurants. The beach here is stony and none too clean, and you'll also have to cope with being centre-stage every time a tram comes past – still, perhaps out of convenience, it remains popular. The second beach, **Platja d'en Repic** (better and bigger with fine white sand but more touristy), is on the bay's western side. If you want to head here, get off the tram at its first stop when it reaches the Port and walk left along pedestrianised, restaurant-lined Passeig de Sa Platja. From here, you can walk (or drive) the couple of kilometres up to the lighthouse; the views across the bay from here are glorious, and there's an excellent restaurant, **Es Faro** (*see p130*).

There are more wonderful views to be had around the other side of the bay from the **Museu de la Mar Sóller**, which explores the importance of the sea in the history of Sóller; it's located in the old fishermen's district of **Santa Caterina**. To reach it, walk up restaurant-lined C/Santa Caterina d'Alexandria, just beyond the tram terminus, and then go right up some steps as C/Mallorca bears left.

Barcos Azules (Passeig Es Través 3, 971 63 01 70, www.barcosazules.com), based at the kiosk at the harbour, runs glass-bottomed boats and catamarans to Sa Calobra and Cala Tuent at 10am, 11am, 1pm and 3pm daily between May and September (a return trip costs €20); a restricted service operates between October and April (Thur and Sat only at 11am and 2pm).

Divers can get kitted out at **Octopus** (C/Canonge Oliver 13, 971 63 31 33, mobile 670 23 58 58, www.octopus-mallorca.com, closed Nov-mid Apr), near the tourist office, while a range of watersports, including sailing, canoeing, water-skiing and windsurfing, can be organised by the **Escola d'Sports Nautics** (Passeig Platja d'En Repic s/n, 971 63 30 18, mobile 609 35 41 32, www.nauticsoller.com, closed Nov-Apr).

The tourist office is on C/Canonge Oliver, which runs parallel to the bay, one street back from the tram terminus. If you're driving, the best place to park is in the car park on your left just before you reach the bay.

Museu de la Mar Sóller

Oratori de Santa Caterina d'Alexandria (971 63 22 04). **Open** *June-Sept* 10am-6pm Tue-Sun. **Admission** €3. **No credit cards.**

Where to eat & drink

On C/Santa Caterina d'Alexandria, near the tram terminus, are a number of other excellent fish restaurants. Informal and laid-back **Es Racó** (No.6, 971 63 36 39, closed Wed mid Nov-end Jan, €) offers excellent fresh fish, salads and tortillas at reasonable prices.

If you want to eat alfresco, bag a table outside one of the places on the strip below. **Ca'n Quirós** (C/Marina 52, no phone, closed dinner Nov-Mar, €€) is a popular, slick tapas joint offering the likes of stuffed aubergines or Galician-style squid (*pulpo a la Gallega*) with paprika, salt and olive oil; there's no phone, but you can call the Sóller branch (971 63 36 08) to make a reservation. Or try **Albatros** (C/ Marina 48, 971 63 32 14), which has been in the local Aloy family for over 100 years. It's a curious combination of hairdresser and tapas bar, so you can try locally caught prawns, slow-cooked rabbit in onion sauce or crispy fried squid while you wait for your short back and sides.

Popular **Restaurant Balear** (C/Santa Catalina 14, 971 63 15 24, closed Wed and mid Dec, Jan, €€) has plenty of toothsome piscine offerings, such as the flavoursome, meaty local fish *denton*. Next is **Ribes** (No.22, 971 63 84 93, closed Dec & Jan, €€), a stylish place with first-rate paella, good salads and quality meat dishes, like shoulder (*palatilla*) of lamb. The last restaurant on the street is **Lua** (No.1, 971 63 47 45, closed Mon, €€€); although at first glance at the menu suggests style over substance, the food here is, in fact, kept simple, with superb results. Try the adventurous salads or great, simply cooked fish, such as sea bream or scorpion fish.

If you're not bothered about sea views, and would rather eat with locals than tourists, try the excellent, family-run **Cellar des Port** (C/Antonio Montis 17, 971 63 06 54, closed Wed and Jan, €€), opposite the entrance to the **Hotel Es Port** (*see p130*). Its delicious Mallorcan food includes *llom con col* (pork with cabbage), which is a lot more tasty and interesting than it sounds. (However, the future of the place was sadly uncertain when this guide went to press.)

Randemar (Passeig Es Través, 16, 971 63 45 78, www.randemar.com, closed Nov-Feb) has a large shaded terrace on the seafront and offers fresh fish, grilled meats and Mediterranean classics like beef carpaccio with rocket and parmesan. Many of the restaurants along the Passeig de Sa Platja, by the Platja d'en Repic, aren't as good as the ones at the other end of the bay, but there are exceptions. **Es Passeig** (No.8, 971 63 02 17, closed Wed and Jan, €€€) excels in simple, well presented modern Mediterranean cuisine. **Es Canyis** (No.32, 971 63 14 06, closed Mon and Dec, Jan, €€) is a prime spot for first-rate fish. **S'Atic** (No.15, 971 63 81 13, closed

Port de Sóller.

Mon, lunch Tue-Sun in Nov, Mar and all Dec-Feb, €€€) is a superb contemporary restaurant with harbour views in the unlikely location of the fourth floor of the modest Hotel Los Geranios. **Agapanto** (Camí des Faro 2, 971 63 38 60, www.agapanto.com, closed Wed, €€) is a cool bar-restaurant with a terrace, offering the likes of penne with chilli and mango sauce or carpaccio of red tuna, and a lively programme (at least during the summer months) of live music, flamenco, tango and art exhibitions.

Prize for best restaurant in town has to go to **Es Faro** (Punta de Jrossa, 971 63 37 52, €€€), however, at the end of the road to the lighthouse, with stunning views over the bay; it serves excellent but pricey fish dishes.

Where to stay

Port de Sóller has numerous places to stay, mainly along the bayside Passeig Es Través or just behind it, but until recently none were outstanding. The **Hotel Espléndido** (Passeig Es Través 5, 971 63 18 50, www.esplendidohotel.com, closed mid Nov-Feb, doubles €150-€240 incl breakfast) had a major revamp a couple of years back and is now the trendiest hotel in town The Swedish owners of the super-chic Hotel Portixol in Palma have breathed fresh life into this classic seaside hotel dating from the 1950s and it now sparkles with a harmonious blend of modern and classic detailing. In the summer holidays it's very popular with familes. Most rooms have views over the bay, there's a chic cocktail bar, a very good restaurant, a spa and two pools, one with a bar that makes it the perfect spot for a laid-back lunch.

Another welcome arrival from the past few years is the **Aimia** (C/Santa María del Camí 1, 971 63 12 00, www.aimiahotel.com, closed Nov-mid Feb, doubles €150-€180 incl breakfast), which was thoroughly revamped in 2004 by the Alcover family in a sleek, contemporary style. Many of its 43 good-value rooms have balconies and look out over the sizeable pool, surrounded by wooden decking; all rooms have internet access. There's also an indoor pool, jacuzzi, sauna, Turkish bath, fitness centre, bar and restaurant. As with Port de Sóller in general, the hotel is popular with a mature crowd.

Situated just 200 metres back from the beach, the **Hotel Es Port** (C/Antonio Montis s/n, 971 63 16 50, www.hotelesport.com, closed mid Nov-Jan, doubles €94-€100 incl breakfast) is a lovely old family-owned hotel with extensive grounds. It boasts indoor and (huge) outdoor pools, tennis courts, gym, spa, jacuzzi, sauna, along with buckets of old-fashioned charm.

The above three hotels are certainly the prime places to stay in the Port. Other options include the **Aparthotel Generoso** (C/Marina 4, 971 63 14 50, www.hotelgeneroso.com, closed Nov-Jan, doubles €70, apartments €120), in a good spot behind the town beach. The building, while not a beauty, is clean and comfortable, and has an old-fashioned charm. If you are here for any length of time, or are with kids, you should consider the apartments, which are a good size, with sea views and include a kitchen and two balconies; there's also a large swimming pool. **Hotel Miramar** (C/Marina 12-14, 971 63 13 50, closed Nov-Jan, doubles €40-€46) is a more basic option with plain rooms, some with a sea view, and a decent restaurant.

Hotel Marina (Passeig de sa Platja, 971 63 14 61, www.hotelmarinasoller.com, closed mid Nov-Jan, doubles €70-€94 incl breakfast) is a neatly kitted-out two-star place backing Platja d'en Repic. Rooms have a sea or mountain view, and there's a large pool and a kids' play area. At night the *terraza* in front of the hotel has live music. **Hotel Los Geranios** (Passeig de sa Platja 15, 971 63 14 40, www.hotel-losgeranios.com, closed 2wks Jan, doubles €110-€150 incl breakfast) offers comfortable rooms with balconies and air-conditioning; some have jacuzzis. No pool, but there's a sauna and a great restaurant, S'Atic (*see p128*), on the top floor.

High up the hillside overlooking the bay (you'll need a car to reach it) is the gorgeous **Muleta de Ca S'Hereu** (Camp de sa Mar s/n, 971 18 60 18, mobile 649 82 13 33, www.muletadecashereu.com, doubles €143-€190), an ancient building that now houses spacious air-conditioned bedrooms furnished with wooden Mallorcan antiques; there's a restaurant and a pool with stunning views.

Resources

Tourist information

Port de Sóller *OIT, C/Canonge Oliver 10 (971 63 30 42/ma.mintour09@bitel.es).* **Open** *Mar-Oct* 9am-12.50pm, 2.40-4.50pm Mon-Fri. Closed *Nov-Apr*.

GETTING THERE

By bus

From Palma, hourly buses Mon-Fri (3 Sat, 2 Sun) run direct to Sóller and Port de Sóller, with a further 7 Mon-Fri (3 Sat, 3 Sun) to Sóller and Port de Sóller via Valldemossa and Deià. There are 5 buses Mon-Fri (3 Sat) to Esporles, 2 buses Mon-Fri to Estellencs via La Granja and Banyalbufar, and 2 buses daily between Port de Sóller and Fornalutx. For services from the west coast to Pollença and the north, *see p147*.

By train

For details of the Palma–Sóller train, *see p126* **Ticket to Ride**.

Northern Serra

Scenic hiking, challenging cycling and enchanting pilgrimages.

The mountains, holm oak forests and tortuous roads that creep through the northern Serra endow this part of Mallorca with a majestic scale that doesn't really belong to the island – Magaluf this ain't. This is home to some of the most spectacular, and spectacularly terrifying, driving in Europe. The northern Tramuntana is also where you'll find some of the island's most outstanding hiking, including the ascent of Massanella, Mallorca's highest climbable peak. It overlooks the island's most famous monastery at Lluc, the hub of this area.

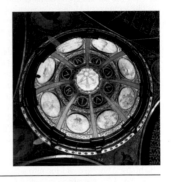

A PEAK EXPERIENCE

Before the advent of tourism, the northern Serra de Tramuntana – named after the northerly Tramuntana winds that buffet it year round – was Mallorca's least desirable and least populated landscape. Precipitous and mostly barren, it is of little use for agriculture and was – and can still be – hazardous for any transport other than the mule. It is the only region of the island to get anything close to a winter; snow often falls in February and March on the highest peaks. Lluc, meanwhile, is the wettest, and possibly the greenest, spot on Mallorca.

Only one road passes through the mountains of the northern Tramuntana. The craggy, soaring peaks hinder access to the coast, but the C710 is a wonderful winding route, linking Sóller to the monastery at Lluc and then to Pollença.

Heading north-east from Sóller, there are fine views down to Port de Sóller and the sea from the **Mirador de ses Barques** (a kilometre after the turn-off to Fornalutx). Continuing onwards, you're soon among the loftiest peaks of the range. The two highest – **Puig Major** (1,445 metres/4,741 feet) and **Massanella** (1,352 metres/4,436 feet) – straddle the road across the stunning **Gorg Blau** (Blue Gorge), which is now home to two reservoirs. A lovely walk around **Tossals Verds**, a 1,000-metre-plus mountain, starts from one of these reservoirs, the **Embassament de Cúber** (*see p133* **Walk**).

There are other hikes to be enjoyed here – it's often just a matter of taking a short stroll from wherever you have bedded down and heading up a path through the farmlands. Puig Major is topped by a military radar station, so Massanella is the highest climbable summit in the Balearics

(for a route up Massanella from Lluc, *see p133*).

Just north of the second of the reservoirs, the **Embassament de Gorg Blau**, the C710 passes through a tunnel and emerges near a turn-off on to the only road to the coast between Port de Sóller and Pollença: the narrow and precipitous 13-kilometre route to the coves of Sa Calobra and Cala Tuent.

Depending on the season, the narrow inlet of **Sa Calobra** can be trying; in summer it is packed with coach parties most of the day. The main draw lies ten minutes' walk from the parking area along the shoreline. A path passes through a narrow, paved tunnel hewn out of the rock before emerging at the bed of the **Torrent de Pareis** (Torrent of the Twins), an impressive canyon with sheer vertical walls that opens into the sea. After heavy rainstorms, the water coming down from the Torrent de Lluc and the Torrent de Gorg Blau streams builds up and the usual trickle of water becomes a genuine torrent. You can swim off the small pebbly beach here. If you want to enjoy the experience in relative peace, it's worth making the effort to come first thing in the morning or in the evening.

After the Torrent de Pareis, the second obligatory stop for coach parties is the monastery of **Lluc** (36 kilometres/22.5 miles north-east of Sóller and 20 kilometres/12.5 miles south-west of Pollença). Stunning for its location rather than its architecture, which mostly dates from the 18th and 19th centuries and is austere in the extreme, the **Monestir de Nostra Senyora de Lluc** (Monastery of Our Lady of Lluc) is the most visited site in the north of Mallorca (though whether its popularity is justified is debatable). Once a place of peace and contemplation, the monastery – also known as the **Santuari de Lluc** – now has a busy daytime scene of incoming tour coaches and resting cyclists. Most people choose to descend on the site between 11am and 5pm (when canny travellers are out exploring the mountains) and at dusk the monastery is eerily calm again.

The location of Mallorca's most important Christian shrine, Lluc was also a significant spiritual site in pagan times. Prehistoric Mallorcans visited a cave here – now known as **Sa Cometa dels Morts** – probably to perform a ritual to the dead. They also deified the holm oak woods, a belief that was later embraced by Roman settlers. The first theory of the origins of the name 'Lluc' is that it comes from *lucus*, Latin for 'sacred wood', and there are still dense swathes of holm oak and cypress on the road leading to Lluc and in the foothills of the rocky slopes that line the wide valleys. After the 13th-century Reconquest, monks migrated to the then remote spot, building a chapel and reworking the historic holiness of Lluc into a miracle.

Today, Lluc remains a site of pilgrimage for religious Mallorcans, who make their devotions to the dark-skinned statue of the Virgin, **La Moreneta**, also known as Our Lady of the Mountains. The legend of the statue's origin is that a young shepherd called Luke ('Lluc' in *Mallorquí*, and thus the second theory about the name of the monastery) found a vividly coloured statue in the woods – perturbed, he sought a monk who was in turn startled when the tiny statue began to glow and play heavenly music.

To see the Virgin, go in through the main doors, walk past the accommodation reception entrance, head down the corridor and cross a small courtyard – in the next, larger courtyard, follow the hand of Bishop Campins (the priest who refurbished Lluc in the 1900s) into the main church, the **Basílica de la Mare de Déu de Lluc** (8.30am-8pm daily, admission free). This plain Renaissance church (built 1622-91) has an elegant façade hemmed in by sober residential buildings. During special services, the Virgin – a small, unprepossessing figure carrying a plump Jesus holding the Book of Life – sits atop a swivelling platform above the high altar. Most of the time, however, this platform is turned to face a small chapel behind the altar where the faithful can kiss the base of the statue. The **Escolania de Lluc** boys' choir, founded almost 500 years ago, sings at mass in the church every day. The choirboys are known as **Els Blauets** (the Blues), after the colour of their cassocks.

With its complex arrangement of buildings and annexes, it takes some time to get your bearings at Lluc. There are two main restaurants (one in the monastery, one at the entrance) and two cafés (one close to the main entrance and another, far quieter one at the rear of the main car park). There are outhouses, an open-air basilica and a small botanical garden (10am-1pm, 3-6pm Mon-Sat, admission free) on the east side of the monastery. A narrow trail runs through the latter, taking visitors through pungent patches of herbs, exotic and native montane trees, and a frenzy of croaking frogs and bees slurping nectar. Behind the monastery complex is the **Camí dels Misteris del Rosari** (Way of the Mysteries of the Rosary) – a broad, winding footpath up to a crucifix; continue down the far side of the hill and the path curves back round to the monastery. The views out west across the Albarca valley are splendid.

On the first floor of the main building is the **Museu de Lluc**, with one floor dedicated to Talayotic and Roman archaeological finds and an assortment of ecclesiastical items, and an upper floor featuring some dimly lit paintings and modern abstract sculptures. The main rooms hold an important collection of coins, ancient bronze items and a sizeable display of ceramics and fans, but there's a distinct lack of information given. A beautiful 18th-century four-poster bed, draped in local lacework, is the outstanding item of furniture, while the most popular attraction, a Talayotic sarcophagus from the fourth century BC, found in Sa Cometa dels Morts, has regrettably had its skeleton removed reportedly because it upset visitors.

If you want to spend a few days exploring the mountains, Lluc makes the best base. One popular walk from here is up to the top of **Massanella**, the island's highest accessible peak (1,352 metres/4,436 feet). The monastery staff will tell you how to get to the road – about 20 minutes' walk – where the hike begins. The owner of the land through which it passes usually charges a small fee for access. Take water and give yourself six to seven hours for the return trip. Red arrows and dots mark the trail where it passes over hard-to-make-out

---

INSIDE TRACK
CROWD-FREE BEACHES

Wanna hit the beach but avoid the coach-party hordes? Take the side road a kilometre back from Sa Calobra that winds down to the beach at Cala Tuent. Though it's stony, this is one of the most uncrowded and serene beaches on this part of the island, with great swimming in crystal water. There's little more here than a smattering of villas, a small 13th-century church, the **Ermita de Sant Llorenç**, overlooking the cove, and a wonderful bar-restaurant (**Es Vergeret**, see p134).

Walk Tossals Verds

Mountainside views define one of Mallorca's most popular hiking routes.

Distance: 13km. Circular.
Time: 4hrs 30mins.
A network of trails criss-crosses Mallorca's high mountains, and the area around the two reservoirs **Cúber** and **Gorg Blau** – in the shadow of the island's tallest peak, **Puig Major** (1,445 metres/4,741 feet) – is one of the most spectacular and popular with hikers. The following walk offers unbeatable views and a great variety of terrain. There's a steepish descent close to the beginning, which passes through a series of tunnels (a small torch is very useful here) down into a serene valley, and then a longish, rocky ascent before the walk levels out for its last hour or so. If you want just a short hour-long stroll (4 kilometres), then there's a road and path that circumnavigate Cúber reservoir.

Park your car in the **Fonts de Noguera** car park, 100 metres or so beyond Cúber reservoir on the main road from Sóller to Pollença. Walk back to the reservoir and through a swing gate by a low gate across the road, and then head along the road.

After 15 minutes you'll come to a dam. Immediately before it, take a rocky track that leads down to the left. Within another 15 minutes you'll have fine views down the gorge, and the rough, rock-strewn path will turn steeply downwards. Ten minutes later you'll reach the bottom. Cross the stream here (it may be dry in summer) and bear left, continuing along for a few minutes and then upwards following a water pipeline.

Fifteen minutes on and the rough path by the pipe bends sharply downwards again. Soon you come to the first of a series of tunnels through which the pipe passes. This is your route, and is where a torch comes in handy. There's plenty of room to walk through, though the floor of the tunnel can be slippery. Ten minutes later and you arrive at the second tunnel. It dips and rises towards its end, so you probably won't be able to see the other end. This emerges by a rusty old cement mixer and a tall concrete water tank.

The path continues steeply down and after another quarter of an hour you'll come to the third tunnel. There's then a mini-tunnel and the fourth and last of the longer variety. This may well be waterlogged at one end, requiring you to either walk along the top of the pipe or get your feet wet.

The path descends gently and swings left at the bottom of the valley, bringing you to a fork. Take the left option, and within five minutes you reach a stile, with a bridge over a stream beyond it. A little further downstream is a great spot for a picnic. You can sit on the rocks and cool your toes in the water (in midsummer it may be dry).

At the bridge, a right turn takes you downwards through a gorge towards **Lloseta**, but you should turn left and follow the metalled road as it snakes upwards along a series of terraces for 25 minutes. Eventually, you'll arrive at the Tossals Verds refuge, where you can get food and drink (and there's a toilet too).

Walk up the left side of the refuge and follow the signed path upwards towards **Cases Valles** and **Font des Noguer** (your destination). After 15 minutes you'll come to a junction, with paths to left and right both heading towards Font des Noguer. Take the right branch (also signed to Cases Velles), which tells you that you're one hour 50 minutes from the end of the walk.

Within 15 or so minutes you'll find that the steepest climbing is over and the path starts to level out. On you come to another sign – carry on towards Font des Noguer. Below to your left are terraces and the remains of some abandoned buildings. A few minutes later you'll see, high above you to your left, a dramatic bare crag (with a shape like an arch eroded into it).

The path now starts to descend a little, and then roughly follows the line of the contour. Soon, on your right, superb views open up down through a precipitous gorge to the plain beyond. After another ten or so minutes you pass through a gate and the gorge starts to narrow. You come to a stream, cross it, turn left, and then almost immediately recross it on a log bridge before continuing upwards on the path.

Ten minutes on, the path splits and you take the left branch, which tells you that Font des Noguer is now an hour away. Another ten minutes and you start to descend, passing through a wooden gate over an aqueduct. The rest of the walk is easy and largely flat. You turn left and follow the aqueduct back to the car park (which should take around 45 minutes), gasping at the sheer, barren mass **Puig Major**, topped by its military radar station.

WEST MALLORCA

Tossals Verds. *See p131.*

rockscapes. The view from the summit on a clear day is breathtaking, and you get the full force of the energising Tramuntana wind.

Museu de Lluc
1st & 2nd floors, Monestir de Nostra Senyora de Lluc (971 87 15 25). **Open** 10am-1.30pm, 2.30-5pm daily. **Admission** €4. **No credit cards.**

WHERE TO STAY & EAT

Es Vergeret (C/Cala Tuent s/n, 971 51 71 05, closed dinner and Nov-Jan, €€) at **Cala Tuent** is a proper restaurant, though only open for lunch; it's thoroughly relaxed and keenly priced with excellent paella. But the real reason everybody comes here is for the views from the terrace over the bay and out to sea.

The monastery at **Lluc** is the only place to stay in the area – 110 'cells' are available for one, two, three, four or six people; there are also more commodious apartments available (971 87 15 25, www.lluc.net, doubles €31). You get an authentically spartan space, with a single bed and a desk and in place of a TV there's a picture of the crucified Christ. It's wonderful and utterly peaceful when the day's coaches have departed, but if you want even more tranquillity head to **Santuari des Puig** above Pollença (*see p141*). There is also a campsite nearby (971 51 70 83).

In terms of eating, as well as two cafés selling

empanadas, sandwiches and drinks, there are two restaurants at Lluc. **Ca S'Amitger** (971 51 70 46, closed Fri, €€€) is at the entrance to the monastery complex and serves seafood starters, meaty mains, plus the likes of paella, sole, hake and the local *emperador* fish. Wines are good and the family-style service is friendly, if slow.

The **Sa Fonda** (971 51 70 22, €€€) restaurant inside the monastery is in an impressive columned and arched room formerly used by the monks. It's a good place to eat, serving plenty of local dishes, such as grilled cuttlefish, lamb with garlic, and rabbit with onion, plus fine wines from Mallorcan, Galician and Riojan bodegas. There's also great, strong coffee to round off a day of hiking, meditation or plain old wandering around Lluc.

By far the finest and best situated restaurant in the area, however, is outside the monastery. Follow the signs to **Inca** (a half-hour walk or five minutes' drive) to **Restaurante Es Guix** (971 51 70 92, closed Tue, Wed, Jan, dinner, €€€). At lunchtimes – it rarely opens in the evenings – its secluded terraces are packed. It's partly the isolation, but mainly the fabulous creative approach to peasant cooking; its *frito Mallorquín* with lamb's liver and *arròs brut* (somewhere between a broth and a paella) are superb and well priced. A good list of mainly Mallorcan wines also presents excellent value. The flower-filled entrance and kids' playground are further pluses, as is the natural rock swimming pool in which diners are allowed a dip.

GETTING THERE

By bus
One bus a day runs from Can Picafort to Sa Calobra via Port d'Alcúdia, Alcúdia, Port de Pollença, Cala Sant Vicenç, Pollença, Lluc (1hr stop). There are 3-4 buses from Palma to Lluc via Inca. For buses from Port de Sóller to Pollença/ Alcúdia via Lluc, *see p147*.

**INSIDE TRACK
DRIVING DOSSIER**

The roads of the northern Serra offer some of the most dramatic driving in Europe, but be warned: while huge un-barriered drops are mercifully few, keeping your eyes on the road in the face of such vistas is difficult. Narrow, impossibly winding roads (one actually turning 270 degrees on itself), storms that hang on the slopes, and a lack of intrepid drivers (thankfully for many) can also turn traffic into a crawling car-snake. And then there are the sheep.

North Mallorca

**Plaça Major,
Pollença.**
See p137.

North Mallorca

9 km
5 miles

EAST MALLORCA (pp191-209)

Massís d'Artà

Artà

Son Morell 564 m

Ermita de Betlem

Ca la Mata

Cala Mata

Cap de Ferrutx

Es Caló

Ca los Cans

Cala de s'Estret

Cala de Menorca

Cap des Pinar

Cala Solana

Cap de Menorca

Punta Sabater

Cap de Formentor

Cap de Formentor

Cala Murta

Cala en Gossalba

Casas Velles de Formentor

Cala Figuera

Cap de Catalunya

El Colomer

Morro de Boquer

Cala Estremer

Cala Sant Vicenç

Illa de Formentor

Cala Pi de la Posada

Punta de l'Avançada

Punta de Manresa

Es Mal Pas

BAY OF POLLENÇA

Fundación Yannick & Ben Jakober

Alcanada

Illa D'Alcanada

Alcúdia

Platja d'Alcúdia

Ses Fotges

BAY OF ALCÚDIA

Punta Llarga de s'Estanyol

Son Serra de Marina

Ses Cabenisses

Punta Llarga de Son Real

Ferrutx 520 m

Morell

Can Canals

Colònia de Sant Pere

S'Estanyol

Port de Pollença

Can Singala

S'Albufera

Port d'Alcúdia

Es Llac Gran

Es Barcarès

Son Fe

Platja de Muro

Can Picafort

Son Bauló

Son Real

MA-12

Santa Margalida

Sa Teulada

Sa Pobla

MA-3410

MA-13

Llubí

Muro

Son Martí

Son Sant Martí

Son Perera Vell

Parc Natural de S'Albufera

BAY OF ALCÚDIA

ALCÚDIA & THE BAY OF ALCÚDIA (pp148-153)

Cala Sant Vicenç

Cala Galera

Punta Galera

Cala Castell

Castell del Rei

Cala Solleric

Es Farallons

Punta Beca

Termelles

L'Horta

Pollença

Puig de Maria 333 m

MA-2220

MA-2220

Can Feliu

Els Rafals

Son Marc

Mortitxó

Puig Gros de Ternelles 838 m

POLLENÇA TO FORMENTOR (pp137-147)

Crestatx

Búger

Campanet

Coves de Campanet

Bujbóna

Moscari

Sant Vicenç

CENTRAL MALLORCA (pp155-176)

Selva

Caimari

MA-2130

Mancor de la Vall

Inca

Lloseta

MA-13

Llubí

Cas Secretari

Binissalem

Consell

Biniali

Alaró

Solleric

Almandrà

Orient

Mancor

Fangar

Puig Tomir 1104 m

Tramuntana

Monestir de Lluc

Sant Macari

MA-10

Puig Roig 1003 m

Racó de Mortitx

Racó de sa Figuera

Oratori de Sant Pere

Arfant

Cala des Codolar

Morro d'en Llobera

Cala es Copellons

Cala des Vaca

Morro de sa Vaca

Torrent de Pareis

Sa Calobra

MA-2141

Puig Major 1445 m

Embassament de Cúber

Embassament des Gorg Blau

Tossals Verds 1118 m

Serra de

Walk (p104)

Massanella 1365 m

WEST MALLORCA (pp99-130)

Pollença to Formentor

Explore north Mallorca's prettiest town and its most dramatic coastline.

The northern reaches of the craggy Serra de Tramuntana mountain range offer some of the most dramatic and beautiful landscapes in all of Mallorca, as well as some great places to stay and eat. The terrain flattens out when it reaches the beautiful historic town of Pollença and the less appealing neighbouring coastal resort of the same name. North-east of here is the Formentor peninsula, the northernmost reaches of the Serra that hugs Mallorca's west coast – literally, a mountain range in the sea.

POLLENÇA

Despite the extensive coastal development nearby, **Pollença** (sometimes written 'Pollensa') remains the prettiest and most characterful town in the north-west. It's tucked into the foothills of the northern Tramuntana, 61 kilometres (38 miles) north-east of Palma and 55 kilometres (34 miles) from Sóller – the former route is vastly quicker, the latter road is one of Europe's most spectacular drives.

There's a Roman stone bridge across the Torrent de Sant Jordi here (built around AD 120), but the town wasn't founded until the 13th century (when its inhabitants confusingly appropriated the name of the Roman town of Pollentia, on the site of today's Alcúdia; *see p148*). It's a small, compact settlement of 14,000 people, built inland from its harbour, as so many Mallorcan towns were, in an attempt to deter pirate raids. Nonetheless, it was attacked – most forcibly in 1550 by the Turkish corsair Dragut. A local hero, Joan Mas, led the resistance and finally overcame the invaders – a victory celebrated every 2 August during the festival of **Mare de Déu dels Àngels** (*see p39*).

The centre's labyrinthine streets – most of them devoid of pavements – are almost the only remaining traces of the medieval town; most of the houses here date from the 17th and 18th centuries. Three imposing churches

dominate the skyline. On Plaça Major rises the vast, austere **Nostra Senyora dels Àngels**; although its origins are in the 13th century, the church was largely rebuilt in Baroque style between 1714 and 1790. It dominates Pollença's pleasantly irregular main square, which buzzes with chatter from its alfresco bars and restaurants in fine weather.

South of Plaça Major lies **Nostra Senyora del Roser**. The Baroque interior of this deconsecrated church contains a superb organ from 1732. In the adjacent cloister of the 16th-century Baroque **Convent de Sant Domingo** is the **Museu de Pollença** (*see p139*), holding a collection of miscellaneous items of archaeological, ecclesiastical and folkloric interest, with some decent Gothic art also on display. The landscapes and depictions of local customs by Argentinian artist Atilio

---

INSIDE TRACK
PORT DE POLLENÇA BEACH

The northern end of the beach, tucked under the pines (and hotels) of the **Passeig Anglada Camarasa**, is the most popular patch for swimming. If you want a bit of space, walk towards the southern (Alcúdia) end, beyond the windsurf hire firms.

Boveri – who visited Pollença in 1912-15 and was also responsible for one of the Via Crucis paintings in the church – are also worth a look.

North of the main square stands the Jesuit church of **Monti-Sion** (completed in 1738), and between it and Plaça Major are clusters of cafés, restaurants and some interesting shops. C/Ombra leads out of Plaça Major to Plaça dels Seglars, with its terrace eateries, and to the foot of the **Via Crucis**, Pollença's most treasured landmark. This steep, straight, 365-step, cypress-lined stairway leads up to a simple chapel on the hilltop of **El Calvarí** (Calvary), from which there are panoramic views of Pollença and its setting between the mountains and the coast. On Good Friday, a figure of Jesus is borne down the Via Crucis in a procession known as the **Davallament** or 'Lowering' (*see p39*).

An even more dramatic vantage point is the top of **Puig de Maria**, the summit of a 333-metre (1,093-foot) hill on the southern edge of town. At the top is a monkless 18th-century monastery, which provides cheap, simple lodgings with absolutely unforgettable views. To reach it from the centre of Pollença, follow C/Alcúdia and Avinguda Pollentia until you hit the main road; turn right and the start of the Puig road is 100 or so metres away on the opposite side of the road.

There is a lively food and crafts market on Plaça Major and the surrounding streets on Sundays. Among the notable shops are **Ceràmiques Monti-Sion** (C/Montesión 19, 971 53 35 00), with its irresistibly colourful selection of hand-painted jugs, tiles, mugs and plates. **Aina** (Plaça Vella 1, 971 53 06 86) stocks wonderfully quirky kids' clothes, from embroidered dresses for parties to stripy Victorian-style swimming costumes with built-in floats, many in technicolour hues. (It has a branch in Port de Pollença at C/Joan XXIII s/n, 971 86 67 81.) **Enseñat** (C/Alcúdia 5, 971 53 36 18) isn't cheap, but it's the smartest place in town to pick up edible Mediterranean goodies (some produced on the shop's estate nearby) – from unusual Binissalem wines to fine olives and oils, hams, sausages and delicate sweets. Come on Sunday mornings for the regular tastings of traditional Mallorcan food and wine.

Pollença is also an artistic hub – the shared legacy of Catalan painter Hermenegild Anglada-Camarasa, who settled in Port de Pollença in 1914 and died there in 1959, and renowned Pollençan intellectual and oil painter Dionís Bennàssar (1904-67). The **Casa Museu Dionís Bennàssar** is the latter's old home and exhibits some of the best of his early academicist and modernist works, as well as figurative studies of everyday life in Pollença.

There are beautiful contemporary textiles and sculpture in the **Museu Martí Vicenç**, a small museum in a 300-year-old building towards the lower end of the Via Crucis that showcases the work of Martí Vicenç (1926-95), an innovative local weaver. If you want to do more than just look, a range of modern art, some of which is for sale, is on view at the **Galeria Maior** (Plaça Major 4, 971 53 00 95, www.galeriamaior.com, closed Monday, free) on the main *plaça*.

Pollença doesn't slack in terms of music either – the annual **Festival de Pollença** (971 53 50 77/40 12, www.festivalpollenca.org), established in 1962, takes place in July and August, with concerts in venues around the

Plaça Major, Pollença.

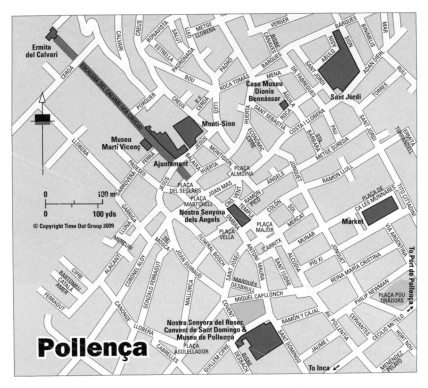

Pollença

town, and attracts international classical musicians and ensembles.

A popular walk from the town is towards the coast and the ruined **Castell del Rei**, passing through the village of **Ternelles** before heading up behind the diminutive **Serra de Sant Vicenç** mountains. The Ternelles valley is popular with birdwatchers, and the seven-kilometre hike from Pollença to the Castell del Rei has long been a favourite with walkers (ask at the tourist office for directions). There are great views from the castle, a coastal fortification established by the Moors in the 11th century and further strengthened by Jaume I; this was the last fort to surrender to Pere of Aragón when Jaume III's short-lived Kingdom of Mallorca came to an end in 1343. You can swim here at the shingly coves of **Cala Castell**, which, being out of the way, are a great, peaceful alternative to the beaches of Port de Pollença and the bay of Alcúdia . The castle is on a private estate and vehicle access is restricted; it should be possible to drive part of the way down the road and then leave your car at a gate, but it's wise to check with the tourist office first.

Casa Museu Dionís Bennàssar

C/Roca 14 (971 53 09 97/ www.museodionis bennassar.com. **Open** 10.30am-1.30pm Tue-Sun. *July-Aug* 10.30am-1.30pm, 6-8.30pm. **Admission** €2. **No credit cards**.

FREE **Museu Martí Vicenç**

C/Calvari 10 (971 53 28 67/www.marti vicens.org). **Open** 10am-2pm, 5-7.30pm Mon; 10am-7pm Tue-Sat; 10am-1.30pm Sun. **Admission** free.

Museu de Pollença

Convento Santo Domingo, C/Guillem Cifre de Colonya s/n (971 53 11 66). **Open** *Oct-June* 10.30am-1pm. *July-Sept* 10am-1pm, 5.30-8.30pm. **Admission** €1.50. **No credit cards**.

Where to eat & drink

One of Pollença's most enjoyable activities is sitting down at one of the cafés in the Plaça Major and drawing out lunch, morning coffee or afternoon tea and pastries for hours at a time. **Ca'n Moixet** (No.2, 971 53 42 14, €), **Bar Juma** (No.9, 971 53 32 58, €), part of

NORTH MALLORCA

Il Giardino.

the eponymous hotel (*see right*), and **L'Illa Café**, with another branch in Port de Pollença, all offer hefty *bocadillos*, salads, croissants, cakes and excellent coffee, and numerous outdoor tables on which to enjoy them.

In terms of bonafide restaurants, the most popular on the square is **Ristorante Il Giardino** (No.11, 971 53 43 02, closed Nov-15 Mar, €€), and understandably so. The staff are delightful, as is the Italian food, which employs high-quality ingredients in classic tricolore salads and carpaccios, good pizzas, meat and fish dishes, and great pastas, such as an unusual black fettucine with king prawns in a rich, tomato-ey sauce; the house Penèdes red is excellent and good value too.

Further up the hill, behind the **Nostra Senyora dels Àngels** church, is another more intimate square, the **Plaça dels Seglars**, which is also full of restaurants with tables outside. For simple Italian lunch fare, **Ristorante La Piazzetta** (No.5, 971 53 44 82, closed Mon Mar-June, Sept, Oct and all Nov-Feb, €€), is a good choice; the French and Italian couple running the tiny restaurant specialise in bruschette and simple but tasty pasta dishes, and there's great *tartuffo* and pannacotta to round off the meal.

For Mallorcan food, try **Bar Nou** (C/Antoni Maura 13, 971 53 00 05, closed Tue and mid Dec-mid Jan, €€), which specialises in hams, cheeses and *pa amb oli*, all prepared with love and care; for bigger appetites, sample the paellas, *chipirones* (baby squid) and outstanding *navajas* (razor clams).

Cantonet (C/Montesión 20, 971 53 04 29, closed lunch, all Tue and Nov-Jan, €€) offers very good Mallorcan and Italian dishes, including lobster and clam spaghetti, lamb bolognese or home-made gnocchi. In fine weather you can eat outside on the lively street against the backdrop of Monti-Sion church.

On the edge of town is **Clivia** (Avda. Pollentia 5, 971 53 36 35, closed lunch Mon & Wed in summer, all Wed in winter, 12 Nov-20 Dec, €€€). It's named after the bright red flowers on its patio and is well loved for its Spanish- and Portuguese-influenced cuisine, with good veal and exceptional fish dishes. Expect welcoming staff and generous portions of cod, monkfish, eel, squid, sea bass in white wine and great spicy fish soups.

At **La Font del Gall** (C/Montesión 4, 971 53 03 96, closed Nov-Feb, €€€) owners have come and gone over the years but it's still popular, showing Scottish influences, with cock-a-leekie soup sitting next to sardines with ginger on the menu.

Another restaurant serious about its food is **Ca'n Costa** (C/Miquel Costa i Llobera 11, 971 53 12 76, closed Sun and Oct-Apr, €€€), set in an old cinema off the main square. Dishes include *queso Mahón* parcels, seared tuna with chilli mash, and lovely lemon sorbet and raspberry mousse.

The Hotel Son Sant Jordi's (*see right*) **La Placeta** (closed Mon, €) is a beautifully located terrace café-restaurant in a quieter part of town, with a short, simple menu of international and Mediterranean dishes.

Where to stay

A lot of the people wandering around Pollença in the day decamp back to their package hotels in Port de Pollença come nightfall, meaning that evenings here are quieter. There are also now a few great places to stay both in the town and nearby.

The place that upped the ante considerably in a town that was lacking in accomodation was three-star **Hotel Juma** (Plaça Major 9, 971 53 50 02, www.hoteljuma.com, closed 15 Nov-15 Dec), founded in 1907, which remains a great spot to lay your head right on the town's main square. Immaculately clean, and in tip-top condition decor-wise, this friendly place has a very Mallorcan feel to it, with simple, spruce (though not cheap) rooms over a bar. Ask for a room with a view of the lovely square (though be prepared for some noise from the nightly gathering of tourists and locals below). At the time of writing the hotel was being sold – be sure to check the website for any rate changes.

Just around the corner is the excellent and great-value **L'Hostal** (C/Mercat 18, 971 53 52 81, www.hostalpollensa.com, closed 15 Nov-15 Dec, which was also changing hands as this guide went to press; check the website for new prices. It's managed by the same family as the Juma (*see above*; enquire there if the doors are locked and you can't seem to get in) and has six stylish and modern rooms, two of which can be connected together to make one big room - ideal for those staying en famille.

In a similar, if slightly more minimalist, vein is the **Desbrull** (C/Marquès Desbrull 7, 971 53 50 55, www.desbrull.com, closed 15 Dec-15 Jan, doubles €75-€96 incl breakfast).

The **Son Sant Jordi** (C/Sant Jordi 29, 971 53 03 89, www.hotelsonsantjordi.com, doubles €60-€186 incl breakfast) is a beautifully restored townhouse hotel with eight rooms, decked out with rough stone walls, cream linen, feng shui-influenced draperies and old Mallorcan touches. The hotel has its own terrace café-restaurant, garden and a swimming pool and sauna. Located five blocks from the main *plaça*, it's a charming and serene spot, and the staff are happy to advise on walks, golf, cycling and nature trips.

The **Posada de Lluc** (C/Roser Vell 11, 971 53 52 20, www.posadalluc.com, closed Dec-Jan, doubles €90-€185 incl breakfast) was built in the 15th century as a nobleman's mansion; the building was donated to the monks of Lluc, so that they had a place to rest when travelling through. It's now a fairly luxurious *hotel del interior*, with eight rooms decked out with Mallorcan furniture and mod cons like satellite TV and minibar. There's a lovely pool too.

If you really want to live it up, the five-star **Son Brull** (Ctra. Palma–Pollença, km49.50, 971 53 53 53, www.sonbrull.com, closed Dec-Jan, doubles €280-€406 incl breakfast, restaurant €€€€) is the poshest place in the area. It's a former 18th-century convent just outside Pollença and is now part of the swanky Relais & Chateau hotel group. Aside from the 23

NORTH MALLORCA

Posada de Lluc Hotel.

NORTH MALLORCA

super high-spec rooms – think Bang & Olufsen TVs, perfect beds and huge bathtubs – there are two pools, a sauna, jacuzzi and Turkish bath. Yoga classes are offered on the verdant lawns and there's a well-regarded modern Mallorcan restaurant, called 365. Helicopter co-ordinates are provided for those who have the luxury of arriving in style.

Further from town is **Can Guillo** (Ctra. Pollença–Palma, km47, mobile 687 89 68 15, www.canguillo.com, doubles €88-€98 incl breakfast), an *agroturismo* set within extensive farmland with space for 16 guests. It's a wonderfully informal place, run by the friendly Salas Comas family, and overflows with friendly animals and various plants; Granny, in particular, loves a cacti and will talk your ear off about them regardless of whether you speak any Spanish. The hotel is upping its eco credentials too, firstly with lots of edible home produce and then through the pool and central heating, which run on solar power and a generator burning almond husks.

Vall De Pollença (Ctra. Pollença–Lluc, km4.8, 971 10 34 00, www.valldepollensa.com) is another *agroturismo* five kilometres out of town off the road to Lluc. The house is full of old Mallorcan character, with exposed beams and even a wooden mill in the breakfast room, but it's the views and peace and quiet of the surrounding countryside that are the real draws. There's also a pool.

Nowhere will you get a better view than the **Santuari Nostra Senyora des Puig** (Puig de Santa María, 971 18 41 32, doubles €22). Perched high above Pollença, this is one of the island's most impressive places to stay and, happily, also one of its cheapest. It's not the easiest of places to get to (unless you've packed your quad bike you'll have to walk up the last 15 minutes of path to get here). There are no TVs or curtains, you make your own bed and bathrooms are shared, but it is a wonderfully silent and truly spiritual place to visit, with astounding views. The chapel and museum are marvellously spooky at night and there's also a restaurant, which offers brilliant stews, paella and sandwiches on request. Highly recommended.

PORT DE POLLENÇA & CALA SANT VICENÇ

While the inland town of Pollença grew to prominence, its nearby beach and fishing port, seven kilometres away, went about its low-key business undisturbed (apart from the odd pirate raid) until the late 19th century, when it began to become popular with artists and aristocrats for a spot of R&R. The gracious Hotel Miramar opened in 1912 and stood more or less alone until the 1960s, when serious tourist development began.

Today's resort of **Port de Pollença** (Puerto Pollensa in Castilian) stretches for three kilometres around the curved **Bay of Pollença**, straying inland for just four blocks of bright, white, medium-height hotels, villas and busy backstreets, set against the dramatic backdrop of the Formentor peninsula. It's an easygoing family destination and less brash than other Mallorcan resorts. It's also deservedly popular, not least for the variety and quality of its restaurants, which range from classic Mediterranean and Mallorcan, to Chinese and Indian.

The northern end of the beach has a pedestrianised promenade, the pine tree-lined Passeig Anglada Camarasa. Along this stretch stand some smartish hotels and some good bars and restaurants. It makes for a lovely pre-dinner stroll.

Diving is well established in the resort, with **Scuba-Mallorca** (C/El Cano 23, 971 86 80 87, www.scubamallorca.com, closed Nov-Apr) among the reliable operators – look out for Turkish wrasse, groupers, barracudas and lovely low coral walls. The Port is also home to the **Real Club Náutico** as well as a busy marina, and there are a number of sailing opportunities, ranging from chilling out on a lavish yacht while people service your every whim to chartering your own unguided boat. There are also half a dozen places to rent a bike near the centre.

Between Pollença town and its port is **Albufereta**, a botanically rich wetland area far smaller than the S'Albufera park south of Alcúdia (*see p153*), but, since 2001, designated as Mallorca's first nature reserve and enjoying a high level of protection. Popular with bird enthusiasts, it is an important stopover on the Europe–Africa migration highway and home to over 100 species, including egrets, herons, bitterns and ospreys.

A popular walking trail (six-kilometre round trip) from Port de Pollença heads inland to the **Vall de Boquer**; it starts from the end of Avinguda Bocchoris.

One of the more attractive resorts in the area is diminutive **Cala Sant Vicenç**, four

Cala Sant Vinçec.

INSIDE TRACK
SANTUARI NOSTRA
SENYORA DES PUIG

If you have a small car, and nerves of steel, you can drive to within 15 minutes' walk of the summit of the *puig*, or hill, leaving the car by the side of the road. Alternatively, you can climb the same route on foot in about 45 minutes.

kilometres off the Pollença–Port de Pollença road. It comprises three tiny sandy beaches (and a rocky cove), a handful of hotels, and a few touristy restaurants and bars. It's a pity that the Hotel Don Pedro hogs the seafront, but it's still a choice spot for a swim (though the sea can get pretty rough here and the red flag is frequently hoisted). Looking right from the main car park you see the rocky hills of the **Serra del Cavall Bernat** and the Formentor peninsula behind it. There are more fine views from the **Puig de l'Àguila** hilltop a few kilometres out of town.

Where to eat & drink

Pollença's eating options are a mixed bag. There are theme pubs and bad fish and chips but also good international restaurants and decent cafés in pleasant surrounds.

One of the best is the **Ivy Garden** (C/Llevant 14, 971 86 62 71, closed Mon, €€€), where dishes such as calf's liver with bacon and sautéed apple, and duck breast with ginger, honey and soy sauce are served in a pretty interior courtyard.

There are plenty of lunch places on the long prom and a block into the town. A good choice is **La Goleta** (Passeig Saralegui 118, 971 86 59 02, closed 15 Nov-15 Feb, €); it sits below a nondescript hotel block, but its steaks, paellas and fish dishes are simple, tasty and cheap, and it's popular with locals.

Pizza is not always top notch in the Balearics, but **Little Italy** (Passeig Voramar 59, 971 86 67 49, closed Nov-Apr, €) follows correct Italian standards of dough thickness, oil, tomato and cheese. **Los Zarzales** (C/Jafuda Cresques, 11, 971 86 51 37) has a cosy interior as well as tables on the street and offers Mallorcan cuisine such as red peppers stuffed with fish and seafood, baked monkfish with king prawns and almond blossom, or roast suckling pig with bay and lemon. The lunchtime and evening *menús* are good value.

La Terrassa, the restaurant of the **Hotel Illa d'Or** (*see right*), nestled under the pines

and overlooking the beach, is a good place for a light lunch or a snack and makes an especially good pit stop on the northern end of the beach.

Popular with well-heeled locals is **Stay** (C/Moll Nou s/n, 971 86 40 13, www.stay restaurant.com, €€€€), which specialises in salmon, lamb, roast duck, pork in apple and calvados sauce, beef with foie gras and port, and a dessert of fresh fig and almond strudel. Stay's aim is to be international with a Mallorcan twist. It sources its ingredients locally where possible, and the vast wine list is a joy. Presentation is verging on art, but the food is honest and tasty, and there are terrace tables out on the quay.

Moneyed folk also eat at the **Real Club Náutico** (Moll Vell s/n, 971 86 56 22/46 35, www.rcnpp.net, €€€€) on the jetty. This is where you can go to sample goose liver pâté, the house special of lobster casserole – all with an excellent vantage point from which to keep a close eye on your yacht.

Corb Mareí (Passeig Anglada Camarassa, 91, 971 86 70 40, closed Nov/Feb, €€€) is another good option with a pretty terrace and warm interior that's been serving good fish and meat since 1967. Try the rabbit or hake kebabs, calamar and mushroom casserole, say, or charcoal-grilled king prawns.

A bucolic option just a couple of kilometres from Port de Pollença is **Ca'n Cuarassa** (Ctra. Port de Pollença–Alcúdia, 971 86 42 66, www.cancuarassa.com, €€€), which has great views over the bay, a lovely shaded terrace, and a gourmet menu of Mediterranean specials and pastas – the rabbit with potato *alioli* is a treat, and the calf's liver ultra-succulent; skewered prawns is a lightweight alternative. Tiramisú and a selection of home-made ice-cream wrap up meals here, and there's a long wine list to explore.

Cala Sant Vicenç concentrates on providing quick lunches for bathers – there are plenty of cafés and snack bars at the top of the bluff and down near the beaches, and many do beans on toast, pizzas, chips and the like. For something more exciting, go along to the restaurants at the Hotel Cala Sant Vicenç (*see p146*) or try the high-quality meats at barbecue restaurant **Modesto Grill** (Avda. Torrent s/n, 971 53 38 49, closed lunch and Nov-Apr, €€).

Where to stay

Much of **Port de Pollença** is made up of boring-looking hotel blocks and villas. The beachside hotels are slightly better, and the older establishments tend to feel more sophisticated, but unfortunately many are block-booked by travel companies.

The *grande dame* is the **Hotel Miramar** (Passeig Anglada Camarasa 39, 971 86 64 00, www.hotel-miramar.net, closed Nov-Mar, doubles €90-€128 incl breakfast). Opened in 1912, the Miramar prides itself on its pedigree. Artists hung out here in the 1960s and, even now, for all the package rep folders you see around, there's still a certain grace to the place. Air-con and double-glazing throughout make it cool and serene, and the terrace café is a people-watchers' fave.

At the posher, eastern end of the pine walk, the smart four-star **Hotel Illa d'Or** (Passeig de Colón 265, 971 86 51 00, www.hotelillador. com, closed 23 Nov-7 Feb, doubles €103-€187 incl breakfast) looks newish but has actually been here, at least in name, since 1929. It's particularly popular with families and those who want everything near to hand – including a gym, nice terrace restaurant (*see left*), indoor and outdoor pools, sauna and jacuzzi. Apartments are available in the same complex and there's a seafront restaurant which is great for a light lunch or an afternoon tea.

For those on a tighter budget, there's the **Hostal Residencia Paris** (C/Magallanes 18, 971 86 40 17, doubles €45). It's located in an ugly medium-height tower, but the location is central and the staff are friendly.

An original alternative to beachside hotels, the finca **Ca'n Cap de Bou** (Bay of Pollença, 971 27 21 59, 971 86 74 03, www. cancapdebou.net, closed Nov-Mar, house for up to 8 people €170-€190, apartments for 2/3 people €85-€95) is a lovely old rural building with room for up to 28 guests. Tennis courts, a swimming pool and even horseriding and the use of sailing dinghies are included in the price. Come dusk it's a welcome refuge from the neon naffness of the town. The sea is less than a kilometre away and you can even travel there by donkey cart on request.

Another superb rural hotel is the luxurious **Hotel Llenaire** (Camí de Llenaire, km3.8, 971 53 52 51, www.hotelllenaire.com, closed Nov-Mar, doubles €275), just south of Port de Pollença, which opened in 2003. It sits within its own estate, offers eight huge suites and three superior doubles, and has good facilities, including a pool, solarium and sauna.

There are several package-type hotels at **Cala Sant Vicenç**, but the most eye-catching is easily the five-star **La Moraleja** (Urb. Los Encinares, 971 53 40 10, www.lamoraleja.net,

NORTH MALLORCA

Mirador des Colomer.

closed Nov-Apr, doubles €283-€321 incl breakfast), which, despite its rather showy faux opulence (note the vintage cars in the folly-cum-showroom and Dallas ranch approach to furnishings), is extremely friendly, has deceptively few bedrooms (17) and is much loved by its guests.

Alternatively, a good option is the more elegant **Hotel Cala Sant Vicenç** (C/Maressers 2, 971 53 02 50, www.hotel cala.com, closed Nov-Mar, doubles €147-€164 incl breakfast). Here you can indulge in the excellent cuisine of its locally revered **Cavall Bernat** (€€€€) restaurant. It also has a trattoria and a poolside grill.

To stay or eat right on the waterfront, try the friendly **Hotel Niu** (Cala Barques, 971 53 05 12, www.hoposa.es, closed Nov-May, doubles €65-€100 incl breakfast). It's simple and comfortable and is owned by a British-Mallorcan couple. The rooms vary according to the view and whether they have a terrace or balcony. A separate building, C'an Franc, houses four smart suites (€130-€180), and there are three different restaurants with varying degrees of formality.

Tucked away among the pine trees above the next beach along, Cala Molins, is the **Hostal Los Pinos** (971 53 12 10, www.hostal-lospinos.com, closed Nov-Apr, doubles €64-€76 incl breakfast), which makes a reasonable stab at looking Mediterranean – with plenty of cats and geraniums – despite its size. There is a decent-sized pool and the views are unbeatable.

FORMENTOR

From Port de Pollença, it's half an hour's drive (21 kilometres/13 miles) up and round the switchbacks of the steep, narrow road to Mallorca's most northerly cape, **Cap de Formentor**, celebrated by poets and artists for its pine forests, its peace and its superlative, dizzying panoramas. It's an essential trip if you're in the area, but make it early or late in the day if you don't want to be part of a honking tourist convoy. The main stops are at the **Mirador des Colomer**, a short pathway on the edge of a 232-metre- (760-foot-) high sheer vertical cliff, and the lighthouse. Further fine views can be had from side journeys up the **Atalaya d'Alberutx** and at **Can es Faro**, but you'll need good nerves and suspension to take on the old, beaten-up roads here.

Like the rest of the Tramuntana, the unwieldy topography of this slender promontory was of little interest to Mallorca's earliest conquerors, though its name (*forment* means wheat) suggests that it was valued at some stage in history by farmers. The first record of a proprietor dates from 1231, two years after

the conquest of Jaume I, and from then until the 20th century the whole of the peninsula changed hands only a few times and development was scant – a few houses, barns, a lighthouse, a single road.

In 1928, Adam Diehl, an Argentinian art-loving dandy who, like many of his contemporaries, made his fortune in the meat trade, bought the whole of the peninsula for half a million pesetas and built a stylish, modernist hotel here for artists and aristocrats (*see below*). Non-residents can visit the **Hotel Formentor** as they drive through and stroll along the lovely public beach, the **Platja de Formentor**.

But there is a more public heritage that the hotel has bequeathed. Neither Diehl nor subsequent owners were keen to downgrade the hotel by allowing large-scale tourist development to take place on their exclusive strip of wilderness. The happy consequence of this has been the preservation of Formentor's ecologies, particularly the seabirds – twitchers report sightings of honey buzzards, black kites and booted eagles as well as Mallorca's star bird of prey, the Eleanora's falcon. The rocky outcrops also provide homes for lizards and smaller birds like martins and swifts, especially at the northern tip.

Where to stay & eat

What was once Mallorca's most famous hotel is the only place to stay on Formentor. The legendary **Hotel Formentor** (Platja de Formentor s/n, 971 89 91 01, www.barcelo.com, closed Oct-Mar, doubles €227-€545 incl breakfast) opened in 1929, and early guests included the Duke of Windsor, the Maharajah of Papurtala and writer Ramón Gomez de la Serna. Later on, Hollywood icons such as Elizabeth Taylor, Ava Gardner, Audrey Hepburn and Gary Cooper would add further lustre, putting Mallorca on the classy tourist map and creating a legacy that, frankly, the hotel can no longer quite live up to. It was bought in 2006 by the Barceló hotel group, which is striving to revive its former glories – difficult given the omnipresent sunken *Titanic* feel in the endless corridors of this vast 122-room complex, though staff work hard to be welcoming. Check out the hairdressing salon, the boutiques and the dining balconies to get a feel for how the other half used to live. There are three in-house restaurants.

The only other option for a bite to eat is the café (mobile 619 74 85 91, open 10am-6pm daily, closed dinner and Nov, €) at the very end of the promontory, near the lighthouse. Here you can tuck into filled baguettes, pizza and ice-cream while you admire the stunning view.

NORTH MALLORCA

Resources

Internet
Pollença *Cafè 1550, Avda. de l'Argentina 1
(971 53 13 30/www.cafe1550.com).* **Open** 6am-
2am daily. **Map** p139.
Port de Pollença *Café Caramba, C/Mestral 7
(971 86 66 46).* **Open** 10am-2am Tue-Sun.
Map p139.

Police station
Pollença *C/Munar 16 (971 53 04 37).*
Map p139.

Post office
Pollença *C/Jonquet 61(971 53 11 25).*
Map p139.
Port de Pollença *C/Levant 15
(971 86 69 71).*

Tourist information
Cala Sant Vicenç OIT *Plaça Sant
Vicenç s/n (971 53 3264/
oitcsv@ajpollenca.net).*
Open *June-Sept* 9.15am-2pm, 3-5pm Mon-Fri;
9.15am-1pm Sat. Closed Oct-May.
Pollença OIT *C/Guillem Cifre de Colonya
s/n (971 53 50 77/oit@ajpollenca.net).*
Open 8am-3pm Mon-Fri; 9am-1pm Sat.
Map p139.
Port de Pollença OIT *Passeig Saralegue
s/n (971 86 54 67/oitport@ajpollenca.net).*

Open *Mar-June* 8am-3pm Mon-Fri; 9am-1pm
Sat. *July-Sept* 8am-8pm, 10am-5pm Sat.
Oct-Feb 8am-3pm Mon-Fri.

Getting there

By bus
Autocares Mallorca (971 54 56 96) runs one
bus (Line 11) Mon-Sat from Palma (departing
at 10.15am) to Formentor via Inca (10.50am),
Alcúdia (11.20am) and Port de Pollença
(11.30am), arriving at Formentor at 11.50am,
and setting off from Formentor for the return
journey at 3.30pm.

Line 3 buses run twice a day Mon-Sat from
Can Picafort (9am, 2.15pm) to Formentor
(arriving 10.20am, 3.20pm) via Port de Alcúdia
(9.30am, 2.40pm), 3 times Mon-Sat from Alcúdia
(9.45am, 11.15am, 2.50pm) to Formentor and
four times Mon-Sat from Port de Pollença (10am,
11.30am, 3pm, 4.30pm) to Formentor.

Line 4 buses run twice a day Mon-Sat between
Port de Sóller (leaving 9am, 3pm) and Can
Picafort (arriving noon, 6pm) via Sóller (9.10am,
3.10pm), Lluc (10.20am, 4.20pm), Pollença
(10.45am, 4.45pm), Cala Sant Vicenç (10.55am,
4.55pm), Port de Pollença (11.10am, 5.10pm),
Alcúdia (11.30am, 5.30pm) and Port d'Alcúdia
(11.35am, 5.35pm). Return buses leave Can
Picafort at 9am and 3pm.

For information on other buses to Alcúdia and
around the Bay of Alcúdia, *see p153.*

NORTH MALLORCA

Hotel Formentor

Alcúdia & the Bay of Alcúdia

Two very different towns and a picture-perfect peninsula.

Tiny, fortified Alcúdia offers an insight into Mallorcan small town life – albeit a gentrified, largely tourist-oriented one. Nevertheless, it's a pretty place to spend some time with some great places to eat and stay. A short hop down to the sea and you come to the bay of Alcúdia's western strip: one row of pubs, lilo shops and fast food outlets after another – all squashed up next to fine, sandy beaches.

It's easy to escape the throngs, though: Alcúdia sits at the neck of an undeveloped peninsula criss-crossed with fine walking trails. Or you can explore the surrounding inland countryside, where you'll find emerald green pasturelands, pretty fruit groves and tracts of ecologically important wilderness.

ALCUDIA

Alcúdia competes with Pollença (*see p137*) for loveliest town in the north of the island. Its quiet winding alleys, dotted with Renaissance mansions, along with a great range of great independent hotels and restaurants, make it a good holiday base.

The town's location on a rise – its name is of Moorish origin, 'al-kudia' meaning 'on the hill' – at the foot of a stubby peninsula between two huge bays made it a strategically key site for most of the island's history. The Phoenicians established a trading post here, and then, following the successful invasion of 123 BC, the Romans built their island capital on this spot. Levelled by the Vandals, it was the Moors who re-established a fortress and settlement, and their Christian successors further developed Alcúdia as an important centre of trade. Today, this neat, trim town of 14,000, 14 kilometres south-east of Port de Pollença and a fast 60-kilometre (38-mile) journey from Palma, remains the main hub of northern Mallorca.

For visitors, the main draw of the place is the compact old centre, contained within the thick, low-slung town wall. This was first erected between 1298 and 1362, by order of Jaume II, though most of what you see now was

reconstructed in recent decades. Some 26 six-metre- (20-foot-) high turreted towers and three gates punctuate the wall. Inside is a network of spruced-up narrow streets, replete with cafés, restaurants and souvenir shops, leading off the central axis of C/Major–Plaça Constitució–C/Moll–Plaça Carles V.

There are few specific sights to admire, but the shady lanes make for an enjoyable wander, particularly on Tuesdays and Sundays when there's a fruit and vegetable, clothes and handicrafts market. Not many visitors venture into the church of **Sant Jaume**. The building originated in the 13th century, but most of the present structure dates from a neo-Gothic remodelling in the 1880s; the Sant Crist chapel is all that remains of the original church – the Sant Crist image is an object of devotion for Alcúdians. The church's organ dates from 1559.

The Romans named their town Pollentia (meaning 'power'; the name was, confusingly, later appropriated by the founders of modern Pollença). To mug up on the town's Roman past, visit the **Museu Monogràfic de Pollentia** – funerary objects, coins, tombstones and marble fragments form the bulk of the collection, garnered from excavations since the 1920s. The town was located just south of the later walled settlement and covered a considerable area. Disappointingly little has survived of Pollentia, but what there is still constitutes the most important Roman remains on Mallorca. There are some scant ruins just south of the church of Sant Jaume over the main road, but the one stand-out is the remains of the amphitheatre, the **Teatre Romà**, which is now part of the **Museu Monogràfic de Pollentia**. Built in the first century AD, with eight tiers and a small stage embedded in the rock, it is still used for alfresco performances today. To reach it, walk up C/Santa Anna. Nearby are the ruins of the Roman **Fòrum**.

Alcúdia boasts the impressive **Auditori d'Alcúdia** (Plaça de la Porta Mallorca 3, 971 89 71 85, www.auditorialcudia.net), a huge theatre and arts space, which houses a library, café and radio station. A range of performing arts is explored each season, from Catalan singing stars to David Hare dramas, with a dance programme for those who can't follow the local lingo.

Despite the weight of tourist development in this part of the island, it's remarkably easy to leave it all behind and escape into nature. Take the minor road that leads from the town north-east along the northern edge of the peninsula (signposted to El Mal Pas, Bonaire, Manresa and La Victòria) towards the **Cap d'es Pinar** (the Cap itself is a military zone and out of bounds to the public). You'll take in fine views across the Bay of Pollença towards Port de Pollença and Formentor, passing the turning for the art collection and sculpture garden of the **Fundación Yannick y Ben Jakober** (*see p152*) and a few little beaches before coming to a large car park at the **Ermita**

de la Victòria. This 17th-century shrine, situated seven kilometres from Alcúdia, provides a home to a revered image of the Virgin – viewable above the Baroque altar inside this dark, sombre church. Every year, on 1 and 2 July, the **Mare de Déu de la Victòria** is celebrated here and *bunyols* (potato doughnuts) and *mistella* – a Mallorcan alcoholic drink – are served at midnight; on the following day the local band gives a concert and almonds are ritually showered on everyone.

For visitors, though, the Ermita is most notable as a starting point for some superb walks into the peninsula's wild hills, chiefly to the peaks of **Penya Rotja** (315 metres/ 1,033 feet) and **Talaia d'Alcúdia** (444 metres/1,457 feet).

Museu Monogràfic de Pollentia

C/Sant Jaume 30 (971 54 70 04). **Open** 10am- 4pm Tue-Fri; 10am-1.30pm Sat, Sun. **Admission** €2; €1.25 reductions. **No credit cards**.

Alcúdia.

NORTH MALLORCA

Where to stay

Alcúdia and its surrounding area are blessed with a number of good places to stay. The more characterful hotels are conversions of 18th- and 19th-century townhouses within the walled old town. The **Nou Hotelet Cas Ferrer** (C/Pou Nou 1, 971 89 75 42, www.nouhotelet.com, closed Jan, doubles €117-€133 incl breakfast) used to be a blacksmith and is now a favourite with trendy thirtysomethings, who lounge on its decked terrace flicking through coffee-table books, while its design mag credentials are lent a real warmth by the effervescent Tolo Llabrés, a mine of information on the town. Another graceful conversion is the **Hotel Sant Jaume** (C/Sant Jaume 6, 971 54 94 19, www.hotelsant jaume.com, closed Dec-Jan, doubles €99-€105 incl breakfast), an elegant, traditional place with much of its original furniture and mosaic flooring, and a pretty Andalucían-style patio where breakfast is served around an old well. Its six rooms are all different, and all have generous bathrooms.

Across the road is **Ca'n Simó** (C/Sant Jaume 1, 971 54 92 60, www.cansimo.com, doubles €96-€106 incl breakfast), with smart, comfortable rooms, a small plunge pool, jacuzzi and sauna. Its restaurant (€€) serves good-value Mediterranean dishes, along with lighter snacks such as *pa amb oli*.

At the other end of the scale, the **Fonda Llabrés** (Plaça Constitució 6, 971 54 50 00, www.fondallabres.com, doubles €36) is an extraordinary bargain, and the oldest hotel in town. It has 21 pristine, simple but attractively furnished rooms above a convivial restaurant and tapas bar (€).

On the road to Palma, **Son Siurana** (Ctra. Palma–Alcúdia, km42.8, 971 54 96 62, www.sonsiurana.com, doubles €112-€171 incl breakfast) is the most lavish of the local finca-type lodgings, set in 100 hectares (245 acres) of pasture land and almond groves. The main house was built in 1784, and now there are six villas, two apartments and one suite. The extensive breakfasts – much of which come from the farm – are taken on the bougainvillea-swamped terrace, overlooking a sizeable pool. Staff are friendly, and sheep, a cocker spaniel and a DVD library add to the homely vibe.

On the way to **Cap d'es Pinar** is a truly marvellous accomodation option, especially if you're not after high-spec frills: the **Ermita de la Victòria** (Ctra. Cap des Pinar, km6, 971 54 99 12, www.lavictoriahotel.com, closed Nov-Jan, doubles €66). The 12 rooms are all en suite and although simply decorated, are far from austere; the real draws, however, are the views and the total silence.

Genestar.

Where to eat & drink

The popular **Restaurante Mirador de la Victòria** (Ctra. Cap des Pinar, 971 54 71 73, €€, closed Mon and 4wks Jan-Feb) is located near the Ermita de la Victòria, serving gutsy Mallorcan fare on a covered terrace with a stunning view across the bay.

A restaurant at the cutting edge of the eating scene is **Genestar** (Plaça Porta de Mallorca 1, 971 54 91 57, www.genestarestaurant.com, closed Wed, Sun evening in winter, Sun lunch in summer, €€); small, bright, monochrome and achingly modern, with food to match. A low-priced *menú degustación* (€25) might include rabbit with apples and pears; monkfish with black olive and spicy tomato sauce; slow-braised pork cheeks with a red wine reduction; and similarly stunning desserts. A short wine list is expertly put together – try Divins, from a tiny bodega in Selva.

Sa Romana (C/Pollentia 81, 971 54 94 28, closed Nov-Mar, €€€€) is built on the site of a Roman villa (parts of which are visible behind glass), out near the Teatre Romà. Beautifully presented meat and fish dishes show a perfect balance of quality and creativity.

Plaça Constitució swarms with hungry tourists at lunch- and dinner time but has some good restaurants – all claim to be 'traditional Mallorcan'; when in reality the only thing Mallorcan about some is their location. **Sa Plaça** (Plaça Constitució 1, 971 54 62 78, closed Wed, €€€) is one of the most popular and has tables on the square. It serves Italian and local cuisine – including a near-perfect beef carpaccio. The €15 *menú* at lunchtime is good value. **Es Canyar** (C/Major 2, 971 54 72 82, €) is almost opposite – walk straight through the unexceptional-looking bar to a gorgeous candlelit, vine-covered terrace, with sofas lining the walls. Food varies from pizzas to modern mediterranean fare.

C'an Costa (C/Sant Viçens, 14, 971 54 53 94, closed Mon, mid Jan-mid Feb) has been in the same family for decades and offers hearty Mallorcan dishes like pork with cabbage or cod cooked in honey – they sound odd, they taste great – in friendly, traditional surroundings.

A quieter option, still in the centre, is **Sa Caseta** (Plaça de les Verdures, 8, 971 54 57 18, €), which serves home-made pizzas and pasta in a beautiful square just behind the Plaça Constitució. For equally straightforward fare, **Sa Portassa** (C/Sant Vicenç 7, 971 54 88 19, closed Mon in winter, €) has a long list of Mallorcan tapas and a popular interior courtyard. Another good, laidback option is **Cas Capella** (C/Serra 26, 971 54 73 14, €). It has tables lining a quiet alley in the old town and is great for *pa amb oli*, simple salads or the good-value lunchtime *menú*.

If you've had your fill of Mediterranean cuisine, **Khun Phanit** (C/Serra, 5, 971 54 77 60, €) offers Thai food in simple surroundings. Try the prawns with peanut, coconut and lime leaves or chicken stir-fry with jasmin and cashew nuts.

PORT D'ALCUDIA & THE BAY OF ALCUDIA

Port d'Alcúdia is the uninspiring coastal sibling of its more refined namesake only a couple of kilometres inland. It doesn't feel like a working port (despite all the ferries to Spain proper), however: the plethora of package hotels called Sol-this and Playa-that leave no doubt that this is a part of the island entirely given over to the tourist trade. There are three wonderful exceptions to the package high-rise slew along the bay: the **S'Albufera** nature reserve (*see p153*), the sublime walks around the **Ermita de Betlem** monastery at the eastern end of the bay and the **Fundación Yannick y Ben Jakober** art collection (*see p152*) up the coast.

Already far larger than Port de Pollença, Port d'Alcúdia's strip of high-rise hotels and villas, immediately south of Alcúdia town, seems intent on extending right around the 15-kilometre shoreline of the Bay of Alcúdia. Tens of thousands of tourist beds are made up each morning, and though the local authorities optimistically rebranded the region an 'ecotouristic municipality' (whatever that might mean) in 1992, the damage has been done. Out of peak season, though, strolling along the prom can feel remarkably pleasant and the beach is a treat. There's money in the coffers here, so the

paving and wooden walkways are kept spruced up, and there are almost as many smartish coffee shops as burger bars and Brit-style pubs.

Every arrow on the main MA12 points towards the 'platja', 'playa', 'strand', 'beach', which is the only reason for the coast road between Alcúdia and Artà. Follow them and you are soon in a dispiriting corridor of multi-storey hotels, expat villa developments, fast food outlets and tat-dispensing shops. Early maps of Mallorca show no road around the Bay of Alcúdia, and even today there's a feeling of pointlessness to the route, unless you own a place here, or know someone who has gone into exile at one-time fishing port **Can Picafort** (favoured by older people and families, despite the proliferation of 'fun pubs') or the smaller **Colònia de Son Serra**. The beaches are nice enough – the **Platja de Muro** is perhaps the best, though **Son Bauló** is quieter – but there's a distinct lack of coherence to the resorts, which feature just the usual services, petrol stations and basic eateries.

Many people go for a ramble over the dunes at Can Picafort to take a look at the **Son Real** necropolis – the walk itself is pleasant when it's not too hot, but the burial site, dating from the seventh century BC to the first century AD and containing 109 tombs, is in a sorry state of disrepair. Since excavations during the 1960s and the prompt removal of the skeletons from the 100-plus tombs, the sea and weather have unfortunately been allowed to erode the walls of the artificial caves, and the protective fence is rusted and ruinous.

At the eastern limit of the Bay of Alcúdia, beyond the final resort development of **Colònia de Sant Pere**, is the **Ermita de Betlem**, a tiny monastery founded in 1805 in what remains a blissfully pristine location. The walk up here takes in woods and a steep hill climb; the stunning views make the effort worthwhile.

The only other bright spot in all this man-made monotony is the incongruous presence of the wonderful **S'Albufera** nature reserve between Port d'Alcúdia and Can Picafort. The

---

INSIDE TRACK
S'ALBUFERA TWITCHING

There have been 271 species of bird recorded in the **S'Albufera** nature reserve, which, unsurprisingly has made the place paradise for birdwatchers. Fans of our feathered friends can geek out on the park's excellent website, which features, among other environmentally informative treats, a list of avian sightings, updated every 15 days.

NORTH MALLORCA

Art Attack Fundación Yannick y Ben Jakober

The island's most unlikely location houses its most unusual collection.

Art is not the first thing that springs to mind when thinking of the Bay of Alcúdia; lobster tans, plastic paella and neon lilos maybe, but a unique art collection housed in a stunningly located gallery? Not really. Which is what makes the **Fundación Yannick y Ben Jakober** all the more special, just a beachball's throw from the glaring lights of the coastal resorts.

It all started when Yannick Vu, the artist daughter of a Vietnamese sculptor and a French pianist, first came to Mallorca in 1963 with her then husband, the Italian painter Domenico Gnoli. They lived near Valldemossa at S'Estaca (built by the Archduke Ludwig Salvator and currently owned by Michael Douglas) until Gnoli's death in 1970. Two years later Yannick married Gnoli's friend Ben Jakober, and, encouraged by his new wife, Ben started working as an artist himself. Since 1992, the couple's sculptures can be seen around the island, including in the Parc de la Mar in front of Palma cathedral, the Anfora at Palma Airport as well as, of course, in their own sculpture garden at the Finca Sa Bassa Blanca.

Over 40 years ago Yannick saw a painting by Mallorcan artist Joan Mestre i Bosch of a young girl holding some cherries, in a shop in Palma. She bought it and as a result unwittingly started what was to become the **Nins Collection** – a remarkable collection of more than 140 portraits of children ('*nins*' is the Mallorcan word for children). Tragedy turned what began as a hobby into an obsession when their daughter Maima died in 1992; the following year they created the Foundation in her memory.

Housed in a former subterranean water cistern, and beautifully lit, the collection offers a fascinating window on to the privileged yet stifling lives of the offspring of royal and noble families. Dating from the 16th to the 19th centuries, the paintings illustrate how relatively recent the concept of a childish childhood is; most of these stern-faced infants are dressed and portrayed as miniature adults. Around 50 paintings are on display at any one time, with the exhibition changing a couple of times a year.

The Jakobers had Finca Sa Bassa Blanca largely rebuilt in the 1970s by well-known Egyptian architect Hassan Fathy, who created for them a *ribat* or classic North African fortified house, constructed around a courtyard, cleverly making it seem far older than its actual years, which now houses a contemporary art collection.

In 2007, the Fundación opened the Sokrates Space, showcasing contemporary work from Jacober and Yannick along with local artists. Highlights include a curtain of 10,000 Swarovski crystals and a full-size, fossilised woolly rhino.

The Foundation is tricky to find. Heading towards Port d'Alcúdia from Alcúdia you come to traffic lights and a left turn before you leave Alcúdia, with signs pointing left to El Mal Pas, Bonaire, Manresa, La Victòria and, enigmatically, 'Fundació'. Take this left and drive for a couple of kilometres before turning right at the Bodega del Sol (there's a further small 'Fundació' sign on its wall). It's then another two kilometres to stone gateposts and an unmade road beyond. Two more kilometres along this brings you to the gates of the Foundation, which open automatically and beckon you onwards to one of Mallorca's least expected and best hidden attractions.

Note that the collection is only open on Tuesdays unless you prebook a guided tour for a group of four or more people.

Parc Natural S'Albufera de Mallorca
(to give it its full name) looks like a Balearic
Everglades and covers 1,708 hectares (4,221
acres) making it their largest and most
important wetlands; nowhere on the islands will
you find greater biodiversity. Among its riches
are 66 species of funghi, 29 of fish, eight of bat,
300 of moth and 200 of bird. It's the latter that
provide the greatest draw for visitors, with
warblers, egrets and sandpipers commonplace.
There are raised observation platforms and
circuits of trails (you can hire bikes at the
visitors' centre) and, in spring, wild flowers
brighten up the yellows, greens and browns
of the reed beds. Try and bring (or borrow)
a pair of binoculars.

Fundación Yannick y Ben Jakober
*Finca Sa Bassa Blanca, Alcúdia (971 54 98 80/
www.fundacionjakober.org).* **Open** 9.30am-12.30pm,
2.30-5.30pm Tue; 9.30am-5.30pm Wed-Sat by
appointment only for guided tours for groups of
4 or more. **Admission** free Tue. Guided tours
(Wed-Sat) €9; free under-10s. **Credit** V, MC.
See p152 Art **Attack**.

Parc Natural S'Albufera de Mallorca
*Ctra. Alcúdia–Artà (971 89 22 50/www.mallorca
web.net/salbufera).* **Open** *Apr-Sept* 9am-6pm
daily. *Oct-Mar* 9am-5pm daily. **Admission** free.

Where to stay, eat & drink

Port d'Alcúdia's hotels tend to be block-
booked by tour operators and as such you're
better off staying in or around Alcúdia (*see
p148*). An exception to the port area's poor
offerings is the **Casal Santa Eulália**
(Ctra. Santa Margalida–Alcúdia, km1.8, 971 85
27 32, www.casal-santaeulalia.com, €€€) near
Can Picafort. It's a beautiful old manor house
with extensive gardens, two pools, an excellent
restaurant, a sauna, plunge pool and a gym.
Try and get a room with a view of the sea,
though beware that in high season the blissful
silence may be somewhat diluted by a lot of
young couples with babies in prams.
    The local area is lacking in outstanding
places to eat as well. Your best bet is to head
to the western part of the harbour where you'll
find a strip of cafés and restaurants. Here
you'll find **La Cabaña** (Passeig Maritim 14,
971 54 61 49) a café serving light snacks and
sandwiches and **Café L'illa** (Passeig Maritim
8, 971 89 74 44), which is good for the same
as well as freshly squeezed orange juice –
surprisingly rare for an island with so many
citrus groves. For fish try **Miramar** (Passeig
Marítim 2, 971 545 293) a local seafood stalwart
with a terrace, or nearby **La Bodega d'es**

Port (C/Teodoro Canet 8, 971 54 96 33,
www.bodegadesport.com, closed Nov-Dec),
which is probably the most formal of the
seaside fish joints.
    Restaurante Jardín (C/Tritones s/n, 971 89
23 91, www.restaurantejardin.com, closed Mon
Jan-Mar, €€€) is classier than most, with tables
in a leafy garden and dishes including cod *al pil
pil*, and roast suckling pig with baked apple.
    As a major resort, Port d'Alcúdia's nightlife
scene is the liveliest in the north. The Roman-
themed **Menta** (Avda. Tucán 5, 971 89 19 72,
www.discomenta.com, closed Sun-Thur Oct-
Apr), which boasts its own swimming pool,
is still the biggest in town and packs them
in a young crowd of locals and tourists for
everything from electro-house nights to
cheesy foam parties.

RESOURCES
Internet
Port d'Alcúdia *Krosan, Avda Tucán 3
(971 89 17 24).* **Open** 7am-10pm daily.

Police station
Bastió de Sant Ferran s/n (971 54 50 66).

Post office
Alcúdia *C/Pollentia s/n (971 54 54 40).*

Tourist information
Can Picafort *OIT, Plaça Enginyer Gabriel
Roca 6 (971 85 03 10).* **Open** *May-Oct* 9am-1pm,
4.30-7.30pm Mon-Fri. *Nov-Apr* 9am-1pm Mon-Fri.
Platja de Muro *OIT, Avda. de S'Albufera
33 (971 89 10 13).* **Open** *May-Oct* 8.30am-
3pm Mon-Fri; 9am-1pm Sat. *Nov-Apr* 8am-
3pm Mon-Fri.
Port d'Alcúdia *OIT, C/Major 17 (971 54 80
71).* **Open** 9.30am-3pm Mon-Fri. *OIT, Ctra. Artà
68 (971 89 26 15).* **Open** *May-Oct* 10am-1.30pm,
3-5.30pm Mon-Fri; 9am-1pm Sat. *OIT* Passeig
Marítim *s/n (971 54 72 57/www.alcudia
mallorca.com).* **Open** *May, June, Sept, Oct* 9am-
8pm Mon-Sat. *July, Aug* 10am-9pm Mon-Sat.

GETTING THERE
By boat
There are regular ferry services between Alcúdia
and Menorca and Barcelona. *See p260.*

By bus
Autocares Mallorca runs 16 buses (Line 1) daily
from Palma to Port d'Alcúdia (1hr 15mins) via
Inca (30mins) and Alcúdia (1hr). There are buses
every 15 mins around the Bay of Alcúdia from
Alcúdia to Can Picafort via Port d'Alcúdia. For
information on buses to Sóller, Port de Sóller,
Lluc, Sa Calobra and Formentor, *see p147.*

Central Mallorca

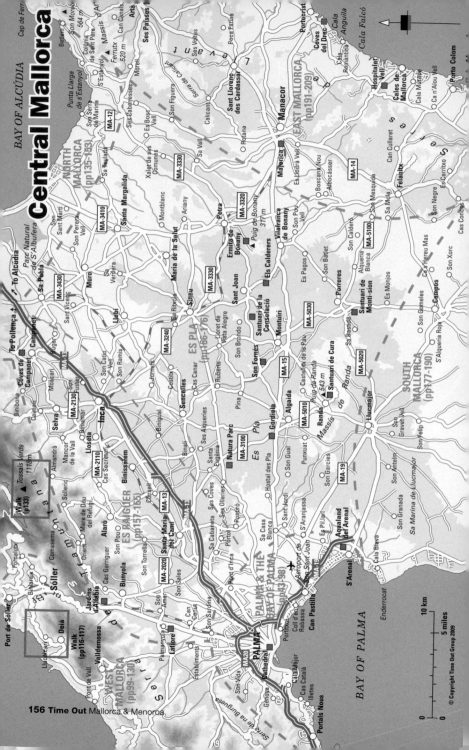

Central Mallorca

© Copyright Time Out Group 2009

Es Raiguer

The foothills of the Tramuntana make a lovely, low-key base.

The area known as Es Raiguer hugs the gentle eastern slopes of the Serra de Tramuntana; its focus is the main route between Palma and Alcúdia via Inca. This is the most fertile land on the island, with almond trees, vineyards, olive groves and sheep and pig breeding aplenty. Each town and village is characterised by its industry, the most famous of which is Inca, famed for its leather. Binissalem and Santa María del Camí are the centre of wine production; Consell is known for its *pa moreno* (unsalted dark bread) and for its blood sausage; Lloseta produces cloth and shoes;

Alaró prides itself on its ceramics. Despite its proximity to Palma and the coast, Es Raiguer is largely *terra incognita* as far as tourism is concerned; *Mallorquí* is spoken here with fierce pride and a foreigner speaking Spanish will often be replied to in the local dialect.

SANTA MARIA DEL CAMÍ, BINISSALEM & LLOSETA

There's not a great deal to see in **Santa Maria del Camí** (17 kilometres/11 miles north-east of Palma), but it is home to a number of architectural gems, including the **Convent del Minims** (Plaça dels Hostals), a beautiful convent and cloisters just off the main square. You can't go inside, alas, but you can look in through the gates at the exquisite 17th-century architecture. South of here is the oldest and prettiest part of town, which has a clutch of 17th-, 18th- and 19th-century buildings in a delightful square, **Plaça de la Vila**. The 17th-century town hall, with its delicate arches and columns, has a stunning Gothic altarpiece inside from 1384, the work of Mallorcan painter Joan Massana, and part of the original parish church. Just around the corner is the impressive Baroque pile of the church of **Santa Maria** (Plaça Caidos), with its distinctive blue-tiled spire and Churrigueresque-style interior.

By far the biggest draw for visitors to Santa Maria is the huge, and hugely popular, Sunday morning open-air market. The clothes won't set many pulses racing, but the caged birds and furry animals are a spectacle, and the fresh fruit and vegetables, sausages and cheeses are superb. Look out for the woman serving up *sobrassada* sandwiches, made with fresh *pa mallorquí*.

If rain stops play, just west of Santa Maria is **Festival Park** (Ctra. Palma–Inca, km7.1, 971 14 09 25, www.festivalpark.es), an American-style mall of fast food outlets, cinemas, bowling alleys, Europe's largest reptilarium, shops and almost 30 factory outlet stores, including Camper (971 22 66 01), Jaime Mascaró (971 22 96 98) and high-street staples like Mango (971 22 96 94). Most shops are open 10am-10pm Monday to Saturday. Bus IB20 between Palma and Inca via Santa Maria, Binissalem and Lloseta stops at Festival Park as well as trains from the Plaça Espanya in Palma.

Press on to **Binissalem** (ten kilometres north-east of Santa Maria), an architectural delight, dominated by its church and packed with 17th- and 18th-century mansions – the highest concentration on Mallorca outside Palma. All this wealth stems from a couple of industries: stone, from which the church was built, and wine. The town was originally a Muslim settlement known as Robines. It was later refounded in 1300 by Jaume II and has long been a focus for powerful, landed families. It is also the centre of the island's wine industry, home to all the big names, including **Vins Ripoll** and **José Luis Ferrer**. *See p162* **Biniculture**.

All roads lead to Plaça Església, where the Friday 'crafts' market is held. Genuine crafts are disappointingly few and far between, but it is fun to come and soak up the atmosphere. The square is dominated by the church of **Nostra**

Senyora de Robines, which has an enormous multi-layered base, started in the 15th century, and topped by a triple-levelled arched spire that was added in 1908. The cockleshell patterns in the walls represent St James; the town now uses the shell as its emblem.

The real architectural delights of Binissalem lie to the east along C/Pere Estruch (just off C/Concepció, which runs south from the main plaça) and its extension, C/Vicenç de Paul, where you'll find a string of Baroque mansions. Unfortunately, none is open to the public and you'll have to make do with admiring their exteriors, characterised by wrought-iron balconies and green wooden shutters.

There are others dotted around town, two of which can be visited. **Can Gelabert de la Portella**, a *casa señorial* converted into a cultural centre, dates originally from the 1500s, though the current structure was built between 1664 and 1837. Inside, over two doorways, are depictions of the destruction of Pompeii. This was home to writer, poet and playwright Llorenç Moyà (1916-81), a leading light in the island's rediscovery of its Catalan literary heritage, who spent much of his life immortalising the house in verse.

Can Sabater was home to another writer, **Llorenç Villalonga** (1897-1980), best known for his novel *The Dolls' Room*, about the decline of a noble family at the end of the 19th century, which is often interpreted as an allegory of the fate of the Mallorcan nobility. It is now the **Fundació Casa Museu Llorenç Villalonga**, a museum and cultural centre, and has preserved some of the rooms in which the writer lived and worked.

Lloseta, a couple of kilometres north-east of Binissalem and the same distance west of Inca, is a dusty little place with little to detain you except a couple of good restaurants and the **Palau d'Aimans**, now a sumptuous hotel (Ca's Comte; *see p159*). The palace was constructed by the Aimans family in the mid 18th century and later enlarged by Joan March, the wealthy banker. It's a stunning building, blending traditional Mallorcan architecture with Italian Renaissance style. Outside in the square are the sculpted gardens and parish church, to which the Aimans' private chapel is adjoined, with a crypt containing their bones. Just outside the village, the 19th-century **Ermita es Cocó** sits in a delightful spot on a rise by the Almadra torrent. The building was paid for by the Count of Aimans, and a pilgrimage takes place here from Lloseta on the first Wednesday after Easter.

FREE **Can Gelabert de la Portella**

C/Portella s/n, Binissalem (971 88 65 31). **Open** 4-9pm Mon-Fri; 5-9pm Sat. **Admission** free.

Santa María Del Camí.

FREE **Fundació Casa Museu Llorenç Villalonga**

C/Bonaire 25, Binissalem (971 88 60 14/65 56/ www.cmvillalonga.org). **Open** *Jan-July, Sept-Dec* 10am-2pm Mon, Wed, Fri, Sat; 10am-2pm, 4-8pm Tue, Thur. **Closed** Aug. **Admission** free.

Where to eat & drink

The recently named **Bacchus** restaurant at **Hotel Reads** in **Santa Maria** (*see p159*; €€€€) is arguably the best on the island and well worth saving up for. The cathedral-like dining room with dazzling trompe l'oeil has become a Mallorcan gastronomic temple, thanks to Michelin-starred chef Marc Fosh and his inspired but consciously healthy cooking. The tasting menu combines new and classic dishes like smoked eel tortellini with salsify, fillet of hare with truffle risotto and parmesan milk, and lemon cream with *ras al hanout* spiced caramel. Sounds wacky; tastes sublime. But hey, maybe you just want a sandwich, in which case head to Santa Maria's main square, where you'll find **C'an Calet** (Plaça dels Hostals 26, 971 62 01 73, €), which also serves reasonably priced dishes including fillet of *cap roig* (a native Mediterranean fish), duck and rabbit on a pretty patio.

Binissalem has a handful of simple bars and pizzeria-type eateries and a good restaurant: **Singló** (Plaça Església 5, 971 87 05 99, €), a smart place in the main square that serves a small selection of tasty and reasonably priced dishes, such as paella, gazpacho and *bocadillos*; it also does a very reasonable lunchtime *menú*. Also on the main square is **Restaurant Robines** (No.25, 971 51 11 36, €€), offering decent Mallorcan staples, including various tasty lamb dishes and Mallorcan soups that, loaded with meat and veg, provide a hearty meal in themselves.

There's not much night-time bar action in Binissalem. What there is takes place in the main square and the streets just off it. One of the best spots is **Café Ca S'Hereu** (C/Pere Estruch 1, 971 88 68 73, closed Mon, €€), which attracts a mixture of resident Brits and locals, drawn by its stylish decor, ambient music, roof terrace, patio and occasional live bands; it serves a small selection of simple dishes, but food is not its forte. **Pub P'dal** (Passeig d'es Born 8, 971 51 10 61, €) has bags of atmosphere, a pool table, table football, excellent music until very late and good pizzas from a wood-fired oven at the back.

For gourmet dining on a budget, **Lloseta** comes up trumps with **Can Carrossa** (C/Nou 28, 971 51 40 23, closed dinner Sun & all Mon, €€€), a pretty restaurant set amid the town's gardens, and where chef Joan Abrines, offers creative three-, four- or five-course set menus at very reasonable prices. Another good bet is **Santi Taura** (C/Guillem Santandreu 38, 971 51 46 22, www.restaurantsantitaura.com, closed Tue & dinner Sun Sept-June, Tue & Sun in July, all Aug, €€), which offers top-notch modern Mallorcan cuisine from a five-course no-choice menu.

Where to stay

This largely unsung corner of the island contains a few excellent places to stay. In **Santa Maria**, **Hotel Reads** (Ctra. Vieja s/n, 971 14 02 61, www.readshotel.com, doubles €198-€417 incl breakfast) is a lavish, always entertaining five-star manor house that indulges just about every luxury you can imagine. From the barn-like indoor swimming pool (which overlooks a still larger outdoor version) to the beautifully laid-out grounds to the dramatically decorated communal rooms (featuring the theatrical frescoes of Tim Bramhill), it's all the vision (and eclectic design sense) of owner and former lawyer Vivian Read. Amazingly for a place of this ilk, the family-run atmosphere endures, even attracting the occasional celeb. Great views of the Tramuntana can be had from here.

A more affordable, but still splendid, alternative near Santa Maria is the seven-bedroom *agroturismo* **Torrent Fals** (Ctra. Santa Maria–Sencelles, km4.5, 971 14 45 84, mobile 696 50 80 03, www.torrentfals.com,

doubles €130-€150 incl breakfast), located within a 15th-century finca. It's been converted with impeccable less-is-more taste and features a fine restaurant and a swimming pool in the midst of a pine forest.

In Binissalem, **Scott's** (Plaça Església 12, 971 87 01 00, www.scottshotel.com, doubles €187-€299 incl breakfast) remains the place that people keep going back to, so reserving well in advance is advised. George and Judy Scott have transformed this 18th-century house on the main square into a delightful hotel, which has the look and feel of a private home. The 17 rooms (six of them suites) are decorated in a homely style, with supremely comfortable beds and well-stocked bathrooms (though no TV, unless you request one); they look on to a pretty patio full of flowers and running water, with a sundeck above and a small heated indoor pool. Welcome touches include the honour bar in the cosy drawing room and small kitchens stocked with tea, coffee and biscuits. George is also an author of crime fiction and has written two novels, both set on the island; you'll find a complimentary copy of *The Bloody Bokhara* awaiting you in your room when you check in. The couple also owns another property in the south-west of the island: Scott's Galilea (*see p108*).

Lloseta's Ca's Comte (C/Comte d'Aimans 11, 971 87 30 77, www.hotelcascomte.com, doubles €120 incl breakfast, restaurant closed lunch, €€) is a surprising stunner in a low-profile village; the conversion of this 18th-century townhouse could grace a *Wallpaper** feature. Juxtaposed with cool stone walls and wooden beams are great sheets of glass and minimalist vases, ornaments and light fittings. There are four doubles and four split-level suites, which come with a lavish lounge and views down over the central *plaça*. The breakfast is an indulgent banquet of fruits, pastries and hot bites. Family-run, this *hotel rural* is ultra-friendly, amazingly helpful for local information and an absolute steal at the price. Its restaurant (for guests only) is also first-rate.

Resources

Police station
Binissalem *C/Concepció 4 (971 51 11 26).*
Lloseta *C/Guillem Santandreu s/n (971 51 94 39).*
Santa Maria del Camí *C/De la Iglesia 1A (971 62 01 31/mobile 608 83 05 37).*

Post office
Binissalem *C/oncepció 5 (971 51 10 51).*
Lloseta *C/Junipero Serra 1 (971 51 40 51).*
Santa Maria del Camí *C/Bernat de Santa Eugènia 41 (971 62 00 26).*

CENTRAL MALLORCA

INSIDE TRACK
FRESHLY SQUEEZED JUICE

For all the citrus groves you'll pass in Mallorca, especially around the Tramuntana mountains, freshly squeezed juice still remains a luxury. Which makes sitting back with a tall glass of fresh lemonade or orange juice in the **Jardins de Alfàbia** all the sweeter. Further joy can be gleamed from the knowledge that your beverage's food miles amount to about seven metres.

ALARÓ, ORIENT & BUNYOLA

The foothills of the Tramuntana, just north of Santa Maria and Binissalem, are the most picturesque part of Es Raiguer, with tiny villages nestled into the landscape. Five kilometres north-west of Consell and the MA-13 is **Alaró**, which makes a pleasant lunch stop. The village is centred on its main square, **Plaça de la Vila**, with a pretty town hall (with some tourist information) and church at the south end and a scattering of restaurants, bars and cafés on or just off it.

Alaró is framed by two molar-shaped outcrops of rock, the **Puig d'Alaró** and the **Puig de s'Alcadena**, which act as the gateway to the higher slopes. The road heading north out of the village passes between the twin peaks, before coming to the turning to the **Castell d'Alaró**, whose ruined battlements appear to grow out of the cliff-face. The first part of the journey up to the castle is not too bad, except on a Sunday, when a snake of traffic heads up to **Es Verger** restaurant (*see p161*). Once you arrive at the restaurant, you can park and hike up the rest of the way (about an hour and a half to the top). The castle's history dates back to Moorish times, but it was beefed up by Jaume I, and although there's not a great deal left, the views from here are quite breathtaking: to the west the valley of **Orient**, to the east the plain and to the south Palma and the coast.

The MA-210 rises up from Alaró towards the mountains for a few kilometres through pine groves and almond trees, before dropping into the brilliant green valley of **Orient** surrounded by vertiginous cliffs. Arguably one of the loveliest hamlets on the island, it has just 26 full-time inhabitants, a very pretty church and some great hotels and restaurants. A popular base for hikers, its origins date back to the 13th century and its name probably derives from the Latin 'aureus', meaning 'golden'. Its high point in terms of population

came in the 18th century, when 100 souls lived here, drawn by the extremely fertile land. Sightseeing is limited to the 17th-century church of **Sant Jordi** on a tiny square reached via steps from the main road. Inside, Sant Jordi (St George) is depicted on the high altar, which is made of gold, donated – so legend has it – by the womenfolk of the village. The church's most significant artefact is the crucifix to the right of the altar, made of cypress wood; it's one of the oldest on the island.

From Orient, it's an 11-kilometre (seven-mile) drive of switchbacks and hairpin bends west to **Bunyola**, a proper market town with a scattering of restaurants and bars around the main *plaça*. It's best known as a stop on the Palma–Sóller railway (*see p126* **Ticket to Ride**) and for the most famous brand of local liqueur *palo*, called Túnel (*see p84* **Made in Mallorca & Menorca**).

A few kilometres from town, just before the entrance to the tunnel to Sóller, lie the prettiest gardens on the island, the **Jardins de Alfàbia**, a blissfully shady oasis of water, lush palms and citrus groves radiating out from an old manor house. Several airy rooms in the house can be visited – there's a splendid ceiling in one; another ceiling in the gatehouse has the distinction of being the only Mudéjar coffered ceiling in Mallorca.

★ Jardins de Alfàbia
Ctra. Palma–Sóller, km17 (971 61 31 23). **Open** *Apr-Sept* 9.30am-6.30pm Mon-Sat. *Oct-Mar* 9.30am-5.30pm Mon-Fri; 9.30am-1pm Sat. **Admission** €4.50. **No credit cards**.

Where to eat & drink

Regarded as the best restaurant in **Alaró**, **Traffic** (Plaça de la Vila 8, 971 87 91 17, closed Tue, €€€) specialises in hearty island cooking done with style. There's some imaginative dishes like monkfish and aubergine pie, and octopus with onions. Inside, it's all wood beams and stone, but if it's warm you'll want to be out on the pretty patio. Next door is **Ca'n Punta** (Plaça de la Vila 9, 971 87 94 40, closed Thur and Nov, €€), which also knocks out quality Mallorcan cooking, though in a slightly less formal setting. Good dishes include the *ensalada de gambas* (prawn salad) and the *cabrito a las finas hierbas* (goat with herbs). You can sit outside on the *terraza*, inside in the rather stuffy *comedor* (dining room) or out at the back on a lovely patio. **Sa Fonda** (C/C'an Ros 4, 971 51 05 83, closed Mon, €€) whips up some good local fare, including fresh fish such as *dorada* (gilthead) and *lubina* (sea bass) and various rice dishes at reasonable prices. Drinking options include **Acros** (Plaça Església, no phone, €), which has a small terrace.

On the road up to **Alaró**'s ruined castle, **Es Verger** (971 18 21 26, €) is one of the island's worst-kept secrets; convoys of 4x4s head up the precarious mountain track every Sunday lunchtime. It's a real spit-and-sawdust place, serving traditional food at low prices in a spectacular setting. Its popularity hasn't changed its (very) basic character. A walk up to the castle to build up your appetite followed by a plateful of shoulder of lamb, slow-cooked in deep cave-like ovens (fired by whole branches of olive wood) is a memorable experience.

In **Orient**, the restaurant at the hotel **Dalt Muntanya** (*see below*; closed Nov-Jan, €€€) has a delightful *terraza* looking out to the mountains and serves meaty local dishes like *pierna de cordero* (leg of lamb), *cochinillo asado* (roast suckling pig) and *conejo* (rabbit), served without fuss in a simple, traditional style. Starters are fancier – the ravioli stuffed with mushrooms and crawfish smothered in Mallorcan cheese is particularly tasty. The warm welcome at **Mandala** (C/Nueva 1, 971 61 52 85, closed lunch Fri & Sat and all Mon in Jan-May, Oct, Nov, closed lunch daily and all Sun June-Sept, closed all Dec, €€) is second only to the cooking. The sweet, cottage-style, Swiss-owned restaurant serves excellent Asian-inspired dishes such as Soba noodle soup, sea bass steamed with ginger, and green curry.

Scott's Hotel. *See p159*.

There's also a first-class restaurant at **L'Hermitage** hotel (*see below*; €€€€).

Adjacent to the Jardins de Alfàbia (*see p160*) is **Restaurante Ses Porxeres** (Ctra. Palma–Sóller 17, 971 61 37 62, www.sesporxeres.com, closed Mon, dinner Sun and July-mid Sept, €€€), a very classy establishment in a wonderful setting that serves excellent Mallorcan cuisine, including pheasant and lamb dishes.

Where to stay

Can Xim (Plaça de la Vila 8, 971 87 91 17, www.canxim.com, closed Nov, doubles €80-€100) on **Alaró**'s main square has eight clean, fresh rooms, all en suite and air-conditioned, and with a good-sized pool.

A few minutes outside the village, on the road to the castle, is the pleasant *agroturismo*, **Son Penyaflor** (Camí del Castell, 971 51 00 71, www.sonpenyaflor.com, doubles €98), with seven simple rooms in its own grounds, nestling below the mountains.

A further accommodation alternative nearby, located between Alaró and Orient, is the classy *hotel rural* **S'Olivaret** (Ctra. Alaró–Orient, km3, 971 51 08 89, www.solivaret.com, closed Nov-Feb, doubles €101 incl breakfast), which has indoor and outdoor pools as well as a jacuzzi. But the super-duper hotel of the area is the fabulous **L'Hermitage** (971 18 03 03, mobile 638 08 82 05, www.hermitage-hotel.com, closed Nov-Feb, doubles €169-€219 incl breakfast, restaurant €€€€), just outside Orient. Whether you go for the (four) older rooms in the monastery or the (20) suite-chalets built out the back – the latter are newer but more spacious and more private – there's little to do here but stare at the fruit trees, play tennis, take a dip in the outdoor pool, detox in the sauna and then tuck into the great food at the hotel's posh rustic-style restaurant.

A much cheaper alternative in **Orient** is the **Dalt Muntanya** (Ctra. Bunyola–Orient, km10, 971 61 53 73, www.daltmuntanya.net, closed Nov-Jan, doubles €105), which has been completely refurbished from the original *hostal* into a modern, stylish and extremely comfortable three-star hotel in its own grounds. The design is rural chic, so it's all big beds, soft duvets, airy rooms, marble bathrooms, stone tiles and wooden shutters. Many of the 18 rooms have great views of the mountains and all are different: No.16 is split-level with a bathroom on the upper floor; No.18 has a tiny skylight; No.1 has a kidney-shaped bath; and No.8 looks out on to the patio. For the quality, this place is a bargain. It's worth opting for half-board: for €18 extra per person you get to eat in the excellent restaurant (*see above*).

CENTRAL MALLORCA

CENTRAL MALLORCA

Biniculture

Binissalem's producers are still the champions of Mallorca's wine industry.

If you've never been to Mallorca, you've probably never sampled Mallorcan wine. And, until fairly recently, you weren't missing very much. Its small-scale production and basic quality in the last century meant that little island wine was exported even as far as mainland Spain, never mind further afield.

During Moorish times, though, wine was produced extensively along the west coast of Mallorca (and, to a lesser extent, in the east too) and widely exported, right up until the islands' vines were wiped out by the phylloxera virus in the 1890s.

The first step in a local viticulture revival came with the founding in the 1930s of the José Luis Ferrer bodega in Binissalem. Progress was slow, however, and it was not until 1991 that the Binissalem area was bestowed a *Denominació de Origen* (DO), and the rebirth began in earnest. In 2000, a second DO was recognised: Pla i Llevant, covering parts of central and eastern Mallorca. Today, you'll find a surprisingly diverse and frequently excellent range of wines on offer in island restaurants and bars.

Some of the grapes used are familiar international varieties; others are indigenous. Mineral-nosed Callet is popular in red blends, though tannin-rich Manto Negro is the most commonly encountered local cultivar (all Binissalem DO reds contain a minimum of 50 per cent Manto Negro). Indigenous white varieties include Giro Blanc, Gargollosa and aromatic Moll (or Prensal Blanc; Binissalem DO whites have at least 70 per cent Moll).

Of the island's 20-plus producers, names to look out for among the Binissalem DO include the ubiquitous José Luis Ferrer (the reds shade the whites; try a reserva, resembling a light Rioja) and Consell's Hereus de Ribas (its red-blend Cabrera is outstanding, if expensive). Among the most interesting Pla i Levant DO producers are Miquel Gelabert from Manacor (who isn't afraid to try unusual grape blends, though his straight Chardonnay is also a winner) and Petra's Miquel Oliver (who made his name with his Muscat Original, an exquisite dry Moscatel).

Don't be afraid to stray from DO bottles. Some of Mallorca's most interesting wines are labelled simply Vin de la Terra. The most celebrated example is multi-award-winning (and consequently pricey and hard-to-find) Anima Negra's An, made with 100 per cent Callet, previously thought to be a grape suitable only for blending.

A tasting tour at one of Binissalem's bodegas makes for a fun afternoon. Those open to visitors include pretty **Vins Nadal** (C/Ramón Llull 2, 971 511 058, www.vinsnadal.net), artsy **Macià Batle** (Camí de Coanegra s/n, Santa María del Camí, 971 140 014, www.maciabatle.com), big players **José Luis Ferrer** (C/Conquistador 103, Binissalem, 971 51 10 50/www.vinosferrer.com) and **Vins Ripoll** (C/Pere Estruch 25, 971 51 10 28), and pint-sized **Can Vinagre** (C/Paborde Jaume 17A, 971 62 03 58) and **Jaume de Puntiró** (Plaça Nova 23, 971 62 00 23). The website www.binissalemdo.com is an excellent resource when it comes to getting to grips with the local vino.

José Luis Ferrer.

The **Son Palou Hotel & Restaurant** (Plaça Eglèsia, 971 14 82 82, www.sonpalou. com, doubles €117-€214 incl breakfast) is also understandably popular. Combining rural chic with a hip atmosphere, the 12 individually decorated rooms have rocking chairs, wood floors, four-poster beds and Berber rugs, while the surrounding sprawling gardens span 100 hectares of land, making it perfect for those who enjoy hiking. It's particularly popular for winter breaks when roaring fires light up the plush living rooms. It also has an excellent, romantic restaurant specialising in suckling pig and home-grown veggies.

If you want to stay near **Bunyola**, try **Finca Sa Màniga** (C/Afores s/n, 971 61 34 28, www.fincasamaniga.com, doubles €95-€130 incl breakfast); it has four spacious, air-conditioned rooms and bikes for guests' use.

Resources

Police station
Alaró *C/Petit 1 (91 51 00 02).*
Bunyola *C/San Jose 2 (mobile 609 35 81 65).*

Post office
Alaró *Avda. Constitució 37 (971 51 03 09).*
Bunyola *C/Mare de Déu de les Neus 8 (no phone).*

INCA

Inca is the island's third-largest town (Manacor is the second) and is predominantly industrial rather than tourist-oriented, with the exception of the Thursday morning market, which brings sightseers in their droves. Traditionally, it was a place famed for its leather goods, though the majority of the leather goods you see for sale in the market today will be from Morocco. The demise of the leather industry, like so many places on the island, sees Inca turning its sights to the tourist euro for salvation, clearly evident in the money being spent to spruce the place up. That said, there are a few notable companies such as **Farrutx** and **Camper** that are still proud to call Inca home. The former sells smart, fashion-conscious leather footwear and bags for men and women, with shops all over Spain and beyond (visit www.farrutx.com); the latter well-known international brand made its name in the 1990s with its funky, chunky yet comfy and practical footwear, but has its roots firmly in the Mallorcan shoemaking tradition. Its **RECamper** outlet shop (*see p157*), which sells end-of-line and one-off shoes at lower prices, is located on the outskirts of town, along with a number of other warehouse stores. If you are in the market for a man bag, a leather jacket, or bag and boots at

a 20 per cent discount, or if you've secretly always coveted a mink stole, head for **Pieles de Mallorca** (Avda. Jaume II 215, 971 88 17 91) on the main road out of town in the direction of Pollença. Next door, **Mumper** is a more upmarket version of the same.

The biggest and best market is on *Dijous Bo* (Good Thursday), the first Thursday in November. The rest of the time, there's a laid-back bustle to the commercial centre, with some interesting boutiques like **Pomelo** (C/Sirena 3, no phone) selling colourful household objects and kimonos, and some wonderfully atmospheric cellar restaurants.

Where to stay, eat & drink

The best of Inca's restaurants are located in old wine cellars. One of the most famous is **Celler Can Amer** (C/Pau 39, 971 50 12 61, closed Sat & Sun June-Oct, closed dinner Sun Nov-May, €€), which has a good reputation, though it's a bit stuck in an old-style haute cuisine time warp of gloopy reductions and overblown combinations. Look for lighter or simpler-sounding dishes, such as quail roasted in honey and orange or salt cod marinated with peppers and tapenade.

Alternatively, **Can Ripoll** (C/Jaume Armengol 4, 971 50 00 24, www.canripoll.com, open 9.30am-4pm, 7.30pm-midnight, closed Sun dinner) has smooth flagstone floors and polished barrels, some papered with black and white photos of patrons gone by. It offers a fairly basic menu of omelettes and salads, as well as more adventurous (sometimes scarily so) offerings. It also has a lovely patio shaded by soaring palm trees.

Celler Sa Travesa (C/Murta 16, 971 50 00 49, 10am-4pm, 7.30-11pm, closed Fri) is more homely feeling, also with a sweet covered patio filled with plants. Everything is home-made and the lunch menu is good value, especially if you're visiting in the cooler months offering

---

INSIDE TRACK
CAN RIPOLL

Visitors to Spain often cower at the nation's culinary timetable of late lunch and late, late dinner. A notable exception to the tardy rule is **Can Ripoll**, where patrons turn up as early as 12.30pm – practically the mid-morning as far as locals are concerned. The sensible luncheon hour means that all you have to get used to is the taste of *frito mallorquín* (all the nasty bits) or battered brains, though kill-joys can order omelettes.

CENTRAL MALLORCA

ribstickers like *potaje de lentils* (lentil soup), marinated fish *escabeche* or stuffed aubergines and pud for under €10.

The **Pambolera** (Sa Plaça 22, no phone), in the adjacent Sa Plaça square, with its stately church Santa Maria La Major and newly renovated arcades, is good for a quick bite; **La Valentina** (Santa Maria La Major 5L, 971 502 929) is more upmarket and does good coffee as well as Latin American dishes such as *ceviche* (raw fish marinated in lime juice), *pico de gallo* (chopped salad with a jalapeño kick), chicken *mole* and margaritas. Next door, **Café Matias** (Santa Maria La Major 10, no phone) has recently had a makeover and is as popular as ever for a coffee and a gossip.

In the summer heat, a pleasant outdoors alternative is to head out of town to **Celler Son Aloy** (Ctra. Inca–Sencelles, km3, 971 88 38 24, www.sonaloy.com, closed dinner Mon, Sun & all Tue, €€), which supplies some of the grapes used by the famous **Bodegas Santa Catarina**. Various meats, including *gazapo* (young rabbit), lamb chops, sausages and belly of pork, are barbecued on a rather spartan patio surrounded by acres of vines. Or if you're just thirsty rather than hungry, you can indulge in a tasting of some of the very reasonably priced Santa Catarina wines.

There's no real reason for staying in Inca, and indeed there isn't really anywhere to stay. However, just outside town there's a very pleasant four-star country manor, which also has an excellent restaurant. **Casa del Virrey** (Ctra. Inca–Sencelles, km2.4, 971 88 10 18, www.casadelvirrey.net, doubles €101-€150 incl breakfast) presents a gracious home to the world, with mature palms and white-cushioned garden furniture in its spacious forecourt. Mature gardens hide a lovely swimming pool. The hotel's 16 rooms are smartly comfortable, with lots of antiques and rich fabrics, and you will feel just as at ease in the welcoming public rooms. The chef at the hotel's **Restaurante Doña Irene** (closed Mon, €€€) produces wonderfully rich dishes, such as quails stuffed with foie gras and truffle sauce.

Another agreeable accommodation option in the area is **Son Vivot** (Ctra. Palma–Alcúdia, km30, 971 88 01 24, www.sonvivot.com, doubles €140 incl breakfast), a functioning agricultural estate that offers four bright guest rooms, a pool and alfresco dinner on request.

Resources

Police station
Inca *Plaça 1 de Maig s/n (971 88 08 18).*

Post office
Inca *Plaça Àngel 12 (971 50 04 23).*

SELVA, CAMPANET, CAIMARI, MOSCARÍ & BINIBONA

North of Inca, in the foothills of the mountains, lies a patchwork of industrious small towns and appealing villages, linked by winding lanes that are popular with cyclists. Just outside town, **Santa Magdalena** is a little-visited hermitage found at the top of a long, winding lane through holm oaks. At the top you're rewarded with 360° views and a pleasantly shaded picnic area with barbecue pits. There's also basic restaurant **Santa Magdalena** (971 50 18 72, closed Tue) with a lunch menu for €10. The main settlements are the leather-working town of **Selva** (four kilometres north of Inca) and ceramics-ville **Campanet** (six kilometres east of Selva).

It also has the area's only real 'sight': the **Coves de Campanet**. This karst cave complex of 3,200 square metres (34,400 square feet) was discovered by workers in 1945 and opened to the public three years later. Several chambers go down as far as 300 metres (984 feet), and the Sala de la Palmera (Palm Tree Chamber) and Sala del Llac (Lake Chamber), which surrounds a crystalline lake, are quite beautiful.

This tiny portion of Es Raiguer takes in the handsome stone-built village of **Caimari**, more run-of-the-mill **Moscari** and the pretty hamlet of **Binibona** (a great base for walking). And, because of its proximity to both the mountains and the wonderful coves of the north-east coast, it has become a hotspot for *agroturismos*.

Coves de Campanet
Ctra. Palma–Alcúdia, km39, Campanet (971 51 61 30/www.covesdecampanet.com). **Open** *Apr-Oct* 10am-7pm daily. *Nov-Mar* 10am-6pm daily. **Admission €9. No credit cards**.

Where to stay & eat

In **Selva**, the six-room **Sa Bisbal** (Plaça Santa Catalina Tomàs 1, 971 51 57 24, www.hotelsa bisbal.com) is located in a lovely 17th-century building at the top of the town. The pick of the rooms has a beamed ceiling, massive windows looking out towards the mountains and its own terrace. There's a pool too.

The prime spot to eat and drink in Selva is **Es Parc** (Parque Recreativo, 971 51 51 45, noon-3.30pm Mon-Thur in winter, noon-3.30pm, 7.30pm-midnight daily in summer), a chic restaurant-bar in the centre of town, with a huge terrace with excellent views of the Tramuntana.

Just north of Selva, the villages of Caimari, Binibona and Moscari are the focus for a clutch of rural hotels and fincas. The jewel in what is a really rather lovely crown is **Can Furiós** (Camí Vell Binibona, 971 51 57 51, www.canfurios.com,

Coves de Campanet.

closed mid Dec-mid Jan, doubles €165-€225). Set in the tiny hamlet of Binibona, with views across fields and orchards to the mountains, it is one of the most relaxed and seductive hotels in Mallorca. Four blissfully comfortable rooms (with vast bathrooms) are in the main building, a converted country house, while there are three suites with terraces in a newer building. Gardens redolent with jasmine, herbs and lemon blossom tumble down to a good-sized pool. The candlelit restaurant, **Sa Tafoneta** (open dinner Tue-Sun, set dinner €40), is also excellent.

Other fine choices in the area include **Finca Albellons** (Parc Natural, Binibona, 971 87 50 69, www.albellons.com, closed mid Nov-mid Feb, doubles €171), **C'an Casetes** (C/Horitzo 14, 971 87 35 62, mobile 657 81 12 97, www.cancasetes. com, doubles €108-€130 incl breakfast) and **C'an Calco** (C/Campanet 1, 971 51 52 60, www.cancalco.com, closed mid Jan-mid Feb, doubles €112 incl breakfast). The latter also has an excellent restaurant, run by two chaps from Alcúdia who own a boat and are happy to take guests fishing (expect a 6am wake-up call) to catch their own dinner. Non-fishermen are also welcome to enjoy the no-choice four-course menu (€€€). Booking is advisable.

Campanet also has its fair share of charming hotels. **Monnàber Nou** (971 87 71 76, www. monnaber.com, doubles €125-€210) is an old manor house that nudges right up against the Sierra d'en Pas d'en Basquera and is surrounded by fig and carob groves. Furnishings are a bit fusty, as is the reception, but the labrynthine gardens and cobbled terraces and patios do give it a magical air. There's a pool, a spa, a shop selling farm produce and an excellent restaurant, **Es Mirador de Monnàber Nou** (€€€€).

A couple of fields over, **Monnàber Vell** (Monnàber Vell s/n, 971 51 61 31, www.monnaber vell.com, closed Dec-Jan, doubles €110-€159 incl breakfast) is a stylish farmhouse with bags more charm and an intimate feel. It has an infinity pool that seems to drop into woodland at the base of the mountains. the restaurant is for guests only.

Nearby, and great for small groups and families, is **Fangar** (Ctra. Antigua de Campanet –Pollença, km5, 971 45 70 44, mobile 610 23 80 55, www.fangar.com, 2 people €99-€135, 4 people €135-€175), a huddle of cute farm cottages, each simply decorated and each boasting a real wood-burning stove (wood supplied free of charge). All have two bedrooms and adequate kitchenettes set in gardens filled with fruit trees and tropical flowers. The shared pool is protected from Tramuntana winds by majestic poplar trees.

Resources

Police station
Campanet *Plaça Major 24 (mobile 650 448 705).*
Selva *Plaça Major 1 (971 87 52 69).*

Post office
Campanet *Sant Miquel (no phone).*
Selva *C/Aires de Montanya 12 (no phone).*

GETTING THERE

By bus
From Palma there are 6 buses Mon-Fri (4 Sat, 3 Sun) to Inca via Santa Maria, Consell, Binissalem and Lloseta, as well as 6-8 buses Mon-Sat (5 Sun) from Palma to Bunyola.

By train
There are 29 trains Mon-Fri and 26 on Sat & Sun between Palma and Inca (36mins), via Marratxi (14mins), Santa Maria (20mins), Alaró-Consell (24mins), Binissalem (28mins) and Lloseta (32mins).

Es Pla

Authentic market towns in a land that time forgot.

The vast central plain is bisected by the MA-15 Palma–Manacor road, which runs through farmland overlooked by the sanctuary-topped minor peaks of the Serra de Randa. A handful of mildly diverting towns – Algaida, Randa, Montuïri, Porreres, Petra – and a couple of worthwhile tourist attractions lie on either side of the main road. Away from it, the only noises you're likely to encounter are birdsong and the swish of a passing phalanx of lycra-clad German cyclists.

Sineu is historically the most important town in the northern Pla, its long-standing importance marked by its direct connection by road to Palma. It's also the most rewarding and lively base in the region. The countryside is criss-crossed by winding roads, lined with honey-stone walls; it's a model-railway landscape of spongy green trees, isolated farm buildings and terraces of citrus groves and vines. Yet the Bay of Alcúdia sands are only 15 minutes' drive away.

SA POBLA, MURO & MARIA DE LA SALUT

The MA-13 between Palma and Alcúdia effectively divides the towns of the foothills from those of the plain. Sizeable **Sa Pobla**, a few kilometres west of hilly Campanet, and just a ten-minute drive from the coast, has that dusty tumbleweed feel typical of an agricultural Es Pla settlement and there's no real reason to visit unless you dig vegetables (literally); there are three harvests a year – of potatoes, haricot beans and a variety of veg – attracting seasonal workers. Surprisingly, Sa Pobla boasts two museums (in the same building), the **Museu d'Art Contemporani i Jugeta Antigua de Sa Pobla** features two collections: one of contemporary works by Mallorcan artists, and the other of toys. It also has its own winery, **Bodegas Crestatx**, which can be visited.

Between here and Muro is Mallorca's windmill graveyard, all stumps and broken sails against a backdrop of deep-red earth. It's worth the drive through just to get a sense of the island before it got 'discovered'. And it's a popular route with cyclists for its ease. **Muro** was declared a town in 1300 by Jaume II (which explains why its street plan has a more organic feel than that of its near-neighbour) and it's the nicer town of this particular bunch, with a pretty oblong central square, **Plaça de Sant Marti**, dotted with fine townhouses, terrace cafés and restaurants; the imposing church of **Sant Joan Baptista** and the 15th-century La Sang chapel are definitely worthy of a peek. The **Museu Etnològic**, a miscellaneous collection of jars, tools, folk music instruments and an old waterwheel, attracts few visitors. There's also a bullring (971 53 73 29) that was

INSIDE TRACK
EMBOTITS ARTESANALS MATAS

Embotits Aretesanals Matas is one of only a few artisanal sausage and cured meat makers in the whole of Spain, never mind the Balearics. Its products are made using high-quality pork from Girona in Catalunya, natural seasonings and no artificial ingredients of any sort. The *sobrassada* covered in pimiento (pepper) and the *camaiot* (pork meat stuffed into skin rather than a stomach) are both Matas-patented and unavailable anywhere else.

chiselled out of the rocky landscape in 1910; it occasionally welcomes big-name matadors. Round the back of Muro is the **Passeig de Sa Riba** – formerly the town walls – with benches looking over the fields and out to sea. It's a good place for a stroll after lunch.

Other towns of the northern Pla, like **Llubí** and **Santa Margalida**, are pleasant for a drinks stop but otherwise contain little of interest. **Maria de la Salut** (eight kilometres south of Muro) is a small, pretty village, its streets surrounded by terraced gardens of cacti and citrus groves, with the odd gamboling sheep adding to the Arcadian air. It's worth passing through (unless you're a vegetarian) in order to visit **Embotits Artesanals Matas** (C/Artà s/n, 971 52 56 21, www.embotits-matas.com, closed Sat & Sun) to stock up on great Spanish deli staples.

Bodegas Crestatx
C/Joan Sindic s/n, Sa Pobla (971 54 07 41/ www.bodegascrestatx.com). **Open** 9am-1pm daily. **Admission** free.

Museu d'Art Contemporani i Jugeta Antigua de Sa Pobla
C/Antoni Maura 6, Sa Pobla (971 54 23 89). **Open** 10am-2pm, 4-8pm Tue-Sat; 10am-2pm Sun. **Admission** (combined) €4; €2.70 reductions; free under-10s. **No credit cards**.

Museu Etnològic
C/Major 15, Muro (971 86 06 47). **Open** 10am-3pm Tue, Wed, Fri, Sat; 10am-3pm, 5-8pm Thur. **Admission** €2.40; €1.20 reductions; free Sat. **No credit cards**.

Where to stay

Of all the villages your best bet for a spot of lunch is probably **Muro**. Plaça de Sant Marti has a handful of cafés popular with cyclists, all offering basic German-inspired dishes such as chicken breast in heavy cream sauce, or hot dogs. If you are looking for something more authentic, head to the main plaza by the ajuntament (town hall), where you'll find **Bar Sa Fonda** (C/Sant Jaume 1, 971 53 79 65), which specialises in typical dishes of the region such as pork and cabbage, and tripe, trotters and slivers of congealed blood skewered around olives and grilled. On the road between Santa Margalida and Petra, **Ses Tarragones** (C/Santa Margalida, km1, 971 85 81 22) does good barbecued food and *pa amb oli* on a pretty terrace. It's popular with families in the summer, and the lunch menu is good value.

Between the village of **Búger** and **Sa Pobla** is a lovely finca: **Son Pons** (Ctra. Búger–Sa Pobla s/n, 971 87 71 52, mobile 649 45 37 76, www.sonpons.com, doubles €100-€200 incl breakfast). It's a characterful 16th-century building that now contains six bedrooms, with a pool outside and a ten-minute drive to the beach.

In **Maria de la Salut**, **Casa Girasol** (Casa Son Roig, 971 85 80 07, www.casagirasol.de, closed Nov-Jan, doubles €139-€179) is a charming home with a rich heritage. The farmhouse was in the hands of the Font i Roig family from the 14th century to 1989. Some of the house's original features are still put to good use, such as the wood-fired bread oven, the well and the tiny chapel, where marriages and christenings can still be held. There are eight

Embotits Artesanals Matas.

Muro. See p166.

tasteful rooms and plenty of space for lounging around the patios, shady gardens and pool.

Another fine place to unwind, located between Sineu and Maria de la Salut, is **Son Fogueró** (Ctra. Sineu–Maria de la Salut, km2, 971 52 53 43, www.sonfoguero.com, closed Nov & Dec, doubles €203-€278), a gorgeous 300-year-old finca. Owned by interior designer Maria Antonia Carbonell and her husband Pere Alemany, Son Fogueró is a super-private haven that attracts creatives. The design of its five suites encompasses natural stone walls, beamed ceilings, antique furniture and striking modern art. There's an honesty bar, a restaurant, a pool and pretty gardens, specked with modern sculptures by the owners' sculptor son.

A few kilometres inland from unappealing Can Picafort on the Bay of Alcúdia, off the road to Muro, is classy **Finca Son Serra** (Predio Son Serra, Ctra. Muro–Can Picafort, km6.5, 971 53 79 80, www.finca-son-serra.de, closed Nov-Apr, doubles €130-€140). This 18th-century house is set in parkland lush with palms, fruit trees and flowering climbing plants, and has a big pool and views out to sea.

Resources

Police station
Muro *Plaça Comte d'Empúries 1 (971 53 76 49)*.
Sa Pobla *Plaça D'es Tren 15 (971 86 22 86)*.

Post office
Muro *C/Gran 99 (971 54 00 85)*.

SINEU

Sineu is the highlight of the central plains, and the geographical heart of Mallorca, located as it is 33 kilometres (21 miles) east of Palma and almost midway between Inca and Manacor. It has a genteel air, evident in the smart streets, spruced-up sandstone townhouses, boutique stores and posh hotels and restaurants (many within historic wine cellars).

During the Middle Ages, Sineu was the key town of the interior, and Jaume II built a royal palace here, though nothing remains. The cute little main square, simply called Sa Plaça, is dominated by the church of **Santa Maria de Sineu** (971 52 00 40), dating from 1549, with its unusual seven-storey pyramidal spire. It's a huge structure, indicating the town's historical significance, with a recently restored interior that is pleasingly simple and light-filled, with modern stained glass. You can visit on Wednesday mornings (market day) and entrance is a measly €1 via the adjoining Plaça de Sant Marc. Here you'll see a bombastic statue of the town's emblem, the winged lion of Sineu, honouring the town's patron St Mark.

Sineu is increasingly being discovered, and though it retains an authentically local air, it seems the whole island comes out for its historic Wednesday market, the oldest on the island, dating back to 1306. It's also the only remaining livestock market on the island where, along with the chickens, turkeys and ducks, you may also see pigs, sheep and occasionally horses on Plaça El Fossar, presided over by a monument to Mallorcan cyclist Francesc Alomar, who trained here. Head for Sa Plaça for a more leisurely amble among stalls sagging beneath piles of fragrant olives, freshly plucked fruit and vegetables, cheese and charcuterie, alongside a mountain of African sarongs and leather handbags. Look out for pretty bundles of *pa de higos* – figs boiled with herbs and lemons, wrapped in fig leaves and tied up with marsh grass.

Like Inca, Sineu is particularly notable for one annual market (and also its spring festival) – the **Sa Fira** – which takes place on the first Sunday in May. Unlike Inca, it is also slowly but surely becoming a boutique haven. **Antik & Deco** (C/Tavernes 1, 971 85 51 42, mornings only) is a real old curiosity shop filled with island antiques ranging from lace and linen tablecloths, to beaded clutch bags, to vintage basketware. Next door, **Pingdai** (Sa Plaça 13, 971 85 52 49) stocks fabulous chunky knits, evening dresses, sparkly tops and glam designer jeans. And over the road **Valldaram** (Sa Plaça 9, 971 85 53 53) is where jewellery designer Martí de Valldaram showcases his own and other small Spanish designers' work. He also has a workshop in Inca (*see p163*). In an old railway station building, the **Centre d'Art S'Estació** art gallery shows an eclectic collection of work by local artists, all for sale.

FREE Centre d'Art S'Estació

C/Estació 2 (971 52 07 50/www.sineuestacio. com). **Open** 9.30am-2pm, 4-7pm Mon-Fri; 10am-1pm Sat. **Admission** free.

Where to stay

Few foreign visitors stay in Sineu, though folk are slowly waking up to its charms. **Can Joan Capo** (C/Degà Joan Rotger 4, 971 85 50 75, www.canjoancapo.com, doubles €160-€234) is a new eight-room boutique on the edge of the old town. Restoration has very cleverly incorporated old and new, salvaging farmhouse furniture and island antiques and turning them into something contemporary and comfortable. The overall look and feel of the place is fresh and modern, laid-back yet elegant, with 21st-century comforts like Wi-Fi providing the cherry on top. The restaurant is excellent too.

The **Hotel Son Cleda** (Plaça Es Fossar 7, 971 52 10 38, www.hotelsoncleda.com, doubles €87 incl breakfast) is 300 years old and retains its original features, including an impressive marble staircase, ornate glass chandelier and Mallorcan antiques. Guests have use of a walled terrace at the back of the house and all the comforts of four-star accommodation (air-con, minibar, internet access) at three-star prices, plus lovely friendly service.

Located on the other side of the hill, the **Hotel León de Sineu** (C/dels Bous 129, 971 52 02 11, www.hotel-leondesineu.com, closed mid Nov-Jan, doubles €104-€125 incl breakfast) has a beautiful, leafy walled garden with a sauna and a small pool. The rooms are light and airy, with white walls and linen and original period tiles on the bathroom floors (ask for one overlooking the garden). In the centre of town, **Celler Ca'n**

Font (Sa Plaça 18, hotel 971 52 02 95, restaurant 971 52 03 13, www.canfont.com, doubles €59 incl breakfast) has basic but pleasant rooms with large bathrooms (all with tubs) right on the square. Downstairs the restaurant is lined with huge, ancient oak barrels and serves traditional country fare.

Just outside of Sineu is **Sa Casa Rotja** (Ctra. Sineu–Muro, km3, 971 18 50 27, www.sacasarotja.com, doubles €75-€90 incl breakfast), located just off the Sineu–Muro road, which offers a variety of cottages with one, two and three double rooms, and a communal pool.

Heading south out of the pretty hamlet of **Lloret de Vista Allegre** towards Montuïri, you'll see a sign for **Finca Sa Rota d'en Palerm** on the left (Ctra. Lloret de Vista Alegre–Montuïri, km0.8, 971 52 11 00, www. sa-rota.com, apartment for 2 or junior suite with terrace €135-€167, house for 4 €223-€279). This friendly, family-run old finca has apartments, junior suites and a house for four with its own private entrance, all kitted out with antique furniture (the owner restores it herself). You can see all the way to the Tramuntana from the secluded apartments' terraces. There are hammocks slung between orange trees and a sheltered outdoor pool. Guests and visitors can eat good home cooking at the finca if they reserve in advance.

Where to eat & drink

Of Sineu's *celler* restaurants, **Celler Es Grop** (C/Major 18, 971 52 01 87, closed Mon and last wk of June, 1st wk of July) is the real deal, serving lots of offal and fried unknowns in an old-fashioned bodega lined with giant barrels strung with chilli peppers and cluttered with ancient wine bottles. **Celler Ca'n Font** (*see above*) is more intimate. Next door is **Cafeteria Sa Plaça** (Sa Plaça 17, 971 52 06 64, closed Mon), a bustling, traditional tapas bar beloved by locals for morning coffee and delicious little dishes.

INSIDE TRACK
CELLER CA'N CASTANYER

Celler Ca'n Castanyer (C/de l'Esperança 1, just off Sa Plaça, no phone) is an unusual picnic spot, hugely popular among locals on market day. Housed in a basement bodega and lined with barrels, the deal is you bring the food, the celler will provide the wine. A ceremonial lighting of the fire takes place on the first Saturday in November.

CENTRAL MALLORCA

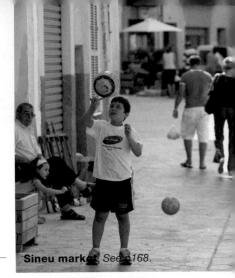
Sineu market. See p168.

Moli d'En Pau (Ctra. Santa Margarita 25, 971 85 51 16, closed Mon, €€) is located in a 16th-century flour mill, over the rail tracks on the road to Maria de la Salut, and not for the faint of heart. Dishes include earthy tongue and tripe concoctions, fresh fish and grilled meats. You can dine to a chorus of songbirds on the garden patio.

In terms of drinking, there's little to choose between the cafés of Plaça Es Fossar, with the notable exception of the terrace of **Hotel Son Cleda** (*see p169*, €), which is by far the chicest spot in town to sip a beer. It also offers an eclectic and keenly priced selection of excellent snacks and light meals – the likes of imaginative salads, Provençal-style hake, lasagne and even Cornish pasties.

Resources

Police station
Sineu *C/Sant Francesc 10 (971 52 00 27/ mobile 639 15 00 15)*.

Post office
Sineu *C/Carril 4 (971 52 02 04)*.

PETRA, SANT JOAN & VILAFRANCA DE BONANY

Between Sineu and Manacor lie three pleasant villages. Ten kilometres south-east of Sineu is **Petra**, a small town with a lot of soul – literally – that's transformed itself into one of the Es Pla highlights in the last couple of years. It is built around the gigantic, cube-shaped **Iglesia de Fray Junipero Serra**. The famous monk was born Miguel José Serra in 1713 at C/Barracar 6, one of the prettiest parts of town. Better known as the missionary **Junípero Serra**, he went on to found a series of missions in California (including the future cities of San Francisco and San Diego), and is seen by many as the most important European pioneer of the southern American Pacific coast. You'll notice tiles bearing the image of Serra everywhere, many of them wreathed in juniper, and it is

INSIDE TRACK
MIGUEL OLIVERA BODEGA

If you're keen to bring some of the local tipple home with you, a great place to pick some up is the Miquel Olivera bodega (*see right*). As well as the wine being great, it can also provide special packaging boxes approved by AENA (the Spanish aviation authority) so that you can check them in when flying home.

worth heading up to Calle Fray Junipero Serra to the small museum (hours variable, donation requested) and his birthplace on C/Barracar.

The museum's three rooms include models of the nine missions he personally founded, plus Native American arrowheads, pictures and documents. A leaflet is available in (idiosyncratic) English. Three doors down from the museum is the humble Serra family house, which was bought by the Rotary Club of Mallorca and given over to the City of San Francisco in 1932, which returned it to the keeping of Petra in 1981. If the museum is closed, a plaque at its entrance tells you which door to knock on to rouse the custodian. On the little street facing the museum is a series of Majolica panels depicting Serra's missionary foundations.

Take a hike up to the **Ermita de Bonany**, a couple of kilometres south-west of Petra. This is where Serra preached his last sermon before heading off to the Americas. It's one of the easier hermitages to reach on foot, but it's still a bit of a climb, rewarded by wonderful views over Es Pla. And then treat yourself to a visit to the **Miquel Olivera** bodega (C/Font 26, 971 561 117, www.miqueloliver.com), right in the centre of town. Pilar Oliver is one of only a few women oenologists on the island, and makes some of its finest wine (2 whites, 2 roses, 6 reds). Her Mont Ferrutx uses three of the island's red grape varieties, resulting in a delightfully fruity, chocolatey red at the bargain price of €6.70 a bottle if you buy direct. Visits to the winery are free and include a tasting. Booking in advance is advised.

Seven kilometres west of Petra is tiny **Sant Joan** – all squat sandstone houses and green shutters. There's a sanctuary here – the

Santuari de la Consolació – built on a knoll overlooking the town. It's in pristine condition, thanks to a restoration undertaken by Sant Joan residents in the 1950s and 1960s.

Just outside Sant Joan is **Els Calderers** (signposted at Ctra. Palma–Manacor, km37). This rambling old manor house used to belong to the noble Verí family, who employed 38 people at one point to oversee the vineyards that surrounded it until the 1870s phylloxera epidemic wiped out the vines. The house, which dates from 1750, has been restored to its late 19th-century condition and the well-organised self-guided tour takes you through more than 20 rooms around a light-filled central courtyard. The restoration is exquisite. Among the rooms are a private chapel and atmospheric wine cellar (where you can sample *vino tinto* from the barrel), a vaulted reception room and the master of the house's office. Outside there are pens containing the types of animals that the family would have kept – a cow, goats, pigs, sheep, hens and turkeys. A café serves snacks; take them outside and enjoy this lovely spot.

The first settlement of any size on the MA-15 Manacor–Palma road, coming from Manacor, is **Vilafranca de Bonany**. The town's shops are famed for their colourful displays of fresh Es Pla produce; look out for curvaceous gourds, the wrinkled deep rust-red tomatoes (*tomatigues de ramallet*) and various different varieties of melon. This is in fact the melon capital of Mallorca and the harvest is celebrated with a festival on the first weekend of September. It's worth coming for the Wednesday morning market to stock up on produce without the crowds, and to take a peak at the extraordinary Iglesia Parroquial with Christ perched on top of the bell tower.

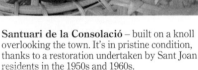

Els Calderers

Ctra. Palma–Manacor, km37 (971 52 60 69/ www.todoesp.es/els-calderers). **Open** *Apr-Oct* 10am-6pm daily. *Nov-Mar* 10am-5pm daily. **Admission** €8; €4 reductions. **No credit cards**.

Where to stay & eat

Petra has a surprising number of good restaurants, including one of the best *celler* restaurants in Es Pla, **Es Celler** (C/Hospital 46, 971 56 10 56, closed Mon, €€), which serves reliably good wood oven-roasted meat in a hearty country style. The complimentary local black olives and rustic brown bread are worth the visit alone. Also good for traditional fare is **Ca Sa Viuda** (C/Pou 37, 971 83 01 00), a charmingly old-fashioned Grandma's kitchen with menus starting at €20. Dishes range from grilled quail and *frito Mallorquín* (fried offal with garlic, pepper and potato) to roast lamb.

Located by Serra's church, the newly opened **Miratar** (971 56 19 20, mobile 661 84 12 32, www.miratar.com, closed Tue and Jan-Feb) is a trendy bar, restaurant and chill-out lounge with a wonderful terrace. From here, head down the slope and take a right to come to Plaça Ramón Llull, the main square for bars. **Café Ca'n Tomeu** (No.47, 971 56 10 23, closed Mon, €€), established in 1945, has terrace tables shaded by umbrellas where you can eat tapas, salads and *pa amb oli*.

The most upmarket place in town is the hotel-restaurant **Sa Plaça Petra** (No.4, 971 56 16 46, www.saplacapetra.com, doubles €80-€110, restaurant closed Tue and all Nov, €€). It has a pretty walled garden with lemon trees and two pint-sized dining rooms dressed with crisp white linen, crystal glassware and island

A Very Big House in the Country

Our pick of the islands' best agroturismos and rural retreats.

Can Guillo.

Cases de Son Barbassa.

Many of the most unusual places to stay on both islands are *agroturismos*, a word that's now become something of a catch-all for rural hideaways. These can range from design mag-type properties – with infinity pools, day spas and trendy restaurants in gutted old fincas – to more homely and basic working farms with a few rooms to rent. The former are perfect for splurging on for a romantic break, the latter are better for those on a budget and those with kids. Mallorca has seen an explosion in *agroturismos* in recent years, symptomatic of the country's aim to move its tourist image away from egg-and-chips-splattered resorts and towards rustic relaxation. Menorca, so far, has been less quick to catch on. There are bargains to be had on both islands, particularly off-season, and it's always worth checking the websites for special offers.

On the north-eastern tip of Mallorca, the **Cases de Son Barbassa** (*see p199*) is modern and close to some of the island's best beaches, set within almond and olive groves. The trendy Ibiza-esque poolside daybeds enclosed in billowing sail-like tents are often featured in the travel supplements of Sunday newspapers. Also in the north-east but just slightly further south you'll find **Can Simoneta** (*see p201*), which continues the style-conscious theme with eye-popping clifftop views, a private beach and decor that's slick enough for the pages of *Wallpaper**.

Luxury like this doesn't come cheap, though, so those looking for somewhere more pocket-friendly to chill out in might like to look south (inland) to **Es Passarell** (*see p174*), a warm and characterful rural retreat with cats, creaky old donkey carts and blooming meadows surrounding five apartments and five rooms.

In the western interior of the island, in the somnolent valley of Orient, you'll find the **Son Palou Hotel & Restaurant** (*see p163*), an elegant mountain hideout for hikers that dates back to the 14th century. It's particularly popular in winter when hikers can explore the surrounding 100 hectares (247 acres) of land and then return to a roaring fire in the rooms. In summer, a drink on the terrace takes some beating, with its views of the mountains.

Son Cosmet (*see p180*), to the south, is a beautiful manor house within extensive grounds. The emphasis here is firmly on character rather than snazzy gadgets – you won't find TVs or minibars in the rooms; what you will find is antique furniture, cool stone interiors and ancient wooden beams, plus a spectacular pool.

Over on the other side of the island near the affluent, boho village of Deià is **Sa Pedrissa** (*see p121*), one of the most beautifully located places to stay on the island. It's a 17th-century estate with just eight rustic rooms. There are splendid gardens but the real selling point is the pool, which appears to float half a kilometre or so above the Mediterranean.

Further north-east, and at the opposite end of the luxury scale, is **Can Guillo** (*see p142*), a ramshackle old farmhouse at the end of a long, long track near Pollença. The vibe is utterly informal, with communal breakfasts, rickety swing-chairs and legions of pets – including a podgy Shetland pony – more than making up for the lack of Bang & Olufsen branded goods and spa treatments. That said, there is a pool.

Another place where you'll get a warm welcome from the resident animals, this time sheep and a soppy spaniel, is **Son Siurana** (*see p150*) near Alcúdia. It's a relaxed and friendly 18th-century estate with six adjacent houses set within 100 hectares (247 acres) of almond groves and meadows.

There are far fewer agroturismos in Menorca, but where you do find them they are largely top quality. **Biniarroca** (*see p226*), in the south-east, within striking distance of Maó and Es Castell, is a labyrinth of gardens containing squat stone bungalows and quiet crannies in which to escape with a book. Not too far away, and equally luxurious, is the **Alcaufar Vell** (*see p226*), dating back to the 14th century; those with aspirations to own their own *castillo* could do worse than to book a room in the main house. As well as 21 rooms and a pool, the hotel sits within 170 hectares (420 acres) of land, the bounty of which can be sampled in its excellent restaurant.

Those on tighter budgets should check out **Binissfullet Vell** (*see p229*), in the same area, run by a ridiculously multilingual (six languages and counting) Mallorcan lady and her son. Highlights are the chatty family atmosphere, pool and vast breakfasts made from the farm's produce.

Alcaufar Vell.

antiques. Dishes are creative Mallorcan such as 'abuela's monkfish from Pollença' and langoustines with chocolate, an all but forgotten old island recipe. The wine cellar is stocked with quality local wines, and offers three beautiful, antique-filled bedrooms with luxurious marble-lined bathrooms. Ask for the large double with a view of the *plaça*.

Another option is to stay in one of the plain double rooms at the hilltop **Ermita de Bonany** (Puig de Bonany, 971 82 65 68, doubles €24), outside Petra.

Resources

Police station
Petra *C/Font 1 (mobile 659 49 15 50).*
Sant Joan *C/Major 61 (971 52 60 03/33 30 03).*
Vilafranca de Bonany *Plaça Major 1 (971 83 21 06).*

Post office
Petra *C/Francesc Torrent (971 56 16 53).*
Sant Joan *C/Consolació 18 (971 52 60 75).*
Vilafranca de Bonany *Ctra. De Palma s/n (971 83 23 00).*

MONTUÏRI & PORRERES

Montuïri, just north of the Palma–Manacor road (eight kilometres east of Algaida and 11 kilometres west of Vilafranca), runs along a ridge, with steeply sloping alleys running off either side. It's remarkable mainly for its ghost town-like emptiness, the crazy paving of the main street and a pretty church dating back to 1649, which forms the centre of life such as it is. Your best hope for action is either the Monday morning market, or the Feast of San Bartomeu on 24 August, when *cossiers* (dancers) don traditional garb and whoop and carouse in a triumph of good over evil.

On the edge of town, the **Museu Arqueológic de Son Fornés** is housed in an old restored flour mill and focuses on the nearby Son Fornés archaeological site, where megalithic talayots and evidence of a medieval settlement have been found (no information in English). The forlorn **Son Fornés** site itself is situated a couple of kilometres west of the town on the Pina–Sencelles road. There's not a lot left of the talayot, though it is of interest in being hollow, and clearly used as a living space or storage room, unlike most of the normally solid talayots on Menorca.

Ten kilometres south-east of Montuïri, **Porreres** sits in pretty countryside, amid pine and almond trees. It's an attractive little place with more life to it than you might expect, most if it centred on a main street that runs between its church (with a distinctive crenellated spire) and the main square, Plaça de la Vila. A general market is held around the *plaça* on Tuesdays. If it's open, it's worth taking a peek at the cathedral-sized church of **Nuestra Señora de la Consolació**, with its spooky, barrel-vaulted interior. Here you'll find a multi-storey gilded Baroque altarpiece and a side chapel as big as most churches.

Just outside Porreres (take the road to Llucmajor then turn left soon after), the small **Santuari de Monti-Sion** (971 64 71 85) perches on top of a low hill, its slopes bristling with pines. The current two-kilometre-long road up to the Santuari was built by the inhabitants of Porreres in just one day in 1954; along it are the Stations of the Cross, dating from 1497. A school was founded up here by Franciscan monks in 1551, which was home, at one time, to more than 500 pupils; it was closed during the 19th century and the buildings fell into disrepair, before being renovated in the 20th century. Only groups can stay overnight, but all visitors can use the picnic area outside the walls. There's a procession up to the Santuari from Porreres on the Sunday after Easter.

Museu Arqueológic de Son Fornés

C/Emili Pou s/n, Montuïri (971 64 41 69/ www.sonfornes.mallorca.museum). **Open** *Mar-Oct* 10am-2pm, 4-8pm Tue-Sun. *Nov-Feb* 10am-2pm Tue-Sun. **Admission** €3.50; €2 reductions. **No credit cards.**

Where to stay & eat

There's nowhere to stay in **Montuïri** itself, but nearby, **Son Manera** (Ctra. Montuïri–Lloret, km0.3, 971 16 15 30, 971 64 67 64, www.son manera.com, €164-€204 incl breakfast) is a modern, comfortable hotel with 21 rooms and the advantage of full spa facilities. Alternatively, **Puig Moltó** (Ctra. Pina–Montuïri, 971 18 17 58, www.espuigmolto.com, closed Nov, Dec, doubles €158-€192 incl breakfast) is one of the oldest estates on Es Pla, surrounded by fig and carob trees, and with ten bright, light suites, and a pool. If you need to stop for lunch in Montuïri, **Ca'n Xorri** (C/Major 2, 971 64 41 33, closed Mon, €) does a hearty menu of *potaje* (chickpea stew with chorizo), baked hake and roast chicken, served on a pleasant rooftop terrace overlooking the plains.

The **Ermita de Sant Miquel** (Puig de Sant Miquel, 971 64 63 14, closed Mon, restaurant €), near Montuïri, has been nicely renovated and houses an excellent café-restaurant.

There are a handful of fincas offering accommodation in and around **Porreres**. **Es Passarell** (Ctra. Porreres–Felanitx, km5.5, 971 18 30 91, www.espassarell.com, doubles €110-€125, apartment €135-€150), just outside Porreres on the road to Felanitx, is the pick. This cosy yet elegant finca is owned and run by Lola, a warm, exuberant woman with a penchant for art, interior design, pets and people. The rooms and apartments have the air of relaxed luxury, with rich fabrics, lots of books and an air of do-as-you-please. There are six apartments, all with a fireplace, garden and terrace, three double rooms with bath, terrace and stove, and one double with a shower. A communal dinner is laid on three times a week. There's a pool too.

In the other direction, towards Llucmajor, you'll find **Finca Son Sama** (Ctra. Llucmajor–Porreres, km3.5, 971 12 09 59, www.sonsama. com, doubles €95 incl breakfast, restaurant closed Sun, €€), a secluded farmhouse dating back to 1531 and stuffed with island antiques. Rooms are large with terracotta-tiled floors. The restaurant, Es Mirador, has endless views of the plains and does bargain-priced suckling lamb and pig. A wonderful rambling garden surrounded by paddocks filled with gambolling horses (it's a stud farm too) adds to the sensation you've really got away, and those of an equine bent can go riding.

More upmarket is **Sa Bassa Rotja** (Finca Son Orell, Camí Sa Pedrera s/n, 971 16 82 25, closed mid Oct-end Jan, www.sabassarotja.com, doubles €166-€190 incl breakfast, restaurant €€), set within a sizeable estate at the foot of the hill crowned by the Monti-Sion sanctuary. It has 25 big rooms, a good restaurant, two pools and tennis courts.

For something a little more homely, the seven-room **Finca Son Mercadal** (Ctra. Porreres–Campos, Camí Son Pau s/n, 971 18 13 07, www. son-mercadal.com, doubles €105 incl breakfast, closed Dec-Feb), which also has a pool, and can be found five kilometres south of Porreres on the road to Campos. Guests are free to make use of the owners' bicycles, horses and even donkeys.

For eating in Porreres, **Restaurant Centro** (Avda. Bisbe Campins 13, 971 16 83 72, closed Sun night, €€€, lunch *menú* €8.50 Mon-Fri, €15 Sun) has a hearty lunchtime *menú* that distinguishes between 'fish' and 'fresh fish' (much of the fish served up on Mallorca is frozen, but the Centro has its own fishing boat, the *Pala Llonga*). The elegant and bustling colonial-style dining hall is a great place to gawp at Es Pla's hearty yeomen. On the main square, **Café Sa Plaça** (Plaça de la Vila 3, 971 16 65 90, €) offers pizzas, decent tapas and has a patio filled with unruly houseplants out back.

Resources

Police station
Montuïri *Plaça Major 1 (900 70 04 50).*
Porreres *Plaça de la Vila 17 (971 64 72 21).*

Post office

Montuïri *C/Corregudes s/n (971 64 61 68).*
Porreres *C/Veiet 17 (971 64 73 19).*

ALGAIDA & RANDA

Algaida (21 kilometres/13 miles east of Palma
and eight kilometres west of Montuïri) is the
first place you come to heading out from the
capital along the Palma–Manacor road. A bit
of a non-event, it is nevertheless an impressive
drive coming in from the Randa, with a huge
wall of mountains pierced by the church steeple
and a couple of windmills. It's also popular
with city folk for Sunday lunch.

On the west side of the town, the massive
mock castle is in fact the factory, museum and
shop of glass-maker **Gordiola**, which has been
producing its wares since 1719. It may look
like a hideously kitsch tour-party magnet
(which it is), but it really is worth a stop. It's
quite something to see the glass-making boys,
clad in shorts and T-shirts (with a couple of
old masters lending some sense of decorum),
producing the goods in front of your eyes.
The setting itself – the heat, the darkness, the
dramatic Gothic atmosphere – is like something
Dante might have penned. Upstairs, in a series
of grand rooms, is Gordiola's glass collection
from around the world. In the shop you can
pick up a souvenir – much of the glassware
is a touch gaudy, but there are some beautiful
(and pricey) modern chandeliers too.

A few kilometres north-west of Algaida, just
outside **Santa Eugènia**, is **Natura Parc**. This
compact, shady nature park boasts mammals
(deer, goats, llamas), birds (most notably black
vultures) and butterflies (in Spain's biggest
enclosed butterfly garden). It's a worthwhile
detour for kids.

The pretty little village of **Randa**, seven
kilometres south-east of Algaida, huddles
beneath the mini-peaks of the **Massís de
Randa**. It has a storybook air, with bright,
blooming flower gardens, alive with the murmur
of bumblebees and the sound of water trickling
through the still-functioning Moorish irrigation
system. Traditionally, this was a stop-off point
for pilgrims on their way to the monasteries
of Gràcia, Sant Honorat and Cura, sited at the
bottom, middle and top, respectively, of the
neighbouring table mountain **Puig de Randa**.
You can walk, cycle or drive to the top (five
kilometres), and, combined with lunch or dinner
at one of the village's restaurants, this makes
for a pleasing half-day excursion.

You can still stay at the handsome **Santuari
de Cura** (*see p176*) with its sandstone walls
and pea-green shutters, and although there's
no escaping the coach parties and cyclists keen
to prove their mettle by day, at night it'll be
just you and the stars. The only blot is a group
of large radio masts next to the monastery.

The illustrious Mallorcan scholar, preacher
and linguist **Ramón Llull** founded the island's
first hermitage here in the 13th century and
it later became an important seat of learning.
For two centuries hundreds of students learned
Latin before heading off to university. You
can see artefacts from this period and Llull's
legacy in the former grammar school hall, now
a free museum (971 66 09 94; ring for opening
hours). The current chapel was built bit by bit
throughout the 17th and 18th centuries. There's

CENTRAL MALLORCA

Gordiola glass factory.

a crib here all year round, according to Franciscan tradition. Because of the monastery's position looking down over hectares of farmland, a 'blessing of the fruits' ceremony is held here every year on the fourth Sunday after Easter.

Gordiola

Ctra. Palma–Manacor, km19 (971 66 50 46/ www.gordiola.com). **Open** *May-Sept* 9am-8pm Mon-Sat; 9am-1pm Sun. *Oct-Apr* 9am-6pm Mon-Sat; 9am-1.30pm Sun. **Admission** free.

Natura Parc

Ctra. Palma–Sineu, km15.4, Santa Eugènia (971 14 40 78/www.naturaparc.net). **Open** *May-Sept* 10am-6.30pm daily. *Oct-Apr* 10am-5.30pm daily. **Admission** €9; €7 reductions. **No credit cards.**

Where to stay & eat

In the centre of **Algaida**, **Apartaments Rurals Raïms** (C/Ribera 24, 971 66 51 57, www.finca-raims.com, suite €105, apartments €115-€130) offers one suite and four apartments in a 17th-century manor house and bodega. Wine is still made here under the Oliver Moragues label and guests can learn about the process (and taste the results). Rooms are light and chic, with white walls and white linen. There's a beautiful garden and a pool with massages available. Bikes are also available and are free to guests.

Join Palma residents for Sunday lunch at one of Algaida's traditional restaurants, such as **Cal Dimoni** (Ctra. Palma–Manacor, km21, 971 66 50 35, closed Wed, €€), for meat *a la brasa*, or **Ca'n Mateu** (Ctra. Palma–Manacor, km21, 971 66 50 36, closed Tue, €€), a birthday cake of a roadside inn, for suckling pig.

North-west of Algaida, in **Santa Eugènia**, is the lovely *agroturismo* **Sa Torre de Santa Eugènia** (C/Alqueries 70, 971 14 40 11, www. sa-torre.com, apartments €144), which has apartments with kitchens and terraces, plus two pools and a hugely atmospheric cellar restaurant.

There's a fine place to eat in the village of Pina: **Es Molí de Pina** (C/Sant Plàcid 3, 971 12 53 03, closed dinner Sun, all Mon & Tue and Aug, €€) is, as its name suggests, in an old windmill, and offers up classic seasonal Mallorcan dishes and first-rate desserts.

A couple of kilometres north of Pina, in the tiny village of **Ruberts**, **Son Jordà** (Ctra. de Sineu, km22, 971 87 22 79, closed Dec-Jan, www.sonjorda.com, doubles €128 incl breakfast, restaurant open daily) provides a slice of manor house living. It's a sizeable 16th-century house consisting of three wings, 21 spacious bedrooms, a chapel, restaurant, pool and tennis court all overlooking rolling countryside. Owner Andreu is ever friendly, smiling and helpful.

In **Randa**, **Es Recó de Randa** (C/Font 21, 971 66 09 97, 971 12 03 02, www.esrecode randa.com, doubles €289, restaurant €€) is situated in a 17th-century building. The gardens are lovely, shaded by giant olive trees and palms with views over the village and across to the Tramuntana. A sauna has recently been installed beneath the pool. It's a good base out of season, when charming owner Manuel Salamanca goes all out to entertain his guests with daily excursions around the island, followed by crackling fires at night and first-rate dinners, such as wood-roasted suckling pig. Added pleasures are tea and coffee in the bedrooms, and an extensive breakfast menu.

Other eating options in Randa include **Ca's Beato** (C/Tanqueta 1, 971 12 03 00, closed Mon), which offers creative dishes, such as cuttlefish stuffed with *sobrassada* or pork steak stuffed with giant prawns in sweet wine, within an old stone-walled dining room and out on the sunny rear terrace; it also organises cycling holidays (visit www.huerzeler.com). Or there's the cheap and cheerful **Celler Bar Randa** (C/Església 24, 971 66 09 89, closed Wed and mid June-mid July, €) further down the slope, a lively locals joint serving good *arroz brut* (a sort of chuck-it-all-in, hearty rice and meat stew), grilled quail and pigeon wrapped in cabbage.

The **Santuari de Cura** (Puig de Randa, 971 12 02 60, www.santuariodecura.com, doubles €51-€64) is more comfortable than you might expect, though possibly not so cheap. You could just stop by at the restaurant (971 12 02 60, €) for a cheap lunch of traditional *pa amb oli* topped with either ham or cheese, local pickles on the side; or take a picnic to have beneath the giant holm oaks while admiring the view.

Resources

Police station

Algaida *C/Rei 6 (971 12 53 35).*

Post office

Algaida *Sa Plaça 2 (971 12 54 56).*

GETTING THERE

By bus

From Palma there are 3 buses Mon-Fri (2 Sat, 2 Sun) to Muro via Inca and Sa Pobla. There are 9 buses Mon-Fri (6 Sat, 5 Sun) between Palma and Felanitx via Algaida and Porreres.

By train

There are 13-14 trains daily between Palma and Sa Pobla (53mins) via Muro (49mins) and Inca, and 13-14 trains daily between Palma and Manacor (1hr 4mins) via Sineu (48mins) and Petra (56mins).

South Mallorca

Cala Figuera.
See p188.

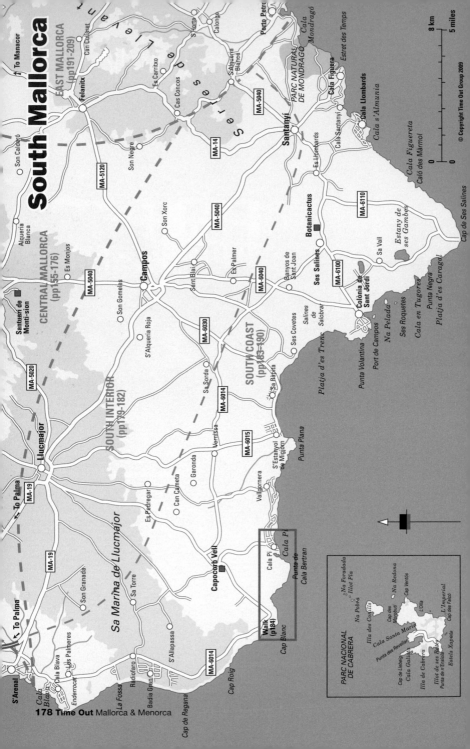

South Mallorca

EAST MALLORCA (pp191-209)

To Manacor

To Palma

To Palma

CENTRAL MALLORCA (pp155-176)

SOUTH INTERIOR (pp179-182)

SOUTH COAST (pp163-190)

Sa Marina de Llucmajor

Santuari de Monti-sion

Felanitx

Es Carritxo

Cas Concos

Son Negre

Son Xorc

Campos

Sant Blai

Es Palmer

Vernissa

Garonda

Sa Sorda

Es Pedregar

Can Calveta

S'Alqueria Roja

Son Gomelis

Es Monjos

Son Caldero

Alqueria Blanca

S'Horta

S'Alqueria
Blanca

Calonge

Porto Petro

Cala
Mondragó

Cala Figuera

Estret des Temps

PARC NATURAL
DE MONDRAGÓ

Cala Llombards

Cala s'Almunia

Cala Figuereta

Caló des Màrmol

Santanyí

Cala-Santanyí

Es-Llombards

Botanicactus

Ses Salines

Banyos de
Sant Joan

Salines
de
Salobra

Sa Vall

Estany de
ses Gambes

**Colònia de
Sant Jordi**

Cap de Ses Salines

Punta Negra

Punta d'es Caragol

Platja d'es Carbó

Ses Roquetes

Cala en Tugores

Na Pelada

Port de Campos

Punta Volantina

Platja d'es Trenc

Ses Covetes

Sa Ràpita

S'Estanyol
de Migjorn

Punta Plana

Vallgornera

Capocorb Vell

Cala Pi

Cala Pi

Punta de
Cala Bertran

Walk (p184)

Cap Blanc

Cap Roig

Cap de Regana

S'Allapassa

S'Arenal

Cala
Blava

Enderrocat

Els Pinarets

Radiofaro

La Fossa

Badia Gran

Cala Blava

Son Granada

Sa Torre

Son Verí

Llucmajor

MA-19
MA-19
MA-19
MA-5020
MA-5120
MA-5040
MA-14
MA-5040
MA-5040
MA-6030
MA-6040
MA-6040
MA-6014
MA-6015
MA-6014
MA-6014
MA-6100
MA-6110
MA-5040

**PARC NACIONAL
DE CABRERA**

Na Foradada

Illot Pla

Na Pobra

Na Redona

Cap Ventós

Illa des Conills

Cap des
Anciola

L'Olla

Cala Santa Maria

Illa de Cabrera

Cala Galiota

Cala Gandulf

L'Imperial

Cap des Falcó

Illot de ses Bledes

Punta de n'Ensiola

Estells Xapats

Punta des Revellar

0   8 km
0   5 miles

© Copyright Time Out Group 2009

South Interior

No need to avoid the crowds – there aren't any.

For such a densely populated island, the sparsely settled south comes as a surprise and a relief. True, it's a relatively harsh, flat, scrubby place, but it provides a welcome window on to a rural Mallorca little affected by decades of tourism. The main towns of Llucmajor and the more attractive Campos and Santanyí have a languid, likeable air, and some of the island's loveliest and most isolated rural hotels provide stylish oases of utter peace that you might have thought impossible to find on the Mediterranean's most popular holiday island. The quiet of the country roads is disturbed only by the swish of massed groups of lycra-clad cyclists.

LLUCMAJOR & CAMPOS

Driving south-east from S'Arenal and Palma the first place you come to is the unremarkable town of **Llucmajor** (27 kilometres/17 miles south-east of Palma), long a centre of the island's shoemaking industry. Today, it is dominated by the handsome 17th-century church of **Sant Bonaventura** and not much else.

Despite its medieval origins there's no charming old quarter to explore, though its main square, **Plaça Espanya**, is attractive and has a couple of decent high-ceilinged old bars for drinks and snacks, populated by old men in berets and checked shirts swatting flies and playing on fruit machines. A fruit and vegetable market takes place here on Wednesdays, Fridays and Sundays – its Friday incarnation also features clothes and bric-a-brac stalls.

In 1349, one of the most decisive events in Mallorcan history took place just outside the town, when the last independent king of Mallorca, Jaume III, was killed at the **Battle of Llucmajor** by the forces of Pere IV of Aragón. The island was never to be independently ruled again.

A further 13 kilometres south-east on the main road is another typical – but distinctly more attractive – rural town, **Campos**. Founded in 1300 by Jaume II on the site of earlier Roman and Arab settlements, it now serves as the market garden for the coast (there's a good fresh produce market on Thursdays and Saturdays). Its narrow streets,

lined by huddled, honey-hued houses, make for an enjoyable short wander.

Fans of the Sevillian artist Bartolomé Esteban Murillo can check out his painting of Christ in the **Museu Parroquial** (C/Bisbe Tellades 17, 971 65 00 03, €2, usually group visits only, but open to public 1st Sat of mth; phone to check) attached to the church of **Sant Julià**. There is also a famed pâtisserie, **Pastisseria Pomar** (C/de sa Plaça 20, 971 65 06 06), which was founded in 1902, plus the

---

THE BEST SOUTHERN SPOTS

For reclining on the sand
Cala Mondragó. See p188. **Platja d'es Trenc.** See p183.

For town strolls
Campos. See p183. **Colònia de Sant Jordi.** See p185. **Santanyí.** See p188.

For rural retreats
Son Bernadinet. See p184. **Cala Llombards.** See p190. **Son Julia.** See p184. **Ses Rotes Velles.** See p187.

For refined refuelling
Ca'n Calent. See p184. **Ca'n Pep.** See p183. **Restaurante Petite Iglesia.** See p190. **Sa Gripia.** See p185. **Villa Lorenzo.** See p190.

---

excellent **Es Brot** restaurant (*see below*) and some superb and seriously off-the-beaten-path places to stay in the surrounding plains.

Where to stay, eat & drink

Ca'n Tià Taleca (C/Campos 115, 971 66 02 79, €€), on the road between Llucmajor and Campos, was founded in the 1970s, with menus from the era making up the decor. You'll find something to suit everyone here from sea bass baked in salt and rabbit with shellfish to pastas and pizzas.

In **Campos**, **Ca'n Calent** (Ronda Estacio 44, 971 65 14 45, www.cancalent.com) has generated waves of late by its inspired use of ingredients, while **Restaurant Es Brot** (C/Ràpita 44, 971 16 02 63, closed dinner Mon and Sun, €€€) is one of the best places in the region for high-grade Mallorcan dishes such as grilled duck liver and *fava de varada* (a typical Mallorcan bean dish); it also serves delectable home-made desserts, including a wonderful *biscuit glace de almendra con chocolate caliente* (almond ice-cream wafer with a hot chocolate sauce).

In terms of places to stay, rural tourism really comes into its own here. For a treat, **Son Julia** (Ctra. S'Arenal a Llucmajor, 971 66 97 00, www.sonjulia.com, doubles €205-€2,900) is everything a luxury getaway should be, with a long sweeping driveway, a fountain in front of the house, gardens, terraces and swimming pools plus huge rooms with Persian rugs, Ezcaray mohair blankets and a seemingly endless supply of chocolates. Food is pricey, but light and excellent, with dishes ranging from steamed seasonal vegetables in a Jamaican pepper vinaigrette to classic *suquet* (monkfish stew). Check online for special package deals.

Time stands still at the country manor of **Son Bernadinet** (Ctra. Campos–Porreres, km5.9, 971 65 06 94, www.son-bernadinet.com, closed Dec-Jan, doubles €219-€257 incl breakfast), which you'll find at the end of a long pine-wooded lane. The farm has been in the family for 200 years and the owners go all out to make you feel like one of the family. With a cool, spacious interior and vast lawns, vegetable gardens and aromatic herb beds outside, the place exudes calm. Not to be missed are the home-produce breakfast and the nightly changing three-course dinner for guests.

South of Campos, **Son Cosmet** (Ctra. Campos–Sa Ràpita, km2, 971 65 16 43, www.soncosmet.com, doubles €156-€201 incl breakfast) is another bucolic idyll; a stunning old manor house in splendid isolation, set amid gardens dotted with terracotta urns of geraniums and fields of grazing horses, where nothing cuts through the silence but birdsong and the tinkle of goat bells. There are no TVs

or minibars, but the house is stuffed with antiques, many of them museum pieces, and there are enough quiet corners and terraces to spend a long weekend here without setting eyes on a soul. Seemingly invisible staff restock a wonderful breakfast buffet and magically replace used beach towels with clean ones by the pool.

Just south of here, **Es Palmer** (Ctra. Campos–Colonia de Sant Jordi, km6.4, 871 18 12 65, closed Nov-Mar, www.espalmer.com, doubles €64-€124 incl breakfast) has ten rooms dotted around a palm grove, each with a terrace and slightly eccentric touches; nicest are the rooms in an old windmill. The restaurant provides simple home cooking and is cosy in winter, when there is a log fire and a wood-fired oven for roast lamb and suckling pig.

If you prefer to go it alone, **Hotel Migjorn** (971 65 06 68, www.thealternativemallorca. com, closed Nov-Mar) is a lovingly restored farmhouse converted into ten self-contained suites with small kitchens, dining areas and living rooms open year round. All have internet, TVs and DVDs.

SANTANYI

The small, pretty town of **Santanyí** was founded in 1300 and lies 14 kilometres south-east of Campos along the MA-17, and the same distance north-east of Colònia de Sant Jordi on the coast. A massive golden sandstone gateway (Sa Porta Murada) leads you to narrow streets lined with pretty townhouses and cottages, which centre on the elongated main square and hilltop church of **Sant Andreu Apostel**. The local honeyed sandstone is much in evidence throughout the town; it was also used in the construction of Palma's cathedral and Sa Llotja. Lately, it's become something of a hotspot with innumerable artists and writers moving in, attracted by the fabulous light and laid-back lifestyle. There's more to it than first meets the eye so it's worth setting aside a couple of hours to explore the many art galleries and craft shops.

Saturday is market day and the best time to visit Santanyí. Its streets throb with life and colour, and Plaça Major bursts with nature's bounty. As well as stalls selling everything from ironmongery to jewellery and cloth (look out for the traditional Mallorcan fabric, the 'cloth of tongues'), there are some interesting shops here, such as **Ceramiques de Santanyí** (C/Guàrdia Civil 22, 971 16 31 28), which produces artisan ceramics and specialises in a unique metallic glaze; all the objects are handmade and are original designs. **Floreta de Mallorca** (C/Constitució 4, 971 64 17 15, www.floretademallorca.com, 10am-2pm,

Market in **Santanyí**.

5pm-8pm Mon-Sat) has some wonderful gift ideas ranging from personalised boxer shorts, bathrobes and bedlinen, to gorgeous Percale cotton pyjamas, embroidered ballet shoes and colourful Kenyan sarongs and beach towels. Everything is fair trade. **Reina Rana** (Plaça Major 15, 971 64 20 75) is a German-run jewellery and accessories shop, dripping with crystals and semi-precious stones. **Vinos Artesanos Binissalem** (C/Pau s/n, mobile 636 40 15 02) is a small, friendly shop with a well-chosen selection of Mallorcan wine at decent prices.

From Santanyí, the beaches and small-scale resorts of the south-east coast are just a few kilometres away (see p188).

Where to stay, eat & drink

The most recent addition to Santanyí is its very own boutique pad, the **Hotel Santanyí** (Plaça de Constitució 7, 971 64 22 14, www.hotel-santanyi.com, doubles €85-€100), which has a handful of individually decorated rooms. The best, Ibiza, is actually the smallest but has its own sizeable terrace. Elsewhere there are big white sofas plumped on to black slate floors, a pavement terrace and a pretty courtyard for drinks and creative dishes.

Probably the best place to eat in town is **Es Cantonet** (Plaça Bernareggi 2, 971 16 34 07, www.es-cantonet.com), a romantic, German-run place serving top-notch rack of lamb, grilled fish and other unpretentious dishes without too much fuss. Plaça Major has several cafés and tapas bars to choose from. **L'Art de Vivre** (Plaça Major 6A, 971 65 38 53) does excellent home-made cakes and quiches to eat in or take away in a cosy atmosphere. **Sa Bodega** (C/de Roser 2, 971 16 30 15) goes in for the Scandinavian country chic look and is hugely popular for brunch-style breakfasts, and salad and pasta at lunchtime. The funky bar-restaurant **Sa Font** (Plaça Major 27, 971 16 34 92, €) has young, friendly staff serving *pa amb oli* alongside crêpes and Galician cider served in traditional ceramic bowls. **Sa Cova Galeria Bar** (Plaça Major 30, 971 16 31 46, mobile 636 71 42 27, closed Nov, €€) is the self-described heart of the town and it's a fair assessment of the place. Everyone meets here to make use of the internet access and twice-weekly live music sessions (Wed & Sat from 9pm) and the free-for-all singalong music session from 5pm on Sundays (providing 'food for the soul', according to co-owner Jean). There are basic salads and sandwiches if you get hungry.

For something more substantial, or simply an atmospheric drink, **Sa Gripia** (C/Obispo Verguer 26, 971 65 38 52, closed Tue, €€€) has an excellent selection of Mallorcan specialities, such as *rodet* (stuffed cabbage leaves) and quail with raisins, cabbage and pine nuts, along with baked fish, paella and steaks. Enter through an art gallery of the same name and emerge into a charming courtyard, where tables are laid out in the shade and the only irritating feature is the piped music.

A short way outside the town, off the MA-14 heading north towards Ca's Concos, you'll find **Sa Galera** (Ctra. Santanyí–Ca's Concos, km6.3, 971 84 20 79, www.hotelsagalera.com, closed 1 Nov-30 Jan, €137-€171 incl breakfast). This lovely 13th-century manor stands within an estate that includes 5,000 almond trees and one of the island's most important centres for the breeding of Mallorcan thoroughbred horses. There are 16 rooms, a big pool and a restaurant.

Off the MA-4012 between Santanyí and Alqueria Blanca is another good *agroturismo*, **Son Marimón** (Ctra. Santanyí–Alqueria Blanca, km1.4, 971 18 17 04, www.sonmarimon. com, closed Nov-Feb, doubles €110-€136 incl breakfast). Outside it resembles a storybook castle, with its mini-crenellated tower; inside it's more fairytale farmhouse (dating from 1832), with white coverlets, fresh flowers and rough stone walls. All five rooms/suites have a view and most of them have terraces.

Resources

Police station
Campos *Ctra. Campos–Felanitx s/n (971 65 16 26)*.
Llucmajor *C/Andalucia s/n (971 66 90 00)*.
Santanyí *Plaça Major 12 (971 65 30 02)*.

Post office
Campos *C/Sa Siquia 15 (971 65 01 64)*.
Llucmajor *C/París 45 (971 66 05 07)*.
Santanyí *C/Palma 33 (971 65 30 48)*.

GETTING THERE

See p190.

Sa Galera.

South Coast

Mallorca's quietest region and the Balearics' best-kept nature reserve.

The relative lack of long sandy beaches (Platja d'es Trenc is a notable exception), together with the almost constant wind and uncompromisingly flat landscape, means that tourist development along the south coast has been relatively ragged, intermittent and unconvincing. Cala Pi probably enjoys the best site, and there's a fine coastal walk from here, but none of the other resorts in the area are particularly enticing. Colònia de Sant Jordi is undoubtedly the liveliest coastal base in the summer, and it's from here that must-do boat trips leave for the pristine islands of the

Cabrera national park. Things pick up when you round the tip of the Cap de Ses Salines, with a scattering of munchkin-sized fishing villages, intimate coves, sapphire waters and secluded farmhouse hotels.

CALA PI, ES TRENC & COLONIA DE SANT JORDI

South of the main MA-717 road running through Llucmajor and Campos to Santanyí is Mallorca's empty quarter – a largely flat, hypnotically desolate, sparsely populated swathe of country that is edged by a smattering of unconvincing little resorts.

Coming from S'Arenal by the coastal road, the first settlement you arrive at is **Cala Blava**, a pleasant enough *urbanización*. From here to **Cap Blanc** it's a wilderness drive, with long tracts of desert-like scrub stretching into the distance among a patchwork of almond and citrus orchards and wild olive groves. You can't access the lighthouse and old watchtower at the cape itself as the area is part of a flyblown military facility, looking much like a neglected holiday camp.

The road turns inland here and, after five or so minutes' driving, sweeps past **Capocorb Vell**, one of the most important prehistoric sites in the Balearics. Spread over an extensive area (though the original village was far larger) are the remains of no fewer than five talayots (two quadrangular, three conical) and 28 dwellings. The settlement was probably founded around 1,000 BC, and continued in use into Roman times. A marked trail takes you around the village, while a leaflet in English explains what you are seeing. Buy tickets at the rustic outdoor bar, which keeps

the same hours as the ruins and which makes a pleasant roadside stop in itself for a beer or an ice-cream.

Heading back towards the coast, a finger-shaped gorge nuzzles its way into the plain from the turquoise bay of **Cala Pi** – the OAP of Mallorca's tourist developments. There's little going on here, but this is its charm, and the largely low-rise villas and hotels have been sensitively landscaped to lessen their environmental impact. From the small beach, walled in by tall limestone cliffs, you can walk to even smaller, more private inlets (*see p184* **Walk**). Climb up the cliffs that rise behind the boathouses, walk around the point and across shallow cliffs dotted with wild flowers for sweeping views across the sea to the island of Cabrera and, on clear days, the hazy outline of Ibiza; it's a fabulous picnic spot.

Continuing along the coast, there's nothing much to detain you in **S'Estanyol de Migjorn** and **Sa Ràpita** – dusty, windswept, low-rise developments that wouldn't look out of place in a western movie – unless you're going to eat at the memorable **Ca'n Pep** (*see p185*). Both towns are good for sailing courses (www.cnestanyol.com, or www.cnrapita.com).

The main draw in this part of the island lies east of here – **Platja d'es Trenc**, the only lengthy stretch of sand on Mallorca that has escaped heavy development. To reach it, head out of Sa Ràpita towards Campos, and you soon come to a badly signed right turn down a bumpy road through flower-filled meadows, passing old windmills and farmhouses, with chickens on the road and poppies on the verges. At the next junction turn right to **Ses Covetes**. Park on the road or pay for the car park near the beach. At the end of this road a rocky coastline is bordered by a few battered holiday homes and a couple of beach bars.

Turn right for a small, relatively quiet beach upon which the only building is the expensive but unbeatably located **Sa Copinya**

Walk Cala Pi to Cap Blanc

Clifftops and wilderness mean a windswept, rugged hike.

Distance: 13km. Linear.
Time: 3hrs 30mins.

The southern coast of Mallorca is far less developed than the Bay of Palma and the northern and eastern shorelines. While this has much to do with its lack of beaches, its reputation as an often bleak, wind-whipped wilderness probably doesn't help. This clifftop walk, however, reveals a wild and ruggedly beautiful side to the south that few visitors see (yet it's little more than 30 minutes' drive from Palma). It has a (very) short climb at the beginning, and some scrambling over rocks, but is otherwise pretty level and easy. As it's a linear walk, you can obviously cut it short at any point. Cala Pi offers plenty of dining and drinking opportunities.

Park in **Cala Pi** and follow the signs to the beach ('Platja'). Descend the steps to the small strand sitting snugly at the end of an inlet, sheltered by cliffs on either side. It's a great setting, though marred a little by the smelly seaweed that sometimes clogs up the beach. On the far side is a line of boathouses. Walk in front of them, in the direction of the sea, and at the last of the row of six solidly built houses turn immediately right and walk up some steps (not easy to see) at the back of the house and on to its flat roof. From here it's a steep but short climb of less than a minute up the rocks (with some rough-hewn steps) to the path at the top of the cliff.

Turn left, and follow the path as it dips into a little gulley, then rises through a gap in a stone wall. As you walk along, take in the views back down the inlet and across to the *atalaya*, one of many 16th-century watchtowers that still stand sentinel over Mallorca's coastline and once warned the islanders of the approach of Muslim pirates. You walk for a while with a drystone wall on your right, bearing left at its end to stay close to the clifftop, before coming to a wider track that heads inland (with a largely broken-down stone wall on its right).

Continue on this path to get around the narrow, snaking **Cala Beltrán** inlet, where you'll meet a wide gravel track. After a couple of minutes on this track, take a rough path to the left (marked by two cairns) for less than a minute before coming up to a clear track leading back towards the cliffs; turn left on to this.

You soon hit the open rocky clifftops at **Punta de Capocorb**. (You should be about half an hour into the walk by this point.) Locals often fish from the rocks. In the distance, on a clear day, you can see the **islands of Cabrera**. From here, it shouldn't be possible to go wrong, providing you keep the sea on your left, though the rock-scrambling can be punishing on the ankles. Cairns mark a route higher up, which is perhaps easier than picking your own. The cliffs gradually rise to more impressive heights as you continue. You'll need to head upwards as they become more sheer, fortified by the tang of the wild rosemary scattered among the rocks.

You may get as high as an unexpected stretch of gravel road. Follow this a short distance and then take a left back on to the cairn-marked path, where someone has helpfully made a big arrow with stones.

It's easier on the feet from here on. Continue along the ever-higher cliff edge, bearing left at a 'gateway' made by two wind-sculpted bushes and a ruined stone building as the path heads around the bay of **Es Carril**. For some time you'll have been able to see the *atalaya* that marks (just beyond) the walk's furthest point on the headland opposite. Follow the cliffs around the bay and then go through a gap in a stone wall that is topped with barbed wire. Ten minutes later you'll arrive at another barbed wire-enhanced stone wall, but, alas, this time there's no gap, just a sign saying 'Stop – Zona Militar'. This is the turnaround point, somewhat frustratingly – the watchtower is only a further five minutes away.

Retrace your steps back to Cala Pi.

SOUTH MALLORCA

bar-restaurant (*see p187*). Alternatively, follow the coast round to the left as you face the sea and you'll come to one of the island's most amazing beaches. Now a nature reserve, it is backed by gently undulating sand dunes sprung with elephant grass and squat pines, and offers a three-and-a-half-kilometre-long, gently curving expanse of soft sand served by a single beach bar with shady tables and great *pomadas* (Menorcan gin with lemon ice).

Behind the beach lie the **Salines de Llevant**, salt pans that attract around 170 migratory bird species; the salt has started to be harvested in recent years, and is now celebrated by gourmets (Flor de Sal d'Es Trenc is the most famous brand; for more info, *see p84* **Made in Mallorca & Menorca**). The other main access to Es Trenc is from the Campos–Colònia de Sant Jordi road, a couple of kilometres north of the latter – there is no development at this end of the beach and fewer tourists.

Colònia de Sant Jordi is the main settlement on this stretch of coast and the best base. The outskirts of this one-time fishing village are undistinguished: a grid of chunky apartment blocks that border the salt pans (good for birdwatching and a gentle stroll, but otherwise not wildly interesting). The port, however, has some charm; modest fishing craft bob in the sheltered bay in front of an arc of bistros and cafés.

From here you can take day-long boat trips to the fantastic offshore nature reserve of **Cabrera** (*see p189* **Island Fever**), or spend long, lazy days exploring the nearby virgin beaches.

A less touristy place than Colònia de Sant Jordi to stop for a break and a meal is **Ses Salines**, a sleepy village five kilometres inland. It's dominated by its church and named for the nearby salt flats; the marshes are a birdwatcher's paradise, and home to species such as cranes, kestrels and ospreys.

Just outside the village is **Botanicactus**, a large but somewhat tired and desultory botanical garden containing a lake, lawns, palms, bamboo and more than 400 species of cactus; one specimen is over 300 years old.

Botanicactus

Ctra. Ses Salines–Santanyí s/n (971 64 94 94). **Open** *May-Sept* 9am-7pm daily. *Nov-Jan* 10.30am-4pm daily. *Feb-Apr* 9am-5pm daily. **Admission** €7.50; €4.20 reductions. **No credit cards**.

Capocorb Vell

Ctra. Llucmajor–Cap Blanc, km23 (971 18 01 55). **Open** 10am-5pm Mon-Wed, Fri-Sun; 10am-2pm Thur. **Admission** €2. **No credit cards**.

INSIDE TRACK
CAP DE SES SALINES WALK

From the **Platja d'es Port** you can walk around the rocks eastwards to the aptly named **Es Dolç** ('Sweet Beach'), or, if you have the energy, all the way to **Cap de Ses Salines** (about seven kilometres away), taking in magnificently secluded beaches en route, such as **Platja d'es Carbó** and **Platja d'es Caragol**. Allow a day to walk to the Cap and back, and bring plenty of water and a picnic: there are no refuelling stops.

Where to stay, eat & drink

After a visit to Capocorb Vell, get back with the living at the bustling roadside diner **Cas Busso** (Ctra. Cap Blanc, km24, 971 12 30 02, €€); it specialises in meats roasted in the wood-fired oven and paella. In **Cala Pi**, the lunchtime €8 *menú* at **Sa Terrassa** (Passeig Cala Pi 391, 971 12 31 65, closed Sat & Sun, €€) is good value, but it's the *piedras* (meat cooked on a hot stone) that everyone comes for. In terms of where to stay, you're much better off heading further round the coast as most of Cala Pi is devoted to timeshares and private villas.

Just about the only reason to visit **Sa Ràpita** is for lunch, and the front is lined with freshly spruced-up low-rise villas, many of which are now fish restaurants. The most famous is **Ca'n Pep** (Avda. Miramar 30, 971 64 01 02, closed Mon and Dec-Feb, €€€), a wonderful seafood restaurant that exudes delicious odours from its justly renowned bouillabaisse and great selection of fish. It's incredibly popular at weekend lunchtimes, so book ahead. The **Restaurant Club Nàutic Sa Ràpita** (971 64 04 13) is a smarter option with its glass-fronted dining room – port on one side, white sand beach with sea-grass parasols on the other. Try the mixed fish grill – a good deal at €47.

Near **Es Trenc** beach, secluded **Can Canals** (Ctra. Campos–Sa Ràpita, km7, 971 64 07 57, www.cancanals.es, junior suites €120-€160 incl breakfast, closed Jan) offers 12 junior suites, a restaurant (in the evening) and a spa. Located just a minute's walk from the southernmost end of the beach, four-star **El Coto** (Avda. Primavera 8, 971 65 50 25, www.elcoto.de, closed Nov-Mar, doubles €116-€170 incl breakfast) has all the usual trimmings, including minibars, air-conditioning and a large pool set in splendid gardens.

At **Ses Covetes**, refreshment can be had at **Restaurant-Café Noray** (C/Murters s/n, mobile 607 98 26 35, closed Oct-Feb, €), or on

The best guides to enjoying London life

(but don't just take our word for it)

'More than 700 places where you can eat out for less than £20 a head... a mass of useful information in a genuinely pocket–sized guide'

Mail on Sunday

'Armed with a tube map and this guide there is no excuse to find yourself in a duff bar again'

Evening Standard

'I'm always asked how I keep up to date with shopping and services in a city as big as London. This guide is the answer'

Red Magazine

'Get the inside track on the capital's neighbourhoods'

Independent on Sunday

'A treasure trove of treats that lists the best the capital has to offer'

The People

Rated 'Best Restaurant Guide'

Sunday Times

the beach to the west at **Sa Copinya**. (Platja de Ses Covetes, no phone, closed Nov-15 Mar, €€).

In terms of accommodation (and food) in **Colònia de Sant Jordi**, a good bet is the **Hostal & Restaurante Playa** (C/Major 25, 971 65 52 56, www.restauranteplaya.com, closed lunch Mon, Nov-Dec, €€€, doubles €72-€80 incl breakfast), a converted fisherman's cottage cluttered with Mallorcan rustic bric-a-brac, china and glassware, overlooking a secluded beach on the north side of town; ask for a room with a balcony looking out to sea. Opened in 1921, it's the oldest hotel in town, with a quiet whitewashed terrace scattered with flowers. Specials here are spanking fresh, salt-baked fish and a fine paella, but prices reflect the lovely location.

Just around the corner, **Hostal Colonial** (C/Ingeniero Gabriel Roca 9, 971 65 52 78, www.hostal-colonial.com, closed Nov-Feb, doubles €56-€72 incl breakfast) has been in the same family for three generations and is one of the best bargains in town for good-value, no-frills accommodation; all rooms are immaculate and have a small balcony or terrace. The owners run a taxi company and can pick up and drop off at the airport. They have made a name for themselves with their home-made ice-cream.

In the centre of town, the modern three-star **Hotel Martorell** (C/Cervantes 2, 971 65 50 30, closed Nov-Mar, doubles €62 incl breakfast) has a mainly German clientele and is another good-value place, with 24 comfortable rooms – all with balconies – and a swimming pool.

Between the beaches of Es Dolç and Es Port, the **Pensión Es Turó** (Plaça Es Dolç, 971 65 50 57, closed Nov-Apr, doubles €42-€52 incl breakfast) has pristine, spartan rooms with balconies in a squat block; prices vary according to the view – street, port or sea. There is a simple restaurant (€) with a comfortable seaside terrace too.

If you had something more rural in mind, **Ses Rotes Velles** (Ctra. Campos–Colònia de Sant Jordi, km8.7, 971 65 61 59, www.sesrotes velles.com, closed Nov-Feb, doubles €120-€145 incl breakfast) is a converted finca just a stone's throw from the bustle of the town, and is very popular among German tourists. Villa-style accommodation gives added privacy, while the pool and shady terraces provide a pleasant focal point for drinks and meeting your neighbours.

The hotel-spa **Hotel Balneario San Juan de la Font Santa** (Ctra. Campos–Colònia de Sant Jordi, km8.2, 971 65 50 16, www.balneario delafont santa.com, closed Nov-Mar, doubles €116-€120 half board) feels more like an old people's home than a place to relax and revitalise – a pity because the 38°c waters are apparently excellent, but here they are siphoned into clinical bath cubicles (19 in all).

The spa is open to the public 9-11am and 4-5.30pm Mon-Fri (€10.50 per session).

For breakfast and picnic fodder in **Colònia de Sant Jordi**, head for **Panadería Pons** (C/Major 29, 971 65 51 71, closed Mon and Nov-15 Jan) for dreamy *ensaïmadas* and other local pastries. On the port, the **Restaurante Sa Llotja** (971 65 65 55, closed Tue and Nov-Mar, €€€) knocks up a fine *mariscada* (a decadent platter of lobster, giant shrimp, prawns, clams, mussels, razor clams and fresh fish) for €32. Or there's **Restaurante Sa Gavina** (C/Lonja 13, 971 65 62 27, closed Thur and Nov-Mar, €€), which serves monster portions of simple dishes, such as onion soup and grilled fish, well and without fuss.

Heading inland a little, **Ses Salines** has taken on a more gentrified air as second-homers have begun to discover this part of the island, and it's become a particularly good place to eat. **Cassai** (C/Sitjar 5, 971 64 97 21,www.cassai.es, closed Mon, 3wks in Jan, €) is a romantic café-cum-tea-room-cum-restaurant with intimate tables lit by giant Chinese lanterns. Produce is local with highlights that include stir-fried scallops with green asparagus, slow-cooked island piglet with Sa Pobla potatoes, and John Dory in a black olive crust with fish risotto. But it's also a fantastic place for tea and cake in the afternoon if you happen to be passing through. It also has an interior design shop across the road.

The cultish Argentinian polo brand La Martina is part of the **Asador Es Teatre** (Plaça San Bartolomé 4, 971 64 95 40, www. asadoresteatre.com, closed Tue); not to be missed if you're a fan of *empanadas* (meat pies), *mollejas* (grilled sweet breads), *asado de tira* (ginormous ribs) and the general tradition of Argentinian meat fests washed down with buckets of lusty red wine. Next door tiny **Casa Manolo** (Plaça Bartomeu 1, 971 64 91 30, closed Mon, Sun evening and Sept, €€€) is something of an island treasure serving 50 superbly fresh and simply cooked tapas. Photos of its customers, running the A-Z list celebrity gamut, from the Crown Prince of Spain and his new bride to German soap actors.

After all that you'll need somewhere to lay your head and **Es Turó** (Camí de Cas Perets, 971 64 95 31, www.esturo.com, closed Nov-Jan, doubles €120-€190 incl breakfast) has ten large and peaceful rooms in buildings that have been owned by the same family for 200 years. The colourful gardens and pool area offer plenty of quiet corners to read or contemplate the view across the plain and beyond to the island of Cabrera. Nearby is **Finca Sa Carrotja** (Sa Carrotja 7, 971 64 90 53, www.sacarrotja.com, closed Dec-Jan, doubles €130-€150 incl breakfast), part of which dates back to the 16th century. There are six inviting bedrooms, with

Cala Mondragó.

air-con and period furniture; five have their own terraces. Genial hosts Guillem and Pilar will rustle you up a fine dinner on request. There's a pool too. Both are peaceful rural getaways.

CALAS LLOMBARDS, SANTANYI, FIGUERA & MONDRÁGO

From the Colònia de Sant Jordi–Ses Salines–Santanyí road (MA-610), a long, straight stretch heads south for ten kilometres through bush and burr to the lighthouse at Mallorca's southernmost point, **Cap de Ses Salines**. This is one of the windiest parts of the island, as the countless fallen trees in the area testify. The lighthouse here is of no great size, age (built in 1993) or beauty, and there's no public access to it, but it's worth making the journey to enjoy the wildness of the spot and to walk the rocky shoreline and gaze out towards Cabrera. The wide shelf of rock littered with cairns and reef makes swimming tricky, but the area is beloved by windsurfers who gather here in droves. Keep walking around the headland to your right when facing the sea and after about 25 minutes you'll come to the beautiful **Platja d'es Caragol**.

You could easily spend a day losing yourself around the laid-back *calas* a few kilometres south-east of Santanyí, which are particularly popular with German tourists. The most westerly, **Cala Llombards**, is a mellow, secluded bay with a seasonal beach bar that has a penchant for 1970s rock music, unnaturally blue water and high cliffs folding gently over themselves; you could almost be in Jamaica.

If things are a little too chilled here, continue on to family-oriented **Cala Santanyí**, the closest these tiny coves get to a resort town. The beach isn't quite so idyllic here, thanks to the hotel that rises along one side of it, but the location is splendid, with sapphire waters lapping on to golden sand through a canyon carved into the limestone. There are plenty of good walks up to the cliffs and the giant natural arch of Portals, created by millennia of persistent waves. Follow signs from the top of the town just above the Hotel Pinos Playa. When you reach the end of the tarmac, bear left down a dirt track until you arrive at an obelisk of sandstone blocks. Continue down the cliff on the footpath and you'll come out just above the arch.

Beyond this, tourist development is far from unknown in **Cala Figuera**, but has yet to completely dominate. There's no beach as such, but you could easily clamber into the sea from the boat slipways, and you frequently see sunbathers toasting themselves on the weathered quay. With a thriving café scene in the summer months, there's no shortage of good places to eat and drink; it's a romantic spot come nightfall. To find the picture-perfect fishing port, with its whitewashed, green-shuttered cottages tumbling down towards the sea, take the unmarked left turn just before town.

If you feel the need for a complete break from tourist development, head across parched, ochre plains from here to the 785-hectare (1,940-acre) **Parc Natural de Mondragó** (Ctra. Alquería Blanca–Mondragó s/n, 971 18 10 22, open 9am-4pm daily, free). The park can be accessed either from the Cala Figuera side or from the

north. Once you've parked, set off on foot to explore pine forests criss-crossed by dusty paths (there are several marked trails, from 20 to 40 minutes long). You'll see plenty of birdlife and, if you're lucky, frolicking hares, rabbits and genets (spotted cat-like relatives of the mongoose), and, on the rocky headlands, sunbathing Balearic lizards – the park's mascot. The rocky coves that protect the southernmost tip of the park are good for sunbathing and snorkelling, though most visitors head for the park's two magnificent white sand beaches. The south beach is the less crowded of the

Island Fever

The Parc Nacional de Cabrera archipelago is a must for Darwin enthusiasts.

One of the best-preserved nature reserves in the whole of the Mediterranean, let alone the Balearics, is the offshore islands of the **Parc Nacional de Cabrera** – Mallorca's answer to the Galápagos Islands.

By far the largest of the archipelago's 17 islands and islets, Isla de Cabrera, lying about 15 kilometres south-west of Cap de Ses Salines, is the only one that can be visited, and then only from March to October (except for groups). **Excursions A Cabrera** (971 64 90 34, www.excursionsacabrera.com) runs daily boat trips from Colònia de Sant Jordi harbour, leaving at 9.30am, 8.45am in July and August; they're pricey, but definitely worth it. Note that pre-booking (online, by phone or at the booth on the harbourside) is essential. You can also take a boat from Porto Petro harbour (971 65 70 12, ring for times and prices), which leaves at 9.30am on Sundays in June, and at 9.30am on Mondays and Fridays from July to September; again, pre-booking is essential.

The Excursions A Cabrera trip consists of an hour's spray-lashed boat ride past seabird-laden smaller islands and into Cabrera's large, peaceful natural harbour, where there's a tiny information centre with leaflets in English and a small bar selling drinks and snacks. However, it's best to bring along your own picnic to have on the beach or in the large covered picnic area. (The lunch offered by the boat company is not recommended.)

You're restricted to wandering on the island along two fairly short paths. One takes you to a castle perched on a cliff, with sweeping views across to the Bay of Palma. It was built in the late 14th

century to stop pirates using the island as a base for raids on Mallorca, and in the 19th century held French prisoners from the Napoleonic Wars. You can still see the soldiers' graffiti on the walls.

The island's other path leads to two wonderful, peaceful beaches – one sandy, the other full of richly teeming rock pools, and both with beautifully clear, enticing waters for swimming.

Because the archipelago is made up of a number of different micro environments, it's a true evolutionary hotspot, with different creatures displaying various adaptations. For instance, Cabrera has 80 per cent of the world population of the Balearic lizard, and around ten different subspecies have developed on these islands. You'll see hundreds of them darting frantically across your path. Further interesting discoveries have been made in one of the island's caves, where scientists have discovered several unique species of crustacea.

This is also a wonderful spot for birdwatching, with many native species of birds, as well as others that stop here on their annual migration or to breed. You could see shags, shearwaters, petrels, the rare Audouin's gull, and birds of prey such as ospreys, kestrels and falcons.

You'll have about four hours to explore and sunbathe on the island, then, on your even wetter return journey to Mallorca (we recommend you sit inside the boat on the way back), there are stops in Sa Cova Blava (Blue Cave), where the water glows a particularly jewel-like blue and you can have a swim. The boat arrives back in Colònia de Sant Jordi at about 5pm.

SOUTH MALLORCA

two, but the north beach tends to be more sheltered on a blustery day and has the advantage of a couple of *chiringuitos* for ice-cold beer and snacks.

For the east coast resorts north of Mondragó, *see p198*.

Where to stay, eat & drink

In **Cala Llombards**, look no further than **Bar Tropical** (mobile 649 41 63 49, closed Nov-Apr, €€), the quintessential beach bar – a dying breed, alas, on this island. There is probably nowhere finer on all Mallorca to eat the freshest, best-quality fish these waters have left to offer, charred on the griddle and served with nothing but a squeeze of lemon juice and maybe some garlic. Up on the hillside, **Casa Poesia** (Avda. Cala Llombards, 971 64 20 62, mobile 626 93 05 65, www.casa-poesia.com, closed Nov-Jan, doubles €54) has 15 ensuite rooms and a good-value, creative restaurant (€€) in a modern block. Despite its unprepossessing exterior it has some colourful touches, and is run with enthusiasm by young Germans.

Cala Santanyí caters largely for (German) families. Accommodation choices include the **Pinos Playa Hotel y Apartamentos** (Costa d'en Nofre 15, 971 16 50 00, www.pinosplaya. com, closed Nov-Apr, doubles €37-€97), which manages to maintain a personal service despite its size. Rooms are large (around half have fine views), and facilities include a diving centre, kindergarten (free), two pools (one heated), squash and tennis courts, a sauna, jacuzzi, three bars and a disco. It's also got a hip new restaurant called the **Buenavista** (€€) that offers a more creative take on the region's fish and seafood dishes.

In **Cala Figuera**, the two-star **Hotel Villa Sirena** (C/Virgen del Carmen 37, 971 64 53 03, www.hotelvillasirena.com, closed Nov-Mar, doubles €67-€75) sticks out on the promontory (from here the houses fall away exposing slate grey cliffs with well-worn paths for strolling – it's a perfect suntrap). The USP of this otherwise fairly ordinary hotel is the way it has made its own beach by carving platforms into the rock and inserting a ladder into the water to make access easy.

The **Restaurante Petite Iglesia** (C/La Marina 11, 971 64 50 09, closed Tue & Wed) is a wonderful new addition to the little town with different foodie delights every day in a stay-a-while atmosphere: oysters and white wine on Fridays, Sunday brunch and special music events for Christmas and New Year. **Restaurante Hostal Cala** (C/Virgen del Carmen 56, 971 64 50 18, apartments €64) is a real bargain, offering apartments with kitchenettes, wicker furniture and fab balconies over the jewel-like gorge, affording excellent views of the small man-made caves chiselled out of the cliffs. Next door, the **Hostal Ca'n Jordi** (C/Virgen del Carmen 58, 971 64 50 35, closed Nov, doubles €43, apartments €47-€75), run by a family from Yorkshire, is smaller and cheaper, but with similar views and rooms with balconies.

Several bars and restaurants line a pedestrianised stretch of road, where you can dine in the shade of the pines to the sound of gently breaking waves. **Café L'Arcada** (C/Virgen del Carmen 80, 971 64 50 32, closed Nov-Mar, €€) offers a good range of Mallorcan dishes along with pizzas and other safe fare. Nearby, **Es Port** (C/Virgen del Carmen 88, 971 16 51 40, €€) also has pizzas, pastas and a handful of basic Spanish dishes.

For somewhere special, head for **Villa Lorenzo** (C/Magallenes 11, 971 64 50 29, www. villalorenzo.com, closed Nov-Jan, restaurant €€€€, doubles €62 incl breakfast), a great place for top-notch Mallorcan cooking. It's located just a few hundred metres from the port and has a beautiful garden terrace dominated by an old-fashioned brick stove and a pleasant pool for a swim before lunch. The attached *hostal* is great for some quality R&R.

Hostal Na Martina (Poligono 7, Cala Mondragó, 971 64 82 50, www.namartina.com, doubles €132-€181) is an 11-room B&B that reopened after a 100-year break in 2005. Clean, comfortable and family run, it's been around since 1900 and yet nobody has ever heard of it. It also does good home-made food, and has a decent-sized pool.

RESOURCES

Police station
Colònia de Sant Jordi *C/Doctor Barraquer 5 (971 16 60 35).*
Ses Salines *Plaça Major 1 (971 64 93 11).*

Tourist information
Colònia de Sant Jordi *OIT, C/Doctor Barraquer 5 (971 65 60 73).* **Open** 8am-2pm Mon-Fri.

GETTING THERE

By bus
From Palma, there are 7 buses a day (5 Sat, 2 Sun) to Colònia de Sant Jordi (1hr), calling at Llucmajor and Campos. Also, 5 buses Mon-Fri (3 Sat, 2 Sun) run to Cala d'Or, calling at Llucmajor, Campos and Santanyi. There are 4 buses Mon-Fri (2 Sat) between Colònia de Sant Jordi and Manacor (1hr) via Campos (25mins) and Porreres (35mins). One bus runs Mon-Sat between Palma and Cala Pi.

SOUTH MALLORCA

East Mallorca

East Mallorca

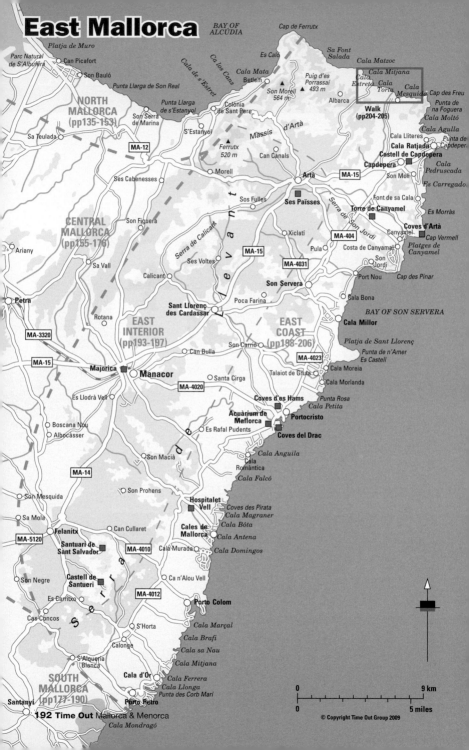

BAY OF ALCÚDIA

Cap de Ferrutx

Platja de Muro
Can Picafort
Son Bauló
Ca los Cans
Cala de s'Estret
Es Caló
Cala Mata
Sa Font Salada
Cala Matzoc
Cala Mitjana
Cala Estreta
Cala Torta
Cala Mesquida
Cap des Freu

Parc Natural de S'Albufera
Punta Llarga de Son Real
Punta Llarga de s'Estanyol
Colònia de Sant Pere
Betlem
Son Morell
Puig d'es Porrassa 564 m ▲
Albarca
Walk (pp204-205)

NORTH MALLORCA (pp135-153)

Sa Teulada
Son Serra de Marina
S'Estanyol
S'Estanyol
Morell
Ferrutx 520 m ▲
Massís d'Artà
Can Canals
Arta
Sos Fulles
Ses Païsses

MA-12

Ses Cabenesses

CENTRAL MALLORCA (pp155-176)

Ariany
Son Figuera
Sa Vall
Calicant
Petra
Rotana
Serra de Calicant
Ses Voltes
Xiclatí
Pula
Costa de Canyamel

Sant Llorenç des Cardassar
Poca Farina
Son Servera

MA-15
MA-404
MA-4031

EAST INTERIOR (pp193-197)

MA-3320
MA-15
Majorica
Manacor
Es Llodrà Vell
Can Bulla
Son Carrió
Santa Cirga
Talaiot de Gruta
Cala Millor
Platja de Sant Llorenç
Punta de n'Amer
Es Castell

EAST COAST (pp198-206)

MA-4023
Cala Moreia
Cala Morlanda
MA-4020
Coves d'es Hams
Acuàrium de Mallorca
Es Rafal Pudents
Portocristo
Coves del Drac
Punta Rosa
Cala Petita

Boscana Nou
Albocàsser
Son Macià
Cala Romàntica
Cala Anguila
Cala Falcó

MA-14
Son Prohens
Son Mesquida
Sa Mola
Hospitalet Vell
Coves des Pirata
Cala Magraner
Cala Bóta
Cales de Mallorca
Cala Antena
Cala Murada
Cala Domingos

MA-5120
Felanitx
Can Cullaret
MA-4010
Ca n'Alou Vell
Santuari de Sant Salvador
Castell de Santueri
Es Carritxo
MA-4012
Porto Colom

Son Negre
Cas Concos
S'Horta
Cala Marçal
Calonga
Cala Brafi
Cala sa Nau
Cala Mitjana
S'Alqueria Blanca
Cala d'Or
Cala Ferrera
Cala Llonga
Punta des Corb Marí

SOUTH MALLORCA (pp177-190)

Santanyí
Porto Petro
Cala Mondragó

Sa Font Salada
Cala Lliteres
Cala Ratjada
Castell de Capdepera
Capdepera
Son Moll
Font de sa Cala
Torre de Canyamel
Coves d'Artà
Canyamel
Cap Vermell
Platges de Canyamel
Son Jordi
Port Nou
Cap des Pinar
Sala Bona

Punta de na Foguera
Cala Moltó
Cala Agulla
Punta de Capdeper
Cala Pedruscada
Es Carregado
Es Morràs

BAY OF SON SERVERA

Serra de Son Jordi

0 — 9 km
0 — 5 miles

192 Time Out Mallorca & Menorca

© Copyright Time Out Group 2009

East Interior

Escape the coastal development for the Serra de Llevant.

Away from the coast, the Serra de Llevant's hills descend gently into the vast central plain, known as Es Pla. To the east of the Serra lies the region's major artery, the MA-14/MA-15, which connects the area's main settlements, including Felanitx, known for its local wine and capers, Manacor, Mallorca's second-largest town and unlikely centre of the artificial pearl-making industry, and the far more appealing Artà, a wonderfully atmospheric and conveniently located town, and a great base for exploring the region.

FELANITX & MANACOR

In **Felanitx**, the most southerly of the east's three towns – Manacor and Artà are the other two – you'll find the 16th-century church of **Sant Miquel**, decorated in florid Churrigueresque style, with an impressive organ. An outer wall of the church was rebuilt after it collapsed on a Palm Sunday procession in 1844, killing 414 people. It also has a small **Cultural Centre** (Plaça de sa Font de Santa Margalida 3, 971 58 22 74, open 6-9pmTue-Sat, 11am-1pm Sun & holidays), showing photography and work by local artists, and folkloric heritage. The town's other claims to fame are the local wine (this is Mallorca's junior wine region, at Binissalem; *see p157*) and 'green pearls' – capers, produced in the surrounding farmland – both of which can be purchased, along with other good picnic fare, at the lively Sunday morning market. Unusually, the covered municipal market is also open for fruit and veg.

It's also claimed locally that Felanitx is the birthplace of Christopher Columbus, that he learned to sail in nearby Porto Colom, and that he named the first land he discovered, San Salvador, after the **Santuari de Sant Salvador** nearby. This sits on the highest peak (516 metres/1,693 feet) at the southern end of the Serra de Llevant. The hair-raising road up to it runs off the Felanitx–Porto Colom road, and the view from the top is certainly amazing enough to inspire world-conquering ambitions. There's a picnic area at the foot of the monastery car park – a wonderful spot for sunsets. You can also spend the night up here in the sanctuary (*see p195*).

To the south, on the neighbouring peak (408 metres/1,339 feet), are the ruins of the **Castell de Santuari**, a 14th-century fortress on the site of an earlier Moorish castle. Ask at the monastery for directions to the footpath (it's about a three-kilometre walk) or, alternatively, you can drive up to the castle from a minor road off the main MA-14. Frustratingly, you have to make do with gazing up at the ramparts as there's no access to the ruins from the road.

Located 18 kilometres (11 miles) north of Felanitx, and 48 kilometres (30 miles) east of Palma, **Manacor** is Mallorca's second-largest town (though a distant second: 34,000 inhabitants as opposed to a third of a million), its size mainly due to its status as a centre of industry. It's an ugly, sprawling place, centred on the church of **Nostra Senyora dels Dolors**, an effective piece of late 19th-century neo-Gothic, with an impressive belfry and altarpiece. Just north of the church is the late 13th-/early 14th-century **Torre del Palau**, the only remaining part of a royal palace built by Jaume II. A couple of minutes' walk north-west of here on Plaça de Convent is the **Convent de Vincenç Ferrer**, with its late 17th-century Baroque church and cloister.

There's a scruffy weekday morning market on Plaça Constitució and a Saturday morning crafts market on Plaça de sa Bassa, but most visitors to the town come for the pearls. Manacor is famed internationally as a centre for the manufacture of **Majorica** pearls, a high-quality artificial pearl that is supposedly all but indistinguishable from the real thing. If you want to learn more about how they are made (it involves an awful lot of fish scales),

Profile Rafael Nadal

The tennis star has injected a little glamour into gritty, grimy Manacor.

Known simply as 'Rafa' to his friends and fans, the great Rafael Nadal has probably done more in a single-handed volley to put Mallorca on the map than all the holidaying Hollywood hotties put together. Despite his tender years, the tennis superstar is already a national treasure.

Born in Manacor in 1986, Rafa was given his first racquet aged four and showed immediate promise. By 12 he had reached the final of Europe's most prestigious under-14s tournament; at 15 he turned professional; in 2000 he was a member of Spain's Davis Cup winning team; in 2003 he became the youngest man since Boris Becker to reach the third round at Wimbledon; in 2004 he won his first ATP title and was again part of the winning Spanish Davis Cup team. But it was 2005 that was truly Rafa's *annus mirabilis*, and the year in which he took his place among the tennis world's elite, with an astonishing eight ATP titles, including the French Open (he beat Roger Federer in the semis), and when he climbed to number two in the world rankings.

By 2008, after winning the Monte Carlo Masters for the fourth time, he had won 98 of 99 finals on clay, earning the more grown-up nickname of 'The King of Clay', while his first ever Wimbledon win had the Spanish press christening him 'El Matador' (the killer). The icing on the cake was his Olympic victory in Beijing, putting him firmly as the World Number One.

Frustratingly for Rafa, the last couple of years have seen this precocious talent take its toll. His seemingly unstoppable winning streak was cut short in the last quarter of 2008 as injuries to his knee caused him to miss both the Masters and the Davis Cup. But that doesn't stop the fans from adoring him. His website is littered with well-wishers, and, although his luminous sports attire, flowing locks and impassioned cries of *vamos!* on court pushed him well into the stratosphere of sports stardom in his late teens, the twentysomething Rafa has a social conscience too.

Fundación Rafa Nadal, launched in January 2008, is located in his hometown of Manacor and uses sport as a means to integrate the disadvantaged into society, both physically and financially. His hands-on approach is making him a hero as much as a star, while his deep-seated family values keep his feet firmly on the ground. As his mum recalls, 'I watch him on court and the way he behaves is the way he behaves in life – all heart, very responsible, hardworking and much more mature than most boys his age. But he is very untidy and disorganised. On the day of the French Open final I went into his room and I was shocked... it was a complete mess.'

FOR THE LATEST NEWS Check out www.rafael nadal.com.

join the coach parties who pile into the Majorica factory. The other notable 'product' of Manacor is tennis pro Rafael Nadal; *see p194* **Profile**.

A kilometre out of town, on the road to Cales de Mallorca, the **Torre dels Enagistes** is a 14th-century fortified enclosure that has been converted into Manacor's archaeological museum, the **Museu de Manacor**.

FREE Majorica

C/Pere Riche s/n, Manacor (971 55 09 00/ www.majorica.com). **Open** 9am-7pm Mon-Fri; 10am-1pm Sat, Sun. **Admission** free.

FREE Torre dels Enagistes – Museu de Manacor

Ctra. Cales de Mallorca, km1.5, Manacor (971 84 30 65/www.manacor.org). **Open** *Mid June-mid Sept* 9.20am-2pm, 6-8pm Mon, Wed-Sat. *Mid Sept-mid June* 10am-2pm, 5-7.30pm Mon, Wed-Sat; 10.30am-7pm Sun. **Admission** free.

Where to stay & eat

Just outside **Felanitx**, off the road to Manacor, **Sa Posada d'Aumallia** (Camí Son Prohens 1027, 971 58 26 57, www.aumallia.com, closed Nov-Jan, doubles €123-€145 incl breakfast), at the end of a fragrant, tree-lined lane, is a sociable place with alfresco piano suppers every night. The decor is smart, if a bit fusty, but staff are friendly. A cheaper option is to stay in one of the 14 rooms at the **Santuari de Sant Salvador** (Puig de Sant Salvador, 971 82 72 82, doubles €68), relatively spruced-up compared to its counterparts, but also with stunning views.

Foodwise, Felanitx is no hottie, but it does boast a handful of old-school noisy bars. **Bar Alhambra** (Plaça d'Espanya 6, mobile 667 35 21 35) packs in the punters on Sundays with the lure of top-notch tapas and crisp cold sherry. If you've kids in tow, the terrace is handily located next to a tots' fun fair. **Can Felia 07** (Plaça d'Espanya 7, 971 82 76 99, closed Sat) does a basic lunchtime *menú* (€7.50 Mon-Sat; €9.50 Sun lunch) consisting of crowd-pleasing salads, roast chicken and crocks of snails.

There's cut-price luxury to be had just five kilometres north of **Manacor** on the road to Artà. **Hotel Rural Son Trobat** (Ctra. Manacor–Sant Llorenç, km4.8, 971 56 96 74, www.sontrobat.com, closed Dec & Jan, doubles €110-€160 incl breakfast) has 25 huge bedrooms and bathrooms, including a suite with a bed tucked under a brick archway. There are charming gardens and patios and a swimming pool.

Even grander is **La Reserva Rotana** (Camí de S'Avall, km3, 971 84 56 85, www. reservarotana.com, closed mid Nov-Jan, €280 incl breakfast), also just north of Manacor

(take the PMV 332-1). This rather aristocratic 17th-century *possessió* is furnished with stags' heads and hunting prints and boasts its own nine-hole golf course (use of which is included in the room price) in addition to a swimming pool and tennis court. If you can live without the grandeur and the golf, then at the same location you'll find the far cheaper *agroturismo* **Es Mayolet** (Camí de S'Avall, km3, 971 84 56 85, www.mayolet.com, €140 incl breakfast).

Another lovely country hideaway is a similar distance from Manacor on the road to Cales de Mallorca. **Son Amoixa Vell Hotel Rural** (Ctra. Cales de Mallorca–Manacor, km5.4, 971 84 62 92, www.sonamoixa.com, closed 1-25 Dec, doubles €188-€255 incl breakfast) is a light, airy, elegant and extremely comfortable German-owned finca. Facilities include a secluded pool, tennis court, small sauna and exercise room. Breakfast is a generous buffet and new guests are warmly welcomed with a complimentary bottle of cava in their room.

Between Manacor and Artà, **Sant Llorenç de Cardassar** is an unremarkable spot except for one great restaurant and a smart new boutique hotel. **Petit Hotel Son Penya** (Camí de Son Berga s/n, 971 82 66 40, www.son penya.com, closed Dec-Mar, double €196-€220) is a getaway to cool in the midst of almond groves. All 12 bedrooms have their own terrace overlooking rolling countryside, and open-plan bathrooms. Mallorcan stone floors, wood beams and exposed stone keep it authentic. A pool, restaurant and library with open fireplace ensure a good time any time of year.

Well worth crossing the island for is Michelin-starred **Es Molí de'n Bou** (C/Lilas s/n, Sa Coma, 971 56 96 63, closed Mon & Tue all year, mid Jan-Feb, €€€€), which was moving to **Sa Coma** at the time of going to press. It serves up perfect, simple Mallorcan peasant dishes with a contemporary twist and has a 200-strong list of Spanish wines. The lunchtime *menú* at just under €50 is a good alternative to eating à la carte.

ARTA

Heading north out of Manacor, the MA-15 runs through picturesque orchards and pastureland until, after 20 kilometres (12.5 miles), you come to **Artà**, the kind of small town that people write books and make movies about. It's rarely troubled by the coastal package tourists and, with a combination of great architecture, some excellent places to eat and stay, an arty community and some of the region's most secluded beaches nearby (*see p198*), it's a true jewel of the east.

The literal high point of the town is the **Santuari de Sant Salvador d'Artà**. It's ringed by metre-thick walls that have stood since Moorish times, giving protection against pirate raids, though the sanctuary itself is a 19th-century neo-classical structure; there's a good café up here.

On the way back down the hill towards town you'll pass the late 16th-century church of the **Transfiguració del Senyor**. Its museum (C/Sant Salvador s/n, 971 83 60 20, open 10am-2pm, 3-5pm Mon-Sat, closed 4wks Dec-Jan, €1.30) has displays of religious artefacts, as well as a video showing the unusual celebrations of the **Festa de Sant Antoni Abat** (mid Jan), when revellers in traditional dress fill the church and behave more like football fans than churchgoers, chanting and jumping around. Other townsfolk dress up as horned and hairy devils, ride horses backwards and generally terrorise the rest of the populace with big sticks. Somehow all this is supposed to protect both the local livestock and local population from harm. A bigger regional museum in the Plaça Espanya was still closed for renovations at the time of going to press, with no date yet known for its reopening.

Artà's main attractions are eating, drinking and shopping. The Tuesday market is a lure for people from all over the island, who come to enjoy live folk music and crafts ranging from artisan jewellery and bags to Alpaca shawls, Panama hats and South African basketware. Note that the covered municipal market was closed for renovation at the time of writing, save for the excellent spit-roasted chicken stand, which is still doing a roaring trade.

The main drag – C/Antoni Blanes and C/Ciutat – is a wide pedestrianised street lined with bars, restaurants and shops, like bakery **Can Matemales** (C/Antoni Blanes 5, no phone, closed Mon), selling wonderful breads, pastries and pies; and **DOMUSart** (C/Ciutat 12, 971 83 69 69), which sells repro tiles, chicken doorstops and furniture. It's great for gifts. Around the corner on the Plaça del Conquistador you'll find **Vino y Más** (C/Montserrat Blanes II, 971 83 50 25), specialising in gourmet Mallorcan products such as aïoli with paprika, olive pâté, jams and preserves, as well as a good selection of local wines. It's great for picnics.

Two kilometres south of town, you can step back in time at the megalithic settlement of **Ses Païsses**. The extensive (but not easily interpreted) ruins date from 1000-800 BC; the main entrance portal, built from three massive stone blocks, is perhaps the most impressive of the remains.

Ses Païsses

Camí de sa Corbaia (619 07 00 10). **Open** *Apr-Oct* 10am-1pm, 3-7pm daily. *Nov-Mar* 9am-1pm, 2-5pm Mon-Fri. **Admission** €2. **No credit cards.**

Where to eat & drink

The main drag C/Antonio Blanes–C/Ciutat with its eye-popping views of the church and castle is lined with numerous bars and restaurants, a mix of old and new. One of the best is **Café Parisien** (C/Ciutat 18, 971 83 54 40, closed Sun and Nov-Feb, €€), a lovely colonial-style townhouse with high ceilings and tiled floors, as well as an enchanting fragrant courtyard shaded by lemon trees and vines. It offers great home-made cakes and pastries as well as a bistro-style menu with the likes of beef salad, goat's cheese and onion tart with fig confit, and mushroom and herb risotto. There's live jazz on Saturday evenings. Across the street, **El Dorada** (C/Ciutat 17, 971 83 50 20, noon-4pm, 7pm-midnight Mon-Sat) is always packed with locals for breakfast, lunch and dinner, offering an extensive menu of crowd-pleasers ranging from tasty crisp-fried croquettes to a variety of tortillas. It also does takeaway. **Café Ciutat** (C/Ciutat 26, 971 56 20 86, open 8am-10pm Mon-Thur, 8am-2am Fri, Sat) has Wi-Fi and knocks out decent coffee.

Artà's most exciting newcomer is the **Club Ca'n Moray** and **Restaurant La Calatrava** (C/Ses Roques 13, 971 82 91 53/mobile 626 59 93 10, www.clubcanmoray.com/www.restaurant lacalatrava.com, closed Nov, €€). The concept was to create a members' club atmosphere without the need for membership or entry fees. As such, anyone is welcome at this old village school built around a tiled courtyard and fountain with three resident goldfish. There's a chill-out lounge for cocktails, a billiard room, a bridge room, a coffee bar, a winter restaurant warmed by a regal fireplace and a wine terrace with 140-year-old vines. There's also a library and work space with Wi-Fi. The restaurant offers a three-course lunch for €19.50 and a more innovative evening *menú* (€48 including wine) of dishes such as beef tartare with wasabi caviar, duck breast with Brussels sprouts and truffles, and green apple cream with champagne sorbet.

INSIDE TRACK
FINCA ES SERRAL

As well as its ethically spotless menu of locally produced, organic fare, **Finca Es Serral** is worth going to for rare Mallorcan sweet treats such as *greixonera dulce* – a sort of bread and butter pudding that really only exists in old-fashioned Mallorcan farmhouse kitchens. Unless your granny's Mallorquí, you're unlikely to have come across it before.

Café Parisien.

Just outside Artà is another of the region's most wonderful restaurants, **Finca Es Serral** (Ctra. Cala Torta, km5, 971 83 53 36, ring for opening times, €€). It's run by a charming couple, Sebastián Amorós and Margarita Lliteras (he toils the land, she cooks its bounty), who are as passionate about saving the planet as they are about their organic produce. Their meat and vegetables are reared and grown within sight of the kitchen window to produce dishes tried and tested by previous generations; the almond soup and tender spring lamb are particularly good.

Where to stay

The prime property in town is the **Hotel Sant Salvador** (C/Castellet 7, 971 82 95 55, www.santsalvador.com, €112-€220 incl breakfast), although service can be a little stuffy. It's a small hotel set within an unusual mansion built in 1890 by a rich textile merchant; locals claim that the wonderful curving interior façade was designed by Gaudí, though there's no written evidence to back this up. Each of the eight spacious rooms is individually designed and combines an inspired mix of the contemporary and traditional, with no holding back in the use of bold, bright colours. There's a small garden with a pool.

Ca'n Moragues (C/Pou Nou 12, 971 82 95 09, www.canmoragues.com, €114-€127) by contrast is a tastefully converted 19th-century townhouse, still in the same family and with much of its original antique furniture. It has a laid-back atmosphere with an honesty bar, outdoor plunge pool, sauna and sun terrace. The family also owns a farm outside the town and can organise hiking and horseriding.

Hotel Restaurante S'Abeurador (C/Abeurador 21, 971 83 52 30, doubles €76-€86 incl breakfast) is another townhouse hotel with lots of charm, replete with old farm furniture and cobblestone floors. Towards the rear are terraces with fountains, fruit trees and the

scent of herbs and flowers. Rooms lead off this secret garden; one is a 100-year-old converted chapel. There is also a restaurant.

For something a little more hip and gay-friendly, try **Hotel Casal d'Artà** (C/Rafael Blanes 19, 971 82 91 63, www.casaldarta.de, doubles €80-€96), which opened in 1936, but has been recently taken over by a German couple. They've done great things with the place, turning the downstairs rooms into a cute breakfast room with a terrace on the plaça (a small bar will also open next year) and a living room with TV area. The eight bedrooms vary in terms of facilities and are all individually decorated in Mallorcan style. There's also a roof terrace with fabulous views over the rooftops.

South of Artà, on the MA-4031 to Son Servera, is **Son Gener** (Ctra. Son Servera–Artà, km3, 971 18 36 12, www.songener.com, closed 1 Dec-20 Jan, junior suites €280 incl breakfast restaurant €€€), an 18th-century farmhouse that has been transformed by a Mallorcan architect-designer into an airy haven of contemporary design. All ten guest rooms are junior suites with their own terraces, and facilities include a pool, spa and restaurant. **Ses Cases de Fetget** (Ctra. Vella Son Servera–Artà, km1, 971 81 73 63, www.sescasesdefetget.com, doubles €120-€155 incl breakfast) offers a similar vibe on a more modest budget, while **Son Cardaix** (Ctra. Palma-Artà, km63.2, 971 82 91 38, www.soncardaix.com, doubles €100-€185) offers the same budget and facilities, designed around the comforts of home, as opposed to the pages of *Wallpaper**.

Resources

Internet
Arta Café Ciutat, C/Ciutat 26 (971 56 20 86).
Open 8am-10pm Mon-Thur; 8am-2am Fri, Sat.

Police station
Artà *Plaça Espanya 1 (971 82 95 95).*
Felanitx *C/Ernest Mestre 64 (971 58 22 00).*
Manacor *Avda. del Parc s/n (971 55 00 48/63).*

Post office
Artà *C/Ciutat 26 (971 83 61 27).*
Felanitx *C/Costa i Llobera 32 (971 58 02 52).*
Manacor *C/Via Palma 100 (971 55 18 39).*

GETTING THERE

By bus
See p206.

By train
There are 13-14 trains daily from Palma to Manacor (1hr 4mins) via Sineu (48mins) and Petra (56mins).

EAST MALLORCA

East Coast

Remarkable natural caves and some remarkably hideous resorts.

The eastern coastline, once marked by pristine coves and specked with fishing villages, has now largely been swallowed up by low-rise Daz-white holiday complexes. However, the resorts here can vary dramatically – from the old-fashioned calm of Porto Colom to the nouveau riche, nouveau Ibiza flash of Cala d'Or and the all-inclusive monster complexes of Cala Millor. The wild north-east, beyond Cala Ratjada, has yet to be developed. Barren it may be, but here's where to head if you want virgin beaches.

THE NORTH-EASTERN BEACHES, CAPDEPERA & CALA RÁTJADA

The north-easterly hook of Mallorca is the east coast's greatest asset, a wild and wind-buffeted stretch of desolate hills and rugged cliffs between **Cap de Ferrutx** and **Cap des Freu**. Dotted along this seemingly inhospitable terrain are some of the best and most secluded beaches in the east. From Artà, head towards Capdepera and almost immediately take a left (north) turn along a steadily rougher and more winding road, through green craggy peaks to the popular but still wild-feeling **Cala Torta**. Camper vans and cars use the back of the beach as a car park/picnic area/campsite, but it's big enough to handle it. Cala Torta is a horseshoe bay with a fine sand beach backed by dunes and pines; there's also a beach bar, **Bar Cala Torta** (*see p199*), that does excellent fish.

Walk over the rocky headland to your left (as you face the sea) to reach **Cala Mitjana**, similar to Torta but a bit smaller and with no bar. Heading straight there by car, it's easier to leave it where the road forks in two – right to Cala Mitjana and left to the narrow inlet of **Cala Estreta**. The latter has no sand, but a deep, beautifully clear natural pool for swimming. Both are a ten-minute walk from the fork, or an uncomfortably potholed drive. If you want even more isolation, you can continue westwards along the coast to a number of increasingly remote beaches, including **Cala Matzoc**, **Sa Font Salada** and **S'Arenalet d'Aubarca**. For details of how to reach these idyllic strands, *see pp204-205* **Walk**.

Travelling from Artà to Cala Ratjada, you can't miss the crenellated battlements of the 14th-century **Castell de Capdepera**, the focal point of the village of **Capdepera**. A local legend recounts that the citizens, under siege from pirates, placed a statue of the Virgin on the battlements, whereupon the invaders were suddenly driven away by a thick fog.

Present-day invaders who don't suffer from vertigo can make a circuit of the walls (the walkway is narrow and there's no safety rail on the inside), which offer fine views, taking in Menorca across the sea to the north-east.

It was from the castle, in 1232, that Jaume I, with a depleted and largely untrained band of men, conquered Menorca without firing a shot. In the dead of night he sent six riders to light 300 fires on the hillsides and along the coast. The Moorish rulers of Menorca were so alarmed and impressed at this apparently mighty army that they surrendered the island and offered themselves as the King's vassals.

There's not much else within the walls to explore beyond the pretty Gothic church of **Nostra Senyora de la Esperança**, but Capdepera itself is a pleasant place for a wander around the Plaça de l'Orient. The village's medieval fair takes place over the third weekend of May and involves hog roasts, market stalls, concerts and much pageantry and it's a far nicer base than nearby Cala Ratjada. One of the few reminders of its basket-weaving past is **Ca'n Cosset** (Pla de'n Cosset 12, 971 56 40 00), which is worth a look for a peek at how its done.

From Capdepera, a minor road runs north to another fine beach, **Cala Mesquida**, once a smuggling centre. The turquoise lapping on virgin white sand backed by windswept dunes is an idyllic scene until you spot the sprawling tourist resort, which crowds one side of the bay.

The main seaside resort on this part of the coast is **Cala Ratjada** (12 kilometres east of Artà), once a small, charming fishing village until it was picked as one of the first places to be developed for tourism on the island. It's now a German- and British-dominated hotspot in season and largely dead out of it.

If you want to stop to swim, the busy town beach, **Platja de Son Moll**, is backed by hotels, bars and restaurants, or there's the smaller **Cala Gat**, a few minutes' walk from the port in the other direction. Across the headland, **Cala Agulla** is a sweeping curve of white sand lapped by blue water. There are developments (a comfortable distance inland) and it has all the usual services, including beach bars and a restaurant, but its collar of pine-backed dunes gives it that all-important wild air.

Castell de Capdepera

Capdepera (971 81 87 46). **Open** *Apr-Oct* 9am-8pm daily. *Nov-Mar* 9am-5pm daily. **Admission** €2; free reductions. **No credit cards**.

Where to stay & eat

If you're heading for the north-east coast beaches, the best (and only) places to get a bite and a drink are **Bar Cala Torta** on **Cala Torta** (no phone, open only in good weather, €€), a simple *chiringuito* (beach shack) on the beach serving excellent boat-fresh fish and seafood, for which it charges princely sums, or the starkly beautiful **Bar-Restaurante Sa Duaia** (Ctra. Artà–Cala Torta, km8, mobile 651 82 64 16, closed Mon and Nov-Mar, €€), which stands alone in the hills over a sea dotted with pristine white sails. Service is slow, and the food is inconsistent, but the view more than makes up for it. If you're eating, you can also use the pool. There's also a well-marked walk of about 45 minutes each way leading off from the car park, if you fancy a stroll before or after lunch, and it has some quite lovely rooms and apartments to rent.

There's unexpectedly good eating to be had in **Capdepera**. For French-style romance, **Renaissance** (C/Nou 29, 971 56 37 13) gets top billing, while **La Fragua** (C/des Pla den Cosset 3, 971 81 94 03, closed Tue, Feb) goes in for stargazing, offering more traditional Mallorcan meals on a handsome rooftop. For lunch, **Es Castell** (C/Major 47, 971 56 57 30, closed Mon and sporadically; call in advance, €), is more rustic, serving generous slabs of *pa amb oli* topped with ham, cheese and salad, along with home-made pâté and superb *sobrassada* and

honey. On the Plaça de l'Orient there are several places to choose from, including lively bars for drinks when the sun goes down. The **Bar Segle XII** offers a range of cocktails including Menorca's famed *pomada* (gin with lemonade), and has the odd party through the summer. Next door the newly refurbished **Café l'Orient** (971 56 30 98) is good for a light bite, and across the way **Kikinda** (971 56 30 14, closed Nov-mid Dec, €) has a trendier vibe for pizza.

Off the road from Capdepera to Cala Mesquida, **Cases de Son Barbassa** (Ctra. Cala Mesquida, 971 56 57 76, www.son barbassa.com, doubles €75-€102, closed mid Nov-mid Feb) is one of the trendiest places to stay in the area. Though parts of it are 500 years old, it offers modern, comfortable rooms decorated in hues of sand and slate, and draped daybeds around a swimming pool and pseudo-Moroccan chill-out lounge, Ibiza-style.

In **Cala Ratjada**, the newest and coolest place to stay is the **Sea Club** (971 56 33 10, www.theseaclub.es, doubles €140-€250), a lavishly restored colonial pad with 12 bedrooms as well as some individual *casitas* and cottages scattered throughout the grounds. Alternatively, if you just want somewhere to lay your head before taking the boat to Menorca, there's **Hostal Ca's Bombu** (C/Leonor Servera 86, 971 56 32 03, www.casbombu.com, closed Nov-Easter, doubles €34-€41 incl breakfast), which has been here since 1885, and which in its day attracted the island's artists and intellectuals. The rooms are simple but appealing; those in the old building have original 19th-century patterned floor tiles. There's also the three-star **Ses Rotges** (C/Rafael Blanes 21, 971 56 31 08, www.sesrotges.com, closed Nov-Apr, doubles €106-€127 incl breakfast) hotel and restaurant. All the bedrooms here have wooden beams, stone tiles and traditional Mallorcan wooden beds, with differences created by stripy or patchwork bedlinen. The restaurant (€€€€) takes inspiration from French cuisine, and has a romantic patio for summer dining.

Other eating options include stylish **El Cactus** (C/Leonor Servera 83, 971 56 46 09,

---

INSIDE TRACK
CALA ROTJA

If you don't want to sit down and eat here, the shallow cliffs that stretch out before it make a great spot for a picnic on the water's edge. Face the sea, turn to the right and you'll see a teeny tiny beach and swimming pool steps into a natural swimming hole.

EAST MALLORCA

closed Mon in Aug and Nov-Feb, €€), with white candles in large glass vases, and milk-fed lamb and good fish dishes on the menu. On the harbour try **La Bodeguita** (Avda. América 14, 971 81 90 62, €), which is open all year round and specialises in Mallorcan dishes, with tables overlooking the seafront and a garden out back; there's a good tapas deal: €8.50 for six tapas.

CANYAMEL, CALA MILLOR, CALA BONA & PORTO CRISTO

Heading south down the coast (though only accessible from the Capdepera–Son Servera road) is **Canyamel**, a more upmarket-feeling resort etched into rugged red-hued cliffs. Development here has been kept in check and consists of a handful of apartment blocks, clusters of villas and a couple of large, 1970s-style hotels. The beach has a pleasant, family-oriented vibe with a couple of *chiringuitos* and beach volley as opposed to jet skis. Come out of season and you'll find a sprinkling of surfers taking advantage of bigger swells. Add one fabulous boutique hotel and a hip lobster restaurant, and Canyamel seems to be making a serious bid to become the most desirable beach town on the east coast.

It's also the closest settlement to the **Coves d'Artà** (often signposted in its Castilian form as Cuevas de Artà). These spectacular caverns make a bold bid for being the island's best caves by dubbing themselves the 'ninth wonder of the world'. Guided tours lead you through the thoroughly sanitised system, but it doesn't take a huge leap of imagination to envisage the awe felt by French geologist Edouard Martel when he first explored it in 1876. They'd been known about for centuries, however – Jaume I supposedly found 2,000 Moors sheltering inside them after his 13th-century conquest of Mallorca. The caves can also be visited by boat from Cala Millor and Cala Ratjada.

The monster developments of **Cala Millor** and **Cala Bona** have little to recommend themselves and are best bypassed. Close by, though, the virgin, scrubby promontory of **Punta de n'Amer**, with low cliffs rising from clear water, has been a protected area since 1986, and so has avoided the scarring tourist developments that have blighted the coastline on either side of it. It's nice for a walk, with an easy footpath leading from the end of Cala Millor beach to a 17th-century defensive tower and a 21st-century bar.

Continuing south, **Porto Cristo** is a lovely bay, granted, but somewhat spoiled by the tacky souvenir shops and touristy restaurants that line it. In sunshine it just about gets away with it, but when the sky is grey it has a

gloomy, slightly depressing air. This may have something to do with its history. In 1936, Republican troops landed here (Mallorca had been taken over by the Nationalists at the outbreak of the Civil War; Menorca remained loyal to the Republic) and made rapid gains before running out of steam and ideas just a couple of weeks later. They were pushed back by a Nationalist counter-attack and were forced to evacuate to the mainland.

In terms of sights, however, Porto Cristo is perfect rainy day material. It has two major cave complexes. The lesser known is the **Coves d'es Hams** (Cuevas dels Hams in Castilian), accessed from the road to Manacor. Discovered in 1905, these modestly sized but beautiful caves (given fanciful names like 'Milton's Lost Paradise' and 'Fairy Cemetery') are famed for their weird tree-like formations. The guided tours in small groups culminate in a short concert of classical music from musicians in boats floating on an underground lake.

The major tourist attraction in these parts, though (and possibly the best-known sight on the island), is the **Coves del Drac** (or Cuevas del Drac in Castilian). The first thing you have to get over is that these positively seethe with coach parties all day every day and have been totally commercialised. What is amazing is that these astonishing caverns are no less remarkable for the intrusion. Not only is

Castell de Capdepera. *See p198.*

their extent impressive (they stretch for 1.7 kilometres), but so is the sheer extravagance of their decoration – with weirdly formed and coloured stalagmites and millions of needle-sharp stalactites covering every inch of their roofs. Visitors shuffle along a path for about a kilometre before sitting in a huge natural amphitheatre in front of one of the world's largest underground lakes and, just as in the Coves d'es Hams, watching a water-borne classical music performance. It should be hopelessly corny, but it's really rather lovely.

Close by is the **Acuàrium de Mallorca**, which seems to have remained as is since it opened in the mid 1970s – as such it's not recommended.

★Coves d'Artà

Ctra. de las Coves s/n, Canyamel (971 84 12 93/www.cuevasdearta.com). **Open** *Apr-Oct* 10am-6pm daily. *Nov-Mar* 10am-5pm daily. **Admission** €10; €5 reductions; free under-6s. **No credit cards**.

★Coves del Drac

Ctra. de les Coves s/n, Porto Cristo (971 82 07 53/www.covesdeldrac.com). **Open** *Mar-Oct* 10am-5pm daily. *Nov-Feb* Guided tours at 10.45am, noon, 2pm & 3.30pm daily. **Admission** €10.50; free under-6s. **No credit cards**.

Coves d'es Hams

Ctra. Porto Cristo–Manacor, km1 (971 82 09 88/www.cuevas-hams.com). **Open** *Summer* 10am-1.30pm, 2-5.30pm daily. *Winter* 10.30am-5pm daily. **Admission** €9.80; free under-12s. **Credit** MC, V.

Torre de Canyamel

Ctra. Artà–Canyamel, km5 (971 84 11 34). **Open** *Apr-Oct* 10am-6pm Tue-Sat; 10am-5pm Sun. **Admission** €3; €1.50 reductions. **No credit cards**.

Where to stay & eat

Just outside **Canyamel**, **Can Simoneta** (Ctra. Artà–Canyamel, km8, 971 81 61 10, www.cansimoneta.com, doubles €185-€375 for the grand suite, incl breakfast, open Feb-Nov) is arguably one of the most spectacular places to stay on the island. The bowling-green lawn stretches down to the edge of the cliff, while handsome pines strung with hammocks line the property. An outdoor lounge area houses an infinity pool; a stroll one way leads to a couple's jacuzzi and usually a pair of love birds, a stroll in the other to a Turkish bath and sauna. Inside it's all champagne marble, white couches, antique pine beams and furniture. But, the pièce de résistance is a secret staircase that

leads down to a rock beach; staff at the hotel are happy to pack you a picnic if you ask.

Off the same road, the more affordable **Na Set Centes** (Ctra. Arta–Canyamel, km2.7, 971 83 54 29, www.nasetcentes.com, doubles €116 incl breakfast) has three doubles and one suite, decorated in warm colours and natural materials; all have their own terraces and fine views. The surrounding gardens are dotted with olive trees and palms and has a lovely family feel to the place, and the owners whip up a wonderful breakfast of *pa amb oli* and delicious omelettes.

In town, the **Cap Vermell Beach Hotel, Club & Restaurant** (Plaça Pins de Ses Vegues 1, 971 84 11 57, www.capvermell-beachclub.com, doubles with sea view €150-€180 incl breakfast) is a recently revamped model of a classic dating back to 1934. The best rooms have sea views and terraces, and all have free Wi-Fi, although the decor is a little dated. The acclaimed restaurant, 1934, boasts its own lobster cellar, where you can go and choose from a variety of species while quieting your conscience with a glass of champagne. If you don't want to eat, the 'Champagne Terrace', which seems to float out at sea, is great for a sundowner.

More modest accommodation can be found at the **Hotel Laguna** (Via Costa I Llobera 16, 971 84 11 50, closed Nov-Feb), a 1970s style block on the beach, newly spruced up with poppy-red shutters and smart balconies.

For eats, continuing past Can Simoneta will take you to **Cala Rotja** (C/Via de las Calas s/n, Urb. Costa Canyamel, 971 84 15 13, www.cala rotja.com, closed Tue), which offers a seaside terrace carefully sheltered from the wind with glass breakers. The menu is a little fussy, but more simple dishes such as Galician octopus salad, gilthead bream with wild garlic shoots, and rice dishes are all good.

Heading back out of town, next to the Torre de Canyamel, the **Porxada de Sa Torre** (971 84 13 10, closed dinner Sun, all Mon and Dec-Jan, €€) is a good-value, simple restaurant,

INSIDE TRACK
TORRE DE CANYAMEL

Off the road between Canyamel and Artà is a 13th-century fortified tower, the Torre de Canyamel, which can be visited. Impressively preserved, notwithstanding the soot marks from the fire that swept through it 30 or so years ago when farm workers still lived here, it houses antique farming implements, a weaving loom, a kneading trough and old guns.

EAST MALLORCA

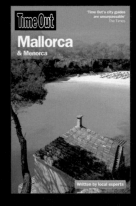

which knocks out straighforward Spanish standards such as baked fish, roast chicken and suckling pig (the house speciality).

Porto Cristo is not well served for hotels and has few decent places to eat. On the promenade, the **THB Felip Hotel** (C/Burdils 41, 971 82 07 50, www.thbhotels.com, doubles €66-€113 incl breakfast) feels a bit like a cheap version of an old-style colonial hotel (it's been around for over a century), with wicker chairs and an airy lounge, and balconies for most of its rooms. Perched on the cliff at the north end of the beach, **Restaurant Flamingo** (C/Burdils s/n, 971 82 22 59, closed Nov-mid Feb, €€) is distinguished by its colourful hand-painted signs featuring cartoon characters and its terrace overlooking the water; home-made *fideuà* (a sort of noodle paella) and paella itself are the highlights of the menu.

By far the classiest place to stay in the area, however, is located five kilometres south of Porto Cristo, just off the road to Porto Colom. **Son Mas** (Camí de Son Mas s/n, 971 55 87 55, www.sonmas.com, closed Dec-Jan, suites €244-€276 incl. breakfast) is an immaculate, tranquil *hotel rural*, centred on a 17th-century watchtower (containing the perfect, circular honeymoon suite) and surrounded by a huge estate of fig, almond, carob and orange trees. All the rooms are immense junior suites, and all are decorated in stunning less-is-more chic, with sandblasted marble floors, huge beds, beamed ceilings, antique wood furniture, soothing earth tones and vast terraces. The public areas are studies in the use of architectural space (the original mill is incorporated in one of them), and are warmed by log fires on cold evenings. There are pools both inside (with massage jets and a sauna) and outside, and a restaurant for guests serving a set menu (except Tuesdays).

PORTO COLOM, CALA D'OR & PORTO PETRO

Sandwiched between Porto Cristo and Porto Colom are the sprawling villa horror resorts collectively known as **Cales de Mallorca**. The only reason to come anywhere near here is to see the serene prehistoric village of **Hospitalet Vell** (signed from the road towards Cales de Mallorca, then a couple of hundred metres' walk off to the right). This is one of the most important talayotic sites on Mallorca, yet has a (not unattractive) air of neglect and decay about it (a rusted sign, in a curious but apt translation, invites visitors to 'locate the forlornness of the village at the end of the second century BC'). Hardly anyone comes here. First settled in the pre-Talayotic period (and partially reoccupied in Roman and Moorish times), it preserves its quadrangular

talayot, a number of dwellings and an impressive chunk of defensive wall.

Porto Colom is the next stop along the coast, 21 kilometres (13 miles) south of Porto Cristo and 11 kilometres south-east of Felanitx. Really it is two harbours: the oldest, serene and lovely is arranged around a pretty little harbour lined by traditional fishing sloops and protected from the Med by an old-fashioned, black and white-striped lighthouse and the headlands Punta de ses Crestes and Punta de sa Bateria. It was originally developed as a port for transporting wine from Felanitx to France (before phylloxera destroyed the wine industry in the 1870s; it has recently revived), and there are still some attractive 19th-century villas overlooking the long and winding promenade. Cutely painted, flat-fronted cottages mingle with lush villas and modern holiday homes. The other is a little more developed, and has most of the town's accommodation. Many Felanitx residents have holiday properties here, giving the summer festivals, such as the sea-based festival of **Mare de Déu del Carme** on 16 June, a more local flavour and vibrancy than is often the case in this area. There is nowhere particularly memorable to stay (yet), but the old fishing harbour has some excellent places to eat (as long as you like fish).

Continuing south, you soon come to **Cala d'Or**, a major tourist development stretching across a series of resorts that cluster around a succession of coves and inlets. Each has its marina jammed with yachts and pleasure cruisers, its blocks of white boxy Ibiza-style holiday apartments and hotels, and low-rise bars and restaurants servicing British resort tastes – pub grub, pizza, curry, Thai. It's billed as a glamorous resort, but this really translate as leathery tans and bad gold jewellery.

Porto Petro, neighbouring Cala d'Or to the south, manages to calm the brashness down a bit. It's more of a traditional harbour, with leafy back roads leading down to whitewashed harbour cottages, most of which have now converted into restaurants. The lack of beach means that development has been more contained than further north. It's also worth heading a just a few kilometres inland from here to the pretty village of Calonge, which has several decent restaurants and a couple of cute interiors shops.

For the enjoyable low-key resorts at Mallorca's south-east tip, *see p188*.

Where to stay & eat

Off the road from Porto Cristo to Porto Colom, inland from Cales de Mallorca, is **Son Josep de Baix** (Ctra. Porto Colom–Porto Cristo, km8.4, 971 65 04 72, www.sonjosepdebaix.com,

Walk North-east Coast

Empty beaches and explorable ruins.

Distance: 9km. Linear.
Time: 2hrs 50mins.

30-plus years of mass tourism have put pay to the possibility of finding an as-of-yet undiscovered beach on Mallorca. But seclusion seekers rejoice – there are still some hard-to-access gems that attract only those willing to walk some distance to reach them, which means that they are never crowded.

This short walk takes in an invigorating stretch of the rugged and blissfully undeveloped coastline north of Artà before arriving at a couple of such beaches. The walking is relatively easy, though some short but steepish ascents and descents are required, and there's almost no shade available (so don't attempt it in the full heat of the summer). Be warned that there are no facilities at these beaches – be sure to bring your own food and water.

To reach the starting point for the walk, take the road from Artà towards Capdepera and Cala Ratjada and, as soon as you've skirted around Artà, turn left where you see a sign pointing the way to Cala Torta. Almost immediately take the next right turn (to Calas Torta, Estreta and Mitjana). Follow this road for ten kilometres until it comes to the sea. The first kilometre is well surfaced, but the rest is rough (getting very rough indeed towards the end), but persevere and park your car at the point where the road reaches the sea by a narrow inlet (Cala Estreta) before it sweeps right to arrive at the beach at Cala Mitjana.

On the other side of the inlet you'll see a footpath rising up a low headland. Scramble down and up the other side of the inlet, and follow this path. After around ten minutes you pass through a rusty gate in a wire fence, before walking around a

closed Nov-Mar, apartment for 2 people €110), an unmissable *agroturismo* with deceptively modern and well-equipped self-catering apartments created in ancient outhouses around a ramshackle farmyard. Amid the flocks of goats, scratching chickens and flowering trees are a secluded pool, a barbecue for guests' use, and several private terraces.

For a small and friendly place to stay south of the harbour in **Porto Colom**, try **Hotel Bahia Azul** (Rda. Crucero Balear 78, 971 82 52 80, www.bahia-azul.de, closed Dec-Mar, doubles €65 incl breakfast), a plain but comfortable spot, run by the German Fecke family and popular with families and young couples. As well as a pool and sauna, this small 15-room

hotel overlooking the water also features a diving centre offering courses at all levels.

Another keenly priced spot to stay is smart **HPC** (C/Cristófal Colóm 5, 971 82 53 23, www.hostalportocolom.com, doubles €54-€96 incl. breakfast, restaurant €€) on the harbour front, which combines *hostal*, bar and decent restaurant, serving pizzas, pastas and more traditional Mallorcan grub.

On Porto Colom's newer waterfront **Bar Restaurant Florian** (C/Cristófal Colóm 11, 971 82 41 71, closed Thur, Nov-mid Dec) is a crisply furnished restaurant with an outdoor terrace facing the sea. Black-uniformed waiting staff serve creative cuisine, such as turbot poached in olive oil with shellfish couscous and cove and climbing up the next headland, from where you'll be able to see the 16th-century watchtower Torre des Matzoc just ahead of you.

The landscapes in this refreshingly virgin part of the island are parched, raw, barren (a series of forest fires has stripped the area of most of its trees) and almost lunar at times, but the sea as it meets the rocks is a translucent, inviting blue – it's certainly a world away from the intensive tourist developments along most of the north and east coasts.

Around 25 minutes after starting out you'll arrive at the beach of Cala Matzoc, which is often seaweed-strewn and, consequently, not that inviting. Continue onwards by climbing up the eroded area towards the front of the far side of the beach and walking through a clump of trees (which provide just about the only shade on the walk).

Ten minutes later you'll reach the watchtower. It's possible to climb up to the top, but the staircase stops short and you'll need to be fairly athletic (and brave) to clamber up the sticks jammed into the walls above it to emerge on the top, where a rusty old cannon has lain for centuries. If you're tempted do, though: the views make it worthwhile with the Talaia de Son Jaumell watchtower visible to the east and Talaia Moreia watchtower to the west on the dramatically jutting Cap de Ferrutx; beyond which it's possible to make out the Formentor peninsula.

Continue on around the next headland, following a rough path that becomes rockier and more indistinct until it passes through some scrubby trees and emerges high above a long, flattish, lower-lying area of rock. You'll see the path stretching away below you. Scramble down and follow it through this other-worldly landscape, passing through a rich vermilion seam of rock.

As you round the next headland you pass through a gate in a wire fence. You can spy a building ahead of you in the distance. This stands behind the beach of S'Arenalet d'Aubarca, the farthest point on this walk.

Around 40 minutes after leaving the watchtower, you arrive at the white-sand beach of Sa Font Salada. It's an idyllic spot, and it's easy to while away an hour or two lying here or swimming in the sea. Though you could also continue onwards for another ten minutes to the equally fine, and wider, beach of S'Arenalet d'Aubarca. School kids often stay in the building backing this beach, so, depending on your luck, you may have more company here than you might have hoped for.

When you've enjoyed all the rest and relaxation you can handle, retrace your steps along the coast and you should be back at the starting point in around one hour 25 minutes. If you feel in need of refreshment, the Bar-Restaurante Sa Duaia (see p199) is located a couple of kilometres from the sea, just off the road you came along. Or you can walk over the headland east of Cala Mitjana to the beach of Cala Torta, where there is a bar serving snacks and drinks.

fennel, and shoulder of lamb with a parmesan crust in black bread and balsamic sauce with aubergine *tumbet* (vegetable bake). For cheaper snacks, try the lunchtime tapas, such as pickled anchovies and shrimp kebabs. The excellent **Restaurante Colón** (C/Cristófal Colóm 7, 971 82 47 83, closed Wed and Jan-mid Feb, €€€) exudes cool, with elegant white candles in the large stone fireplace, leather sofas in the bar area and smooth service from the smart waiting staff. Dishes include *solomillo* of beef and duck liver, and marinated pig's trotters.

Over in the fishing harbour **La Llotja** (C/Pescadores s/n, 971 82 51 65, closed Mon and Nov-Dec) has a smart roof terrace overlooking the port and a lunch menu for €32. If you're after locally caught fish, though, stay à la carte and opt for *rape* (monkfish), *gallo* (John Dory) and *gambas rojas de Sóller* (Sóller red prawns). Further along, **Sa Sinia** (C/Pescadores s/n, 971 82 43 23, closed Mon, Nov-Jan) is a serious fish joint in a wood-panelled dining room, recommended by Michelin in 2008. **Club Nautic** (C/Pescadores 31, 971 82 46 90, closed Tue in winter) does a daily special such as *suquet* (a generous fish stew) for €18.90 (with many dishes costing less than this). If you walk round to the old town, built on top of a knoll that juts slightly out to sea and crowned by a church with no name, you'll find a handy bar serving cold beers from a hatch to drink on the harbour's edge, on the Plaça de Sant Jaume.

If you haven't got your own luxury yacht at **Cala d'Or**, staying at the **Hotel Cala d'Or** (Avda. de Belgica 33, 971 65 72 49, www.hotel calador.com, closed Nov-Mar, doubles €112 incl breakfast) is a fine alternative. This lovely 1930s whitewashed villa has light and airy lounges with comfy sofas. The rooms are slightly less chic, but all are comfortable, smart and clean, with views of the gardens or the sea. The hotel is right next to Cala d'Or's tiny beach, but you can avoid the hordes by swimming in the heated outdoor pool.

A family-oriented hotel in **Porto Petro** is the **Hostal Nereida** (C/Patrons Martina 3, 971 65 72 23, www.hostalnereida.com, closed Nov-Apr, call for prices), just back from the harbour, which has decent-sized, no-nonsense rooms, a large swimming pool and garden, table tennis and swings.

At the edge of Porto Petro's furthermost inlet, you can sit on the first-floor terrace of **Rafael y Flora**'s eponymous restaurant (C/Far 12, 971 65 78 09, closed Nov-Apr, €€) and stuff yourself with perfect paella or sole with ginger and onions. If you're feeling really greedy, start with some of Filipina Flora's oriental/Spanish tapas, such as satay chicken and Mallorcan spinach croquettes. On the edge of the harbour, **Ca'n Martina** (Passeig des Port 56, 971 65 75 17, €€, closed Nov-Feb) does a good breakfast but otherwise offers good value paella and seafood.

Five kilometres inland from Cala d'Or, in **Calonge**, you'll find **Zab** (Cala Llonga 4, 971 16 29 28, closed Nov-Feb), which fuses Thai and Italian cooking in a smart, converted townhouse. The next town along is **Alqueria Blanca** and a good place to enjoy rural accommodation. In the town itself, the **Hotel Son Llorenç** (C/Ramón Llull 7, 971 16 11 61, www.hotelsonllorenc.com, closed Nov, doubles €120 incl breakfast) has eight rooms in a sensitively converted townhouse. Breakfast is served on a charming, flower-filled terrace and there is a small library with a log fire in winter. Keep your eyes peeled on the road from here to Ca's Concos for **Es Pujol** (Camí des Pujols, 971 16 40 65/mobile 649 47 58 91, www.espujol.com, doubles €95-€100), a beautifully peaceful house, parts of which date back to the 13th century. There are four double rooms (one with its own kitchen) or the whole house can be rented. As well as a tennis court and small pool, Es Pujol also boasts its own tiny Gothic chapel.

In Alqueria Blanca itself you'll find the area's most upmarket restaurant, the intimate **Es Clos** (C/Convento 17, 971 65 34 04, www. es-clos.com, closed lunch and all Mon and Jan-Mar, €€€€), which specialises in creative cooking. Expect mains such as suckling pig with pumpkin and rabbit with cauliflower mousseline and mushrooms.

RESOURCES

Internet
Porto Cristo *Academia Porto Cristo, C/Sementera 43, Baixos (971 82 26 18).* **Open** 9am-1pm, 4-8pm Mon-Fri.
Son Servera *Rótulos, C/Juana Roca 119 (971 56 76 83).* **Open** 10am-1pm, 3.30-8.30pm Mon-Sat.

Police station
Cala Millor
C/Lloret 1 (971 81 40 76).
Cala Ratjada/Capdepera
C/Roses s/n (971 56 54 63).

Post office
Cala d'Or *Centre Civic 1 (971 65 94 64).*
Cala Ratjada *C/Magallanes 29 (971 81 86 22).*
Capdepera *C/Llum s/n (no phone).*
Porto Cristo *C/Zanglada s/n (no phone).*

Tourist information
Cala Millor *OIT, C/Parc de la Mar 2 (971 58 54 09/www.visitcalamillor.com).* **Open** *Apr-Oct* 9am-5pm Mon-Fri. *Nov-Mar* 9am-2pm Mon-Fri.
Cala d'Or *OIT, Avda. Perico Pomar 10 (971 65 74 63).* **Open** 8.15am-2.15pm Mon-Fri; 9am-2pm Sat.
Cala Ratjada/Capdepera *OIT, C/Castellets 5 (971 56 30 33).* **Open** 9.30am-1.30pm, 3.30-6pm Mon-Fri; 9am-2pm Sat.
Cales de Mallorca *OIT, Passeig de Manacor s/n (971 83 41 44/www.manacor.org).* **Open** 9am-4pm Mon-Fri. Closed Nov-Apr.
Porto Colom *OIT, Avda. Cala Marçal 15 (971 82 60 84/turisme@felanitx.org).* **Open** *Apr-Oct* 9am-1pm, 4-8pm Mon-Fri; 10am-7pm Sat. Closed Nov-Mar.
Porto Cristo *OIT, C/Moll s/n, Baixos (971 81 51 03/turisme@manacor.org).* **Open** *May-Oct* 9am-4pm Mon-Fri. *Oct-May* 9am-3pm Mon-Fri.
Son Servera *OIT, Avda. Joan Servera Camps s/n (971 58 58 64/www.sonservera.cat).* **Open** *May-Oct* 9am-5pm Mon-Sat. *Nov-Apr* 9am-3pm Mon-Fri; 10am-1pm Sat.

GETTING THERE

By bus
From Palma, there are 6 buses Mon-Sat (3 Sun) to Cala d'Or; 6 buses Mon-Sat (3 Sun) to Cala Millor; 3 buses Mon-Fri, Sun (2 Sat to Porto Colom; 2 buses Mon-Sat to Cales de Mallorca; 6 buses Mon-Sat (3 Sun) to Porto Cristo via Manacor and 4 buses Mon-Sat (2 Sun) to Cala Ratjada via Artà and Capdepera.

Menorca

Cala Macarella.
See p230.

Menorca

NORTH MENORCA (pp240-245)

CENTRAL MENORCA (pp234-229)

SOUTH MENORCA (pp221-233)

CIUTADELLA & WEST MENORCA (pp246-258)

MEDITERRANEAN SEA

Ciutadella
Maó
MAÓ
Alaior
Es Mercadal
Ferreries
Es Migjorn Gran
Sant Agustí
Sant Tomàs
Sant Climent
Es Castell
La Mola
Fort Sant Felip
Fort Marlborough
Torre d'en Penjat
Trebalúger
Sant Lluís
Es Consell
S'Algar
Cala d'Alcalfar
Punta Prima
Binibèquer Vell
Binissafúller
S'Ullastrar
Torret
Biniancolla
Binidalí
Es Canutells
Cala en Porter
Cales Coves
Torre d'en Gaumès
Son Vitamina
So na Caçana
Torralba d'en Salort
Torre-solí Nou
Rafal-Rubí
Talatí de Dalt
Torrellonet Vell
Fornàs de Torelló
Trepucó
Lluchassanès
Binissafúller
Sant Esteve
Sant Lluís
Es Grau
Sa Torre Blanca
Cala Tortuga
Cala d'en Colom
Illa d'en Colom
Walk (p242)
Centre de Na Torreta

Cap de Favàritx
Platja d'en Tortuga
Cap de Montsenyor Vives
Port d'Addaia
Illes d'Addaia
Na Macaret
Arenal de Son Saura
Son Parc
Arenal d'en Castell
Platges de Fornells
Ses Salines
Cala Tirant
Fornells
Sa Nitja
Ecomuseu de Cap de Cavalleria
Cap de Cavalleria
Cap de Fornells
Cap de Cavalleria
Platja de Cavalleria
Bay of Fornells
Puig de sa Roca
El Toro 357 m
Hort de Sant Patrici
Castell de Santa Agueda
Torrellafuda
Torretrencada
Naveta des Tudons
Pedreres de s'Hostal
Son Catlar
Cala Blanca
Cala de Santandria
Cala Morell
Cala en Brut
Cala en Blanes
Cala en Forcat
Punta Nati
Cap Gros
Cala Morell
Cala d'Algaiarens
Cala en Pilar
Cala Pregonda
Cala Pública Binimel·la
Illes Bledes
Illa des Porros
Cala Macarella
Cala en Turqueta
Cala Galdana
Cala Mitjana
Son Saura
Son Xoriguer
Cala d'Artrutx
Cap d'Artrutx
Cap d'en Font
Cap Negre
Illa de l'Aire
Illa de l'Addaia
Es Macar de sa Llosa
Na Mesquida
Cala Llonga
Sant Jaume Mediterrani
Son Bou
So na Caçana

Parc Natural de S'Albufera de Grau

CAMÍ DE CAVALLS
CAMÍ D'EN KANE

Me-1, Me-2, Me-5, Me-7, Me-8, Me-12, Me-13, Me-16, Me-18, Me-20, Me-22, Me-24

N

8 kms
5 miles

© Copyright Time Out Group 2009

Maó

Welcome to Europe's most manageable capital.

Shaped by the Moors, Catalans, British, French and Spanish, the harbour town of Maó, or Mahón in Spanish, once so strategically important during centuries of Mediterranean power struggles, is now simply a great place to spend a few days. Though it's Menorca's capital, the city lacks the usual swagger of a port town, and although the harbourside is given over almost entirely to tourism, it has none of the hedonistic horrors associated with other Balearic tourist towns. It's also tiny, making strolling round easy and ensuring that it's all but impossible to get lost.

When two rival towns compete for prime billing, one of them invariably falls shy of the other. In the case of Menorca, Ciutadella was undeniably top dog until the occupying British switched the island capital to Maó in the 18th century; a fact that still rankles with Ciutadella's inhabitants. Almost 300 years later, Ciutadella still feels more like the coherent, organic town, while Maó continues to have the whiff of a colonial naval base. Its dominant feature is its magnificent, snaking harbour, the second largest in the world after Pearl Harbor, and the reason the maritime Brits were so keen to establish a presence here; it provided the key to naval domination of the western Mediterranean in the 18th century.

The town, which is impressively arrayed along cliff-tops on the harbour's northern side, may not be as instantly appealing as its rival across the island, but it has a more complex charm, amply repaying a leisurely exploration of its small squares and narrow streets. These roads and plazas are gradually being smartened up, the old walls are being scrubbed and buffed and cleaned, and the utilitarian starkness that characterised Maó of old is slowly being replaced with a more stylish and contemporary sensibility. Maó clearly bears the imprints of the various cultures that have occupied the island over the centuries, particularly the British. Even today, it feels more cosmopolitan than its western cousin (though its population is a mere 22,000), both in atmosphere and architecture, though there seems to be a curious mutual ambivalence between town and port, land and sea.

SIGHTSEEING

The most logical, but certainly not the prettiest, place to start a tour of Maó is the **Plaça de s'Esplanada**. Originally the town's parade ground, it was laid out by the British during their second period of occupation (1763-82), and the original barracks still runs along one side of the square. The colonial façade, painted wine red with white window and door frames, sparked off a trend for British colonial architecture throughout the island that is still very much in evidence today. Nowadays the barracks is looking a little shabby, hidden away behind a Franco-era war memorial, a thick hedge and a concrete row of lock-ups serving snacks, sweets and even British fish and chips. In fact, the square is so cluttered with wretched architecture it is sometimes difficult to appreciate its former charm. At weekends and on summer evenings, though, it is transformed as kids play on the swings among the pine trees, adolescents zoom their scooters around the perimeter roads, and pensioners and holidaymakers fill the café terraces.

To get to the heart of the old town, follow C/Ses Moreres down the hill past the monument to Dr Mathieu Orfila (1787-1853), the father of modern toxicology; the street changes name to Costa de sa Plaça (also known as C/Hannover), and runs past the small, cobbled **Plaça Colón**, with its palm trees and twee statue of the Menorcan singer Pilar Alonso as a young girl.

To the right, C/Àngel runs from the square to Costa d'en Deià, where an arched passage straight ahead leads, unexpectedly, to **Parc**

d'es Freginal, a largish, scruffy, pine-filled park hidden away behind the houses; Maó's expat Latin American residents gather here to play volleyball at weekends. Up the hill, at the top of Costa d'en Deià, a large, modern statue of a female nude clutching the masks of comedy and tragedy marks the town's theatre, the **Teatre Principal**, built in 1829.

Back at Plaça Colón, the pedestrianised street continues down to another small, cobbled square, **Plaça de la Constitució**, the administrative heart of Maó. It is dominated by the monolithic edifice of the church of **Santa Maria**, built during the second half of the 18th century on the site of an earlier church erected by Alfons III. The brightly painted interior consists of a single nave beneath a high, Gothic-arched ceiling, with small chapels along each side; there's a fine organ, dating from 1810.

The smaller, ornate building next door is the **Ajuntament** (town hall), built in 1789. Visitors are free to wander in up the stairs, past the statue of St Sebastian, Maó's second patron saint after the Verge de Gràcia (Our Lady of Grace), to look around the council chamber – a rather sombre hall lined with portraits of Spanish dignitaries from the time of the final British handover of the island in 1802 onwards.

Between the town hall and the church, a short alley leads to **Plaça de sa Conquesta**, a large, quiet square containing a statue of Alfons III and one of a number of balconies in Maó that provides great views down over the port. The elegant mansion on the square's north side, **Can Mercadal**, was built by Joan Mercadal in 1761; nowadays it houses the public library. On the opposite side of the square, steps take you down snaking Costa de ses Voltes to the harbour.

Returning to the Ajuntament, C/Sant Roc heads uphill to Plaça Bastió and the **Pont de Sant Roc**, the only surviving medieval gateway into the city. Built under Pere IV in 1359, the impressive structure is almost all that is left of the second city wall.

The narrow white belltower with stained-glass windows beside the Ajuntament is part of the Franciscan convent, founded in 1623, though the tower and most of the chapel date from the end of the 19th century. Access is restricted (unless you're a nun), but the wooden door on the left inside the entrance porch leads to the simple chapel.

From here, C/Isabel II leads off parallel to the port. This is one of the most attractive streets on the island, lined with elegant 18th-century mansions, some featuring Maó's famous bow windows or *boinders*; a British legacy. **Palau Febrer** (at No.5, about halfway along) is one such mansion; you can see its ground-floor

vaulted rooms by visiting the antique furniture shop around the corner (at C/Bonaire 33), which has access to the courtyard with a well at its centre. Since natural water sources on the island are scarce, wells are a ubiquitous feature of Menorcan architecture, both urban and rural, connecting with subterranean water cisterns that store rainwater via elaborate collection systems. They are even present in many talayotic settlements.

On the opposite side of C/Isabel II, another alleyway, Pont des General, leads down long ramps and stairs to the port, via Costa ses General and Costa ses Muret, and offers great views of the ramparts above.

A short way beyond the entrance to this alley is the island's main military headquarters, the **Gobierno Militar**, a small, domestic-looking structure around a courtyard that looks more like a converted stable block than a barracks. Originally called the Casa del Rei (King's House), it initially functioned as a fortress at the north-western corner of the ramparts, and was where the governor stayed when he visited from the then capital, Ciutadella. When the capital was moved to Maó in 1722, Governor Richard Kane moved in and had what was once a rather primitive building extended.

C/Isabel II ends at the beautiful, if somewhat worn, red sandstone façade of the church of **Sant Francesc**, built between 1719 and 1792 on the site of an earlier Gothic church. Inside, the church is gloomy and badly in need of restoration, while the murals above the altar give it a black and white cartoon-like feel. The main structure is neo-Gothic, though it has a fine, if faded, Baroque altarpiece. Far lighter than the main part of the church is the large, octagonal Chapel of the Immaculate Conception (1745) set into the east wall, complete with cupola and lantern.

The bright, white sandstone cloisters next door form the centrepiece of the **Museu de Menorca** (*see p214*), the largest and most comprehensive museum on the island.

INSIDE TRACK
MAONAISE

A local legend surrounds the origins of mayonnaise. The most likely story is that the chef of the Duc de Richelieu created the sauce in celebration of the French capture of Maó and Fort Sant Felip from the British in 1756. (It was originally spelt 'mahonnaise'.) Local claims that the Duc stole the recipe from the Menorcans are, alas, unlikely to be true.

MENORCA

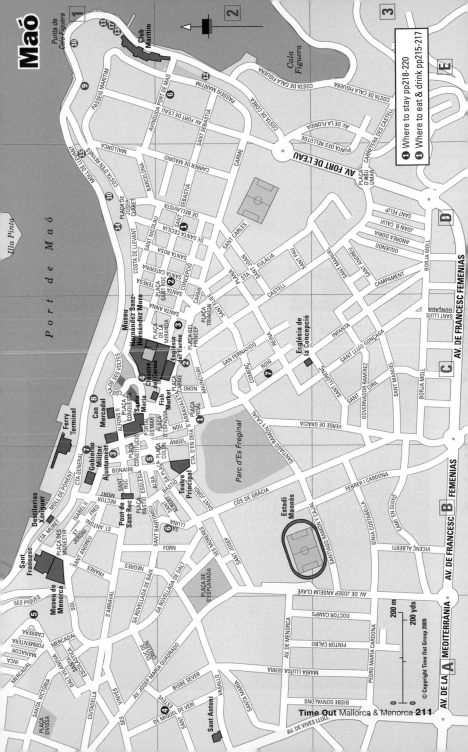

Maõ

Punta de Cala-Figuera

1

2

3

Club Marítim

Illa Pinta

Port de Maõ

PASSEIG MARÍTIM

MOLL DE LLEVANT

COSTA D'EN REYNÉS

PLAÇA DE JOSEP CLARET

Ferry Terminal

Destilerías Xoriguer

Sant Francesc

Museu de Menorca

SES PIQUES

PLAÇA DES MONESTIR

CTA MURET

MOLL DE PONENT

CTA GENERAL

Gobierno Militar

Ajuntament

Can Mercadal

Museu Sanz-Hernández Mora

Claustre del Carme

Fish Market

Santa Maria

PLAÇA CONQUESTA

ALFONS II

PLAÇA D'ESPANYA

PORTAL DE MAR

PLAÇA CONSTITUCIÓ

Teatre Principal

Pont de Sant Roc

Esglèsia del Carme

PLAÇA DE MIRANDA

PLAÇA BEL PRÍNCEP

PLAÇA TRIANGA

Parc d'Es Freginal

Estadi Maonès

AV. DE JOSEP ANSELM CLAVÉ

Esglèsia de la Concepció

COSTA DE CALA FIGUERA

Cala Figuera

AV. FORT DE L'EAU

AVINGUDA PORT DE MAÓ

CARRER DE MADRID

CARME

PLAÇA DES RELLOTGE

PUNTA DES CASTELL

CARRETERA DES CASTELL

AV. FORT DE L'EAU

PLAÇA D'ABÚ UMARÍ

SANT FELIP

JOAN B. CALVÓ

ANDREA DORIA

OQUENDO

CAMPAMENT

BORJA MOLL

AV. DE FRANCESC FEMENIAS

AV. DE FRANCESC FEMENIAS

AV. DE LA MEDITERRÀNIA

① Where to stay pp218-220
② Where to eat & drink pp215-217

200 m
200 yds

© Copyright Time Out Group 2009

Time Out Mallorca & Menorca **211**

Retracing your steps back to the centre of town, the slight hill beyond Plaça d'Espanya is dominated by the façade of the Carmelite **Església del Carme**, built in 1750, much to the disgust of the town's existing Franciscan community, who held up construction for as long as they could. Next to it, the cloisters (**Claustre del Carme**) have been variously used as prison, law courts and school, and now house the local market, a rather antiseptic affair, with little of the life and colour of most Spanish food markets, though it's still a good place to stock up on picnic fodder. More authentic in feel is the little fish market that sits atop a bastion just down from the church. Get there before 1pm if you plan to do any buying.

The exit on the far side of the cloisters leads to Plaça de la Miranda, with more views over the port, and also gives access to the small **Museu Hernández Sanz-Hernández Mora** (*see p214*).

From Plaça d'Espanya, a long flight of steps leads down to the harbour, criss-crossed on its descent by the serpentine **Costa de ses Voltes**. At the harbour you'll often find at least one ferry or cruise ship docked, plus glass-bottomed tourist boats and a long line of restaurants and bars stretching along the waterside. Close to the ferry terminal is the **Destilerias Xoriguer** (*see p214*), within which is made Menorca's Xoriguer gin, one of the more positive aspects of British rule.

From the harbour, there is a good view of the naval base and dockyards on the far side of the port, including **Illa Pinta**, an artificial island created by the British. For a closer look at these, and the port's other islands and landmarks, take one of the tourist boats that offer trips around the harbour (such as Yellow Catamarans; *see p214*). These include the **Illa del Rei**, named after Alfons III, who landed and camped here for 12 days before launching his successful conquest of the island in 1287; it's also known as 'Bloody Island', after the 18th-century British military hospital built here.

The next island, flat **Illa Plana** or **Illa Quarentena**, was the original quarantine station, until demand in the 18th century necessitated the building of a big hospital for infectious diseases on the larger neighbouring **Illa del Llatzeret**. This has only been an island since 1900, when a canal was cut to provide more sheltered access to the massive **Fortaleza de Isabel II**, more commonly known as **La Mola** (*see p214*), which once guarded the entrance to the port.

The harbour boat trips also give visitors a good view of the gracious British colonial mansion known as the **Golden Farm**. Set high up the hillside on the northern side of the port, the house may have been used (very briefly) by Admiral Nelson during the third British occupation of Menorca (1798-1802), but, alas, was certainly not, as a local legend has it, the scene of love trysts with Emma Hamilton. Look out also for a little whitewashed house accessible only by a jetty – it's informally called 'Little Venice' and is owned by Richard Branson, whose connections with Menorca go back to his childhood.

MENORCA

The port.

If you want to pedal your way around Maó and the surrounding area, bikes can be hired for €12 a day from **Velo Rent Bike** (C/S'Arravaleta 52, 971 35 37 98, www.bikemenorca.com, open 10am-1.30pm, 5-8pm Mon-Fri, 10am-1.30pm Sat).

Alternatively, take to the open seas – which is one of the best ways of seeing the island – with the **Menorca Cruising School** (971 35 41 03, www.menorcasailing.co.uk), a reliable and friendly company that offers great-value luxury day sails on board its 36-foot Bavaria yachts with gourmet lunch from €125 per head (maximum of seven people per yacht); the company also runs two- to five-day sailing courses.

And finally, if you want to head to the beach, **Cala Mesquida** is four kilometres north-east of Maó (*see p240*). It's a rugged but pretty spot with golden sand, though those with their own transport might want to head to the wonderful beaches on the south coast (*see pp221-233*).

FREE Destilerias Xoriguer

Moll de Ponent 91 (971 36 21 97/www. xoriguer.es). **Open** *May-Oct* 8am-7pm Mon-Fri; 9am-1pm Sat. *Nov-Apr* 9am-1pm, 4-6pm Mon-Fri. **Admission** free. **Map** p211 B1.

Introduced to Menorca during the British occupation, gin has been distilled here ever since, using juniper berries that are imported from around the Mediterranean. The Xoriguer Distillery is really just a glorified shop aimed at tour groups and cruise passengers. Windows at the back look into the distillery, though there's not a great deal to see except a handful of copper stills. On the plus side, you can try various Xoriguer products, as well as the gin itself. In summer, particularly during the festival of Sant Joan, Xoriguer gin is mixed with lemonade, preferably home-made, to create a refreshing *pomada*.

Fortaleza de Isabel II (La Mola)

Ctra. de la Mola (971 36 40 40/www. fortalesalamola.com). **Open** *June-Sept* 10am-8pm daily; guided tours 10.30am, 12.30pm & 5.30pm daily. *May & Oct* 10am-6pm daily; guided tours 10.30am & 12.30pm daily. Closed last 2wks Dec,

---

INSIDE TRACK
CAFE MIRAMAR

Café Mirador, great though it is, is best avoided when cruise ships are in town. Your view will be obscured by 5,000 tonnes of steel and the restaurant swamped by a similar number of the vessel's passengers, desperate for a beer after their schlep up from the ferry terminal, just underneath the café.

1st wk Jan. **Admission** €7.50; reductions €4.75; free under-12s. Guided tours €2.50 per person. **Credit** MC, V. **Map** p211 B1.

Built in the mid 19th century, this extensive fortress guards the northern side of the entrance to Maó harbour. After the Spanish Civil War it became notorious as one of Franco's high-security political prisons. The guided tours listed above are in English (booking advisable); audio guides (in English) are an alternative for those wishing to stroll around these impressive fortifications at their own speed. Booking in advance is advised.

FREE Museu Hernández Sanz-Hernández Mora

Plaça Claustre del Carme 5 (971 35 05 97). **Open** *Museum* 10am-1pm Mon-Sat. *Library* 10am-1pm Mon-Fri. **Admission** free. **Map** p211 C1.

This private collection consists of four rooms of furniture, paintings and maps from the 18th, 19th and 20th centuries, with a library on the top floor.

Museu de Menorca

Plaça des Monastir (971 35 09 55). **Open** *Apr-Oct* 10am-2pm, 6-8.30pm Tue-Sat; 10am-2pm Sun. *Nov-Mar* 9.30am-2pm Tue-Fri; 10am-2pm Sat, Sun. **Admission** €2.40; free-€1.20 reductions. **No credit cards. Map** p211 B1..

On the first floor, after a brief but informative video introduction (available in various languages; ask at the desk), there is a collection of artefacts from prehistoric, Roman, Moorish and Catalan Menorca, plus a skeleton of *Myotragus Balearicus*, Menorca's indigenous but long-extinct goat-like mammal – a cheeky chappy with a devilish smile, short horns and eyes mounted in the front of his head (like a chimpanzee), rather than the side (like modern goats and sheep). Upstairs is an extensive collection of maps and paintings, mostly from the 18th and 19th centuries. It's free to get in on Sundays, and on Saturday afternoons in the summer.

Yellow Catamarans

Port de Maó, at foot of Costa de ses Voltes (971 35 23 07/mobile 639 67 63 51). **Departures** *Mid Apr-Oct* 10.30am & every 45 mins approx until 4pm Mon-Sat; 10.45am, 12.15pm, 1.45pm Sun. No service Nov-Apr. **Tickets** €10; €5 reductions; free under-5s. **Credit** MC, V. **Map** p211 C1.

Call in advance to check where they're leaving from.

WHERE TO EAT & DRINK

Maó has some really great places to eat and some truly dreadful ones. There are top-class seafood restaurants, locals' tapas bars, excellent Italian restaurants and great Asian ones, as well as the ever-present egg and chips tourist dives, and all often within metres of each other.

MENORCA

There are plenty of fish restaurants along the port, varying considerably in price and quality – bear in mind, though, that unless it says on the menu or you ask, what you might assume was fished locally may in fact have been imported. Restaurants in the old town tend to be more individual, often with more of a local clientele; unsurprisingly the portside tends to see more tourists. The old town is great for coffee and people watching while the port is better for drinking. The Moll de Llevant, further out to sea, so to speak, feels more grown-up than the younger, more up-for-it Moll de Ponent.

Old Town

American Bar

Plaça Reial 8 (971 36 18 22). **Open** *June-Sept* 7am-1am Mon-Sat. *Oct-May* 7am-10pm Mon-Sat. **Average** €. **No credit cards. Map** p211 C2 **❶** Café

American Bar is a large, popular French-style café with a pavement terrace and refurbished interior hung with black and white photos that show how characterful it was before the decorators were let loose. It's still popular with locals and tourists of all ages, and serves decent coffee, continental breakfasts, sandwiches and snacks.

★ Ars Café

Plaça del Príncep 12B (971 35 18 79). **Open** 8.30am-midnight Mon-Sat. Closed Aug. **Average** €. **Credit** AmEx, DC, MC, V. **Map** p211 C2 **❷** Café

There's not a whole bunch of artsy, bohemian places to hang out in in Maó, so Ars Café is deservedly popular with those who like their *jámon* with conversation. Housed in what was once the casino's 'summer bar' this small and atmospheric café-restaurant serves tapas such as Spanish chorizo or *jamón serrano* as well as sandwiches, salads and dishes like tuna carpaccio, and the no-choice lunch *menú* is excellent and provides good value for money. In summer, there are just two, highly coveted tables outside and there's a club/disco in the cellar.

€ Cristanal y Gradinata

C/Isabel II 1 (971 36 33 16). **Open** 8.30am-3pm Mon; 8.30am-3pm, 7.30pm-midnight Tue-Fri; noon-3pm, 7.30pm-midnight Sat. Closed 3wks Sept. **Average** €. **Credit** MC, V. **Map** p211 B1 **❸** Café

On a quiet corner tucked away from the crowds sits this stylish jazz bar with red velvet couches and glass-topped wooden tables. Ella's on the sound system and there are antique radios galore along the walls. It serves excellent coffee and simple sandwiches, with a short menu of more elaborate *torrades* and sandwiches available for a couple of hours in the evening.

★ € Café Mirador

Plaça d'Espanya 2 (971 35 21 07). **Open** *June-Oct* 10am-2am Mon-Sat. *Nov-May* noon-midnight Mon-Sat. **Average** €. **Credit** V. **Map** p211 C1 **❹** Café

Tucked down a side street halfway up the cliffside above the port, Café Mirador is one of the stalwarts of the Maó scene. In summer, a terrace offers vistas over the ramparts and the harbour, or occasionally the starboard wall of a cruise ship, many of whose passengers scramble up here for a beer, but don't let that put you off. At night it's a different story – the vibe is more local dreadlocked youth loafing about enjoying the tunes. A good range of tapas, sandwiches and salads are available all day.

Ses Palmeras

Plaça Colon 6 (971 36 47 17). **Open** 9am-8pm Mon-Sat. Closed 2wks Nov. **Average** €. **Credit** V. **Map** p211 B1 **❺** Café

This non-intimidating locals' bar is not going to win any prizes for decor, though it might for its chummy atmosphere and its location, squeezed into the corner of the Plaça Colon. It does a brisk trade in decent coffee and delicious bacon and tomato sandwiches. Indeed, it's one of the best places in town for cheap, simple fare with a bargain-priced lunchtime *menú*. Inside, it's usually loud and bustling; outside, the tables in the square offer a calm oasis, set a little back from the activity of the town's main pedestrianised street. If you can't grab a table in summer, try the Bracafé next door.

La Tropical

C/Sa Lluna 36 (971 36 05 56). **Open** 7.30am-midnight Mon, Tue, Thur-Sun. Closed mid Feb-mid Mar. **Average** €. **Credit** AmEx, DC, MC, V. **Map** p211 B2 **❻** Café-restaurant

A good, unpretentious Spanish café-restaurant close to Plaça de s'Esplanada and open at all hours of the day for coffee, snacks and more substantial meals.

Port

★ Akelarre

Moll de Ponent 41 (971 36 85 20/www. akelarrejazz.es). **Open** *June-Sept* 8am-4am daily. *Oct-May* 8pm-4am daily. **Admission** €10 incl 1 drink. **No credit cards. Map** p211 B1 **❼** Bar

This is the city's leading venue for good quality blues and jazz, with stone arches, a paved floor and the bare rock of the cliff-face dominating the tiny courtyard at the back. It's a great place to start a night on the tiles – the surrounding bars and clubs at this end of Moll de Ponent constitute most of Maó's nightlife. *Photo p216.*

€ Café Baixamar

Moll de Ponent 17 (971 36 58 96). **Open** *May-Oct* 8am-3am daily. *Nov-Apr* noon-midnight

Akelarre. *See p215.*

Mon-Thur, Sun; noon-3am Fri, Sat. Closed mid Jan-mid Feb. **Average** €. **Credit** MC, V. **Map** p211 C1 ❽ **Café**
A friendly, hip *modernista* café with original wood panelling, an old, ornate bar, and tables inside and out. Open all day, it's great for a morning coffee, a late-night drink or anything in between. Like so many of Spain's decent nightlife spots, it suffers from a little too much Bob Marley on the jukebox; but the goat's cheese and sultana salad or brie and *jamón serrano* sandwich, washed down with an excellent home-made milkshake, more make up for the slightly clichéd music.

Café Mambo
Moll de Llevant 209 (971 35 67 82). **Open** *Apr-Sept* 6pm-4am daily. *Oct-May* 8pm-2am daily. **Average** €. **Credit** V. **Map** p211 E1 ❾ **Bar**

**INSIDE TRACK
ILLA DEL REI**

No long-term plans have been finalised for the decrepit former hospital island in Maó's harbour. And although a group of volunteers assembles here every Sunday to tug out weeds and shovel dirt, the island's only permanent resident continues to be *Podarcis lilfordi balearica*, a species of lizard found nowhere else in the world.

A range of its own CDs, a decent terrace and a relaxed party vibe (this and Akelarre are the locals' faves as far as nights out go) have helped to make this one of Maó's most reputable bar stalwarts. It's as popular with locals as it is with visitors and positively heaves with people in the summer months. Good cocktails, cold beers and well-pitched tunes keep it buzzing along till the wee hours.

€ Elefant
Moll de Llevant 106 (no phone). **Open** afternoons. **Average** €. **No credit cards**. **Map** p211 D1 ❿ **Tapas**
Another establishment that leans toward the neo-hippie end of the atmosphere spectrum; this cosy harbourside lounge serves a good range of tapas, salads, dips – still a rarity in Spain – and sandwiches. Avoid the deep, deep-fried offerings (prawns, squid rings and the like) and leave room for something that actually merits heart failure: the excellent chocolate cheesecake. Service maybe slowwww but at least it comes with a smile.

★ S'Espigó
Moll de Llevant 267 (971 36 99 09). **Open** 1-3.30pm, 8-11.30pm Tue-Sun. Closed Jan. **Average** €€€. **Credit** AmEx, DC, MC, V. **Map** p211 E1 ⓫ **Seafood**
Widely thought to be one of the town's best fish restaurants, serving classic, simply prepared fresh fish in an intimate, rather formal setting. The food is generally excellent, though the service can be a little wayward at times. In high season it's worth booking in advance.

★ Itake

Moll de Llevant 317 (971 35 45 70). **Open**
1-3.30pm, 8-11.30pm Tue-Sun. Closed mid Dec-
Jan. **Average** €€. **Credit** AmEx, DC, MC, V.
Map p211 E2 ⑫ **Basque**
The main drawback with Itake is the fact that it
doesn't have any tables outside. It's also quite small,
but that tends to add to the eccentric atmosphere
nodded to with non-matching crockery and glassware. The food is no less individual, with a whole
range of hearty, atypical dishes, including pancakes,
brochettes, filled baked potatoes, duck, rabbit stew
and grilled vegetables, all served in a friendly, low-
key atmosphere.

La Mar

Moll de Llevant 275 (971 43 65 51). **Open**
7.30pm-1am daily. Closed Jan. **Average** €.
Credit MC, V. **Map** p211 E1 ⑬ **Bar**
Same name, different owners and quite different
atmosphere. The yachting crowd has been replaced
or at least budged over by anyone who's in town
after a cocktail or a beer in vaguely upbeat surroundings. La Mar now lies somewhere between
McTrendily designed bar – flat-screen TV with fish-
tank imagery, and the like – and a genuinely cool
place you'd want to have a drink in – the tunes, especially, tend to be well chosen for a pre-party drink.

Minerva

Moll de Llevant 87 (971 35 19 95). **Open**
Apr-Sept 1-3.30pm, 7-11.30pm daily. *Oct-Mar*
1-3.30pm, 7-11.30pm Tue-Sat; 1-3.30pm Sun.
Average €€€. **Credit** AmEx, DC, MC, V.
Map p211 D1 ⑭ **Seafood**
There's not much to differentiate the myriad seafood
places along this harbour strip in terms of cuisine,
quality, decor or price. Minerva's selling point is the
floating pontoon moored to the quay and as such it
can be something of a lottery in July and August
when the restaurant is often bursting at the seams.
There are usually two set lunch *menús*.

Nashville

Anden de Levante 143-147 (971 36 79 56).
Open 7-11.30pm Tue-Fri; 1-3pm, 7-11pm Sat,
Sun. **Average** €-€€. **Credit** AmEx, DC, MC, V.
Map p211 D1 ⑮ **Pizzeria/steakhouse**
This pizzeria and steakhouse is not the place to come
for a formal meal. For a start, it's not exactly authentic *cuina menorquina*. And with Sting on the stereo,
a Darth Vader cut-out perched in the corner and a
loud crowd (mainly Spanish), it's not too far-fetched
to call it the Menorcan equivalent of Planet
Hollywood. But to be snobby about the place miss-
es the point, as it's fun, silly and really quite tasty.

Il Porto

Moll de Llevant 225 (971 35 44 26). **Open** *Feb-*
June, Sept, Oct 1-3.30pm, 7pm-midnight Mon,
Tue, Thur-Sun. *July, Aug* 6.30pm-1am Mon, Tue;

1-3.30pm, 7pm-midnight Wed-Sun. Closed Nov-
Jan. **Average** €-€€. **Credit** AmEx, MC, V.
Map p211 E1 ⑯ **Italian**
It's difficult to miss this large, yellow-hued Italian
restaurant, serving a variety of excellent, authentic
meat, pasta and pizza dishes, including deliciously
tender lamb, large platters of grilled vegetables and
good home-made desserts. The main dining room
inside has a maritime feel, with bright wood and
large, arched windows looking out on to the harbourside; next door there's an airier overspill.

★ Thai Country

Moll de Llevant 274 (971 35 39 34). **Open**
12.30-3.30pm, 8-11pm Mon, Wed-Sun; 8-11pm
Tue. **Average** €€. **Credit** MC, V. **Map** p211 E1
⑰ **Thai**
You won't find many Thai restaurants on Menorca
– on our last count there was, erm, one. So it's reassuring to find that Thai Country, while dominating
the Thai market, pretty much blows the island's
other Asian restaurants out of the water too. It's a
hit with long-term expats who come here for authentic fare, executed with flare. Try the sticky prawns
with chilli sauce or the pad thai.

NIGHTLIFE

Let's be honest – whoever tapped Ibiza with
their magic clubbing wand and turned it into
a party paradise clearly had it in for Menorca.
And, while it's not fair to say that the island is
dead nightlife-wise, it's not far off, and certainly
outside of the summer season the clubs, like
their patrons, disappear. Do not come here for
Balearic hedonism of lore – there isn't any; the
spoilsport local council, perhaps in an attempt
to prevent Menorca ending up like Ibiza, has
imposed a 4am curfew on all bars and clubs.
But that's not to say that it's all early nights or
there isn't a party to be had somewhere, it's just
a question of finding it. Bars and clubs change
from season to season but all the ones we've
listed above are here for the long haul. Good
nights out often start at **Akelarre** (*see p215*),
Mambo (*see p216*), **La Mar** (*see above*) or
Café Baixamar (*see p216*). From there it's

INSIDE TRACK
CLUBBING AT COVAS

If you feel let down by Maó's lack of
places to large it, fear not. Grab a gang,
a cab and your best dancing shoes and
head over to **Cova D'en Xoroi** (*see p229*)
in Cala En Porter, a half hour away – one
of the most impressively positioned clubs
in the world. Just make sure you check
online first to see who's playing.

either a question of asking the locals or the barstaff, or following the throng – usually a couple of steps away round to the end of the Moll de Ponent, where there's often something going on, though it can be a little seedy: **Aura** at No.22 is a safe bet.

Those with more subdued tastes can investigate Maó's jazz scene, with its own festival that starts in April and lasts all summer, featuring live bands in bars and on *plaças* across town. Again **Akelarre** (*see p215*) is the best spot for live music, attracting an impressive array of international artists as well as local talent. Nearby **Sant Climent** (*see p224*) – on the road from Maó to **Cala en Porter** – is a surprise hub for jazz-lovers also, and has achieved something of a reputation for its excellent jam sessions (Tuesday nights at the old **Casino** from May to October).

SHOPPING

Most of the main clothes, sports, shoe and accessories chains, as well as a few smaller, more individual outlets, are concentrated around C/Ses Moreres, Costa de sa Plaça and C/Nou. In general, though, Maó is not as good a bet for shops as Ciutadella. For locally made goods, including shoes, bags, jewellery and clothes, there are several boutiques interspersed among the restaurants in the port, particularly along Moll de Ponent. These have more character than their counterparts in the old town, and in high season stay open late for the pre- and post-dinner crowd.

The main market, selling mostly shoddy clothes, is held in Plaça de s'Esplanada every Tuesday and Saturday.

The place to buy the obligatory pair of *albarcas* (Menorcan leather sandals with soles made of old car tyres) is **S'Avarca de Menorca** (C/Àngel 14, 971 36 63 41), the oldest factory on the island. If peasant clobber isn't quite your thing, **Jaime Mascaró** (C/Ses Moreres 29, 971 36 05 68), Menorca's poshest shoemaker, offers highly covetable butter-soft leather pumps and stilettos for ladies, and brogues and dress shoes for gents (*see p238* **Profile**).

If you want to stock up on *fuet* (Catalan chorizo or *sobrassada*), wine or smoked ham, try **Colmado La Palma** (C/Hannover 15, 971 36 34 63), which has more variety and better quality produce than the covered market nearby in the **Claustre del Carme**. The Claustre also has a large branch of the Spar supermarket underneath it – useful for stocking up on staples.

For summer garb, swimwear and boating goods, a far better option than the tourist shops is the new **Aqua** (Moll de Llevant 325,

no phone), a Croatian label – somewhere between Petit Bateau and Gap – with lovely striped sailor T-shirts, towels and beach bags.

WHERE TO STAY

Menorca's capital has not experienced the designer hotel boom of its big sister Palma, and most of its hotels are uninspiring to say the least. If you've come to relax in real comfort we advise staying outside of town in one of the *agroturismos*, which have heaps of character, excellent food and, more than likely, a swimming pool. The south of the island (*see pp221-233*) has a range of great places to stay, all within 20 minutes or less of Maó, and with distances on the island short and roads excellent, driving around the countryside is a pleasure.

Eurohotel

C/Santa Cecilia 41 (971 36 48 55). Closed Oct-mid Apr. **Rates** €58-€104 double. **No credit cards. Map** p211 D2 ❶

One block in from the harbour, this bright, reasonably priced hotel down a quiet side street was refurbished in 1997. Its 22 rooms are a little small and bland but all are clean and comfortable and have balconies, and there's a large terrace on the roof with views over Maó. It's been for sale for years, though the plan is for it to remain a hotel regardless.

La Isla

C/Santa Caterina 4 (971 36 64 92). Closed mid Dec-mid Jan. **Rates** (incl breakfast) €42-€50 double. **Credit** MC, V. **Map** p211 E2 ❷

A modest, 24-room *hostal* above a bar-restaurant of the same name. It's a little bare and dingy, but the owners are friendly and the rooms are clean and quiet, and all have en suite bathrooms.

Jume

C/Concepció 6 (971 36 32 66). Closed mid Dec-mid Jan. **Rates** (incl breakfast) €55-€68 double. **Credit** MC, V. **Map** p211 C2 ❸

A classic old-style *pensión*, run by a sweet and chirpy old Menorcan couple, with 39 simple but comfortable rooms, all with en suite bathrooms, TVs and a cosy breakfast room. It's not the lap of luxury, but it's not depressing like some of the other cheaper options in the city and attracts its fair share of budget business travellers. There is also a room adapted for wheelchair users.

Hotel Capri

C/Sant Esteve 8 (971 36 14 00/www.rtmhotels. com). **Rates** (incl breakfast) €70-€146 double; €51-€130 apartment per person. **Credit** AmEx, DC, MC, V. **Map** p211 A2 ❹

Just round the corner from the Plaça de s'Esplanada, Hotel Capri is a large, popular and comfortable mid-range hotel with 75 well-equipped, spacious rooms,

MENORCA

Rule Britannia

Seven decades of Brits left forts, roads, drink and a lot of weird words.

Brits make up 29 per cent of foreign visitors to Mallorca, but 60 per cent in Menorca. Relations with Blighty have always been strong: for 71 of the 94 years between 1708 and 1802 the British ruled Menorca. It was a period of great European significance for the island and one that hasn't been without its legacies.

Firstly, and most obviously, the fondness of British holidaymakers for the island. From the Maó to Ciutadella, Son Bou to Fornells, the scenery might change a great deal but one thing is pretty much certain, you're bound to bump into Brits. But it doesn't stop there.

The island's most far-sighted governor, Richard Kane introduced numerous innovations and improvements to the island in the first half of the 18th century, the most significant of which was probably the Camí d'en Kane (Kane's Road) between Maó and Ciutadella. Much of the current main road between the towns still follows its course. Defensive works such as Fort Marlborough and 11 coastal watchtowers are more evidence of the British presence.

Kane was responsible for introducing several species of livestock and crop. He brought in apples, still called Pomes d'en Quen, and the ubiquitous Friesian cows to make all that cheese. Later, to feed them, the British also introduced the clover that fills the hedgerows each spring. There are even plums called Prunes de Neversó, after Kane allegedly declared one day, 'I never saw such plums.'

Another legacy is the famous bow windows, or *boinders* in Menorcan, that adorn many of the elegant townhouses on the island, and the sash technology to open them. There are the door latches too, the kind with a thumb lever on one side of the door, the latch on the other, and so foreign on much of the Continent that even today many guidebooks offer instructions on how to use them.

Not all British contributions to the island were due to official policy. There was a huge garrison stationed on the island, and with prostitution banned and windsurfing still not invented, there wasn't a lot for a homesick sailor to do but drink. And what sailors drank in the 18th century was gin, and plenty of it. So enterprising local tradesmen imported juniper berries from around the Mediterranean and set about distilling gin, as they do to this day.

The Brits also contributed to Menorcan vocabulary, and while a lot of it is the language of commerce, carpentry and ship-building (a *tornescrú* is a screwdriver, *moguin* or *mòguini* is mahogany, a *rul* is a ruler) a lot came from less formal sources. When a scuffle breaks out between two or more *mens* (men), or even *bois* (boys), it's called *fàitim*, from 'fight him', the result of which could be an *ull blèc* (black eye), though it's a good idea to patch it up with a *xaquèns* (handshake). Alternatively, you could go down to the port and *fer un berguin*, which is to make a deal, but came to mean contracting the services of a prostitute (Kane's ban notwithstanding). You drink from a *moc* (mug) or a *bòtil*, boil water in a *quíter* or *quítel* (kettle), and serve rum, gin, grog, *punx* (punch) or *xèri* (sherry) on your *saidbord* (sideboard). Lower down the ranks, you're a *mitjamen*, from 'midshipman', which is someone foolish, unknown or middle-class, but if you're a gentleman, you might be a *milord*, married to a *miledi*. Since a *milord* is also a yacht, and a *miledi* can mean a strange, ugly (British) lady, clearly not all British imports met with local approval.

MENORCA

---

almost all with balconies (on to the street or the court-yard at the back). There's also a small gym, jacuzzi, sun deck and pool with retractable roof, with views over Maó and the surrounding area. Massages and beauty treatments are available. The Restaurant Capri downstairs serves excellent pizzas. *Photo p220.*

Hotel Catalonia Mirador d'es Port

Dalt Vilanova 1 (971 36 00 16/www.hoteles-catalonia.com). Rates €76-€186 double. **Credit** AmEx, DC, MC, V. **Map** p211 A1 **❺**

Hotel Catalonia Mirador d'es Port is a fair three-star hotel, located at the western end of the ramparts, and close to the Museu de Menorca. It has a good view of the port (albeit the more industrial end) from its dining room and terrace. The decor is corporate smart, with lots of blonde wood and Scandinavian blues. Rooms are comfortable if on the unremarkable side and most have at least a partial view of the port, as well as looking down on attractive gardens, complete with swimming pool, jacuzzi and the rooftops of the old town.

★ Hotel Port-Mahón

Avda. Fort de l'Eau 13 (971 36 26 00/
www.sethotels.com). **Rates** (incl breakfast)
€110-€170 double. **Credit** AmEx, MC, V.
Map p211 E2 **❻**

Perched back on the hill above the Moll de Llevant
is this grand old dame of Maó, by far the nicest hotel
in town. It's a large, smart airy place with an odd
whiff of a colonial past – though the place actually
dates from 1956 rather than 1756. The views from
the terrace, the pool and the rooms at the front are
all wonderful, and it's a stone's throw – literally –
from the port.

€ Posada Orsi

C/Infanta 19 (971 36 47 51). **Rates** €39-€48
double. **No credit cards. Map** p211 C2 **❼**

The best budget option in Maó is this bright, cheerful *hostal*, a perennial favourite close to the market.
Rooms are airy and very brightly painted in a variety of bold colours, while upstairs there is a small
sitting room and kitchen. Three of the double rooms
have en suite bathrooms; otherwise washing facilities are communal, but were given a major overhaul
in 2003, with fresh paint and fittings. There's also a
cute three-person apartment.

RESOURCES

Police station

Plaça Constitució 21 (971 36 98 00).
Map p211 C1. Ring 112 in emergency.

Post office

C/Bonaire 2 (971 35 66 29). **Open**
8am-8pm Mon-Fri. **Map** p211 B1.

Tourist information

Moll de Llevant 2 (971 35 59 52/www.e-menorca.
org). **Open** *May-Oct* 8am-1pm Mon, Sun; 8am-
8.30pm Tue-Sat. **Map** p211 D1.
Maó Airport (971 15 71 15/www.e-menorca.org).
Open *May-Oct* 8am-10pm Mon, Wed-Fri, Sun;
8am-1pm Tue, Sat.

GETTING THERE

For air and sea links to Maó, *see p260.*

By bus

Local buses stop in Maó at Plaça de s'Esplanada,
while island-wide services operate from Avda. JM
Quadrado. There are 7 buses Mon-Sat and 6 on
Sun between Maó and Ciutadella (1hr), via Alaior
(20mins), Es Mercadal (30mins) and Ferreries
(40mins). Other services from Maó include 26
buses Mon-Sat (20 Sun) to Es Castell (10mins), 13
buses Mon-Sat (12 Sun) to Sant Lluís (10mins), 6
buses daily to Alcaufar (20mins), 12 buses Mon-
Sat (4 Sun) to Sant Climent (10mins), 7 buses Mon-
Sat to Cala en Porter (20mins), 5 buses Mon-Sat
(4 on Sun) to Cala Galdana (1hr) via Ferreries
(40mins), 6 buses Mon-Sat to Son Bou (35mins)
via Alaior, 2 buses Mon-Fri to Sant Tomás
(40mins), 2 buses Mon-Sat to Fornells (35mins).

Hotel Capri. *See p218.*

South Menorca

Fine dining, splendid beaches and a whole lot of history.

Menorca's south is the most visited part of the island and it's easy to see why. Its south-east corner is a privileged bastion of pretty, white-washed villages, holiday villas and gourmet restaurants – beloved of wealthy Spaniards and Brits with second-home aspirations, and with a strip nicknamed the 'golden mile' owing to the amount of great places to eat and stay. Further west you'll find some of Menorca's, if not Europe's, most beautiful beaches, as well as, unfortunately, some of the island's biggest and least attractive resorts. The interior is quite a

different story, with quiet, gently rolling hills dotted with wild olive trees, holm oaks, donkeys and drystone walls, and development that has largely been sympathetic – this is where to come for a perfect rural retreat.

PREHISTORIC SOUTH-EAST

If you want to check out some of Menorca's talayotic settlements (*see pp20-21* **Site-seeing Guide**), the south-east is great for a gander, both in terms of how many there are and how well they are preserved.

The most impressive in terms of size and conservation is **Trepucó**, a kilometre south of Maó. The base of the talayot here is in very good condition, as is the taula precinct, with a particularly tall taula (its support stone has now been replaced by a concrete block). This was once a sizeable settlement, though only a small portion of it has been excavated.

Further south, a kilometre east of Sant Lluís, **Trebalúger** is less well preserved, though it offers good views over the surrounding area. The same distance the other side of Sant Lluís is **Binisafullet**, located in an attractive grove, but in very poor condition and it makes little sense unless you have previously seen a more complete ruin. **So na Caçana**, four kilometres west of Sant Climent, is more interesting, with two taula precincts, one of which is sited right next to the talayot.

A few minutes' drive north of here, on the road to Alaior, lies **Torralba d'en Salort**; it's far more complete and impressive, with a tall taula within its sanctuary, two well-preserved talayots, a hypostyle room (a chamber with a roof supported by pillars) and the ruins of several prehistoric buildings (plus an even more

ruined 17th-century chapel, providing evidence of continuing use of the site over almost 3,000 years). Archaeological excavations and pathways make the remains more easily comprehensible than many Menorcan sites, though these, plus the refreshment kiosk/ticket office, take away some of the mystery. The explanatory leaflet you can pick up here is useful, however.

Midway between Maó and Alaior, the two *navetas* of **Rafal Rubí** stand just north of the main road. Though they are not as well preserved as the **Naveta d'es Tudons** near Ciutadella, their rural setting is evocative. The northern naveta has an interesting doorway, made from a single stone with a square hole cut into it, including a flange to hold the door itself.

A couple of kilometres back towards Maó, **Talatí de Dalt** (sometimes referred to as simply Talatí), just off the Maó–Ciutadella road, is one of the most comprehensive sites on the island. It has been partially excavated, and a useful explanatory pamphlet is available from the hut at the entrance. Within a lovely bucolic setting, you can wander around the remains of its talayot, taula (with a fallen pillar resting against one end of it), dwellings and defensive wall.

Nearby, on an extremely narrow lane just east of Sant Climent, off the Sant Climent – Maó road, is the talayot of **Torellonet Vell**. Further up this lane are the remains of the basilica of **Fornàs de Torelló**, an early

Christian church similar to the one at Son Bou. Little remains of the structure other than its impressive mosaic floor, now enclosed in a huge roofed cage to protect it from the weather, vandals and thieves.

With the exception of Talatí de Dalt and Torralba d'en Salort, all the prehistoric sites mentioned above are open access.

Talatí de Dalt

Ctra. Maó–Ciutadella, km4 (mobile 607 90 08 86/www.arqueomenorca.com). **Open** 9.30am-sunset daily. **Admission** €3; €2 reductions. **No credit cards**.

Torralba d'en Salort

Ctra. Alaior–Cala en Porter (mobile 696 21 76 64). **Open** *June-Sept* 10am-8pm daily. Closed 1st Sat of mth. *Oct-May* 10am-1pm, 3-6pm Mon-Sat. **Admission** €3; €1.50 reductions. **No credit cards**.

ES CASTELL & SANT ESTEVE

Es Castell, a couple of kilometres east of Maó, has a bizarre history of having its name and location changed by whoever happens to be in charge. When British soldiers and their families (during the first period of occupation – 1708-56) built their homes in the lee of the castle of Sant Felip, their settlement was known as Philipstown. During their second period of occupation (1763-82), the British decided to move the town further from the castle to its present site, which they called Georgetown after George III. When the Spanish took over in 1782, they changed the town's name again, to Vilacarlos, after Carlos III. Nowadays, it's simply called 'The Castle', to pre-empt any future changes to its name.

Except there is no castle. With a sense of perverse logic, the Spanish tore the castle down, thinking that if there were no defences the British wouldn't be interested in the island (overlooking the fact that it was the port of Maó that had always been the primary draw). When the British returned in 1798, they landed at Fornells and Addaia on the north of the island.

Today, Es Castell is an attractive place, built along a regimented grid with a large parade ground at its centre, edged by barracks buildings along the east and west sides. The town hall – a low, red building with a clock tower – is on the northern side, with a small military museum, the **Museu Militar de Menorca**, standing opposite. It contains weapons and various maps from the last three centuries, plus scale models of fortresses and ancient ruins, portraits of British admirals and period furniture.

From the main square, it's a short downhill walk to the picturesque fishing boat-specked little bay of **Cales Fonts**. Edged by restaurants and bars, it's a lovely spot for a stroll, a meal or an evening drink. Boat trips around the port leave from here.

Further west towards Maó is Es Castell's second bay, the narrower, quieter **Cala Corb**.

The scant remains of **Fort Sant Felip** stand on a headland above the lovely inlet of **Cala Sant Esteve**, a five-minute drive south-east of Es Castell. They can only be visited by guided tour and consist of little more than earth ramparts, though these, especially seen in aerial photographs, show how impressive the whole site would once have been.

This is also the most easterly point of the island (aptly named Sol del Este) and it's well worth shaking yourself out of bed to witness memorable sunrises from here.

A more worthwhile visit than Fort Sant Felip is to **Fort Marlborough**, on the southern side

Trepucó. *See p221.*

Cales Fonts.

of the inlet, just above the charming village of **Sant Esteve**. This unusual subterranean fortress, built by the British between 1710 and 1726 and named after John Churchill, Duke of Marlborough, is almost entirely below the level of the surrounding hill. An introductory audio-visual show (available in English) gives some good background on the fort and its history, before visitors follow a marked path through the fort's gloomy, claustrophobic and hugely atmospheric rock-hewn tunnels. It suffered two long sieges – by the French in 1756 and the Spanish in 1781 – and an impressive use of life-size figures and sound and light effects make it all too easy to imagine just how scary it would have been inside the fort at such times.

During the sieges the French and Spanish bombarded the fort from the hill just to the south. To prevent any repeat of this, the British built the sturdy **Torre d'en Penjat** in 1798; it's sometimes known as **Torre Stuart**, after General Stuart, who ordered its construction.

Fort Marlborough

Cala de Sant Esteve (971 36 04 62). **Open** *Mid May-Sept* 9.30am-2.15pm Mon, Sun; 9.30am-7.45pm Tue-Sat. *Apr-mid May, Oct-mid Dec* 9.30am-2.15pm Tue-Sat. Closed mid Dec-Mar. **Admission** €3; €1.80 reductions; free under 7s, Sun. **No credit cards**.

Fort Sant Felip

Nr Cala Sant Esteve (971 36 21 00). **Open** (Guided tour only) *June-Oct* 10am Mon, Thur. *Nov-Dec, Mar-May* 10am Sat. Closed Jan-Mar. **Admission** €5; €2.50 reductions; free under 12s. **No credit cards**.

Museu Militar de Menorca

Plaça de s'Esplanada 19, Es Castell (971 36 21 00/www.museomilitarmenorca.com). **Open** *June-Oct* 11am-1pm Mon-Fri & 1st Sun of mth. *Nov-May* 10am-1pm Mon, Wed, Fri & 1st Sun of mth. **Admission** €3; €1.50 reductions; free under 12s. **No credit cards**.

Where to eat & drink

When it comes to eating out, the pedestrianised bay of **Cales Fonts** in **Es Castell** is a calm alternative to the sometimes hectic feel of Maó's portside strip. It's also much smaller, lending itself well to wandering along and looking at menus, all of which feature lots of seafood and some of which offer good-value lunchtime *menús*. There are a handful that stand out. **El Trébol** (Cales Fonts 43, 971 36 70 97, closed mid Oct-Mar) is well known locally as one of the best seafood restaurants in the area, and **Miramar** (Cales Fonts 15, 971 36 46 43, closed Mon-Fri Dec-Feb and all Mar & Nov, €€) is the oldest restaurant on the bay, serving good tapas. **Club Náutico** (Camí de Baix 8, 971 38 11 46, €€), above the harbour at the western end, has a great view and is popular with locals, as is **Sa Foganya** (Àngel Ruiz i Pablo, 97, 971 35 49 50, €€), perched up at the end the bay, by the Club Náutico, which serves grilled fish, vegetables and meat and has a good lunchtime menu. Afterwards, **Dinkums** (Cales Fonts 20, 971 36 70 17, closed Nov-Mar), an American-run café at the beginning of the bay, is as good a spot as any for a drink. The large terrace at **Sa Sinia** (C/San José 9, 971 36 41 33), up near the roundabout at the top of town, is where everybody ends up later, being the only place where you can dance.

Where to stay

Es Castell is a great place to stay for those who don't want to be in Maó but don't have their own transport. There are three large, decent chain hotels all on the waterfront and all with pools – be sure to ask for a room with a sea view. The hotel **Agamenón** (C/Agamenón 16, 971 36 21 50, www.sethotels.com, closed Nov-Apr, doubles €95-€159 incl breakfast) has been renovated recently and can organise water taxis to Maó – a fun and convenient way to begin an evening out. The **Barceló Hamilton** (Passeig de Santa Agueda 6, 971 36 20 50, www.barcelo.com, doubles €77-€110) and **Rey Carlos III** (C/Carlos III 2-4, 971 36 31 00, www.reycarlosiii.com, closed Nov-Apr, doubles €74-€104 incl breakfast) also look out over the harbour, and the rooms are comfortable too if, again, a little dull.

To stay somewhere with more character you have to leave town. Just outside, on the road to Sant Lluís, are two gems. The splendid **Son Granot** (Ctra. Sant Felip s/n, 971 35 55 55, www.songranot.com, doubles €128-€245) was built during the first British occupation by Scot Patrick Mackellar and proudly lords it over the surrounding landscape in fine colonial style. It changed ownership in 2007 and now has eight rooms (one adapted for disabled guests) and two suites, both with terraces. The place is straight out of an interiors magazine yet the atmosphere is resolutely down to earth, with large gardens, an orchard and a variety of animals – including the much-celebrated Menorcan horses. The owners are veritable goldmines of historical information and the pool and classy restaurant (€€€) are additional attractions.

The first thing you'll encounter at the excellent **Sant Joan de Binissaida** (Camí de Binissaida 108, 971 35 55 98, www.binissaida.com, closed Nov-Mar, doubles €120-€280 incl breakfast), a beautifully renovated farmhouse dating back to 1887, are sheep roaming the car park. It's a charming spot and inside a very classy affair; 11 rooms, a large pool, a popular restaurant and a kid-friendly atmosphere are some of the attractions.

A more economical choice is the lovely **Hotel del Almirante** in Collingwood House (Port de Maó s/n, 971 36 27 00, www.hoteldel almirante.com, closed Nov-Apr, doubles €72-€115 incl breakfast), halfway between Es Castell and Maó. Built in the 18th century for Admiral Collingwood, much of the original house has been left more or less untouched, so it's a little like staying in a museum, although most of the rooms are in an adjacent modern extension. It's charmingly bizarre and has a tennis court and a small pool.

SANT LLUIS & SANT CLIMENT

Just south of Maó, **Sant Lluís**, its church standing like a beacon over the surrounding countryside, is a convenient hub for the south-east corner of the island (a signpost just outside the village names four different destinations, all four kilometres away).

Like Es Castell, its strict grid plan layout suggests its origins as another garrison town, though a French rather than a British one; it was built by the Duc de Richelieu in the late 1750s, and named after the 13th-century crusading French king Louis IX. It is essentially a two-street town – driving through the centre can be a pain in wide cars – with three windmills, one of which, the **Molí de Dalt**, still works and houses a small museum of rural tools and machinery. Halfway up C/Comte Lannion, one block over from the main street, there is an interesting donkey-powered well (now unused) opposite No.44. Aside from these minor attractions there's not much to see here, though you could always check out the **Maó Hippodrome** (Ctra. Maó–Sant Lluís 400, 971 36 57 30, €3), halfway between Maó and Sant Lluís, which hosts trotting races every Saturday from May to October at 6pm, and every Sunday from November to April at 2pm.

Four kilometres south-west of Maó is tiny **Sant Climent**, whose only attraction for visitors is its restaurants and, less obviously, a thriving jazz scene.

Molí de Dalt

C/Sant Lluís 4, Sant Lluís (971 15 10 84). **Open** *May-Nov* 10am-2pm, 6-8pm Mon-Fri; 10am-1pm Sat; 11am-1pm Sun. *Dec-Apr* 10am-2pm Mon-Fri; 10am-1pm Sat. **Admission** €1.20; €0.60 reductions. **No credit cards**.

Where to eat & drink

Sant Lluís has a couple of reasonable restaurants, including **La Rueda** (C/Sant Lluís 30, 971 15 03 49, closed Tue and Nov, €€), which has a locals' feel – avoid the interior, with its blaring TV, and bag a table on the terrace for great tapas. **La Bolla** (C/Sant Lluis 56, no phone) has an even more authentic feel – the only concession to tourist palates is a menu in English. On the roundabout at the end of the road, **La Venta de Paco** (Avda. de sa Pau 158, 971 15 09 95, closed dinner Mon, Sun in Nov-Mar, €€) is also a bit garish and very popular – come here for grilled fish and meat. The area just south of Sant Lluís, along a snaking stretch of road through the hamlets of **Torret** and **S'Ullastrar**, has a number of fine eateries. In high season, reservations are essential.

Paradise Platjas

South Menorca's coastline features some of Europe's most idyllic beaches.

Had your fill of talayotic rubble? Traipsed around Ciutadella looking for those *albarcas* for your mum? Now it's time to do what you really came to do – absolutely nothing. And, guess what, you came to the right place. Unbeknown to many, Menorca has some of Europe's most beautiful unspoilt beaches: idyllic strands with white limestone sand and transparent waters to rival those of the Caribbean.

Beware, however, that during high season some of these swathes are practically standing room only. If it's solitude you want, be sure to come early, come late or come out of season with a jumper. Alternatively, head to one of the more popular beaches below and walk along to one of the less accessible and hence less busy bays.

South-east of Ciutadella, and easily accessible from the town by car are three of the most celebrated stretches of sand in the Balearics, all backed by fragrant pine forests and all with car parks. The twin beaches of **Cala Macarella** and **Cala Macarelleta**, and **Cala en Turqueta** are all stunning and have free car parks, whose capacities are handily indicated in advance on electronic billboards when leaving Ciutadella. Leave your car, empty of course, and it's a ten- to 15-minute stroll through the forest and down to the beach.

If they are too busy, from Cala en Turqueta you can continue walking west along the Camí de Cavalls bridlepath that

Cala en Turqueta.

hugs the coast and you'll end up at **Cala des Talaier**, a tiny patch no bigger than a basketball court, or walk further on and you'll find **Son Saura**, a double bay and the largest of the beaches, which usefully also has its own car park.

Alternatively, these beaches can all be reached by walking west from the town of **Cala Galdana** (*see p230*) – a good option if the aforementioned beach car parks are full. Take the sharp right after the Hotel Audax in town, climb the steps and head up on the rough track through the trees. Carry on along the path on top of the headland and eventually you'll reach some wooden steps that lead down to the beach of Cala Macarella, which has a beach bar. Keep going in the same direction and 20 minutes later you'll end up at Cala en Turqueta.

Further secluded spots can be found by walking east from Cala Galdana along the footpath to **Cala Mitjana** and then **Cala Trebalúger**.

Other beaches, not in the south but which merit an excursion, include **Cala Pregonda** (*see p245*), **Cala d'Algairens** (*see p258*) and **Cala en Pilar** (*see p245*) in the North. Further east there's **Caló d'es Moro** on Illa d'en Colom (*see p240*), **Platja Tortuga** and **Cala Presili** (*see p241*).

With all these excursions it's worth bringing a picnic and plenty of water – beach shacks are few and far between – and, of course, a camera.

Cala Macarella.

MENORCA

Pan y Vino (Camí de la Coixa 3, Torret, 971 15 02 01, closed lunch and Tue in Apr-Sept; closed lunch Mon-Fri and dinner Mon-Thur, Sun in Oct-mid Dec, mid Feb-Mar and all mid Dec-mid Feb, €€€) is now owned by a French-Catalan couple and offers a five-course taster menu of seasonal international dishes for €32, and is deservedly popular.

La Caraba (C/S'Ullastrar 78, 971 15 06 82, closed Sun in June, July & Sept and all Oct-May, €€€) is one of the most appealing places to have a meal in Menorca, offering a short menu of extremely fresh, impressively prepared Menorcan food in a traditional cottage with a small, charming garden.

Another farmhouse – this time modern – houses **Sa Pedrera d'es Pujol** (Camí d'es Pujol 14, 971 15 07 17, closed dinner Mon-Fri, Sun Nov-Apr, lunch May-Oct, €€€). The main dining room is cosy, with a roaring fire in the winter, while two conservatory-style rooms offer sunlight and privacy for small groups or dinner à deux. In the summer, though, most visitors opt for the walled terrace, presided over by a giant dragon tree. Owners Daniel and Nuria offer an impeccable and inspired menu from their home region, Asturias – itself undergoing a boom as a culinary tiger – while maintaining a strong focus on island staples: succulent beef, *presalé* lamb, vegetables, seafood and cheese.

A pretty wine-red villa in leafy gardens, with wide verandas at the front and back for dining alfresco, is home to **Villa Madrid** (Ctra. S'Uestrá 46, 971 15 04 64, closed Nov-May, €€). It used to be a swanky restaurant, now it's an Italian-run joint that knocks out great pizzas. Even if you're not staying at either place, it's still worth popping over to both **Biniarroca** (€€€, *see below*) and **Alcaufar Vell** (€€€, *see below*) for dinner. Both offer some of the island's best food, and as such, you'll need to reserve a table in high season.

Sant Climent has an inordinate number of restaurants for such a small place, ranging from smart to simple. At the top end of the scale is **Es Molí de Foc** (C/Sant Llorenç 65, 971 15 32 22, closed Jan, all Mon & dinner Sun Feb-May & Sept-Dec, all Mon June-Aug, €€€), a smart affair in a bright townhouse. Tellingly, the menu outside is not in English and this isn't somewhere to come to in your beachwear, but it's friendly and the food is excellent, with a fairly adventurous menu – king prawn carpaccio in Mahón cheese sauce, say, or *magret de canard* with strawberry salsa. At the other end of the scale, the recently refurbished **Casino** (C/Sant Jaume 4, 971 15 34 18, closed Wed and 2wks Feb, €€) is a typical village restaurant, serving everything from steamed mussels to sandwiches. There are two English

pubs, both authentic in their own way: the **Coach & Horses** (C/Sant Jaume 38, 971 15 33 34, closed evening Sun, €) and **Sa Taverna** across the road (C/Sant Jaume 25, no phone). The former is a better bet for English-style pub food, wraps and roasts on Sundays.

Where to stay

The area contains two of the best places to stay in Menorca, both wonderfully peaceful and with excellent restaurants. Firstly, **Biniarroca** (Sant Lluís Camí Vell 57, 971 15 00 59, www. biniarroca.com, closed Nov-Apr, doubles €128-€187 incl breakfast), which is run by two English women – a painter and a fashion designer – is a tranquil, rustic hideaway. It's popular with everyone from José María Aznar to *madrileño* chaps getting hitched (the local mayor performs civil partnerships) and it's not hard to see why. There's a lovely pool, labyrinth-like gardens, roaming pet tortoises and cool, comfy stone bungalows. The restaurant also deserves a special mention, serving classic European fare with a Menorcan slant on a candlelit garden terrace.

The **Alcaufar Vell** rural hotel (Ctra. Cala d'Alcalfar, km7.3, 971 15 18 74, www. alcaufarvell.com, closed Jan & Feb, doubles €142-€250 incl breakfast) is also a great place to unwind. The rooms in the converted stables are straight out of the pages of *Wallpaper**: huge sleek bathtubs, massive beds and subdued lighting. They also have their own terraces, which are great for kids or a spot of nude sunbathing. The rooms in the main house, parts of which date back to the 14th century, are akin to staying in a castle and are fantastically romantic, though again extremely comfortable. If you really want to splash the cash, the penthouse suite has a private terrace at the top of the building with stunning 360-degree views of the surrounding countryside. Finally, the restaurant – which opened in 2007 serving imaginative modern European food with a Menorcan twist – is excellent.

Not quite as snazzy but still a worthwhile place to stay is the **Son Tretze** (C/Binifadet 20, 971 15 09 43, www.hotelmenorca.com, doubles €87-€156), just outside Sant Lluís, close to the windmill. It has typically rustic rooms as well as a pool and a restaurant serving Menorcan cuisine.

Nearer the airport is **Matxani Gran** (Ctra. Binidali km1, 971 15 33 00/37, www. menorcacountryhouse.com, closed Nov-Apr, €110-€230). It's an informal, self-catering B&B run by a British couple. It has a pool, gardens and even its own well; though those with children should note that they do not allow under-14s.

Another option in the village of **Llucmaçanes** is **Llucmaçanes Gran** (Es Plà Sant Gaietà 10, 971 35 21 17, www.llucmagran.com, €72-€93), dating back to 1859, and now a small, relaxed hotel with seven double rooms. There is a swimming pool and a strip on which to play pétanque.

SOUTH-EAST COAST

You're hard pressed to find a solitary spot on this part of the coast – it's pretty much all been developed now. If you want untouched beaches, you'll need to head west of **Cala Galdana** (*see p230*) or to the north coast west of Fornells (*see p243*). Working from east to west, **S'Algar** is the most built up, with two four-star hotels and several purpose-built estates and villas. The nearest (small) beach is at **Cala d'Alcalfar**, a charming inlet with emerald waters, boathouses built into the side of the cliff and, on its far side, a watchtower guarding the point, surrounded by low vegetation and bare rock.

From here there is a pleasant walk along the old **Camí de Cavalls** (Horse Road), which follows the line of the cliffs to **Punta Prima**, a largish, unappealing resort clustered around a popular sandy beach that looks out to the green and white lighthouse on **Illa de l'Aire**. From here, holiday developments and villas are more or less continuous until you reach **Cap d'en Font** – though happily, for much of the way, the road passes in front of the smug ranks of white houses, giving great views over the rocks out to sea and offering possibilities for clambering down to swim or snorkel.

Cala Torret has a diving and sailing school from which you can explore the depths of the south coast, or, if you don't want to get (too) wet, you can rent kayaks and dinghies. Further on, **Binibèquer** has a pretty beach, surrounded by a small grove of pine trees and thick shrubs, and protected to the west by fins of rock sharking down into the water, with fine white sand and the most photogenic beach bar on the island, **Los Bucaneros** (no phone).

A little further on, the self-proclaimed 'fisherman's village' of **Binibèquer Vell** is neither a fishing village, nor particularly 'vell' (old). In fact, it's a holiday apartment complex built in 1972 as a composite of Mediterranean architecture. The result is a higgledy-piggledy heap of whitewashed houses with wooden beams and balconies, clinging together like shipwreck survivors. Pale imitations can be seen throughout the island, from Platges de Fornells to Son Bou, and to seal its fate, it is now an obligatory stop for every bus tour of the island.

West of here, the only sizeable beaches (by Menorcan standards) are **Binissafúller** and **Canutells**, which is like a smaller version

of Cala en Porter (*see below*). There are also some small patches of sand at the end of **Binidalí** and **Biniparratx** coves, both of which are worth the trek, with clear waters and low cliffs, and wild undergrowth threatening the dirt paths that lead down their respective narrow gorges.

A truly wonderful place for a dip is the rocky bay of **Cales Coves**; grab a picnic and spend the day clambering about the rocks and swimming in the sheltered, clear water. Access is down a very rough dirt road from just outside the development of Son Vitamina – take the signposted track by the roundabout located halfway along the Sant Climent–Cala en Porter road. Drive down the bumpy track and leave the car among the bushes in the makeshift car park, and continue down the track for around 25 minutes – eventually you'll end up with a view that has changed little over the last 2,000 years. Cales Coves is home to the largest necropolis on the island, with over 100 prehistoric burial caves carved into the sides of the cliffs, some impossibly high up and hard to reach.

The double bay was used by the Romans, who got their water from a small spring that emerges from the rocks just to the left of the tiny beach. It's possible to scramble over the rocks around the right-hand side of the beach to reach the bay's second fork. The Romans also constructed a road from here to Porta Magonis (Maó), which doubtless explains why the road to Sant Climent and Maó is the straightest on the island.

The next resort west is **Cala en Porter** (sometimes contracted to Cala'n Porter), at the end of the gorge of the same name. High, steep cliffs create a sheltered, almost rectangular bay with a beach at the end. Small villas and apartments cling to the eastern cliff, with paths and steps leading up to a sprawling, unlovely holiday resort at the top. The other side of the gorge is thankfully untouched,

MENORCA

Profile Cova D'en Xoroi

The island's clifftop clubbing experience defies Menorca's tame reputation.

One of Menorca's most spectacular sights, and an exception to the island's rather poor offerings when it comes to nightlife, is **Cova D'en Xoroi**: a tourist attraction by day, a fantastically positioned and atmospheric *discoteca* by night, which is also home to a local legend.

Located in a system of natural caves high up in the cliffs overlooking the sea at **Cala en Porter**, it's not the place to visit if you suffer from vertigo – the main dancefloor and the various terrace bars perch precariously high above the crashing waves. The setting is so spectacular that during the day the place packs with visitors who drop by for the tremendous views out over the Med; plenty pay the steep entry fee (mercifully, it includes a drink) just to sit and enjoy the vista, accompanied by (slightly clichéd) Balearic ambient beats.

Come nightfall and it's a different story. Folk come from far and wide for international DJ line-ups, with names like **Krafty Cuts**, **Martin Solveig** or even the **Utah Saints** flying in to play for a rave-starved crowd. Do bear in mind, however, that this ain't Fabric: turn up off-season and the only thing you'll be hearing is the wind whipping the rocks. Which is exactly how the legendary pirate Xoroi would have felt when he first set foot in the caves. According to the story, a shipwrecked pirate named Xoroi came to the caves with a girl whom he'd kidnapped in Cala en Porter. For three years the locals had no clue as to what had happened to the local lass until an unexpected flurry of snow left tracks leading to the Cova. An armed mob entered the caves and found Xoroi, his belle and their three kids. Xoroi and his eldest son jumped into the sea, never to be seen again. The damsel of the story, horrified, either by her kidnap ordeal or by the villagers' meddling in her lovelife, moved to Alaior where she spent the rest of her days.

GETTING THERE
A cab to the Cova from Maóshould take about 20 minutes and cost around €20.

LINE-UPS
Don't trek out here for a DJ dud – check online to see who's playing first.

WINDCHILL
In the early hours, in low season, it can get a little cold up here – bring a jumper.

so there are great views over the rugged countryside and down to the sandy bay, where the water is so clear that boats moored there seem to float on air.

Just round the tip of the bay, in the south-facing cliffs, the **Cova d'en Xoroi** is a spectacularly located pirate cave that is now a tourist attraction by day and a club by night (*see p228* **Profile**).

Cova d'en Xoroi

Cala en Porter (971 37 72 36/www.covaden xoroi.com). **Open** *Visits* 10.30am-9pm daily. *Club* 11pm-5am daily. Club closed Oct-June. **Admission** *Visits* €5 (incl 1 drink). *Club* €20-€25. **Credit** MC, V. *See p228* **Profile**.

Triton Diving Center

Cala Torret (971 18 85 28/www.tritondiving center). **Open** *Apr-Sept* 9am-6pm daily. *Shop* Apr-Sept 10am-6pm, 9-11pm daily.

Where to eat & drink

While there are a lot of places in which to eat here, on the most developed part of the island's coast, many of the restaurants serve lacklustre seaside fare or greasy spoon classics; but there are exceptions. In **Cala d'Alcalfar**, the bar-restaurant of the **Hostal Xuroy** (€€; *see below*) serves fresh fish, grilled meats and snacks on a charming, pine-shaded terrace overlooking the small bay and across to the watchtower, a pleasant stroll away.

Further south, **Son Ganxo** (Urb. Son Ganxo s/n, 971 15 90 75, closed Tue and all Nov, €€), in the development of the same name, seems an unlikely option, but has a sea view from the patio at the back and serves simple but decent seafood, meat dishes and salad.

A little further along the coast, on the road between Biniancolla and Cala Torret, **En Caragol** (Marina de Torret s/n, mobile 630 57 35 90, closed Tue and all Nov-Mar, €€) knocks out very good fresh fish, overlooking the rocks and the sea beyond.

In **Cala Torret**, the bar attached to the diving school (*see above*), **Bar Paupa**, has that laid-back, sunbleached watersports vibe and serves sandwiches and snacks. Try the goat's cheese, walnut and apple salad.

In **Punta Prima**, the pedestrianised strip adjacent to the beach is a good spot for lunch with restaurants serving fish and seafood; it's just a shame that chips seem to be an obligatory side order. **Manolo** (Passeig de s'Arenal, 8, 971 15 95 42) serves good-value grilled sardines and swordfish, while **Santi** (Passeig de s'Arenal 4, 971 15 91 70) has sandwiches, paella, grilled prawns and squid.

Where to stay

With one exception, the accommodation options around this particular stretch are largely uninspiring, so those who have their own transport are better off staying further inland. In **S'Algar** there are two large hotels, much used by tour operators: the **Hotel S'Algar** (Urb. S'Algar, 971 05 54 00, closed Nov-Mar, doubles €120-€180), which is close to the bay, and its sister operation the **Hotel San Luís** (Urb. S'Algar, 971 15 07 50, www. salgarhotels.com, closed Nov-Mar, doubles €110-€175), situated further up the hill.

In nearby **Cala d'Alcalfar**, the **Hostal Xuroy** (C/Llevant 1, 971 15 18 20, www.xuroy menorca.com, closed Nov-Apr, doubles €60-€128 incl breakfast) claims to be the oldest hotel on the island and certainly retains some 1950s charm. Most of the rooms have balconies; ask for one with a view of the bay. Be warned, though, that it's often taken over by package groups.

In **Punta Prima**, the five-star apart-hotel **Insotel Club Punta Prima** (971 15 92 00, www.insotel.com, closed Nov-Apr, €83-€384 incl breakfast) dominates the northern edge of town, while just by the beach, the three-star **Xaloc Playa** (C/Major s/n, 971 15 91 20, www.xalocplaya.es, closed Nov-Apr, doubles €58-€156 half board) is usually filled up by tour operators.

In **Binibèquer**, the **Binibeca Club** (Passeig del Mar s/n, 971 15 10 75, www. eden-hotels.com, closed Nov-Apr, doubles €64-€170 incl breakfast) is an example of postmodernism gone nuts, looking like the Aztec zone of the *Crystal Maze*. Lucky patrons have a great view of the sea and Binibèquer Vell from their asymmetric pool; from Binibèquer Vell it's an eyesore.

For apartments in **Binibèquer Vell** itself, call **Apartamentos Binivell Park** (971 15 06 08, www.hlghotels.com, closed Oct-Apr, phone for details of prices).

For places to hire in **Binibèquer Nou**, closer to the beach, visit www.redorka.com or call 971 15 16 18. Further inland, **La Boyera** (Binisafua Roters s/n, 971 15 17 86, mobile 637 52 54 77, closed Nov-May, apartments €39-€120) is a cheaper option, with pleasant bungalows around a pool and a good restaurant.

The most characterful option is the **Binissafullet Vell** (Ctra. Binissafuller 64, 971 15 66 33, www.binissafullet.com, double €80-€200 incl breakfast), one of Menorca's slowly growing number of *agroturismos*. It's less remote and more basic than some of its equivalents, but what it lacks in Italian design classics it makes up for in the personal touch of owner Geni. Breakfasts are a feast of Menorcan specialities from the hotel's

MENORCA

INSIDE TRACK
KAYAKING FROM
CALA GALDANA

A great way to escape Cala Galdana and explore the local caves that are tucked into the nearby coastal cliffs is to hire a canoe. If the sea is calm enough, it's also a great way of getting to spectacular nearby beaches, including Cala en Turqueta, Cala Mitjana, Cala Macarella and Son Saura, all of which are unspoilt (*see p225* **Paradise Platjas**).

adjacent farm: excellent home-made *sobrassada* sausages, jams and bread. And dinner, if you ask for for it, will be whatever is good in the garden right now. As well as the dining room terrace, there's a lovely pool, by which you can thumb through stacks of beaten-up old mags from *Vice* to *Hola!*, which reflect the place's demographic. In winter, the action moves inside to the living room, which has wrinkly old sofas and a log fire.

SOUTH COAST

The south coast is where you'll find many of Menorca's most beautiful beaches. However, it's also where you'll find some of the island's least appealing resorts. But fear not, there are still some secluded beaches (*see p225* **Paradise platjas**). Aside from the development, another, albeit less threatening, viper in this paradise is the sea grass posidonia that gets washed up on the shore; floating in an ankle-tickling band a metre or so wide where the waves break, it's unsightly and irritating rather than anything else, and during peak season the local authorities usually clear it away from the most popular beaches.

The high, sheer cliffs that rise up south of Sant Climent continue along most of the southern coastline, interrupted only by the stretch from **Son Bou** to **Sant Tomàs**, and then tailing off towards **Cap d'Artrutx** at Menorca's south-western point. Son Bou and Sant Tomàs together share the longest, straightest beaches on the island, separated by a rocky outcrop between Punta de Talis and Punta Rodona.

West of here the cliffs resume, broken by occasional gorges that harbour small inlets and quiet beaches. The largest and most accessible of these is **Cala Galdana**, a well-protected horseshoe curving between the pine-topped cliffs on either side, but marred by the high-rise hotel on the beach. West of here are the pristine beaches of **Cala**

Mitjana, Cala Macarella and Cala en Turqueta (*see p225* **Paradise platjas**).

Finally, the coastline ends with a flourish of package hotels and restaurants, ruining the inherent beauty of **Cala en Bosc** (*see p258*) and its natural marina, and nearby **Son Xoriguer**.

Almost every photograph of **Son Bou** features the ruins of an early Christian church in the foreground and miles of virgin beach in the background. It is a shot that evokes wonder at the beauty of the location, a few metres from the water. This and the fact that upon entering the beach a sign reads 'you are entering an unspoilt protected area', is mendacious to say the least. Just out of shot, almost adjacent to the ruins, rise the twin monoliths of the **Sol Milanos Pingüinos** hotel, destroying any atmosphere or magic the site must once have had and dominating the landscape, even from several kilometres away.

It could have been worse. There were plans in the 1970s to build no fewer than 20 hotels here, the theory being that this would concentrate tourism in one spot on the island, and leave everywhere else untouched. This would also have meant draining the large area of marshlands behind the dunes, which is an important stopping point for migrating birds. Fortunately, the plan was shelved, much to the relief of nature-lovers, migrating birds and the mosquitoes that enjoy the marsh (and the tourists) to the full. Behind the marshlands, which are impenetrable, the hillside is dotted with villa developments (which spread westwards, merging into the neighbouring resort of **Sant Jaume Mediterrani**). Though hardly inconspicuous, they are certainly less offensive to the eye than a line of tower blocks.

The beach at Son Bou is long. As access is only available at the eastern end, relative calm (and the liberty to sunbathe nude) rewards anyone willing to trudge west, though go too far west and you will find yourself meeting fellow trudgers trudging east from Sant Tomàs, just beyond the rocky outcrop.

The ruins of the church at Son Bou consist of an outline of low stones that show the precise floor plan of the church, including the location of the altar and three narrow naves. It dates back to the end of the fifth century and is one of six early Christian churches on the island – others have been excavated at **Es Fornàs de Torelló** (*see p221*), **Fornells** and on the **Illa del Rei** (*see p211 and 216*), while two more, at Sanitja and on the Illa d'en Colom, have yet to be excavated.

Halfway between Son Bou and Alaior, about 1.5 kilometres down a well-signposted lane, is the largest talayotic village on the island, **Torre d'en Gaumés**. An early

Cala Galdana.

example of suburban sprawl, it is spread over a hillside with good views to the coast (and of any marauding invaders sailing in from the south). Remarkable mainly for its size, the individual buildings are in similar condition to others on the island. Key aspects here are the presence of three large talayots. The central talayot has a taula precinct beside it, although at some point the T-bar was removed and used as a sarcophagus, possibly by the Romans or the Moors, both of whom also inhabited the village. There is a hypostyle chamber with large slabs forming the roof, although whatever filled in the spaces between them has long since disappeared.

The road to **Sant Tomàs** rolls gently down from Es Migjorn Gran through attractive farmland and avenues of tall pines, meeting the coast at the western end of the resort. To the east, a group of hotels, none more than four storeys high, hog the shoreline, their gardens separated from the beach by a pathway, while behind them the hillside is covered with private villas.

To the west stretch various untouched beaches, separated by low rocks and edged with dunes and pine woods. **Platja de Binigaus**, at the western end, where the Binigaus gorge opens out into the sea, is the widest and wildest section, and one of the more accessible nudist beaches on the island.

A farm road on the west side of the gorge heads inland from the remains of a house dug into the rock, past the large meadow where the gorge opens out, and up the west side of the gorge to the farmhouses of Binigaus Nou and Binigaus Vell. The former has an interesting prehistoric hypostyle (pillared) chamber beside it. Along the way you pass

two elaborate rain collection systems, which channel the water to large cisterns equipped with a bucket suspended from a pulley.

Nearby, but difficult to reach from the gorge itself, are the remains of the talayotic settlement at **Sant Agustí**, standing on the eastern clifftop. The easiest access to the site, though, is from the Sant Tomàs–Es Migjorn road. A dirt layby between km8 and km9 conceals an unmarked farm road leading to the farmhouse of Sant Agustí Vell. The only indication that you are in the right place is a board 100 metres in from the road telling you to leave your car there, but with no other clues or directions. Continue along the metalled road to the farmhouse, branching off right through the gate and along the stony farm path that passes directly in front of the first outbuildings. Almost a kilometre further on you will come to the next clue: a rubbish bin. The site is a little further along, and well worth the walk: it features two talayots and a taula, as well as subterranean water cisterns. What is

> ### INSIDE TRACK
> ### COVA DELS COLOM
>
> Halfway between Es Migjorn Gran and Binigaus beach in the Binigaus gorge is a huge natural cave, the Cova dels Coloms. To get there take either the path at the bottom of the gorge, a couple of hundred metres from the beach, or the path close to the top, soon after Binigaus Nou. Both are clearly signposted. Once you're in it you'll need a torch to explore.

MENORCA

particularly interesting is that you can still enter the pillared chamber inside the northernmost talayot, which is supported by a huge, ancient juniper beam.

At first sight, **Cala Galdana**, the next resort to the west after Sant Tomàs, comes as something of a shock: a beautiful horseshoe beach marred by the huge white hotel that stands almost upon it, and by the resort that has sprung up within the natural amphitheatre between the cliffs. Again, you'll feel overzealous planning has blighted what is some of Europe's most enchanting coastline. But, with a gently sloping beach, not to mention the availability of pedaloes, kayaks and the like, the bay is ideal for those with young children. A tallish outcrop of rock jutting out into the bay, and accessible via a newly constructed bridge, has a bar on it, and gives an alternative view. Until recently, the outcrop was part of the adjacent hillside, before the connecting rock was dynamited away a couple of years ago so the river that flows down the gorge would run straight into the bay, rather than curling round and taking up too much precious beach. What the planners had not foreseen was that this would allow the ubiquitous sea grass to be washed straight up the river, trapping dead sealife and filling the area around the new canal with the pungent aroma of rotting fish.

While the resort itself is limited in size because of the natural obstacles on each side, there are plenty of options for walking, mountain biking and sea kayaking nearby. The coastal cliffs harbour numerous caves that can be explored by kayak, especially when there is no wind and the sea is pond-still. It's also a great way of getting to the nearby beaches, including **Cala en Turqueta**, **Cala Mitjana**, **Cala Macarella** and **Son Saura**, all of which are unspoilt. **Audax Sports & Nature** (Urb. Cala Galdana s/n, 971 15 45 48, www.rtmhotels.com, closed Nov-Mar), beside the Hotel Audax, rents bikes and kayaks, as well as running various types of guided excursions on land and sea.

Where to eat & drink

If you want to watch the football with a plate of egg and chips and a Guinness, you'll be spoilt for choice in **Son Bou**, **Sant Tomàs** and **Cala Galdana**, all of which cater for package tourists. Unfortunately, when it comes to other eating options, the pickings are thin on the ground. That said, all three resorts have beach shacks serving at least reasonable snacks – **Es Bruc** (no phone, €) in **Sant Tomàs** is particularly good for fresh, grilled sardines and lovely views (if you turn your back on the concrete hotels).

Restaurant Cala Mitjana (Passeig des Riu 1, 971 15 45 66, closed dinner Sat, Sun and all Nov-Apr, €€), in **Cala Galdana**, bucks the local trend for draught Guinness and fish and chips with grilled fish, meat and even daiquiris and mojitos, all on a pleasant terrace. Alternatively, if you're allergic to the resortiness of the area, **Es Migjorn Gran** or **Es Mercadal** have some great restaurants.

Another alternative, a couple of kilometres south of Ferreries on the road to Cala Galdana, is **El Gallo** (Ctra. Cala Galdana, km1.5, 971 37 30 39, closed Mon and all Dec & Jan, €€), a sizeable old farmhouse serving delicious grilled meat and good paella; or try **Es Forn** (Urb. Torres Soli Nou 28, 971 37 28 98, closed Tue, €€€), a couple of kilometres from Son Bou on the Torre Soli Nou road towards Alaior, another venerable farmhouse serving modern cuisine.

Where to stay

If you don't like holiday resorts, you're stumped for places to stay on the south coast, unless you want to camp (*see p233*). Your best bet is to head inland from Cala Galdana to **Son Triay** (Ctra. Cala Galdana, km3, 971 55 00 78, mobile 600 07 44 41, www.sontriay.com, closed Nov-Mar, double €66-€106), a lovingly restored neo-colonial mansion set in formal

Son Saura.

gardens complete with nubile statues and yet more idyllic rural scenery. The current family bought the house, which dates back to the 1800s, after the Civil War and have turned it into an *agroturismo* in an attempt to save their heritage. It has just six large, cool bedrooms in the main house and two apartments (one old-fashioned with a wood-burning fire and cobbled terrace shaded by a 200-year-old fig tree; the other more modern, with views over the fields), while the pleasantly rustic breakfast room, where home-produced food is served, has a walk-in fireplace. There's also a swimming pool and tennis courts.

The only two campsites on the south coast are three kilometres outside Son Bou and Cala Galdana respectively. **Camping Son Bou** (Ctra. Sant Jaume, km3.5, 971 37 26 05/ 27 27, www.campingsonbou.com, closed mid Oct-mid Apr, tents €3.60-€14, adults €6.40-€7.75, bungalows €56-€78, mobile homes €79-€122) has a pool and a tennis court and accepts both tents and caravans. **Camping S'Atalaia** (Ctra. Cala Galdana, km4, 971 37 42 32, www.campingsatalaia.com, closed mid Oct-mid Apr, tents €2.80-€8.35, adults €5.25-€6.30) is reserved for tents only.

Son Bou has just two hotels, the doubly monolithic **Sol Pingüinos** (Platja de Son Bou s/n, 971 37 12 00, www.solmilanospinguinos.solmelia.com, closed Nov-Apr, doubles €75-€131 incl breakfast) and the **Royal Club Son Bou** (Platja de Son Bou s/n, 971 37 23 58, www.royalsonbou.com, closed Nov-Mar, doubles €69-€184), which is aimed at families with young children. For apartments, try **Apartamentos Son Bou Gardens** (971 37 12 16, www.menorcarentals.com, closed Nov-Apr, phone for prices).

Sant Tomàs has four hotels and three hotel-like apartment blocks, and all receive large numbers of package tourists. The best is the **Santo Tomas** (Platja de Sant Tomàs s/n, 971 37 00 25, www.sethotels.com, closed Nov-Mar, doubles €100-€238 incl breakfast), a comfortable hotel with balconies overlooking the palm-filled garden and pool and the beach, a few steps away. It also has a small indoor pool and jacuzzi for when Menorcan weather turns grey, as well as sauna and steam rooms, a gym and massages. A close second, and very similar in almost every respect, is the **Sol Menorca** next door (Platja de Sant Tomàs s/n, 971 37 00 50, www.solmelia.com, closed Nov-Apr, doubles €70-€214 incl breakfast), with sea views, a sizeable gym and a decent swimming pool. On the same strip is the **Lord Nelson** (Platja de Sant Tomàs s/n, 971 37 01 25, www.hihotels.net, closed Nov-Feb, doubles €71-€149 incl breakfast). For apartments, try the **Hamilton Court** (971 37 00 00, www.hamiltoncourt.com,

closed Nov-Apr) or **Mestral & Llebeig** (Urb. Sant Tomàs s/n, 971 37 03 70, www.set hotels.com, closed Nov-Apr, apartments €74-€164), which also has some villas to rent.

Cala Galdana has three hotels around the bay. The immense **Sol Gavilanes** (Urb. Cala Galdana s/n, 971 15 45 45, www.solgavilanes.solmelia.com, closed Nov-Apr, doubles €75-€225 incl breakfast) is impossible to miss, being right on the beach. A better alternative is the **Hotel Audax** (Urb. Serpentona s/n, 971 15 46 46, www.rtmhotels.com, closed Nov-mid Mar, doubles €90-€200 half board), on the western side of the beach, which is far more discreet and still has a great view of the bay. Further back, the **Hotel Cala Galdana** (Urb. Cala Galdana s/n, 971 15 45 00, www.infotelecom.es/galdana, closed Nov-Apr, doubles €124-€150 incl breakfast) is a huge, colonial-style mansion. Up the hill behind the Audax, the **FloraMar** (Urb. Serpentona, 971 15 45 12, www.comitashotels.com, closed Nov-Apr, apartments €50-€180) has apartments and studios.

RESOURCES

Internet
Cala Galdana *Snack-Bar Alaska, Urb. Cala Galdana (971 15 45 77).* **Open** *May-Oct* 11am-11pm daily. Closed Nov-Apr.

Police station
Es Castell *Plaça de l'Esplanada 5 (971 36 27 47).*
Sant Lluís *C/d'Allemand 97 (971 15 17 17).*

Post office
Es Castell *C/Llevant 2 (971 36 71 07).*
Sant Lluís *C/Sant Esteve 14 (971 15 12 87).*

Tourist information
Sant Lluís *OIT, C/Sant Lluís 4 (971 15 10 84).* **Open** 10am-2pm Mon-Sat; 10am-1pm Sun.

GETTING THERE

By bus
From Maó, there are 26 buses Mon-Sat (20 Sun) to Es Castell (10mins), 13 buses Mon-Sat (12 Sun) to Sant Lluís (10mins), 12 buses Mon-Sat (4 Sun) to Sant Climent (10mins), 3 buses daily to Binibèquer (20mins), 7 buses Mon-Sat to Cala en Porter (20mins), and 6 buses Mon-Sat to Son Bou (35mins), 4 buses Mon-Fri (3 Sat) to Sant Tomàs (40mins) and 5 buses daily (4 Sun) to Cala Galdana (1hr) via Ferreries (20mins). From Ciutadella, there are 7 buses daily (3 Sun) to Cala Galdana (40mins) via Ferreries (not all stop), 4 buses Mon-Fri (3 Sat) to Sant Tomàs (40mins) and 1 Mon-Sat to Son Bou (1hr). Note that there are fewer services to the resorts Nov-Apr.

Central Menorca

Escape the coastal frenzy to Menorca's quiet quarter.

The small, sleepy towns of **Alaior**, **Es Mercadal** and **Ferreries**, numbering fewer than 15,000 inhabitants between them, are a welcome break from the crowds of the rest of the island and pleasant places for a wander. All three also have at least one unexpected gem in terms of eating. The central region also acts as a gateway to the resorts on the south coast – Son Bou, Sant Tomàs and Cala Galdana respectively (*see p221-233*), all of which have pretty beaches of fine white sand and turquoise water – as well as garish high-rise developments.

ALAIOR

Perched on a hill around its pretty sandstone church, Alaior (12 kilometres north-west of Maó) is the largest, but also the quietest, of the towns of the interior, and a focus for local cheese making. Originally just a quiet maze of narrow streets woven around the church, it has a couple of interesting buildings and an attractive cemetery just outside the town on the **Camí d'en Kane**. Due largely to the cheese- and shoe making industries, the town now sprawls southwards in unlovely industrial and housing estates, which are all too visible from the main road.

Standing proudly above the rest of the town, the 17th-century sandstone church of **Santa Eulàlia** is similar in style to the cathedral in Ciutadella; it's desperately gloomy within, thanks to its lack of natural light. Just down the hill from here is **Plaça Constitució**, a diminutive square, just large enough for a pavement café and the self-important **Casino**, looking like a South American small-town hall. The real town hall is in C/Major, to the right of the pavement café; it's a compact building with a beautiful carved façade, a covered courtyard and a sweeping stone staircase. Almost opposite is **Can Salort**, a 17th-century mansion, similar to those in Ciutadella, which now contains a libary and an outpost of the University of the Balearics.

Leading north from the Casino, C/Es Forn contains a number of interesting townhouses and the old Franciscan church of **Sant Didac** (San Diego), with its adjoining monastery.

Now used as a cultural centre, it is a large, whitewashed building dating back to 1629, with palm trees in its forecourt giving it a North African flavour. The carved stone doorway features a sculpture of the saint himself; above it is the crest of the Order of St Francis.

To the north of the town is another small chapel, **Sant Pere Nou**, with a small pine-filled park and play area in front. From here, **Es Cós**, the narrow road leading to the walled, cypress-filled cemetery, is remarkable for still being the course for horse races, held during the local festivities, the **Festes de Sant Llorenç**. The continuous drystone walls on either side of the road are topped by a whitewashed step that acts as a single long seat for spectators, while towards the far end, close to the cemetery, is a small tribune for the judges. As architect Joan J Gomila points out in his excellent *Menorca Architecture Guide*, 'the two white lines that mark the path delineate a magical space which, as well as being a racecourse, could perhaps also be a connection between the city of the living and the city of the dead.'

On Camí de Binifabini, the road from Alaior to Addaia, you'll find **Subaida**, a farm with a shop where you can see Menorcan cheese being made. Or on the road to Maó is the **Lloc de Menorca** zoo, a hit with kids who can get up close and personal with goats, pigs, parrots and horses of all shapes and sizes.

Lloc de Menorca

Urb. l'Argentina, Alaior (917 37 24 03/www. llocdemenorca.es). **Open** *Apr-Oct* 10am-8pm

daily. *Nov, Feb, Mar* 10am-6pm daily. Closed
Jan & Dec. **Admission** €8; €5 reductions.
Credit MC, V.

Subaida

*Camí de Binifabini s/n (971 37 90 86/www.
subaida.com).* **Open** *May-Sept* 9am-2pm, 4-8pm
Mon-Fri; 9am-1pm Sat. *Oct-Apr* 9am-3pm Mon-
Fri; 9am-1pm Sat. Call in advance to book tours.
Admission *Tours* €7 (incl tasting); free under-
10s. **Credit** MC, V.

Where to eat & drink

Most visitors are day-trippers staying at
the southern beaches, which is why there
are no hotels in town, and relatively few
restaurants. The best place to eat is still the
Cobblers (C/San Macario 6, 971 37 14 00,
www.thecobblers.es, closed lunch Mon-Sat,
dinner Sun and mid Dec-mid Apr, €€-€€€), an
English-run brasserie in a gorgeous townhouse
with exposed beams, arched doorways and, in
summer, tables in the airy courtyard; the menu
offers the likes of poached pear salad, tomato
and basil soup with cheesey croutons, or
Argentinian fillet steak. For something more
local, try **C'an Jaumot** (C/San Juan Bautista
6A, 971 37 82 94, closed Sun, €), a traditional
village restaurant, pizzeria and bar in front
of a park full of palms, pines and sycamores
just down from the church of Sant Didac.

For coffee or a light lunch head to Plaça de
la Constitució, a square with two cafés. **Ca Na
Divina** (Sa Placa, 971 37 13 48, €) is the more
popular option, serving sandwiches and tapas.

ES MERCADAL & EL TORO

Located almost exactly at the centre of
the island, **Es Mercadal** (eight kilometres
north-west of Alaior) has always been the
place where people stop off on the way to
somewhere else, so might perhaps be excused
a certain lack of identity. It is redeemed (just)
by a handful of good restaurants, and by its
proximity to El Toro, the highest point on the
island. It's unfortunate too that the town's most
interesting monument, the **Aljub**, or water
reservoir (at the western end of the town, a
couple of minutes' walk from the town hall) is
closed to the public. Built under the orders of
the tireless Governor Kane in 1735, it was
designed to catch rainwater for his parched
troops as they marched from one end of the
island to the other. Although rather
unprepossessing from ground level, it has a
surface area of 800 square metres (8,611 square
feet), and can store 273,000 litres (60,060
gallons) of water behind walls one and a half
metres thick. Its key feature is the long, straight
staircase (visible through a gate), which is like
the proverbial stairway to heaven, topped by a
typical Menorcan olive-wood gate. To the north
of the Aljub are various walled allotments, still
used for growing fruit and vegetables, while to
the south a couple of picturesque streets around
the town hall and church attempt to make up
for the banality of the rest of the town.

To the east, a steep road snakes up **El Toro**,
whose modest summit (357 metres/1,171 feet),
bristling with a cathedral of telecommunications
towers, is visible from most of the island. Beside

MENORCA

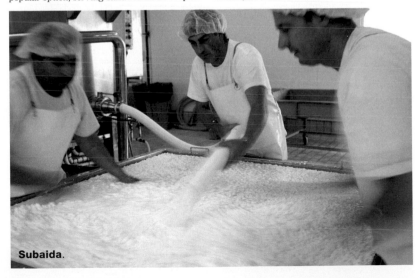

Subaida.

it, an immense statue of Christ welcomes you to the **Església del Toro**, with its plant-filled courtyard, souvenir shop and snack bar. Much of the church was destroyed by fire and rebuilt during the Civil War, and is now a bright, scrubbed space with interesting tapestries and an ornate gold altarpiece. Next door is the much-rebuilt fortress/barracks block that is all that remains of the stronghold that once stood on this site. On a clear day you can just about make out the entire coast of Menorca, though it is the Bay of Fornells and Cap de Cavalleria to the north that are most easily distinguished.

Where to stay, eat & drink

The **Hostal Jeni** (Mirada del Toro 81, 971 37 50 59, www.hostaljeni.com, doubles €50-€90 incl breakfast), a bright, spick-and-span place that was revamped in 2006 and that now includes a sauna and jacuzzi alongside the pool and terrace. The 56 rooms are comfortable if a little lacking in character. Another option is the **Hotel Es Mercadal** (C/Nou 49, 971 15 44 39, www.hoteles mercadal.com, doubles €75-€161 incl breakfast), a townhouse on the main street that was refurbished and opened as a hotel in 2007. Its six rooms are bright, modern and spotless.

Es Mercadal is blessed with more than its fair share of good places to eat. **N'Aguadet** (C/Lepanto 30, 971 37 53 91, €€€) has been owned by the Mariano family since 1936, and specialises in traditional Menorcan cuisine in a setting that is formal without being starchy; the sprightly elderly mother of the family bustles between the tables offering culinary tips, and wine from the restaurant's vineyards. King Juan Carlos's late father, Joan de Borbó, often used to slip in here unannounced for lunch. **Ca'n Olga** (Pont da na Macarrana s/n, 971 37 54 59, closed lunch Mon, all Tue and Nov-Mar, €€) is smaller, more modern and less formal and run by the Crispin siblings from

a charming cottage (it's named after their late mother). It's widely agreed to be one of the best restaurants on the island, serving excellent Menorcan cuisine, though with wider influences – particularly modern Catalan, French and Basque. The menu changes regularly. In spring and autumn, the dining room, with its lurid paintings, is often full, and classical music provides the background tempo. In summer, diners are moved outside to the pleasant, flower-filled garden, a lovely, romantic spot.

It's difficult to miss **Es Molí d'es Racó** (Ctra Maó–Ciutadella, km21, 971 37 53 92, €-€€), the converted windmill beside the main road. The downstairs rooms have been turned into snug dining areas, while outside a vine provides shade for the terrace overlooking the main road. The cheap daily €10-€15 *menú* is popular among local labourers and truck drivers, while the à la carte Menorcan menu is a more formal affair, and attracts diners from across the island.

Tast (Plaça Pare Camps 21, 971 37 55 87, www.tastmercadal.es, closed Mon, €€) serves modern light dishes in a slick restaurant-café on the square. Think squid stuffed with vegetables and black rice, or local gammon in red wine.

Sa Plaça (Plaça de la Constitució 2, 971 37 50 48) is a down-to-earth locals joint on the town's main drag, serving good sandwiches, tapas and gazpacho.

FERRERIES

The town of Ferreries (eight kilometres west of Es Mercadal and 16 kilometres east of Ciutadella), set among the rolling hills in the centre of the island, is not the liveliest of towns; most people come for the factory outlet shops (notably the Jaime Mascaró shop; *see p238* **Profile**) and then leave. With just one dull hotel and a handful of bars and restaurants, the place only really comes alive on Saturday mornings when there is a handicrafts market in the main square, **Plaça Espanya**. It's a fairly small, dispiriting affair out of season, notwithstanding the odd troupe of adolescents dancing to traditional live folk music. In summer, however, there are many more stalls, many more people, and the dancers wear traditional costume.

Further up the hill is a small square of whitewashed buildings, including the tiny but attractive town hall and the 18th-century church of **Sant Bartomeu**, with its pretty neo-classical belltower (dating from the late 19th century) and doorways picked out in yellow. There are a couple of quiet, attractive bars here, though Plaça Espanya is where the real action is. Nearby, there is a very small natural history and ethnographic museum, the **Centre de la Natura**, which features changing seasonal exhibitions on local animal and plant life and

INSIDE TRACK
CAMI D'EN KANE

If you're not in a particular hurry, the old Camí d'en Kane makes for a far more rewarding drive than the main motorway that crosses the islands; this was the original road built by British Governor Richard Kane in the early 18th century between Menorca's two main towns. Largely traffic-free, it branches off the ME-7 Maó–Fornells road and then runs parallel to the main highway, bypassing the town of Alaior and rejoining the main ME-1 just before Es Mercadal.

Ferreries.

other aspects of Menorca's natural history (those in spring/summer tend to be geared towards tourists, while autumn and winter exhibitions are aimed at schoolchildren). There is also a short stretch of the ancient Ciutadella road, the **Camí Vell** (Old Way) or **Camí Real** (Royal Way), that has been restored and is a pleasant spot for a short stroll – pick up a leaflet from the town hall with a map and points of interest.

Just north of Ferreries, **Hort de Sant Patrici** is one of the island's 52 official cheese-makers, producing around 100 cheeses a day. In the morning you can see fresh cheese being made, while in the afternoon the staff tend to the cheese being cured, rubbing it regularly with olive oil. Menorcan cheese, known generically as 'queso Mahón', comes in fresh, semi-cured and cured varieties; each cheese needs between 30 and 40 litres (53-70 pints) of milk, which, conveniently, is about how much you get from a cow each day. The place doubles as a cheese museum and also has an interesting sculpture garden. An audio tour is available.

At **Son Martorellet**, on the road south to Cala Galdana, there are twice-weekly Menorcan dressage displays.

FREE Centre de la Natura

C/Mallorca 2 (971 37 45 05/www. gobmenorca.com). **Open** *May-Oct* 10.30am-1.30pm, 5.30-8.30pm Tue-Sat. *Oct-Apr* 10am-1pm, 5.30-8.30pm Sat, some afternoons; call for information. **Admission** free. **No credit cards**.

FREE Hort de Sant Patrici

Camí Ruma–Sant Patrici s/n (971 37 37 02/ www.santpatrici.com). **Open** *May-Oct* 9am-1.30pm, 4.30-8pm Mon-Sat. *Nov-Apr* 9am-1pm, 4-6pm Mon-Fri; 9am-1pm Sat. **Admission** free; €4.50 audio tour, (audio tour) free under-15s. **Credit** AmEx, DC, MC, V.

Jaime Mascaró

(Poligono Industrial/971 37 38 37/www. mascaro.com). **Open** *Mid May-mid Oct* 9.30am-8.30pm Mon-Sat; 10am-2pm Sun. *Mid Oct-mid May* 9.30am-8pm Mon-Sat. **Credit** AmEx, DC, MC, V. *See p238* **Profile**.

Son Martorellet

Ctra. Cala Galdana, km1.7 (971 37 71 15/ mobile 639 15 68 51/www.sonmartorellet.com). **Shows** *May-Oct* 8.30pm, 10pm Tue, Thur. Closed Nov-Apr. **Tickets** €17.50-€25; €11.50-€15 reductions. **No credit cards**. Ring in advance to check showtimes.

Where to stay, eat & drink

The **Loar** (C/Verge del Toro 2, 971 37 41 81, doubles €64-€130, restaurant €€) is the only hotel in town, with 24 bright and modern rooms that are popular with business travellers. The hotel was refurbished in 2007 and contains one of only a handful of restaurants in town, offering wholesome food, including plenty of meat and seafood. Its USP is the rooftop pool, sundeck and jacuzzi from which you can survey the town's terracotta skyline and the surrounding mountains.

Another good acccommodation option is the recently opened *agroturismo* from the cheese-making owners of **Hort de Sant Patrici** (*see above*): **Ca Na Xini** (Camí Ruma–Sant Patrici s/n, 971 37 37 02, www. canaxini.com, doubles €100-€230). It's a small but slick affair with eight double bedrooms and a pool, surrounded by the vineyards and outhouses of the queso Mahón factory.

The best restaurant in town, and a favourite among island residents, is the **Liorna** (C/Dalt 9, 971 37 39 12, www.liorna.com, closed Mon

MENORCA

Profile Jaime Mascaró

Fashion-forward Ferreries.

Ferreries-may seem like an unlikely spot from which to launch an attack on the catwalks of Milan, New York and London, but try telling that to the Mascaró family. They've been making shoes here since 1918, and their Jaime Mascaró brand is going great guns in shopping hubs the world over.

The company ethos remains firmly grounded in local tradition, however; for though Menorca – and sleepy central Menorca at that – may not be on most people's fashion radars, what it lacks in armies of style bloggers and rows of boutiques (there's barely even a street in Ferreries that's busy enough to strut your stuff on) it has always made up for in its heritage of good old-fashioned craftsmanship.

Established by Jaime Mascaró's uncle and his father in 1918, the business is today run by Jaime himself, along with his sisters Ursula and Lina; Ursula's husband even takes care of marketing the shoes in the UK. And 90 years on, the shoes – from smart men's loafers to stylish ballet pumps – all continue to be made in the town's factory, overseen by the Mascarós themselves. Suffice to say this is a family affair.

The company branched out into the belts, bags and coats market a while back, too, but it's the itsy-bitsy ballet pumps that have been a roaring success of late. As the craze for simple slip-ons invaded highstreets, workplaces and nightclubs from Brussels to Beijing, with 90 years of experience, Jaime Mascaró could eleiver the real deal – celebrity endorsements have rolled in, with everyone from Lindsay Lohan to Claudia Schiffer declaring themselves fans of Ferreries' finest.

A Jaime Mascaró shop opened in London's Marylebone, an exclusive shopping enclave if ever there was one, in 2007, selling the company's popular Pretty Ballerina range.

Female readers in need of some retail therapy who are finding that queso Mahón, gin Xoriguer and *sobrassada* sausages don't quite cut the mustard when it comes to shopping satisfaction will be delighted to learn that the factory's outlet shop stocks many different lines at knock-down prices.

Chaps in tow needn't fret though, as there's plenty of mens' shoes, leather jackets, bags and belts too, though, if we're honest it's all about the ladies shoes. Besides, a shopping excursion here begins and ends here. This ain't Bluewater, folks – you won't be traipsing around for hours simply because there's nowhere to traipse to – save for a couple of uninspiring factory shops next door, there's nowhere else to part with your cash. Apart from the on-site café, that is, which offers up a light, modern Menorcan *menú*.

SALES
Seasonal restocking is usually preceeded by a sale of last season's lines.

May-Oct and Mon-Thur, Sun Nov-Apr, €€€), a bright, minimalist shrine that combines classic and more modern Mediterranean cuisine with international influences – tuna steak with wasabi purée, say, or Thai-style mussels.

Vimpi (Plaça Príncipe Juan Carlos 5, 971 37 31 99, €), at the entrance to the village, is a kitsch, very Spanish café-restaurant that serves hearty, good-value tapas, as well as more substantial meals. Alternatively, **El Gallo** (Ctra. Cala Galdana, km1.5, 971 37 30 39, www.mesonelgallo.com, closed Mon and Dec-Jan) is a 200-year-old farmhouse and something of an island institution for its delicious paella and steak melts with Mahon cheese. It is situated just a couple of kilometres down the road to Cala Galdana and is at its most atmospheric for Sunday lunch.

Most of the town's bars are located around the main square, Plaça Espanya, which gets pretty lively on Friday and Saturday nights, when they act as a general meeting point for local youths. All the bars have tables out on the square, and almost without exception are gloomy and overbearing inside. Far nicer than these are the two bars situated further up the hill: **Bar Can Marc** (no phone) and **Bar Ca'n Bernat** (971 37 31 10) in Plaça de s'Església, the square beside the church.

ES MIGJORN GRAN

Equidistant from Es Mercadal, Ferreries and Sant Tomàs (*see p230*), Es Migjorn Gran is a village with a couple of decent places to eat, and while not actually very 'gran' at all, it does have a certain calm appeal. An attractive church, a town hall that looks as if it might have taken over the local stables and a couple of streets of whitewashed houses highlighted in cornflower blue and buttermilk yellow make it a pleasant place to stop for lunch on the way to the beach at **San Tomàs** (*see p230*). Uniquely, the church has a grandfather clock ticking away beside the altar.

Where to stay, eat & drink

S'Engolidor (C/Major 3, 971 37 01 93, www.sengolidor.com, closed Nov-Apr, doubles €47-€53, restaurant closed Mon in May-Sept and Mon & Tue in Oct, €€), a converted cottage in the centre of the village, is the best place to stay and eat, with four, cosy and characterful rooms (the best look over the patio at the back) above a small, eccentric but excellent Menorcan restaurant. The short menu features interesting salads and starters such as stuffed aubergine and tomato and leek soup followed by a couple of meat and fish dishes (stingray with capers, pork with prunes), and is excellent value.

In the summertime try to bag one of the tables (complete with candelabra) on the lovely flower-filled terrace.

Another place to eat is **Ca Na Pilar** (Avda. de la Mar 1, 971 37 02 12, closed dinner Wed, Thur & Sun, all Mon, Tue and Dec-Mar, €€), serving local and Mediterranean cuisine in a pretty, rustic restaurant. The focal point for village nightlife (and daylife) is **Bar Peri** (Sa Plaça 1, 971 37 01 15), on a corner, in the centre of the village.

RESOURCES

Internet
Es Mercadal *Ca'n Internet, Avda. Mestre Gari 48 (971 37 53 59/www.esmercadal.com/ www.caninternet.net).* Open 10.30am-2pm, 5-10.30pm Tue-Sat; 5-11.30pm Sun.

Police station
Alaior *C/de la Sala s/n (971 37 13 20).*
Ferreries *Plaça de s'Església 1 (971 15 51 77/ mobile 606 37 23 55).*
Es Mercadal *C/Major 18 (971 37 52 51).*
Es Migjorn *Mirada del Toro 20 (971 37 05 05/ mobile 676 99 11 27).*

Post office
Alaior *C/Sant Pere Nou s/n (971 37 19 71).*
Ferreries *Plaça Constitució s/n (971 37 41 00).*
Es Mercadal *C/Lepanto 43 (971 37 53 37).*
Es Migjorn Gran *Plaça de s'Ajuntament (971 37 53 37).*

GETTING THERE

By bus
The 7 buses that run Mon-Sat (6 on Sun) between Maó and Ciutadella stop at Alaior, Es Mercadal and Ferreries. In addition, there are 4 buses daily between Ferreries and Maó (40mins), 7 buses daily between Ferreries and Cala Galdana (20mins), 13 buses Mon-Sat between Alaior and Son Bou (15mins) and 4 buses Mon-Fri (3 on Sat) from Es Migjorn Gran to Sant Tomàs (10mins). Note that there are fewer services to the resorts out of season (Nov to Apr).

> ### INSIDE TRACK
> ### BINIGAUS GORGE
>
> 'Es Migjorn' (as the village is often signposted) is also a possible starting point for walking 4.5 kilometres down the Binigaus Gorge, ending up at the beach of Sant Tomàs. It takes about an hour and is fairly easygoing, but be sure to take plenty of water in summer.

North Menorca

Welcome to the rugged quarter.

Menorca's north is a great antidote to the development found elsewhere, and the region gives a taste of what the island was like before the tour operators moved in. Among its treasures are virgin beaches, some on islands only accessible by boat; therapeutic mud; the alluring fishing village of Fornells; and jagged cliffs and bizarre rock formations carved by the harsh Tramuntana wind – it's a far cry from the postcard depiction of the Med. Indeed, in the summer, the interior, with its gentle hills, hedges and clusters of white cottages, looks like a parched Cornwall.

THE NORTH-EAST COAST

The road from Maó to Fornells is a lovely drive through picturesque farmland, fertile pastures, thick woods and rolling hills before reaching the pines and salt flats of the **Bay of Fornells**. Tributaries branch off to the various villages of the north-east coast. Four kilometres north-east of Maó, **Sa Mesquida** has the closest beach to the city (Cala Mesquida), sheltered by a rocky outcrop and once protected by a now much-eroded defence tower, built by the British in 1799. In 1781, a combined French-Spanish force landed here to launch their attack on the island.

Further north, the fishing village of **Es Grau** retains much of its charm and is where many Maó families come for the summer. From here you can get a boat to the **Illa d'en Colom**, an island with two small, pretty beaches – ideal for a day's picnicking. Es Grau itself lies at the edge of the island's only officially protected nature reserve, **S'Albufera des Grau**, which was dubbed a 'Parc Natural' in 1993 when the island as a whole was declared a UNESCO Biosphere Reserve (which means further building on the island is forbidden). The park includes bays, beaches, farmland (including the winery of Sa Cudia, which makes Menorca's first white wine, an excellent 100 per cent malvasia, created with the lobsters of Fornells in mind) and the wetlands of **S'Albufera des Grau**, and is an important staging post for migratory birds. Three short, well-marked walks lead visitors through different parts of the reserve, one starting at the beach and two more from the visitor centre, a couple of

minutes' drive outside the village. There is also a hut in the village car park with information. Excellent free guided tours in Spanish and/or Catalan (but not English) are held every Tuesday and Wednesday at 10am, as well as on Thursdays at 6pm and Saturdays at 10am during the summer months (reservations essential: 971 35 63 02, mobile 609 60 12 49).

This is one of the few places on the island where you can easily follow the old **Camí dels Cavalls** (Horse Path), which used to connect the island's outposts and watchtowers. Beyond the far end of the beach, you can walk to **Cala Tamarells** and **Cala de sa Torreta**, separated by the badly eroded watchtower **Torre del Tamarells**. From Cala de sa Torreta the path continues inland through meadows and woodland to the farm at **Sa Torre Blanca**, which has a magnificent taula and the remains of a talayot, made all the more impressive by the tranquillity of

---

INSIDE TRACK
BINIMEL.LA BEACH

Driving to Binimel.la beach can be quite an experience. It lies at the end of a long, extremely dusty track the width of a motorway, and as such, expect to be raced by tourists playing the 'let's ruin the hire car' game and locals on dirt bikes re-enacting scenes from *Mad Max*. If you didn't bring your flying goggles, you'll need to wind up the windows.

the surrounding countryside. For a detailed description of the walk to Sa Torre Blanca, *see p242* **Walk**.

From here you can see the lighthouse at **Cap de Favàritx**, a bare, windswept promontory that marks the north-eastern corner of the island. To get there by car, take the recently resurfaced road signed 'Favàritx' from the main Maó–Fornells road, passing through lush farmland that grows increasingly rough and desperate the closer you get to the point. Ignore the 'Propriedad Privada' sign and continue as the road deteriorates. Finally, all vegetation disappears to leave a blasted landscape of stark, desolate black slate, which is especially dramatic in stormy weather. When it's fine, though, there are a couple of nice beaches east of the lighthouse – the nearest is **Cala Presili**, followed by **S'Arenal de Morella** and then the shingly **Platja d'en Tortuga** (Tortoise Beach) – though you need stamina and stout shoes to reach them.

Between Cap de Favàritx and Fornells, the coast is made up of rocky headlands and sheltered bays of various sizes, including the long, sheltered **Port d'Addaia**, where the English landed in 1798, and which ends in wild salt flats. North-west of here there are various holiday developments of differing degrees of intrusion. **Addaia** itself has a small, working marina, a defence tower at the tip of the headland and small villas overlooking the bay and across to the featureless but picturesque **Illes d'Addaia** and **Punta de Montgofra**. There's great diving to be had in these parts (*see p38*).

Further on, **Na Macaret** consists of private holiday homes and a tiny beach with three palm trees. To the west, **Arenal d'en Castell** is a beautiful horseshoe bay with emerald waters and white sand, though it is dominated by the resort that stretches around it. A couple of lovely, quieter beaches, accessible only on foot, can be found to the west at **Es Macar de sa Llosa**. Finally, the grim holiday village of **Son Parc** smears itself through the woods like a virulent weed, emerging from the trees to overlook yet another beautiful white beach, **Arenal de Son Saura**. To escape the crowds, head around the rock at the western edge of the main beach to the small inlet of **Cala Pudent**.

Where to eat & drink

For wonderful views over the bay, and barren, rocky headlands typical of this stretch of coast, try **Cap Roig** (Urb. Cala Mesquida, 971 18 83 83, closed Mon and all Dec-Mar, €€) at the entrance to **Sa Mesquida**. It has a great reputation for grilled sardines, prawns and *escopiñas* (giant clams usually served raw). Arrive by 1.30pm for lunch as it soon gets jam-packed.

Lovely **Es Grau** has four small bars, three of which are on the waterfront, with great views over the beach and bay. **Es Moll** (Moll Magatzems 17, 971 35 91 67, closed Oct-Mar, €), at the far end of the village, is the quietest and serves delicious home-made snacks and sardines. In the same vein is **Tamarindo** (971 35 91 67, closed Oct-May), which overlooks the bay with a terrace on stilts.

Cap de Favàritx.

MENORCA

Walk Es Grau to Sa Torre Blanca

Into the wild… with sandy coves and prehistoric ruins along the way.

Distance: 9km. Circular.
Time: 2hrs 45mins.

The north-east coast of Menorca contains some of the wildest and most beautiful landscapes on the island. This relatively easy but varied walk starts at the cute little resort of **Es Grau** and follows the rugged coastline north past countless (often deserted) sandy coves, before turning inland to reach the isolated and little-visited prehistoric site of **Sa Torre Blanca**, and returning to Es Grau via the northern edge of the **Albufera lagoon**. There's nowhere to get refreshments along the way, so take a picnic, or start mid-morning if you want to be back in Es Grau in time for a leisurely lunch at one of the resort's waterside bar-restaurants (*see p241*).

Leave your car at the car park by the side of the beach at the edge of Es Grau, and walk around the long, wide arc of sand. At the far end of the beach ignore a sign pointing off to the left to Albufera and climb up the wide rocky path, which gives lovely views back over the bay and the small whitewashed village.

Fifteen minutes after starting the walk, the main path dips down to the left (ignore a lesser path off to the right at this point), and then follows the contours of the densely shrub-packed hillside. On a hot day, the scents of the plants – camomile and rosemary among them – are intoxicating.

The path, now sandy, heads inland through trees (including the most common Menorcan native species, the Aleppo pine), before emerging on to a headland. Ahead of you along the coast you'll see the **Torre dels Tamarells**, an 18th-century defensive tower. At this point the path splits – ignore the right-hand branch and take the left fork down a rocky path.

After ten minutes you come to a small sandy beach, **Cala Tamarells**. Climb up the rocks at its far side, and within five minutes you arrive at a stone stile over a wall next to a fire warning sign. (From here, you'll walk in a loop that returns to this spot.) Climb over the stile and head towards the tower. The sandy path zigzags and splits amid the trees and shrubs, but it doesn't matter which branch you take as long as you keep going towards the tower.

In eight or so minutes you'll come to the first of a couple of lovely beaches side by side. If you want to check out the tower, pass them both and climb the rocks to reach it. If you're not bothered, then walk to the back of the first beach, where you'll come across a dirt track wide enough for a vehicle. Take this, heading roughly in the direction in which you've been walking, with the tower on your right.

After five minutes you'll arrive at another bay. The track becomes narrower as it meets a stone wall, then widens again as it rises, following the wall, and dipping again as it passes an old cottage. You come to another beach, **Cala de Sa Torreta**, and follow the path as it bends away from the sea to the left. Almost immediately a wide sandy track crosses the path. Turn right here, through trees, to the back of another bay (with an old boat house on its far side), before following the path as it swings inland.

Around eight minutes after leaving the sea, the track heads through a field of thistles and exits by a gateway in a stone wall as it starts to climb. After a further five or so minutes you pass through another stone gateway and immediately see a group of old farm buildings ahead of you.

As you approach you pass through another stone gateway. You'll take the track to the left here on returning from **Sa Torre Blanca**, which is just a minute's walk away. For now, head straight up to a rusty gate next to a more modern breeze block-built building, and take the path that runs in front of it to the right. This emerges at the small and overgrown prehistoric site, complete with taula and ruined talayot. Scramble to the top of the latter for lovely panoramas of the surrounding countryside.

When you've had your fill of history, return to the spot mentioned earlier, and now turn right on to the track, passing through a wooden gate and returning to open country. Within a few minutes you'll come to two gates. Go through (or climb over) the right-hand one. After a quarter of an hour of walking you'll get your first glimpse of the **Albufera lagoon**.

Keep following the track as it descends gently through a number of stone gates and past a stone cattle trough on your left, keeping the lagoon on your right. By this point the track becomes somewhat overgrown, though still easy to follow.

Just as you reach the level of the lagoon, the path curves round to the left. Pass through a double stone gateway with another cattle trough between it and walk steadily upwards, away from the water and back towards the sea.

After five minutes of climbing you again spy the sea and the tower, and start to descend. A further eight or so minutes and you reach a point where the main path bears round to the left before a clump of trees. You take a right here on to a path that is somewhat overgrown and tricky to make out. This spot is marked by some red markings on a rock on the path and also by a small cairn.

Soon you're back at the stone stile next to the fire warning sign. From here, retrace your steps back to Es Grau.

Of the three restaurants in **Na Macaret**, **Acuario** (Plaça Macaret s/n, 971 35 98 58, closed Mon and all Nov-Apr, €€) has the nicest view being practically on the beach; it offers tapas and snacks at lunchtime, and a wider selection of more substantial dishes at dinner. **Biosphera** (Plaça de Na Macaret, 971 35 96 14, phone for opening hours) is a laid-back and friendly bar-restaurant with light lunches – try the mountainous tomato and mozzarella salad or satisfying *jamón serrano* baguette with fries.

In **Arenal d'en Castell**, **Restaurante Alcalde** (Avda. Central s/n, 971 35 80 93, closed Dec-Feb, €€) is good value with a terrace overlooking the beach.

FORNELLS

The small fishing village of **Fornells** is one of the most popular villages on the island, let alone on the north coast. But despite being almost totally given over to tourism, it manages to remain quiet, appealing and Menorcan. This could be due to its size: it amounts to no more than a couple of streets running parallel to the palm-lined waterfront, with a small walled harbour and a tiny church. But it's also down to the fact that any development there has strayed little from the quaint fishing village blueprint. Beyond the village, a rocky promontory dominates the entrance to the bay and is topped by the best-preserved watchtower on the island, built by the English in 1801. The village is well known for its seafood restaurants and its watersports centres – the Bay of Fornells and the surrounding coast is a great place to learn to windsurf, sail or dive (*see p38*).

Sheltered from the worst of the Tramuntana wind, the bay has been strategically important throughout Menorcan sea faring history. Nowadays it provides the perfect place for sailing and windsurfing. There is nowhere to swim easily, though, and most people head for **Cala Tirant**, just to the west. The short route leads to a newish resort, **Platges de Fornells**, while the longer route passes through beautiful marshlands before arriving at the quieter end. For watersports, try **Windsurf Fornells** (C/Nou 33, 971 18 81 50, www.windfornells.com, closed Nov-Apr).

Where to eat & drink

Per square foot, **Fornells** probably has more decent places to eat than anywhere else on the island – if you like seafood that is. The most famous dish, and the reason for many people's culinary pilgrimage here, is *caldereta de llagosta* – spiny lobster stew (some menus erroneously translate it as 'crayfish stew') prepared with tomato, onion and peppers. It was formerly food

MENORCA

for poor fishermen who couldn't afford to eat most of their catch, which was destined for noblemen's tables. Lobsters, in contrast, were considered unworthy fare. Nowadays you practically need to be a nobleman to afford it – €80 a head is about the going rate. Much less and the lobster is likely to be frozen, or the *caldereta* frozen once cooked, which amounts to the same thing. Alternatively, *caldereta de marisco* (made with assorted seafood, rather than just lobster) is delicious and a third of the price.

With one very notable exception, all the restaurants are along the waterfront and have similar menus, including fresh fish and paella as well as *caldereta*. If you want something more straightforward, both of the *hostales* in the centre have tapas, *platos combinados* and home cooking. Alternatively, **Ca Na Marga** (Urb. Ses Salines 1, 971 37 64 10, ww.canamarga. com, closed lunch and all Nov-Apr, €) in nearby **Ses Salines** is a good choice for picky kids, serving good pizzas and grilled fish and meat.

The only restaurant not on the waterfront, **Es Cranc** (C/Escoles 31, 971 37 64 42, closed Wed Sept-July and Nov-mid Mar, €€€) deserves its reputation as the best dining spot in Fornells, and is certainly the place to eat *caldereta*, though at peak times (mid July-end Aug) you need to book at least a week in advance. In low season there is an excellent set menu available, offering simple fish dishes cooked to perfection and delicious desserts.

To avoid the feeding frenzy at the centre of the village, head for **Es Cranc Pelut** (Passeig Maritim 98, 971 37 67 43, closed Tue Sept-July and Nov-Feb, €€€) at the southern end of the waterfront, run by Juan Vicente Flores, who owns an olive grove in his native Andalucía that provides oil for the restaurant, and local chef Diego Coll Petrus, ex-chef at Es Cranc. The specialities are paella, fish, *caldereta de llagosta* and a delicious *caldereta de marisco*, which gets better with each serving as the thick, rich sauce cools and deepens in flavour. Don't decline the 'bib' the waiter will proffer you – you'll need it.

Unlike most of the restaurants in Fornells, **Sa Llagosta** (C/Gabriel Gelabert 12, 971 37 65 66, closed Oct-Easter, €€€), in an old cottage in front of the harbour, is small, quiet and intimate, with wooden beams and pretty blue and white decor. A shortish menu features seasonal local dishes as well as a few more modern additions, such as hake with honey and garlic sauce, green risotto with squid, and scorpion fish with shallots. Again, like the Es Cranc and Es Cranc Pelut, it's not cheap – a main of grilled prawns alone will set you back €40.

Es Pla (Passatge d'Esplá s/n, 971 37 66 55) probably has the best location in town, with a terrace so close to the water that the waiters toss the remains of your bread to the fish.

Curiously, given the mediocre interior and tourist-oriented menu, King Juan Carlos *y familia* are fans. Though we doubt they stick to the good-value set meals. Order local staples: grilled squid, paella or the *caldereta*, and you can't go far wrong.

As an alternative to Menorcan seafood dishes, **Thai Country** (Menorca Country Club, Urb. Platges de Fornells, 971 37 68 60, closed Nov-Apr, €) is an opulent affair, decorated with intricate teak furniture and Buddhas, and offering some excellent, authentic Thai food.

In terms of drinking, the bars outside the **S'Algaret** and **La Palma** (for both, *see below*) *hostals* are pretty busy all the time. For a cocktail try **Bar Sa Taula** (C/Major 1, 971 37 68 79), about 30 metres up the hill away from the square, which has a younger, trendier vibe. You won't find caipirinhas this spot-on outside of Ipanema. The rooftop terrace is one of the best places in town to watch the sun go down.

Where to stay

There are only three places to stay in **Fornells** itself, all mid-range but pleasant *hostales* right in the centre of the village. **S'Algaret** (Plaça S'Algaret 7, 971 37 65 52, www.hostal-salgaret.com, doubles €35-€90), which also has a restaurant, and **La Palma** (Plaça S'Algaret 3, 971 37 64 87, www.hostallapalma.com, closed

Es Pla.

end Oct-Mar, doubles €45-€90) are next to each other, opposite the harbour, on the town's central square. Both have rooms overlooking their respective swimming pools and also double up as the two main village bars, serving reasonably priced food.

A few metres up the slight hill is **Hostal Fornells** (C/Major 17, 971 37 66 76, closed Nov-Mar, www.hostalfornells.com, doubles €37-€118 incl breakfast), which has a little more character than the other two, and certainly more stylish flare than one normally expects with a three-star hotel. Rooms are priced according to view, the cheapest is a very small interior room with no view. We advise booking well in advance and splurging on a room at the top with a terrace overlooking the pool, the village and the bay. There's a bar by the pool and all rooms have en suite bathrooms, air-conditioning, TV, safe and telephone, and the staff are young and friendly.

One- and two-bedroom apartments, some with a view of the bay, are available at **Can Digus** (C/Vivers s/n, 971 37 65 12, www.can digus.com, closed Nov-Mar, apartments €55-€98), which also has its own pool.

If you can't find anywhere in Fornells, **Hostal Port Fornells** (C/d'es Port Fornells s/n, 971 37 63 73, www.hostalportfornells.com, closed late Oct-late Apr, doubles €80-€90), down the road at **Ses Salines**, has simple, clean rooms, half of which look out over the bay. It has a small pool and is popular with people staying at the sailing school at the end of the road, which means it has a noisy, slightly school trip atmosphere, but it's also very friendly.

CAP DE CAVALLERIA TO CALA GROS

West of Fornells lie some of Menorca's most beguiling and deserted landscapes: hilly pastures and long, dusty tracks leading to some of the great beaches. **Cap de Cavalleria** is a small, low headland with nothing but an unmanned lighthouse and a herd of goats. At the base of the isthmus that connects it to the rest of the island is an optimistic 'eco-museum', **Ecomuseu Cap de Cavalleria**, which displays artefacts from the nearby Roman settlement of **Sanitja**. It's a beautiful spot to visit, though there is little to see as most of the ruins have either been excavated and covered over again, or have yet to be dug up.

The beaches in this part of the island are almost entirely unspoilt, with reddish-brown sand between weather-beaten cliffs. **Platja de Cavalleria** is easy to get to, as is **Platja de Binimel.la** (where you'll find the only place to eat on this stretch of coast; *see below*). Once you're there, if it's heaving with people, **Cala Pregonda** is a 20-minute walk over the

headland. You'll be rewarded with turquoise water surrounding a beautifully harsh rocky bay with a sandy beach. There's also a small lunar-like island – normally covered in children – which you can snorkel around.

Cala en Pilar is also only accessible on foot – there's a car park midway down the side road leading off the main Maó–Ciutadella highway (around km34); from here it's about a three-kilometre walk down to the beach. Alternatively, you can approach it from the side road off the highway between km31 and km32, signed to the **Castell de Sant Agueda**. This ruined Moorish fortress stands atop the island's third highest hill. Built in the tenth century, the fortress was abandoned following Alfons III's conquest of the island and is now little more than an outline, although the medieval track to the top is still in good condition and it's a lovely 45-minute walk through glades of holm oaks up to the peak.

Ecomuseu Cap de Cavalleria
Camí de Sa Cavalleria, Fornells (971 35 99 99/ www.ecomuseodecavalleria.com). **Open** *May-Oct* 10am-8pm daily. **Admission** €3; free under-8s. **Credit** MC, V.

Where to eat

The only beach on this coast with any facilities is **Platja Binimel.la**, where, perched up above the sand, you'll find **Restaurante Binimel.la** (971 35 92 75, closed dinner and all Nov-Apr, €€). It's a laid-back place with a great, occasionally windswept, garden terrace – watch out for the flying plastic chairs. Service outside, when there is any, is unbearably slow and you're better off muscling your way to the bar. Inside it's a more formal affair – or rather, as formal as it gets in swimming trunks – with beachgoers tucking into local roast lamb and grilled fish.

GETTING THERE

By bus
There are 2 buses Mon-Sat between Fornells and Maó (35mins) and 1 bus Mon-Fri to Es Mercadal (15mins).

MENORCA

Ciutadella & West Menorca

Menorca's second city is its most enchanting

As the island's capital, Maó might be better kitted-out for visitors in terms of facilities, but for straightforward appeal Menorca's second city, Ciutadella, wins hands down. Elegant mansions of pink-tinged sandstone, narrow cobbled streets, pastel houses with bright shutters and a small, attractive working port make it an instant hit.

Outside of town it's a mixed bag: the countryside is a relaxed place to kick back with several prehistoric monuments dotted about the harsh, rocky but enticing terrain, while the west coast, on the other hand, is home to some of the island's least appealing egg-and-chips resort ghettos.

CIUTADELLA
Sightseeing

Ciutadella doesn't feel like a city at all, with hardly more than 20,000 inhabitants and a pace that's about as far from frenetic as it gets. Apart from during the island's San Joan festivities, that is, when Ciutadella's residents stuff themselves with hazelnuts, gallons of *pomada* (Xoriguer gin and lemonade) and watch the *jaleo* (horsemen charging round the streets and rearing up in the crowded squares). It does, however, have a cathedral at its centre, along with two large, adjoining squares – one laid-back and bucolic, the other poised and formal. Plaça de s'Esplanada is better known as the **Plaça dels Pins**, with tall pine trees that turn the sandy square into an oasis of shade, filled with park benches, play areas and cafés. Beside it, the **Plaça d'es Born** is an open expanse bordered by buildings straight from a theatre set, including the town hall, an actual theatre and 19th-century palaces. The obelisk at the centre commemorates the bloodthirsty Turkish attack of 1558, which culminated in a three-day rampage of rape, murder and pillage, the razing of the town and the kidnapping of 3,452 men and women to work as galley slaves and courtesans respectively in Constantinople.

The tallest and most arresting building on the Plaça d'es Born is the **Ajuntament** (town hall) in the north-west corner, with an arcaded sandstone façade. Built on the site of the old Moorish Real Alcázar, or royal citadel, the building incorporates references to both Moorish and military architecture. Inside the town hall, a stone stairway leads up to the impressive first floor, where the Gothic council chamber is worth a quick visit. Round the back, the remains of the old **Governor's Palace** can still be visited (9am-2pm Mon-Fri, admission free) to give a better idea of the building's military past.

A road beside the town hall leads down to the port, while on its other side, a balustrade overlooking the port tops all that is left of the city's medieval ramparts, which were demolished at the end of the 19th century and replaced by the wide avenues that now circumscribe the old town. Looking up from the port, though, these ramparts still give a good idea of the Ciutadella's one-time defences.

Alongside them, on the square's north side, is the old 19th-century **Teatre d'es Born** (Plaça d'es Born 20). To the right of the theatre, C/Sa Muradeta leads to the Bastió de sa Font, a blind stone edifice built in 1677 as part of the town's defences (and doubling up as a warehouse for storing tithes). Nowadays it contains the small

MENORCA

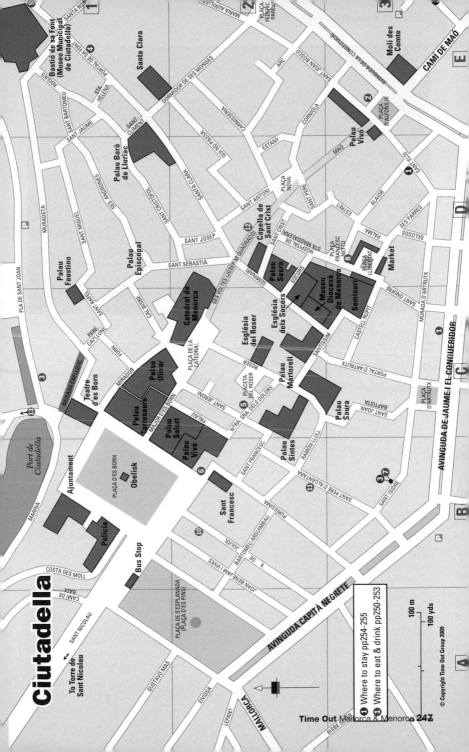

Ciutadella

To Torre de Sant Nicolau

Port de Ciutadella

Bastió de sa Font
(Museu Municipal
de Ciutadella)

PORTAL DE SA FONT

Santa Clara

Santa Clara

PLAÇA
FEDERIC
PAREJU

PLAÇA
MARIA AUXILIA

Molí des
Comte

CAMÍ DE MAÓ

Palau Baró
de Lluriac

AVINGUDA DE LA CONSTITUCIÓ

Palau
Vivó

PLAÇA
D'ALFONS III

Palau
Faustino

Palau
Episcopal

Capella de
Sant Crist

PLAÇA
NOVA

Catedral de
Menorca

Palau
Saura

HOSPITAL DE
STA MAGDALENA

PLAÇA
FRANCESC
NETTO

PLAÇA
LLIBERTAT

Market

Museu
Diocesà
de Menorca

Seminari

Església
del Roser

Església
dels Socors

Teatre
d'es Born

Palau
Olivar

PLAÇA DE LA
CATEDRAL

PLAÇETA
DEL ROSER

Palau
Martorell

Palau
Saura

PORTAL D'ARTRUTX

PLAÇA
D'ARTRUTX

Ajuntament

Palau
Torresaurà

Palau
Salort

Palau
Vivó

PLAÇA D'ES BORN

Obelisk

Palau
Sintes

AVINGUDA DE JAUME I EL CONQUERIDOR

Policia

Sant
Francesc

Bus Stop

PLAÇA DE S'ESPLANADA
(PLAÇA D'ES PINS)

AVINGUDA CAPITÀ NEGRETE

MALLORCA

① Where to stay pp254-255
⑪ Where to eat & drink pp250-253

100 m
100 yds

© Copyright Time Out Group 2009

Time Out Mallorca & Menorca **247**

Ciutadella.

MENORCA

but interesting **Museu Municipal de Ciutadella** (*see p249*). Below here is the Pla de Sant Joan, a sandy area at the end of the port where jousting games take place during the **Festes de Sant Joan** in June (*see p39* **Festivals and Events**).

Back in the Plaça d'es Born, the eastern side of the square is taken up by three palaces, all built in the 19th century. To the left as you face them is the **Palau Torresaura**, the most impressive of the three, with a fine neo-classical façade, complete with two triple-arched, double-height galleries that were added later to bring the building in line (physically and architecturally) with the **Palau Salort** next door. These days you have to screw up your eyes and ignore the ground-floor shops selling tourist trinkets to see it at its best.

In the south-east corner of the square stands the large, simple church of **Sant Francesc**, most of which was built at the end of the 16th century (1583-1607) to replace the one that had been destroyed (with its adjoining monastery) during the Turkish sacking of the city in 1558. The sedate, unadorned main façade dates from the 19th century. The site of the monastery, which was active until 1835, is now hidden beneath the modern monstrosity that is the post office.

Between the Palaus Torresaura and Salort, pedestrianised C/Major d'es Born leads up past yet another palace, the 17th-century (with an 18th-century façade) **Palau Olivar**, to the **Catedral de Menorca** (*see p249*), a beautiful, monolithic hulk of a building

of creamy-pink sandstone that changes colour throughout the day as the sun moves across the sky.

Next to the cathedral's south entrance, a wooden door leads to the pleasant, plant-filled courtyard of the **Palau Episcopal**, which gives a different perspective of the cathedral and the three subsequent side chapels. Also of interest is the bakery opposite, where bread and Menorcan 'pasties' are baked in a wood-fired oven, concealed behind the guillotine-like oven door behind the counter.

Just to the south of the cathedral, down C/del Roser, is the elaborately carved entrance of the **Església del Roser**, a small, pretty baroque church built at the beginning of the 18th century, which has now been converted into an exhibition hall. The red sandstone façade is one of the most ornate on the island, despite being badly damaged by erosion.

Back in Plaça de la Catedral, the square narrows, leading to the charming **C/Ses Voltes**, an arcaded pedestrianised street with low, whitewashed arches; it's best seen at night, when the surrounding shops have packed away their wares and the arches can be fully appreciated.

At the start of C/Ses Voltes, C/d'es Seminari leads south to the dilapidated Renaissance **Església del Socors**, built between 1619 and 1670. Beside it, and now housing the seminary and the **Museu Diocesà de Menoria** (*see p250*), is the Augustine monastery, added in the mid 17th century, with airy cloisters that offer a good view of the church's two belltowers. The Diocesan Museum itself fills five small rooms around the courtyard, giving a rapid tour of Menorcan history that complements the Museu Municipal de Ciutadella.

Directly behind the seminary, and now tucked in beneath its walls, is the small but quaint marketplace in Plaça de la Llibertat, a charming square with tall arcades and a fish market (that looks rather like a fish tank) right in the middle.

Meanwhile, Ses Voltes continues east through pretty Plaça Nova before reaching Plaça d'Alfons III, more usually referred to as **Plaça de ses Palmeres** (on account of the palm trees), which has a great tapas restaurant, **Aurora** (*see p250*). Standing above the square is the town's only remaining windmill, the **Molí des Comte**, with a handicraft centre beside it and the atmospheric **Bar El Molí** (971 38 33 08) occupying the ground floor. The windmill marks the start of the Maó road, and can be visited by appointment.

The windmill's geographical and architectural mirror image, the **Torre de Sant Nicolau**, stands on the low cliffs at the western tip of Ciutadella, guarding the mouth of the port at the end of Passeig Sant Nicolau. Built in the 17th century, it is the most elegant of the island's watchtowers and, although there is little to see inside, the view from the roof is excellent. The rocks around its base were used as defences during the Civil War. Nearby is a statue to Admiral David Glasgow Farragut

(1801-70), son of a Ciutadella emigrant, hero of the American Civil War and the first four-star admiral of the US Navy.

On the port in Ciutadella there are a couple of places for aspiring seadogs to get their hands on a boat. Anything from a small dinghy (no licence required) to swish powerboats can be rented from **Mestral Rent a Boat & Boat Trips** (Moll Comercial 46-48, 971 38 14 85, mobile 619 67 30 39, www.menorca digital.com/mestral.htm, €170-€380 per day). Proper sail boats can be rented from **Arrayan** (Apdo. Correos 366, mobile 649 82 90 72, www.veleroarrayan.com, €300-€2,800). There are also tourist boat trips that set off from the port.

Bikes can be hired from **Tot Velo** (C/Ibiza 59, 971 48 11 48, www.totvelo.com) for €10 per day.

[FREE] Catedral de Menorca

Plaça de la Catedral (971 38 07 39). **Open** 8am-1pm, 6-9pm daily. **Admission** free. **Map** p247 C2.

From the outside, the lower half of the cathedral appears as a single, unadorned base, supporting an upper half of buttresses and stained-glass windows – though once inside it becomes clear that there are, in fact, shrines between each of the support columns. Following the Turkish raid of 1558, the lower parts of the buttresses were encased in stone to guard against future attack. Originally one of four chapels ordered by Alfons III to celebrate his conquest of the island, work started in 1303 under Jaume II on the

MENORCA

El Jardí. *See p252.*

MENORCA

site of an existing mosque, and incorporated the mosque's minaret as the belltower. The south entrance, facing C/Roser, retains its original Gothic portal, while at the main entrance, the original west doorway is now hidden behind a neo-classical entrance that was added at the beginning of the 19th century, perhaps to celebrate the church's newly awarded status as a cathedral in 1795. Inside, the cathedral consists of a single Gothic nave flanked by small chapels, although three other slightly larger chapels have been added along the left-hand side over the centuries. The Capilla de las Ànimas (Chapel of the Souls) is one of Menorca's most impressive examples of the Baroque.

Museu Diocesà de Menoría

C/Seminari 7 (971 48 12 97). **Open** 10.30am-1.30pm Tue-Sat. Closed end Oct-Apr. **Admission** €3.50; €2.50 reductions; free under-12s. **No credit cards. Map** p247 C2.
The Diocesan Museum contains various talayotic artefacts and bones, human skulls that show evidence of early experiments in trepanning, a single skull of the extinct but still grinning local goat-like *Myotragus Balearicus*, and Roman jars and jewellery. There is also a room dedicated to religious paraphernalia and another to the paintings of Pere Daura y Garcia, a sub-Cézanne with only a tenuous link to Menorca.

Museu Municipal de Ciutadella

Plaça de sa Font s/n (971 38 02 97/www. ciutadella.org/museu). **Open** *Oct-Apr* 10am-2pm Tue-Sat. *May-Sept* 10am-2pm, 6-9pm daily. **Admission** €2.25; reductions free-€1.13. Free to all Wed. **No credit cards. Map** p247 E1.
This absorbing little museum focuses on the history of the city and the island, particularly from prehistoric times until its integration with the Crown of Aragón in 1287.

Where to eat & drink

Ciutadella is a great place to eat out. The old town is scattered with a variety of restaurants, from decent pizzerias hidden down alleyways to fine tapas bars in leafy squares. The port, being predominantly tourist-oriented, is home to some mediocre fish restaurants, but also some excellent ones and it's also where most of the town's nightlife can be found, though don't go expecting much in the way of clubbing.

All of the seafood restaurants along the port have outside terraces, a few feet from the moored yachts. Offering almost identical menus, including fresh fish, meat and pricey *caldereta de llagosta* (spiny lobster stew), they are tourist-oriented and most offer set *menús* in the region of €15. Remember, though, that you get what you pay for, and here you're paying for the setting as much as anything. Remember

too that the ubiquitous grilled salmon is not indigenous to the Mediterranean.

As well as the places we've listed below, **Sa Figuera** (C/Marina 99, 971 38 21 12, closed dinner mid Nov-Mar and 1mth Dec-Mar, €€€) is a reliable port spot, offering a range of set menus from €15 to €50. If it's kitsch cuisine you're after, then **Es Forat** (Passeig del Port s/n, 971 48 08 30, closed lunch Sun and all Oct-Apr, €€€) won't disappoint, with its romanticised paintings of horses hanging on the stone walls above the tables on the terrace. Next to that, **Corb Marí** (C/Marina 43, 971 38 42 93, €€) is smaller and much less formal, with a few tables in its cavern. **Triton** (Moll Comercial 55, 971 38 00 02, open year round, €) is a fisherman's caff nestling alongside the port. It serves unexceptional tapas all day and good sandwiches – a fine *jamón serrano* baguette, particularly, but you can just come for a drink and enjoy the view. Most of the locals, though, head for **Café Balear**.

Anny's

Avda. Conqueridor 71 (971 38 46 67). **Open** *June-Oct* 8am-midnight Mon-Sat. *Nov-May* 8am-midnight Mon-Sat; 8am-5pm Sun. **Average** €-€€. **Credit** MC, V. **Map** p247 C3 **❶** International
If you can manage to ignore the laminated signs outside and the faux-rustic decor inside – somewhat ubiquitous in Ciutadella – Anny's is friendly and offers tasty, good-value food. Generous portions and competent, unfussy cuisine attract the locals in ravenous hordes. Due to the fact that it's off the tourist trail the lunchtime *menú* is €9, which might feature the likes of gazpacho followed by grilled cuttlefish, with bread and dessert – a deal indeed.

★ € Aurora

Plaça Ses Palmeres 3 (971 38 00 29). **Open** *June-Oct* 8am-midnight Mon-Sat. *Nov-May* 8am-5pm Mon-Thur; 8am-midnight Fri, Sat. **Average** €. **Credit** MC, V. **Map** p247 E3 **❷** Tapas
A great way to start a night on the tiles is at this tapas bar in the square off the Avinguda de la Constitució, opposite the windmill. It specialises in *Montaditos* (slices of bread covered in numerable toppings). Ignore the restaurant proper, sit yourself in the tapas section with all the locals, grab the menu (handily illustrated) and get ordering. With these prices (roughly just over a euro each) you can and should be adventurous; try the *sobrassada* with honey, the oven-baked squid or the *jamón serrano* with cheese and onion.

★ Café Balear

Passeig de Sant Joan 15 (971 38 00 05). **Open** *June-Sept* 1-4pm, 7.30pm-midnight Mon-Sat. *Oct, Dec-May* 1-4pm, 7.30pm-midnight Tue-Sat; 1-4pm

Profile Pedreres de s'Hostal

Turning holes in the ground into tourist attractions.

Just a couple of kilometres outside the town, on the Camí Vell, lies one of Menorca's strangest attractions, the **Pedreres de s'Hostal**. It's a network of old, and not so old, quarries, which have been turned into a scenic tourist attraction-cum-culture centre.

The colossal bizarre shapes, slashes and steps left in the rock from over 200 years of excavation have left a space that's halfway between an Escher drawing and the setting for a James Bond fight. There are some almighty drops, some incredible views and countless hidden crannies.

The quarry was converted into a tourist attraction in 1994 when an organisation called **Líthica** was set up with the aim of saving South Menorca's sandstone quarries from being turned into rubbish tips. The not-for-profit association was started by architect and sculptor Laetitia Lara and now has over 200 members, and connections to various cultural and artistic organisations both in Spain and abroad.

The pits are split into two areas, the maze-like older quarry, which was cut by hammers, chisels and handsaws and has irregular shaped, overhanging façades, and the newer shafts, which are much deeper, wider and symetrically scarred by mechanical cutting machines. The former zone is greener and largely overgrown, though with a perfectly manicured medieval garden and orchard; it's also home to a variety of lizards, snakes and birds of prey. The latter is like two giant stone bath tubs: austere but quite awe-inspiring, which is why they're used for concerts and catwalk fashion shows. Plans are also afoot to build four

FIESTA
The quarry throws a party to celebrate August's full moon. It's a family bash – don't expect mayhem.

different labyrinths on the site – somewhat fitting for a space that would lend itself so well to getting lost, were it not for the maps and signposts.

Such is the overwhelming size and layout of the place that it's closed when storms are rolling in (to avoid the risk of people panicking and hurting themselves) and visitors are advised not to come at midday in the summer due to the intense heat (the crater acts like a white, glaring oven under the sun). The best time to arrive in the summer is at about 5pm, when it's cooler and the shadows are long across the chasms (*see p255*).

MENORCA

Sun. Closed Nov. **Average** €€-€€€. **Credit** AmEx, MC, V. **Map** p247 C1 ❸ **Seafood**
This is one of the island's most famous and therefore most consistently packed restaurants – folk descend from across Menorca for the set lunch *menú* of house specialities and Menorcan and Spanish seafood staples, much of it caught by the restaurant's mini-fleet. In summer, either reserve a table inside or queue up along the quayside for one outdoors (reservations are not taken for the terrace).

Cas Ferrer
Portal de sa Font 16 (971 48 07 84). **Open** *Sept-Feb, Apr-mid July* 1-3.30pm, 8pm-midnight Tue-Sat. *Mid July-Aug* 8pm-midnight Mon, Sun; 1-3.30pm, 8pm-midnight Tue-Sat. Closed Mar. **Average** €€€€. **Credit** MC, V. **Map** p247 E1 ❹ **Menorcan**
If you're fed up with some of the same old, same old restaurant offerings of the port, come to this old blacksmith's, complete with forge, anvil and bellows, tucked away behind the Bastió. It's an intimate warren of rooms with original beams and tiles, and food that's a mix of influences. The place is well regarded locally, even if it doesn't always hit the mark.

La Guitarra
C/Dolors 1, Bajos (971 38 13 55). **Open** 12.30-3.30pm, 7.30-11.30pm Mon-Sat. Closed Feb. **Average** €€€. **Credit** MC, V. **Map** p247 C2 ❺ **Menorcan**
A discreet doorway leads to a flight of steps down to a vaulted stone cellar, where this atmospheric restaurant offers homely food. The lunch menu can be a little too homely quality-wise, but there's also a €39 evening menu of traditional Menorcan tapas: *frito Menorquín* (mixed, fried fish) and *embutidos* (a selection of local sausages) followed by the ubiquitous *caldereta de llagosta* is actually good value. There's also a much cheaper lunchtime *menú*.

★ El Imperi
Plaça d'es Born 5 (971 38 22 20). **Open** 7.30pm-midnight daily. **No credit cards**. **Map** p247 B2 ❻ **Café**
Wedged in the corner of the Plaça d'es Born, El Imperi is one of the town's main meet-up bars. It has bags of character, from the wonderful beamed bar with marble tables to the stone arches of the back room and the pretty courtyard beyond. The tables out front are great for people watching and if you get peckish it sells great hot sandwiches and pies.

El Jardí
C/Sant Isidre 33 (971 48 05 16). **Open** 1.30-3.30pm, 8-11.30pm daily. **Average** €-€€. **No credit cards**. **Map** p247 B3 ❼ **International**
Built around a pretty terrace shaded by a giant umbrella pine, El Jardí is a peaceful courtyard next to the Hostal Oasis in the old town. Come here for new wave *Menorquí* and international cuisine, from

goat's cheese and bacon salads to Argentinian steaks. The €15 *menú* is good value. *Photo p252.*

Look al Plaça
Plaça de la Llibertat 1 (971 38 58 67). **Open** *Apr-Oct* 9am-midnight daily. *Nov-Mar* 9am-2pm, 5-10pm Mon-Sat. **No credit cards**. **Map** p247 D3 ❽ **Café**
There are various small bars clustered around the market; this one's a real treat. Small, simple and laidback, it is open all day and evening, and offers decent music, delicious coffee and plenty of tables on the pavement outside. Tapas are also served in the summer.

Oristano
Borja Moll 1 (971 38 41 97). **Open** 7pm-1am Thur-Sun. Closed Jan-Mar. **Average** €. **Credit** MC, V. **Map** p247 E1 ❾ **Pizzeria**
The pizzas here, cooked in a wood-fired oven and deliciously thin and crisp, have a deserved reputation. Other items on the menu should be treated with circumspection. It's a pleasant building overlooking the port, but somewhat lacking in atmosphere.

Pa amb Oli
C/Nou de Juliol 4 (971 38 36 19). **Open** noon-5pm, 7.30pm-1am Mon-Sat. **Average** €€. **Credit** MC, V. **Map** p247 B2 ❿ **Menorcan**
Inadvertently kitsch, from the perplexed bull and stag heads to the artificial barrels, and with gruesome displays of red meat to greet you, Pa amb Oli is actually reasonably good and, surprisingly, one of the better options for vegetarians. There's a selection of grilled vegetable dishes on offer, alongside (literally) all the grilled meats, hams, cheeses and seafood. Unpretentious and friendly, though not especially cheap, it is rightly popular with the locals.

€ Pizzeria Roma
C/Sant Pere d'Alcantara 18 (971 38 47 18). **Open** noon-4pm, 7pm-1am Mon, Wed-Sun. Closed mid Sept-mid Oct. **Average** €. **No credit cards**. **Map** p247 B2 ⓫ **Pizzeria**
This decent pizzeria is a safe bet for crisp pizzas and decent pasta. It's down a sidestreet near the Plaça d'es Born – the two tables outside seem quiet enough until the delivery bikes get going every evening; you're better off sitting inside or on the terrace.

€ Ses Voltes
Jose María Quadrado 16 (971 381 498). **Open** *Apr-Oct* 9am-midnight daily. *Nov-Mar* 9am-2pm, 5-10pm Mon-Sat. **Average** €. **Credit** MC, V. **Map** p247 D2 ⓬ **Tapas**
It might be on one of the main tourist drags but this slick Barcelona-esque tapas bar is rammed with Menorcans (if the seats out the front are taken, try the second-floor terrace). There's a good range of salads, sandwiches and tapas, or, if you're not peckish, it's as good a spot as any for a coffee and a gawp.

★ La Taberna

Port de Ciutadella (no phone). **Open** 1pm-late daily. **Average** €-€€. **No credit cards. Map** p247 B1 ⓭ **Seafood**

Standing alone opposite the hectic throng of eateries on the south side of the port is this relaxed and friendly fish restaurant. Bag an outdoor table at lunch to catch its lobster boats arriving (usually between 12.30pm and 1pm) with what's soon to end up on your plate – reassuringly, if it hasn't been caught it won't be on the blackboard menu. The paella is very good as is the *tumbet* (baked vegetable stew).

Nightlife

We've said it before and we'll say it again: Menorca is no Ibiza. Though there is fun to be had; at weekends and during the summer there are a dozen or so bars and clubs, many with terraces, clustered around the Pla de Sant Joan at the inland end of the port, offering tunes from pop to techno by way of lounge, jazz, funk and rock. It's all fairly low-key, with no cover charge, which makes bar-hopping effortless and enjoyable. **Jazzbah** (Pla de Sant Joan 3, 971 48 29 53, open June-Sept 11pm-6am daily, Oct-May 11pm-6am Fri, Sat) is the most serious musically, attracting a crowd as good-looking as the club itself, which has several terraces, high-priced drinks and some very good live jazz music (it's probably the most reliable big-night-out in town).

There is also a handful of small, smart late-night bars on Baixada Capllonc, the slope that runs from the town down to the port: **Cactus Bar** (No.15, mobile 662 06 02 28) is German-run and the only proper cocktail bar on the port, with a gigantic terrace for drinks. At the bottom of the hill, cave-like **Sa Clau** (C/Marina 93, 971 38 48 63, www.saclau.com, closed mid Sept-mid May Mon-Thur, Sun and all mid Dec-mid Jan) is a minuscule jazz bar that could easily be a pirate's lair and certainly makes up in atmosphere what it lacks in size. But the place that really gets the party started is **Martin's Bar** (no phone), one of the only places on Menorca with a gay/straight mix.

Shopping

Don't come to Ciutadella for the shopping. Many of the centre's shopping options stock either tourist tat or high-street labels which you'll find a greater selection back home. That said, there's a clutch of boutiques around C/Maó and C/Santa Clara, the extension to Ses Voltes, which is where the main shopping drag is.

For local shoes, especially *albarcas*, the leather sandals with car tyre soles (check the sides of the soles – if they are made from genuine tyres, they have a wire thread running through them), try any of the shops on the main tourist drag part of the marina.

Movedra Nou. *See p256.*

MENORCA

MENORCA

Pine wood of **Son Àngel**. *See p258.*

Ciutadella scores higher for food than fashion, though, and local produce makes great gifts. For local cheese, cured meat and wine, there are several small grocers around the marketplace, all of which have a good selection. **Ca na Riera** (Hospital Santa Magdalena 7, no phone) is chaotic but very good. **Ca'n Padet** next door (Plaça Francesc Netto s/n, 971 38 00 91) is less atmospheric but better organised. **Moll Pastisseria Bomboneria** (C/Maó 8, 971 38 40 81 and C/Roser 1, 971 38 10 85) sells wonderful artisan preserves including *figat de Menorca* (fig jam), home-cured *alcaparras* (capers) and *amargos* (sweet almond cakes). For wine, Xoriguer gin and other local concoctions, **Ses Industries** (C/Santa Clara 4, 971 38 28 82) is small but irresistible. Not to be missed either is the **Horno Montaner** (C/Obispo Torres 11, 971 38 08 32), the oldest continuing functioning bakery on the island (the Montaner family has had it for five generations, though the house it's located in is at least 400 years old) and the old-fashioned bread oven has become an attraction in itself. It's excellent for picnic fodder: home-made bread, cheese and meat pies and pastries.

Where to stay

If you want to stay somewhere truly memorable, you'll need to leave town and head out of town to one of the *agroturismos* (*see p256*). As with Maó, Ciutadella is not well served for accommodation; the boutique hotel boom that has swept through Palma has still yet to reach Menorcan towns.

€ Hostal Paris

Camí Santandria 4 (971 38 16 22). **Rates** (incl breakfast) €36-€75 double. Closed Oct-Apr. **Credit** MC, V.
Run by a Basque woman, this youthful, laid-back *hostal* is ideal for solo travellers. Of the 13 brightly painted rooms, the six singles all have sunny balconies facing west. Most of the doubles look out on to the main road south, which can get quite busy in high season, and only two rooms have en suite bathrooms.

Hostal Residencia Ciutadella

C/Sant Eloi 10 (971 38 34 62/www. alojarseenmenorca.com). **Rates** €52-€102 double. **Credit** MC, V. **Map** p247 D3 ❶
It's easy to miss this large, old-fashioned hotel right in the old town, just off Plaça Alfons III. Rooms are reasonably comfortable, spick and span and excellent value, and many of them look out on to the narrow street. The hotel is open all year round.

Hostal Residencia Menurka

C/Domingo Savio 6 (971 38 14 15/www. menurka.com). **Rates** (incl breakfast) €40-€78 double. **Credit** MC, V. **Map** p247 E3 ❷
A simple, family-run *pensión* with 21 rooms, close to the bus station and a few minutes' walk to the old town. Internal rooms are dim and a little noisy; external ones are quiet, bright and spacious, and some have a balcony.

Hotel Balear

Camí de Maó 178 (971 48 23 41). **Rates** (incl breakfast in high season) €42-€72 double. **Credit** MC, V.

This 16-room hotel on the road out of Ciutadella is a touch inconvenient, but it is friendly, with clean, comfortable ensuite rooms, making it a reasonable budget option – if you don't mind the ten-minute walk to the centre of town.

Hotel Geminis

C/Josepa Rossinyol 4 (971 38 46 44/www.hotel geminismenorca.com). **Rates** (incl breakfast) €53-€96 double. Closed 10 Dec-end Feb. **Credit** MC, V.

A pastel-pink building down a quiet side street just outside the old town, the Geminis is light, bright and friendly. Half the rooms look out on to a small swimming pool and the overgrown garden next door, complete with palm trees. The other half look out on to the street. Comfortable sofas are strewn around the bar and reception.

Hotel Hesperia Patricia

Passeig de Sant Nicolau 90-92 (971 38 55 11/ www.hoteles-hesperia.es). **Rates** €48-€175 double. **Credit** AmEx, MC, V.

The largest non-seasonal hotel in Ciutadella is comfortable, close to the port and convenient for the centre of town, which lies a five-minute walk away. Though slightly corporate in style, it reaches beyond the business market, attracting a combination of holidaymakers as well as business travellers. There's an outdoor chlorine-free pool.

Hotel Playa Grande

C/Obispo Juano 2 (971 48 08 64/www.grupo andria.com). **Rates** (incl breakfast) €60-€110 double. Closed 15 Dec-15 Jan. **Credit** MC, V.

Located in Ciutadella's city centre this large, corporate-style chain hotel does not quite overlook the ironically named beach (it's in fact minuscule) from which it takes its name, though many of the rooms have balconies from which can be seen a little sand and water (just).

★ Hostal Sa Prensa

Plaça de Madrid s/n (971 38 26 98). **Rates** €35-€70 double. Closed 1mth in winter. **No credit cards.**

Close to Castell de Sant Nicolau, four of the rooms here have great views of the sea from their generous balconies and are usually booked up several months in advance. The other three have no balcony and look out on to drab apartment blocks.

Oasis

C/Sant Isidre 33 (971 38 21 97). **Rates** (incl breakfast in high season) €40-€50. Closed 16 Oct-31 Mar. **No credit cards.** **Map** p247 B3 ❸

This small, simple *pensión* really is an oasis, hidden away in the middle of the old town, but opening out into a bright, peaceful courtyard filled with flowers. The bedrooms are quite small and simply furnished, with old-fashioned fittings, but are nevertheless clean and comfortable.

Resources

Internet

Café Internet, Plaça dels Pins 37 (971 38 42 15/www.elcafenet.net). **Open** June-Oct 9am-1am Mon-Sat. *Nov-May* 9am-11pm Mon-Sat. **Map** p247 A2.

Police station

Carretera ME-1 km43,700 (971 38 07 87).

Post office

Plaça d'es Born 9 (971 38 00 81). **Map** p247 B1.

Tourist information

OIT (Oficina d'Informació Turística), Plaça Catedral 5 (971 38 26 93/www.e-menorca.org). **Open** *May-Oct* 9am-8.30pm Mon-Sat. *Nov-Apr* 9am-1pm, 4-7pm Mon-Fri; 9am-1pm Sat. **Map** p247 C2.
OMIT (Oficina Municipal d'Informació Turística), Plaça dels Pins (971 48 41 55). **Open** *June-Sept* 9am-1pm, 6-8pm Mon-Sat. *Jan-May, Oct-Dec* 9am-1pm Mon-Fri.

WEST INTERIOR

The beautiful countryside surrounding Ciutadella is rich in prehistoric remains and also has one of the island's most bizarre and original tourist attractions: **Pedreres de s'Hostal** *(see below)*. All these are easily reachable from town and a half-day tour makes for an enjoyable excursion.

Also in the vicinity, albeit on the south coast, are some of the islands's finest beaches: **Son Saura**, **Cala en Turqueta** and **Cala Macarella**. For more on how to get to these beaches, *see p225* **Paradise platjas**.

INSIDE TRACK
SOUTH-WEST CYCLING

The west of the island is flat, pretty, well signposted and dotted with places worth visiting by bike; hire one in Ciutadella and head out to any of the local prehistoric monuments (*see left*), up to **Punta Nati** (*see p258*), or even down to the south coast beaches (*see left*).

Seven kilometres south of the town, on the way to Son Saura, is Menorca's largest prehistoric settlement, **Son Catlar**. It's hard to make out most of its internal structure beyond four talayots and a taula (without its T stone), but its outstanding feature is an 870-metre (2,854-foot) encircling defensive wall studded with defensive towers – the only one of its kind to survive in its entirety on Menorca.

Off the main Ciutadella to Maó highway are two interesting sites. The most photographed of all the island's prehistoric remains is the **Naveta d'es Tudons**, close to the road, situated around five kilometres east of Ciutadella. This superbly preserved burial monument, used between 1200 and 750 BC, consists of two large compartments, one on top of the other. When it was excavated and restored in the 1950s, it was found to contain the remains of more than 100 people and a wide variety of burial objects; these are now displayed in the island's museums.

A further three kilometres east is the far less frequently visited and romantically overgrown site of **Torrellafuda**, which sits in lovely countryside, bathed in sunlight and birdsong. Here you'll find a huge *talayot*, a couple of *taulas* and the remains of houses, plus fragments of the encircling wall.

Nearby, but only accessible from the road running parallel and to the south of the main highway (known as the Camí Vell), is the small site of **Torretrencada**, which contains a fine *taula* (with a rib carved down the back of the main pillar, rather than a separate supporting stone) and rock-cut burial chambers. It's a five-minute walk from the car park.

To the north, near the Biniatram *agroturismo*, is **Cavalls Son Àngel** (call Toni or Catalina on mobiles 609 83 39 02 or 649 48 80 98 or email cavallssonangel@yahoo.es), which offers horseriding through the pine forest which flanks this part of the north coast and runs down to the cliffs. The stables cater for beginners with docile, sure-footed animals that wouldn't harm a fly, though more experienced riders should make it clear in advance that they don't just want to plod along. The farm also provides an opportunity to check out the Menorcan pure breed horses, though given the incredible amount of stamping and snorting going on, you'd have be Frankie Dettori – or nuts – to mount one.

Pedreres de s'Hostal

Camí Vell, km1 (971 48 15 78/www.lithica.es). **Open** *May, Sept, Oct* 9.30am-sunset daily. *June-Aug* 9.30am-2.30pm, 4.30pm-sunset daily. *Nov-Apr* 10am-1pm Mon-Fri; 10am-5pm Sat, Sun. **Admission** €4; reductions €2-free. Free to all Nov-Apr. **No credit cards**.

Where to stay & eat

Two of the loveliest places to stay on the island lie between Ciutadella and Cala Morell. **Hotel Sant Ignasi** (Ctra. Ciutadella–Cala Morell s/n, 971 38 55 75, www.santignasi.com, closed 9 Dec-9 Jan, €120-€250 double), a couple of kilometres from Ciutadella, comes straight from the pages of a design magazine, with its mustard yellow colonial façade and elegant rooms, each one different – all very 'designer rural'. If you can afford it, it's a wonderfully peaceful place to stay, with nice gardens, a pool and the excellent **Es Lloc** restaurant (phone to check opening times, closed Oct-Mar, €€€€) next door. The food is stylishly presented Mediterranean cuisine, with just a handful of starters followed by three meat and three fish dishes. Nouveau-fiddling is kept to a minimum (a foam here, an emulsion there), and the results are delicious. The hotel and restaurant are located up a very long, very narrow rural lane off the Ciutadella to Cala Morell road.

For some rural peace and quiet, the 500-year-old **Biniatram** farmhouse (Ctra. Ciutadella–Cala Morell, km6, 971 38 31 13, www.biniatram. com, doubles €55-€115) is a more down-to-earth option. With the donkeys, chickens and horses it feels a little like if Old McDonald had an *agroturismo,* and Toni, the manager, will most likely hop down from his tractor to show you your room. It's close enough to Ciutadella for a night on the town, yet just a kilometre from the coast and set in acres of farmland. There's a pool, tennis court, table tennis, and a large, baronial sitting room, as well as a kitchen for self-catering, plus a couple of self-contained apartments. All rooms have TVs and air-conditioning. Pleasant walks wind through the fields to the beach at La Vall (*see 258*), or just across the fields is the Cavalls Son Àngel riding stables (*see p255*).

South-east of Ciutadella is **Movedra Nou** (Camí de Sant Joan de Missa, km7, 971 35 95 21, www.morvedranou.es, doubles €106-€169), a 17th-century farmhouse turned into a rural hotel. The 18 rooms are rustic rather than designer, but they are all comfortable and all have terraces (two of which have splendid views). There is a swimming pool and lovely gardens but the real USP is that it's only eight kilometres from the idyllic beaches of the south coast (photo p256).

THE NORTH-WEST & WEST COASTS

Isolated as it is, the settlement of **Cala Morell** – built around a small, pretty bay between high cliffs – has a stormy, end-of-the-earth atmosphere. It's the only development on

Punta Nati. *See p258.*

MENORCA

MENORCA

the north-west coast and has a sizeable but
not overbearing estate of holiday apartments.
It is also the site of an interesting prehistoric
necropolis of 15 caves dug from the rock,
which is known too as Cala Morell.

East of here lies the pretty bay and beach of
Cala d'Algairens, also known as **La Vall**. It's
a better, bigger beach than that at Cala Morell
and remains undeveloped, though you have to
pay to use the car park. On the road here from
Ciutadella, you pass the medieval defence tower
at **Torre d'en Quart** and go through the pine
woods of **Son Àngel** (photo p254).

Further west, Menorca drops down into a
flat, rough plain that ends abruptly in low cliffs,
as if the land has been snapped off by divine
forces and hurled into the sea – it's beautiful.
From the lighthouse at Punta Nati in the north-
west corner down to its counterpart at **Cap
d'Artrutx** in the south-west, there are no
more than half a dozen narrow rocky inlets, the
largest being the port of Ciutadella. The rest are
now dominated by holiday resorts, from Cala en
Blanes in the north down to Cala en Bosc and
Son Xoriguer just round the corner in the south.

English-dominated ghetto **Cala en Blanes**,
just north of Ciutadella, is an encampment
of hotel-apartments built around leisure
complexes filled with English pubs. It's a
miserable place, especially as the two 'beaches',
Cala en Forcat and **Cala en Brut**, are
nothing more than pocket handkerchiefs of
sand less than a dozen metres across at the end
of their respective inlets. The beach of Cala en
Blanes itself, surrounded by independent villas,
is slightly larger and a lot more pleasant, with a
herd of elephant-footed palms clustered around
its landward end. Trotting races take place at
the **Torre del Ram** racetrack in Cala en
Blanes every Sunday from April to November.

From here, the road back to Ciutadella
passes along the top of the low cliffs, in front of
interesting villas, some a century old. North of
Cala en Blanes the coastline is wild, rocky and
almost entirely devoid of human habitation.
For lovers of the romantically barren, it's well
worth driving up to the **Punta Nati** lighthouse

(photo p257) and clambering about on the rocks
above the crashing waves. This is also where
you can see some of the best examples of ponts
and *barracas*, the stone cattle shelters that look
like ancient dwellings but actually date from
the mid 19th century (*see p20* **Site-seeing
guide**). The former are usually oblong, while
the latter are circular pyramids, with a single
entrance and a bare interior, with a stone lintel
that sometimes has the construction date
carved into it. Watch out for perilous open
shafts while walking around.

South of Ciutadella, the inlets at **Cala de
Santandria** and **Cala Blanca** are larger and
much nicer than their counterparts to the north.
Both are surrounded by villas, with a couple of
hotels and snack bars on or overlooking the
beach. From Cala Blanca the road runs a mile
inland, through attractive grazing land neatly
separated into plots by drystone walls and
dotted with pine copses and the occasional
farmhouse. Alternatively, a beautiful but
rugged coastal path leads over the top of the
cliffs, with great views inland and out to sea.

Around the tip of **Cap d'Artrutx**, with
its unprepossessing lighthouse, the beaches
of **Cala en Bosc** and **Son Xoriguer** are
stunning, with fine white sand, turquoise
waters and more of the low cliffs that dominate
this end of the island. Unfortunately, this is
another package holiday ghetto and although
the hotels are no more than a few storeys high,
they still cover every inch of land. The once-
attractive natural lagoon at Cala en Bosc is now
a malodorous marina, lined with more pubs.

Where to stay

Almost every hotel on the west coast is the
preserve of package tours, and none can be
recommended. You're better off staying in
Ciutadella and making forays to the coast, or
try any of the nearby places recommended in
the West Interior section (*see p256*).

GETTING THERE

By bus

Buses to and from Ciutadella leave from Plaça
dels Pins. There are buses every hour between
Ciutadella and Maó (reduced service at the
weekend), via Ferreries (20mins), Es Mercadal
(30mins) and Alaior (40mins). Other services from
Ciutadella include 7 daily buses (3 on Sun) to Cala
Galdana (40mins) via Ferreries, 3 buses Mon-Fri
(2 Sat) to Sant Tomàs (40mins) and 1 bus Mon-
Sat to Son Bou (1hr). There are also hourly buses
along the west coast from Cala en Forcat (via
Ciutadella) to Cala Blanca and Cap d'Artrutx
(25mins). Note that there are fewer services
on some routes Nov-Apr.

Directory

Cap de
Formentor.
See p146.

Getting There & Around

ARRIVING & LEAVING

By air

Visit www.aena.es for details on all Spanish airports and live departure and arrival details.

Maó airport, Menorca
971 15 70 00/airport tourist office 971 15 71 15.
Menorca's international airport is four kilometres south-west of Maó. From mid May to October, services from Maó bus station to the airport run every 30mins 5.45am-10.25pm, then at 11.15pm and 12.15am. From November to mid May, buses run every 30mins, 6am-10.30pm weekdays, and hourly 6am-10.30pm at weekends and public holidays.
A single fare is €1.60. For details, phone 902 07 50 66, Torres bus company (www.e-torres.net) on 971 38 64 61 or the airport tourist office on 971 15 71 15. A taxi into Maó shouldn't cost more than €12.

Palma airport, Mallorca
971 78 90 00/airport tourist office 971 78 95 56.
Son Sant Joan airport lies eight kilometres east of Palma.
Bus 1 runs between the airport and the bay-side Passeig Maritim via Plaça Espanya every 15mins from around 6am to around 2.15am every day. The single fare is €1.85 (971 21 44 44, 900 700 710).
A taxi will cost around €22 to the city centre. There are fixed-rate taxi fares to other places on the island.

Airlines Below are listed the major airlines flying to Palma and Maó. Some only offer charter flights and may have a reduced timetable or no service out of the summer season.

Air Berlin *UK 0871 500 0737/ www.airberlin.com.*
BMI British Midland *UK 0870 60 70 555/Palma 971 78 94 75/ 78 92 69/www.flybmi.com.*
BMIbaby *UK 0871 224 0224/ Spain 902 10 07 37/ www.bmibaby.com.*

EasyJet *www.easyjet.com.*
Excel Airways *UK 0870 169 0169/www.xl.com.*
First Choice *UK 0871 200 7799/www.firstchoice.co.uk/flights.*
flybe *UK 0871 700 2000/ www.flybe.com.*
flyglobespan *UK 0871 971 1440/ www.flyglobespan.com.*
British Airways *UK 0870 850 9850/Spain 902 11 13 33/Palma 971 26 51 88/26 51 74/Maó 971 15 70 25/www.ba.com.*
Iberia *UK 0870 609 0500/Spain 902 40 05 00/Maó 971 36 90 15/ www.iberia.com.*
Jet2 *UK 0871 226 1737/Spain 902 02 00 51/Palma 971 78 95 80/ www.jet2.com.*
Monarch *UK 0870 040 5040/ Spain 91 414 15 00/Palma 971 78 95 80/Maó 971 36 38 00/ 15 70 87/www.flymonarch.com.*
Thomsonfly *UK 0871 231 4691/ Spain 91 414 14 81/www.thomson fly.com.*

By boat

Baleària *Spain 902 16 01 80/ Palma 971 40 53 60/ www.balearia.com.*
Standard and high-speed passenger and car ferries between Barcelona and Valencia and the Balearics.
From Barcelona, there's a daily service to Ciutadella on Menorca (3hrs 45mins), going on to Alcúdia on Mallorca (5hrs 30mins; 1hr from Ciutadella to Alcúdia), and three slow ferries a week to Maó (9hrs). From Dénia, a twice-daily service runs to Palma via Ibiza (5hrs or 8hrs 45mins; 2hrs or 4hrs from Palma to Ibiza).
Between Mallorca and Menorca, ferries run daily between Alcúdia and Ciutadella (1hr) and three times a week (July-Sept only) between Alcúdia and Maó (1hr 30mins).
Single passenger tickets from mainland Spain to the Balearics are €66 (standard ferry) and €90 (high-speed ferry). Single fares between Mallorca and Menorca are €59.60, and €49 between Palma and Ibiza.

Iscomar *Spain 902 11 91 28/ www.iscomar.com.*
Iscomar operates car and passenger ferries between Alcúdia on Mallorca and Ciutadella on Menorca (2hrs 30mins; twice daily Mon-Fri, once daily Sat, Sun, with an extra service on Sat from mid June to Sept), as well as a daily passenger service between Barcelona and Palma (8hrs 30mins) and six boats a week between Valencia and Palma (9hrs).
A single passenger fare between Alcúdia and Ciutadella is €39; Barcelona and Palma is €29; and Valencia and Palma is €25.

Trasmediterranea *902 45 46 45/www.trasmediterranea.es.*
Services from Barcelona and Valencia to the Balearics on both high-speed and standard passenger and car ferries. There are daily departures in high season from Barcelona to Palma (3hrs 45mins or 7hrs) and six a week during high season to Maó (8hrs). In summer, daily services run from Valencia to Palma (6hrs or 7hrs 15mins) and one a week (on Sat) to Maó (14hrs). There's a weekly ferry every Sun between Palma and Maó (5hrs 30mins), and twice-daily service between Palma and Ibiza (2hrs).
One-way fares between mainland Spain and the Balearics start at €68 (standard ferry) and €98 (high-speed ferry) . A single fare between palma and Maó is €56.

PUBLIC TRANSPORT

For all forms of transport on and to the Balearics, see www.tib.caib.es.

Bus

Mallorca is well served by buses, the easiest means of getting around the island if you don't have your own transport. Many buses to and from tourist areas only offer limited services out of season.
The main companies operating bus services are: **Empresa Municipal de Transportes Urbanos de Palma** (971 21 44

44, www.emtpalma.es) has more than 20 routes in and near Palma; **Autocares Levante** (971 81 80 76, www.autocareslevante.com) runs airport transfers and excursions; and **Autocares Mallorca** (971 54 56 96, www.autocaresmallorca.com) offers 11 routes around Mallorca.

Buses are the only form of public transport on Menorca. Services to resort areas are more frequent in high season. **Transportes Menorca** (971 36 04 75, www. tmsa.es) is the main operator; its website shows timetables. Other operators include **Torres Allés Autocares** (971 38 64 61, www. e-torres.net) and **Autocares Norte** (971 48 00 48, www.norbus.es).

For details of specific routes, *see* **Getting there** sections at the end of individual chapters.

Train

On Mallorca, there are two rail lines. The picturesque old narrow-gauge Palma to Sóller railway now exists largely for tourists. *See p126* **Ticket to ride**. Locals are far more likely to use the Palma to Inca line (run by SFM: 971 75 22 45), which has stops at Marratxi, Santa Maria del Cami, Consell, Binissalem and Lloseta. In 2003, its extension to Manacor via Sineu was reopened, 26 years after it had been closed down. Another branch line extends from Inca to Llubi, Muro and Sa Pobla. In Palma, the stations for both lines are in Plaça Espanya. Menorca has no rail services.

DRIVING

Driving (on the right) on the islands is straightforward, and you'll rarely encounter a serious traffic jam outside Palma, though the busy cross-Mallorca routes and the Maó–Ciutadella road on Menorca are largely single carriageways and you can get stuck behind slow-moving traffic. The main problem you are likely to encounter will be parking (*see below*).

Car rental

Renting a car is cheap compared to the rest of Europe. There's lots of competition, so it pays to shop around. The local firms tend to be cheaper than the big international names, but make sure you check about hidden extras.

At Palma airport, there's a huge choice of companies. You should be able to find the cheapest compact for around €130 a week all-inclusive.

One of the cheapest brokers in Spain is **CarJet** (1279 770 450, www.carjet.com). It's notable for its no extras policy, which means extra drivers, car seats and damage excess are all included in the price. Another competitively priced broker is **Holiday Autos** (UK 0870 606 0100, www.holidayautos. com). A toll-free number from the UK 0870 606 0100), Palma airport (971 78 91 87), Palma city, Passeig Maritim 16 (971 73 07 20/ 73 07 35), Maó city, Moll de Ponent 61 (971 36 47 78). There is also **Europcar** (902 10 50 55/www. europcar.com), **Hertz** (www.hertz. es) Palma airport (971 78 96 70/ Palma city, Passeig Maritim 13 (971 26 99 73) Maó airport 971 35 40 92 Maó city, C/Son Cremat 10 (971 36 15 12). **National-Atesa** www.atesa.es Palma airport (971 26 60 01), Palma city, Maó airport (971 36 62 13).

Legal requirements

In order to drive in Spain you'll need a valid driving licence and third-party motor insurance. Theoretically, all valid UK licences should be accepted; but, in fact, older non-photocard licences and Northern Ireland licences issued prior to 1 January 1991 do not conform to the EU model and may cause confusion. Drivers from the US and other non-EU countries should obtain an international driving permit.

The minimum age at which you may drive a temporarily imported car or motorcycle (over 75cc) is 18. Most rental companies require the driver to be at least 21 years old and to have held a full driving licence for at least a year. Drivers under 25 often have to pay a supplementary charge.

The minimum age for hiring a scooter (up to 49cc) is 16; no driving licence is required. For motorbikes over 250cc drivers must hold a driving licence and be aged 21 or over.

Severe penalties, including fines and the withdrawal of your driving licence, may be enforced if the level of alcohol in your bloodstream is found to be 0.05 per cent or above. Fines are issued on the spot and can be steep; always ask for an official receipt.

Seatbelts are compulsory for both front and rear seat occupants, if fitted. Children under 12 cannot travel as front seat passengers unless a suitable restraint system is in place.

● By law you must carry a fluorescent warning triangle, which must be set up on the hard shoulder some way behind the car if you break down. You must also carry a spare set of headlight bulbs.

Motorbikes/scooters

Scooters are fine for pottering along the coast, but you'll need something more powerful to explore the mountains.

Helmets are compulsory. Speed limits are enforced on an ad hoc basis. The police are hot on headlights, which should be set on half-beam at all times.There are motorbike rental places all over the islands, including: **Rent A Bike** C/Joan Miró 330D, San Augustin, Palma (971 40 18 21).

Parking

The Spanish drive everywhere and there are never enough parking spaces, particularly in Palma.

Road classifications

All roads in Mallorca are now prefixed MA (replacing the former PM and C prefixes), while Menorca's roads are prefixed ME. So the letters now bear no relation to the size or quality. For example, the four main autopistas, all of them on Mallorca, are prefixed MA, but so are many of the secondary roads. The number of numerals after the letter is a clue to the road's size – generally, the more numerals, the narrower the road.

Note that the ring road around Palma is known as the Via de Cintura.

Signs

Cedeixi el pas/cede el paso – give way. *Vosté no té prioritat/usted no tiene la prioridad* – you don't have the right of way. *Sentit únic/unico sentido* – one way. *Canvi de sentit/cambio de sentido* – a junction that allows you to change direction. *Recordi/recuerde* – remember (warning).

Speed limits

On major roads and motorways the speed limit is 120km/h (75mph), though many local drivers don't seem to take much notice of this. The minimum speed on motorways is 60km/h (37mph). In urban areas the speed limit is 50km/h (31mph); on other roads it is 90km/h (56mph)

Where to Stay

Mallorca is blessed with a vast number of places to stay. The package crowds stick to the coasts, while inland you can find small, boutique-style hotels with designer prices, and *casas rurales*: former farmhouses or private residences turned into accommodation.

Menorca is lagging some way behind its bigger neighbour, with the boutique and *agroturismo* boom only just starting to make its presence felt. Pickings are fewer for those on a budget, with standard resort hotels often offering the keenest prices but little character.

Book ahead in high season (mid June to mid September). Many of the hotels in the coastal resorts are likely to be block-booked by tour operators months ahead, and finding a room on spec in July and August can be nigh on impossible. There shouldn't be problems at other times of the year, except during Semana Santa (Easter Week), but many places close for the winter months.

The **Spanish National Tourist Office** (SNTO) publishes the *Guía de Hoteles, Campings y Apartamentos*, which is available from the major tourist offices and SNTO office abroad (*see p269*). It lists every officially recognised place to stay on the islands, and prints prices in both high and low seasons.

Value-added tax, known as IVA, will be added to your bill at the rate of seven per cent. Always check whether IVA is included in the quoted room price. Breakfast (*desayuno*) may or may not be included in the rate.

In this guide we have added IVA to prices for accommodation. Bear in mind, however, that although the prices were correct at the time of writing, most of the establishments raise their rates each year.

AGROTURISMOS & RURAL HOTELS

Turismo rural or *agroturismo* is the Balearic government's way of getting more tourists away from the coast and into the countryside. There has been a significant growth in this area in recent years.

The Balearic government divides the accommodation into three different types:

● *Agroturismo* – farms and country estates with a maximum of 11 rooms.
● *Hotel rural* – generally more upmarket with 12 or more rooms.
● *Turismo de interior* – renovated historic houses in towns and villages.

The website for the **Associació Agroturisme Balear** (www. topfincas.com) lists around 100 *agroturismos* with lots of photos. Nine fincas have broken away from the association and maintain their own site (www.fincaturismo.com). Menorca's fledgling *agroturismos* and *hoteles rurales* can be found on the Menorca Rural website (www.menorca-rural.com).

See also p172 **A Very Big House in the Country**.

CAMPING

Very few people camp on Mallorca and Menorca, and there are only three official campsites. On Mallorca: **Club Nautico San Pedro** (Passeig de la Mar s/n, near Artà, 971 58 91 18, www.cncoloniasp.com, open all year round). On Menorca: **Camping Son Bou** and **Camping S'Atalaia** (for both, *see p233*). You can camp elsewhere, but it's important to use your judgement – city centres, private farmland and tourist beaches are off-limits; if you camp here you are liable for a fine.

HOSTALES & PENSIONES

These are a rarity on the islands, with just a handful in Palma and the odd one in larger inland towns. *Hostales* (and *hostal-residencias*) are graded in the same way as hotels, with one or two stars. Most offer simple rooms with en suite facilities at reasonable prices. Most are family-run. '*Residencia*' simply means that no meal other than breakfast is served.

HOTELS

The Balearic government has banned any new hotels of fewer than three stars and is trying to upgrade the remainder, so you'll find the majority of places to be three-star and up, although there are still a handful of one and two star places.

The appellation 'GL' beside five star hotels means that the place is

'*Gran Lujo*' ('grand luxury'). The stars correspond to the hotel's facilities, size of room, whether it has a lift, etc, but do not reflect levels of service, atmosphere or location.

'HA' denotes Apartment-Hotels, which are graded from one to four keys and offer self-catering facilities. These are very good value if you are travelling as a family.

MONASTERIES

These offer simple accommodation, often in stunning surroundings and at very low prices. See individual chapters for details. You can obtain a full list from tourist offices.

REFUGIOS

There are a handful of mountain refuges dotted around the *serras* at strategic points along trails, offering spartan accommodation, simple food and cheap prices.

Villa rental

Among the companies offering villas are:

James Villa Holidays *UK 0800 074 0122/www.jamesvillas.co.uk*. Almost 200 villas on Mallorca, most in the Pollença area, and around 180 on Menorca, the majority on the south coast. All have pools.
Mallorca Farmhouse Holidays *UK 0845 800 8080/ from outside the UK +44 118 947 3001/www.mfh.co.uk*
MNK Villas *902 36 99 02/www.mnkvillas.com*.
Owners Direct *www.ownersdirect.co.uk*.
Villa Retreats *UK 0800 988 558/www.villaretreats.com*.

YOUTH HOSTELS

Youth hostels on Mallorca can be found in **S'Arenal** (Albergue Playa de Palma, C/Costa Brava 13, 971 26 08 92, reserves@tjove.caib.es, closed Nov-Jan, €9.74-€15.52 per person) and just outside **Alcúdia** (Albergue de la Victoria, Ctra. Cabo de Pinar, km4.9, 971 54 53 95, 971 54 55 42, reserves@tjove.caib.es, closed Nov-Jan, €9.74-€15.52 per person). Visit www.reaj.com.

Sport & Activity Holidays

The Balearics are paradise for those looking for active holidays. As islands, watersports – and in particular sailing and diving – are popular pursuits here, but you are also spoilt for choice on land, with Mallorca's Tramutana mountain range attracting hikers and cyclists in every increasing numbers.

See the **Outdoor Pursuits** chapter on pages 34-38 for a general overview of activities. You will also find sports club listings in individual chapters.

GOLF

There are 21 courses on Mallorca, and one on Menorca. The prices listed below are subject to change.

Golf Alcanada *Ctra. del Faro s/n, Port d'Alcúdia (971 54 95 60/ www.golf-alcanada.com).* **Green fees** (9/18 holes) €55/€105.
Opened in 2003, and designed by Robert Trent Jones Sr and Jr, this challenging course is the closest to a links course you'll find on the island, with magnificent views.
Golf Pollença *Ctra. Palma– Pollença, km49.3, Pollença (971 53 32 16/www.golfpollensa.com).* **Green fees** (9/18 holes) €40/€70.
Expect good fairways, lots of sand, a couple of lakes and wonderful views to the coast.
Golf de Poniente Ctra *Cala Figuera s/n, Calvià (971 13 01 48/ www.ponientegolf.com).* **Green fees** (9/18 holes) €45/€88.
The 18 holes, opened in 1978, were designed by J Harris. Don't believe other guidebooks that suggest that this is the island's toughest course; it isn't.
Golf Santa Ponça I *Urbanización Santa Ponça, Calvià (971 69 02 11/www.habitatgolf.es).* **Green fees** (9/18 holes) €40/€88.
Opened in 1992 and designed by Jose Gancedo, this is a good course for less confident golfers, with generous flat fairways and no dramatic rough.
Golf Son Parc *Urbanización Son Parc, Es Mercadal (971 18 88 75/*

35 90 59/www.golfsonparc.com).* **Green fees** (18 holes) €60.
Extended in the past few years from nine to 14 holes, with the final four holes completed in summer 2006. So far the only course on Menorca.
Golf Son Termens *Ctra. S'Esglaieta, km10, Bunyola (971 61 78 62/www.golfson termens.com).* **Green fees** (9/18 holes) €45/€78.
This fabulous course is set at the foot of the Serra de Tramuntana and offers wondrous views. It's a hard walk, so lazy golfers should hire a buggy.
Marriott Hotel & Golf Resort *Llucmajor (971 12 92 00/ www.marriotthotels.com/pmigs).* **Green fees** (9/18 holes) €37/€65 (€42 twilight fee). NB 9 holes only available 9-9.30am or late afternoon.
The East is the older course and the West benefits from some creative landscaping. Perfect for golfers who don't enjoy uphill fairways and elevated tees.
Pula Golf *Ctra. Son Servera– Capdepera, km3, Son Servera (971 81 70 34/reservas@pulagolf.com).* **Green fees** (18 holes) €80.
Not easy for beginners, Pula Golf has plenty of challenging narrow fairways and small greens. Smart dress a must.
Real Golf de Bendinat *Urb. Bendinat, C/Campoamor s/n, Calvià (971 40 52 00/www.real golfbendinat.com).* **Green fees** (18 holes) €80.
Good golfing along pine-lined fairways, with beautiful views across the Bay of Palma.
Son Vida Golf *Urbanización Son Vida, Palma (971 79 12 10/ www.golfsonvida.com).* **Green fees** (9/18 holes) €45-€70.
This excellent, varied course was the first on Mallorca when it opened in 1964.
Vall d'Or Golf *Ctra. Porto Colom–Cala d'Or, km7.7, S'Horta (971 83 70 01/www. valldorgolf.com).* **Green fees** (18 holes) €98.

An excellent, challenging course, facing south across Porto Colom and Cala d'Or, which offers plenty for all abilities. Several uphill fairways and elevated greens.

HORSERIDING

For general information and a list of all horse riding clubs on the islands, contact the Federació Hipica de les Illes Balears (Recinto Ferial d'Es Mercadal, Menorca, 971 15 42 25, www.hipica baleares.com).

Llevant Riding Club *C/Aurora 5A, Manacor, Mallorca (mobile 610 42 71 86).*
Mallorca Riding School *Real Club Escola Equitació de Mallorca, Ctra. de Sóller, km12.2, Bunyola, Mallorca (971 61 31 57).*
Offers riding for the handicaped.
Alaior Riding School *Es Cos s/n, Alaior, Menorca (971 37 82 43).*
Ciutadella Riding Club *Camino Caracol s/n, Ciutadella, Menorca (971 38 54 78/clubhipic ciutadella@hotmail.com).*

SCUBA DIVING

The following are the top diving centres on Menorca; we have listed other smaller outfits in individual chapters.

S'Algar Diving *Passeig Marítim, S'Algar (971 15 06 01/www.salgar diving.com).* **Prices** try dive €78; 1 boat dive €60; 7 boat dives €378; PADI Open Water Course €499.
7 Fathoms Dive Centre *Local 6, Parcela 410, C/Canal, Calas Picas, Ciutadella (971 38 87 63/ www.7fathoms.com).* **Prices** try dive €59; 1 boat dive €45; 7 boat dives €315; PADI Open Water Course €430.
Ulmo Diving *Zona Comercial, Addaia (971 35 90 05/www. ulmodiving.com).* **Prices** try dive €99; 1 boat dive €35; 5 boat dives €160; PADI Open Water Course €460.

Resources A-Z

TRAVEL ADVICE

For up-to-date information on travel to a specific country – including the latest on safety and security, health issues, local laws and customs – contact your home country government's department of foreign affairs. Most have websites with useful advice for would-be travellers.

AUSTRALIA
www.smartraveller.gov.au

CANADA
www.voyage.gc.ca

NEW ZEALAND
www.safetravel.govt.nz

REPUBLIC OF IRELAND
www.foreignaffairs.gov.ie

UK
www.fco.gov.uk/travel

USA
www.state.gov/travel

ADDRESSES

These are written street first, number second. In other words: C/Palma 7. Apartment addresses are written according to the floor and which side of the block the flat is on, and may be written in Catalan or Castilian, so 'dcha' = *dreta/derecha* (right); 'izda' = *esquerra/izquierda* (left); 'cto' = *centre/centro* (centre). 'Piso 1° dcha' would therefore translate as 'first-floor flat on the right'. The odd moniker s/n stands for '*sin número*', or 'no number'. *Código postal* is the five-figure postcode and should always be included.

Most Spanish street names are preceded by 'Carrer' ('Calle' in Castilian), meaning 'street', often abbreviated to 'C/' and not marked at all on many street maps. We've used the following common abbreviations in addresses in this guide: Avda. = *avinguda* (Catalan)/*avenida* (Castilian) (avenue), and Ctra. = *carretera* (road). Other common words that you may come across in either Catalan or Castilian are *passeig/paseo* (boulevard), *passatge/pasaje* (alley, passageway) and *placeta/plazuela* (small square).

Addresses outside of towns are often designated by a kilometre mark. For example, 'Ctra. Palma–Manacor, km4' means 'at the 4km mark on the Palma to Manacor road'.

AGE RESTRICTIONS

The minimum legal age for smoking and drinking is 16. The age of consent for both hetero- and homosexuals is just 13, one of the lowest in Europe. To drive a car or

motorbike/scooter above 125cc you need to be 18; to drive a scooter up to 50cc you must be 14; to drive one up to 125cc you must be 16.

ATTITUDE

The Spanish are far more tactile than northern Europeans; the common greeting between members of the opposite sex and between two women is a kiss on both cheeks. Personal space is much less guarded than in the UK or USA, so do not be fazed if you find someone crowding you or bumping into you without apologising. However, the Balearics have been welcoming and dealing with the foibles of foreigners for so long that you're unlikely to be subject to any sort of significant culture shock.

CHILDREN

The Spanish love children – so much so that they take them with them wherever they go, at almost any time of day or night. Do not be surprised to see a baby asleep in a pushchair in a bar at 1am. The Spanish are also much less strict about keeping control of their kids than northern European parents. Bars and restaurants will bend over backwards to look after children or babies, even if they have no special facilities or kids' menus, and almost all hotels are happy to accommodate children at reduced rates.

CONSUMER

The Govern de les Illes Balears has a freephone number (900 16 60 00, 8am-8pm Mon-Fri, 9am-2pm Sat, operators speak English) dedicated to consumer issues. Its website

(www.caib.es) contains details of offices around the islands (five on Mallorca, one on Menorca) that can offer consumer help and advice (see http://web2.caib.es/pcnfront/do/serveis/xarxa).

CONSULATES

British Consulate *Plaça Major 3D, Palma, Mallorca (971 71 24 45/971 71 60 48/www.fco.gov.uk).* **Open** 8.30am-1.30pm Mon-Fri.
British Consulate *SA Casa Nova, Camí de Biniatap 30, Es Castell, Menorca (971 36 78 18/www.fco.gov.uk).* **Open** 10am-noon Mon-Fri.
US Consular Office *Edificio Reina Constanza, C/Porto Pi 8, 9th floor, Palma (971 40 37 07).* **Open** 10.30am-1.30pm Mon-Fri.

CUSTOMS

There are no restrictions on the import/export of duty-paid goods into Spain from any other EU country, provided the goods are for personal consumption only. Amounts qualifying as personal consumption are as follows. (If you import more than these amounts, you may be asked to prove that the goods are solely for you.)

● up to 800 cigarettes, 400 small cigars, 200 cigars or 1kg loose tobacco.
● 10 litres of spirits (over 22% alcohol), 90 litres of wine (under 22% alcohol) or 110 litres of beer.

If you are travelling into Spain from outside the EU, the limits are as follows.
● 200 cigarettes, 100 small cigars, 50 cigars or 250g loose tobacco.

● 1 litre of spirits (over 22% alcohol) or 2 litres of wine and beer (under 22% alcohol).
● 50g perfume.
● 500g coffee, 100g tea.

DISABLED

The main towns and the resorts are fairly well geared up for disabled travellers, but rural areas are not. Many new buses are of the low-floor type, and wheelchairs should be available at most train stations. Many of the major car hire companies offer specially adapted cars for hire. Disabled parking bays are denoted by a blue wheelchair sign.

Most public buildings and monuments, certainly in the cities, have disabled access and facilities by law. This also applies to larger hotels, but smaller places are unlikely to be equipped for disabled visitors. Larger restaurants and service stations in tourist areas will also have disabled access, but in smaller villages facilities are scarce. Most toilets, outside of the resorts and big hotels, are similarly unadapted.

Organisations

Get a list of wheelchair-friendly accommodation and useful tips about Mallorca and Menorca for disabled visitors before you go from Spanish National Tourist Offices around the world. For your nearest office, see p269 **Tourist information**.

Asprom C/Pascual Ribot 6A, Palma (971 28 90 52/ www.asprom.net).
This is the main association on Mallorca for people with disabilities, and can offer basic information on accessibility by phone or via email.
Holiday Care Service 7th Floor, Sunley House, 4 Bedford Park, Croydon, Surrey CR0 2AP (from UK 0845 124 9971/from outside UK 00 44 208 760 0072/ www.holidaycare.org.uk).
Information on travel for the disabled; its Mallorca factsheet (£2.50) has lots of useful details on wheelchair accessibility around the island and can be ordered online.

DRUGS

Tolerance towards soft drugs has become stricter since the heady days of the late 1980s when it was perfectly acceptable to smoke in parks, public spaces and many bars and cafés. Today, you might see people smoking joints (porros) in certain areas such as El Terreny in Palma, but it's not as commonplace. Cannabis possession is illegal in Spain and can result in a fine and a possible court appearance.

If you are found in possession of any other drugs, you are looking at big fines and a prison sentence.

ELECTRICITY & GAS

Spain operates on a 220V, 50-cycle AC grid and uses two-pin plugs. You will need an adaptor if you are bringing British electrical appliances with you. Visitors from the USA will need to bring an adaptor and a transformer to use appliances from home.

EMERGENCIES

The general 24-hour emergency number is 112. Multilingual operators can then co-ordinate the necessary police, fire or ambulance services.

GAY & LESBIAN

There's not much of a scene outside Palma (see p81) and, in season, Magaluf. For information (though only if you speak Spanish/Catalan), contact Ben Amics.

Ben Amics C/Conquistador 2 Principal, 07001 Palma (971 71 56 70, 9am-3pm Mon-Fri, 6-9pm Thur-Fri/www.benamics.com). This is the Balearic gay and lesbian association. Its website is only in Catalan and Castilian.

HEALTH

All travellers are strongly advised to take out comprehensive travel health insurance that will cover medical costs and repatriation, if required. Visitors can obtain emergency care through the public health service. EU nationals are entitled to free basic medical attention if they have the European emergency health card, also known as the EU health insurance card. This card replaced the E111 form and is valid for one year. Contact the health service in your country of residence for further details. For non-emergencies, it's usually quicker to use private travel/ medical insurance rather than the state system.

For further information about health matters visit the Balearic government website (www.caib.es).

Accident & emergency

In a serious medical emergency requiring an ambulance, call the general emergency number 112. For lesser injuries, pharmacists are highly knowledgeable and can offer advice. See below.

Contraception

Condoms (condons/preservativos) can be bought from pharmacies and vending machines in the toilets of some bars. The female contraceptive pill (la píndola/la píldora) can be bought at most pharmacies without prescription, but women travellers are advised to bring their own supply with them. Local doctors are also able to write prescriptions for female contraceptive pills, and you'll usually need a prescription to get the morning-after pill (la píndola del dia seguent/la píldora del día siguiente). If you want a pregnancy test, ask a pharmacist for a 'Predictor' (a brand name, but the word everyone uses).

Doctors & dentists

Medical treatment covered by the European emergency health card (EU health insurance card; see the introduction to the Health section above) is only provided by practitioners within the Spanish national health service at a participating surgery (consultori metge/consultorio), health centre (centre sanitari/centro sanitario) or hospital clinic (ambulatori/ ambulatorio).

If you require treatment, you will need to have your card available to show to the doctor. Anyone without such a card who gets medical treatment in Spain (including all non-EU visitors) will need a doctor's signature in order to make an insurance claim.

In Spain, doctors, health centres and hospitals have separate surgery times for private patients. If you are asked to pay for treatment, be aware that you are not being treated under the national health service and your emergency health card will not be accepted. If you need to call out a doctor in an emergency, make it clear you have an EU emergency health card and that you want to be treated under the EU arrangements.

Note that dental treatment is not usually available free of charge and you are unlikely to be able to claim the costs unless you have comprehensive travel insurance.

DIRECTORY

Hospitals

Hospital Manacor *Ctra. Manacor–Alcúdia s/n (general 971 84 70 00/emergencies 971 84 70 60/http://fundacion.hospital manacor.org).*
Hospital Son Llàtzer *Ctra. Palma–Manacor, km4 (871 20 20 00/www.hsll.es).*
Hospital Son Dureta *C/Andrea Doria 55, Palma (971 17 50 19/ www.hsd.es).*
Hospital Mateu Orfila *Ronda de Malbuguer 1 (971 48 70 00)*

Opticians

You can get a replacement pair of spectacles or order new contact lenses at any opticians (*optica*) as long as you have your prescription with you.

Pharmacies & prescriptions

Farmàcies/farmacias, denoted by an illuminated green cross, can be found in most villages and all towns and cities. Pharmacists are highly knowledgeable and will often be able to save you a trip to the doctor. Pharmacies are usually open 10am to 2pm and 5pm to 8pm Monday to Saturday, but also operate a rota system so there is always one in the vicinity that is open 24 hours, as listed at the back of the local paper under '*Farmàcies de guàrdia*'.

Holders of an EU health insurance card will pay 40 per cent less than the full price for a prescription; other visitors must pay full prescription charges.

STDs, HIV & AIDS

Spain has the highest number of AIDS cases and deaths in the EU, according to UN statistics. Most cases are caused by the use of infected needles by drug abusers, rather than by sexual contact. However, this is largely confined to mainland Spain, particularly in the big cities and the south. The Spanish national AIDS helpline can provide information in English (freephone 900 11 10 00, www.fase.es).

HELPLINES

Alcoholics Anonymous *mobile 616 08 88 83/www.alcoholicos- anonimos.org.*
There are regular meetings held in English in Mallorca and in Ibiza but none currently in Menorca.

Narcotics Anonymous *902 11 41 47/www.na-esp.org/ engnaesp@yahoo.es.*
The email address above is for queries from English speakers. There are currently no English-language meetings.

ID

You are meant to carry some form of ID with you at all times in Spain; the Spanish have identity cards but a passport is ideal for most foreign visitors. If you are stopped by the police and are not carrying valid ID, you will probably get a warning, although you may be liable to an on-the-spot fine. This is, however, very rare. Valid ID (passport) is essential when you're checking into a hotel, hiring a car, changing or paying with travellers' cheques and collecting poste restante.

INSURANCE

All travellers should take out personal travel insurance to cover trip cancellation, emergency medical costs and loss or theft of baggage, money or travellers' cheques. Don't forget to add on 'dangerous sports' cover if you're planning on horseriding, scuba diving, etc. Keep a record of your policy number and the emergency telephone number with you at all times.

INTERNET

There is usually an internet café or at least a *locutori/locutorio* offering internet access in most towns and resorts. See the listings under 'Resources' in individual chapters of this guide. For useful websites on Mallorca and Menorca, *see p274*.

LEGAL HELP

Consulates (*see p264*) can help tourists in emergencies, and can provide a list of English-speaking lawyers/interpreters.

LIBRARIES

Municipal libraries are open 9am to 9pm Monday to Friday and 9am to 2pm on Saturday.

LOST PROPERTY

If you lose something in your hotel, report it to the staff. If you lose something on public transport or in the street, go to your nearest police station. See the listings under 'Resources' in each chapter.

MAPS

All tourist offices supply free local maps. If you're planning on driving, get the **Michelin Baleares** map (no.579). The **Spanish Cycling Federation** publishes cycling maps on its website (www.rfec.com).

MEDIA

Newspapers & magazines

In Spain newspapers and magazines are sold from *quioscos/ kioscos* – kiosks on the street. The Spanish press is largely serious and pretty dry; you won't find anything equivalent to the British tabloids. The biggest seller on a national level, with a circulation of about 400,000, is the left-of-centre **El País**, which has the best foreign coverage and political analysis. The regional edition has a daily Baleares section inside. **El Mundo** and **Diario 16** are both good centrist alternatives, while **ABC** is solidly conservative and reactionary.

The islands have a couple of good local papers: **Diario de Mallorca**, which is a serious tabloid, and **Ultima Hora**, which is a bit more populist. Its English equivalent is the **Majorca Daily Bulletin** (www.majorcadaily bulletin.es), which keeps expat residents updated on local and UK news, and includes an extensive classified section.

Mallorca Reporter is a good weekly free paper, distributed in various resorts, which has news, features and classifieds.

The glossy English-language mag **Island Life** (www.island lifemallorca.com) carries features on everything from cool new hotels to celebs living on the islands.

The free fortnightly Spanish-language **Youthing** publication has listings guides to gigs and youth-slanted events all over the island. It's available from many bars, music shops, etc.

The glossy mag **In Palma** (www.inpalma.com), often to be found in boutique hotel rooms, has interesting articles on cultural issues in both Spanish and English.

Otherwise, most British and US newspapers are available the same day in the larger towns (many print a Spanish edition on Mallorca), and the following day in villages.

Celebrity gossip is confined to the magazines; Spain pioneered the genre with the sycophantic glitz of **¡HOLA!**.

Parents should note that Spain's laissez-faire attitude towards pornography means that you will often find hard-core porn magazines within easy reach of children.

Radio

The Spanish are avid radio fans; you'll hear radios blaring out in bars, cafés, buses and taxis. **Radio Nacional de España** is the main public broadcaster, with four stations. The main commercial broadcaster is **SER** (Sociedad Española de Radiofusión), which controls four networks. There are an enormous number of talk radio-style stations with endless discussions about current affairs, including **Onda Cero**.

The best pop stations are **Cadena Cuarenta Mallorca** and **Cadena 100**, which plays about two Spanish songs to every three British or American ones and is littered with ad breaks. **Radio Clasical** is a relaxing alternative. The local stations include **Ultima Hora Radio 98.8 FM**, **Somràdio** (in Catalan) and **Radio Balear**. You'll also find a few English channels including **Sunshine Capital Radio**, which is on the same frequency as its namesake in London – 95.8 FM.

Television

Spanish television is poor, but you'll find it dominating almost every bar or café you visit. There are five main channels, which pump out an endless diet of tacky game shows, talk shows, hilariously dreadful imported *telenovelas* (soaps) from South/Central America and badly dubbed American movies. The only redeeming feature is the news coverage.

The local TV channel in Mallorca is **Canal 4** (Palma). **TVE** (Televisión España) has a Balearic outpost in Palma, broadcasting in Catalan and Castilian; **m7 Televisió de Mallorca**, also in both languages, is another Mallorca-specific channel.

In most three-star and above hotels you should be able to get **BBC World** and **CNN**. Cable channel Canal Plus offers premium sport and music.

MONEY

Spain's currency is the euro. Each euro (€) is divided into 100 cents (¢), known as céntimos/céntimos. Notes come in denominations of €500, €200, €100, €50, €20, €10 and €5.

Coins come as €2, €1, 50¢, 20¢, 10¢, 5¢, 2¢ and 1¢. Euro travellers' cheques are widely accepted.

Banks & ATMs

You will find a bank in even the tiniest rural community. Banks invariably offer better rates of exchange than bureaux de change. For opening hours, *see below*.

Almost every bank has an ATM (Automated Teller Machine) that can be used to withdraw cash. ATMs accept most credit cards, as well as debit cards that display the Cirrus symbol; they're usually the most convenient way to get hold of local currency. For both credit and debit cards you will need a valid PIN number in order to withdraw money. Your card issuer is likely to charge you a fee for using an ATM while abroad.

Credit cards

Credit cards, especially MasterCard and Visa, will be accepted in all major hotels and many upmarket restaurants on the islands, as well as in supermarkets and petrol stations. However, smaller shops, bars, *hostales* and restaurants in rural areas will often not have credit card facilities. Note too that many places will be reluctant to accept AmEx due to the cost to the retailer. If your card has a Maestro symbol on it, you can use it in major department stores and hotels.

Natural hazards

In summer, beware of the strength of the sun. In the mountains watch out for rockfalls, flash flooding and getting caught up in a snowfall in the winter.

OPENING HOURS

Banks Opening hours are 9am to 2pm Monday to Friday. Banks in towns and cities are also open 9am-1pm on Saturdays from October to April.

Bars & cafés Bars and cafés usually open at lunchtime and stay open until midnight or 1am. However, some cafés may open as early as 5.30am or 6am, depending on their clientele. *Bares de copa*, where the emphasis is more on drinking than eating, rarely open before 7pm and may continue serving until 4am. *Discoteca*-bars start later still and often do not close until after dawn (*madrugada*) at 6/7am. Note

that few bars and cafés have strict closing times.

Museums & monuments Opening hours vary, although a siesta period in the afternoon is not uncommon. Many sights are also closed on a Monday.

Restaurants Restaurants are generally open from 1/2pm until 4/5pm and again from 8/9pm until midnight or 1am at weekends. In tourist areas, UK opening hours are more common. Note: most restaurants have a *día de descans/descanso* (rest day), usually Monday or Wednesday. Away from the coast they may close for the summer holidays in August (*tancat per vacances/cerrado por vacaciones*).

Post offices *Correus/correos* are open from 8am to noon and again from 5pm to 7.30pm, although the ones in big cities do not close in the afternoon. Some offices are also open on Saturdays.

Shops Most shops are open from about 9.30/10am until 1/2pm, when they close for a siesta until 5pm. In the evening they stay open until 8pm. Some smaller shops, such as bakers (*forn de pa/panadería*) and greengrocers (*fruiteria/frutería*), will open much earlier at 7/8am, and department stores and supermarkets stay open all day, sometimes until 10pm.

Police & crime There are three types of police in Spain: the Guàrdia Urbana, the municipal police, operate on a city or town level, directing traffic and dealing with intra-urban crime; the Policía Nacional, who wear brown uniforms, patrol the areas outside the cities; while the green-uniformed paramilitary Guàrdia Civil spend most of their time on highway patrol handing out speeding tickets.

Postal services There is usually just one post office (*correus/correos*) per urban area, often characterised by endless queues; so if you are only after stamps (*segells/sellos*), you are better off going to a tobacconist (*estanc/estanco*), recognisable by its brown and yellow *tabacs/tabacos* sign. They also sell phonecards. For opening times, *see above*. At the time of going to press stamps for letters or postcards up to 20g within Spain were €0.28, €0.53 within the EU and €0.78 for other international destinations. Post can take days just to go to the next town. Airmail within Europe takes at least five days, but often much longer, and it will take at least ten days to a destination outside Europe.

DIRECTORY

DIRECTORY

POSTE RESTANTE

Poste restante is available at any post office. Letters should be addressed to the recipient at *'Llistat de correus'/'Lista de correos'*. You will need your passport to collect your post. American Express offers the same service.

PUBLIC HOLIDAYS

The Spanish enjoy more public holidays than any other European nation. On Mallorca and Menorca there are also holidays specific to the islands and local *fiestas* (*see pp39-42* **Calendar**). If a holiday falls midweek, the Spanish will often take the following day(s) as holiday too, turning it into a long weekend or *pont/puente* (bridge).

On public holidays, banks, post offices and public buildings close and many museums operate Sunday opening times. Note too that many Spaniards take the whole of August off as holiday and that many shops and restaurants away from the resorts close for the whole month.

The following are public holidays on both islands:

1 Jan *Cap d'Any/Día de Año Nuevo* (New Year's Day)
6 Jan *Epifanía del Senyor/Día de Los Reyes Magos (Epifanía del Señor)* (Epiphany)
1 Mar *Día de les Illes Balears/Día de las Islas Baleares* (Balearics Day)
19 Mar *Día de Sant Josep/San José* (St Joseph's Day)
9 Apr 2009/1 Apr 2010 *Dijous Sant/Jueves Santo* (Maundy Thursday)
10 Apr 2009/2 Apr 2010 *Divendres Sant/Viernes Santo* (Good Friday)
1 May *Festa del Treball/Día del Trabajo* (Labour Day)
15 Aug *Assumpció/Día de la Asunción* (Assumption)
12 Oct *Día de la Hispanidad* (Spanish National Day)
1 Nov *Tots Sants/Todos los Santos* (All Saints' Day)
6 Dec *Día de la Constitució/ Constitución* (Constitution Day)
8 Dec *Immaculada Concepció/Inmaculada Concepción* (Immaculate Conception)
25 Dec *Nadal/Navidad* (Christmas Day)
26 Dec *Segona Feste de Nadal/ Día de San Esteban* (Boxing Day)

RELIGION

Although officially a Catholic country, as elsewhere in Europe Spain's church-going is dominated by the older generation. Many religious festivals on the islands, such as Semana Santa (Easter Week), are as much about civic pride and spectacle as they are about religious devotion.

SAFETY & SECURITY

Serious crime is rare on the islands. If you are unlucky, call the general emergency line 112. The only type of crime you are likely to be the victim of is petty crime, such as bag-snatching, pickpocketing, particularly in Palma, and breaking into hire cars. Another common crime involves cutting handbag straps or camera straps (especially around the cathedral in Palma).

For this reason you should take reasonable precautions when you're out and about:

● Don't flash around wads of cash or, indeed, carry a lot of cash on your person; lock it in your hotel safe instead.
● Conceal cameras and valuables.
● Keep a firm hold of your handbag both when walking along and when sitting in a café or restaurant, especially outside. (A good tip is to slip the strap of your bag under your chair leg.)
● Theft from hotel rooms is more common in cities in the lower-end establishments. Again, it generally tends to be opportunistic, so don't leave valuables lying around when you leave your room. Either put them in the safe or give them to the hotel reception for safe-keeping.
● Cars are vulnerable when parked or in stationary traffic with the window open, when scooter riders can snatch belongings from the passenger seat, though this is rare. Overnight, try and park in a hotel garage or a patrolled public garage.
● If you are the victim of a theft, head straight to the nearest police station to report it (see under 'Resources' in each chapter). You're unlikely to ever see your possessions again, but you'll need the police report in order to make an insurance claim. Be warned: outside the main tourist areas the police often don't speak English, and the form-filling (which is likely to be in Spanish) takes ages.

If you have your passport stolen, contact your consulate (*see p264*).

SMOKING

Cigarettes in Spain – both international and local brands – are cheap by UK standards and it is estimated that 30% of Spaniards smoke. In 2006, it became illegal to light up in shops, offices, on public transport and in cultural centres. Many hotels now have no smoking floors.

STUDY

If you want to learn Spanish in Spain, your best resource is to visit the **Instituto Cervantes** website (www.cervantes.es). This provides a full list of the various courses on offer and a description of the places where they are run.

The Palma-based **Universitat de les Illes Balears** (information office 971 17 29 39, 917 17 29 39, www.uib.es) was founded in 1978 in an attempt to prevent a mass migration of bright local youngsters to the mainland; it now has 15,000 students. In addition to a range of degree courses, it also offers Spanish courses for foreigners (www.uib.es/depart/dfe/curso/curso.htm).

It operates the Erasmus student exchange scheme, as part of the EU's Socrates programme to help students move between member states. Interested students should contact the Erasmus co-ordinator at their home college. Information is available in the UK from the UK Socrates-Erasmus Council, Rothford, Giles Lane, Canterbury, Kent CT2 7LR (01227 762712, www.erasmus.ac.uk).

TAX

Value-added tax (IVA) at seven per cent is included in the price of all consumer goods and will be added on to the total bill in hotels and restaurants. (Be aware that it is often not included in initial quotes for rates in hotels.) IVA is non-recoverable for EU citizens. Visitors residing outside the EU should pick up a form at the airport and keep all receipts to get an IVA refund.

TELEPHONES

The Spanish telephone network is efficient and fairly cheap to use. Telephone numbers in Mallorca and Menorca consist of nine digits. The area code for the Balearics is 971, which is followed by six digits. You always need to dial the area code, even when you are on the islands.

Freephone calls are prefixed with 900, cheap rate calls are prefixed with 902 and premium rates are prefixed with 906. Any number starting with a 6 will be a mobile.

International calls

When calling Mallorca or Menorca from abroad, you need to dial the international access code (0011 from Australia; 00 from Ireland, New Zealand and the UK; 011 from the USA and Canada), followed by the country code for Spain (34), followed by the nine-digit number.

To make a call abroad from Mallorca and Menorca, dial 00 (the international access code) plus the international country code, area code and number. Remember to omit the initial 0 from the area code unless you are calling the United States.

International country codes: Australia 61; Canada 1; Ireland 353; New Zealand 64; South Africa 27; United Kingdom 44; United States 1.

Mobile phones

Most European mobile phones (*telefons mòbils/telefonos moviles*) work in Spain (once you have set them up for roaming), but be warned that even if you are making a local call you will be charged at international roaming rates. You will also be charged for incoming calls. Contact your service provider for details.

US handsets are not GSM-compatible and will not work in Europe. If you plan on being on the islands for more than a few weeks, you might be better off buying a pay-as-you-go package when you arrive.

Mobile phone shops include ONO, C/Francisco Sancho 2A, Palma (971 90 36 36, www.ono.es). See below for a list of service providers.

Orange 1474
Movistar 1485
Vodafone 607 13 33 33

Public phones

It's much cheaper to make a call from a phone box than a hotel. There are plenty of phone boxes in towns and villages; most will take coins (you'll need a fistful) and phonecards (*tarja telefónica/ tarjeta telefonica*). Phonecards are the simplest option and can be bought at most *quioscos/kioscos* (kiosks) and *estancs/estancos* (tobacconists), as well as from phone shops. Many bars have payphones.

To make a call from a public phone: lift the receiver, insert the card or coins, then dial the number (not forgetting the area code). If you wish to make another call and you have change left, press the 'R' button and dial the next number rather than hanging up the receiver.

You can also make calls from *locutoris/locutorios*, which are small rooms full of phone booths where you sit down to talk and then pay for your call at the end. These often double up as internet cafés and you can also send faxes. Faxes may also be sent from hotels and stationery shops (*papereries/papelerias*).

Operator services

In most phone boxes operator services will be denoted by little buttons with signs on the main phone panel. You will usually have to insert a coin even to make a free call, although it will be returned when you hang up.

Note that English is not commonly spoken by Spanish phone operators; none of the following is in English.

Useful numbers

National operator 1004
International operator 11880
Directory enquiries 11811
International directory enquiries 11880
Weather reports www.aemet.es
Talking clock 1212

TIME

Spain is an hour ahead of Greenwich Mean Time and six ahead of Eastern Standard Time. Clocks go back in the last week of October and forward in the last week of March.

TIPPING

Spaniards aren't tippers and rarely do more than round up bills. In smarter restaurants you may find a service charge of ten per cent is added to the bill. It's not obligatory, and don't feel you have to pay it if you're not happy with the service you've received. In tourist areas, however, there's a greater expectation of tipping in restaurants. You are not expected to tip at a bar. Taxi drivers expect a small tip for longer journeys. Hotel staff don't rely on tips to supplement their wage and will not expect them. Having said that, it is perfectly acceptable to reward particularly good service.

TOILETS

Toilets (*serveis/servicios*) are generally of a good standard, except in the older bars or restaurants in rural areas. They are much less private than in the UK or USA, with usually just one door rather than two giving on to the facilities. Public toilets are fairly rare, but most bars will be happy to let you use their facilities. They are also known as *aseos, banys/baños* or *lavabos*, and are usually denoted by 'S' for ladies (*senyores/señoras*), and sometimes 'D' (*dones/damas*) or 'M' (*mujeres*), and 'C' for gentlemen (*cavallers/caballeros*). Sometimes, however, you'll find an 'S' on both doors, denoting *senyores/señoras* and *senyors/señores*.

TOURIST INFORMATION

Despite the enormous number of tourists who visit the islands, Mallorca and Menorca have just a small network of *turismos* run by the **Conselleria de Turisme**, confined chiefly to the tourist areas (for details see the relevant area chapters under 'Resources').

Tourist office staff are usually helpful and will often speak a little English. As well as supplying (usually free) maps and pamphlets with information on the local area, they can also help you find accommodation and provide you with lists of hotels and restaurants. In the larger towns *turismos* open throughout the day and at weekends. In villages they often close for siesta and at weekends. Out of season, village and resort *turismos* may operate to a winter timetable with reduced hours, or close altogether.

If there is no actual tourist office in the place you are visiting, try the *Ajuntament* (town hall), which should be able to supply you with basic information and maps.

For tourist information before you leave your own country, contact the local **Spanish National Tourist Office**:

Canada *2 Bloor Street West, Suite 3402, Toronto, Ontario M4W 3E2 (416 961 3131/4079/ www.tourspain.toronto.on.ca).*
UK *PO Box 4009, London W1A 6NB (020 7486 8077/www. tourspain.co.uk).*
USA *8383 Wilshire Boulevard, Suite 960, Beverly Hills, CA 90211 (323 658 7188/www.okspain.org); Water Tower Place, Suite 915 East,*

DIRECTORY

845 North Michigan Avenue, Chicago, IL 60611 (312 642 1992); 1395 Brickell Avenue, Miami, FL 33131 (305 358 1992); 666 Fifth Avenue, 35th floor, New York, NY 10103 (212 265 8822).

VISAS & IMMIGRATION

If you are a citizen of the EU, Norway, Iceland, the USA, Japan, Canada, Australia or New Zealand, you do not need a visa to enter Spain and stay for 90 days. All other nationals should contact their local Spanish consulate for information. Regulations do change, so all visitors should check with their local Spanish consulate for the latest information prior to travelling.

To stay longer you need to obtain a *permiso de residencia* (residency permit) at a police station and prove that you can support yourself financially. If you have found employment within this time, your employer will often sort out the red tape for you (*see below* **Working**).

WEIGHTS & MEASURES

Spain uses the metric system.

1 kilometre (km) = 0.62 miles
1 litre (l) = 1.76 UK pints/
2.12 US pints
1 gram (g) = 28 ounces
1 kilogram (kg) = 2.2 pounds
(9/5 Celsius temperature) +32
= temperature in Fahrenheit

WHEN TO GO

The Balearics enjoy a Mediterranean climate with a year-round average temperature of 21°C in Mallorca on the coast and 20°C in Menorca, and an average of more

than 300 days of sunshine throughout the year. For average monthly temperatures, *see below* **The Local Climate**.

The best time to visit the islands is in the spring, when the blossom and wild flowers are out, the sun is not too fierce and the *fiesta* season is just beginning. At this time, prices (except during Easter Week) are still low, but the weather is often warm enough to enjoy a beach holiday. Inland, however, it can still be a bit damp and cold, especially in the mountains, so come prepared.

From mid June prices and temperatures rise steeply, and by July and August the islands are a furnace, with temperatures regularly hitting the mid 40s.

By mid September high season is officially over and prices and temperatures start to fall. This is also a good time to visit as the fine, mild weather often stretches into late October.

November to February is officially winter, and many hoteliers and restaurants choose to close for a few months. It can snow during this period, especially in the high mountains, and it gets very cold in towns like Valldemossa. This is also rainy season, and sudden downpours after months of near drought can lead to flash floods and rock falls.

WOMEN

The Balearics (and Catalunya in general) have probably the most enlightened attitudes to women in Spain, and you are unlikely to encounter any more harassment than you would at home. Women encounter few problems travelling solo; you may be approached if you are on your own in a bar or café, but if you make it clear that you are not

interested, you are likely to be left alone. Sex crimes are very rare.

WORKING

Queries regarding residency and legal requirements for foreigners working in Spain can be addressed to the Ministry of Interior's helpline on 060 (there are English-speaking operators). Its website (www.mir.es) lays out the regulations in force on these matters (not in English).

It's a great deal easier for EU citizens to find (legal) work in the Balearics than those from non-EU countries. By far the easiest and most usual way of finding work on the islands is working on yachts, both taking them out with their owners in season and keeping them polished and well maintained while they languish in the harbour. Your best bet is to simply turn up at any port or marina and ask around.

Close second is as an English teacher, a great way to meet locals and learn Spanish. The majority of *academias de inglés* are based in Palma and Maó, but you will also find them in some smaller towns and villages. You do not even have to speak Spanish to become an English teacher (many schools prefer it, in fact, if you don't), but most want you to be qualified in TEFL (Teaching English as a Foreign Language). Many of the bigger English language institutions, such as Wall Street and Opening, advertise in the UK in the British Council newspaper and sometimes in the job sections of the national newspapers. Many will also have a website.

You may also find seasonal work in bars and restaurants, particularly in the English-dominated resorts such as Santa Ponça and Magaluf.

THE LOCAL CLIMATE

Average temperatures, hours of sunshine, monthly rainfall and humidity in Mallorca.

	High (°C / °F)	Low (°C / °F)	Sunshine (hrs)	Rainfall (mm/in)	Humidity (%)
Jan	15 / 59	3 / 38	5.3	37 / 1.5	79
Feb	15 / 60	4 / 39	5.5	34 / 1.3	77
Mar	17 / 62	4 / 40	6.2	36 / 1.4	75
Apr	19 / 66	6 / 43	7.2	39 / 1.5	74
May	23 / 73	10 / 50	8.8	30 / 1.2	71
June	27 / 81	14 / 58	10.2	14 / 0.6	67
July	31 / 87	17 / 63	10.7	10 / 0.4	65
Aug	31 / 87	18 / 64	10.0	20 / 0.8	69
Sept	28 / 82	16 / 60	7.4	50 / 2.0	75
Oct	23 / 74	12 / 54	6.6	63 / 2.5	78
Nov	19 / 66	7 / 45	5.6	47 / 1.9	79
Dec	16 / 61	5 / 41	5.0	44 / 1.7	80

Catalan Vocabulary

The official language of the Balearics is Catalan (*català*), of which *mallorquí* and *menorquí* are dialects. Though every Spanish native on the islands will speak Castilian Spanish, Catalan is the mother tongue of the majority. It was banned under Franco, and for many is a badge of pride, identity and independence. You might find that some locals will prefer to speak to you in English rather than Castilian. Most of the road signs, street names, etc, that you'll see on the islands will be written in Catalan.

There are differences between the Catalan spoken in the Balearics and that of the Barcelona region (one of the more obvious is the use of the articles es, sa, ses rather than el, la, els, les), but most of them are fairly minor. The information given below is standard Catalan.

For food and menu terms, *see pp28-33* **Food & Drink**.

PRONUNCIATION

In Catalan, words are run together, so *si us plau* (please) is more like *sees-plow*.

● **ç**, and **c** before an i or an e, are like a soft **s**, as in **s**it; **c** in all other cases is as in **cat**
● **e**, when unstressed as in *cerves*es (beers), or Jaume I, is a weak sound, like centre or comfortable
● **g** before i or e and **j** are pronounced like **s** in plea**s**ure; **tg** and **tj** are similar to **dg** in ba**dg**e
● **g** after an i at the end of a word (*Puig*) is a hard ch sound, as in wat**ch**; otherwise, **g** is as in **g**et
● **h** is silent
● **ll** is somewhere between the **y** in **y**es and the **lli** in mi**lli**on
● **l·l** has a slightly stronger stress on a single l sound; *paral·lel* sounds similar to the English paral**l**el
● **o** at the end of a word is like the **u** sound in fl**u**; **ó** at the end of a word is similar to the **o** in tomat**o**; **ò** is like the **o** in h**o**t
● **r** beginning a word and **rr** are heavily rolled; but at the end of many words is almost silent, so *carrer* (street) sounds like carr-ay
● **s** at the beginning and end of words and **ss** between vowels are soft, as in **s**it; a single **s** between two vowels is a **z** sound, as in la**z**y

● **t** after l or n at the end of a word is almost silent
● **v** is more like an English **b**
● **x** at the beginning of a word, or after a consonant or the letter i, is like the **sh** in **sh**oe, at other times like the English e**x**pert
● **y** after an n at the end of a word or in **nys** is not a vowel but adds a nasal stress and a y-sound to the n

BASICS

● **please** *si us plau*; **thank you (very much)** *(moltes) gràcies*; **very good/great/OK** *molt bé*; **you're welcome** *de res*
● **hello** *hola*; **hello** (when answering the phone) *hola, digui'm*
● **goodbye/see you later** *adéu/ fins després*
● **excuse me/sorry** *perdoni/disculpi*; **excuse me, please** *escolti* (literally, 'listen to me'); **OK/fine** *val/d'acord*
● **open** *obert*; **closed** *tancat*; **entrance** *entrada*; **exit** *sortida*; **very** *molt*; **and** *i*; **or** *o*; **with** *amb*; **without** *sense*; **enough** *prou*

MORE EXPRESSIONS

● **good morning, good day** *bon dia*; **good afternoon/evening** *bona tarda*; **good evening** (after dark), **good night** *bona nit*
● **do you speak English?** *parla anglès?*; **I'm sorry, I don't speak Catalan** *ho sento, no parlo català*; **I don't understand** *no ho entenc*; **speak more slowly, please** *parli més a poc a poc, si us plau*; **can you say that in Spanish, please?** *m'ho pot dir en castellà, si us plau?*; **how do you say that in Catalan?** *com es diu això en català?*
● **what's your name?** *com es diu?*; **my name is…** *em dic…*
● **Sir/Mr** *senyor (sr)*; **Madam/Mrs** *senyora (sra)*; **Miss** *senyoreta (srta)*
● **where is…?** *on és…?*; **why?** *perquè?*; **who?** *qui?*; **when?** *quan?*; **what?** *què?*; **where?** *on?*; **how?** *com?*; **who is it?** *qui és?*; **is/are there any…?** *hi ha…?/n'hi ha de…?*
● **I would like…** *vull…* (literally, 'I want'); **how much is it?** *quant val?*
● **price** *preu*; **free** *gratuit/de franc*; **change, exchange** *canvi*
● **I don't want** *no vull*; **I like** *m'agrada*; **I don't like** *no m'agrada*

● **good** *bo/bona*; **bad** *dolent/a*; **well/badly** *bé/malament*; **small** *petit/a*; **big** *gran*; **expensive** *car/a*; **cheap** *barat/a*; **hot** (food, drink) *calent/a*; **cold** *fred/a*
● **toilet** *el bany/el servei/el lavabo*
● **airport** *aeroport*; **rail station** *estació de tren*
● **car** *cotxe*; **bus** *autobús*; **train** *tren*; **bus stop** *parada d'autobús*; **the next stop** *la propera parada*
● **a ticket** *un billet*; **return** *d'anada i tornada*
● **left** *esquerra*; **right** *dreta*
● **here** *aquí*; **there** *allà*; **straight on** *tot recte*; **near** *a prop*; **far** *lluny*; **at the corner** *a la cantonada*; **as far as** *fins a*; **towards** *cap a*; **is it far?** *és lluny?*

TIME

● **now** *ara*; **later** *més tard*
● **yesterday** *ahir*; **today** *avui*; **tomorrow** *demà*; **tomorrow morning** *demà pel matí*
● **morning** *el matí*; **midday** *migdia*; **afternoon** *la tarda*; **evening** *el vespre*; **night** *la nit*
● **at what time…?** *a quina hora…?*; **in an hour** *en una hora*

NUMBERS

● **0** *zero*; **1** *u, un, una*; **2** *dos, dues*; **3** *tres*; **4** *quatre*; **5** *cinc*; **6** *sis*; **7** *set*; **8** *vuit*; **9** *nou*; **10** *deu*; **11** *onze*; **12** *dotze*; **13** *tretze*; **14** *catorze*; **15** *quinze*; **16** *setze*; **17** *disset*; **18** *divuit*; **19** *dinou*; **20** *vint*; **21** *vint-i-u*; **22** *vint-i-dos, vint-i-dues*; **30** *trenta*; **40** *quaranta*; **50** *cinquanta*; **60** *seixanta*; **70** *setanta*; **80** *vuitanta*; **90** *noranta*; **100** *cent*; **200** *dos-cents, dues-centes*; **1,000** *mil*; **1,000,000** *un milló*

DATES & SEASONS

● **Monday** *dilluns*; **Tuesday** *dimarts*; **Wednesday** *dimecres*; **Thursday** *dijous*; **Friday** *divendres*; **Saturday** *dissabte*; **Sunday** *diumenge*
● **January** *gener*; **February** *febrer*; **March** *març*; **April** *abril*; **May** *maig*; **June** *juny*; **July** *juliol*; **August** *agost*; **September** *setembre*; **October** *octobre*; **November** *novembre*; **December** *desembre*
● **spring** *primavera*; **summer** *estiu*; **autumn** *tardor*; **winter** *hivern*

Spanish Vocabulary

Spanish is generally referred to as *castellano* (Castilian) rather than *español*. The Spanish familiar form for 'you' – *tú* – is used very freely, but it's safer to use the more formal *usted* with older people and with strangers (verbs below are given in the *usted* form unless stated otherwise).

PRONUNCIATION

● **c** before an i or an e and z are like **th** in **thin**
● **c** in all other cases is as in **cat**
● **g** before an i or an e and j are pronounced with a guttural **h**-sound that doesn't exist in English – like **ch** in Scottish 'lo**ch**', but much harder
● **g** in all other cases is as in **get**
● **h** at the beginning of a word is normally silent
● **ll** is pronounced almost like a **y**
● **ñ** is like **ny** in ca**ny**on
● a single **r** at the beginning of a word and **rr** elsewhere are heavily rolled
● **v** is more like an English **b**
● In words ending with a vowel, **n** or **s**, the penultimate syllable is stressed: eg *barato*, *viven*, *habitaciones*.
● In words ending with any other consonant, the last syllable is stressed: eg *exterior*, *universidad*.
● An accent marks the stressed syllable in words that depart from these rules: eg *estación*, *tónica*.

BASICS

● **please** *por favor*; **thank you** (very much) (*muchas*) *gracias*; **you're welcome** *de nada*
● **hello** *hola*; **hello** (when answering the phone) *hola, diga*
● **goodbye/see you later** *adiós/hasta luego*
● **excuse me/sorry** *perdón*;
● **excuse me, please** *oiga* (the standard way to attract attention, politely; literally, 'hear me')
● **OK/fine/**(to a waiter) **that's enough** *vale*
● **open** *abierto*; **closed** *cerrado*
● **entrance** *entrada*; **exit** *salida*
● **very** *muy*; **and** *y*; **or** *o*; **with** *con*; **without** *sin*; **enough** *bastante*
● **How are you?** *¿cómo está/estás?* (polite/informal)
● **I'm fine, thanks** *estoy bien, gracias*

MORE EXPRESSIONS

● **good morning/good day** *buenos días*; **good afternoon/good evening** *buenas tardes*; **good evening** (after dark)/**good night** *buenas noches*
● **do you speak English?** *¿habla inglés?*; **I'm sorry, I don't speak Spanish** *lo siento, no hablo castellano*; **I don't understand** *no lo entiendo*; **speak more slowly, please** *hable más despacio, por favor*; **wait a moment** *espere un momento*; **can you say that in Catalan?** *¿Cómo se dice eso en catalán?*
● **what's your name?** *¿cómo se llama?* **my name is… me llamo…**
● **Sir/Mr** *señor* (sr); **Madam/Mrs** *señora* (sra); **Miss** *señorita* (srta)
● **where is…?** *¿dónde está…?*; **why?** *¿porqué?*, **who?** *¿quién?*, **when?** *¿cuándo?*, **what?** *¿qué?*, **where?** *¿dónde?*; **how?** *¿cómo?*; **who is it?** *¿quién es?*; **is/are here any…?** *¿hay…?*
● **what time does it open/close?** *¿a qué hora abre/cierra?*
● **pull** (on signs) *tirar*; **push** *empujar*
● **I would like** *quiero*; **how many would you like?** *¿cuántos quiere?*; **how much is it?** *¿cuánto vale?*
● **price** *precio*; **free** *gratis*; **discount** *descuento*; **do you have any change?** *¿tiene cambio?*
● **I don't want** *no quiero*; **I like** *me gusta*; **I don't like** *no me gusta*
● **good** *bueno/a*; **bad** *malo/a*; **well/badly** *bien/mal*; **small** *pequeño/a*; **big** *gran, grande*; **expensive** *caro/a*; **cheap** *barato/a*; **hot** (food, drink) *caliente*; **cold** *frío/a*;
● **bank** *banco*; **to rent** *alquilar*; **(for) rent, rental** (en) *alquiler*; **post office** *correos*; **stamp** *sello*; **postcard** *postal*; **toilet** *el baño, el servicio, el lavabo*
● **airport** *aeropuerto*; **rail station** *estación de ferrocarril/estación de RENFE* (Spanish railways); **metro station** *estación de metro*; **car** *coche*; **bus** *autobús*; **train** *tren*; **bus stop** *parada de autobus*; **the next stop** *la próxima parada*; **a ticket** *un billete*; **return** *de ida y vuelta*
● **excuse me, do you know the way to…?** *¿oiga, señor/señora, sabe cómo llegar a…?*

● **left** *izquierda*; **right** *derecha*
● **here** *aquí*; **there** *allí*; **straight on** *recto*; **near** *cerca*; **far** *lejos*; **it is far?** *¿está lejos?*

ACCOMMODATION

● **do you have a double/single room for tonight?** *¿tiene una habitación doble/para una persona/para esta noche?*
● **we have a booking** *tenemos reserva*; **an inside/outside room** *una habitación interior/exterior*
● **with/without bathroom** *con/sin baño*; **shower** *ducha*; **double bed** *cama de matrimonio*; **with twin beds** *con dos camas*; **breakfast included** *desayuno incluido*; **air-conditioning** *aire acondicionado*

TIME

● **now** *ahora*; **later** *más tarde*
● **yesterday** *ayer*; **today** *hoy*; **tomorrow** *mañana*; **tomorrow morning** *mañana por la mañana*
● **morning** *la mañana*; **midday** *mediodía*; **afternoon/evening** *la tarde*; **night** *la noche*
● **at what time…?** *¿a qué hora…?*

NUMBERS

● 0 *cero*; 1 *un, uno, una*; 2 *dos*; 3 *tres*; 4 *cuatro*; 5 *cinco*; 6 *seis*; 7 *siete*; 8 *ocho*; 9 *nueve*; 10 *diez*; 11 *once*; 12 *doce*; 13 *trece*; 14 *catorce*; 15 *quince*; 16 *dieciséis*; 17 *diecisiete*; 18 *dieciocho*; 19 *diecinueve*; 20 *veinte*; 21 *veintiuno*; 22 *veintidós*; 30 *treinta*; 40 *cuarenta*; 50 *cincuenta*; 60 *sesenta*; 70 *setenta*; 80 *ochenta*; 90 *noventa*; 100 *cien*; 200 *doscientos*; 1,000 *mil*; 1,000,000 *un millón*

DATES & SEASONS

● **Monday** *lunes*; **Tuesday** *martes*; **Wednesday** *miércoles*; **Thursday** *jueves*; **Friday** *viernes*; **Saturday** *sábado*; **Sunday** *domingo*
● **January** *enero*; **February** *febrero*; **March** *marzo*; **April** *abril*; **May** *mayo*; **June** *junio*; **July** *julio*; **August** *agosto*; **September** *septiembre*; **October** *octubre*; **November** *noviembre*; **December** *diciembre*
● **spring** *primavera*; **summer** *verano*; **autumn** *otoño*; **winter** *invierno*

DIRECTORY

Further Reference

BOOKS

There are surprisingly few books in print in English on Mallorca and Menorca (there is, for instance, no dedicated account of Mallorcan history currently available). A number of the books listed below are either out of print or only available on the islands.

Mallorca

David Abulafia *A Mediterranean Emporium: the Catalan Kingdom of Mallorca*
A detailed dissection of independent Mallorca during the Middle Ages, concentrating on its role in trade in the western Mediterranean.
Mossèn Antoni Alcover *Folk Tales of Mallorca*
This enormous compendium of island folk stories was gathered by a 19th-century priest.
Vicky Bennison *The Taste of a Place: Mallorca*
Excellent culinary guide to the island and its cuisine, including recommended restaurants, markets, shops and recipes.
David & Ros Brawn *Discovery Walking Guides*
The Brawns produce a series of excellent walking guides to various different areas of Mallorca (and also Menorca).
Raymond Carr *Spain: A History*
In the absence of a dedicated history of Mallorca, this is the best short survey of the history of the country as a whole; it touches on the Balearics.
Henry L Carrigan *Romancing God: Contemplating the Beloved*
A short introduction to the life of scholar, linguist, poet and missionary Ramón Llull.
Barbara Catoir *Miró on Mallorca*
Catalan artist Joan Miró always held Mallorca in special affection (his mother was a native and it was his permanent home from the mid 1950s until his death). This book focuses largely on the techniques and themes of Miró's later works, many inspired by the piercing blue light of his adopted island.
Valerie Crespí-Green *Sunflower Guides: Mallorca*
Containing more than 20 detailed walks on the island, plus

suggestions for six driving tours and picnics.
Lucia Graves *A Woman Unknown*
A compelling memoir of life in Francoist Mallorca and Catalunya by the daughter of Robert Graves. In beautifully measured prose it tells the story of a woman caught between two cultures, and of the unsung lives of many of the quietly heroic women she came into contact with during that period.
Robert Graves *Majorca Observed*
The poet's thoughts and fancies on his adopted island just as the first waves of mass tourism were breaking upon the shores that he thought of as his own. Though snobbish at times, it's an interesting portrait of a society on the cusp of monumental change.
Tomás Graves *Bread & Oil: Majorcan Culture's Last Stand*
Still resident in Deià, to where his father Robert moved in 1929, son Tomás is a passionate supporter of traditional Mallorcan culture, and this absorbing and idiosyncratic exploration of the classic Mallorcan peasant dish of *pa amb oli* (bread and oil) is also part autobiography and part cultural history of the island during the last few decades.
Tomás Graves *Tuning Up at Dawn: A Memoir of Music and Majorca*
Published in 2004, this is Graves's affectionate portrait of the island, its history and the central role that music has played in his life. Better written and with a more general appeal than *Bread & Oil*, it's particularly interesting when dealing with Deià's bohemian past and the many colourful characters who have passed through the village over the years.
William Graves *Wild Olives*
Another book by another son of Robert Graves, this account is chiefly concerned with the author's childhood, his difficult relationship with his father and their less than harmonious family life.
Graham Hearl & Jon King *A Birdwatching Guide to Mallorca*
The island is a favourite haunt of twitchers, and this is the best guide available to what you can see and where.

Herbert Heinrich *Twelve Classic Hikes through Mallorca*
There is a far wider range of quality guides to Mallorca in German than in English; this translation details some superb walks in the Serra de Tramuntana.
Roderic Jeffries *An Enigmatic Disappearance*
This is one of Jeffries' Inspector Alvarez series of detective novels, set on Mallorca.
Peter Kerr *Snowball Oranges/ Mañana Mañana/Viva Mallorca!/ A Basketful of Snowflakes*
Enjoyable if predictable accounts of the author's attempts to set up a new life in south-west Mallorca in the *Year in Provence/Driving Over Lemons* style.
Könemann (publisher) *Majorca: Culture and Life*
This large-format picture-packed book by German publisher Könemann is by far the best and most comprehensive general introduction to the island.
Santiago Rusiñol *Majorca: The Island of Calm*
Possibly the best-known book by the Catalan writer and humorist, this series of vignettes on subjects such as 'The men of Palma' and 'Eulogy of the ensaïmada' now seems somewhat dated and rather cloying in style, but it is still an intriguing document of an early 20th-century Mallorca that four decades of mass tourism have long since eradicated. Available in English on Mallorca.
George Sand *A Winter in Majorca*
Sand's notorious demolition of the Mallorcans, sparked by the miserable winter (1838-39) she spent in Valldemossa with her children and companion Frédéric Chopin, is, ironically, widely available throughout the island in a number of different editions. Though she was unimpressed by the islanders, she loved the scenery, and the book remains a highly entertaining and valuable (if biased) account of an isolated agricultural society.
George Scott *The Bloody Bhokara*
Written by the co-owner of Scott's Hotel in Binissalem, this enjoyable crime fiction romp provides plenty of interesting background detail on

expat life on the island along the way; its follow-up is *The Chewed Caucasian*.

Miranda Seymour *Robert Graves: Life on the Edge*
A detailed but rarely dynamic account of Graves's long life and turbulent relationships. The book was written with the full co-operation of Graves's family.

Llorenç Villalonga
The Dolls' Room
Published in the 1950s, this sharply observed portrayal of the declining fortunes of the 19th-century Mallorcan nobility was written by one of the island's best-known authors.

Gordon West
Jogging Round Majorca
This easygoing, entertaining account of the author's slow progression around the island in the 1920s paints a fascinating portrait of a Mallorca before mass tourism.

MENORCA

Amics del Museu de Menorca *Guide of Menorca: Historical and Natural Patrimony*
This haltingly translated island guide produced by the Museu de Menorca contains lots of interesting details that you won't find in most other guidebooks.

Rodney Ansell *Sunflower Guides: Menorca*
Contains more than 20 detailed walks on the island, plus various suggestions for driving tours and picnics.

Desmond Gregory *Minorca, the Illusory Prize: History of the British Occupation of Minorca between 1708 and 1802*
An expensive, exhaustive, academic survey of the 18th-century British occupations of the island.

Bruce Laurie *The Life of Richard Kane: Britain's First Lieutenant-Governor of Minorca*
Overview of the life of the most influential foreigner in Menorca's history. Pricey.

Rev Fernando Marti
History of Menorca
Though dated in some respects (it was published in the late 1970s) and idiosyncratic in style, this is a treasure trove of facts, figures and stories on the island, covering everything from Menorcan surnames to ancient rock paintings and the shoe industry.

Micaela Mata *Conquests and Reconquests of Menorca*
There's a heavy pro-Catalan bias to this exploration of Menorca

between the 13th and 18th centuries. Nevertheless, it's full of interesting detail, particularly regarding the devastating pirate attacks on the island during the 16th century, and the British and (brief) French occupations of the 18th century. The book is easiest to find in Maó and Ciutadella.

Enric Ramos
The Birds of Menorca
This excellent title provides a detailed description of all the species of birds recorded in Menorca. Reader-friendly and full of handsome illustrations.

WEBSITES

a2zMallorca
www.a2zmallorca.com
Heaps of information on just about every subject and every town and village on the island.

Ajuntament de Palma
www.a-palma.es
Palma city council website. Good listings for public libraries, bus timetables and all things municipal, and has a useful interactive street finder and city map.

Consell de Mallorca
www.conselldemallorca.net
The Mallorcan council's website, with road, walking and cycling maps, and other useful information.

Consell Insular de Menorca
www.emenorca.org
The island council's website, with a handy events and activities search facility as well as useful opening hours.

Discover Menorca
www.discovermenorca.co.uk
Located in the UK, this agent rents villas on the island as well as arranging travel insurance and car hire. It also offers useful information on activities and guided tours.

Govern de les Illes Balears
www.caib.es
Official Balearic government website with useful links, including a directory of local products and tourist information.

Fauna Ibérica
http://faunaiberica.org
Conservation-led guide to the islands' native fauna. In Spanish only.

hot-maps
www.hot-maps.de
www.hot-maps.de/europe/spain/balearen/palma_de_mallorca/homede.htm
German site with access to a detailed interactive map of Palma.

Illes Balears
www.visitbalears.com
Official tourist office site for the Balearics, with everything from the weather to what's on.

Magalluf-Palmanova/ Santa Ponsa.com
www.magalluf-palmanova.com
www.santa-ponsa.com
Listings for everything from bookies to lawn bowls in Mallorca's party capital, and its slightly more sedate near-neighbour.

Majorca Daily Bulletin
www.majorcadailybulletin.es
Online version of the English-language paper.

MallorcaWeb
www.mallorcaweb.com/eng
General Mallorca search engine.

Menorca Private Owners
www.villanet.co.uk
An independent organisation run by villa owners who want to rent their properties direct to holidaymakers.

Menorca The Guide
www.menorca-net.co.uk/
Free registration to an online guide with information on everything from the biosphere, beaches, car hire and accommodation to learning Spanish.

Minorca
www.islandofminorca.info
An updated e-book version of David Wilson Taylor's detailed 1970s guide to Menorca's history and culture.

PuertoPollensa.com
www.puertopollensa.com
Guide to the resort of Port de Pollença (Puerto Pollensa).

Sollernet.com
www.sollernet.com
Guide to the town of Sóller and sister resort Port de Sóller.

Spain for Visitors
http://spainforvisitors.com
A useful resource with cultural info.

Think Spain
www.thinkspain.com
A comprehensive website covering travel and accommodation to useful local news and the environment.

STRIANET
http://nibis.ni.schule.de/~trianet/mallorca/physic3.htm
If you like graphs, you'll enjoy this educational site that delves beneath the tourist tat to look at the physical character of the Balearics.

Ultimate Guide to Menorca
www.ultimateguide-menorca.com
Good all-round guide to the island.

VisitMenorca.com
www.visitmenorca.com
Website of the Menorca Hotel Association with an online search facility.

Index

INDEX

Advertisers' Index

Palma Street Index

STREET INDEX